RACIAL
AND ETHNIC
DIVERSITY

American Consumer Series

RACIAL AND ETHNIC DIVERSITY

Asians, Blacks, Hispanics, Native Americans, and Whites

BY CHERYL RUSSELL

New Strategist Publications, Inc.

Ithaca, New York

New Strategist Publications, Inc.
P.O. Box 242, Ithaca, New York 14851
607/273-0913
www.newstrategist.com

ISBN 1-885070-15-2

Printed in the United States of America

Table of Contents

List of Tables

Chapter 4. Native Americans

Chapter 5. Whites

Health

Households

Housing

Income

List of Charts

Chapter 5. Whites

Chapter 6. Total Population

About the Author

Cheryl Russell is a business demographer, editor-in-chief of New Strategist Publications, and executive editor of *The Boomer Report*. She has authored a number of books on demographic trends, including *The Master Trend: How the Baby-Boom Generation Is Remaking America* (Plenum Publishing) and two editions of *Racial & Ethnic Diversity* (New Strategist Publications). Prior to joining New Strategist, she was a contributing editor of *Money* magazine and editor-in-chief of *American Demographics* magazine. Ms. Russell's articles about demographic trends have appeared in a wide variety of publications, including *Barron's, The Wall Street Journal, Family Circle*, and *TV Guide*. She has appeared on CBS Evening News, NBC Nightly News, and PBS. She holds an M.A. in Demography from Cornell University.

Introduction

The diversity of the American population is growing rapidly. It has become vital for researchers—whether from business, government, or academia—to keep track of the wants and needs of America's racial and ethnic groups. The second edition of *Racial and Ethnic Diversity* provides the building blocks for understanding the similarities and differences between whites and blacks, Hispanics and non-Hispanics, Asians and Native Americans.

For many researchers, to examine statistics for the total population falls far short of what they need to keep up with trends because the total figures mask differences by racial and ethnic group. The living arrangements of Hispanics are different from those of whites and blacks in ways that affect consumer behavior. The educational level of several Asian ethnic groups makes them more sophisticated consumers than the average American.

Racial and Ethnic Diversity presents in a single volume the most important characteristics of Asians, blacks, Hispanics, Native Americans, and whites. It is designed for easy use in locating the latest demographic information about each racial and ethnic group, and to provide quick comparisons between groups. *Racial and Ethnic Diversity* is as complete and up-to-date as possible, given the constraints of the data. In a perfect world, the kinds of demographic data available for each group would be identical and all would be available for the same point in time. In the real world, this is not possible since the government collects information on the smaller racial and ethnic groups less frequently and in less detail. There are no spending or wealth data for Asians or Native Americans, for example, and the government has only just begun to examine non-Hispanic whites separately from the white population as a whole. For Native Americans, and for Asian and Hispanic ethnic groups, many of the latest available data are from the 1990 census—now eight years old. *Racial and Ethnic Diversity* uses this information only when no other data are available and when the patterns they reveal are not likely to have changed much over the decade.

Racial/Ethnic Classifications

Racial and Ethnic Diversity examines the latest demographic characteristics of the four racial groups in the U.S.: Asians, blacks, Native Americans, and whites. The book also examines the demographic characteristics of Hispanics, who may be of any race.

The government classifies Americans by race and Hispanic origin through self-identification. In both census and Current Population Survey, which are the sources for most of the data in the book, respondents themselves indicate their race and Hispanic origin on questionnaires. They are allowed to specify only one racial group, although they may be multiracial. Beginning with the 2000 census, Americans will be allowed to identify themselves as multiracial. In a separate question, respondents are asked to specify whether they are Hispanic or non-Hispanic. The racial and Hispanic-origin groups created by these Census Bureau procedures and described in *Racial and Ethnic Diversity* are defined as follows:

Asian The term "Asian" includes both Asians and Pacific Islanders. The Current Population Survey classifies as Asian or Pacific Islander anyone who identifies him- or herself as "Asian or Pacific Islander." The 1990 census goes further, asking Asians and Pacific Islanders to specify their ethnic origin, such as Chinese, Filipino, Japanese, Asian Indian, Korean, Vietnamese, Samoan, Tahitian, and so on. The Census Bureau then classifies as "Asian or Pacific Islander" anyone who named a Far Eastern or Pacific Island nation as their origin. The only exception to this definition of Asian occurs in the immigration tables in the Asian and Total Population chapters. The Immigration and Naturalization Service includes people from the Middle East—such as Israel, Lebanon, Iran, and so on—as immigrants from the Asian world region. They are included as Asian immigrants in the immigration tables.

Black The black racial category includes those who identified themselves as "black" on the Current Population Survey, or as "black or Negro" in the 1990 census, or who wrote in an ancestry or ethnic origin on the 1990 census that included African American, Jamaican, Nigerian, West Indian, or Haitian.

Native American The Native American statistics in this book include people who indicated they were American Indian, Eskimo, or Aleut on the 1990 census. The American Indian category includes persons who reported their race as American Indian or entered the name of an American Indian tribe. The tribal data shown in this book are from the written entries on the 1990 census questionnaire.

White The white racial category includes those who identified themselves as "white" in the Current Population Survey or in the 1990 census. In addition, those who report an ancestry or ethnic origin that includes Canadian, German, Polish, Italian, Lebanese, Near Easterner, Arab, or another country made up primarily of whites, are considered white. The only exception to this definition of white occurs in the immigration tables in the Asian and Total Population chapters because the Immigration and Naturalization Service classifies people from the Middle East as from the Asian world region. They are included as Asian immigrants in the immigration tables, although the Census Bureau would classify them as white.

Hispanic The government classifies people as Hispanic through self-identification in questions separate from those about race. Because "Hispanic" is an ethnic origin rather than a race, Hispanics may be of any race. While most are white, there are black, Asian, and Native American Hispanics. The Hispanic statistics in this book include anyone who identified him- or herself as Hispanic in the Current Population Survey or the 1990 census. Hispanics include those who identify themselves as Mexican, Puerto Rican, Cuban, or of "other" Spanish/Hispanic origin. Persons of "other" Hispanic origin include those from Spain, the Spanish-speaking countries of Central and South America, and the Dominican Republic. They also include those who identify themselves as Spanish, Spanish American, Latino, and so on. The only exception to this definition of Hispanic occurs in the immigration table in the Hispanic chapter,

Hispanic Composition of Racial Groups, 1998

(number and percent distribution of persons by race and Hispanic origin, 1998; numbers in thousands)

	total	white	black	Asian	Native American
Total persons	**270,002**	**222,648**	**34,537**	**10,480**	**2,337**
Non-Hispanic	240,436	195,786	32,789	9,856	2,005
Hispanic	29,566	26,862	1,748	624	332
Total persons	**100.0%**	**100.0%**	**100.0%**	**100.0%**	**100.0%**
Non-Hispanic	89.0	87.9	94.9	94.0	85.8
Hispanic	11.0	12.1	5.1	6.0	14.2

Racial Composition of Hispanics, 1998

(number and percent distribution of Hispanics by race, 1998; numbers in thousands)

	Hispanic number	Hispanic percent
Total persons	**29,566**	**100.0%**
White	26,862	90.9
Black	1,748	5.9
Asian	624	2.1
Native American	332	1.1

Source: Bureau of the Census, Population Projections of the United States by Age, Sex, Race, and Hispanic Origin: 1995 to 2050, Current Population Reports, P25-1130, 1996; calculations by New Strategist

where people from Brazil are classified as Hispanic because they are from South America.

Non-Hispanic People who did not indicate they were Hispanic in the Current Population Survey or the 1990 census are classified as non-Hispanic. Most of the non-Hispanic statistics shown in this book are for whites only and can be found in the White chapter. There are few statistics available for non-Hispanic blacks, Asians, or Native Americans.

A breakdown of the Hispanic composition of racial groups and the racial composition of Hispanics is shown on page 3.

How to Use This Book

Racial and Ethnic Diversity is divided into seven chapters: Asians, Blacks, Hispanics, Native Americans, Whites, Total Population, and Attitudes.

Except for Attitudes, each chapter includes nine sections arranged alphabetically: Education, Health, Households, Housing, Income, Labor Force, Population, Spending, and Wealth. Each chapter includes an introductory text describing the most important trends for that particular racial or ethnic group, including what to expect in the future. Wherever possible, identical tables of data are shown for each group. If identical tables are not present, then identical data are not available for one or more of the groups. No spending or wealth data are available for Asians or Native Americans.

The Total Population chapter allows readers to compare statistics for a racial or ethnic group with those for the nation as a whole. When comparable statistics for the total population are included in the individual racial or ethnic chapters, no table on the topic is included in the Total Population chapter.

The Attitudes chapter examines what Americans think about a range of diversity issues. The data are from the 1996 General Social Survey (GSS) of the National Opinion Research Center of the University of Chicago. The GSS is conducted every two years using a nationally representative sample of noninstitutionalized English-speaking persons aged 18 or older living in the United States. Because the GSS divides respondents into three racial groups (white, black, and other), responses to diversity questions can only be shown for those three groups. It is important to remember that the "other" race category includes Asians, Native Americans, and Hispanics who did not identify themselves as white or black.

Most of the tables in the book are based on data collected by the federal government, in particular the Bureau of the Census, the Bureau of Labor Statistics, the National Center for Education Statistics, and the National Center for Health Statistics.

The federal government continues to be the best source of up-to-date, reliable information on the changing characteristics of Americans.

As we publish *Racial and Ethnic Diversity,* dramatic technological change is reshaping the demographic reference industry. The government's detailed demographic data, once widely available to all in printed reports, are now accessible only to Internet users or in unpublished tables, which can be obtained only by calling the appropriate government agency with a specific request. The government's web sites, which house enormous spreadsheets of data, are of great value to researchers with the time and skills to first download the appropriate sheets and then extract the important nuggets of information. The shift from printed reports to web sites—while convenient for number-crunchers—has made demographic analysis a bigger chore.

With this volume, the editors of New Strategist have done the extraction and analysis for you. While most of the data in *Racial and Ethnic Diversity* were collected by the government, the tables published here are not reprints of the government's tabulations. Each table is individually compiled and created, with statistical calculations performed to reveal trends. Each table tells a story about blacks, Asians, Hispanics, whites, or Native Americans. If you need more information than the tables provide, you can locate the original datasets by exploring the source listed at the bottom of each table.

Racial and Ethnic Diversity also contains a list of tables to help you locate the information you need. For a more detailed search, use the index at the back of the book. Also at the back of the book you will find a bibliography of data sources and a glossary defining the terms used in the tables and text.

With *Racial and Ethnic Diversity* in hand, researchers will be able to discover the many ways in which Americans are the same—and different. As the diversity of the population grows, this kind of understanding will be critical to success in any endeavor, whether business, government, or academia.

—Cheryl Russell

1

Asians

■ The Asian population is projected to grow from 10.5 million in 1998 to nearly 20 million by 2020, when Asians will account for 6 percent of the total U.S. population.

■ Asians are much better educated than the population as a whole. Forty-two percent were college graduates in 1996, versus 24 percent of the total population.

■ Regarding all but a few health conditions, Asians fare much better than the average American. At birth, life expectancy for Asian males is seven years longer than average, while for females it is five years longer.

■ Asian households are more likely to be headed by married couples than the average household—61 versus 54 percent. Only 24 percent of Asian households are not families. This compares with 30 percent of households nationally.

■ The median income of Asian households fell 9 percent between 1990 and 1995, after adjusting for inflation. Despite this decline, the median income of Asian households remains higher than the median income of all households.

■ Fifty-three percent of Asian households have at least two earners. This compares with 45 percent of all households and is the highest proportion among all racial groups.

■ Note: There are no spending or wealth data for Asians.

Asian Americans are 4 percent of the U.S. population

(percent distribution of total persons by race and ethnicity, 1998)

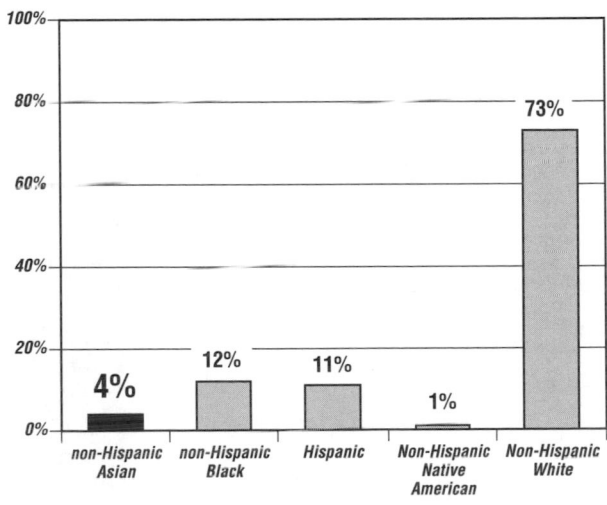

Asians: Education

Asian Americans are far better educated than the average American.

Asians are much better educated than the population as a whole. As of 1996, 83 percent of Asians were high school graduates, versus 82 percent of the total population. Fully 42 percent of Asians were college graduates, a much higher share than the 24 percent of the total population that has a bachelor's degree. Among Asians, Vietnamese Americans are the least educated because many are refugees who fled Vietnam after the war. Only 61 percent of Vietnamese Americans had a high school diploma as of 1990.

Not only are Asians better educated than the average person, they are more likely to be enrolled in school. While just 4 percent of the total population is Asian, 6 percent of all college students and 10 percent of those enrolled in first-professional degree programs are Asian. More than 60,000 bachelor's degrees were awarded to Asian Americans in 1994–95. Asians earned 13 percent of bachelor's degrees awarded in biological sciences and 11 percent in engineering. They also earned from 13 to 19 percent of first-professional degrees in the fields of dentistry, medicine, optometry, and pharmacy.

■ The educational level of Asians is much higher than that of the average American because many are highly educated immigrants with professional jobs. The educational level of Asians could fall in the future if more immigrants arrive from countries such as Vietnam, where adults have little education.

Nearly half of Asians are college graduates

(percent of Asians and total persons aged 25 or older who are high school or college graduates, 1996)

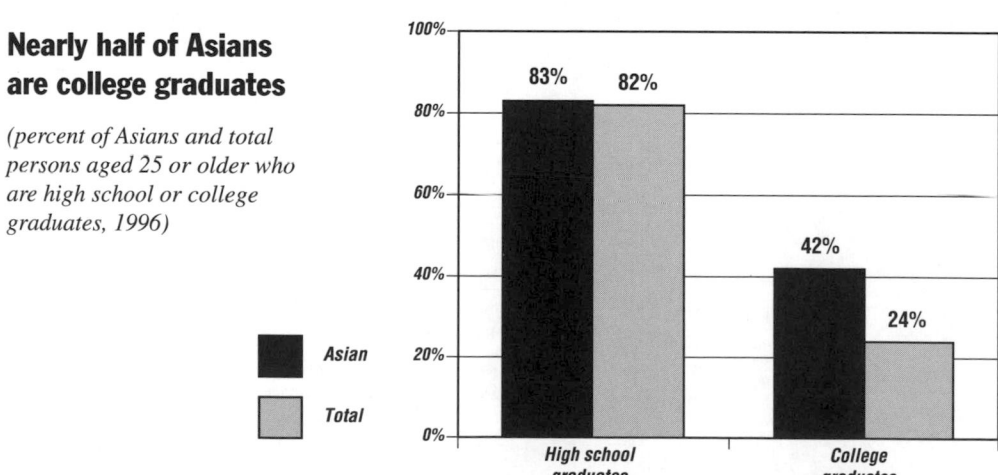

Asian
Total

High school graduates — Asian 83%, Total 82%
College graduates — Asian 42%, Total 24%

Educational Attainment of Asians by Sex, 1996

(number and percent distribution of Asians aged 25 or older by educational attainment and sex, 1996; numbers in thousands)

	total		men		women	
	number	percent	number	percent	number	percent
Total, aged 25 or older	**5,677**	**100.0%**	**2,738**	**100.0%**	**2,939**	**100.0%**
Not a high school graduate	579	10.2	214	7.8	367	12.5
High school graduate or more	4,723	83.2	2,355	86.0	2,372	80.7
Some college or assoc. degree	1,124	19.8	542	19.8	579	19.7
Bachelor's degree or more	2,367	41.7	1,270	46.4	1,096	37.3

Source: Bureau of the Census, The Asian and Pacific Islander Population in the United States: March 1996 (Update), *detailed tables for Current Population Reports P20-503, PPL-77, 1997; calculations by New Strategist*

Educational Attainment of Asians by Ethnicity and Sex, 1990

(total number of Asians aged 25 or older and percent who are high school or college graduates, by ethnicity and sex, 1990; numbers in thousands)

	total	high school	college
TOTAL			
Total, aged 25 or older	**4,316**	**77.5%**	**36.6%**
Chinese	1,077	73.6	40.7
Filipino	865	82.6	39.3
Japanese	626	87.5	34.5
Asian Indian	464	84.7	58.1
Korean	456	80.2	34.5
Vietnamese	304	61.2	17.4
MEN			
Total, aged 25 or older	**2,034**	**81.5**	**41.9**
Chinese	525	77.2	46.7
Filipino	372	84.2	36.2
Japanese	276	89.9	42.6
Asian Indian	257	89.4	65.7
Korean	186	89.1	46.9
Vietnamese	157	68.5	22.3
WOMEN			
Total, aged 25 or older	**2,283**	**74.0**	**31.8**
Chinese	551	70.2	35.0
Filipino	493	81.4	41.6
Japanese	350	85.6	28.2
Asian Indian	208	79.0	48.7
Korean	269	74.1	25.9
Vietnamese	147	53.3	12.2

Note: Numbers will not add to total because not all ethnicities are shown.
Source: U.S. Bureau of the Census, Asians and Pacific Islanders in the United States, *1990 Census of Population, 1990 CP-3-5, 1993*

Asian High School and College Graduates by State, 1990

(percent of Asians aged 25 or older who are high school or college graduates, by state, 1990)

	high school graduate or more	college graduate		high school graduate or more	college graduate
United States	**77.5%**	**36.6%**	Missouri	81.5%	47.3%
Alabama	78.9	43.7	Montana	78.5	32.1
Alaska	75.4	20.5	Nebraska	80.0	39.5
Arizona	80.2	37.5	Nevada	74.1	21.9
Arkansas	66.4	24.6	New Hampshire	82.7	26.1
California	77.2	34.1	New Jersey	86.8	57.1
Colorado	78.3	32.1	New Mexico	80.8	38.7
Connecticut	81.9	50.8	New York	72.4	38.7
Delaware	86.1	55.9	North Carolina	77.9	39.3
District of Columbia	80.2	50.9	North Dakota	83.7	37.8
Florida	77.8	33.6	Ohio	83.5	53.2
Georgia	77.5	38.6	Oklahoma	76.1	34.7
Hawaii	74.7	19.4	Oregon	79.4	32.3
Idaho	80.3	27.6	Pennsylvania	77.1	45.2
Illinois	83.9	49.8	Rhode Island	59.6	30.6
Indiana	85.8	53.1	South Carolina	77.4	34.4
Iowa	76.4	47.3	South Dakota	74.3	33.1
Kansas	73.6	39.9	Tennessee	79.3	42.6
Kentucky	77.9	44.2	Texas	79.1	41.3
Louisiana	68.1	31.4	Utah	80.7	29.4
Maine	74.3	44.9	Vermont	87.1	52.1
Maryland	84.8	50.3	Virginia	82.1	40.2
Massachusetts	74.1	44.9	Washington	77.3	30.2
Michigan	83.3	54.1	West Virginia	88.8	63.3
Minnesota	69.7	33.5	Wisconsin	71.5	40.4
Mississippi	68.2	35.1	Wyoming	77.5	28.6

Source: National Center for Education Statistics, Digest of Education Statistics 1993, NCES 93-292, 1993

School Enrollment of Asians by Age and Ethnicity, 1990

(number and percent of Asians aged 3 or older enrolled in school, by age and ethnicity, April 1990; numbers in thousands)

	total		Chinese		Filipino		Japanese		Asian Indian		Vietnamese	
	number	*percent*	*number*	*percent*	*number*	*percent*	*number*	*percent*	*number*	*percent*	*number*	*percent*
Total, aged 3 or older	**2,553**	**37.1%**	**590**	**37.3%**	**445**	**32.7%**	**229**	**27.3%**	**285**	**38.1%**	**252**	**44.7%**
Aged 3 and 4	71	30.4	17	41.3	9	21.9	9	46.4	9	34.5	4	18.9
Aged 5 to 14	1,060	93.0	198	94.6	202	92.8	82	94.6	127	94.7	98	91.3
Aged 15 to 19	533	90.2	115	94.5	103	87.5	41	90.9	54	93.2	64	91.0
Aged 20 to 24	356	58.6	93	70.6	54	46.4	39	63.5	41	62.4	37	59.5
Aged 25 to 34	316	22.4	105	30.4	37	14.5	33	19.6	35	21.4	29	23.6
Aged 35 or older	218	7.5	61	8.3	40	6.6	25	5.5	20	6.6	20	11.1

Note: Numbers by ethnicity will not add to total because not all ethnicities are shown.
Source: U.S. Bureau of the Census, Asians and Pacific Islanders in the United States, 1990 Census of Population, 1990 CP-3-5, 1993; calculations by New Strategist

College Enrollment of Asians by Sex, 1995

(number of Asians enrolled in institutions of higher education by level of study and sex, and Asian enrollment as a percent of total enrollment, fall 1995; numbers in thousands)

	total		men		women	
	number	percent of total enrollment	number	percent of total men enrolled	number	percent of total women enrolled
Total enrolled	**797**	**5.8%**	**393**	**2.8%**	**404**	**2.9%**
Undergraduate	692	5.8	338	2.8	354	3.0
Graduate	76	4.9	39	2.5	37	2.4
First-professional	30	10.2	16	5.6	13	4.6

Source: National Center for Education Statistics, Digest of Education Statistics 1997, *NCES 98-015, 1997; calculations by New Strategist*

Bachelor's, Master's, and Doctoral Degrees Earned by Asians by Field of Study, 1994–95

(number and percent of bachelor's, master's, and doctoral degrees earned by Asians, by field of study, 1994–95)

	bachelor's		master's		doctoral	
	number	percent	number	percent	number	percent
Total degrees	**60,478**	**5.2%**	**16,842**	**4.2%**	**2,690**	**6.1%**
Agriculture and natural resources	424	2.1	129	3.0	71	5.6
Architecture and related programs	704	8.0	282	7.2	4	2.8
Area, ethnic, and cultural studies	558	9.8	86	5.2	5	2.7
Biological and life sciences	7,208	12.9	431	8.0	407	8.8
Business, management, and admin. services	13,174	5.6	4,924	5.2	82	5.9
Communications	1,378	2.9	171	3.3	15	4.7
Communications technologies	16	2.3	14	3.0	–	–
Computer and information sciences	2,425	9.9	1,329	12.9	92	10.4
Construction trades	2	1.8	–	–	–	–
Education	1,381	1.3	1,706	1.7	151	2.2
Engineering	6,939	11.1	2,732	9.6	635	10.4
Engineering-related technologies	714	4.6	46	4.1	2	11.1
English language and literature	1,755	3.4	192	2.4	35	2.2
Foreign languages and literature	591	4.3	112	3.6	33	3.6
Health professions and related sciences	3,563	4.5	1,590	5.1	153	7.4
Home economics	459	3.0	76	2.7	9	2.3
Law and legal studies	66	3.2	59	2.3	1	1.1
Liberal arts and sciences	1,091	3.3	39	1.5	2	2.2
Library science	–	–	146	2.9	5	9.1
Mathematics	984	7.2	257	6.1	95	7.7
Mechanics and repairers	2	3.0	–	–	–	–
Multi- and interdisciplinary studies	1,478	5.7	75	3.1	14	5.9
Parks, recreation, leisure, fitness	183	1.4	20	1.1	6	4.0
Philosophy and religion	346	4.8	27	2.0	13	2.6
Physical sciences	1,387	7.2	307	5.3	438	9.8
Precision production trades	12	3.4	–	–	–	–
Protective services	420	1.7	33	1.9	3	11.5
Psychology	3,404	4.7	310	2.2	104	2.7
Public administration and services	467	2.5	593	2.5	16	2.9
R.O.T.C. and military sciences	1	3.7	7	5.6	–	–
Social sciences and history	6,626	5.2	485	3.3	196	5.3
Theological studies and religious vocations	151	2.7	230	4.4	51	3.2
Transportation and material moving	101	2.7	18	2.2	–	–
Visual and performing arts	2,468	5.1	416	4.0	52	4.8

Note: (–) means no degrees were awarded.
Source: National Center for Education Statistics, Digest of Education Statistics 1997, *NCES 98-015, 1997; calculations by New Strategist*

First-Professional Degrees Earned by Asians by Field of Study, 1994–95

(number and percent of first-professional degrees earned by Asians by field of study, 1994-95)

	number	percent
Total degrees	**6,397**	**8.4%**
Dentistry (D.D.S. or D.M.D.)	589	15.1
Medicine (M.D.)	2,485	16.0
Optometry (O.D.)	157	13.2
Osteopathic medicine (D.O.)	185	10.0
Pharmacy (Pharm. D.)	434	19.2
Podiatry (Pod. D., D.P., or D.P.M.)	57	10.5
Veterinary medicine (D.V.M.)	37	1.7
Chiropractic medicine (D.C. or D.C.M.)	125	4.2
Law (LL.B. or J.D.)	2,011	5.1
Theology (M.Div., M.H.L., B.D., or Ord.)	317	5.3
Other	–	–

Note: (–) means no degrees were awarded.
Source: National Center for Education Statistics, Digest of Education Statistics 1997, *NCES 98-015, 1997; calculations by New Strategist*

Asians: Health

Asians are healthier than average and can expect to live longer.

For all but a few health conditions, Asians fare much better than the average American. Infant mortality and death rates for accidents, heart disease, and cancer are all far lower for Asians than for the population as a whole. The incidence of tuberculosis is above average for Asians, however. Many Asians are immigrants living in cramped quarters where tuberculosis spreads easily. Because Asians are more metropolitan than other racial or ethnic groups in the U.S., they are more likely to live in counties with poor air quality.

More than 167,000 babies were born to Asian American women in 1996, or just over 4 percent of all babies born that year. This proportion should rise to 7 percent by 2020. Asians accounted for 70 percent of all births in Hawaii in 1996 and for 11 percent of those in California.

The death rate for Asians is lower than that for the total population. Consequently, life expectancy for Asians is well above average. At birth, Asian males can expect to live to age 80, or seven years longer than average. Asian females can expect to live to age 85, five years longer than average. Even at age 65, Asian life expectancy remains three to four years greater than the life expectancy of the average American.

■ The Asian health advantage could diminish if immigrants with low levels of education and income become a bigger share of the Asian American population as a whole.

Asians live longer

(life expectancy of Asians and total persons at birth, 1996; in years)

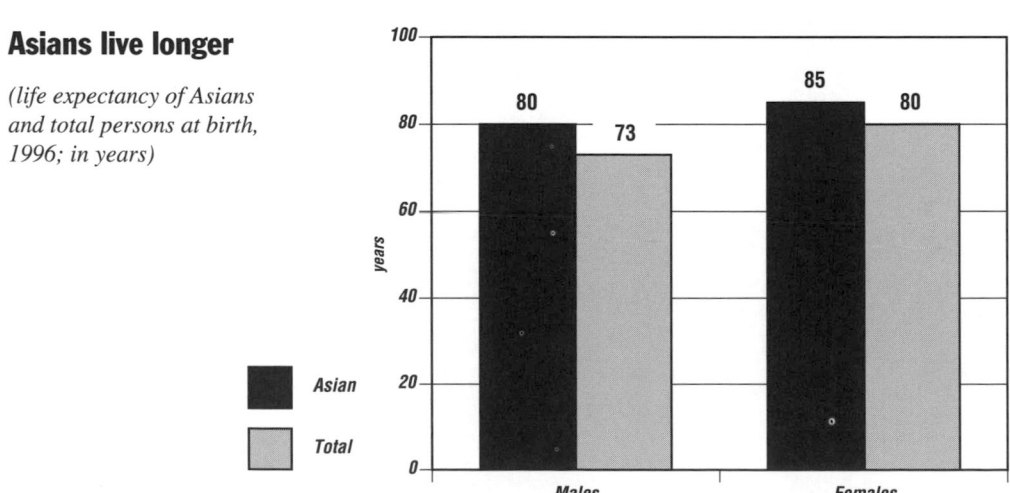

Health Indicators for Asians, 1993 and 1994

(selected indicators of total population and Asian health status, and index of Asian health indicators to total, 1993 and 1994)

	total population indicator	Asian indicator	index
Infant mortality rate (deaths before age 1 per 1,000 live births), 1993	8.4	5.8	69
Total deaths per 100,000 population, 1993	513.3	295.9	58
Motor vehicle crash deaths per 100,000 population, 1993	16.0	9.5	59
Work-related injury deaths per 100,000 people aged 16 or older, 1994	3.3	2.9	88
Suicides per 100,000 population, 1993	11.3	6.4	57
Homicides per 100,000 population, 1993	10.7	6.4	60
Lung cancer deaths per 100,000 population, 1993	39.3	18.5	47
Female breast cancer deaths per 100,000 population, 1993	21.5	9.5	44
Cardiovascular disease deaths per 100,000 population, 1993	181.8	109.7	60
Heart disease deaths per 100,000 population, 1993	145.3	79.0	54
Stroke deaths per 100,000 population, 1993	26.5	24.5	92
Reported incidence of AIDS per 100,000 population, 1994*	26.9	6.6	25
Reported incidence of tuberculosis per 100,000 population, 1994*	9.4	45.3	482
Reported incidence of syphilis per 100,000 population, 1994*	8.1	0.9	11
Prevalence of low birth weight, as percent of total live births, 1994	7.3	6.8	93
Births to girls aged 10 to 17, as percent of total live births, 1994	5.3	2.2	42
Percent of mothers without care, first trimester of pregnancy, 1994	19.8	20.3	103
Percent under age 18 living in poverty, 1994	21.8	–	–
Percent living in counties exceeding U.S. air quality standards, 1994	24.9	44.4	178

* Data are for the non-Hispanic Asian population.
Note: (–) means data are not available. The index for each indicator is calculated by dividing the Asian figure by the total population figure and multiplying by 100. For example, the index of 69 in the first row indicates that Asian infant mortality is 31 percent below the rate for all infants.
Source: National Center for Health Statistics, Health Status Indicators by Race and Hispanic Origin, *Healthy People 2000 Review, 1995–96; calculations by New Strategist*

Births to Asian Women by Age, 1996

(number and percent distribution of births to Asian women, by age, 1996)

	number	*percent*
Total births	**167,444**	**100.0%**
Under age 15	237	0.1
Aged 15 to 19	8,853	5.3
Aged 20 to 24	27,672	16.5
Aged 25 to 29	51,161	30.6
Aged 30 to 34	50,617	30.2
Aged 35 to 39	23,521	14.0
Aged 40 or older	5,383	3.2

Source: National Center for Health Statistics, Births and Deaths: United States, 1996, *Monthly Vital Statistics Report, Vol. 46, No.1, Supplement 2, 1997; calculations by New Strategist*

Births to Asian Teenagers and Unmarried Women by Ethnicity, 1995

(percent of Asian births to women under age 20, and percent to unmarried women, by ethnicity; 1995)

	percent of births to women	
	under age 20	unmarried
Total Asian births	**5.6%**	**16.3%**
Chinese	0.9	7.9
Filipino	6.2	19.5
Japanese	2.5	10.8
Hawaiian	19.1	49.0
Other	6.3	16.2

Source: National Center for Health Statistics, Advance Report of Final Natality Statistics: 1995, *Monthly Vital Statistics Report, Vol. 45, No.11(S), 1997; calculations by New Strategist*

Births to Asian Women by Age and Ethnicity, 1992

(number and percent distribution of births to Asian women, by age and ethnicity, 1992)

	total	Chinese	Filipino	Japanese	Korean	Asian Indian	Vietnamese
Total births	**108,295**	**19,497**	**24,482**	**7,383**	**8,772**	**9,173**	**10,870**
Under age 15	162	–	17	1	–	3	6
Aged 15 to 19	5,781	144	1,353	194	110	135	639
Aged 20 to 24	18,841	1,426	4,474	581	883	1,599	2,582
Aged 25 to 29	33,309	6,122	6,959	1,819	3,499	3,821	3,060
Aged 30 to 34	32,002	7,648	6,816	2,964	3,222	2,648	2,646
Aged 35 to 39	15,098	3,561	4,046	1,555	933	849	1,500
Aged 40 or older	3,102	596	817	269	125	118	437
Percent distribution by ethnicity							
Total births	**100.0%**	**18.0%**	**22.6%**	**6.8%**	**8.1%**	**8.5%**	**10.0%**
Under age 15	100.0	0.0	10.5	0.6	0.0	1.9	3.7
Aged 15 to 19	100.0	2.5	23.4	3.4	1.9	2.3	11.1
Aged 20 to 24	100.0	7.6	23.7	3.1	4.7	8.5	13.7
Aged 25 to 29	100.0	18.4	20.9	5.5	10.5	11.5	9.2
Aged 30 to 34	100.0	23.9	21.3	9.3	10.1	8.3	8.3
Aged 35 to 39	100.0	23.6	26.8	10.3	6.2	5.6	9.9
Aged 40 or older	100.0	19.2	26.3	8.7	4.0	3.8	14.1
Percent distribution by age							
Total births	**100.0**	**100.0**	**100.0**	**100.0**	**100.0**	**100.0**	**100.0**
Under age 15	0.1	0.0	0.1	0.0	0.0	0.0	0.1
Aged 15 to 19	5.3	0.7	5.5	2.6	1.3	1.5	5.9
Aged 20 to 24	17.4	7.3	18.3	7.9	10.1	17.4	23.8
Aged 25 to 29	30.8	31.4	28.4	24.6	39.9	41.7	28.2
Aged 30 to 34	29.6	39.2	27.8	40.1	36.7	28.9	24.3
Aged 35 to 39	13.9	18.3	16.5	21.1	10.6	9.3	13.8
Aged 40 or older	2.9	3.1	3.3	3.6	1.4	1.3	4.0

Note: Asian births by ethnicity are for the seven reporting states—California, Hawaii, Illinois, New Jersey, New York, Texas, and Washington. Together they account for 72 percent of all Asian and Pacific Islander births. Numbers will not add to total because not all Asian ethnicities are shown. (–) means sample is too small to make a reliable estimate.
Source: National Center for Health Statistics, Birth Characteristics for Asian or Pacific Islander Subgroups, 1992, Monthly Vital Statistics Reports, *Vol. 43, No. 10 Supplement, 1995; calculations by New Strategist*

Births to Asian Women by State and Ethnicity, 1992

(number and percent distribution of Asian births by state and ethnicity, for the seven reporting states; 1992)

	total	Chinese	Filipino	Japanese	Korean	Asian Indian	Vietnamese
Total, 7 reporting states	**108,295**	**19,497**	**24,482**	**7,383**	**8,772**	**9,173**	**10,870**
California	59,519	11,673	15,669	3,497	4,449	3,375	7,410
Hawaii	13,258	737	3,700	2,421	422	10	179
Illinois	5,367	654	955	260	527	1,255	252
New Jersey	5,384	889	1,068	269	576	1,442	181
New York	13,252	4,087	1,376	487	1,512	2,075	370
Texas	6,953	1,032	801	175	748	866	1,817
Washington	4,562	425	913	274	538	150	661
Percent distribution by ethnicity							
Total, 7 reporting states	**100.0%**	**18.0%**	**22.6%**	**6.8%**	**8.1%**	**8.5%**	**10.0%**
California	100.0	19.6	26.3	5.9	7.5	5.7	12.4
Hawaii	100.0	5.6	27.9	18.3	3.2	0.1	1.4
Illinois	100.0	12.2	17.8	4.8	9.8	23.4	4.7
New Jersey	100.0	16.5	19.8	5.0	10.7	26.8	3.4
New York	100.0	30.8	10.4	3.7	11.4	15.7	2.8
Texas	100.0	14.8	11.5	2.5	10.8	12.5	26.1
Washington	100.0	9.3	20.0	6.0	11.8	3.3	14.5
Percent distribution by state							
Total, 7 reporting states	**100.0%**	**100.0%**	**100.0%**	**100.0%**	**100.0%**	**100.0%**	**100.0%**
California	55.0	59.9	64.0	47.4	50.7	36.8	68.2
Hawaii	12.2	3.8	15.1	32.8	4.8	0.1	1.6
Illinois	5.0	3.4	3.9	3.5	6.0	13.7	2.3
New Jersey	5.0	4.6	4.4	3.6	6.6	15.7	1.7
New York	12.2	21.0	5.6	6.6	17.2	22.6	3.4
Texas	6.4	5.3	3.3	2.4	8.5	9.4	16.7
Washington	4.2	2.2	3.7	3.7	6.1	1.6	6.1

Note: The seven reporting states accounted for 72 percent of all Asian births in 1992; number of births by ethnic group will not add to total Asian births by state because not all ethnic groups are shown.
Source: National Center for Health Statistics, Birth Characteristics for Asian or Pacific Islander Subgroups, 1992, *Monthly Vital Statistics Reports, Vol. 43, No. 10 Supplement, 1995; calculations by New Strategist*

Births to Asian Women by State, 1996

(number and percent distribution of Asian births by state, and Asian births as a percent of total births by state, 1996)

	number	percent	Asian share of total births
United States	**167,444**	**100.0%**	**4.3%**
Alabama	577	0.3	0.9
Alaska	400	0.2	3.9
Arizona	1,504	0.9	1.9
Arkansas	338	0.2	0.9
California	58,420	34.9	10.8
Colorado	1,575	0.9	2.8
Connecticut	1,227	0.7	2.8
Delaware	215	0.1	2.1
District of Columbia	147	0.1	1.8
Florida	3,869	2.3	2.0
Georgia	2,115	1.3	1.8
Hawaii	12,853	7.7	70.1
Idaho	247	0.1	1.3
Illinois	6,043	3.6	3.3
Indiana	920	0.5	1.1
Iowa	748	0.4	2.0
Kansas	894	0.5	2.2
Kentucky	449	0.3	0.9
Louisiana	1,083	0.6	1.6
Maine	145	0.1	1.1
Maryland	2,417	1.4	3.5
Massachusetts	3,548	2.1	4.4
Michigan	2,561	1.5	1.9
Minnesota	2,677	1.6	4.2
Mississippi	376	0.2	0.9
Missouri	1,143	0.7	1.5
Montana	108	0.1	1.0
Nebraska	413	0.2	1.8
Nevada	1,381	0.8	5.3
New Hampshire	161	0.1	1.1
New Jersey	7,166	4.3	6.3
New Mexico	391	0.2	1.4
New York	17,747	10.6	6.5
North Carolina	1,999	1.2	1.9
North Dakota	103	0.1	1.2

(continued)

(continued from previous page)

	number	percent	Asian share of total births
Ohio	1,959	1.2%	1.3%
Oklahoma	778	0.5	1.7
Oregon	1,655	1.0	3.8
Pennsylvania	3,310	2.0	2.2
Rhode Island	396	0.2	3.2
South Carolina	635	0.4	1.2
South Dakota	96	0.1	0.9
Tennessee	1,020	0.6	1.4
Texas	8,872	5.3	2.7
Utah	1,140	0.7	2.8
Vermont	53	0.0	0.8
Virginia	3,949	2.4	4.3
Washington	5,529	3.3	6.9
West Virginia	141	0.1	0.7
Wisconsin	1,887	1.1	2.8
Wyoming	62	0.0	1.0

Source: National Center for Health Statistics, Births and Deaths: United States, 1996, *Monthly Vital Statistics Report, Vol. 46, No. 1, Supplement 2, 1997; calculations by New Strategist*

Projections of Births to Asian Women, 1998 to 2020

(number of births to Asian women, and Asian births as a percent of total births, 1998–2020; numbers in thousands)

	number	Asian share of total births
1998	176	4.5%
1999	181	4.6
2000	186	4.8
2001	191	4.9
2002	196	5.0
2003	202	5.1
2004	207	5.2
2005	212	5.3
2006	218	5.4
2007	224	5.5
2008	230	5.6
2009	236	5.6
2010	243	5.7
2011	249	5.8
2012	256	5.9
2013	262	6.0
2014	269	6.1
2015	275	6.2
2016	282	6.3
2017	288	6.4
2018	295	6.5
2019	302	6.6
2020	308	6.7

Source: Bureau of the Census, Population Projections of the United States, by Age, Sex, Race, and Hispanic Origin: 1995 to 2050, *Current Population Reports, P25-1130, 1996; calculations by New Strategist*

Asians with Disabilities by Type of Disability, 1994–95

(number and percent distribution of Asians with a disability by type of disability, 1994–95; numbers in thousands)

	number	percent
Total Asians	**6,184**	**100.0%**
With any disability	903	14.6
Severe	444	7.2
Not severe	459	7.4
Uses wheelchair	28	0.5
Used cane/crutch/walker for six or more months	75	1.2
Difficulty with or unable to perform one or more functional activities	557	9.0
Difficulty with or unable to perform one or more ADLs	132	2.1
Difficulty with or unable to perform one or more IADLs	218	3.5
Needs personal assistance with an ADL or an IADL	148	2.4

Note: Functional activities are seeing, hearing, speaking, lifting, climbing stairs, and walking. An ADL is an activity of daily living and includes getting around inside the house, getting in and out of bed or chair, bathing, dressing, eating, and using the toilet. An IADL is an instrumental activity of daily living and includes going outside alone, keeping track of money and bills, preparing meals, doing light housework, taking prescribed medicines, and using the telephone.
Source: Bureau of the Census, Internet web site, http://www.census.gov

Life Expectancy of Asians at Birth and Age 65, 1998 to 2020

(average number of years of life remaining at birth and at age 65 for Asians by sex, selected years 1998–2020; difference between Asian and total life expectancy at birth and at age 65 by sex, 1998 and 2020)

	life expectancy (years)	
	males	*females*
AT BIRTH		
1998	79.5	85.0
2000	79.5	85.0
2005	79.8	85.2
2010	80.2	85.5
2015	80.6	85.8
2020	81.1	86.2
Life expectancy of Asians minus		
life expectancy of total Americans		
1998	6.7	5.4
2020	8.1	6.5
AT AGE 65		
1998	18.9	23.0
2000	19.0	23.0
2005	19.2	23.2
2010	19.5	23.4
2015	19.8	23.6
2020	20.1	23.9
Life expectancy of Asians minus		
life expectancy of total Americans		
1998	3.2	3.7
2020	4.2	4.4

Source: Bureau of the Census, Population Projections of the United States, by Age, Sex, Race, and Hispanic Origin: 1995 to 2050, *Current Population Reports, P25-1130, 1996; calculations by New Strategist*

Asians: Households

Asian households are more likely to be headed by married couples than the average American household.

Because many of the Asians immigrating to the U.S. are young adults, Asian householders are much younger than average. Only 10 percent were aged 65 or older in 1990, just half the share among households nationally.

Partly because of their younger age, Asian householders are more likely to be married couples than householders in the nation as a whole—61 versus 54 percent. While only about one in four households nationally is a nuclear family (a married couple with children under age 18), the proportion is 54 percent for Asian Indian households. Because married couples are more common among Asians, Asian children are more likely to live with both parents than the average American child, 83 versus 72 percent.

Asians are more likely to be married than men and women in the U.S. as a whole. Overall, 60 percent of Asian men and women aged 15 or older are married. This proportion peaks at 70 percent among Asian Indian women and 65 percent among Asian Indian men.

■ Asian households are more likely to be nuclear families than the average American household because many Asians are immigrants from countries with traditional lifestyles. As the children and grandchildren of immigrants adopt the more freewheeling American lifestyle, their family structure is likely to change.

Asian households are more traditional

(percent distribution of Asian and total households by type, 1996)

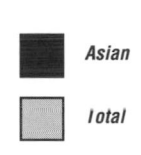

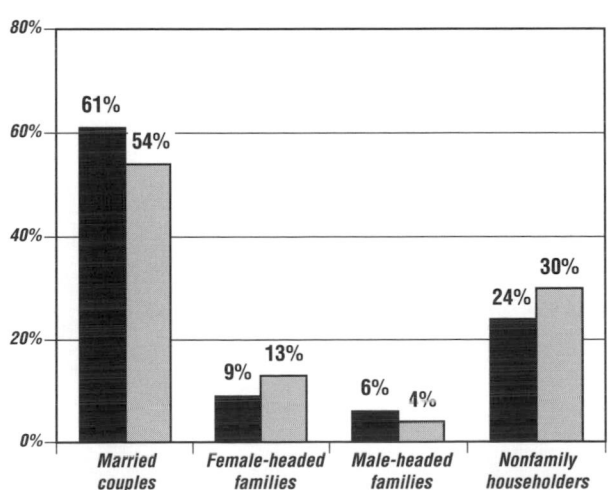

Asian Households by Age of Householder, 1990

(number and percent distribution of Asian households by age of householder, 1990; numbers in thousands)

	number	*percent*
Total households	**2,020**	**100.0%**
Under age 25	111	5.5
Aged 25 to 34	516	25.5
Aged 35 to 44	592	29.3
Aged 45 to 54	384	19.0
Aged 55 to 64	220	10.9
Aged 65 to 74	132	6.5
Aged 75 or older	66	3.3

Source: Bureau of the Census, 1990 census STF3 CD-ROM, and TGE Demographics, Inc., Honeoye Falls, New York

Asian Households by Household Type, 1996

(number and percent distribution of Asian households by type, 1996; numbers in thousands)

	number	percent
Total households	**2,777**	**100.0%**
Family households	**2,124**	**76.5**
Married-couple families	1,691	60.9
Female householder, no spouse present	258	9.3
Male householder, no spouse present	172	6.2
Nonfamily households	**653**	**23.5**
Female householder	319	11.5
Male householder	333	12.0

Source: Bureau of the Census, The Asian and Pacific Islander Population in the United States: March 1996 (Update), *detailed tables for Current Population Reports P20-503, PPL-77, 1997; calculations by New Strategist*

Asian Households by Household Type and Ethnicity, 1990

(number and percent distribution of Asian households by type of household and ethnicity of house-holder, 1990; numbers in thousands)

	total	Chinese	Filipino	Japanese	Asian Indian	Korean	Vietnamese
TOTAL, NUMBER	**2,020**	**509**	**356**	**316**	**234**	**202**	**141**
Family households	**1,578**	**390**	**293**	**208**	**193**	**163**	**118**
With children under age 18	938	209	176	87	132	102	82
Without children under age 18	640	181	117	121	61	61	36
Married-couple families	**1,295**	**331**	**231**	**174**	**175**	**137**	**85**
With children under age 18	816	190	148	76	126	90	65
Without children under age 18	479	141	83	98	49	47	20
Female householder,							
no spouse present	**186**	**37**	**44**	**25**	**9**	**18**	**19**
With children under age 18	94	14	22	8	5	10	12
Without children under age 18	92	23	22	17	4	8	7
Male householder,							
no spouse present	**97**	**22**	**18**	**9**	**9**	**8**	**14**
Nonfamily households	**443**	**120**	**63**	**108**	**41**	**39**	**22**
People living alone	325	90	44	88	28	29	14
TOTAL, PERCENT	**100.0%**	**100.0%**	**100.0%**	**100.0%**	**100.0%**	**100.0%**	**100.0%**
Family households	**78.1**	**76.6**	**82.3**	**65.8**	**82.5**	**80.7**	**83.7**
With children under age 18	46.4	41.1	49.4	27.5	56.4	50.5	58.2
Without children under age 18	31.7	35.6	32.9	38.3	26.1	30.2	25.5
Married-couple families	**64.1**	**65.0**	**64.9**	**55.1**	**74.8**	**67.8**	**60.3**
With children under age 18	40.4	37.3	41.6	24.1	53.8	44.6	46.1
Without children under age 18	23.7	27.7	23.3	31.0	20.9	23.3	14.2
Female householder,							
no spouse present	**9.2**	**7.3**	**12.4**	**7.9**	**3.8**	**8.9**	**13.5**
With children under age 18	4.7	2.8	6.2	2.5	2.1	5.0	8.5
Without children under age 18	4.6	4.5	6.2	5.4	1.7	4.0	5.0
Male householder,							
no spouse present	**4.8**	**4.3**	**5.1**	**2.8**	**3.8**	**4.0**	**9.9**
Nonfamily households	**21.9**	**23.6**	**17.7**	**34.2**	**17.5**	**19.3**	**15.6**
People living alone	16.1	17.7	12.4	27.8	12.0	14.4	9.9

Note: Numbers by ethnicity will not add to total because not all ethnicities are shown.
Source: Bureau of the Census, Asians and Pacific Islanders in the United States, *1990 Census of Population, 1990 CP-3-5, 1993; calculations by New Strategist*

Asian Households by Size, 1996

(number and percent distribution of Asian households by size, 1996; numbers in thousands)

	number	percent
Total households	**2,777**	**100.0%**
One person	483	17.4
Two persons	655	23.6
Three persons	517	18.6
Four persons	628	22.6
Five persons	292	10.5
Six persons	111	4.0
Seven or more persons	89	3.2

Source: Bureau of the Census, The Asian and Pacific Islander Population in the United States: March 1996 (Update), *detailed tables for Current Population Reports P20-503, PPL-77, 1997; calculations by New Strategist*

Living Arrangements of Asian Children, 1996

(number and percent distribution of Asian children under age 18 by living arrangement, 1996; numbers in thousands)

	number	percent
Total children	**2,886**	**100.0%**
Living with two parents	2,381	82.5
Living with one parent	465	16.1
Mother only	369	12.8
Father only	95	3.3
Living with neither parent	40	1.4

Source: Bureau of the Census, The Asian and Pacific Islander Population in the United States: March 1996 (Update), *detailed tables for Current Population Reports P20-503, PPL-77, 1997; calculations by New Strategist*

Marital Status of Asians by Sex and Ethnicity, 1990

(number and percent distribution of Asians aged 15 or older by sex, marital status, and ethnicity, 1990; numbers in thousands)

	total	*Chinese*	*Filipino*	*Japanese*	*Asian Indian*	*Korean*	*Vietnamese*
Men, number	**2,649**	**656**	**490**	**329**	**322**	**253**	**231**
Never married	984	234	171	121	101	89	118
Married	1,519	392	286	185	209	153	101
Separated	34	6	8	3	3	3	5
Divorced	79	15	18	14	6	6	5
Widowed	33	9	8	6	3	2	2
Men, percent	**100.0%**	**100.0%**	**100.0%**	**100.0%**	**100.0%**	**100.0%**	**100.0%**
Never married	37.1	35.7	34.9	36.8	31.4	35.2	51.1
Married	57.3	59.8	58.4	56.2	64.9	60.5	43.7
Separated	1.3	0.9	1.6	0.9	0.9	1.2	2.2
Divorced	3.0	2.3	3.7	4.3	1.9	2.4	2.2
Widowed	1.2	1.4	1.6	1.8	0.9	0.8	0.9
Women, number	**2,864**	**675**	**610**	**403**	**266**	**340**	**205**
Never married	769	189	164	95	58	81	72
Married	1,709	404	358	241	187	211	108
Separated	50	8	13	5	3	5	6
Divorced	132	22	31	26	6	18	8
Widowed	203	51	43	36	13	24	12
Women, percent	**100.0%**	**100.0%**	**100.0%**	**100.0%**	**100.0%**	**100.0%**	**100.0%**
Never married	26.9	28.0	26.9	23.6	21.8	23.8	35.1
Married	59.7	59.9	58.7	59.8	70.3	62.1	52.7
Separated	1.8	1.2	2.1	1.2	1.1	1.5	2.9
Divorced	4.6	3.3	5.1	6.5	2.3	5.3	3.4
Widowed	7.1	7.6	7.0	8.9	4.9	7.1	5.9

Note: Numbers by ethnicity will not add to total because not all ethnicities are shown.
Source: Bureau of the Census, Asians and Pacific Islanders in the United States, 1990 Census of Population, 1990 CP-3-5, 1993; calculations by New Strategist

Asians: Housing

Half of Asian householders own their home.

Asian Americans own some of the most highly valued homes in the nation, in large part because so many live in the two states with the most expensive housing—Hawaii and California. Overall, homes owned by Asians had a median value of $178,300 in 1990 compared to a median value of $78,300 for the average American home. But Asians are less likely to own a home than the average American. Just 53 percent of Asian householders own their homes, versus a homeownership rate of 65 percent for all Americans. Although Asians are less likely to own homes than the average American, they are more likely to be homeowners than are blacks, Hispanics, and Native Americans.

As of 1990, the largest number of Asian households in any one metropolitan area was in Los Angeles–Long Beach, California, followed by New York City, Honolulu, and San Francisco. These four metropolitan areas accounted for 35 percent of all Asian households in the nation. Among the 25 metropolitan areas with the most Asian households, the homeownership rate was highest in Nassau-Suffolk, New York, at 77 percent. The value of Asian homes was highest in San Francisco, with a median of $304,100.

■ The Asian homeownership rate could fall in the years ahead if immigrants from poor Asian countries such as Vietnam become a larger share of the overall Asian population.

Most Asian households are in the West

(percent distribution of Asian households by region, 1995)

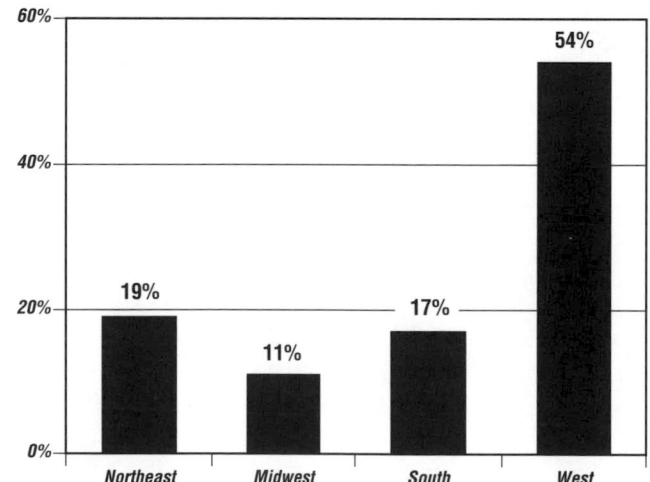

Region of Residence and Metropolitan Status of Housing Units Occupied by Asians, 1995

(number, percent distribution, and percent of housing units occupied by Asians, by regional, metropolitan, and homeownership status, 1995; numbers in thousands)

	total		owner			renter		
	number	percent distrib.	number	percent distrib.	percent of total	number	percent distrib.	percent of total
Total occupied housing units	**2,430**	**100.0%**	**1,295**	**100.0%**	**53.3%**	**1,135**	**100.0%**	**46.7%**
Home built in past four years	152	6.3	123	9.5	80.9	30	2.6	19.7
Mobile home	17	0.7	12	0.9	70.6	5	0.4	29.4
Northeast	466	19.2	230	17.8	49.4	236	20.8	50.6
Midwest	256	10.5	129	10.0	50.4	127	11.2	49.6
South	406	16.7	217	16.8	53.4	189	16.7	46.6
West	1,302	53.6	719	55.5	55.2	583	51.4	44.8
In metropolitan areas	2,378	97.9	1,264	97.6	52.0	1,114	98.1	45.8
In central cities	1,121	46.1	439	33.9	39.2	682	60.1	60.8
In suburbs	1,257	51.7	825	63.7	65.6	432	38.1	34.4
Outside metropolitan areas	52	2.1	31	2.4	59.6	21	1.9	40.4

Source: Bureau of the Census, American Housing Survey for the United States in 1995, *Current Housing Reports, H150/95, 1997; calculations by New Strategist*

Asian Homeownership in the 25 Metropolitan Areas with the Most Asian Households, 1990

(number of Asian households, percent of total households that are Asian, percent of Asian households that are owner occupied, and median value of Asian owner-occupied houses, in the U.S. and in the 25 metropolitan areas with the most Asian households, ranked alphabetically, 1990; numbers in thousands)

	number	Asian share of total households	owner occupied percent	owner occupied median value
Total Asian households	**2,014**	**2.2%**	**52.2%**	**$178,300**
Anaheim–Santa Ana, CA	64	7.7	60.2	256,300
Atlanta, GA	14	1.3	46.7	98,500
Bergen-Passaic, NJ	18	3.9	52.8	247,700
Boston, MA	27	2.5	39.2	203,900
Chicago, IL	66	3.0	52.6	140,000
Dallas, TX	20	2.1	43.9	92,300
Detroit, MI	16	1.0	59.1	111,000
Honolulu, HI	155	58.5	62.2	274,000
Houston, TX	36	3.1	55.2	68,100
Los Angeles–Long Beach, CA	277	9.3	51.3	246,300
Middlesex–Somerset–Hunterdon, NJ	15	4.2	66.5	194,700
Minneapolis–St. Paul, MN-WI	15	1.6	41.7	92,500
Nassau-Suffolk, NY	15	1.7	76.8	224,400
New York, NY	167	5.1	32.6	220,700
Newark, NJ	14	2.2	61.2	221,900
Oakland, CA	77	9.9	61.3	240,600
Philadelphia, PA	28	1.6	56.1	121,000
Riverside–San Bernardino, CA	26	3.0	64.6	162,500
Sacramento, CA	32	5.8	55.4	140,000
San Diego, CA	48	5.4	53.2	177,200
San Francisco, CA	96	15.0	50.7	304,100
San Jose, CA	70	13.4	60.4	282,000
Seattle, WA	40	5.1	54.7	134,200
Stockton, CA	14	8.8	47.4	111,600
Washington, DC-MD-VA	56	3.8	61.1	183,600

Source: Bureau of the Census, Housing in Metropolitan Areas—Asian or Pacific Islander Households, Statistical Brief, SB/05-6, 1995; calculations by New Strategist

Asians: Income

Asian incomes fell in the first half of the 1990s, but remain above average.

The median income of Asian households fell 9 percent between 1990 and 1995 as the recession cut into earnings and growing numbers of Asian immigrants depressed incomes. Despite the decline, the median household income of Asians is significantly higher than that of the average household because so many Asian households have two or more earners.

Twenty percent of Asian households had incomes of $75,000 or more in 1995. Asian couples had the highest incomes, with a median of over $50,000. More than one in four Asian couples had incomes of $75,000 or more.

Asian men who worked full-time earned a median of $35,788 in 1996, up 9 percent since 1990 after adjusting for inflation. Asian women earned a median of $26,313, down slightly since 1990. Asian men and women earn slightly more than the average full-time worker because they are better educated.

Because many Asians are recent immigrants, poverty is more common among Asians than among the population as a whole.

■ The future affluence of the Asian population depends on immigration patterns. If growing numbers of immigrants arrive from countries with little education, such as Vietnam, Asian incomes could drop. But if a growing share hail from countries with high educational levels, such as India, then Asian incomes could rise.

Asian households have higher-than-average incomes

(percent distribution of Asian households by household income, 1995)

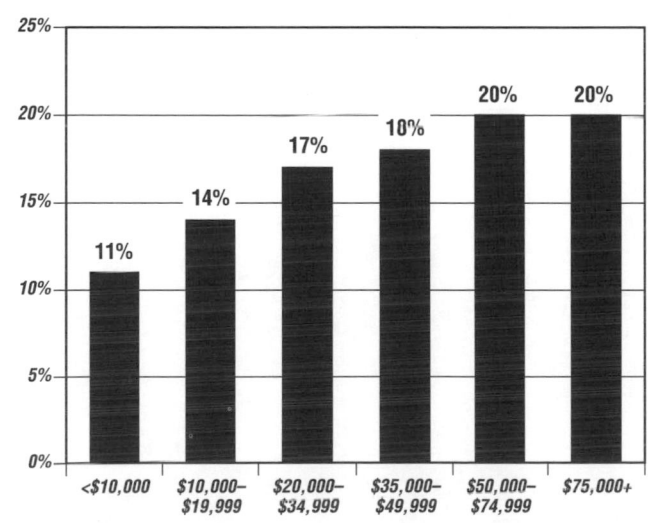

Median Income of Asian Households, 1988 to 1996

(median income of Asian households, and ratio of Asian to total households' median income, 1988–96; percent change in income and ratio, selected years; in 1996 dollars)

	median income	ratio Asian/total
1996	$43,276	1.22
1995	41,813	1.19
1994	42,858	1.25
1993	41,638	1.23
1992	42,274	1.23
1991	41,989	1.21
1990	46,158	1.28
1989	45,681	1.25
1988	42,795	1.19
Percent change		
1990–1996	–6.2%	–4.7%
1988–1996	1.1	2.5

Note: Ratios are calculated by dividing median income of Asian households by median of total households.
Source: Bureau of the Census, unpublished tables from the 1997 Current Population Survey; calculations by New Strategist

Income Distribution of Asian Households, 1995

(number and percent distribution of Asian households by household income, 1995; households in thousands as of 1996)

	number	percent
Total households	**2,777**	**100.0%**
Under $10,000	308	11.1
$10,000 to $19,999	380	13.7
$20,000 to $34,999	480	17.3
$35,000 to $49,999	494	17.8
$50,000 to $74,999	558	20.1
$75,000 or more	555	20.0
Median income	$40,613	–

Source: Bureau of the Census, The Asian and Pacific Islander Population in the United States: March 1996 (Update), *detailed tables for Current Population Reports P20-503, PPL-77, 1997; calculations by New Strategist*

Income Distribution of Asian Families by Family Type, 1995

(number and percent distribution of Asian families by family income and family type, 1995; families in thousands as of 1996)

	total	married couples	female householder, no spouse present	male householder, no spouse present
Total, number	**2,125**	**1,692**	**260**	**173**
Under $10,000	166	93	57	15
$10,000 to $19,999	259	188	54	17
$20,000 to $34,999	342	257	41	43
$35,000 to $49,999	383	293	47	43
$50,000 to $74,999	482	396	45	41
$75,000 or more	495	465	16	15
Median income	$46,356	$50,626	$26,552	$38,817
Total, percent	**100.0%**	**100.0%**	**100.0%**	**100.0%**
Under $10,000	7.8	5.5	21.9	8.7
$10,000 to $19,999	12.2	11.1	20.7	9.6
$20,000 to $34,999	16.1	15.2	15.9	24.9
$35,000 to $49,999	18.0	17.3	18.2	24.7
$50,000 to $74,999	22.7	23.4	17.2	23.8
$75,000 or more	23.3	27.5	6.2	8.5

Source: Bureau of the Census, The Asian and Pacific Islander Population in the United States: March 1996 (Update), *detailed tables for Current Population Reports P20-503, PPL-77, 1997; calculations by New Strategist*

Income Distribution of Asians by Work Status and Sex, 1995

(number and percent distribution of Asians aged 15 or older with income, by income, work status, and sex, 1995; persons in thousands as of 1996)

	total persons		year-round, full-time workers	
	men	*women*	*men*	*women*
Total with income, number	**3,095**	**3,025**	**1,882**	**1,304**
Under $10,000	752	1,240	58	77
$10,000 to $19,999	644	690	390	370
$20,000 to $34,999	786	620	597	463
$35,000 to $49,999	415	290	373	241
$50,000 to $74,999	288	133	263	108
$75,000 or more	210	51	196	44
Median income	$22,163	$12,862	$32,046	$25,505
Total with income, percent	**100.0%**	**100.0%**	**100.0%**	**100.0%**
Under $10,000	24.3	41.0	3.1	5.9
$10,000 to $19,999	20.8	22.8	20.7	28.4
$20,000 to $34,999	25.4	20.5	31.7	35.5
$35,000 to $49,999	13.4	9.6	19.8	18.5
$50,000 to $74,999	9.3	4.4	14.0	8.3
$75,000 or more	6.8	1.7	10.4	3.4

Source: Bureau of the Census, The Asian and Pacific Islander Population in the United States: March 1996 (Update), *detailed tables for Current Population Reports P20-503, PPL-77, 1997; calculations by New Strategist*

Median Earnings of Asians Who Work Full-Time by Sex, 1988 to 1996

(median earnings of Asians who work year-round, full-time by sex; ratio of Asian to total population median earnings, and Asian female earnings as a percent of Asian male earnings, 1988–96; percent change in earnings and ratios for selected years; in 1996 dollars)

	Asian men		Asian women		Asian women's earnings as a percent of Asian men's earnings
	median earnings	ratio Asian/total	median earnings	ratio Asian/total	
1996	35,788	1.07	26,313	1.06	73.5
1995	32,992	1.00	26,258	1.07	79.6
1994	34,397	1.03	26,463	1.07	76.9
1993	33,972	1.01	27,188	1.11	80.0
1992	34,580	1.00	26,996	1.09	78.1
1991	35,923	1.03	24,876	1.02	69.2
1990	32,770	0.94	26,449	1.07	80.7
1989	37,505	1.04	27,292	1.10	72.8
1988	37,238	1.03	26,323	1.07	70.7
Percent change					
1990–1996	9.2%	13.3%	–0.5%	–1.4%	–8.9%
1988–1996	–3.9	3.9	–0.0	–1.4	4.0

Note: Asian/total ratios are calculated by dividing median earnings of Asian men and women by median of total men and women.
Source: Bureau of the Census, unpublished tables from the 1997 Current Population Survey; calculations by New Strategist

Earnings Distribution of Asians Who Work Full-Time by Sex and Education, 1995

(total number and percent distribution of Asians aged 25 or older with earnings who work year-round full-time, by sex, earnings, and educational attainment, 1995; persons in thousands as of 1996)

	total	not a high school graduate	high school graduate only	some college or associate's degree	bachelor's degree or more
Men with earnings	**1,769**	**167**	**330**	**348**	**924**
Percent	**100.0%**	**100.0%**	**100.0%**	**100.0%**	**100.0%**
Under $10,000	3.1	7.2	5.1	1.3	2.1
$10,000 to $19,999	20.4	39.8	28.9	28.0	10.8
$20,000 to $34,999	30.8	37.3	40.4	37.9	23.6
$35,000 to $49,999	20.8	13.4	14.3	20.9	24.1
$50,000 to $74,999	14.8	1.8	9.7	9.9	20.7
$75,000 or more	10.4	0.5	1.6	1.7	18.5
Median earnings	$32,236	$20,673	$25,011	$27,686	$41,375
Women with earnings	**1,240**	**110**	**262**	**320**	**548**
Percent	**100.0%**	**100.0%**	**100.0%**	**100.0%**	**100.0%**
Under $10,000	5.3	11.0	9.5	7.6	0.8
$10,000 to $19,999	30.1	71.9	47.2	26.8	15.5
$20,000 to $34,999	34.6	10.1	30.1	38.8	38.9
$35,000 to $49,999	17.9	6.8	10.6	18.7	23.1
$50,000 to $74,999	9.1	–	2.5	7.5	15.1
$75,000 or more	3.1	–	–	0.5	6.7
Median earnings	$25,280	$15,136	$18,218	$24,712	$32,451

Note: (–) means sample is too small to make a reliable estimate
Source: Bureau of the Census, The Asian and Pacific Islander Population in the United States: March 1996 (Update), *detailed tables for Current Population Reports P20-503, PPL-77, 1997; calculations by New Strategist*

Median Income of Asians Who Work Full-Time by Occupation and Sex, 1995

(median income of Asians aged 16 or older who work year-round, full-time by occupation and sex, and women's income as a percent of men's, 1995)

	men	women	Asian women's income as a percent of Asian men's income
Executive, administrative, and managerial	$41,521	$33,552	80.8%
Professional specialty	50,409	36,852	73.1
Technical and related support	33,651	32,772	97.4
Sales	32,074	20,630	64.3
Administrative support, including clerical	30,586	25,310	82.8
Private household	–	11,592	–
Protective service	14,861	–	–
Service, except private household	19,093	15,521	81.3
Farming, fishing, and forestry	19,115	–	–
Precision production, craft, and repair	26,624	16,957	63.7
Machine operators, assemblers, and inspectors	20,842	16,886	81.0
Transportation and material moving	25,376	–	–
Handlers, equipment cleaners, helpers, and laborers	17,992	15,817	87.9

Note: (–) means sample is too small to make a reliable estimate.
Source: Bureau of the Census, The Asian and Pacific Islander Population in the United States: March 1996 (Update), *detailed tables for Current Population Reports P20-503, PPL-77, 1997; calculations by New Strategist*

Asian Families below the Poverty Level, 1995

(total number of Asian families with a householder aged 15 or older, and number and percent below poverty level by type of family and educational attainment of householder, 1995; families in thousands as of 1996)

	total	in poverty	
		number	percent
Family type			
Total families	**2,125**	**264**	**12.4%**
Married couples	1,692	181	10.7
Female householder, no spouse present	260	67	26
Male householder, no spouse present	173	15	8.6
Educational attainment of householder			
Not a high school graduate	326	108	33.1
High school graduate	438	78	17.8
Bachelor's degree or more	934	39	4.1

Source: Bureau of the Census, The Asian and Pacific Islander Population in the United States: March 1996 (Update), *detailed tables for Current Population Reports P20-503, PPL-77, 1997; calculations by New Strategist*

Asians: Labor Force

Over one-third of Asian men and women who work full-time are managerial or professional specialty workers.

More than 4.6 million Asians were in the civilian labor force in 1996, or 66 percent of all Asian Americans aged 16 or older. Seventy-four percent of Asian men are in the labor force, as are 59 percent of Asian women. Over half of Asian men and women who work full-time are in managerial or professional specialty occupations.

Among Asian men in 1990, the labor force participation rate was highest for Asian Indians, at 84 percent. Among Asian women, the rate was highest for Filipinos, at 72 percent.

A 53 percent majority of Asian households have at least two earners. This compares with 45 percent of total households and is the highest proportion among all racial groups.

The number of workers who are Asian or of "other" race (primarily Native American) will grow 41 percent between 1996 and 2006, according to projections by the Bureau of Labor Statistics. The Asian and "other" share of the labor force will reach 5.4 percent by 2006.

■ The occupational distribution of Asians will become more like that of the total population in the years ahead if less-educated immigrants become a larger share of the Asian American population.

Asian households are more likely to have two or more earners

(percent distribution of Asian households by number of earners, 1996)

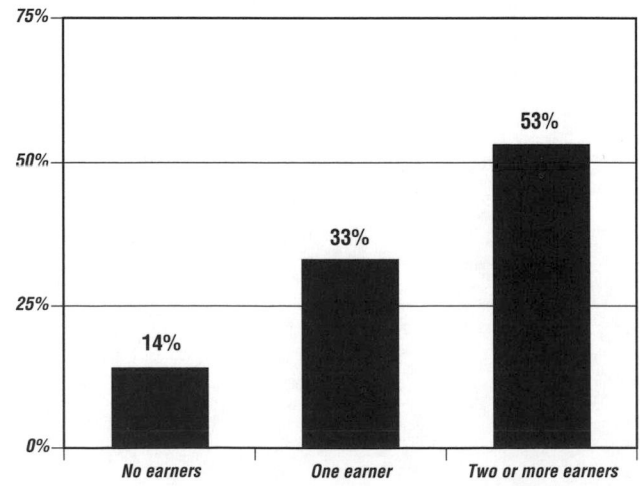

Employment Status of Asians by Sex, 1996

(employment status of the civilian noninstitutionalized Asian population aged 16 or older, by sex, 1996; numbers in thousands)

	total	*men*	*women*
Civilian labor force	**4,641**	**2,516**	**2,125**
Employed	4,408	2,376	2,032
Unemployed	233	140	93
Not in labor force	**2,402**	**902**	**1,501**
Percent in labor force	**65.9%**	**73.6%**	**58.6%**
Percent unemployed	5.0	5.6	4.4
Percent not in labor force	**34.1**	**26.4**	**41.4**

Note: The civilian labor force equals the number of employed plus the number of unemployed persons. The civilian population equals the number of persons in the labor force plus the number of those not in the labor force.
Source: Bureau of the Census, The Asian and Pacific Islander Population in the United States: March 1996 (Update), detailed tables for Current Population Reports P20-503, PPL-77, 1997; calculations by New Strategist

Employment Status of Asians by Sex and Ethnicity, 1990

(employment status of the civilian noninstitutionalized Asian population aged 16 or older, by sex and ethnicity, 1990; numbers in thousands)

	Chinese	Filipino	Japanese	Asian Indian	Korean	Vietnamese
MEN						
Civilian labor force	**468**	**359**	**242**	**263**	**180**	**160**
Employed	447	339	237	251	172	148
Unemployed	21	20	6	12	8	13
Not in labor force	**174**	**99**	**80**	**52**	**65**	**62**
Percent in labor force	72.9%	79.3%	75.5%	83.5%	73.8%	72.3%
Percent unemployed	4.5	5.6	2.4	4.5	4.3	8.0
Percent not in labor force	**27.1**	**20.7**	**24.5**	**16.5**	**26.2**	**27.7**
WOMEN						
Civilian labor force	**393**	**432**	**221**	**153**	**185**	**111**
Employed	373	411	215	141	173	101
Unemployed	20	20	6	12	11	10
Not in labor force	**271**	**166**	**178**	**108**	**148**	**88**
Percent in labor force	59.2%	72.0%	55.4%	58.6%	55.5%	55.8%
Percent unemployed	5.0	4.7	2.7	7.6	6.1	8.9
Percent not in labor force	**40.8**	**27.7**	**44.5**	**41.4**	**44.5**	**44.2**

Note: The civilian labor force equals the number of employed plus the number of unemployed persons. The civilian population equals the number of persons in the labor force plus the number not in the labor force.
Source: Bureau of the Census, Asians and Pacific Islanders in the United States, 1990 Census of Population, 1990 CP-3-5, 1993; calculations by New Strategist

Occupations of Asians by Sex, 1996

(number and percent distribution of employed Asians aged 16 or older by occupation and sex, 1996; numbers in thousands)

	men		women	
	number	*percent*	*number*	*percent*
Total employed	**2,376**	**100.0%**	**2,032**	**100.0%**
Managerial and professional specialty	836	35.2	628	30.9
Technical, sales, and administrative support	630	26.5	768	37.8
Service	240	10.1	337	16.6
Farming, forestry, and fishing	45	1.9	8	0.4
Precision production, craft, and repair	283	11.9	67	3.3
Operators, fabricators, and laborers	342	14.4	226	11.1

Source: Bureau of the Census, The Asian and Pacific Islander Population in the United States: March 1996 (Update), *detailed tables for Current Population Reports P20-503, PPL-77, 1997; calculations by New Strategist*

Asian Share of Workers by Occupation, 1996

(total number of persons aged 16 or older employed by occupation, number of Asians employed, and Asian share of total employment by occupation, 1996; numbers in thousands)

		Asian	
	total	*number*	*percent*
Total employed	**124,513**	**4,408**	**3.5%**
Managerial and professional specialty	35,851	1,464	4.1
Technical, sales, and administrative support	31,225	1,398	4.5
Service	16,882	577	3.4
Farming, forestry, and fishing	3,296	53	1.6
Precision production, craft, and repair	12,994	350	2.7
Operators, fabricators, and laborers	17,783	568	3.2

Note: The total number of employed shown here is different from that shown in other labor force tables because this figure is for March 1996 whereas the others are 1996 averages, and because this figure is unadjusted for seasonal changes in employment.
Source: Bureau of the Census, The Asian and Pacific Islander Population in the United States: March 1996 (Update), *detailed tables for Current Population Reports P20-503, PPL-77, 1997; calculations by New Strategist*

Occupations of Asian Full-Time Workers by Sex, 1995

(number and percent distribution of Asians aged 16 or older who work year-round, full-time by occupation and sex, 1995; persons in thousands as of 1996)

	men		women	
	number	*percent*	*number*	*percent*
Total year-round, full-time workers	**1,745**	**100.0%**	**1,240**	**100.0%**
Managerial and professional specialty	659	37.8	441	35.6
Executive, administrative, and managerial	266	15.2	185	14.9
Professional specialty	393	22.5	256	20.6
Technical, sales, and administrative support	464	26.6	459	37.0
Technical and related support	83	4.8	88	7.1
Sales	208	11.9	126	10.2
Administrative support, including clerical	173	9.9	245	19.8
Service	137	7.9	162	13.1
Private household	–	–	11	0.9
Protective service	18	1.0	4	0.3
Service, except private household	119	6.8	147	11.9
Farming, fishing, and forestry	39	2.2	2	0.2
Precision production, craft, and repair	216	12.4	50	4.0
Operators, fabricators, and laborers	230	13.2	127	10.2
Machine operators, assemblers, and inspectors	113	6.5	117	9.4
Transportation and material moving occupations	68	3.9	–	–
Handlers, equipment cleaners, helpers, and laborers	49	2.8	10	0.8

Note: (–) means sample is too small to make a reliable estimate.
Source: Bureau of the Census, The Asian and Pacific Islander Population in the United States: March 1996 (Update), *detailed tables for Current Population Reports P20-503, PPL-77, 1997; calculations by New Strategist*

Asian Households by Number of Earners, 1996

(number and percent distribution of Asian households by number of earners, 1996; numbers in thousands)

	number	percent
Total households	**2,777**	**100.0%**
No earners	392	14.1
One earner	922	33.2
Two or more earners	1,461	52.6
Two earners	1,052	37.9
Three earners	272	9.8
Four or more earners	136	4.9

Source: Bureau of the Census, The Asian and Pacific Islander Population in the United States: March 1996 (Update), *detailed tables for Current Population Reports P20-503, PPL-77, 1997; calculations by New Strategist*

Projections of the Asian Labor Force by Sex, 1996 to 2006

(number of Asians in the civilian labor force in 1996 and 2006, and percent change in number; labor force participation rate of Asians and Asian share of total labor force in 1996 and 2006; by sex; numbers in thousands)

| | number in labor force | | percent change |
	1996	2006	1996–2006
Total	**5,703**	**8,041**	**41.0%**
Men	3,039	4,222	38.9
Women	2,664	3,818	43.3

| | labor force participation rate | | percentage point change |
	1996	2006	1996–2006
Total	**65.8%**	**64.3%**	**–1.5**
Men	73.4	71.7	–1.7
Women	58.8	57.8	–1.0

| | percent of total labor force | | percentage point change |
	1996	2006	1996–2006
Total	**4.3%**	**5.4%**	**1.1**
Men	4.2	5.4	1.2
Women	4.3	5.4	1.1

Note: These figures are for Asians and "others," some of whom are Native Americans.
Source: Bureau of Labor Statistics, Monthly Labor Review, *November 1997; calculations by New Strategist*

Asians: Population

The Asian population will double between 1998 and 2020, growing from 10 million to 20 million.

Despite the rapid growth of the Asian population, Asians will account for just 6 percent of the U.S. population in 2020. Blacks and Hispanics will continue to greatly outnumber Asians for decades to come.

Behind the growth of the Asian population is immigration. Asia dispatched 34 percent of all immigrants to the U.S. in 1996; the largest numbers came from the Philippines, India, Vietnam, and China.

Fully 63 percent of Asians in this country are foreign born, according to the 1990 census. Asians with ethnic origin in Vietnam, India, and Korea are most likely to be foreign born. The Asians least likely to be foreign born are those whose ethnic origin is Japan.

Most Asian Americans speak English "very well." Only 38 percent of those aged 5 or older do not speak English fluently. But more than half of Asians aged 65 or older do not speak English "very well."

A great number of Asian Americans live in the West, where they account for about 13 percent of the population of the Pacific division. California is home to about 39 percent of the nation's Asian population, including 52 percent of Filipinos and 46 percent of Vietnamese. Los Angeles has more Asians than any other metropolitan area.

■ While the Asian share of the population is much bigger in some states and cities than others, the Asian influence on American culture can be felt in all parts of the United States.

The Asian American population will grow to nearly 20 million by 2020

(number of Asian Americans, 1998 and 2020)

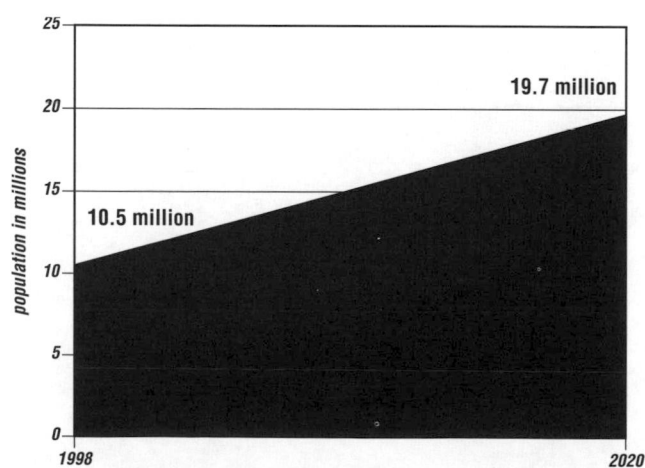

Asians by Age, 1995 to 2020

(number of Asians by age, selected years 1995–2020; percent change 1995–2000 and 2000–2010; numbers in thousands)

	1995	*1998*	*2000*	*2010*	*2020*	percent change	
						1995–2000	*2000–2010*
Total persons	**9,357**	**10,480**	**11,245**	**15,265**	**19,651**	**20.2%**	**35.7%**
Under age 5	834	885	926	1,170	1,476	11.0	26.3
Aged 5 to 9	729	855	925	1,145	1,440	26.9	23.8
Aged 10 to 14	771	842	901	1,233	1,524	16.9	36.8
Aged 15 to 19	690	825	894	1,248	1,502	29.6	39.6
Aged 20 to 24	745	750	811	1,141	1,473	8.9	40.7
Aged 25 to 29	815	894	895	1,164	1,515	9.8	30.1
Aged 30 to 34	879	919	968	1,119	1,452	10.1	15.6
Aged 35 to 39	846	931	975	1,148	1,417	15.2	17.7
Aged 40 to 44	754	856	919	1,142	1,298	21.9	24.3
Aged 45 to 49	616	720	779	1,065	1,238	26.5	36.7
Aged 50 to 54	435	544	630	941	1,153	44.8	49.4
Aged 55 to 59	337	398	447	779	1,043	32.6	74.3
Aged 60 to 64	280	322	356	633	913	27.1	77.8
Aged 65 to 69	238	269	290	457	748	21.8	57.6
Aged 70 to 74	182	211	232	345	582	27.5	48.7
Aged 75 to 79	109	140	159	246	384	45.9	54.7
Aged 80 to 84	61	73	83	160	241	36.1	92.8
Aged 85 or older	37	46	55	130	250	48.6	136.4
Aged 18 to 24	1,007	1,059	1,158	1,632	2,058	15.0	40.9
Aged 18 or older	6,595	7,382	7,946	10,961	14,292	20.5	37.9
Aged 65 or older	627	739	819	1,338	2,206	30.6	63.4

Source: Bureau of the Census, Population Projections of the United States, by Age, Sex, Race, and Hispanic Origin: 1995 to 2050, Current Population Reports, P25-1130, 1996; calculations by New Strategist

Asian Share of the Total Population by Age, 1995 to 2020

(Asians as a percent of the total population by age, selected years 1995–2020)

	1995	*1998*	*2000*	*2010*	*2020*
Total persons	**3.6%**	**3.9%**	**4.1%**	**5.1%**	**6.1%**
Under age 5	4.3	4.6	4.9	5.8	6.7
Aged 5 to 9	3.8	4.3	4.6	5.9	6.7
Aged 10 to 14	4.1	4.3	4.5	6.1	7.1
Aged 15 to 19	3.8	4.2	4.5	5.7	7.0
Aged 20 to 24	4.2	4.3	4.4	5.4	6.9
Aged 25 to 29	4.3	4.8	5.1	5.9	7.0
Aged 30 to 34	4.0	4.6	5.0	6.0	6.8
Aged 35 to 39	3.8	4.1	4.4	6.2	6.9
Aged 40 to 44	3.7	3.9	4.1	5.7	6.8
Aged 45 to 49	3.5	3.8	3.9	4.9	6.7
Aged 50 to 54	3.2	3.5	3.7	4.3	6.0
Aged 55 to 59	3.0	3.2	3.4	4.1	4.9
Aged 60 to 64	2.8	3.1	3.3	3.9	4.4
Aged 65 to 69	2.4	2.8	3.1	3.8	4.3
Aged 70 to 74	2.1	2.4	2.7	3.9	4.2
Aged 75 to 79	1.6	1.9	2.1	3.5	4.1
Aged 80 to 84	1.4	1.5	1.7	2.9	4.1
Aged 85 or older	1.0	1.2	1.3	2.3	3.9
Aged 18 to 24	4.0	4.2	4.4	5.4	6.9
Aged 18 or older	3.4	3.7	3.9	4.9	5.8
Aged 65 or older	1.9	2.2	2.4	3.4	4.1

Source: Calculations by New Strategist based on Census Bureau data in Population Projections of the United States, by Age, Sex, Race, and Hispanic Origin: 1995 to 2050, *Current Population Reports, P25-1130, 1996*

Non-Hispanic Asians by Age, 1995 to 2020

(number of non-Hispanic Asians by age, selected years 1995–2020; percent change 1995–2000 and 2000–2010; numbers in thousands)

	1995	1998	2000	2010	2020	percent change 1995–2000	2000–2010
Total persons	**8,788**	**9,856**	**10,584**	**14,402**	**18,557**	**20.4%**	**36.1%**
Under age 5	773	826	867	1,093	1,381	12.2	26.1
Aged 5 to 9	672	790	859	1,072	1,347	27.8	24.8
Aged 10 to 14	716	781	834	1,158	1,427	16.5	38.8
Aged 15 to 19	642	769	835	1,166	1,411	30.1	39.5
Aged 20 to 24	694	700	756	1,063	1,385	8.9	40.6
Aged 25 to 29	758	833	836	1,089	1,418	10.3	30.3
Aged 30 to 34	825	862	907	1,052	1,362	9.9	16.0
Aged 35 to 39	800	880	921	1,085	1,338	15.1	17.8
Aged 40 to 44	715	812	873	1,080	1,230	22.1	23.7
Aged 45 to 49	587	687	742	1,013	1,177	26.4	36.5
Aged 50 to 54	415	520	602	898	1,096	45.1	49.2
Aged 55 to 59	322	381	428	745	996	32.9	74.1
Aged 60 to 64	268	309	342	608	875	27.6	77.8
Aged 65 to 69	229	259	278	440	719	21.4	58.3
Aged 70 to 74	174	202	222	331	559	27.6	49.1
Aged 75 to 79	104	133	152	235	368	46.2	54.6
Aged 80 to 84	58	69	79	152	231	36.2	92.4
Aged 85 or older	34	43	51	123	237	50.0	141.2
Aged 18 to 24	939	989	1,081	1,521	1,933	15.1	40.7
Aged 18 or older	6,228	6,978	7,514	10,372	13,539	20.6	38.0
Aged 65 or older	600	706	783	1,281	2,113	30.5	63.6

Source: Bureau of the Census, Population Projections of the United States, by Age, Sex, Race, and Hispanic Origin: 1995 to 2050, *Current Population Reports, P25-1130, 1996; calculations by New Strategist*

Asians by Age and Sex, 1998

(number of Asians by age and sex, and sex ratio by age, 1998; numbers in thousands)

	total	male	female	sex ratio*
Total persons	**10,480**	**5,035**	**5,445**	**92**
Under age 5	885	452	433	104
Aged 5 to 9	855	438	417	105
Aged 10 to 14	842	428	414	103
Aged 15 to 19	825	415	410	101
Aged 20 to 24	750	367	384	96
Aged 25 to 29	894	426	468	91
Aged 30 to 34	919	438	481	91
Aged 35 to 39	931	447	483	93
Aged 40 to 44	856	403	453	89
Aged 45 to 49	720	332	388	86
Aged 50 to 54	544	250	294	85
Aged 55 to 59	398	186	212	88
Aged 60 to 64	322	146	176	83
Aged 65 to 69	269	113	157	72
Aged 70 to 74	211	87	124	70
Aged 75 to 79	140	58	82	71
Aged 80 to 84	73	30	43	70
Aged 85 or older	46	17	29	59
Aged 18 to 24	1,059	522	539	97
Aged 18 or older	7,382	3,455	3,927	88
Aged 65 or older	739	305	434	70

* The sex ratio is the number of males per 100 females.
Source: Bureau of the Census, Population Projections of the United States, by Age, Sex, Race, and Hispanic Origin: 1995 to 2050, *Current Population Reports, P25-1130, 1996; calculations by New Strategist*

Asians by Ethnicity, Age, and Ability to Speak English, 1990

(number and percent of Asians aged 5 or older who do not speak English "very well" by ethnicity and age, for the six largest Asian ethnic groups, 1990; numbers in thousands)

	total	*5 to 17*	*18 to 64*	*65 to 74*	*75 or older*
Total aged 5 or older, number	**2,555**	**379**	**1,912**	**168**	**96**
Chinese	777	90	589	64	34
Filipino	318	32	228	34	24
Japanese	206	21	148	21	17
Korean	376	40	308	20	8
Asian Indian	169	25	133	9	3
Vietnamese	331	67	249	10	5
Total aged 5 or older, percent	**38.4%**	**25.7%**	**40.4%**	**56.9%**	**65.4%**
Chinese	50.5	32.6	52.1	73.1	76.8
Filipino	24.2	11.2	24.4	56.6	60.2
Japanese	25.2	18.8	24.5	28.0	53.0
Korean	51.6	22.5	59.5	81.9	85.2
Asian Indian	23.5	14.7	24.9	55.3	59.3
Vietnamese	60.8	44.6	66.1	88.2	87.0

Source: Bureau of the Census, Asians and Pacific Islanders in the United States, *1990 Census of Population, CP-3-5, 1990; calculations by New Strategist*

Characteristics of the Asian Foreign-Born Population, 1996

(number and percent distribution of Asian foreign-born persons by age, sex, income, and education, selected countries of origin, 1996; countries listed by size of foreign-born population; numbers in thousands)

	Philippines	China	India	Vietnam	Korea
Total foreign born, number	**1,164**	**801**	**757**	**740**	**550**
Age					
Under age 5	5	3	8	9	10
Aged 5 to 15	82	49	50	43	65
Aged 16 or 17	31	10	16	42	27
Aged 18 to 24	72	53	71	85	62
Aged 25 to 29	114	50	132	113	34
Aged 30 to 34	118	108	90	65	68
Aged 35 to 44	297	163	184	152	122
Aged 45 to 64	308	255	172	191	115
Aged 65 or older	136	111	34	40	46
Sex					
Male	534	409	375	383	265
Female	630	392	382	357	286
Income in 1995					
Total with income	**959**	**654**	**613**	**574**	**377**
Under $10,000	219	236	154	218	149
$10,000 to $19,999	228	158	117	149	75
$20,000 to $34,999	261	125	125	129	75
$35,000 to $49,999	149	44	92	47	45
$50,000 or more	102	91	125	31	33
Education					
Total aged 25 or older	974	687	612	562	385
Not a high school graduate	127	165	59	165	47
High school grad. or some college	427	218	158	307	163
Bachelor's degree	353	163	173	79	120
Graduate/professional degree	67	141	222	11	55

(continued)

(continued from previous page)

	Philippines	China	India	Vietnam	Korea
Total foreign born, percent	**100.0%**	**100.0%**	**100.0%**	**100.0%**	**100.0%**
Age					
Under age 5	0.4	0.4	1.1	1.2	1.8
Aged 5 to 15	7.0	6.1	6.6	5.8	11.8
Aged 16 or 17	2.7	1.2	2.1	5.7	4.9
Aged 18 to 24	6.2	6.6	9.4	11.5	11.3
Aged 25 to 29	9.8	6.2	17.4	15.3	6.2
Aged 30 to 34	10.1	13.5	11.9	8.8	12.4
Aged 35 to 44	25.5	20.3	24.3	20.5	22.2
Aged 45 to 64	26.5	31.8	22.7	25.8	20.9
Aged 65 or older	11.7	13.9	4.5	5.4	8.4
Sex					
Male	45.9	51.1	49.5	51.8	48.2
Female	54.1	48.9	50.5	48.2	52.0
Income in 1995					
Total with income	**100.0**	**100.0**	**100.0**	**100.0**	**100.0**
Under $10,000	22.8	36.1	25.1	38.0	39.5
$10,000 to $19,999	23.8	24.2	19.1	26.0	19.9
$20,000 to $34,999	27.2	19.1	20.4	22.5	19.9
$35,000 to $49,999	15.5	6.7	15.0	8.2	11.9
$50,000 or more	10.6	13.9	20.4	5.4	8.8
Education					
Total aged 25 or older	100.0	100.0	100.0	100.0	100.0
Not a high school graduate	13.0	24.0	9.6	29.4	12.2
High school grad. or some college	43.8	31.7	25.8	54.6	42.3
Bachelors degree	36.2	23.7	28.3	14.1	31.2
Graduate/professional degree	6.9	20.5	36.3	2.0	14.3

Source: Bureau of the Census, Internet web site, http://www.census.gov; calculations by New Strategist

Asian Immigrants by Country of Birth, 1996

(total number of immigrants, number of Asian immigrants, and Asian share of total and Asian immigrants, by country of birth, 1996; ranked by number of immigrants)

	number	share of total immigrants	share of Asian immigrants
Total immigrants	**915,900**	**100.0%**	–
Total Asian immigrants	**307,807**	**33.6**	**100.0%**
Philippines	55,876	6.1	18.2
India	44,859	4.9	14.6
Vietnam	42,067	4.6	13.7
Mainland China	41,728	4.6	13.6
Korea	18,185	2.0	5.9
Taiwan	13,401	1.5	4.4
Pakistan	12,519	1.4	4.1
Iran	11,084	1.2	3.6
Bangladesh	8,221	0.9	2.7
Hong Kong	7,834	0.9	2.5
Japan	6,011	0.7	2.0
Iraq	5,481	0.6	1.8
Jordan	4,445	0.5	1.4
Lebanon	4,382	0.5	1.4
Thailand	4,310	0.5	1.4
Turkey	3,657	0.4	1.2
Israel	3,126	0.3	1.0
Syria	3,072	0.3	1.0
Laos	2,847	0.3	0.9
Yemen	2,209	0.2	0.7
Cambodia	1,568	0.2	0.5
Malaysia	1,414	0.2	0.5
Burma	1,320	0.1	0.4
Sri Lanka	1,277	0.1	0.4
Afghanistan	1,263	0.1	0.4
Kuwait	1,202	0.1	0.4
Saudi Arabia	1,164	0.1	0.4
Indonesia	1,084	0.1	0.4
Other Asia	2,201	0.2	0.7

Note: (–) means not applicable.
Source: U.S. Immigration and Naturalization Service, 1996 Statistical Yearbook of the Immigration and Naturalization Service, 1997; calculations by New Strategist

Asians by Region, Division, and Ethnicity, 1990

(number and percent distribution of Asians by region, division, and ethnicity, 1990; numbers in thousands)

	total	Chinese	Filipino	Japanese	Asian Indian	Korean	Vietnamese
UNITED STATES	**7,274**	**1,645**	**1,407**	**848**	**815**	**799**	**615**
Northeast	**1,335**	**445**	**143**	**74**	**285**	**182**	**61**
New England	232	72	15	15	36	21	22
Middle Atlantic	1,104	373	128	59	249	161	39
Midwest	**768**	**133**	**113**	**63**	**146**	**109**	**52**
East North Central	573	103	97	50	123	80	26
West North Central	195	30	17	13	23	29	26
South	**1,122**	**204**	**159**	**67**	**196**	**153**	**169**
South Atlantic	631	114	108	39	114	101	62
East South Central	84	15	9	9	15	12	10
West South Central	407	76	43	20	67	40	97
West	**4,048**	**863**	**991**	**643**	**189**	**355**	**334**
Mountain	217	40	32	34	15	28	20
Pacific	3,831	823	960	609	173	327	314

Percent distribution by region and division

UNITED STATES	100.0%	100.0%	100.0%	100.0%	100.0%	100.0%	100.0%
Northeast	**18.4**	**27.1**	**10.2**	**8.7**	**35.0**	**22.8**	**9.9**
New England	3.2	4.4	1.1	1.8	4.4	2.6	3.6
Middle Atlantic	15.2	22.7	9.1	7.0	30.6	20.2	6.3
Midwest	**10.6**	**8.1**	**8.0**	**7.4**	**17.9**	**13.6**	**8.5**
East North Central	7.9	6.3	6.9	5.9	15.1	10.0	4.2
West North Central	2.7	1.8	1.2	1.5	2.8	3.6	4.2
South	**15.4**	**12.4**	**11.3**	**7.9**	**24.0**	**19.1**	**27.5**
South Atlantic	8.7	6.9	7.7	4.6	14.0	12.6	10.1
East South Central	1.2	0.9	0.6	1.1	1.8	1.5	1.6
West South Central	5.6	4.6	3.1	2.4	8.2	5.0	15.8
West	**55.7**	**52.5**	**70.4**	**75.8**	**23.2**	**44.4**	**54.3**
Mountain	3.0	2.4	2.3	4.0	1.8	3.5	3.3
Pacific	52.7	50.0	68.2	71.8	21.2	40.9	51.1

(continued)

(continued from previous page)

Percent distribution by ethnicity

	total	Chinese	Filipino	Japanese	Asian Indian	Korean	Vietnamese
UNITED STATES	100.0%	22.6%	19.3%	11.7%	11.2%	11.0%	8.5%
Northeast	100.0	33.3	10.7	5.5	21.3	13.6	4.6
New England	100.0	31.0	6.5	6.5	15.5	9.1	9.5
Middle Atlantic	100.0	33.8	11.6	5.3	22.6	14.6	3.5
Midwest	100.0	17.3	14.7	8.2	19.0	14.2	6.8
East North Central	100.0	18.0	16.9	8.7	21.5	14.0	4.5
West North Central	100.0	15.4	8.7	6.7	11.8	14.9	13.3
South	100.0	18.2	14.2	6.0	17.5	13.6	15.1
South Atlantic	100.0	18.1	17.1	6.2	18.1	16.0	9.8
East South Central	100.0	17.9	10.7	10.7	17.9	14.3	11.9
West South Central	100.0	18.7	10.6	4.9	16.7	9.8	23.8
West	100.0	21.3	24.5	15.9	4.7	8.8	8.3
Mountain	100.0	18.4	14.7	15.7	6.9	12.9	9.2
Pacific	100.0	21.5	25.1	15.9	4.5	8.5	8.2

Source: Bureau of the Census, General Population Characteristics, *1990 Census of Population, CP-1-1, 1992; calculations by New Strategist*

Asians by Region and Division, 1995 to 2020

(number and percent distribution of Asians and Asian share of the total population by region and division, selected years 1995–2020; percent change in number and percentage point change in distribution and share, 1995–2000 and 2000–2010; numbers in thousands)

	1995	2000	2010	2020	percent change 1995–2000	2000–2010
Number						
UNITED STATES	**9,348**	**11,246**	**15,265**	**19,650**	**20.3%**	**35.7%**
Northeast	**1,718**	**2,104**	**2,894**	**3,702**	**22.5**	**37.5**
New England	300	384	558	739	28.0	45.3
Middle Atlantic	1,417	1,721	2,337	2,964	21.5	35.8
Midwest	**966**	**1,215**	**1,614**	**1,979**	**25.8**	**32.8**
East North Central	726	885	1,172	1,435	21.9	32.4
West North Central	261	330	443	545	26.4	34.2
South	**1,542**	**1,902**	**2,556**	**3,195**	**23.3**	**34.4**
South Atlantic	867	1,070	1,445	1,811	23.4	35.0
East South Central	112	138	178	210	23.2	29.0
West South Central	564	692	934	1,173	22.7	35.0
West	**5,100**	**6,022**	**8,202**	**10,775**	**18.1**	**36.2**
Mountain	312	418	566	691	34.0	35.4
Pacific	4,788	5,604	7,634	10,063	17.0	36.2

	1995	2000	2010	2020	percentage point change 1995–2000	2000–2010
Percent distribution						
UNITED STATES	**100.0%**	**100.0%**	**100.0%**	**100.0%**	**–**	**–**
Northeast	**18.4**	**18.7**	**19.0**	**18.8**	**0.3**	**0.3**
New England	3.2	3.4	3.7	3.8	0.2	0.3
Middle Atlantic	15.2	15.3	15.3	15.1	0.1	0.0
Midwest	**10.3**	**10.8**	**10.6**	**10.1**	**0.5**	**–0.2**
East North Central	7.8	7.9	7.7	7.3	0.1	–0.2
West North Central	2.8	2.9	2.9	2.8	0.1	0.0
South	**16.5**	**16.9**	**16.7**	**16.3**	**0.4**	**–0.2**
South Atlantic	9.3	9.5	9.5	9.2	0.2	0.0
East South Central	1.2	1.2	1.2	1.1	0.0	0.0
West South Central	6.0	6.2	6.1	6.0	0.2	–0.1
West	**54.6**	**53.5**	**53.7**	**54.8**	**–1.1**	**0.2**
Mountain	3.3	3.7	3.7	3.5	0.4	0.0
Pacific	51.2	49.8	50.0	51.2	–1.4	0.2

(continued)

(continued from previous page)

	1995	2000	2010	2020	percentage point change 1995–2000	percentage point change 2000–2010
Percent share						
UNITED STATES	**3.6%**	**4.1%**	**5.1%**	**6.1%**	**0.5%**	**1.0%**
Northeast	**3.3**	**4.0**	**5.4**	**6.6**	**0.7**	**1.4**
New England	2.3	2.8	3.9	4.9	0.5	1.1
Middle Atlantic	3.7	4.5	5.9	7.2	0.8	1.4
Midwest	**1.6**	**1.9**	**2.4**	**2.9**	**0.3**	**0.5**
East North Central	1.7	2.0	2.6	3.0	0.3	0.6
West North Central	1.4	1.7	2.2	2.6	0.3	0.5
South	**1.7**	**1.9**	**2.4**	**2.7**	**0.2**	**0.5**
South Atlantic	1.8	2.1	2.6	3.0	0.3	0.5
East South Central	0.7	0.8	1.0	1.1	0.1	0.2
West South Central	2.0	2.3	2.7	3.1	0.3	0.4
West	**8.9**	**9.8**	**11.6**	**13.2**	**0.9**	**1.8**
Mountain	2.0	2.4	2.8	3.1	0.4	0.4
Pacific	11.4	12.8	15.2	16.9	1.4	2.4

Note: Numbers will not add to total due to rounding. (–) means not applicable.
Source: Bureau of the Census, Population Projections for States, by Age, Sex, Race, and Hispanic Origin: 1995 to 2025, Current Population Reports, PPL-47, 1996; calculations by New Strategist

Asians by State and Ethnicity, 1990

(number of Asians by state and ethnicity, 1990; numbers in thousands)

	total	Chinese	Filipino	Japanese	Asian Indian	Korean	Vietnamese
United States	**7,274**	**1,645**	**1,407**	**848**	**815**	**799**	**615**
Alabama	22	4	2	2	4	3	2
Alaska	20	1	8	2	–	4	1
Arizona	55	14	8	6	6	6	5
Arkansas	13	2	2	1	1	1	2
California	2,846	705	732	313	160	260	280
Colorado	60	9	5	11	4	11	7
Connecticut	51	11	5	4	12	5	4
Delaware	9	2	1	1	2	1	–
District of Columbia	11	3	2	1	2	1	1
Florida	154	31	32	9	31	12	16
Georgia	76	13	6	6	14	15	8
Hawaii	685	69	169	247	1	24	5
Idaho	9	1	1	3	–	1	1
Illinois	285	50	64	22	64	42	10
Indiana	38	7	5	5	7	5	2
Iowa	25	4	2	2	3	5	3
Kansas	32	5	3	2	4	4	7
Kentucky	18	3	2	3	3	3	2
Louisiana	41	5	4	2	5	3	18
Maine	7	1	1	1	1	1	1
Maryland	140	31	19	7	28	30	9
Massachusetts	143	54	6	9	20	12	15
Michigan	105	19	14	11	24	16	6
Minnesota	78	9	4	4	8	12	9
Mississippi	13	3	2	1	2	1	4
Missouri	41	9	6	3	6	6	4
Montana	4	1	1	1	–	1	–
Nebraska	12	2	1	2	1	2	2
Nevada	38	7	12	4	2	4	2
New Hampshire	9	2	1	1	2	2	1
New Jersey	273	59	53	17	79	39	7
New Mexico	14	3	2	2	2	1	1
New York	694	284	62	35	141	96	16
North Carolina	52	9	5	5	10	7	5
North Dakota	3	1	1	–	–	1	–
Ohio	91	19	10	10	21	11	5

(continued)

(continued from previous page)

	total	Chinese	Filipino	Japanese	Asian Indian	Korean	Vietnamese
Oklahoma	34	5	3	2	5	5	7
Oregon	69	14	7	12	4	9	9
Pennsylvania	137	30	12	7	28	27	16
Rhode Island	18	3	2	1	2	1	1
South Carolina	22	3	6	2	4	3	2
South Dakota	3	–	1	–	–	1	–
Tennessee	32	6	3	3	6	5	2
Texas	319	63	34	15	56	32	70
Utah	33	5	2	7	2	3	3
Vermont	3	1	–	–	1	1	–
Virginia	159	21	35	8	20	30	21
Washington	211	34	44	34	8	30	19
West Virginia	7	1	2	1	2	1	–
Wisconsin	54	7	4	3	7	6	2
Wyoming	3	1	–	1	–	–	–

Note: (–) means less than 500. Numbers may not add to total because not all Asian ethnicities are shown.
Source: U.S. Bureau of the Census, Internet web site, http://www.census.gov

Distribution of Asians by State and Ethnicity, 1990

(percent distribution of Asians by state and ethnicity, 1990)

	total	Chinese	Filipino	Japanese	Asian Indian	Korean	Vietnamese
United States	100.0%	100.0%	100.0%	100.0%	100.0%	100.0%	100.0%
Alabama	0.3	0.2	0.1	0.2	0.5	0.4	0.4
Alaska	0.3	0.1	0.6	0.2	0.1	0.5	0.1
Arizona	0.8	0.9	0.6	0.7	0.7	0.7	0.9
Arkansas	0.2	0.1	0.1	0.1	0.2	0.1	0.4
California	39.1	42.8	52.0	36.9	19.6	32.5	45.6
Colorado	0.8	0.5	0.4	1.3	0.5	1.4	1.2
Connecticut	0.7	0.7	0.4	0.4	1.4	0.6	0.7
Delaware	0.1	0.1	0.1	0.1	0.3	0.2	0.1
District of Columbia	0.2	0.2	0.1	0.1	0.2	0.1	0.1
Florida	2.1	1.9	2.3	1.0	3.9	1.6	2.7
Georgia	1.0	0.8	0.4	0.8	1.7	1.9	1.3
Hawaii	9.4	4.2	12.0	29.2	0.1	3.1	0.9
Idaho	0.1	0.1	0.1	0.3	0.1	0.1	0.1
Illinois	3.9	3.0	4.6	2.6	7.9	5.2	1.7
Indiana	0.5	0.4	0.3	0.6	0.9	0.7	0.4
Iowa	0.4	0.3	0.1	0.2	0.4	0.6	0.5
Kansas	0.4	0.3	0.2	0.2	0.5	0.5	1.1
Kentucky	0.2	0.2	0.2	0.3	0.4	0.4	0.2
Louisiana	0.6	0.3	0.3	0.2	0.6	0.3	2.9
Maine	0.1	0.1	0.1	0.1	0.1	0.1	0.1
Maryland	1.9	1.9	1.4	0.8	3.5	3.8	1.4
Massachusetts	2.0	3.3	0.4	1.0	2.4	1.5	2.5
Michigan	1.4	1.2	1.0	1.3	2.9	2.0	1.0
Minnesota	1.1	0.5	0.3	0.4	1.0	1.4	1.5
Mississippi	0.2	0.2	0.1	0.1	0.2	0.1	0.6
Missouri	0.6	0.5	0.4	0.4	0.7	0.7	0.7
Montana	0.1	0.0	0.1	0.1	0.0	0.1	0.0
Nebraska	0.2	0.1	0.1	0.2	0.1	0.2	0.3
Nevada	0.5	0.4	0.9	0.5	0.2	0.5	0.3
New Hampshire	0.1	0.1	0.1	0.1	0.2	0.2	0.1
New Jersey	3.7	3.6	3.8	2.0	9.7	4.8	1.2
New Mexico	0.2	0.2	0.1	0.2	0.2	0.2	0.2
New York	9.5	17.3	4.4	4.2	17.3	12.0	2.5
North Carolina	0.7	0.5	0.4	0.6	1.2	0.9	0.8
North Dakota	0.0	0.0	0.1	0.0	0.1	0.1	0.0
Ohio	1.3	1.2	0.7	1.2	2.6	1.4	0.8

(continued)

(continued from previous page)

	total	Chinese	Filipino	Japanese	Asian Indian	Korean	Vietnamese
Oklahoma	0.5%	0.3%	0.2%	0.3%	0.6%	0.6%	1.2%
Oregon	1.0	0.8	0.5	1.4	0.4	1.1	1.5
Pennsylvania	1.9	1.8	0.9	0.8	3.5	3.4	2.6
Rhode Island	0.3	0.2	0.1	0.1	0.2	0.2	0.1
South Carolina	0.3	0.2	0.4	0.2	0.5	0.3	0.3
South Dakota	0.0	0.0	0.0	0.0	0.0	0.1	0.0
Tennessee	0.4	0.3	0.2	0.4	0.7	0.6	0.3
Texas	4.4	3.8	2.4	1.7	6.8	4.0	11.3
Utah	0.5	0.3	0.1	0.8	0.2	0.3	0.5
Vermont	0.0	0.0	0.0	0.0	0.1	0.1	0.0
Virginia	2.2	1.3	2.5	0.9	2.5	3.8	3.4
Washington	2.9	2.1	3.1	4.1	1.0	3.7	3.0
West Virginia	0.1	0.1	0.1	0.1	0.2	0.1	0.0
Wisconsin	0.7	0.4	0.3	0.3	0.8	0.7	0.4
Wyoming	0.0	0.0	0.0	0.1	0.0	0.1	0.0

Source: Calculations by New Strategist based on Census Bureau data from the 1990 Census at Internet web site, http://www.census.gov

Ethnic Share of Asian Population by State, 1990

(Asian ethnic groups as a percent of total Asian population, by state, 1990)

	total Asian	Chinese	Filipino	Japanese	Asian Indian	Korean	Vietnamese
United States	**100.0%**	**22.6%**	**19.3%**	**11.7%**	**11.2%**	**11.0%**	**8.4%**
Alabama	100.0	18.0	8.3	9.3	19.9	15.8	10.4
Alaska	100.0	6.8	40.4	10.5	2.4	21.1	3.0
Arizona	100.0	25.6	14.3	11.4	10.3	10.6	9.5
Arkansas	100.0	13.8	12.5	7.6	10.6	8.3	18.7
California	100.0	24.8	25.7	11.0	5.6	9.1	9.8
Colorado	100.0	14.5	9.1	19.0	6.4	18.9	12.0
Connecticut	100.0	21.9	10.2	7.5	23.2	10.1	8.1
Delaware	100.0	25.4	14.6	7.6	24.1	13.6	3.8
District of Columbia	100.0	28.0	18.6	9.2	14.3	7.3	6.7
Florida	100.0	19.9	20.7	5.5	20.4	8.0	10.6
Georgia	100.0	16.7	7.7	8.4	18.4	20.2	10.3
Hawaii	100.0	10.0	24.6	36.1	0.1	3.6	0.8
Idaho	100.0	15.2	11.6	29.0	5.1	10.0	6.4
Illinois	100.0	17.5	22.5	7.7	22.5	14.5	3.6
Indiana	100.0	19.6	12.6	12.5	18.9	14.6	6.6
Iowa	100.0	17.4	6.3	6.4	11.9	18.1	11.3
Kansas	100.0	16.8	8.0	6.4	12.5	12.6	20.7
Kentucky	100.0	15.4	12.3	14.1	16.4	16.7	8.5
Louisiana	100.0	13.2	9.1	3.7	12.4	6.7	42.8
Maine	100.0	18.9	15.8	8.8	9.1	12.8	9.6
Maryland	100.0	22.1	13.9	4.7	20.3	21.7	6.3
Massachusetts	100.0	37.5	4.3	6.1	13.8	8.2	10.8
Michigan	100.0	18.2	13.1	10.2	22.7	15.5	5.8
Minnesota	100.0	11.5	5.4	4.6	10.6	14.9	12.1
Mississippi	100.0	19.3	12.0	5.4	14.4	8.6	29.3
Missouri	100.0	20.9	13.6	8.2	14.8	13.9	10.6
Montana	100.0	15.4	17.3	19.5	5.8	15.7	3.7
Nebraska	100.0	14.3	11.1	12.7	9.8	15.6	14.5
Nevada	100.0	17.4	31.6	10.6	4.8	11.3	5.1
New Hampshire	100.0	24.8	9.4	8.0	18.2	16.1	5.9
New Jersey	100.0	21.7	19.5	6.3	29.2	14.1	2.7
New Mexico	100.0	18.5	14.3	13.4	11.3	10.4	10.5
New York	100.0	41.0	9.0	5.1	20.3	13.8	2.2
North Carolina	100.0	17.0	10.2	9.7	18.9	13.9	10.0
North Dakota	100.0	16.1	20.5	7.1	13.9	15.2	8.1
Ohio	100.0	21.3	11.3	11.5	22.9	12.3	5.4

(continued)

(continued from previous page)

	total Asian	Chinese	Filipino	Japanese	Asian Indian	Korean	Vietnamese
Oklahoma	100.0%	15.5%	9.0%	7.1%	13.5%	14.1%	21.8%
Oregon	100.0	19.7	10.7	17.0	5.1	12.5	13.1
Pennsylvania	100.0	21.5	8.8	4.8	20.7	19.5	11.6
Rhode Island	100.0	17.3	10.0	4.1	10.8	7.1	4.2
South Carolina	100.0	13.6	24.7	8.4	17.4	11.5	7.8
South Dakota	100.0	12.3	17.0	9.2	9.2	16.8	8.6
Tennessee	100.0	17.8	9.5	10.8	18.6	14.2	6.5
Texas	100.0	19.8	10.8	4.6	17.5	9.9	21.8
Utah	100.0	15.9	5.7	19.5	4.7	7.9	8.4
Vermont	100.0	21.1	7.9	11.6	16.5	17.5	7.3
Virginia	100.0	13.4	22.0	5.0	12.9	19.0	13.0
Washington	100.0	16.1	20.8	16.3	3.9	14.1	8.9
West Virginia	100.0	15.7	21.5	10.5	26.6	10.4	2.5
Wisconsin	100.0	13.7	6.9	5.2	12.9	10.5	4.7
Wyoming	100.0	19.7	14.5	20.8	8.6	14.3	4.4

Note: Numbers will not add to total because not all ethnicities are shown.
Source: Calculations by New Strategist based on Census Bureau data from the 1990 census at Internet web site, http://www.census.gov

Asians by State, 1995 to 2020

(number of Asians by state, selected years 1995–2020; percent change 1995–2000 and 2000–2010; numbers in thousands)

	1995	2000	2010	2020	percent change 1995–2000	percent change 2000–2010
United States	**9,348**	**11,246**	**15,265**	**19,650**	**20.3%**	**35.7%**
Alabama	28	34	44	52	21.4	29.4
Alaska	28	46	96	158	64.3	108.7
Arizona	80	107	143	176	33.8	33.6
Arkansas	15	19	24	30	26.7	26.3
California	3,627	4,289	5,969	8,001	18.3	39.2
Colorado	82	108	147	181	31.7	36.1
Connecticut	67	80	115	151	19.4	43.8
Delaware	12	15	19	24	25.0	26.7
District of Columbia	17	15	21	27	-11.8	40.0
Florida	218	267	366	472	22.5	37.1
Georgia	112	142	187	225	26.8	31.7
Hawaii	755	796	920	1,093	5.4	15.6
Idaho	13	17	22	26	30.8	29.4
Illinois	358	423	543	661	18.2	28.4
Indiana	48	60	78	91	25.0	30.0
Iowa	34	43	58	69	26.5	34.9
Kansas	41	50	64	77	22.0	28.0
Kentucky	24	29	37	43	20.8	27.6
Louisiana	53	62	83	102	17.0	33.9
Maine	8	9	13	17	12.5	44.4
Maryland	185	223	296	368	20.5	32.7
Massachusetts	190	246	361	476	29.5	46.7
Michigan	132	163	215	263	23.5	31.9
Minnesota	106	139	196	248	31.1	41.0
Mississippi	16	19	25	30	18.8	31.6
Missouri	54	63	80	94	16.7	27.0
Montana	5	7	9	11	40.0	28.6
Nebraska	17	23	31	39	35.3	34.8
Nevada	61	85	111	130	39.3	30.6
New Hampshire	11	14	21	27	27.3	50.0
New Jersey	373	475	681	889	27.3	43.4
New Mexico	21	29	41	52	38.1	41.4
New York	867	1,028	1,359	1,703	18.6	32.2
North Carolina	74	96	128	157	29.7	33.3
North Dakota	4	6	7	9	50.0	16.7
Ohio	115	140	186	229	21.7	32.9

(continued)

(continued from previous page)

	1995	2000	2010	2020	percent change 1995–2000	percent change 2000–2010
Oklahoma	42	51	65	81	21.4%	27.5%
Oregon	92	116	155	195	26.1	33.6
Pennsylvania	178	218	296	371	22.5	35.8
Rhode Island	22	28	41	55	27.3	46.4
South Carolina	29	33	42	52	13.8	27.3
South Dakota	4	5	7	9	25.0	40.0
Tennessee	44	57	72	85	29.5	26.3
Texas	452	562	762	962	24.3	35.6
Utah	46	62	85	103	34.8	37.1
Vermont	4	6	8	10	50.0	33.3
Virginia	212	267	370	467	25.9	38.6
Washington	288	358	496	639	24.3	38.5
West Virginia	9	11	15	19	22.2	36.4
Wisconsin	73	100	147	189	37.0	47.0
Wyoming	3	4	7	10	33.3	75.0

Note: Numbers may not add to total due to rounding.
Source: Bureau of the Census, Population Projections for States, by Age, Sex, Race, and Hispanic Origin: 1995 to 2020, *Current Population Reports, PPL-47, 1996; calculations by New Strategist*

Distribution of Asians by State, 1995 to 2020

(percent distribution of Asians by state, selected years 1995–2020)

	1995	*2000*	*2010*	*2020*
United States	100.0%	100.0%	100.0%	100.0%
Alabama	0.3	0.3	0.3	0.3
Alaska	0.3	0.4	0.6	0.8
Arizona	0.9	1.0	0.9	0.9
Arkansas	0.2	0.2	0.2	0.2
California	38.8	38.1	39.1	40.7
Colorado	0.9	1.0	1.0	0.9
Connecticut	0.7	0.7	0.8	0.8
Delaware	0.1	0.1	0.1	0.1
District of Columbia	0.2	0.1	0.1	0.1
Florida	2.3	2.4	2.4	2.4
Georgia	1.2	1.3	1.2	1.1
Hawaii	8.1	7.1	6.0	5.6
Idaho	0.1	0.2	0.1	0.1
Illinois	3.8	3.8	3.6	3.4
Indiana	0.5	0.5	0.5	0.5
Iowa	0.4	0.4	0.4	0.4
Kansas	0.4	0.4	0.4	0.4
Kentucky	0.3	0.3	0.2	0.2
Louisiana	0.6	0.6	0.5	0.5
Maine	0.1	0.1	0.1	0.1
Maryland	2.0	2.0	1.9	1.9
Massachusetts	2.0	2.2	2.4	2.4
Michigan	1.4	1.4	1.4	1.3
Minnesota	1.1	1.2	1.3	1.3
Mississippi	0.2	0.2	0.2	0.2
Missouri	0.6	0.6	0.5	0.5
Montana	0.1	0.1	0.1	0.1
Nebraska	0.2	0.2	0.2	0.2
Nevada	0.7	0.8	0.7	0.7
New Hampshire	0.1	0.1	0.1	0.1
New Jersey	4.0	4.2	4.5	4.5
New Mexico	0.2	0.3	0.3	0.3
New York	9.3	9.1	8.9	8.7
North Carolina	0.8	0.9	0.8	0.8
North Dakota	0.0	0.1	0.0	0.0
Ohio	1.2	1.2	1.2	1.2

(continued)

(continued from previous page)

	1995	2000	2010	2020
Oklahoma	0.4%	0.5%	0.4%	0.4%
Oregon	1.0	1.0	1.0	1.0
Pennsylvania	1.9	1.9	1.9	1.9
Rhode Island	0.2	0.2	0.3	0.3
South Carolina	0.3	0.3	0.3	0.3
South Dakota	0.0	0.0	0.0	0.0
Tennessee	0.5	0.5	0.5	0.4
Texas	4.8	5.0	5.0	4.9
Utah	0.5	0.6	0.6	0.5
Vermont	0.0	0.1	0.1	0.1
Virginia	2.3	2.4	2.4	2.4
Washington	3.1	3.2	3.2	3.3
West Virginia	0.1	0.1	0.1	0.1
Wisconsin	0.8	0.9	1.0	1.0
Wyoming	0.0	0.0	0.0	0.1

Source: Calculations by New Strategist based on Census Bureau data in Population Projections for States, by Age, Sex, Race, and Hispanic Origin: 1995 to 2025, *Current Population Reports, PPL-47, 1996*

Asian Share of State Populations, 1995 to 2020

(Asians as a percent of state populations, selected years 1995–2020; percentage point change, 1995–2020)

	1995	2000	2010	2020	percentage point change 1995—2020
United States	**3.6%**	**4.1%**	**5.1%**	**6.1%**	**2.5**
Alabama	0.7	0.8	0.9	1.0	0.4
Alaska	4.6	7.0	12.9	18.9	14.2
Arizona	1.9	2.2	2.6	2.9	1.0
Arkansas	0.6	0.7	0.8	1.0	0.4
California	11.5	13.2	15.9	17.7	6.2
Colorado	2.2	2.6	3.2	3.6	1.4
Connecticut	2.0	2.4	3.4	4.2	2.1
Delaware	1.7	2.0	2.3	2.8	1.2
District of Columbia	3.1	2.9	3.8	4.3	1.3
Florida	1.5	1.8	2.1	2.4	0.9
Georgia	1.6	1.8	2.1	2.4	0.8
Hawaii	63.6	63.3	63.9	65.2	1.6
Idaho	1.1	1.3	1.4	1.5	0.4
Illinois	3.0	3.5	4.3	5.0	2.0
Indiana	0.8	1.0	1.2	1.4	0.6
Iowa	1.2	1.5	2.0	2.3	1.1
Kansas	1.6	1.9	2.2	2.5	0.9
Kentucky	0.6	0.7	0.9	1.0	0.4
Louisiana	1.2	1.4	1.8	2.0	0.8
Maine	0.6	0.7	1.0	1.2	0.6
Maryland	3.7	4.2	5.2	6.1	2.4
Massachusetts	3.1	4.0	5.6	7.1	3.9
Michigan	1.4	1.7	2.2	2.6	1.2
Minnesota	2.3	2.9	3.8	4.6	2.3
Mississippi	0.6	0.7	0.8	1.0	0.4
Missouri	1.0	1.1	1.4	1.5	0.5
Montana	0.6	0.7	0.9	1.0	0.4
Nebraska	1.0	1.3	1.7	2.1	1.0
Nevada	4.0	4.5	5.2	5.8	1.8
New Hampshire	1.0	1.1	1.6	1.9	1.0
New Jersey	4.7	5.8	7.9	9.6	4.9
New Mexico	1.2	1.6	1.9	2.1	0.9
New York	4.8	5.7	7.3	8.8	4.0
North Carolina	1.0	1.2	1.5	1.7	0.7
North Dakota	0.6	0.9	1.0	1.3	0.6
Ohio	1.0	1.2	1.6	2.0	0.9

(continued)

(continued from previous page)

	1995	2000	2010	2020	percentage point change 1995–2020
Oklahoma	1.3%	1.5%	1.8%	2.1%	0.8
Oregon	2.9	3.4	4.1	4.7	1.7
Pennsylvania	1.5	1.8	2.4	3.0	1.5
Rhode Island	2.2	2.8	3.9	5.0	2.8
South Carolina	0.8	0.9	1.0	1.2	0.4
South Dakota	0.5	0.6	0.8	1.1	0.5
Tennessee	0.8	1.0	1.2	1.3	0.5
Texas	2.4	2.8	3.3	3.7	1.3
Utah	2.4	2.8	3.3	3.7	1.3
Vermont	0.7	1.0	1.2	1.5	0.8
Virginia	3.2	3.8	4.9	5.7	2.5
Washington	5.3	6.1	7.4	8.6	3.3
West Virginia	0.5	0.6	0.8	1.0	0.5
Wisconsin	1.4	1.9	2.6	3.3	1.8
Wyoming	0.6	0.8	1.2	1.5	0.9

Source: Calculations by New Strategist based on Census Bureau data in Population Projections for States, by Age, Sex, Race, and Hispanic Origin: 1995 to 2020, *Current Population Reports, PPL-47, 1996*

Metropolitan Areas with the Most Asians, 1990

(metropolitan areas with at least 100,000 Asians ranked by size of Asian population; number of Asians and Asian share of total metropolitan population, 1990; numbers in thousands)

		number	percent
1.	Los Angeles–Riverside–Orange County, CA	1,339	9.2%
2.	San Francisco–Oakland–San Jose, CA	927	14.8
3.	New York–Northern New Jersey–Long Island, NY-NJ-CT-PA	898	4.6
4.	Honolulu, HI	526	63.0
5.	Chicago–Gary–Kenosha, IL-IN-WI	258	3.1
6.	Washington–Baltimore, DC-MD-VA-WV	248	3.7
7.	San Diego, CA	198	7.9
8.	Seattle–Tacoma–Bremerton, WA	181	6.1
9.	Boston–Brockton–Nashua, MA-NH-ME-CT	137	2.5
10.	Houston–Galveston–Brazoria, TX	132	3.5
11.	Philadelphia–Wilmington–Atlantic City, PA-NJ-DE-MD	119	2.0
12.	Sacramento–Yolo, CA	115	7.7

Source: Bureau of the Census, Statistical Abstract of the United States 1993; *calculations by New Strategist*

2

Blacks

■ The black population is projected to grow from 35 million in 1998 to more than 45 million by 2020. Blacks will remain the largest minority in the U.S. until 2009, when Hispanics will outnumber them.

■ Seventy-four percent of blacks were high school graduates in 1996. While this share is less than that of the total population, blacks are rapidly gaining on whites in educational attainment.

■ A 57 percent majority of blacks say they are in excellent or very good health. Only 15 percent say they are in fair or poor health.

■ Just 18 percent of black households consist of married couples with children. Fifty-eight percent of black children live with their mother only.

■ Few blacks think their neighborhood has a crime problem—only 10 percent of homeowners and 17 percent of renters say crime is a problem in their area.

■ Black household income was just 66 percent of the median for all households in 1996. Behind the lower household income of blacks is the fact that only 32 percent of black households are married couples—typically the most affluent household type.

■ The median net worth of nonwhite and Hispanic households was just $16,500 in 1995. Net worth is low for blacks because most do not own homes.

Blacks are 12 percent of the U.S. population

(percent distribution of total persons by race and ethnicity, 1998)

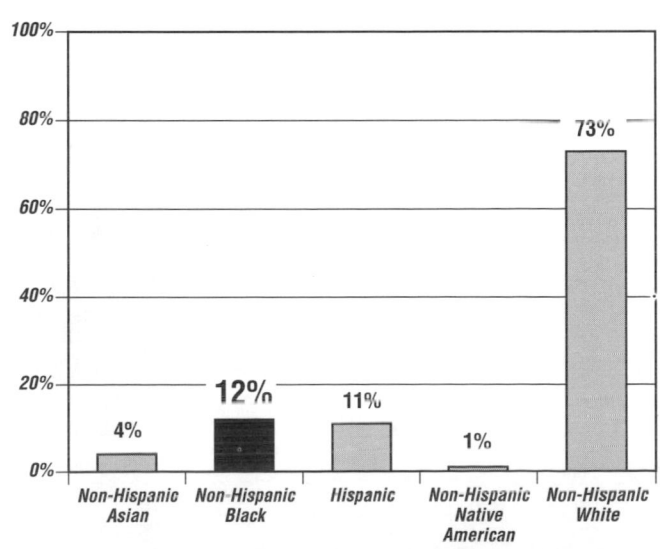

Blacks: Education

Blacks are gaining on whites in educational attainment.

Seventy-four percent of blacks aged 25 or older are high school graduates. While this figure is 9 percentage points lower than the share of the total population with a high school diploma, blacks are rapidly gaining on whites.

As recently as 1980, barely half of blacks had graduated from high school. The surge in educational attainment is due to the much greater educational level of younger blacks. Among blacks aged 25 to 39, from 84 to 87 percent are high school graduates.

Fourteen percent of blacks aged 25 or older had a bachelor's degree in 1996, compared with 24 percent of the total population. Among black families with children aged 18 to 24, 29 percent have a child in college full-time. This proportion rises to 52 percent among black families with incomes of $75,000 or more. Nearly 2 million blacks were in college in 1995, 39 percent of them full-time students at four-year schools.

Blacks earned 7.5 percent of bachelor's degrees, 6 percent of master's degrees, and 4 percent of doctorates awarded in 1994–95. Blacks earned 8 percent of first-professional degrees in theology and 10 percent of those in pharmacy.

■ The proportion of blacks with a college education is likely to surge in the next decade thanks to changes in the tax code which make it easier for low- and middle-income families to afford college tuition.

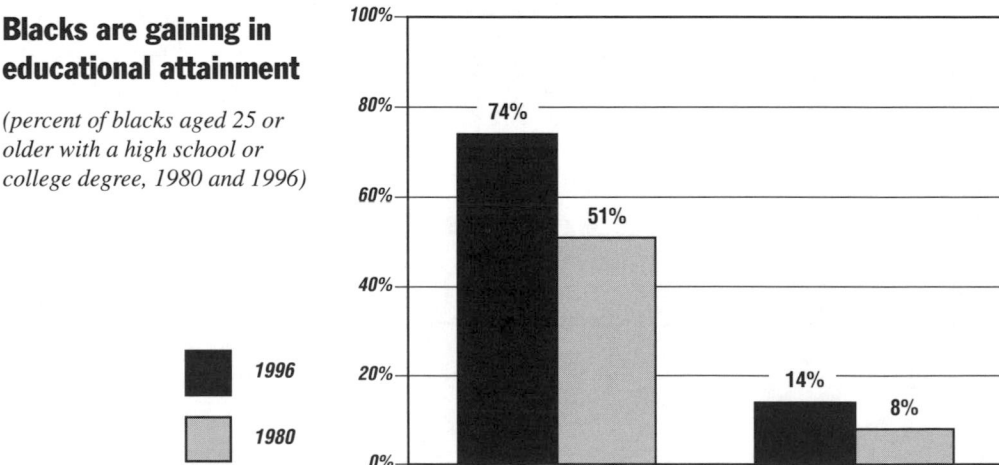

Blacks are gaining in educational attainment

(percent of blacks aged 25 or older with a high school or college degree, 1980 and 1996)

■ 1996
▨ 1980

Educational Attainment of Blacks by Sex, 1996

(number and percent distribution of blacks aged 25 or older by educational attainment and sex, 1996; numbers in thousands)

	total		men		women	
	number	*percent*	*number*	*percent*	*number*	*percent*
Total, aged 25 or older	**18,715**	**100.0%**	**8,286**	**100.0%**	**10,429**	**100.0%**
Not a high school graduate	4,819	25.7	2,133	25.7	2,687	25.8
High school graduate or more	13,896	74.3	6,154	74.3	7,742	74.2
High school graduate only	6,576	35.1	3,107	37.5	3,468	33.3
Some college or assoc. degree	4,769	25.5	2,020	24.4	2,750	26.4
Bachelor's degree or more	2,551	13.6	1,027	12.4	1,524	14.6
Bachelor's degree only	1,868	10.0	715	8.6	1,153	11.1
Master's degree	530	2.8	225	2.7	305	2.9
Professional degree	78	0.4	36	0.4	42	0.4
Doctoral degree	75	0.4	51	0.6	24	0.2

Source: Bureau of the Census, Educational Attainment in the United States: March 1996, *Current Population Reports, P20-493, 1997; calculations by New Strategist*

Black High School and College Graduates by Sex, 1980 to 1996

(percent of blacks aged 25 or older who are high school or college graduates, by sex, selected years 1980–96)

	total	men	women
High school graduates			
1996	74.3%	74.3%	74.2%
1990	66.2	65.8	66.5
1985	59.8	58.4	60.8
1980	51.2	51.1	51.3
College graduates			
1996	13.6	12.4	14.6
1990	11.3	11.9	10.8
1985	11.1	11.2	11.0
1980	7.9	7.7	8.1

Source: Bureau of the Census, Educational Attainment in the United States: March 1996, *Current Population Reports, P20-493, 1997; and Internet web site,* http://www.census.gov

Black High School and College Graduates by Age and Sex, 1996

(percent of blacks aged 25 or older who are high school or college graduates by age and sex, 1996)

	total	*men*	*women*
High school gradutes			
Total, aged 25 or older	**74.3%**	**74.3%**	**74.2%**
Aged 25 to 29	85.6	87.2	84.2
Aged 30 to 34	83.5	83.3	83.7
Aged 35 to 39	87.3	86.0	88.3
Aged 40 to 44	82.3	78.1	85.9
Aged 45 to 49	76.9	77.4	76.4
Aged 50 to 54	69.7	68.4	70.8
Aged 55 to 59	62.3	59.0	64.9
Aged 60 to 64	58.0	58.9	57.3
Aged 65 and over	41.5	39.9	42.4
College graduates			
Total, aged 25 or older	**13.6**	**12.4**	**14.6**
Aged 25 to 29	14.6	12.4	16.4
Aged 30 to 34	12.9	10.0	15.2
Aged 35 to 39	17.6	15.1	19.6
Aged 40 to 44	16.0	14.6	17.2
Aged 45 to 49	15.5	16.0	15.1
Aged 50 to 54	13.0	12.8	13.2
Aged 55 to 59	11.1	9.4	12.5
Aged 60 to 64	11.8	12.3	11.4
Aged 65 and over	7.3	6.5	7.8

Source: Bureau of the Census, Educational Attainment in the United States: March 1996, *Current Population Reports, P20-493, 1997*

Black High School and College Graduates
by Age and Region, 1996

(percent of blacks aged 25 or older who are high school or college graduates, by age and region, 1996)

	Northeast	Midwest	South	West
High school graduates				
Total, aged 25 or older	**74.4%**	**78.6%**	**71.3%**	**82.8%**
Aged 25 to 34	82.5	86.5	83.3	91.9
Aged 35 to 44	83.8	87.8	83.9	87.6
Aged 45 to 54	72.5	78.2	71.3	84.5
Aged 55 to 64	63.9	73.1	52.8	69.6
Aged 65 or older	51.9	49.5	33.2	54.9
College graduates				
Total, aged 25 or older	**12.4**	**12.2**	**13.2**	**21.8**
Aged 25 to 34	12.6	12.1	13.4	19.8
Aged 35 to 44	16.2	13.3	16.7	24.3
Aged 45 to 54	11.2	12.6	14.0	30.6
Aged 55 to 64	9.1	15.2	9.8	18.1
Aged 65 or older	9.2	6.5	6.3	11.2

Source: Bureau of the Census, Educational Attainment in the United States: March 1996, *Current Population Reports, P20-493, 1997*

Black High School and College Graduates by State, 1990

(percent of blacks aged 25 or older who are high school or college graduates, by state, 1990)

	high school graduate or more	college graduate		high school graduate or more	college graduate
United States	**63.1%**	**11.4%**	Missouri	65.1%	11.2%
Alabama	54.6	9.3	Montana	80.9	18.4
Alaska	88.2	14.1	Nebraska	73.2	12.4
Arizona	75.1	14.3	Nevada	70.8	9.0
Arkansas	51.5	8.4	New Hampshire	86.1	25.7
California	75.6	14.8	New Jersey	67.0	13.6
Colorado	80.8	17.1	New Mexico	74.7	14.2
Connecticut	67.0	12.3	New York	64.7	12.6
Delaware	63.2	10.6	North Carolina	58.1	9.5
District of Columbia	63.8	15.3	North Dakota	95.9	17.1
Florida	56.4	9.8	Ohio	64.6	9.1
Georgia	58.6	11.0	Oklahoma	70.1	12.0
Hawaii	94.2	15.2	Oregon	75.0	9.1
Idaho	82.8	15.8	Pennsylvania	63.5	10.0
Illinois	65.2	11.4	Rhode Island	65.9	12.7
Indiana	65.4	9.3	South Carolina	53.3	7.6
Iowa	70.1	12.8	South Dakota	82.2	24.1
Kansas	71.0	11.6	Tennessee	59.4	10.2
Kentucky	61.7	7.7	Texas	66.1	12.0
Louisiana	53.1	9.1	Utah	77.0	15.9
Maine	87.6	22.3	Vermont	82.9	30.5
Maryland	70.6	16.1	Virginia	60.3	11.1
Massachusetts	70.0	17.0	Washington	81.2	15.4
Michigan	64.9	10.1	West Virginia	64.7	10.9
Minnesota	76.2	17.5	Wisconsin	61.3	8.3
Mississippi	47.3	8.8	Wyoming	81.2	9.5

Source: National Center for Education Statistics, Digest of Education Statistics 1993, *NCES 93-292, 1993*

School Enrollment of Blacks by Age and Sex, 1995

(number and percent of blacks aged 3 or older enrolled in school, by age and sex, October 1995; numbers in thousands)

	total		male		female	
	number	*percent*	*number*	*percent*	*number*	*percent*
Total, aged 3 or older	**10,753**	**33.9%**	**5,313**	**36.2%**	**5,440**	**31.9%**
Aged 3 and 4	657	47.5	351	51.5	306	43.6
Aged 5 and 6	1,305	95.5	649	94.7	656	96.3
Aged 7 to 9	1,867	97.7	956	98.2	911	97.2
Aged 10 to 13	2,441	99.2	1,239	99.5	1,202	99.0
Aged 14 and 15	1,223	99.0	621	99.6	602	98.3
Aged 16 and 17	1,127	92.9	602	95.2	525	90.4
Aged 18 and 19	631	57.4	307	59.1	325	55.9
Aged 20 and 21	363	37.4	157	36.1	206	38.5
Aged 22 to 24	309	19.9	143	20.3	166	19.5
Aged 25 to 29	254	10.0	69	6.1	185	13.0
Aged 30 to 34	217	7.8	85	6.7	133	8.7
Aged 35 to 44	230	4.4	98	4.1	132	4.7
Aged 45 to 54	97	2.9	28	1.9	69	3.8
Aged 55 or older	32	0.7	9	0.5	23	0.8

Source: Bureau of the Census, School Enrollment—Social and Economic Characteristics of Students: October 1995, *Current Population Reports, P20-492, 1997*

Black Families with Children in College, 1995

(total number of black families, number with children aged 18 to 24, and number and percent with children aged 18 to 24 attending college full-time as of October 1995, by household income in 1994; numbers in thousands)

| | total | with children aged 18–24 | with one or more children attending college full-time | | |
			number	percent of total families	percent of families with children 18–24
Total families	**8,446**	**1,472**	**422**	**5.0%**	**28.7%**
Under $20,000	3,508	544	102	2.9	18.8
$20,000 to $29,999	1,251	244	87	7.0	35.7
$30,000 to $39,999	880	149	53	6.0	35.6
$40,000 to $49,999	535	94	37	6.9	39.4
$50,000 to $74,999	812	151	54	6.7	35.8
$75,000 or more	379	90	47	12.4	52.2

Source: Bureau of the Census, School Enrollment—Social and Economic Characteristics of Students: October 1995, *Current Population Reports, P20-492, 1997; calculations by New Strategist*

College Enrollment of Blacks by Age, 1995

(number and percent distribution of blacks aged 15 or older enrolled in college by age, type of school, and attendance status, October 1995; numbers in thousands)

| | | undergraduate | | | | | | | graduate | | |
| | total | total | two-year college | | | four-year college | | | total | full-time | part-time |
			total	full-time	part-time	total	full-time	part-time			
Total enrolled	1,772	1,475	573	318	255	902	692	211	297	107	190
Aged 15 to 17	24	22	6	6	–	16	16	–	2	2	–
Aged 18 and 19	344	344	111	94	18	233	216	17	–	–	–
Aged 20 and 21	339	334	107	71	36	227	207	20	5	5	–
Aged 22 to 24	305	260	88	49	39	172	130	42	46	32	14
Aged 25 to 29	233	169	82	43	40	87	57	31	63	32	31
Aged 30 to 34	193	139	80	26	54	59	32	27	54	16	38
Aged 35 to 39	126	79	35	20	15	44	17	27	47	9	38
Aged 40 to 44	91	60	24	4	19	36	12	24	31	4	27
Aged 45 to 49	72	45	30	4	27	15	3	12	27	8	19
Aged 50 to 54	17	6	4	–	4	2	–	2	11	–	11
Aged 55 or older	27	17	6	2	4	11	1	9	11	–	11

(continued)

(continued from previous page)

| | | undergraduate | | | | | | | graduate | | |
| | | | two-year college | | | four-year college | | | | | |
Percent distribution by age	total	total	total	full-time	part-time	total	full-time	part-time	total	full-time	part-time
Total enrolled	100.0%	100.0%	100.0%	100.0%	100.0%	100.0%	100.0%	100.0%	100.0%	100.0%	100.0%
Aged 15 to 17	1.4	1.5	1.0	1.9	–	1.8	2.3	–	0.7	1.9	–
Aged 18 and 19	19.4	23.3	19.4	29.6	7.1	25.8	31.2	8.1	–	–	–
Aged 20 and 21	19.1	22.6	18.7	22.3	14.1	25.2	29.9	9.5	1.7	4.7	–
Aged 22 to 24	17.2	17.6	15.4	15.4	15.5	19.1	18.8	19.9	15.5	29.9	7.4
Aged 25 to 29	13.1	11.5	14.3	13.5	15.7	9.6	8.2	14.7	21.2	29.9	16.3
Aged 30 to 34	10.9	9.4	14.0	8.2	21.2	6.5	4.6	12.8	18.2	15.0	20.0
Aged 35 to 39	7.1	5.4	6.1	6.3	5.9	4.9	2.5	12.8	15.8	8.4	20.0
Aged 40 to 44	5.1	4.1	4.2	1.3	7.5	4.0	1.7	11.4	10.4	3.7	14.2
Aged 45 to 49	4.1	3.1	5.2	1.3	10.6	1.7	0.4	5.7	9.1	7.5	10.0
Aged 50 to 54	1.0	0.4	0.7	–	1.6	0.2	–	0.9	3.7	–	5.8
Aged 55 or older	1.5	1.2	1.0	–	1.6	1.2	–	4.3	3.7	–	5.8

(continued)

(continued from previous page)

Percent distribution by type of school and attendance status

	total	undergraduate							graduate		
		total	two-year college			four-year college			total	full-time	part-time
			total	full-time	part-time	total	full-time	part-time			
Total enrolled	**100.0%**	**83.2%**	**32.3%**	**17.9%**	**14.4%**	**50.9%**	**39.1%**	**11.%**	**16.8%**	**6.0%**	**10.7%**
Aged 15 to 17	100.0	91.7	25.0	25.0	–	66.7	66.7	–	8.3	8.3	–
Aged 18 and 19	100.0	100.0	32.3	27.3	5.2	67.7	62.8	4.9	–	–	–
Aged 20 and 21	100.0	98.5	31.6	20.9	10.6	67.0	61.1	5.9	1.5	1.5	–
Aged 22 to 24	100.0	85.2	28.9	16.1	12.8	56.4	42.6	13.8	15.1	10.5	4.6
Aged 25 to 29	100.0	72.5	35.2	18.5	17.2	37.3	24.5	13.3	27.0	13.7	13.3
Aged 30 to 34	100.0	72.0	41.5	13.5	28.0	30.6	16.6	14.0	28.0	8.3	19.7
Aged 35 to 39	100.0	62.7	27.8	15.9	11.9	34.9	13.5	21.4	37.3	7.1	30.2
Aged 40 to 44	100.0	65.9	26.4	4.4	20.9	39.6	13.2	26.4	34.1	4.4	29.7
Aged 45 to 49	100.0	62.5	41.7	5.6	37.5	20.8	4.2	16.7	37.5	11.1	26.4
Aged 50 to 54	100.0	35.3	23.5	–	23.5	11.8	–	11.8	64.7	–	64.7
Aged 55 or older	100.0	63.0	22.2	7.4	14.8	40.7	3.7	33.3	40.7	0.0	40.7

Note: (–) means sample is too small to make a reliable estimate.
Source: Bureau of the Census, School Enrollment—Social and Economic Characteristics of Students: October 1995, Current Population Reports, P20-492, 1997; calculations by New Strategist

Bachelor's, Master's, and Doctoral Degrees Earned by Non-Hispanic Blacks by Field of Study, 1994–95

(number and percent of bachelor's, master's, and doctoral degrees earned by non-Hispanic blacks, by field of study, 1994–95)

	bachelor's		master's		doctoral	
	number	percent	number	percent	number	percent
Total degrees	**87,203**	**7.5%**	**24,171**	**6.1%**	**1,667**	**3.8%**
Agriculture and natural resources	472	2.4	116	2.7	13	1.0
Architecture and related programs	345	3.9	142	3.6	6	4.3
Area, ethnic, and cultural studies	650	11.4	121	7.4	22	11.8
Biological and life sciences	3,303	5.9	169	3.1	87	1.9
Business, management, and admin. services	20,286	8.7	5,165	5.5	41	2.9
Communications	4,036	8.4	376	7.3	14	4.4
Communications technologies	86	12.3	34	7.3	–	–
Computer and information sciences	2,563	10.5	372	3.6	9	1.0
Construction trade	8	7.1	3	42.9	–	–
Education	6,658	6.3	8,163	8.1	620	9.0
Engineering	2,908	4.7	706	2.5	76	1.2
Engineering-related technologies	1,262	8.1	58	5.2	–	–
English language and literature	3,303	6.4	300	3.8	37	2.4
Foreign languages and literature	498	3.6	75	2.4	8	0.9
Health professions and related sciences	5,806	7.3	1,682	5.4	90	4.3
Home economics	1,051	6.8	238	8.3	28	7.2
Law and legal studies	211	10.4	89	3.5	1	1.1
Liberal arts and sciences	3,155	9.5	158	6.2	8	8.9
Library science	2	4.0	227	4.5	7	12.7
Mathematics	1,011	7.4	162	3.9	5	0.4
Mechanics and repairers	2	3.0	–	–	–	–
Multi- and interdisciplinary studies	1,893	7.3	131	5.3	13	5.5
Parks, recreation, leisure, and fitness	715	5.5	64	3.6	5	3.4
Philosophy and religion	326	4.5	44	3.2	14	2.8
Physical sciences	1,056	5.5	156	2.7	45	1.0
Precision production trades	43	12.2	–	–	–	–
Protective services	3,702	15.3	252	14.8	4	15.4
Psychology	5,878	8.2	898	6.5	154	4.0
Public administration and services	3,026	16.3	2,702	11.5	59	10.6
R.O.T.C. and military sciences	–	–	7	5.6	–	–
Social sciences and history	10,562	8.2	874	5.9	119	3.2
Theological studies and religious vocations	243	4.4	274	5.2	150	9.4
Transportation and material moving	168	4.5	30	3.6	–	–
Visual and performing arts	1,975	4.1	383	3.7	32	3.0

Note: (–) means no degrees were awarded.
Source: National Center for Education Statistics, Digest of Education Statistics 1997, *NCES 98-015, 1997;* calculations by New Strategist

First-Professional Degrees Earned
by Non-Hispanic Blacks by Field of Study, 1994–95

(number and percent of first-professional degrees earned by blacks by field of study, 1994–95)

	number	percent
Total degrees	**4,747**	**6.3%**
Dentistry (D.D.S. or D.M.D.)	180	4.6
Medicine (M.D.)	929	6.0
Optometry (O.D.)	27	2.3
Osteopathic medicine (D.O.)	51	2.8
Pharmacy (Pharm. D.)	233	10.3
Podiatry (Pod. D., D.P., or D.P.M.)	28	5.1
Veterinary medicine (D.V.M.)	52	2.4
Chiropractic medicine (D.C. or D.C.M.)	50	1.7
Law (LL.B. or J.D.)	2,699	6.9
Theology (M.Div., M.H.L., B.D., or Ord.)	496	8.3
Other	2	2.7

Source: National Center for Education Statistics, Digest of Education Statistics 1997, *NCES 98-015, 1997; calculations by New Strategist*

Blacks: Health

Most blacks say their health is very good or excellent, but their life expectancy remains below average.

While blacks fare poorly on many health indicators, a 57 percent majority say they are in excellent or very good health. This compares with 66 percent of the total population who rate their health as excellent or very good.

Just under 600,000 babies were born to black women in 1996, accounting for 15 percent of all babies born that year. Fully 70 percent of black babies are born to unmarried women, the highest proportion among all racial and ethnic groups.

The disability rate among blacks is about average, with 26 percent of blacks aged 15 or older having been disabled in 1994–95. This compares with a disability rate of 24 percent for the total population.

Heart disease, cancer, and cerebrovascular disease are the three leading killers of blacks, just as they are for the population as a whole. But AIDS ranks fourth as a cause of death among blacks, while it is the eighth leading cause of death nationally. Black life expectancy is well below average.

■ While blacks have made significant gains in income and education over the past few decades, their health status is lagging. Behind the lower life expectancy of blacks are much higher rates of infant mortality and homicide.

Blacks rate their own health highly

(percent distribution of blacks by self-assessed health status, 1994)

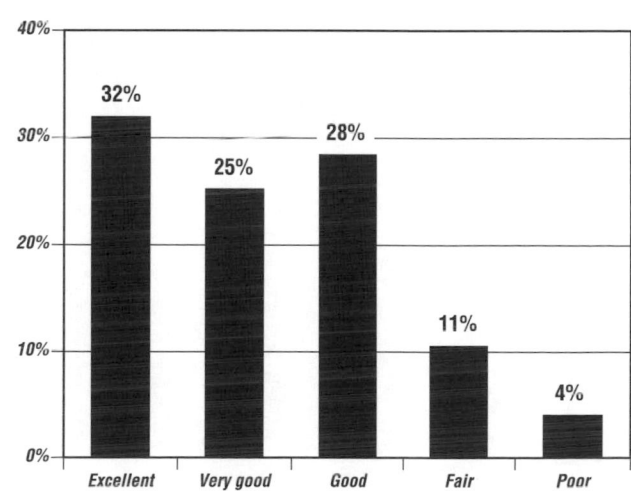

Health Status of Blacks by Age, 1994

(percent distribution of self-assessed or parent-assessed health status of blacks, by age, 1994)

	total	excellent	very good	good	fair	poor
Total persons	**100.0%**	**31.9%**	**25.2%**	**28.4%**	**10.5%**	**4.0%**
Under age 5	100.0	46.6	25.6	23.2	4.0	0.6
Aged 5 to 17	100.0	41.7	25.8	27.4	4.4	0.8
Aged 18 to 24	100.0	36.6	28.7	27.4	5.8	1.4
Aged 25 to 44	100.0	31.0	27.4	28.9	10.0	2.7
Aged 45 to 64	100.0	16.4	21.2	32.2	20.2	10.0
Aged 65 or older	100.0	10.4	16.3	30.4	26.6	16.2

Source: National Center for Health Statistics, Current Estimates from the National Health Interview Survey, 1994, *Series 10, No. 193, 1995*

Health Indicators for Blacks, 1993 and 1994

(selected indicators of total population and black health status, and index of black health indicators to total, 1993 and 1994)

	total population indicator	black indicator	index
Infant mortality rate (deaths before age 1 per 1,000 live births), 1993	8.4	16.5	196
Total deaths per 100,000 population, 1993	513.3	785.2	153
Motor vehicle crash deaths per 100,000 population, 1993	16.0	16.3	102
Work-related injury deaths per 100,000 people aged 16 or older, 1994	3.3	3.1	94
Suicides per 100,000 population, 1993	11.3	7.2	64
Homicides per 100,000 population, 1993	10.7	40.9	382
Lung cancer deaths per 100,000 population, 1993	39.3	48.9	124
Female breast cancer deaths per 100,000 population, 1993	21.5	27.1	126
Cardiovascular disease deaths per 100,000 population, 1993	181.8	269.6	148
Heart disease deaths per 100,000 population, 1993	145.3	208.9	144
Stroke deaths per 100,000 population, 1993	26.5	45.0	170
Reported incidence of AIDS per 100,000 population, 1994*	26.9	93.3	347
Reported incidence of tuberculosis per 100,000 population, 1994*	9.4	26.8	285
Reported incidence of syphilis per 100,000 population, 1994*	8.1	59.5	735
Prevalence of low birth weight, as percent of total live births, 1994	7.3	13.2	181
Births to girls aged 10 to 17, as percent of total live births, 1994	5.3	10.8	204
Percent of mothers without care, first trimester of pregnancy, 1994	19.8	31.7	160
Percent under age 18 living in poverty, 1994	21.8	43.8	201
Percent living in counties exceeding U.S. air quality standards, 1994	24.9	29.6	119

* Data are for the non-Hispanic black population.
Note: The index for each indicator is calculated by dividing the black figure by the total population figure and multiplying by 100. For example, the index of 196 in the first row indicates that black infant mortality is 96 percent above the rate for all infants.
Source: National Center for Health Statistics, Health Status Indicators by Race and Hispanic Origin, Healthy People 2000 Review, 1995–96; calculations by New Strategist

Births to Black Women by Age, 1996

(number and percent distribution of births to black women, by age, 1996)

	number	*percent*
Total births	**596,039**	**100.0%**
Under age 15	5,227	0.9
Aged 15 to 19	131,059	22.0
Aged 20 to 24	180,093	30.2
Aged 25 to 29	133,437	22.4
Aged 30 to 34	94,256	15.8
Aged 35 to 39	43,614	7.3
Aged 40 or older	8,352	1.4

Source: National Center for Health Statistics, Births and Deaths: United States, 1996, *Monthly Vital Statistics Report, Vol. 46, No.1, Supplement 2, 1997; calculations by New Strategist*

Births to Unmarried Black Women by Age, 1995

(number and percent of births to unmarried black women, by age; 1995)

	number	percent of total black births
Births to unmarried blacks	**421,489**	**69.9%**
Under age 15	5,876	99.1
Aged 15 to 19	127,241	95.2
Aged 20 to 24	145,134	79.1
Aged 25 to 29	75,815	56.8
Aged 30 to 34	44,690	46.5
Aged 35 to 39	19,271	45.3
Aged 40 or older	3,462	43.5

Source: National Center for Health Statistics, Births and Deaths: United States, 1996, *Monthly Vital Statistics Report, Vol. 46, No.1, Supplement 2, 1997; calculations by New Strategist*

Births to Black Women by State, 1996

(number and percent distribution of births to black women by state, and black births as a percent of total births by state, 1996)

	number	percent	black share of total births
United States	**596,039**	**100.0%**	**15.2%**
Alabama	19,833	3.3	32.3
Alaska	425	0.1	4.2
Arizona	2,447	0.4	3.1
Arkansas	7,921	1.3	21.8
California	37,695	6.3	7.0
Colorado	2,579	0.4	4.6
Connecticut	5,224	0.9	11.8
Delaware	2,391	0.4	23.3
District of Columbia	6,123	1.0	73.5
Florida	42,288	7.1	22.3
Georgia	38,777	6.5	33.8
Hawaii	508	0.1	2.8
Idaho	76	0.0	0.4
Illinois	36,499	6.1	19.8
Indiana	9,024	1.5	10.8
Iowa	1,047	0.2	2.8
Kansas	3,006	0.5	7.6
Kentucky	4,862	0.8	9.2
Louisiana	26,860	4.5	40.6
Maine	85	0.0	0.6
Maryland	22,349	3.7	32.1
Massachusetts	7,329	1.2	9.1
Michigan	24,873	4.2	18.1
Minnesota	3,034	0.5	4.8
Mississippi	19,288	3.2	46.3
Missouri	11,091	1.9	15.0
Montana	37	0.0	0.3
Nebraska	1,203	0.2	5.2
Nevada	1,972	0.3	7.6
New Hampshire	112	0.0	0.8
New Jersey	20,101	3.4	17.6
New Mexico	467	0.1	1.7
New York	55,805	9.4	20.6
North Carolina	27,462	4.6	26.0
North Dakota	87	0.0	1.0
Ohio	21,705	3.6	14.2

(continued)

(continued from previous page)

	number	percent	black share of total births
Oklahoma	4,486	0.8%	9.7%
Oregon	893	0.1	2.0
Pennsylvania	20,791	3.5	13.9
Rhode Island	931	0.2	7.4
South Carolina	17,861	3.0	35.2
South Dakota	83	0.0	0.8
Tennessee	16,029	2.7	21.7
Texas	38,708	6.5	11.8
Utah	331	0.1	0.8
Vermont	17	0.0	0.3
Virginia	20,920	3.5	22.6
Washington	3,187	0.5	4.0
West Virginia	744	0.1	3.6
Wisconsin	6,425	1.1	9.6
Wyoming	49	0.0	0.8

Source: National Center for Health Statistics, Births and Deaths: United States, 1996, *Monthly Vital Statistics Report, Vol. 46, No.1, Supplement 2, 1997; calculations by New Strategist*

Projections of Births to Black Women, 1998 to 2020

(number of births to black women, and black births as a percent of total births, 1998–2020; numbers in thousands)

	number	black share of total births
1998	677	17.4%
1999	681	17.5
2000	685	17.6
2001	690	17.7
2002	695	17.7
2003	702	17.8
2004	709	17.9
2005	718	17.9
2006	728	18.0
2007	738	18.0
2008	748	18.1
2009	758	18.1
2010	767	18.1
2011	776	18.1
2012	783	18.1
2013	791	18.1
2014	797	18.1
2015	804	18.1
2016	810	18.1
2017	816	18.1
2018	822	18.1
2019	828	18.2
2020	834	18.2

Source: Bureau of the Census, Population Projections of the United States, by Age, Sex, Race, and Hispanic Origin: 1995 to 2050, *Current Population Reports, P25-1130, 1996; calculations by New Strategist*

Acute Health Conditions among Blacks by Age, 1994

(number of acute conditions and rate per 100 blacks, by type of acute condition and age, 1994; numbers in thousands)

	total conditions		under age 18		aged 18 to 44		aged 45 or older	
	number	rate	number	rate	number	rate	number	rate
Total acute conditions	**50,855**	**153.9**	**20,850**	**184.5**	**21,633**	**153.6**	**8,372**	**109.4**
Infective/parasitic diseases	**6,665**	**20.2**	**3,738**	**33.1**	**2,353**	**16.7**	**574**	**7.5**
Common childhood diseases	689	2.1	498	4.4	191	1.4	–	–
Intestinal virus	1,746	5.3	823	7.3	713	5.1	211	2.8
Viral infections	2,438	7.4	1,202	10.6	1,035	7.3	202	2.6
Other	1,791	5.4	1,216	10.8	414	2.9	161	2.1
Respiratory conditions	**21,714**	**65.7**	**8,597**	**76.1**	**9,170**	**65.1**	**3,948**	**51.6**
Common cold	9,680	29.3	4,725	41.8	3,628	25.8	1,326	17.3
Other acute upper respiratory infections	2,333	7.1	925	8.2	893	6.3	516	6.7
Influenza	7,668	23.2	1,934	17.1	3,952	28.1	1,782	23.3
Acute bronchitis	795	2.4	360	3.2	279	2.0	156	2.0
Pneumonia	575	1.7	226	2.0	230	1.6	119	1.6
Other respiratory conditions	664	2.0	427	3.8	187	1.3	50	0.7
Digestive system conditions	**2,939**	**8.9**	**1,103**	**9.8**	**1,500**	**10.7**	**335**	**4.4**
Dental conditions	853	2.6	443	3.9	271	1.9	138	1.8
Indigestion, nausea, vomiting	1,611	4.9	417	3.7	1,080	7.7	114	1.5
Other digestive conditions	474	1.4	243	2.2	148	1.1	83	1.1
Injuries	**6,798**	**20.6**	**2,070**	**18.3**	**3,453**	**24.5**	**1,274**	**16.6**
Fractures and dislocations	719	2.2	312	2.8	145	1.0	262	3.4
Sprains and strains	1,349	4.1	51	0.5	1,063	7.5	235	3.1
Open wounds and lacerations	1,174	3.6	599	5.3	468	3.3	106	1.4
Contusions/superficial injuries	1,719	5.2	696	6.2	500	3.6	523	6.8
Other current injuries	1,836	5.6	412	3.6	1,276	9.1	148	1.9

(continued)

(continued from previous page)

	total conditions		under age 18		aged 18 to 44		aged 45 or older	
	number	*rate*	*number*	*rate*	*number*	*rate*	*number*	*rate*
Selected other acute								
conditions	**8,233**	**24.9**	**4,024**	**35.6**	**2,951**	**21.0**	**1,258**	**16.4**
Eye conditions	481	1.5	115	1.0	117	0.8	249	3.3
Acute ear infections	2,512	7.6	2,315	20.5	188	1.3	8	0.1
Other ear conditions	488	1.5	257	2.3	231	1.6	–	–
Acute urinary conditions	573	1.7	55	0.5	466	3.3	52	0.7
Disorders of menstruation	261	0.8	163	1.4	98	0.7	–	–
Other disorders of female								
genital tract	445	1.3	–	–	302	2.1	143	1.9
Delivery and other conditions								
of pregnancy	725	2.2	37	0.3	688	4.9	–	–
Skin conditions	472	1.4	384	3.4	–	–	87	1.1
Acute musculoskeletal								
conditions	978	3.0	–	–	523	3.7	454	5.9
Headache, excluding migraine	619	1.9	116	1.0	238	1.7	265	3.5
Fever, unspecified	680	2.1	582	5.2	99	0.7	–	–
All other acute conditions	**4,507**	**13.6**	**1,317**	**11.7**	**2,207**	**15.7**	**983**	**12.8**

Note: The acute conditions shown here are those that caused people to restrict their activity for at least half a day or to contact a physician about the illness or injury. (–) means not applicable or sample is too small to make a reliable estimate.
Source: National Center for Health Statistics, Current Estimates from the National Health Interview Survey, 1994, Series 10, No. 193, 1995

Chronic Health Conditions among Blacks by Age, 1994

(number of chronic conditions and rate per 1,000 blacks, by type of chronic condition and age, 1994; numbers in thousands)

	under age 45		aged 45 to 64		aged 65 to 74		aged 75 or older	
	number	rate	number	rate	number	rate	number	rate
Selected skin and musculoskeletal conditions								
Arthritis	723	28.5	1,318	257.0	756	486.8	633	651.9
Gout, including gouty arthritis	75	3.0	141	27.5	54	34.8	86	88.6
Intervertebral disc disorders	68	2.7	130	25.3	61	39.3	–	–
Bone spur/tendinitis, unspecified	40	1.6	58	11.3	–	–	8	8.2
Disorders of bone or cartilage	46	1.8	–	–	–	–	–	–
Trouble with bunions	210	8.3	126	24.6	22	14.2	4	4.1
Bursitis, unclassified	79	3.1	343	66.9	87	56.0	56	57.7
Sebaceous skin cyst	57	2.2	5	1.0	20	12.9	–	–
Trouble with acne	547	21.6	43	8.4	–	–	–	–
Psoriasis	30	1.2	57	11.1	12	7.7	32	33.0
Dermatitis	544	21.4	167	32.6	7	4.5	18	18.5
Trouble with dry skin, unclassified	364	14.3	164	32.0	91	58.6	6	6.2
Trouble with ingrown nails	195	7.7	130	25.3	98	63.1	46	47.4
Trouble with corns/calluses	304	12.0	232	45.2	120	77.3	58	59.7
Impairments								
Visual impairment	595	23.4	295	57.5	68	43.8	153	157.6
Color blindness	118	4.6	113	22.0	5	3.2	–	–
Cataracts	42	1.7	86	16.8	178	114.6	280	288.4
Glaucoma	95	3.7	108	21.1	146	94.0	175	180.2
Hearing impairment	753	29.7	361	70.4	233	150.0	178	183.3
Tinnitus	227	8.9	161	31.4	53	34.1	58	59.7
Speech impairment	620	24.4	108	21.1	35	22.5	8	8.2
Absence of extremities	45	1.8	59	11.5	93	59.9	18	18.5
Paralysis of extremities, complete or partial	130	5.1	57	11.1	33	21.2	21	21.6
Deformity or orthopedic impairment	1,985	78.2	954	186.0	140	90.1	169	174.0
Back	1,170	46.1	416	81.1	69	44.4	119	122.6
Upper extremities	121	4.8	113	22.0	4	2.6	37	38.1
Lower extremities	972	38.3	556	108.4	70	45.1	91	93.7

(continued)

(continued from previous page)

	under age 45		aged 45 to 64		aged 65 to 74		aged 75 or older	
	number	*rate*	*number*	*rate*	*number*	*rate*	*number*	*rate*
Selected digestive conditions								
Ulcer	336	13.2	221	43.1	127	81.8	18	18.5
Hernia of abdominal cavity	219	8.6	62	12.1	89	57.3	18	18.5
Gastritis or duodenitis	211	8.3	26	5.1	26	16.7	40	41.2
Frequent indigestion	260	10.2	126	24.6	60	38.6	6	6.2
Enteritis or colitis	79	3.1	9	1.8	–	–	–	–
Spastic colon	108	4.3	17	3.3	10	6.4	–	–
Diverticula of intestines	–	–	33	6.4	16	10.3	–	–
Frequent constipation	362	14.3	89	17.4	78	50.2	125	128.7
Selected conditions of the genitourinary, nervous, endocrine, metabolic, and blood and blood-forming systems								
Goiter/other thyroid disorders	123	4.8	73	14.2	43	27.7	11	11.3
Diabetes	260	10.2	740	144.3	242	155.8	164	168.9
Anemias	1,030	40.6	150	29.2	31	20.0	8	8.2
Epilepsy	159	6.3	43	8.4	2	1.3	32	33.0
Migraine headache	916	36.1	298	58.1	26	16.7	22	22.7
Neuralgia/neuritis, unspecified	20	0.8	–	–	–	–	13	13.4
Kidney trouble	107	4.2	75	14.6	–	–	70	72.1
Bladder trouble	350	13.8	64	12.5	19	12.2	101	104.0
Diseases of prostate	42	1.7	43	8.4	44	28.3	38	39.1
Diseases of female genital organs	489	19.3	102	19.9	–	–	7	7.2
Selected circulatory conditions								
Rheumatic fever with or without heart disease	118	4.6	83	16.2	6	3.9	–	–
Heart disease	659	26.0	696	135.7	184	118.5	323	332.6
Ischemic heart disease	73	2.9	209	40.7	94	60.5	94	96.8
Heart rhythm disorders	425	16.7	276	53.8	41	26.4	90	92.7
Tachycardia or rapid heart	22	0.9	87	17.0	15	9.7	32	33.0
Heart murmurs	378	14.9	146	28.5	6	3.9	35	36.0
Other and unspecified heart rhythm disorders	26	1.0	42	8.2	21	13.5	24	24.7
Other selected diseases of heart, excl. hypertension	161	6.3	211	41.1	49	31.6	138	142.1
High blood pressure (hypertension)	1,205	47.5	1,733	337.9	682	439.2	528	543.8
Cerebrovascular disease	61	2.4	157	30.6	74	47.6	104	107.1
Hardening of the arteries	–	–	62	12.1	17	10.9	40	41.2
Varicose veins of lower extremities	120	4.7	186	36.3	40	25.8	38	39.1
Hemorrhoids	414	16.3	273	53.2	32	20.6	35	36.0

(continued)

(continued from previous page)

	under age 45		aged 45 to 64		aged 65 to 74		aged 75 or older	
	number	*rate*	*number*	*rate*	*number*	*rate*	*number*	*rate*
Selected respiratory conditions								
Chronic bronchitis	825	32.5	108	21.1	66	42.5	58	59.7
Asthma	1,495	58.9	255	49.7	65	41.9	47	48.4
Hay fever or allergic rhinitis								
without asthma	1,887	74.3	436	85.0	166	106.9	49	50.5
Chronic sinusitis	2,989	117.8	986	192.2	155	99.8	70	72.1
Deviated nasal septum	61	2.4	30	5.8	–	–	–	–
Chronic disease of tonsils								
or adenoids	342	13.5	55	10.7	–	–	–	–
Emphysema	–	–	22	4.3	31	20.0	7	7.2

Note: Chronic conditions are those that last longer than three months or belong to a group of conditions considered chronic regardless of when they began. (–) means not applicable or sample is too small to make a reliable estimate. Source: National Center for Health Statistics, Current Estimates from the National Health Interview Survey, 1994, Series 10, No. 193, 1995

Blacks with Disabilities by Type of Disability and Age, 1994–95

(total number of blacks aged 15 or older, and percent with a disability by type of disability and age, 1994–95; numbers in thousands)

	15 or older	15 to 21	22 to 44	45 to 54	55 to 64	65 to 79	80 or older
Total persons	23,805	4,058	12,010	3,138	2,015	2,040	544
With any disability	**26.4%**	**10.9%**	**18.9%**	**29.6%**	**46.0%**	**61.8%**	**81.4%**
Severe	17.3	4.1	11.8	18.4	35.0	44.3	63.2
Not severe	9.1	6.8	7.1	11.2	11.0	17.4	18.1
With a mental disability	6.4	3.8	5.6	6.5	7.0	12.2	24.4
Uses wheelchair	1.2	0.3	0.3	0.6	3.2	4.3	12.7
Used cane/crutch/walker for six or more months	3.3	0.1	0.9	2.2	7.4	15.0	28.5
Difficulty with or unable to perform one or more functional activities	**18.0**	**4.5**	**9.8**	**21.1**	**34.4**	**57.0**	**75.2**
Seeing words and letters	5.5	0.5	2.2	8.1	11.3	20.4	28.4
Hearing normal conversation	3.2	0.5	1.3	2.8	5.6	12.9	26.7
Having speech understood	1.4	1.1	1.0	0.8	2.4	3.5	3.6
Lifting, carrying 10 pounds	9.7	1.7	4.2	10.9	23.7	34.1	47.9
Climbing stairs without resting	11.7	1.8	5.2	12.9	25.5	42.6	61.7
Walking three city blocks	11.1	2.1	5.3	11.0	22.7	40.5	58.4
Difficulty with or unable to perform one or more ADLs	**5.3**	**0.8**	**2.3**	**4.1**	**10.8**	**19.7**	**34.7**
Getting around inside the home	2.6	0.4	0.7	1.8	4.6	11.8	24.2
Getting in/out of bed or chair	3.4	0.6	1.5	2.8	7.2	12.5	26.3
Bathing	3.0	0.3	1.1	2.0	5.9	12.9	25.8
Dressing	2.2	0.4	1.0	1.5	4.4	7.7	18.6
Eating	0.8	0.4	0.3	0.5	1.3	3.2	4.1
Getting to/using toilet	1.5	0.4	0.4	1.0	2.7	5.4	17.5
Difficulty with or unable to perform one or more IADLs	**7.7**	**1.3**	**3.8**	**6.4**	**14.9**	**26.8**	**50.9**
Going outside alone	5.0	0.7	1.7	3.0	10.9	21.7	42.3
Keeping track of money/bills	2.9	0.9	1.9	2.5	3.4	8.8	19.7
Preparing meals	2.9	0.5	1.5	1.7	4.6	11.7	22.3
Doing light housework	4.6	0.5	2.2	3.1	8.6	18.5	34.5
Taking prescribed medicines	2.2	0.8	1.1	2.1	2.4	7.7	18.6
Using the telephone	1.4	0.5	0.7	0.8	2.1	5.0	14.0
Needs personal assistance with an ADL or an IADL	**5.9**	**1.0**	**3.0**	**4.7**	**10.7**	**20.4**	**43.1**

Note: An ADL is an activity of daily living; an IADL is an instrumental activity of daily living.
Source: Bureau of the Census, Internet web site, http://www.census.gov

Health Insurance Coverage of Blacks by Age, 1996

(number and percent distribution of blacks by age and health insurance coverage status, 1996; numbers in thousands)

	total	covered by private or government health insurance							not covered
		total	private health insurance		government health insurance				
			total	group health	total	Medicaid	Medicare	Champus	
Number									
Total persons	34,110	26,732	17,705	16,344	13,263	8,521	3,385	1,357	7,378
Under age 18	11,338	9,231	5,157	4,865	5,228	4,609	168	451	2,106
Aged 18 to 24	3,700	2,407	1,609	1,379	1,004	819	39	146	1,294
Aged 25 to 34	5,350	3,803	2,904	2,775	1,200	912	107	181	1,547
Aged 35 to 44	5,415	4,178	3,270	3,151	1,189	794	166	229	1,237
Aged 45 to 54	3,524	2,820	2,355	2,251	773	449	166	158	703
Aged 55 to 64	2,166	1,753	1,323	1,193	797	386	315	96	414
Aged 65 or older	2,616	2,540	1,086	730	3,074	552	2,425	97	76
Percent distribution by health insurance coverage status									
Total persons	**100.0%**	**78.4%**	**51.9%**	**47.%9**	**38.9%**	**25.0%**	**9.9%**	**4.0%**	**21.6%**
Under age 18	100.0	81.4	45.5	42.9	46.1	40.7	1.5	4.0	18.6
Aged 18 to 24	100.0	65.1	43.5	37.3	27.1	22.1	1.1	3.9	35.0
Aged 25 to 34	100.0	71.1	54.3	51.9	22.4	17.0	2.0	3.4	28.9
Aged 35 to 44	100.0	77.2	60.4	58.2	22.0	14.7	3.1	4.2	22.8
Aged 45 to 54	100.0	80.0	66.8	63.9	21.9	12.7	4.7	4.5	19.9
Aged 55 to 64	100.0	80.9	61.1	55.1	36.8	17.8	14.5	4.4	19.1
Aged 65 or older	100.0	97.1	41.5	27.9	117.5	21.1	92.7	3.7	2.9
Percent distribution by age									
Total persons	**100.0%**	**100.0%**	**100.0%**	**100.0%**	**100.0%**	**100.0%**	**100.0%**	**100.0%**	**100.0%**
Under age 18	33.2	34.5	29.1	29.8	39.4	54.1	5.0	33.2	28.5
Aged 18 to 24	10.8	9.0	9.1	8.4	7.6	9.6	1.2	10.8	17.5
Aged 25 to 34	15.7	14.2	16.4	17.0	9.0	10.7	3.2	13.3	21.0
Aged 35 to 44	15.9	15.6	18.5	19.3	9.0	9.3	4.9	16.9	16.8
Aged 45 to 54	10.3	10.5	13.3	13.8	5.8	5.3	4.9	11.6	9.5
Aged 55 to 64	6.4	6.6	7.5	7.3	6.0	4.5	9.3	7.1	5.6
Aged 65 or older	7.7	9.5	6.1	4.5	23.2	6.5	71.6	7.1	1.0

Note: Numbers will not add to total because some persons have more than one type of health insurance.
Source: Bureau of the Census, unpublished tables from the 1997 Current Population Survey; calculations by New Strategist

Physician Contacts by Blacks, 1994

(total number of physician contacts by blacks and number per person per year, by age and type of contact, 1994)

	total	telephone	office	hospital	other
Total contacts	**178,612**	**13,714**	**83,626**	**34,961**	**44,678**
Under age 18	39,253	3,131	19,600	8,573	7,686
Aged 18 to 44	69,807	6,484	32,441	13,934	16,243
Aged 45 to 64	39,348	3,023	18,733	8,521	8,921
Aged 65 or older	30,204	1,076	12,851	3,933	11,828
Contacts per person	**5.4**	**0.4**	**2.4**	**1.1**	**1.4**
Under age 18	3.5	0.3	1.7	0.8	0.7
Aged 18 to 44	5.0	0.5	2.3	1.0	1.2
Aged 45 to 64	7.7	0.6	3.7	1.7	1.7
Aged 65 or older	12.0	0.4	5.1	1.6	4.7

Source: National Center for Health Statistics, Current Estimates from the National Health Interview Survey, 1994, *Series 10, No. 193, 1995*

Leading Causes of Death for Blacks, 1995

(total number of deaths among blacks, and number and percent accounted for by ten leading causes of death, 1995)

		number	percent
	All causes	**286,401**	**100.0%**
1.	Diseases of heart	78,643	27.5
2.	Malignant neoplasms	60,603	21.2
3.	Cerebrovascular diseases	18,537	6.5
4.	Human immunodeficiency virus infections	17,139	6.0
5.	Unintentional injuries	12,748	4.5
6.	Homicides and legal intervention	10,783	3.8
7.	Diabetes mellitus	10,402	3.6
8.	Pneumonia and influenza	7,803	2.7
9.	Chronic obstructive pulmonary diseases	6,667	2.3
10.	Certain conditions originating in the perinatal period	4,952	1.7
	All other causes	58,124	20.3

Source: National Center for Health Statistics, Health, United States, 1996–97; *calculations by New Strategist*

Life Expectancy of Blacks at Birth and Age 65, 1998 to 2020

(average number of years of life remaining at birth and at age 65 for blacks by sex, selected years 1998–2020; difference between black and total life expectancy at birth and at age 65 by sex, 1998 and 2020)

	life expectancy (years)	
	males	*females*
AT BIRTH		
1998	64.7	74.6
2000	64.6	74.7
2005	64.5	75.0
2010	65.1	75.5
2015	65.8	76.0
2020	66.5	76.5
Life expectancy of blacks minus life expectancy of total Americans		
1998	–8.1	–5.0
2020	–9.0	–5.0
AT AGE 65		
1998	13.7	17.7
2000	13.8	17.8
2005	14.0	18.0
2010	14.3	18.3
2015	14.6	18.5
2020	14.8	18.8
Life expectancy of blacks minus life expectancy of total Americans		
1998	–2.0	–1.6
2020	–2.8	–1.8

Source: Bureau of the Census, Population Projections of the United States, by Age, Sex, Race, and Hispanic Origin: 1995 to 2050, *Current Population Reports, P25-1130, 1996; calculations by New Strategist*

Blacks: Households

Female-headed families slightly outnumber married couples.

Black householders are younger than householders in the nation as a whole. Only 15 percent are aged 65 or older, versus 22 percent of all householders. Thirty percent of black householders are under age 35 versus 25 percent nationally.

Female-headed families are the dominant household type among blacks, accounting for 33 percent of all black households. Only 32 percent of black households are married couples. Nuclear families—married couples with children—represent just 18 percent of black households, while female-headed families with children are a larger 25 percent.

Only 37 percent of black children live with both parents. A 58 percent majority live with only their mother. Among black children under age 6, fully 46 percent live with a never-married mother.

Only 38 percent of black women are currently married, versus 56 percent of women in the nation as a whole. The proportion of black women who are married rises above 50 percent only among those aged 35 to 64. In contrast, the majority of all women between the ages of 25 and 74 are married.

■ The living arrangements of blacks directly affect their incomes. Because so many black households are female-headed families, the poorest household type, the income of black households is well below average. Blacks will not close this gap until their household composition is similar to the average.

Female-headed families account for the largest share of black households

(percent distribution of black households by type, 1996)

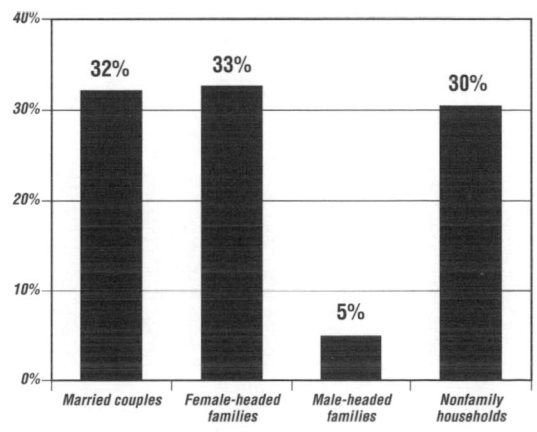

Black Households by Age of Householder, 1996

(number and percent distribution of black households by age of householder, 1996; numbers in thousands)

	number	percent
Total households	**11,577**	**100.0%**
Under age 25	774	6.7
Aged 25 to 29	1,180	10.2
Aged 30 to 34	1,454	12.6
Aged 35 to 39	1,549	13.4
Aged 40 to 44	1,340	11.6
Aged 45 to 54	2,118	18.3
Aged 55 to 64	1,385	12.0
Aged 65 to 74	1,064	9.2
Aged 75 or older	713	6.2

Source: Bureau of the Census, Household and Family Characteristics: March 1996, *Current Population Reports, P20-495 (Update), 1997; calculations by New Strategist*

Black Households by Household Type, 1996

(number and percent distribution of black households by type, 1996; numbers in thousands)

	number	percent
Total households	**11,577**	**100.0%**
Family households	**8,055**	**69.6**
Married couple families	3,713	32.1
With children under age 18	2,119	18.3
Without children under age 18	1,594	13.8
Female householder, no spouse present	3,769	32.6
With children under age 18	2,884	24.9
Without children under age 18	885	7.6
Male householder, no spouse present	573	4.9
Nonfamily households	**3,521**	**30.4**
Female householder	1,989	17.2
Living alone	1,810	15.6
Male householder	1,532	13.2
Living alone	1,235	10.7

Source: Bureau of the Census, Household and Family Characteristics: March 1996, *Current Population Reports, P20-495 (Update), 1997; calculations by New Strategist*

Black Households by Age of Householder and Household Type, 1996

(number and percent distribution of black households by age of householder and household type, 1996; numbers in thousands)

		family households				nonfamily households	
	total	total	married couples	female householder no spouse present	male householder no spouse present	female householder	male householder
Total households, number	**11,577**	**8,055**	**3,713**	**3,769**	**573**	**1,989**	**1,532**
Under age 20	104	84	14	49	20	13	8
Aged 20 to 24	670	461	91	321	49	110	99
Aged 25 to 29	1,180	842	259	510	73	153	185
Aged 30 to 34	1,454	1,107	438	586	83	155	191
Aged 35 to 39	1,549	1,200	527	608	65	150	199
Aged 40 to 44	1,340	1,086	527	470	89	129	124
Aged 45 to 54	2,118	1,481	853	546	82	326	311
Aged 55 to 64	1,385	904	539	327	38	291	190
Aged 65 to 74	1,064	599	319	226	54	318	147
Aged 75 to 84	563	245	125	100	21	244	73
Aged 85 or older	150	46	21	25	–	99	6
Total households, percent	**100.0%**	**69.6%**	**32.1%**	**32.6%**	**4.9%**	**17.2%**	**13.2%**
Under age 20	100.0	80.8	13.5	47.1	19.2	12.5	7.7
Aged 20 to 24	100.0	68.8	13.6	47.9	7.3	16.4	14.8
Aged 25 to 29	100.0	71.4	21.9	43.2	6.2	13.0	15.7
Aged 30 to 34	100.0	76.1	30.1	40.3	5.7	10.7	13.1
Aged 35 to 39	100.0	77.5	34.0	39.3	4.2	9.7	12.8
Aged 40 to 44	100.0	81.0	39.3	35.1	6.6	9.6	9.3
Aged 45 to 54	100.0	69.9	40.3	25.8	3.9	15.4	14.7
Aged 55 to 64	100.0	65.3	38.9	23.6	2.7	21.0	13.7
Aged 65 to 74	100.0	56.3	30.0	21.2	5.1	29.9	13.8
Aged 75 to 84	100.0	43.5	22.2	17.8	3.7	43.3	13.0
Aged 85 or older	100.0	30.7	14.0	16.7	–	66.0	4.0

Note: (–) means sample is too small to make a reliable estimate.
Source: Bureau of the Census, Household and Family Characteristics: March 1996, Current Population Reports, P20-495 (Update), 1997; calculations by New Strategist

Black Households by Size, 1996

(number and percent distribution of black households by size, 1996; numbers in thousands)

	number	percent
Total households	**11,577**	**100.0%**
One person	3,055	26.4
Two persons	3,034	26.2
Three persons	2,197	19.0
Four persons	1,715	14.8
Five persons	919	7.9
Six persons	366	3.2
Seven or more persons	291	2.5

Source: Bureau of the Census, Household and Family Characteristics: March 1996, *Current Population Reports, P20-495 (Update), 1997; calculations by New Strategist*

Black Married Couples by Presence of Children and Age of Householder, 1996

(number and percent distribution of black married couples by presence and number of own children under age 18 at home and age of householder, 1996; numbers in thousands)

	total	< age 20	20–24	25–29	30–34	35–39	40–44	45–54	55–64	65+
Married couples, number	**3,713**	**14**	**91**	**259**	**438**	**527**	**527**	**853**	**539**	**465**
Without children <18	1,811	6	28	86	82	61	140	470	484	455
With children <18	1,901	8	63	173	357	465	387	383	55	10
One	778	4	40	81	118	123	158	202	43	10
Two	692	4	11	74	151	194	134	119	5	–
Three or more	433	–	12	18	89	148	96	62	7	–
Married couples, percent	**100.0%**	**100.0%**	**100.0%**	**100.0%**	**100.0%**	**100.0%**	**100.0%**	**100.0%**	**100.0%**	**100.0%**
Without children <18	48.8	–	30.8	33.2	18.7	11.6	26.6	55.1	89.8	97.8
With children <18	51.2	57.1	69.2	66.8	81.5	88.2	73.4	44.9	10.2	2.2
One	21.0	28.6	44.0	31.3	26.9	23.3	30.0	23.7	8.0	2.2
Two	18.6	–	12.1	28.6	34.5	36.8	25.4	14.0	0.9	–
Three or more	11.7	–	13.2	6.9	20.3	28.1	18.2	7.3	1.3	–

Note: (–) means sample is too small to make a reliable estimate.
Source: Bureau of the Census, Household and Family Characteristics: March 1996, *Current Population Reports, P20-495 (Update), 1997; calculations by New Strategist*

Black Female-Headed Families by Presence of Children and Age of Householder, 1996

(number and percent distribution of black female-headed families by presence and number of own children under age 18 at home and age of householder, 1996; numbers in thousands)

	total	< age 20	20–24	25–29	30–34	35–39	40–44	45–54	55–64	65+
						age of householder				
Female-headed families, number	**3,769**	**49**	**321**	**510**	**586**	**608**	**470**	**546**	**327**	**351**
Without children <18	1,365	20	33	31	39	69	161	362	303	347
With children <18	2,404	30	287	479	547	540	309	184	24	4
One	1,007	24	116	148	175	205	180	134	22	4
Two	731	2	71	165	173	205	78	37	–	–
Three or more	666	4	99	167	200	129	52	13	2	–
Female-headed families, percent	**100.0%**	**100.0%**	**100.0%**	**100.0%**	**100.0%**	**100.0%**	**100.0%**	**100.0%**	**100.0%**	**100.0%**
Without children <18	36.2	40.8	10.3	6.1	6.7	11.3	34.3	66.3	92.7	98.2
With children <18	63.8	61.2	89.4	93.9	93.3	88.8	65.7	33.7	7.3	1.8
One	26.7	49.0	36.1	29.0	29.9	33.7	38.3	24.5	6.7	1.8
Two	19.4	4.1	22.1	32.4	29.5	33.7	16.6	6.8	–	–
Three or more	17.7	8.2	30.8	32.7	34.1	21.2	11.1	2.4	0.6	–

Note: (–) means sample is too small to make a reliable estimate.
Source: Bureau of the Census, Household and Family Characteristics: March 1996, *Current Population Reports, P20-495 (Update), 1997; calculations by New Strategist*

Black Single-Person Households by Age of Householder, 1996

(number and percent distribution of black single-person households and single-person households as a percent of total black households, by age of householder, 1996; numbers in thousands)

	number	percent	percent of total black households
Total households	**3,055**	**100.0%**	**26.4%**
Under age 25	142	4.6	18.3
Aged 25 to 29	234	7.7	19.8
Aged 30 to 34	302	9.9	20.8
Aged 35 to 39	301	9.9	19.4
Aged 40 to 44	224	7.3	16.7
Aged 45 to 54	568	18.6	26.8
Aged 55 to 64	431	14.1	31.1
Aged 65 to 74	449	14.7	42.2
Aged 75 or older	405	13.3	56.8
Median age (years)	50.6		

Source: Bureau of the Census, Household and Family Characteristics: March 1996, *Current Population Reports, P20-495 (Update), 1997; calculations by New Strategist*

Living Arrangements of Black Children by Age, 1995

(number and percent distribution of black children by living arrangement, marital status of parent, and age of child, 1995; numbers in thousands)

	total	under age 6	aged 6 to 11	aged 12 to 17
Number with one or both parents	**10,085**	**3,611**	**3,353**	**3,122**
Living with both parents	3,746	1,169	1,363	1,214
Living with mother only	5,881	2,270	1,832	1,778
Never married	3,255	1,663	980	612
Divorced	1,204	269	411	524
Married, spouse absent	1,212	306	373	533
Widowed	210	32	69	109
Living with father only	458	171	157	130
Never married	211	123	62	27
Divorced	97	15	43	39
Married, spouse absent	115	31	40	44
Widowed	35	2	13	20
Percent with one or both parents	**100.0%**	**100.0%**	**100.0%**	**100.0%**
Living with both parents	37.1	32.4	40.7	38.9
Living with mother only	58.3	62.9	54.6	57.0
Never married	32.3	46.1	29.2	19.6
Divorced	11.9	7.4	12.3	16.8
Married, spouse absent	12.0	8.5	11.1	17.1
Widowed	2.1	0.9	2.1	3.5
Living with father only	4.5	4.7	4.7	4.2
Never married	2.1	3.4	1.8	0.9
Divorced	1.0	0.4	1.3	1.2
Married, spouse absent	1.1	0.9	1.2	1.4
Widowed	0.3	–	0.4	0.6

Note: (–) means sample is too small to make a reliable estimate.
Source: Bureau of the Census, Marital Status and Living Arrangements: March 1995, Current Population Reports, P20-491, 1996; calculations by New Strategist

Living Arrangements of Black Men by Age, 1995

(number and percent distribution of black men aged 18 or older by living arrangement and age, 1995; numbers in thousands)

	total	18 to 19	20 to 24	25 to 29	30 to 34	35 to 39	40 to 44	45 to 54	55 to 64	65 to 74	75 or older
Black men, number	**9,922**	**518**	**1,202**	**1,208**	**1,270**	**1,282**	**1,106**	**1,441**	**896**	**646**	**353**
Family householder or spouse	3,515	12	121	293	436	510	455	719	458	356	155
Child of householder	2,451	421	752	378	296	260	193	90	44	3	14
Other member of family household	1,617	59	113	193	216	209	221	240	171	108	87
Nonfamily householder	1,654	8	106	191	194	235	179	311	185	148	97
Other member of nonfamily house	683	18	110	153	128	68	58	81	36	31	–
Group quarters*	2	–	–	–	–	–	–	–	2	–	–
Black men, percent	**100.0%**	**100.0%**	**100.0%**	**100.0%**	**100.0%**	**100.0%**	**100.0%**	**100.0%**	**100.0%**	**100.0%**	**100.0%**
Family householder or spouse	35.4	2.3	10.1	24.3	34.3	39.8	41.1	49.9	51.1	55.1	43.9
Child of householder	24.7	81.3	62.6	31.3	23.3	20.3	17.5	6.2	4.9	0.5	4.0
Other member of family household	16.3	11.4	9.4	16.0	17.0	16.3	20.0	16.7	19.1	16.7	24.6
Nonfamily householder	16.7	1.5	8.8	15.8	15.3	18.3	16.2	21.6	20.6	22.9	27.5
Other member of nonfamily house	6.9	3.5	9.2	12.7	10.1	5.3	5.2	5.6	4.0	4.8	–
Group quarters*	0.0	–	–	–	–	–	–	–	0.2	–	–

The Current Population Survey does not include people living in institutions such as prisons, the military, or college dormitories. It defines people living in group quarters as those in noninstitutional living arrangements that are not conventional housing units, such as rooming houses, staff quarters at a hospital, and halfway houses.

Note: (–) means sample is too small to make a reliable estimate.

Source: Bureau of the Census, Marital Status and Living Arrangements: March 1995, Current Population Reports, P20-491, 1996; calculations by New Strategist

Living Arrangements of Black Women by Age, 1995

(number and percent distribution of black women aged 18 or older by living arrangement and age, 1995; numbers in thousands)

	total	18 to 19	20 to 24	25 to 29	30 to 34	35 to 39	40 to 44	45 to 54	55 to 64	65 to 74	75 or older
Black women, number	**12,220**	**561**	**1,403**	**1,435**	**1,534**	**1,504**	**1,297**	**1,754**	**1,174**	**895**	**663**
Family householder or spouse	7,460	55	520	830	1,135	1,124	987	1,332	781	473	223
Child of householder	1,616	403	563	254	165	113	64	44	8	2	–
Other member of family household	863	80	131	100	83	88	48	67	73	86	107
Nonfamily householder	1,903	12	118	168	100	131	152	285	288	322	327
Other member of nonfamily household	374	11	71	83	47	48	46	26	24	12	6
Group quarters*	4	–	–	–	4	–	–	–	–	–	–
Black women, percent	**100.0%**	**100.0%**	**100.0%**	**100.0%**	**100.0%**	**100.0%**	**100.0%**	**100.0%**	**100.0%**	**100.0%**	**100.0%**
Family householder or spouse	61.0	9.8	37.1	57.8	74.0	74.7	76.1	75.9	66.5	52.8	33.6
Child of householder	13.2	71.8	40.1	17.7	10.8	7.5	4.9	2.5	0.7	0.2	–
Other member of family household	7.1	14.3	9.3	7.0	5.4	5.9	3.7	3.8	6.2	9.6	16.1
Nonfamily householder	15.6	2.1	8.4	11.7	6.5	8.7	11.7	16.2	24.5	36.0	49.3
Other member of nonfamily household	3.1	2.0	5.1	5.8	3.1	3.2	3.5	1.5	2.0	1.3	0.9
Group quarters*	0.0	–	–	–	0.3	–	–	–	–	–	–

* The Current Population Survey does not include people living in institutions such as prisons, the military, or college dormitories. It defines people living in group quarters as those in noninstitutional living arrangements that are not conventional housing units, such as rooming houses, staff quarters at a hospital, and halfway houses.

Note: (–) means sample is too small to make a reliable estimate.

Source: Bureau of the Census, Marital Status and Living Arrangements: March 1995, Current Population Reports, P20-491, 1996; calculations by New Strategist

Marital Status of Black Men by Age, 1995

(number and percent distribution of black men aged 15 or older by age and marital status, 1995; numbers in thousands)

	total	never married	married	divorced	widowed
Total, number	**10,825**	**5,031**	**4,632**	**852**	**310**
Aged 15 to 19	1,422	1,413	–	9	–
Aged 20 to 24	1,202	1,087	107	7	–
Aged 25 to 29	1,208	785	387	36	–
Aged 30 to 34	1,270	584	607	78	–
Aged 35 to 39	1,282	451	695	132	5
Aged 40 to 44	1,106	277	628	189	12
Aged 45 to 54	1,441	254	957	209	22
Aged 55 to 64	896	114	613	113	57
Aged 65 to 74	646	31	442	64	108
Aged 75 to 84	296	30	166	16	85
Aged 85 or older	57	6	29	–	21
Total, percent	**100.0%**	**46.5%**	**42.8%**	**7.9%**	**2.9%**
Aged 15 to 19	100.0	99.4	–	0.6	–
Aged 20 to 24	100.0	90.4	8.9	0.6	–
Aged 25 to 29	100.0	65.0	32.0	3.0	–
Aged 30 to 34	100.0	46.0	47.8	6.1	–
Aged 35 to 39	100.0	35.2	54.2	10.3	0.4
Aged 40 to 44	100.0	25.0	56.8	17.1	1.1
Aged 45 to 54	100.0	17.6	66.4	14.5	1.5
Aged 55 to 64	100.0	12.7	68.4	12.6	6.4
Aged 65 to 74	100.0	4.8	68.4	9.9	16.7
Aged 75 to 84	100.0	10.1	56.1	5.4	28.7
Aged 85 or older	100.0	10.5	50.9	–	36.8

Note: (–) means sample is too small to make a reliable estimate.
Source: Bureau of the Census, Marital Status and Living Arrangements: March 1995, *Current Population Reports, P20-491, 1996*

Marital Status of Black Women by Age, 1995

(number and percent distribution of black women aged 15 or older by age and marital status, 1995; numbers in thousands)

	total	never married	married	divorced	widowed
Total, number	**13,097**	**5,250**	**4,942**	**1,525**	**1,380**
Aged 15 to 19	1,437	1,421	15	1	–
Aged 20 to 24	1,403	1,178	201	23	2
Aged 25 to 29	1,435	836	503	95	–
Aged 30 to 34	1,534	615	729	170	19
Aged 35 to 39	1,504	460	754	269	22
Aged 40 to 44	1,297	283	681	287	46
Aged 45 to 54	1,754	248	987	374	145
Aged 55 to 64	1,174	109	620	164	281
Aged 65 to 74	895	67	343	112	373
Aged 75 to 84	478	22	97	24	334
Aged 85 or older	185	10	13	6	156
Total, percent	**100.0%**	**40.1%**	**37.7%**	**11.6%**	**10.5%**
Aged 15 to 19	100.0	98.9	1.0	–	–
Aged 20 to 24	100.0	84.0	14.3	1.6	0.1
Aged 25 to 29	100.0	58.3	35.1	6.6	–
Aged 30 to 34	100.0	40.1	47.5	11.1	1.2
Aged 35 to 39	100.0	30.6	50.1	17.9	1.5
Aged 40 to 44	100.0	21.8	52.5	22.1	3.5
Aged 45 to 54	100.0	14.1	56.3	21.3	8.3
Aged 55 to 64	100.0	9.3	52.8	14.0	23.9
Aged 65 to 74	100.0	7.5	38.3	12.5	41.7
Aged 75 to 84	100.0	4.6	20.3	5.0	69.9
Aged 85 or older	100.0	5.4	7.0	3.2	84.3

Note: (–) means sample is too small to make a reliable estimate.
Source: Bureau of the Census, Marital Status and Living Arrangements: March 1995, *Current Population Reports, P20-491, 1996*

Blacks: Housing

Black homeownership is below average, but a majority of blacks are satisfied with their homes and neighborhoods.

Forty-four percent of the nation's 12 million black householders own their home. This compares with a homeownership rate of 65 percent for all Americans. Black homeowners paid a median of $34,108 for their homes, and most used savings as the down payment. Their homes are now worth a median of $64,372.

Most black householders are satisfied with their homes. On a scale of 1 to 10, with 1 being the worst and 10 the best, 65 percent of blacks rate their homes an eight or higher. Even among black renters, 56 percent rate their homes at least an eight. Few blacks think their neighborhood has a crime problem—only 10 percent of homeowners and 17 percent of renters say crime is a problem in their area. Fully 57 percent of black householders say their neighborhood has no problems.

Nineteen percent of blacks moved between 1995 and 1996, versus 16 percent of the total population. The most common reason for moving among blacks was to establish their own household.

Among the 50 metropolitan areas with the most black households, New York has the largest number—over 700,000 in 1990. Blacks account for the largest share of households—37 percent—in Jacksonville, Florida.

■ The low rate of homeownership among blacks can be explained by the composition of black households. Because so many black households are female-headed families—one of the household types least likely to own a home—black homeownership is well below average.

Most black households are in the South

(percent distribution of black households by region, 1995)

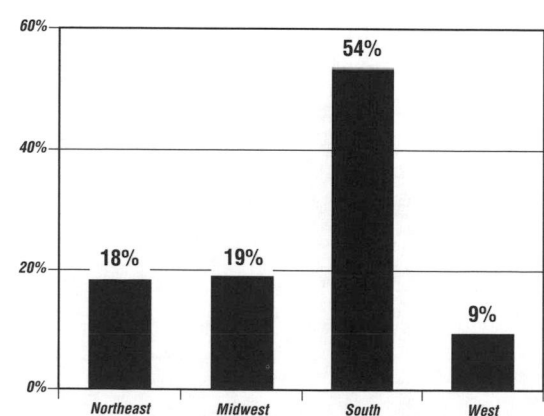

Region of Residence and Metropolitan Status of Housing Units Occupied by Blacks, 1995

(number, percent distribution, and percent of housing units occupied by blacks, by regional, metropolitan, and homeownership status, 1995; numbers in thousands)

	total		owner			renter		
	number	percent distrib.	number	percent distrib.	percent of total	number	percent distrib.	percent of total
Total occupied housing units	**11,773**	**100.0%**	**5,137**	**100.0%**	**43.6%**	**6,637**	**100.0%**	**56.4%**
Northeast	2,147	18.2	647	12.6	30.1	1,500	22.6	69.9
Midwest	2,227	18.9	918	17.9	41.2	1,309	19.7	58.8
South	6,295	53.5	3,150	61.3	50.0	3,145	47.4	50.0
West	1,104	9.4	422	8.2	38.2	682	10.3	61.8
In metropolitan areas	10,156	86.3	4,198	81.7	41.3	5,957	89.8	58.7
In central cities	6,699	56.9	2,429	47.3	36.3	4,270	64.3	63.7
In suburbs	3,457	29.4	1,769	34.4	51.2	1,687	25.4	48.8
Outside metropolitan areas	1,618	13.7	938	18.3	58.0	680	10.2	42.0

Source: Bureau of the Census, American Housing Survey for the United States in 1995, *Current Housing Reports, H150/95, 1997; calculations by New Strategist*

Characteristics of Housing Units Occupied by Blacks, 1995

(number and percent distribution of housing units occupied by blacks, by selected housing characteristics and homeownership status, 1995; numbers in thousands)

	total number	total percent	owner-occupied number	owner-occupied percent	renter-occupied number	renter-occupied percent
Total occupied housing units	**11,773**	**100.0%**	**5,137**	**100.0%**	**6,637**	**100.0%**
Units in structure						
One, detached	5,601	47.6	4,131	80.4	1,471	22.2
One, attached	1,071	9.1	407	7.9	663	10.0
Two to four	1,754	14.9	163	3.2	1,591	24.0
Five to nine	988	8.4	40	0.8	948	14.3
10 to 19	742	6.3	38	0.7	705	10.6
20 to 49	495	4.2	18	0.4	477	7.2
50 or more	724	6.1	33	0.6	690	10.4
Mobile home or trailer	398	3.4	307	6.0	91	1.4
Median number of rooms in unit	**5.0**	–	**6.0**	–	**4.3**	–
Median square footage of unit	**1,433**	–	**1,537**	–	**1,183**	–
Number of bathrooms						
None	95	0.8	41	0.8	54	0.8
One	7,102	60.3	1,984	38.6	5,119	77.1
One and one-half	1,842	15.6	1,102	21.5	740	11.1
Two or more	2,734	23.2	2,010	39.1	724	10.9
Primary heating fuel						
Housing units with heating fuel	11,658	100.0	5,109	100.0	6,549	100.0
Electricity	3,438	29.5	1,318	25.8	2,120	31.9
Piped gas	6,105	52.4	2,871	56.2	3,234	48.7
Bottled gas	375	3.2	261	5.1	114	1.7
Fuel oil	1,209	10.4	374	7.3	836	12.6
Kerosene or other liquid fuel	163	1.4	106	2.1	57	0.9
Coal or coke	8	0.1	5	0.1	3	0.0
Wood	272	2.3	164	3.2	107	1.6
Solar energy	–	–	–	–	–	–
Other	88	0.8	10	0.2	78	1.2

(continued)

(continued from previous page)

	total		owner-occupied		renter-occupied	
	number	percent	number	percent	number	percent
Selected equipment						
Dishwasher	3,466	29.4%	1,852	36.1%	1,614	24.3%
Washing machine	7,148	60.7	4,518	88.0	2,630	39.6
Clothes dryer	5,700	48.4	3,850	74.9	1,850	27.9
Disposal in kitchen sink	3,487	29.6	1,467	28.6	2,020	30.4
Air conditioning	4,609	39.1	2,291	44.6	2,318	34.9
Porch, deck, balcony, or patio	7,925	67.3	4,052	78.9	3,873	58.4
Telephone	10,404	88.4	4,874	94.9	5,529	83.3
Usable fireplace	1,992	16.9	1,438	28.0	554	8.3
Garage or carport	3,975	33.8	2,804	54.6	1,171	17.6
Cars and trucks available						
No cars, trucks, or vans	2,913	24.7	538	10.5	2,375	35.8
One car, with or without						
trucks or vans	5,575	47.4	2,399	46.7	3,176	47.9
Two or more cars	2,920	24.8	1,999	38.9	921	13.9
Overall opinion of housing unit						
1 (worst)	175	1.5	38	0.7	137	2.1
2	110	0.9	12	0.2	98	1.5
3	158	1.3	26	0.5	132	2.0
4	201	1.7	51	1.0	151	2.3
5	985	8.4	267	5.2	748	11.3
6	813	6.9	256	5.0	558	8.4
7	1,491	12.7	484	9.4	1,007	15.2
8	2,842	24.1	1,225	23.8	1,616	24.3
9	1,486	12.6	814	15.8	672	10.1
10 (best)	3,359	28.5	1,947	37.9	1,411	21.3

Note: (−) means not applicable or sample is too small to make a reliable estimate.
Source: Bureau of the Census, American Housing Survey for the United States in 1995, *Current Housing Reports,*
H150/95RV, 1997; calculations by New Strategist

Telephone Availability in Non-Hispanic Black Households, 1996

(number and percent distribution of total and non-Hispanic black households by telephone availability, 1996; numbers in thousands)

	total	black
Total households	**99,627**	**11,333**
Telephone in household	91,705	9,599
Telephone available to household	1,777	353
Telephone not available	6,146	1,381
Total households	**100.0%**	**100.0%**
Telephone in household	92.0	84.7
Telephone available to household	1.8	3.1
Telephone not available	6.2	12.2

Source: Bureau of the Census, Internet web site http://www.census.gov

Neighborhood Characteristics of Housing Units Occupied by Blacks, 1995

(number and percent distribution of housing units occupied by blacks, by selected neighborhood characteristics and homeownership status, 1995; numbers in thousands)

	total		owner-occupied		renter-occupied	
	number	*percent*	*number*	*percent*	*number*	*percent*
Total occupied housing units	**11,773**	**100.0%**	**5,137**	**100.0%**	**6,637**	**100.0%**
Overall opinion of neighborhood						
1 (worst)	443	3.8	101	2.0	342	5.2
2	189	1.6	39	0.8	150	2.3
3	255	2.2	60	1.2	196	3.0
4	280	2.4	77	1.5	203	3.1
5	1,249	10.6	422	8.2	827	12.5
6	800	6.8	307	6.0	492	7.4
7	1,410	12.0	608	11.8	801	12.1
8	2,522	21.4	1,161	22.6	1,360	20.5
9	1,277	10.8	661	12.9	616	9.3
10 (best)	3,125	26.5	1,619	31.5	1,506	22.7
Neighborhood problems						
No problems	6,711	57.0	2,994	58.3	3,717	56.0
With problems*	4,756	40.4	2,028	39.5	2,728	41.1
Crime	1,649	14.0	521	10.1	1,127	17.0
Noise	1,148	9.8	385	7.5	763	11.5
Traffic	712	6.0	292	5.7	420	6.3
Litter or housing deterioration	750	6.4	336	6.5	414	6.2
Poor city or county services	206	1.7	103	2.0	103	1.6
Undesirable commercial, institutional, industrial	167	1.4	92	1.8	75	1.1
People	1,680	14.3	613	11.9	1,067	16.1
Other	1,113	9.5	589	11.5	524	7.9
Not reported	82	3	33	2	49	3

* Numbers will not add to total because more than one problem could be cited.
Source: Bureau of the Census, American Housing Survey for the United States in 1995, *Current Housing Reports, H150/95RV, 1997; calculations by New Strategist*

Housing Value and Purchase Price
for Black Homeowners, 1995

(number and percent distribution of black homeowners by value of home, purchase price, and major source of down payment, 1995; numbers in thousands)

	number	percent
Total homeowners	**5,137**	**100.0%**
Value of home		
Under $50,000	1,862	36.2
$50,000 to $79,999	1,502	29.2
$80,000 to $99,999	597	11.6
$100,000 to $149,999	673	13.1
$150,000 to $199,999	304	5.9
$200,000 to $299,999	123	2.4
$300,000 or more	77	1.5
Median	$64,372	–
Purchase price*		
Home purchased or built	4,877	94.9
Under $50,000	2,519	49.0
$50,000 to $79,999	729	14.2
$80,000 to $99,999	272	5.3
$100,000 to $149,999	231	4.5
$150,000 to $199,999	79	1.5
$200,000 to $299,999	41	0.8
$300,000 or more	27	0.5
Received as inheritance or gift	236	4.6
Median purchase price	$34,108	–
Major source of down payment*		
Sale of previous home	452	8.8
Savings of cash on hand	2,890	56.3
Sale of other investment	15	0.3
Borrowing, other than mortgage on this property	172	3.3
Inheritance or gift	76	1.5
Land where built used for financing	56	1.1
Other	232	4.5
No down payment	489	9.5

* Numbers may not add to total because "not reported" is not shown.
Note: (–) means not applicable.
Source: Bureau of the Census, American Housing Survey for the United States in 1995, *Current Housing Reports, H150/95RV, 1997; calculations by New Strategist*

Geographical Mobility of the Black Population by Age, 1995–96

(total number of blacks aged 1 or older, and number and percent of those who moved between March 1995 and March 1996, by age of person and type of move; numbers in thousands)

			different house in the U.S.							moved from abroad
					different county					
							different state			
	total	same house (non-movers)	total	same county	total	same state	total	same region	different region	
Number										
Total, aged 1 or older	**33,294**	**27,040**	**6,149**	**4,511**	**1,637**	**987**	**651**	**291**	**360**	**106**
Aged 1 to 4	2,649	1,873	765	622	143	90	52	24	29	11
Aged 5 to 9	3,358	2,603	744	564	180	95	85	31	54	11
Aged 10 to 14	3,074	2,513	552	422	129	68	62	27	35	10
Aged 15 to 19	2,959	2,505	430	332	98	65	33	21	11	23
Aged 15 to 17	1,844	1,585	247	183	64	47	17	6	10	11
Aged 18 and 19	1,115	920	183	149	34	18	16	15	1	11
Aged 20 to 24	2,540	1,821	706	510	196	138	58	27	31	13
Aged 25 to 29	2,614	1,776	834	564	270	162	108	39	70	4
Aged 30 to 34	2,740	2,056	678	474	203	119	84	38	46	6
Aged 35 to 39	2,820	2,284	519	354	165	93	72	43	29	17
Aged 40 to 44	2,483	2,112	364	264	100	56	44	13	32	7
Aged 45 to 49	2,046	1,838	204	151	53	35	18	3	16	4
Aged 50 to 54	1,412	1,291	121	94	27	25	2	2	–	–
Aged 55 to 59	1,148	1,047	100	58	42	24	18	18	–	–
Aged 60 to 64	977	936	41	34	6	5	1	1	1	–
Aged 60 and 61	414	400	15	11	3	3	–	–	–	–
Aged 62 to 64	563	537	26	23	3	2	1	1	1	–
Aged 65 to 69	849	828	21	17	5	3	2	2	–	–
Aged 70 to 74	632	611	22	19	3	–	3	2	1	–
Aged 75 to 79	471	443	28	18	10	4	6	2	4	–
Aged 80 to 84	295	280	15	9	6	3	2	–	2	–
Aged 85 or older	230	224	6	4	2	2	–	–	–	–
Median age	29.0	31.0	24.1	23.1	26.4	26.2	26.6	27.0	26.4	19.7

(continued)

(continued from previous page)

Percent	total	same house (non-movers)	different house in the U.S.							moved from abroad
			total	same county	different county		different state			
					total	same state	total	same region	different region	
Total, aged 1 or older	**100.0%**	**81.2%**	**18.5%**	**13.5%**	**4.9%**	**3.0%**	**2.0%**	**0.9%**	**1.1%**	**0.3%**
Aged 1 to 4	100.0	51.3	21.0	17.0	3.9	2.5	1.4	0.7	0.8	0.3
Aged 5 to 9	100.0	77.5	22.2	16.8	5.4	2.8	2.5	0.9	1.6	0.3
Aged 10 to 14	100.0	81.8	18.0	13.7	4.2	2.2	2.0	0.9	1.1	0.3
Aged 15 to 19	100.0	84.7	14.5	11.2	3.3	2.2	1.1	0.7	0.4	0.8
Aged 15 to 17	100.0	86.0	13.4	9.9	3.5	2.5	0.9	0.3	0.5	0.6
Aged 18 and 19	100.0	82.5	16.4	13.4	3.0	1.6	1.4	1.3	0.1	1.0
Aged 20 to 24	100.0	71.7	27.8	20.1	7.7	5.4	2.3	1.1	1.2	0.5
Aged 25 to 29	100.0	67.9	31.9	21.6	10.3	6.2	4.1	1.5	2.7	0.2
Aged 30 to 34	100.0	75.0	24.7	17.3	7.4	4.3	3.1	1.4	1.7	0.2
Aged 35 to 39	100.0	81.0	18.4	12.6	5.9	3.3	2.6	1.5	1.0	0.6
Aged 40 to 44	100.0	85.1	14.7	10.6	4.0	2.3	1.8	0.5	1.3	0.3
Aged 45 to 49	100.0	89.8	10.0	7.4	2.6	1.7	0.9	0.1	0.8	0.2
Aged 50 to 54	100.0	91.4	8.6	6.7	1.9	1.8	0.1	0.1	–	–
Aged 55 to 59	100.0	91.2	8.7	5.1	3.7	2.1	1.6	1.6	–	–
Aged 60 to 64	100.0	95.8	4.2	3.5	0.6	0.5	0.1	0.1	0.1	–
Aged 60 and 61	100.0	96.6	3.6	2.7	0.7	–	–	–	–	–
Aged 62 to 64	100.0	95.4	6.4	4.1	0.5	0.4	0.2	0.2	0.2	–
Aged 65 to 69	100.0	97.5	2.5	2.0	0.6	0.4	0.2	0.2	–	–
Aged 70 to 74	100.0	96.7	3.5	3.0	0.5	–	0.3	0.3	0.2	–
Aged 75 to 79	100.0	94.1	5.9	3.8	2.1	–	0.4	0.4	–	–
Aged 80 to 84	100.0	94.9	5.1	3.1	2.0	1.0	–	–	0.7	–
Aged 85 or older	100.0	97.4	2.6	1.7	0.9	–	–	–	–	–

Note: (–) means sample is too small to make a reliable estimate.
Source: Bureau of the Census, Geographical Mobility: March 1995 to March 1996, *Current Population Reports, P20-497(Update), 1997; calculations by New Strategist*

Reasons for Moving among Black Households
by Homeownership Status, 1995

(number and percent distribution of black households that moved in the past 12 months by reason for move and for choosing new neighborhood and house, and by comparison with previous home and neighborhood, by homeownership status, 1995; numbers in thousands)

	total		owner-occupied		renter-occupied	
	number	percent	number	percent	number	percent
Total movers	**2,595**	**100.0%**	**419**	**100.0%**	**2,177**	**100.0%**
Reasons for leaving previous unit*						
Private displacement	128	4.9	6	1.4	122	5.6
Government displacement	47	1.8	6	1.4	41	1.9
Disaster loss	21	0.8	4	1.0	16	0.7
New job or job transfer	175	6.7	28	6.7	147	6.8
To be closer to work, school, other	201	7.7	21	5.0	181	8.3
Other, financial- or employment-related	125	4.8	3	0.7	121	5.6
To establish own household	525	20.2	62	14.8	463	21.3
Needed larger house or apartment	387	14.9	59	14.1	328	15.1
Married	27	1.0	2	0.5	25	1.1
Widowed, divorced, or separated	75	2.9	13	3.1	62	2.8
Other, family- or person-related	261	10.1	36	8.6	225	10.3
Wanted better home	397	15.3	57	13.6	340	15.6
Change from owner to renter	19	0.7	–	–	19	0.9
Change from renter to owner	123	4.7	123	29.4	–	–
Wanted lower rent or maintenance	150	5.8	7	1.7	142	6.5
Choice of present neighborhood*						
Convenient to job	544	21.0	55	13.1	489	22.5
Convenient to friends or relatives	515	19.8	64	15.3	451	20.7
Convenient to leisure activities	83	3.2	18	4.3	65	3.0
Convenient to public transportation	145	5.6	17	4.1	128	5.9
Good schools	187	7.2	26	6.2	160	7.3
Other public services	66	2.5	17	4.1	49	2.3
Looks or design of neighborhood	379	14.6	94	22.4	284	13.0
House was most important consideration	588	22.7	126	30.1	462	21.2
Neighborhood search						
Looked at just this neighborhood	1,019	39.3	145	34.6	874	40.1
Looked at other neighborhoods	1,468	56.6	245	58.5	1,223	56.2

(continued)

(continued from previous page)

	total		owner-occupied		renter-occupied	
	number	*percent*	*number*	*percent*	*number*	*percent*
Choice of present home*						
Financial reasons	962	37.1%	144	34.4%	819	37.6%
Room layout or design	473	18.2	103	24.6	369	16.9
Kitchen	46	1.8	14	3.3	31	1.4
Size	427	16.5	70	16.7	357	16.4
Exterior appearance	160	6.2	44	10.5	116	5.3
Yard, trees, view	132	5.1	39	9.3	93	4.3
Quality of construction	91	3.5	30	7.2	61	2.8
Only one available	365	14.1	34	8.1	331	15.2
Other reasons	740	28.5	106	25.3	634	29.1
Comparison to previous home						
Better home	1,369	52.8	284	67.8	1,085	49.8
Worse home	430	16.6	26	6.2	404	18.6
About the same	696	26.8	77	18.4	619	28.4
Comparison to previous neighborhood						
Better neighborhood	1,056	40.7	226	8.7	830	32.0
Worse neighborhood	324	12.5	19	0.7	304	11.7
About the same	958	36.9	116	4.5	842	32.4
Same neighborhood	156	6.0	24	0.9	132	5.1

* Numbers may not add to total because more than one category may apply and unreported reasons are not shown.
Note: (–) means not applicable.
Source: Bureau of the Census, American Housing Survey for the United States in 1995, *Current Housing Reports, H150/95RV, 1997; calculations by New Strategist*

Black Homeownership in the 50 Metropolitan Areas with the Most Black Households, 1990

(number of black households, percent of total households that are black, percent of black households that are owner occupied, and median value of black owner-occupied houses, in the U.S. and in the 50 metropolitan areas with the most black households, ranked alphabetically, 1990; numbers in thousands)

	number	black share of total households	owner-occupied percent	owner-occupied median value
Total black households	**9,976**	**10.8%**	**43.4%**	**$50,700**
Atlanta, GA	254	24.0	40.4	66,700
Augusta, GA	40	28.2	51.7	47,700
Baltimore, MD	207	23.5	39.4	57,100
Baton Rouge, LA	49	26.1	52.8	45,900
Birmingham, AL	85	24.6	53.3	38,900
Boston, MA	71	6.5	24.7	160,200
Buffalo, NY	43	11.3	34.2	38,500
Charleston, SC	47	26.7	57.1	52,800
Charlotte–Gastonia–Rock Hill, NC-SC	78	17.6	43.8	49,900
Chicago, IL	440	19.8	37.1	64,100
Cincinnati, OH	71	13.0	33.1	54,400
Cleveland, OH	132	18.5	42.2	45,500
Columbia, SC	42	26.0	50.3	53,200
Columbus, OH	58	11.1	38.9	50,400
Dallas, TX	140	14.7	37.9	57,000
Dayton–Springfield, OH	46	12.6	47.3	42,100
Detroit, MI	329	20.3	48.7	29,200
Fort Lauderdale–Hollywood–Pompano Beach, FL	59	11.1	44.9	67,300
Fort Worth–Arlington, TX	49	9.9	43.9	47,600
Gary-Hammond, IN	40	18.7	50.8	34,200
Greensboro–Winston-Salem–High Point, NC	66	17.7	41.3	53,700
Houston, TX	209	17.6	43.1	43,200
Indianapolis, IN	62	12.9	42.5	41,000
Jackson, MS	62	18.0	50.2	41,500
Jacksonville, FL	52	36.9	54.0	42,100
Kansas City, MO-KS	71	11.7	46.7	37,600
Los Angeles–Long Beach, CA	353	11.8	36.5	143,500
Louisville, KY-IN	46	12.4	42.7	34,800

(continued)

(continued from previous page)

	number	black share of total households	owner-occupied percent	owner-occupied median value
Memphis, TN	129	36.0%	47.9%	$44,500
Miami–Hialeah, FL	120	17.4	43.7	62,800
Milwaukee, WI	62	11.5	30.3	40,600
Mobile, AL	42	24.3	54.8	38,500
Nashville, TN	54	14.3	41.7	57,100
Nassau–Suffolk, NY	52	6.0	61.5	152,600
New Orleans, LA	141	30.9	40.9	56,300
New York, NY	762	23.4	20.8	159,900
Newark, NJ	141	21.6	30.9	132,400
Norfolk–Virginia Beach–Newport News, VA	132	26.7	42.3	66,300
Oakland, CA	111	14.3	36.7	138,100
Orlando, FL	41	10.3	46.0	59,400
Philadelphia, PA-NJ	316	17.8	55.5	36,200
Pittsburgh, PA	64	7.7	38.9	36,200
Raleigh–Durham, NC	65	22.8	41.4	63,400
Richmond–Petersburg, VA	89	26.8	49.0	57,300
Riverside–San Bernardino, CA	54	6.2	45.5	127,900
San Diego, CA	50	5.7	28.4	129,700
San Francisco, CA	44	6.9	31.5	223,200
St. Louis, MO-IL	144	15.6	45.3	43,800
Tampa–St. Petersburg–Clearwater, FL	63	7.2	45.4	47,000
Washington, DC-MD-VA	371	25.4	41.1	111,700

Source: Bureau of the Census, Housing in Metropolitan Areas—Black Households, *Statistical Brief, SB/95-5, 1995; calculations by New Strategist*

Blacks: Income

Black incomes are growing as blacks make gains in education and jobs.

The median income of black households rose 5 percent between 1990 and 1996, to $23,482 after adjusting for inflation. This was the largest increase among all racial and ethnic groups. Since 1980, the median household income of blacks has grown 14 percent.

Despite these gains, median household income for blacks stood at just 66 percent of the median for all households in 1996. This is because just 32 percent of all black households are married couples—typically the most affluent household type. Black couples had a median income of $42,069 in 1996, while the slightly more numerous black female-headed families had a median income of just $16,256.

For black men and women, incomes peak in the 45-to-54 age group. Black men who work full-time had a median income of $27,136 in 1996, while their female counterparts had a median income of $21,990. The earnings of blacks rise steadily with education. Black men with at least a bachelor's degree who work full-time earned a median of $36,001 in 1996, while similarly educated black women earned $29,806.

Black families are more likely to be poor than the average American family, but the percentage of blacks in poverty fell from 31 percent in the early 1990s to 26 percent in 1996.

■ Blacks should continue to see income gains in the years ahead as more get a college education. But the household income of blacks will remain far below average as long as female-headed families remain the dominant household type.

Black household income peaks for householders aged 45 to 54

(median income of black households by age of householder, 1996)

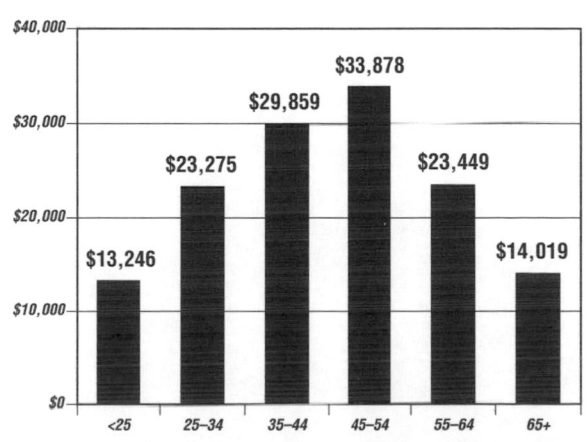

Median Income of Black Households, 1980 to 1996

(median income of black households, and ratio of black to total households' median income, 1980–96; percent change in income and ratio, selected years; in 1996 dollars)

	median income	ratio black/total
1996	$23,482	.66
1995	23,054	.66
1994	22,261	.65
1993	21,209	.63
1992	20,974	.61
1991	21,665	.62
1990	22,420	.62
1989	22,881	.63
1988	21,760	.60
1987	21,646	.60
1986	21,588	.61
1985	21,609	.63
1984	20,343	.60
1983	19,579	.60
1982	19,642	.59
1981	19,693	.59
1980	20,521	.61
Percent change		
1990–1996	4.7%	6.1%
1980–1996	14.4	8.9

Note: Ratios are calculated by dividing median income of black households by median of total households.
Source: Bureau of the Census, unpublished tables from the 1997 Current Population Survey; calculations by New Strategist

Income Distribution of Black Households by Age of Householder, 1996

(number and percent distribution of black households by household income and age of householder, 1996; households in thousands as of 1997)

	total	< age 25	25–34	35–44	45–54	55–64	65+
Total households, number	**12,109**	**871**	**2,687**	**3,095**	**2,210**	**1,428**	**1,818**
Under $10,000	2,794	335	606	495	376	337	646
$10,000 to $19,999	2,513	224	564	568	306	297	556
$20,000 to $29,999	1,893	129	516	491	328	218	210
$30,000 to $39,999	1,512	90	344	489	246	174	172
$40,000 to $49,999	994	35	219	297	245	127	69
$50,000 to $59,999	804	28	177	261	197	83	58
$60,000 to $69,999	557	8	104	197	164	52	33
$70,000 to $79,999	297	–	60	86	93	42	18
$80,000 to $89,999	240	7	38	78	85	20	14
$90,000 to $99,999	175	5	27	39	52	32	17
$100,000 or more	328	9	31	95	117	50	26
Median income	$23,482	$13,246	$23,275	$29,859	$33,878	$23,449	$14,019
Total households, percent	**100.0%**	**100.0%**	**100.0%**	**100.0%**	**100.0%**	**100.0%**	**100.0%**
Under $10,000	23.1	38.5	22.6	16.0	17.0	23.6	35.5
$10,000 to $19,999	20.8	25.7	21.0	18.4	13.8	20.8	30.6
$20,000 to $29,999	15.6	14.8	19.2	15.9	14.8	15.3	11.6
$30,000 to $39,999	12.5	10.3	12.8	15.8	11.1	12.2	9.5
$40,000 to $49,999	8.2	4.0	8.2	9.6	11.1	8.9	3.8
$50,000 to $59,999	6.6	3.2	6.6	8.4	8.9	5.8	3.2
$60,000 to $69,999	4.6	0.9	3.9	6.4	7.4	3.6	1.8
$70,000 to $79,999	2.5	–	2.2	2.8	4.2	2.9	1.0
$80,000 to $89,999	2.0	0.8	1.4	2.5	3.8	1.4	0.8
$90,000 to $99,999	1.4	0.6	1.0	1.3	2.4	2.2	0.9
$100,000 or more	2.7	1.0	1.2	3.1	5.3	3.5	1.4

Note: (–) means sample is too small to make a reliable estimate.
Source: Bureau of the Census, unpublished tables from the 1997 Current Population Survey; calculations by New Strategist

Income Distribution of Black Households by Household Type, 1996

(number and percent distribution of black households by household income and household type, 1996; households in thousands as of 1997)

	total households	family households				nonfamily households				
		total	married couples	female hh, no spouse present	male hh, no spouse present	total	female hh total	female hh living alone	male hh total	male hh living alone
Total households, number	**12,109**	**8,455**	**3,851**	**3,947**	**657**	**3,654**	**1,985**	**1,823**	**1,669**	**1,303**
Under $10,000	2,794	1,509	157	1,280	73	1,283	840	819	444	396
$10,000 to $19,999	2,513	1,691	504	1,059	128	824	452	416	371	328
$20,000 to $29,999	1,893	1,259	547	606	107	634	304	257	332	263
$30,000 to $39,999	1,512	1,154	608	423	124	359	176	165	184	136
$40,000 to $49,999	994	759	422	248	89	235	87	77	147	98
$50,000 to $59,999	804	648	460	137	53	154	63	45	93	51
$60,000 to $69,999	557	510	407	81	22	47	11	5	36	14
$70,000 to $79,999	297	259	201	39	18	40	11	7	29	–
$80,000 to $89,999	240	227	179	33	16	13	5	3	8	4
$90,000 to $99,999	175	150	127	14	9	26	13	10	12	8
$100,000 or more	328	290	243	28	19	38	22	14	16	6
Median income	$23,482	$27,496	$42,069	$16,256	$30,995	$15,454	$12,434	$11,529	$20,525	$16,447
Total households, percent	**100.0%**	**100.0%**	**100.0%**	**100.0%**	**100.0%**	**100.0%**	**100.0%**	**100.0%**	**100.0%**	**100.0%**
Under $10,000	23.1	17.8	4.1	32.4	11.1	35.1	42.3	44.9	26.6	30.4
$10,000 to $19,999	20.8	20.0	13.1	26.8	19.5	22.6	22.8	22.8	22.2	25.2
$20,000 to $29,999	15.6	14.9	14.2	15.4	16.3	17.4	15.3	14.1	19.9	20.2
$30,000 to $39,999	12.5	13.6	15.8	10.7	18.9	9.8	8.9	9.1	11.0	10.4
$40,000 to $49,999	8.2	9.0	11.0	6.3	13.5	6.4	4.4	4.2	8.8	7.5
$50,000 to $59,999	6.6	7.7	11.9	3.5	8.1	4.2	3.2	2.5	5.6	3.9
$60,000 to $69,999	4.6	6.0	10.6	2.1	3.3	1.3	0.6	0.3	2.2	1.1
$70,000 to $79,999	2.5	3.1	5.2	1.0	2.7	1.1	0.6	0.4	1.7	–
$80,000 to $89,999	2.0	2.7	4.6	0.8	2.4	0.4	0.3	0.2	0.5	0.3
$90,000 to $99,999	1.4	1.8	3.3	0.4	1.4	0.7	0.7	0.5	0.7	0.6
$100,000 or more	2.7	3.4	6.3	0.7	2.9	1.0	1.1	0.8	1.0	0.5

Note: (–) means sample is too small to make a reliable estimate.
Source: Bureau of the Census, unpublished tables from the 1997 Current Population Survey; calculations by New Strategist

Income Distribution of Black Men by Age, 1996

(number and percent distribution of black men aged 15 or older by income and age, 1996; men in thousands as of 1997)

	total	< age 25	25–34	35–44	45–54	55–64	65+
Total men, number	**11,113**	**2,667**	**2,414**	**2,483**	**1,587**	**948**	**1,014**
Without income	1,702	1,052	247	188	91	73	51
With income	9,410	1,615	2,167	2,295	1,496	875	963
Under $10,000	3,080	1,123	527	454	305	270	404
$10,000 to $19,999	2,246	318	576	532	300	197	323
$20,000 to $29,999	1,584	132	481	467	280	112	113
$30,000 to $39,999	1,149	34	303	380	214	160	61
$40,000 to $49,999	654	–	148	231	185	66	22
$50,000 to $74,999	488	5	106	157	153	47	17
$75,000 to $99,999	116	3	17	33	34	19	11
$100,000 or more	92	–	8	42	25	5	12
Median income of men with income	$16,491	$5,761	$19,585	$22,895	$24,744	$17,166	$11,628
Total men, percent	**100.0%**	**100.0%**	**100.0%**	**100.0%**	**100.0%**	**100.0%**	**100.0%**
Without income	15.3	39.4	10.2	7.6	5.7	7.7	5.0
With income	84.7	60.6	89.8	92.4	94.3	92.3	95.0
Under $10,000	27.7	42.1	21.8	18.3	19.2	28.5	39.8
$10,000 to $19,999	20.2	11.9	23.9	21.4	18.9	20.8	31.9
$20,000 to $29,999	14.3	4.9	19.9	18.8	17.6	11.8	11.1
$30,000 to $39,999	10.3	1.3	12.6	15.3	13.5	16.9	6.0
$40,000 to $49,999	5.9	–	6.1	9.3	11.7	7.0	2.2
$50,000 to $74,999	4.4	0.2	4.4	6.3	9.6	5.0	1.7
$75,000 to $99,999	1.0	0.1	0.7	1.3	2.1	2.0	1.1
$100,000 or more	0.8	–	0.3	1.7	1.6	0.5	1.2

Note: (–) means sample is too small to make a reliable estimate.
Source: Bureau of the Census, unpublished tables from the 1997 Current Population Survey; calculations by New Strategist

Income Distribution of Black Women by Age, 1996

(number and percent distribution of black women aged 15 or older by income and age, 1996; women in thousands as of 1997)

	total	< age 25	25–34	35–44	45–54	55–64	65+
Total women, number	**13,514**	**2,888**	**2,936**	**2,932**	**1,937**	**1,219**	**1,603**
Without income	1,698	905	206	183	183	158	62
With income	11,817	1,983	2,730	2,749	1,754	1,061	1,541
Under $10,000	5,252	1,407	1,029	810	500	425	1,081
$10,000 to $19,999	3,060	378	872	763	437	304	302
$20,000 to $29,999	1,845	142	526	556	353	174	95
$30,000 to $39,999	879	34	199	327	207	87	24
$40,000 to $49,999	407	9	64	171	115	37	12
$50,000 to $74,999	297	14	31	99	111	26	15
$75,000 to $99,999	36	–	5	13	9	5	4
$100,000 or more	37	–	5	8	20	–	4
Median income of women with income	$11,772	$5,827	$13,769	$17,606	$18,442	$12,337	$7,231
Total women, percent	**100.0%**	**100.0%**	**100.0%**	**100.0%**	**100.0%**	**100.0%**	**100.0%**
Without income	12.6	31.3	7.0	6.2	9.4	13.0	3.9
With income	87.4	68.7	93.0	93.8	90.6	87.0	96.1
Under $10,000	38.9	48.7	35.0	27.6	25.8	34.9	67.4
$10,000 to $19,999	22.6	13.1	29.7	26.0	22.6	24.9	18.8
$20,000 to $29,999	13.7	4.9	17.9	19.0	18.2	14.3	5.9
$30,000 to $39,999	6.5	1.2	6.8	11.2	10.7	7.1	1.5
$40,000 to $49,999	3.0	0.3	2.2	5.8	5.9	3.0	0.7
$50,000 to $74,999	2.2	0.5	1.1	3.4	5.7	2.1	0.9
$75,000 to $99,999	0.3	–	0.2	0.4	0.5	0.4	0.2
$100,000 or more	0.3	–	0.2	0.3	1.0	–	0.2

Note: (–) means sample is too small to make a reliable estimate.
Source: Bureau of the Census, unpublished tables from the 1997 Current Population Survey; calculations by New Strategist

Median Earnings of Blacks Who Work
Full-Time by Sex, 1980 to 1996

(median earnings of blacks who work year-round, full-time by sex; ratio of black to total population median earnings, and black female earnings as a percent of black male earnings, 1980–96; percent change in earnings and ratios for selected years; in 1996 dollars)

	black men		black women		black women's earnings as a percent of black men's earnings
	median earnings	ratio black/total	median earnings	ratio black/total	
1996	$27,136	.81	$21,990	.88	81.0%
1995	25,530	.77	21,701	.89	85.0
1994	25,838	.77	21,839	.89	84.5
1993	25,588	.76	22,058	.90	86.2
1992	25,711	.75	22,655	.92	88.1
1991	26,067	.75	22,042	.90	84.6
1990	25,787	.74	22,261	.90	86.3
1989	26,197	.73	22,613	.91	86.3
1988	27,475	.76	22,371	.91	81.4
1987	26,963	.73	22,068	.91	81.8
1986	26,865	.72	21,422	.89	79.7
1985	26,205	.72	21,275	.90	81.2
1984	25,586	.71	21,196	.91	82.8
1983	25,851	.73	20,479	.90	79.2
1982	25,915	.73	20,312	.91	78.4
1981	26,093	.72	19,918	.92	76.3
1980	26,452	.72	20,809	.94	78.7
Percent change					
1990–1996	5.2%	9.2%	−1.2%	−2.1%	−6.1%
1980–1996	2.6	11.8	5.7	-6.3	3.0

Note: Black/total ratios are calculated by dividing median earnings of black men and women by median for total men and women.
Source: Bureau of the Census, unpublished tables from the 1997 Current Population Survey; calculations by New Strategist

Median Earnings of Blacks Who Work Full-Time by Education and Sex, 1996

(median earnings of blacks aged 25 or older who work year-round, full-time, by educational attainment and sex, 1996)

	men	women	black women's earnings as a percent of black men's earnings
Total persons	**$23,275**	**$17,957**	**77.2%**
Less than 9th grade	14,057	9,694	69.0
9th to 12th grade, no diploma	16,307	10,369	63.6
High school graduate	21,376	15,050	70.4
Some college, no degree	25,890	19,640	75.9
Associate's degree	29,748	22,020	74.0
Bachelor's degree or more	36,001	29,806	82.8
Bachelor's degree	32,413	27,534	84.9
Master's degree	38,650	37,100	96.0
Professional degree	71,986	27,323	38.0
Doctoral degree	69,639	40,070	57.5

Source: U.S. Bureau of the Census, unpublished tables from the 1997 Current Population Survey, Internet web site, http://www.census.gov; calculations by New Strategist

Black Families below the Poverty Level, 1980 to 1996

(total number of black families, and number and percent below poverty level by type of family and presence of children under age 18 at home, 1980–96; percent change in numbers and rates for selected years; families in thousands as of March the following year)

	total families			married couples			female hh, no spouse present		
		in poverty			in poverty			in poverty	
	total	number	percent	total	number	percent	total	number	percent
With and without children under age 18									
1996	8,455	2,206	26.1%	3,851	352	9.1%	3,947	1,724	43.7%
1995	8,055	2,127	26.4	3,713	314	8.5	3,769	1,701	45.1
1994	8,093	2,212	27.3	3,842	336	8.7	3,716	1,715	46.2
1993	7,993	2,499	31.3	3,715	458	12.3	3,828	1,906	49.9
1992	7,982	2,484	31.1	3,777	490	13.0	3,738	1,878	50.2
1991	7,716	2,343	30.4	3,631	399	11.0	3,582	1,834	51.2
1990	7,471	2,193	29.3	3,569	448	12.6	3,430	1,648	48.1
1989	7,470	2,077	27.8	3,750	443	11.8	3,275	1,524	46.5
1988	7,409	2,089	28.2	3,722	421	11.3	3,223	1,579	49.0
1987	7,202	2,117	29.4	3,681	439	11.9	3,089	1,577	51.1
1986	7,096	1,987	28.0	3,742	403	10.8	2,967	1,488	50.1
1985	6,921	1,963	28.7	3,680	447	12.2	2,874	1,452	50.5
1984	6,778	2,094	30.9	3,469	479	13.8	2,964	1,533	51.7
1983	6,681	2,161	32.3	3,454	535	15.5	2,871	1,541	53.7
1982	6,530	2,158	33.0	3,486	543	15.6	2,734	1,535	56.2
1981	6,413	1,972	30.8	3,535	543	15.4	2,605	1,377	52.9
1980	6,317	1,826	28.9	3,392	474	14.0	2,634	1,301	49.4
Percent change									
1990–1996	13.2%	0.6%	−11.0%	7.9%	−21.4%	−27.5%	15.1%	4.6%	−9.2%
1980–1996	33.8	20.8	−9.7	13.5	−25.7	−34.7	49.8	32.5	−11.6

(continued)

(continued from previous page)

	total families			married couples			female hh, no spouse present		
		in poverty			in poverty			in poverty	
	total	*number*	*percent*	*total*	*number*	*percent*	*total*	*number*	*percent*
With children									
under age 18									
1996	5,695	1,941	34.1%	2,174	239	11.0%	3,120	1,593	51.1%
1995	5,340	1,821	34.1	2,119	209	9.9	2,884	1,533	53.2
1994	5,439	1,954	35.9	2,147	245	11.4	2,951	1,591	53.9
1993	5,525	2,171	39.3	2,147	298	13.9	3,084	1,780	57.7
1992	5,448	2,132	39.1	2,229	343	15.4	2,971	1,706	57.4
1991	5,143	2,016	39.2	2,129	263	12.4	2,771	1,676	60.5
1990	5,069	1,887	37.2	2,104	301	14.3	2,698	1,513	56.1
1989	5,031	1,783	35.4	2,179	291	13.3	2,624	1,415	53.9
1988	5,010	1,802	36.0	2,181	272	12.5	2,583	1,452	56.2
1987	4,880	1,788	36.6	2,205	290	13.2	2,453	1,437	58.6
1986	4,806	1,699	35.4	2,236	257	11.5	2,386	1,384	58.0
1985	4,636	1,670	36.0	2,185	281	12.9	2,269	1,336	58.9
1984	4,512	1,758	39.0	2,001	331	16.6	2,335	1,364	58.4
1983	4,482	1,789	39.9	2,052	369	18.0	2,244	1,362	60.7
1982	4,470	1,819	40.7	2,093	360	17.2	2,199	1,401	63.7
1981	4,455	1,652	37.1	2,202	357	16.2	2,118	1,261	59.5
1980	4,465	1,583	35.5	2,154	333	15.5	2,171	1,217	56.0
Percent change									
1990–1996	12.3%	2.9%	−8.4%	3.3%	−20.6%	−23.1%	15.6%	5.3%	−9.0%
1980–1996	27.5	22.6	−4.0	0.9	−28.2	−29.1	43.7	30.9	−8.8

Source: Bureau of the Census, unpublished tables from the 1997 Current Population Survey; calculations by New Strategist

Blacks in Poverty by Sex and Age, 1996

(total number of blacks, and number and percent below poverty level by sex and age, 1996; persons in thousands as of 1997)

		in poverty	
	total	*number*	*percent*
Total persons	**34,110**	**9,694**	**28.4%**
Under age 18	11,338	4,519	39.9
Aged 18 to 24	3,700	1,095	29.6
Aged 25 to 34	5,350	1,276	23.8
Aged 35 to 44	5,415	1,053	19.4
Aged 45 to 54	3,524	584	16.6
Aged 55 to 59	1,184	257	21.7
Aged 60 to 64	982	250	25.4
Aged 65 to 74	1,570	357	22.8
Aged 75 or older	1,046	303	29.0
Females, total	**18,203**	**5,771**	**31.7**
Under age 18	5,614	2,328	41.5
Aged 18 to 24	1,963	686	35.0
Aged 25 to 34	2,936	893	30.4
Aged 35 to 44	2,932	701	23.9
Aged 45 to 54	1,937	370	19.1
Aged 55 to 59	660	156	23.7
Aged 60 to 64	558	160	28.6
Aged 65 to 74	926	266	28.7
Aged 75 or older	677	211	31.2
Males, total	**15,908**	**3,923**	**24.7**
Under age 18	5,724	2,192	38.3
Aged 18 to 24	1,738	409	23.5
Aged 25 to 34	2,414	383	15.9
Aged 35 to 44	2,483	352	14.2
Aged 45 to 54	1,587	214	13.5
Aged 55 to 59	524	100	19.2
Aged 60 to 64	424	90	21.2
Aged 65 to 74	644	92	14.2
Aged 75 or older	369	92	24.9

Source: Bureau of the Census, unpublished tables from the 1997 Current Population Survey

Blacks: Labor Force

One in five black workers is a manager, administrator, or professional.

Sixty-eight percent of black men and 62 percent of black women were in the labor force in 1997. The labor force participation rate of black men is below the 75 percent rate for all men, while the rate for black women is slightly higher than average.

Twenty percent of black workers are in managerial or professional specialty jobs, accounting for 7 percent of the employed in those occupations. For comparison, among all workers, 29 percent are managers or professionals. The largest share of blacks (29 percent) are employed in technical, sales, or administrative support jobs. Blacks account for 11 percent of all workers, but for 29 percent of dietitians, 22 percent of guards, and 26 percent of taxicab drivers.

In 58 percent of black couples, both husband and wife are in the labor force. Nevertheless, only 37 percent of black households have two or more earners, well below the national average of 45 percent. A smaller-than-average share of black households have two or more earners because relatively few are headed by married couples.

Between 1996 and 2006, the number of black workers will grow 14 percent. The black share of the labor force will rise only slightly during those years, from 11.3 to 11.6 percent.

■ Younger, better-educated blacks are making inroads on high-paying white-collar occupations, but it will take another few decades until their progress is captured by the labor force statistics for black workers as a whole.

Blacks are more likely than Hispanics to be managers or professionals

(percent of employed blacks and Hispanics aged 16 or older in managerial or professional specialty occupations, 1997)

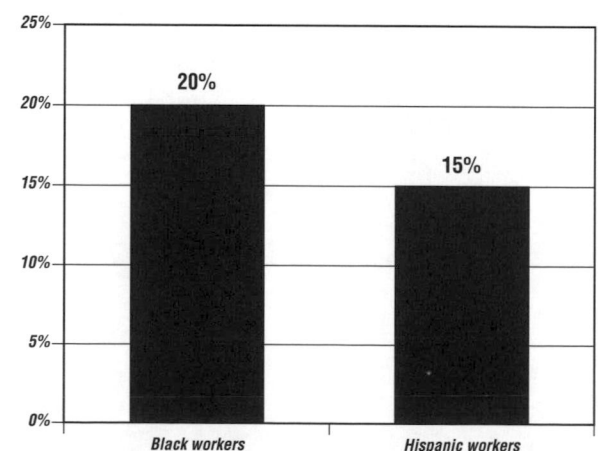

Employment Status of Blacks by Sex and Age, 1997

(employment status of the civilian noninstitutionalized black population aged 16 or older, by sex and age, 1997; numbers in thousands)

	civilian labor force						not in labor force	
	total	percent of population	employed	percent of labor force	unemployed	percent of labor force	total	percent of population
Total persons	**15,529**	**64.7%**	**13,969**	**90.0%**	**1,560**	**10.0%**	**8,474**	**35.3%**
Aged 16 to 19	933	38.7	631	67.6	302	32.4	1,479	61.3
Aged 20 to 24	1,783	70.9	1,456	81.7	327	18.3	732	29.1
Aged 25 to 34	4,329	82.0	3,903	90.2	426	9.8	949	18.0
Aged 35 to 44	4,401	81.4	4,094	93.0	307	7.0	1,009	18.7
Aged 45 to 54	2,724	76.3	2,588	95.0	136	5.0	847	23.7
Aged 55 to 64	1,093	50.5	1,048	95.9	45	4.1	1,070	49.4
Aged 65 or older	265	10.0	249	94.0	16	6.7	2,388	90.0
Total men	**7,354**	**68.3**	**6,607**	**89.8**	**747**	**10.2**	**3,409**	**31.7**
Aged 16 to 19	444	37.4	282	63.5	162	36.5	744	62.6
Aged 20 to 24	832	72.1	668	80.3	165	19.8	321	27.8
Aged 25 to 34	2,052	86.8	1,874	91.3	178	8.7	311	13.2
Aged 35 to 44	2,096	84.8	1,955	93.3	141	6.7	375	15.2
Aged 45 to 54	1,287	80.1	1,215	94.4	72	5.6	320	19.9
Aged 55 to 64	508	54.3	487	95.9	22	4.2	427	45.6
Aged 65 or older	134	12.9	127	94.8	7	5.5	911	87.2
Total women	**8,175**	**61.7**	**7,362**	**90.1**	**813**	**9.9**	**5,066**	**38.3**
Aged 16 to 19	489	39.9	349	71.4	140	28.7	736	60.1
Aged 20 to 24	951	69.9	789	83.0	163	17.1	411	30.2
Aged 25 to 34	2,277	78.1	2,029	89.1	248	10.9	638	21.9
Aged 35 to 44	2,305	78.4	2,139	92.8	166	7.2	634	21.6
Aged 45 to 54	1,437	73.2	1,373	95.5	64	4.4	527	26.8
Aged 55 to 64	585	47.6	561	95.9	24	4.1	643	52.4
Aged 65 or older	131	8.2	122	93.1	9	6.6	1,477	91.9

Note: The civilian labor force equals the number of employed plus the number of unemployed persons. The civilian population equals the number of persons in the labor force plus the number of those not in the labor force.
Source: Bureau of Labor Statistics, Employment and Earnings, *January 1998; calculations by New Strategist*

Black Workers by Occupation, 1997

(total number of employed persons aged 16 or older in the civilian labor force; number and percent distribution of employed blacks, and black share of total employed, by occupation, 1997; numbers in thousands)

	total	black number	black percent	black share of total employed
Total employed, number	**129,558**	**13,969**	**100.0%**	**10.8%**
Managerial and professional specialty	**37,686**	**2,764**	**19.8**	**7.3**
Executive, administrative, and managerial	18,440	1,267	9.1	6.9
Professional specialty	19,245	1,497	10.7	7.8
Technical, sales, and administrative support	**38,309**	**4,032**	**28.9**	**10.5**
Technicians and related support	4,214	410	2.9	9.7
Sales occupations	15,734	1,271	9.1	8.1
Administrative support, including clerical	18,361	2,352	16.8	12.8
Service occupations	**17,537**	**3,092**	**22.1**	**17.6**
Private household	795	129	0.9	16.2
Protective service	2,300	430	3.1	18.7
Service, except private household and protective	14,442	2,533	18.1	17.5
Precision production, craft, and repair	**14,124**	**1,144**	**8.2**	**8.1**
Mechanics and repairers	4,675	370	2.6	7.9
Construction trades	5,378	381	2.7	7.1
Other precision production, craft, and repair	4,071	393	2.8	9.7
Operators, fabricators, and laborers	**18,399**	**2,781**	**19.9**	**15.1**
Machine operators, assemblers, and inspectors	7,962	1,178	8.4	14.8
Transportation and material moving occupations	5,389	819	5.9	15.2
Handlers, equipment cleaners, helpers, and laborers	5,048	784	5.6	15.5
Farming, forestry, and fishing	**3,503**	**156**	**1.1**	**4.5**

Source: Bureau of Labor Statistics, Employment and Earnings, *January 1998; calculations by New Strategist*

Black Worker Share by Detailed Occupation, 1997

(total number of employed persons aged 16 or older in the civilian labor force; and black share of total employed, by selected occupation, 1997; numbers in thousands)

	total	*percent black*
Total employed	**129,558**	**10.8%**
Managerial and professional specialty	**37,686**	**7.3**
Executive, administrative, and managerial	18,440	6.9
Officials and administrators, public administrators	606	11.9
Financial managers	688	5.6
Personnel and labor relations managers	108	7.5
Purchasing managers	114	6.4
Managers, marketing, advertising, and public relations	711	3.7
Administrators, education and related fields	733	10.7
Managers, medicine and health	701	7.4
Managers, food serving and lodging establishments	1,408	9.1
Managers, property and real estate	535	7.1
Professional specialty	19,245	7.8
Architects	169	1.7
Engineers	2,036	3.9
Mathematical and computer scientists	1,494	7.5
Natural scientists	529	5.1
Physicians	724	4.2
Dentists	138	2.6
Registered nurses	2,065	8.3
Pharmacists	200	4.1
Dietitians	101	28.5
Therapists	455	6.6
Teachers, college and university	869	6.5
Teachers, except college and university	4,798	10.2
Librarians, archivists, and curators	217	6.3
Economists	135	6.6
Psychologists	256	9.2
Social, recreation, and religious workers	1,357	17.2
Lawyers and judges	925	2.8
Writers, artists, entertainers, and athletes	2,234	5.0
Technical, sales, and administrative support	**38,309**	**10.5**
Technicians and related support	4,214	9.7
Health technologists and technicians	1,693	13.0
Engineering and related technologists and technicians	960	7.4
Science technicians	287	9.4

(continued)

(continued from previous page)

	total	percent black
Technicians, except health, engineering, and science	1,275	7.1%
Airplane pilots and navigators	120	1.8
Computer programmers	626	5.9
Legal assistants	346	9.8
Sales occupations	15,734	8.1
Supervisors and proprietors	4,635	4.8
Sales representatives, finance and business services	2,613	6.9
Sales representatives, commodities, except retail	1,507	3.0
Sales workers, retail and personal services	6,887	11.9
Administrative support, including clerical	18,361	12.8
Supervisors	685	14.4
Computer equipment operators	392	15.4
Secretaries, stenographers, and typists	3,692	9.8
Information clerks	1,993	11.3
Records processing occupations, except financial	935	15.3
Financial records processing	2,196	7.1
Service occupations	**17,537**	**17.6**
Private household	795	16.2
Protective	2,300	18.7
Firefighting and fire prevention	233	11.9
Police and detectives	1,005	18.1
Guards	881	21.6
Service occupations, ex. private hh and protective services	14,442	17.5
Food preparation and service occupations	5,999	11.6
Health service occupations	2,447	30.8
Cleaning and building service occupations	3,108	21.5
Personal service occupations	2,888	14.3
Precision production, craft, and repair	**14,124**	**8.1**
Mechanics and repairers	4,675	7.9
Construction trades	5,378	7.1
Extractive occupations	145	8.6
Precision production occupations	3,926	9.7
Operators, fabricators, and laborers	**18,399**	**15.1**
Machine operators, assemblers, and inspectors	7,962	14.8
Transportation and material moving occupations	5,389	15.2
Motor vehicle operators	4,089	15.3
Truck drivers	95	19.3
Bus drivers	472	23.3
Taxicab drivers and chauffers	248	25.8
Material moving equipment operators	1,125	15.4
Handlers, equipment cleaners, helpers, and laborers	5,048	15.5
Farming, forestry, and fishing	**3,503**	**4.5**

Source: Bureau of Labor Statistics, Employment and Earnings, *January 1998*

Black Workers by Industry, 1997

(total number of employed persons aged 16 or older in the civilian labor force; number and percent distribution of employed blacks, and black share of total employed, by industry, 1997; numbers in thousands)

	total	black number	black percent	black share of total employed
Total employed	**129,558**	**13,969**	**100.0%**	**10.8%**
Agriculture	3,399	117	0.8	3.4
Mining	634	26	0.2	4.1
Construction	8,302	563	4.0	6.8
Manufacturing	20,835	2,162	15.5	10.4
Durable goods	12,437	1,096	7.8	8.8
Nondurable goods	8,399	1,066	7.6	12.7
Transportation, communications, and other public utilities	9,182	1,368	9.8	14.9
Wholesale and retail trade	26,777	2,372	17.0	8.9
Wholesale trade	4,907	307	2.2	6.3
Retail trade	21,869	2,065	14.8	9.4
Finance, insurance, and real estate	8,297	802	5.7	9.7
Services	46,393	5,611	40.2	12.1
Private households	921	163	1.2	17.7
Other service industries	45,472	5,449	39.0	12.0
Professional and related services	30,935	3,813	27.3	12.3
Public administration	5,738	948	6.8	16.5

Source: Bureau of Labor Statistics, Employment and Earnings, *January 1998; calculations by New Strategist*

Black Households by Number of Earners, 1996

(number and percent distribution of black households by number of earners, 1996; numbers in thousands)

	number	percent
Total households	**12,109**	**100.0%**
No earners	2,800	23.1
One earner	4,867	40.2
Two or more earners	4,442	36.7
Two earners	3,512	29.0
Three earners	745	6.2
Four or more earners	185	1.5

Source: Bureau of the Census, Money Income: 1996, *Current Population Reports, P60-197, 1997; calculations by New Strategist*

Labor Force Status of Black Married Couples, 1996

(number and percent distribution of black married couples by age of householder and labor force status of husband and wife, 1996; numbers in thousands)

	total married couples	husband and/or wife in labor force			neither husband nor wife in labor force
		husband and wife	husband only	wife only	
Total couples, number	**3,713**	**2,136**	**714**	**349**	**514**
Under age 20	14	10	4	–	–
Aged 20 to 24	91	53	28	3	7
Aged 25 to 29	259	201	48	7	2
Aged 30 to 34	438	368	52	16	3
Aged 35 to 39	527	385	94	36	12
Aged 40 to 44	527	348	125	45	9
Aged 45 to 49	512	368	88	40	16
Aged 50 to 54	341	190	82	49	21
Aged 55 to 59	276	107	96	36	37
Aged 60 to 64	263	72	48	63	80
Aged 65 to 74	319	34	45	48	191
Aged 75 to 84	125	–	2	4	118
Aged 85 or older	21	–	–	3	18
Total couples, percent	**100.0%**	**57.5%**	**19.2%**	**9.4%**	**13.8%**
Under age 20	100.0	71.4	28.6		
Aged 20 to 24	100.0	58.2	30.8	3.3	7.7
Aged 25 to 29	100.0	77.6	18.5	2.7	0.8
Aged 30 to 34	100.0	84.0	11.9	3.7	0.7
Aged 35 to 39	100.0	73.1	17.8	6.8	2.3
Aged 40 to 44	100.0	66.0	23.7	8.5	1.7
Aged 45 to 49	100.0	71.9	17.2	7.8	3.1
Aged 50 to 54	100.0	55.7	24.0	14.4	6.2
Aged 55 to 59	100.0	38.8	34.8	13.0	13.4
Aged 60 to 64	100.0	27.4	18.3	24.0	30.4
Aged 65 to 74	100.0	10.7	14.1	15.0	59.9
Aged 75 to 84	100.0	–	1.6	3.2	94.4
Aged 85 or older	100.0	–	–	14.3	85.7

Note: (–) means sample is too small to make a reliable estimate.
Source: Bureau of the Census, Household and Family Characteristics: March 1996, *Current Population Reports, P20-495(Update), 1997; calculations by New Strategist*

Union Membership of Blacks, 1997

(number of employed black wage and salary workers aged 16 or older, number and percent who are represented by unions or are union members, and median weekly earnings by union membership status; by sex, 1997; numbers in thousands)

	total	men	women
Total employed	**13,346**	**6,201**	**7,145**
Represented by unions*	2,688	1,378	1,309
Percent of employed	20.1%	22.2%	18.3%
Members of unions**	2,394	1,251	1,143
Percent of employed	17.9%	20.2%	16.0%
Median weekly earnings, total***	$400	$432	$375
Represented by unions*	523	573	496
Members of unions**	533	577	504
Non-union	371	396	349

* Members of a labor union or an employee association similar to a union as well as workers who report no union affiliation but whose jobs are covered by a union or an employee association contract.
** Members of a labor union or an employee association similar to a union.
*** Full-time wage and salary workers.
Source: Bureau of Labor Statistics, Employment and Earnings, *January 1998*

Projections of the Black Labor Force by Sex, 1996 to 2006

(number of blacks in the civilian labor force in 1996 and 2006, and percent change in number; labor force participation rate of blacks in 1996 and 2006, and black share of total labor force in 1996 and 2006; by sex; numbers in thousands)

| | number in labor force | | percent change |
	1996	2006	1996–2006
Total	**15,134**	**17,225**	**13.8%**
Men	7,264	7,996	10.1
Women	7,869	9,229	17.3

| | labor force participation rate | | percentage point change |
	1996	2006	1996–2006
Total	**64.1%**	**64.9%**	**0.8**
Men	68.7	69.6	0.9
Women	60.4	61.3	0.9

| | percent of total labor force | | percentage point change |
	1996	2006	1996–2006
Total	**11.3%**	**11.6%**	**0.3**
Men	10.1	10.2	0.1
Women	12.7	13.1	0.3

Source: Bureau of Labor Statistic, Monthly Labor Review, *November 1997; calculations by New Strategist*

Blacks: Population

Blacks are still the largest minority in the U.S., a position they will hold until 2009.

The black population is projected to grow from 35 million in 1998 to 45 million in 2020, when blacks will account for 14 percent of the U.S. population. Blacks will remain the largest minority in the U.S. until 2009, when Hispanics will finally outnumber them, according to projections by the Census Bureau.

Blacks account for a larger share of children and young adults than of older Americans because black fertility and mortality are above average. While only 7.5 percent of people aged 85 or older are black, fully 16 percent of children under age 5 are black.

More than half of blacks live in the South, where they account for 19 percent of the population. In Mississippi, 36 percent of the population is black, as is at least 30 percent of the population of Louisiana and South Carolina. No single state is home to more than 10 percent of the black population.

Among metropolitan areas, New York has the largest number of blacks, over 3.4 million in 1990. Blacks account for 18 percent of the population in the greater New York metropolitan area. Overall, there are 51 metropolitan areas with more than 100,000 blacks. Among them, the black share of the population is highest in Jackson, Mississippi, at 42.5 percent.

■ Unlike Hispanics or Asians, most of whom are concentrated in only a few states, blacks are an important segment of the population throughout the country. This adds to their cultural influence and political power.

The black population will climb to 45 million by 2020

(number of blacks in the population, 1998 and 2020)

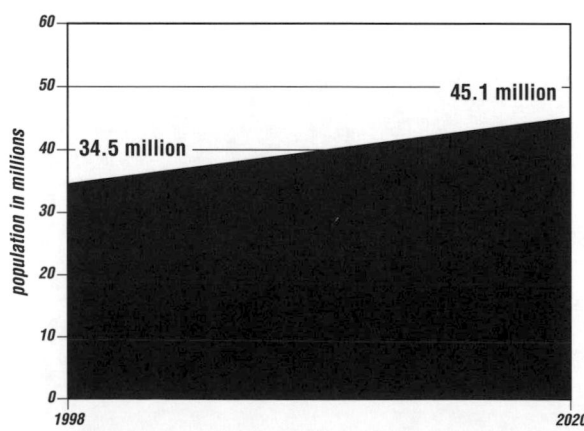

Blacks by Age, 1995 to 2020

(number of blacks by age, selected years 1995–2020; percent change 1995–2000 and 2000–2010; numbers in thousands)

	1995	1998	2000	2010	2020	percent change 1995–2000	percent change 2000–2010
Total persons	**33,144**	**34,537**	**35,454**	**40,109**	**45,075**	**7.0%**	**13.1%**
Under age 5	3,107	3,098	3,127	3,454	3,818	0.6	10.5
Aged 5 to 9	3,021	3,177	3,158	3,296	3,717	4.5	4.4
Aged 10 to 14	2,873	2,995	3,175	3,338	3,677	10.5	5.1
Aged 15 to 19	2,817	3,003	3,032	3,494	3,639	7.6	15.2
Aged 20 to 24	2,636	2,598	2,742	3,245	3,399	4.0	18.3
Aged 25 to 29	2,594	2,598	2,551	2,830	3,242	−1.7	10.9
Aged 30 to 34	2,829	2,711	2,621	2,659	3,126	−7.4	1.4
Aged 35 to 39	2,792	2,870	2,868	2,605	2,879	2.7	−9.2
Aged 40 to 44	2,392	2,659	2,781	2,632	2,673	16.3	−5.4
Aged 45 to 49	1,856	2,148	2,307	2,735	2,493	24.3	18.6
Aged 50 to 54	1,381	1,585	1,804	2,591	2,466	30.6	43.6
Aged 55 to 59	1,138	1,246	1,325	2,150	2,565	16.4	62.3
Aged 60 to 64	989	1,027	1,081	1,651	2,399	9.3	52.7
Aged 65 to 69	918	929	933	1,200	1,966	1.6	28.6
Aged 70 to 74	697	721	742	833	1,289	6.5	12.3
Aged 75 to 79	510	547	554	606	788	8.6	9.4
Aged 80 to 84	319	324	336	395	455	5.3	17.6
Aged 85 or older	275	300	317	396	482	15.3	24.9
Aged 18 to 24	3,726	3,805	3,974	4,747	4,888	6.7	19.5
Aged 18 or older	22,417	23,471	24,186	27,957	31,679	7.9	15.6
Aged 65 or older	2,718	2,822	2,883	3,430	4,981	6.1	19.0

Source: Bureau of the Census, Population Projections of the United States, by Age, Sex, Race, and Hispanic Origin: 1995 to 2050, *Current Population Reports, P25-1130, 1996; calculations by New Strategist*

Black Share of the Total Population by Age, 1995 to 2020

(blacks as a percent of the total population by age, selected years 1995–2020)

	1995	1998	2000	2010	2020
Total persons	**12.6%**	**12.8%**	**12.9%**	**13.5%**	**14.0%**
Under age 5	15.9	16.2	16.5	17.3	17.4
Aged 5 to 9	15.7	15.9	15.9	16.9	17.2
Aged 10 to 14	15.2	15.5	15.8	16.5	17.2
Aged 15 to 19	15.6	15.5	15.3	16.0	17.0
Aged 20 to 24	14.7	14.9	15.0	15.4	16.0
Aged 25 to 29	13.7	14.0	14.4	14.4	15.0
Aged 30 to 34	12.9	13.4	13.4	14.3	14.6
Aged 35 to 39	12.5	12.7	12.9	14.1	14.0
Aged 40 to 44	11.8	12.2	12.4	13.2	14.0
Aged 45 to 49	10.6	11.4	11.6	12.5	13.6
Aged 50 to 54	10.1	10.1	10.5	12.0	12.7
Aged 55 to 59	10.3	10.0	10.0	11.3	12.1
Aged 60 to 64	9.8	10.0	10.1	10.2	11.7
Aged 65 to 69	9.3	9.7	9.9	9.9	11.2
Aged 70 to 74	7.9	8.2	8.5	9.3	9.3
Aged 75 to 79	7.6	7.6	7.5	8.5	8.4
Aged 80 to 84	7.1	6.9	6.9	7.1	7.7
Aged 85 or older	7.6	7.5	7.4	7.0	7.5
Aged 18 to 24	14.9	15.1	15.1	15.8	16.3
Aged 18 or older	11.6	11.7	11.9	12.4	12.9
Aged 65 or older	8.1	8.2	8.3	8.7	9.4

Source: Calculations by New Strategist based on Census Bureau data in Population Projections of the United States, by Age, Sex, Race, and Hispanic Origin: 1995 to 2050, *Current Population Reports, P25-1130, 1996*

Non-Hispanic Blacks by Age, 1995 to 2020

(number of non-Hispanic blacks by age, selected years 1995–2020; percent change 1995–2000 and 2000–2010; numbers in thousands)

	1995	1998	2000	2010	2020	percent change 1995–2000	percent change 2000–2010
Total persons	**31,598**	**32,789**	**33,568**	**37,466**	**41,538**	**6.2%**	**11.6%**
Under age 5	2,929	2,910	2,929	3,187	3,466	0.0	8.8
Aged 5 to 9	2,863	2,995	2,966	3,054	3,391	3.6	3.0
Aged 10 to 14	2,738	2,837	2,997	3,104	3,370	9.5	3.6
Aged 15 to 19	2,687	2,854	2,872	3,252	3,342	6.9	13.2
Aged 20 to 24	2,508	2,460	2,592	3,023	3,121	3.3	16.6
Aged 25 to 29	2,448	2,451	2,405	2,635	2,973	–1.8	9.6
Aged 30 to 34	2,680	2,552	2,458	2,476	2,875	–8.3	0.7
Aged 35 to 39	2,661	2,720	2,706	2,428	2,655	1.7	–10.3
Aged 40 to 44	2,287	2,532	2,641	2,448	2,469	15.5	–7.3
Aged 45 to 49	1,779	2,053	2,199	2,563	2,307	23.6	16.6
Aged 50 to 54	1,326	1,516	1,723	2,446	2,279	29.9	42.0
Aged 55 to 59	1,094	1,193	1,267	2,036	2,388	15.8	60.7
Aged 60 to 64	954	985	1,034	1,565	2,249	8.4	51.4
Aged 65 to 69	888	893	894	1,135	1,845	0.7	27.0
Aged 70 to 74	677	697	714	786	1,206	5.5	10.1
Aged 75 to 79	498	532	536	573	732	7.6	6.9
Aged 80 to 84	311	315	327	375	420	5.1	14.7
Aged 85 or older	270	295	310	381	449	14.8	22.9
Aged 18 to 24	3,547	3,607	3,749	4,354	4,459	5.7	16.1
Aged 18 or older	21,420	22,342	22,963	26,201	29,306	7.2	14.1
Aged 65 or older	2,644	2,732	2,781	3,249	4,651	5.2	16.8

Source: Bureau of the Census, Population Projections of the United States, by Age, Sex, Race, and Hispanic Origin: 1995 to 2050, *Current Population Reports, P25-1130, 1996; calculations by New Strategist*

Blacks by Age and Sex, 1998

(number of blacks by age and sex, and sex ratio by age, 1998; numbers in thousands)

	total	male	female	sex ratio*
Total persons	**34,537**	**16,378**	**18,159**	**90**
Under age 5	3,098	1,571	1,527	103
Aged 5 to 9	3,177	1,614	1,563	103
Aged 10 to 14	2,995	1,521	1,474	103
Aged 15 to 19	3,003	1,524	1,479	103
Aged 20 to 24	2,598	1,280	1,318	97
Aged 25 to 29	2,598	1,241	1,357	91
Aged 30 to 34	2,711	1,271	1,440	88
Aged 35 to 39	2,870	1,346	1,524	88
Aged 40 to 44	2,659	1,240	1,419	87
Aged 45 to 49	2,148	980	1,168	84
Aged 50 to 54	1,585	710	874	81
Aged 55 to 59	1,246	546	700	78
Aged 60 to 64	1,027	439	588	75
Aged 65 to 69	929	396	533	74
Aged 70 to 74	721	293	428	68
Aged 75 to 79	547	211	336	63
Aged 80 to 84	324	110	214	51
Aged 85 or older	300	86	215	40
Aged 18 to 24	3,805	1,887	1,918	98
Aged 18 or older	23,471	10,755	12,716	85
Aged 65 or older	2,822	1,096	1,726	63

* The sex ratio is the number of males per 100 females.
Source: Bureau of the Census, Population Projections of the United States, by Age, Sex, Race, and Hispanic Origin: 1995 to 2050, Current Population Reports, P25-1130, 1996; calculations by New Strategist

Blacks by Region and Division, 1995 to 2025

(number and percent distribution of blacks and black share of the total population by region and division, selected years 1995–2025; percent change in number and percentage point change in distribution and share, 1995–2005 and 2000–2010; numbers in thousands)

	1995	2000	2010	2020	percent change 1995–2000	percent change 2000–2020
United States	**33,134**	**35,456**	**40,110**	**45,075**	**7.0%**	**13.1%**
Northeast	**6,247**	**6,575**	**7,300**	**8,140**	**5.3**	**11.0**
New England	734	811	982	1,172	10.5	21.1
Middle Atlantic	5,513	5,764	6,318	6,968	4.6	9.6
Midwest	**6,197**	**6,553**	**7,199**	**7,866**	**5.7**	**9.9**
East North Central	5,197	5,449	5,914	6,408	4.8	8.5
West North Central	1,002	1,103	1,285	1,459	10.1	16.5
South	**17,495**	**18,983**	**21,779**	**24,575**	**8.5**	**14.7**
South Atlantic	9,987	10,931	12,675	14,393	9.5	16.0
East South Central	3,184	3,367	3,673	3,957	5.7	9.1
West South Central	4,324	4,685	5,432	6,225	8.3	15.9
West	**3,194**	**3,343**	**3,831**	**4,493**	**4.7**	**14.6**
Mountain	490	601	755	887	22.7	25.6
Pacific	2,704	2,742	3,075	3,606	1.4	12.1

	1995	2000	2010	2020	percentage point change 1995–2000	percentage point change 2000–2020
Percent distribution						
United States	**100.0%**	**100.0%**	**100.0%**	**100.0%**	–	–
Northeast	**18.9**	**18.5**	**18.2**	**18.1**	**–0.4**	**–0.3**
New England	2.2	2.3	2.4	2.6	0.1	0.1
Middle Atlantic	16.6	16.3	15.8	15.5	–0.3	–0.5
Midwest	**18.7**	**18.5**	**17.9**	**17.5**	**–0.2**	**–0.6**
East North Central	15.7	15.4	14.7	14.2	–0.3	–0.7
West North Central	3.0	3.1	3.2	3.2	0.1	0.1
South	**52.8**	**53.5**	**54.3**	**54.5**	**0.7**	**0.8**
South Atlantic	30.1	30.8	31.6	31.9	0.7	0.8
East South Central	9.6	9.5	9.2	8.8	–0.1	–0.3
West South Central	13.1	13.2	13.5	13.8	0.1	0.3
West	**9.6**	**9.4**	**9.6**	**10.0**	**–0.2**	**0.2**
Mountain	1.5	1.7	1.9	2.0	0.2	0.2
Pacific	8.2	7.7	7.7	8.0	–0.5	0.0

(continued)

(continued from previous page)

Percent share	1995	2000	2010	2020	percentage point change 1995–2000	percentage point change 2000–2020
United States	**12.6%**	**12.9%**	**13.5%**	**14.0%**	**0.3%**	**0.6%**
Northeast	**12.1**	**12.6**	**13.6**	**14.5**	**0.5**	**1.0**
New England	5.5	6.0	6.9	7.8	0.5	0.9
Middle Atlantic	14.5	15.0	16.0	16.9	0.5	1.0
Midwest	**10.0**	**10.3**	**10.9**	**11.5**	**0.3**	**0.3**
East North Central	12.0	12.3	12.9	13.6	0.3	0.6
West North Central	5.5	5.8	6.4	6.9	0.3	0.6
South	**19.0**	**19.4**	**20.2**	**21.0**	**0.4**	**0.8**
South Atlantic	21.3	21.8	22.9	23.8	0.5	1.1
East South Central	19.8	19.9	20.3	20.8	0.1	0.4
West South Central	15.0	15.3	16.0	16.5	0.3	0.7
West	**5.5**	**5.4**	**5.4**	**5.5**	**–0.1**	**0.0**
Mountain	3.1	3.4	3.7	4.0	0.3	0.3
Pacific	6.4	6.3	6.1	6.1	–0.3	–0.2

Note: (–) means not applicable.
Source: Bureau of the Census, Population Projections for States, by Age, Sex, Race, and Hispanic Origin: 1995 to 2025, PPL-47, 1996; calculations by New Strategist

Blacks by State, 1995 to 2020

(number of blacks by state, selected years 1995–2020; percent change 1995–2000 and 2000–2010; numbers in thousands)

	1995	2000	2010	2020	percent change 1995–2000	percent change 2000–2010
United States	**33,134**	**35,456**	**40,110**	**45,075**	**7.0%**	**13.1%**
Alabama	1,087	1,137	1,227	1,318	4.6	7.9
Alaska	26	29	33	37	11.5	13.8
Arizona	146	177	222	263	21.2	25.4
Arkansas	394	409	434	457	3.8	6.1
California	2,414	2,425	2,702	3,176	0.5	11.4
Colorado	164	196	246	287	19.5	25.5
Connecticut	300	324	384	455	8.0	18.5
Delaware	131	147	169	190	12.2	15.0
District of Columbia	352	321	329	366	-8.8	2.5
Florida	2,078	2,326	2,820	3,318	11.9	21.2
Georgia	2,019	2,279	2,724	3,128	12.9	19.5
Hawaii	29	31	35	40	6.9	12.9
Idaho	6	8	12	15	33.3	50.0
Illinois	1,813	1,865	1,971	2,105	2.9	5.7
Indiana	471	502	551	594	6.6	9.8
Iowa	56	62	76	86	10.7	22.6
Kansas	158	173	203	234	9.5	17.3
Kentucky	274	287	310	332	4.7	8.0
Louisiana	1,382	1,448	1,600	1,767	4.8	10.5
Maine	5	5	7	8	0.0	40.0
Maryland	1,347	1,489	1,724	1,958	10.5	15.8
Massachusetts	373	417	508	606	11.8	21.8
Michigan	1,379	1,435	1,539	1,649	4.1	7.2
Minnesota	127	158	210	257	24.4	32.9
Mississippi	968	1,012	1,078	1,134	4.5	6.5
Missouri	589	628	696	766	6.6	10.8
Montana	3	3	6	6	0.0	100.0
Nebraska	64	72	88	103	12.5	22.2
Nevada	109	138	171	192	26.6	23.9
New Hampshire	8	9	10	14	12.5	11.1
New Jersey	1,151	1,239	1,422	1,622	7.6	14.8
New Mexico	41	48	63	79	17.1	31.3
New York	3,192	3,299	3,563	3,885	3.4	8.0
North Carolina	1,598	1,738	1,957	2,151	8.8	12.6
North Dakota	3	5	5	5	66.7	0.0
Ohio	1,250	1,320	1,452	1,590	5.6	10.0

(continued)

(continued from previous page)

	1995	2000	2010	2020	percent change 1995–2000	percent change 2000–2010
Oklahoma	257	282	341	403	9.7%	20.9%
Oregon	56	65	80	93	16.1	23.1
Pennsylvania	1,168	1,224	1,334	1,462	4.8	9.0
Rhode Island	48	54	68	83	12.5	25.9
South Carolina	1,103	1,156	1,255	1,354	4.8	8.6
South Dakota	3	5	6	7	66.7	20.0
Tennessee	853	929	1,057	1,170	8.9	13.8
Texas	2,292	2,543	3,058	3,597	11.0	20.3
Utah	18	22	29	35	22.2	31.8
Vermont	2	2	4	6	0.0	100.0
Virginia	1,298	1,416	1,637	1,862	9.1	15.6
Washington	180	192	224	261	6.7	16.7
West Virginia	57	58	60	64	1.8	3.4
Wisconsin	283	326	400	469	15.2	22.7
Wyoming	3	6	8	8	100.0	33.3

Note: Numbers may not add to total due to rounding.
Source: Bureau of the Census, Population Projections for States, by Age, Sex, Race, and Hispanic Origin: 1995 to 2025, *PPL-47, 1996; calculations by New Strategist*

Distribution of Blacks by State, 1995 to 2020

(percent distribution of blacks by state, selected years 1995–2020)

	1995	*2000*	*2010*	*2020*
United States	**100.0%**	**100.0%**	**100.0%**	**100.0%**
Alabama	3.3	3.2	3.1	2.9
Alaska	0.1	0.1	0.1	0.1
Arizona	0.4	0.5	0.6	0.6
Arkansas	1.2	1.2	1.1	1.0
California	7.3	6.8	6.7	7.0
Colorado	0.5	0.6	0.6	0.6
Connecticut	0.9	0.9	1.0	1.0
Delaware	0.4	0.4	0.4	0.4
District of Columbia	1.1	0.9	0.8	0.8
Florida	6.3	6.6	7.0	7.4
Georgia	6.1	6.4	6.8	6.9
Hawaii	0.1	0.1	0.1	0.1
Idaho	0.0	0.0	0.0	0.0
Illinois	5.5	5.3	4.9	4.7
Indiana	1.4	1.4	1.4	1.3
Iowa	0.2	0.2	0.2	0.2
Kansas	0.5	0.5	0.5	0.5
Kentucky	0.8	0.8	0.8	0.7
Louisiana	4.2	4.1	4.0	3.9
Maine	0.0	0.0	0.0	0.0
Maryland	4.1	4.2	4.3	4.3
Massachusetts	1.1	1.2	1.3	1.3
Michigan	4.2	4.0	3.8	3.7
Minnesota	0.4	0.4	0.5	0.6
Mississippi	2.9	2.9	2.7	2.5
Missouri	1.8	1.8	1.7	1.7
Montana	0.0	0.0	0.0	0.0
Nebraska	0.2	0.2	0.2	0.2
Nevada	0.3	0.4	0.4	0.4
New Hampshire	0.0	0.0	0.0	0.0
New Jersey	3.5	3.5	3.5	3.6
New Mexico	0.1	0.1	0.2	0.2
New York	9.6	9.3	8.9	8.6
North Carolina	4.8	4.9	4.9	4.8
North Dakota	0.0	0.0	0.0	0.0
Ohio	3.8	3.7	3.6	3.5

(continued)

(continued from previous page)

	1995	2000	2010	2020
Oklahoma	0.8%	0.8%	0.9%	0.9%
Oregon	0.2	0.2	0.2	0.2
Pennsylvania	3.5	3.5	3.3	3.2
Rhode Island	0.1	0.2	0.2	0.2
South Carolina	3.3	3.3	3.1	3.0
South Dakota	0.0	0.0	0.0	0.0
Tennessee	2.6	2.6	2.6	2.6
Texas	6.9	7.2	7.6	8.0
Utah	0.1	0.1	0.1	0.1
Vermont	0.0	0.0	0.0	0.0
Virginia	3.9	4.0	4.1	4.1
Washington	0.5	0.5	0.6	0.6
West Virginia	0.2	0.2	0.1	0.1
Wisconsin	0.9	0.9	1.0	1.0
Wyoming	0.0	0.0	0.0	0.0

Source: Calculations by New Strategist based on Census Bureau data in Population Projections for States, by Age, Sex, Race, and Hispanic Origin: 1995 to 2025, *PPL-47, 1996*

Black Share of State Populations, 1995 to 2020

(blacks as a percent of state populations, selected years 1995 to 2025; percentage point change in share, 1995–2020)

	1995	*2000*	*2010*	*2020*	*percentage point change 1995–2020*
United States	**12.6%**	**12.9%**	**13.5%**	**14.0%**	**1.4%**
Alabama	25.6	25.5	25.6	25.8	0.3
Alaska	4.3	4.4	4.4	4.4	0.1
Arizona	3.5	3.7	4.0	4.3	0.8
Arkansas	15.9	15.5	15.3	15.2	-0.6
California	7.6	7.5	7.2	7.0	-0.6
Colorado	4.4	4.7	5.3	5.7	1.3
Connecticut	9.2	9.9	11.3	12.6	3.4
Delaware	18.3	19.1	20.7	22.4	4.2
District of Columbia	63.5	61.4	58.8	58.6	-5.0
Florida	14.7	15.3	16.2	16.9	2.2
Georgia	28.0	28.9	30.9	32.7	4.7
Hawaii	2.4	2.5	2.4	2.4	-0.1
Idaho	0.5	0.6	0.8	0.9	0.4
Illinois	15.3	15.5	15.7	16.0	0.7
Indiana	8.1	8.3	8.7	9.2	1.0
Iowa	2.0	2.1	2.6	2.8	0.9
Kansas	6.2	6.5	7.1	7.7	1.6
Kentucky	7.1	7.2	7.4	7.8	0.7
Louisiana	31.8	32.7	34.2	35.4	3.6
Maine	0.4	0.4	0.5	0.6	0.2
Maryland	26.7	28.2	30.5	32.3	5.5
Massachusetts	6.1	6.7	7.9	9.0	2.9
Michigan	14.4	14.8	15.6	16.5	2.0
Minnesota	2.8	3.3	4.1	4.8	2.0
Mississippi	35.9	35.9	36.2	36.7	0.8
Missouri	11.1	11.3	11.9	12.5	1.4
Montana	0.3	0.3	0.6	0.5	0.2
Nebraska	3.9	4.2	4.9	5.4	1.5
Nevada	7.1	7.4	8.0	8.6	1.4
New Hampshire	0.7	0.7	0.8	1.0	0.3
New Jersey	14.5	15.2	16.5	17.6	3.1
New Mexico	2.4	2.6	2.9	3.2	0.8
New York	17.6	18.2	19.2	20.1	2.5
North Carolina	22.2	22.3	22.9	23.6	1.4
North Dakota	0.5	0.8	0.7	0.7	0.2
Ohio	11.2	11.7	12.6	13.6	2.4

(continued)

(continued from previous page)

	1995	2000	2010	2020	percentage point change 1995–2020
Oklahoma	7.8%	8.4%	9.4%	10.3%	2.4%
Oregon	1.8	1.9	2.1	2.2	0.4
Pennsylvania	9.7	10.0	10.8	11.6	2.0
Rhode Island	4.8	5.4	6.6	7.5	2.7
South Carolina	30.0	30.0	29.8	30.0	-0.1
South Dakota	0.4	0.6	0.7	0.8	0.4
Tennessee	16.2	16.4	17.1	17.9	1.7
Texas	12.2	12.6	13.4	14.0	1.7
Utah	0.9	1.0	1.1	1.3	0.3
Vermont	0.3	0.3	0.6	0.9	0.6
Virginia	19.6	20.2	21.5	22.7	3.1
Washington	3.3	3.3	3.4	3.5	0.2
West Virginia	3.1	3.2	3.2	3.5	0.3
Wisconsin	5.5	6.1	7.2	8.1	2.6
Wyoming	0.6	1.1	1.3	1.2	0.6

Source: Calculations by New Strategist based on Census Bureau data in Population Projections for States, by Age, Sex, Race, and Hispanic Origin: 1995 to 2025, *PPL-47, 1996*

Metropolitan Areas with the Most Blacks, 1990

(metropolitan areas with at least 100,000 blacks ranked by size of black population; number of blacks and black share of total metropolitan population, 1990; numbers in thousands)

		number	percent
1.	New York–Northern New Jersey–Long Island, NY-NJ-CT-PA	3,439	17.8%
2.	Washington–Baltimore, DC-MD-VA-WV	1,696	25.2
3.	Chicago–Gary–Kenosha, IL-IN-WI	1,564	19.0
4.	Los Angeles–Riverside–Orange County, CA	1,230	8.5
5.	Philadelphia–Wilmington Atlantic City, PA-NJ-DE-MD	1,083	18.4
6.	Detroit–Ann Arbor-Flint, MI	1,061	20.5
7.	Atlanta, GA	747	25.2
8.	Houston–Galveston-Brazoria, TX	668	17.9
9.	Miami–Fort Lauderdale, FL	591	18.5
10.	Dallas–Fort Worth, TX	566	14.0
11.	San Francisco–Oakland–San Jose, CA	538	8.6
12.	New Orleans, LA	447	34.8
13.	Cleveland–Akron, OH	445	15.6
14.	St. Louis, MO-IL	424	17.0
15.	Memphis, TN-AR-MS	410	40.7
16.	Norfolk–Virginia Beach–Newport News, VA-NC	409	28.3
17.	Boston–Brockton–Nashua, MA-NH-ME-CT	261	4.8
18.	Richmond–Petersburg, VA	252	29.2
19.	Birmingham, AL	241	28.7
20.	Charlotte–Gastonia–Rock Hill, NC-SC	232	19.9
21.	Milwaukee–Racine, WI	214	13.3
22.	Raleigh–Durham–Chapel Hill, NC	207	24.2
23.	Cincinnati–Hamilton, OH-KY-IN	204	11.2
24.	Greensboro–Winston–Salem–High Point, NC	203	19.3
25.	Kansas City, MO–KS	201	12.7
26.	Tampa–St. Petersburg–Clearwater, FL	186	9.0
27.	Indianapolis, IN	182	13.2
28.	Jacksonville, FL	181	20.0
29.	Pittsburgh, PA	180	7.5
30.	Jackson, MS	168	42.5
31.	Columbus, OH	163	12.1
32.	San Diego, CA	159	6.4
33.	Charleston–North Charleston, SC	153	30.2
34.	Nashville, TN	152	15.5

(continued)

(continued from previous page)

		number	*percent*
35.	Orlando, FL	147	12.0%
36.	Greenville–Spartansburg–Anderson, SC	145	17.4
37.	Baton Rouge, LA	143	30.5
38.	Columbia, SC	138	30.4
39.	Seattle–Tacoma–Bremerton, WA	133	4.5
40.	Mobile, AL	131	27.4
41.	Shreveport–Bossier City, LA	130	34.6
42.	Dayton–Springfield, OH	126	13.3
43.	Augusta–Aiken, GA-SC	125	31.6
44.	Louisville, KY–IN	122	12.9
45.	Buffalo–Niagara Falls, NY	122	10.3
46.	West Palm Beach–Boca Raton, FL	108	12.5
47.	Montgomery, AL	105	36.0
48.	Sacramento–Yolo, CA	102	6.9
49.	Little Rock–North Little Rock, AR	102	19.9
50.	Macon, GA	102	35.0
51.	Oklahoma City, OK	101	10.5

Source: Bureau of the Census, Statistical Abstract of the United States 1993*; calculations by New Strategist*

Blacks: Spending

Black spending is rising as blacks earn higher incomes.

The nation's 10.2 million black consumer units spent an average of $23,442 in 1995, according to the Consumer Expenditure Survey. With a spending index of 73, blacks spend 27 percent less than the average consumer unit.

While black spending is below average in many categories, it is above average on a wide variety of items—despite blacks' lower incomes. Blacks spend more than the average consumer unit on such things as rice; meats, poultry, fish, and eggs; oranges; fresh fruit juice; telephone services; bedroom furniture; infants' furniture; boys' and girls' clothes; women's pants and suits; footwear; new cars; and color TV consoles.

■ With the incomes of blacks rising faster than those of other racial or ethnic groups, black spending should approach or exceed the average on more items in the years ahead. Blacks will become an increasingly important market for many businesses— especially those targeting children and young adults.

Blacks spend 27 percent less than the average consumer unit

(average annual spending of consumer units by race and Hispanic origin of householder, 1995)

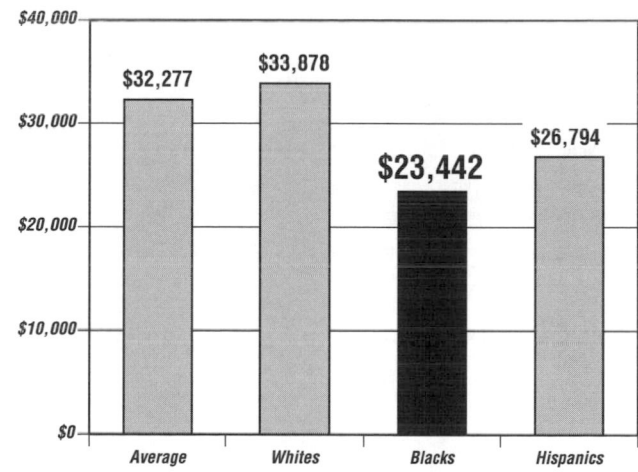

Average and Indexed Spending of Black Households, 1995

(average annual expenditures of total and black consumer units, and indexed expenditures of black consumer units, 1995)

	average spending of total consumer units	black consumer units	
		average spending	indexed spending*
Number of consumer units	103,024,000	10,246,000	–
Average before-tax income of consumer unit	$36,948.00	$25,447.00	69
Average spending of consumer unit, total	32,276.59	23,442.02	73
FOOD	**$4,505.34**	**$3,321.62**	**74**
FOOD AT HOME	2,802.91	2,367.40	84
Cereals and bakery products	**441.13**	**361.21**	**82**
Cereals and cereal products	165.23	157.63	95
Flour	8.42	9.02	107
Prepared flour mixes	12.80	11.78	92
Ready-to-eat and cooked cereal	97.00	85.57	88
Rice	20.17	29.46	146
Pasta, cornmeal, and other cereal products	26.84	21.80	81
Bakery products	275.90	203.58	74
Bread	75.70	65.36	86
White bread	36.77	35.38	96
Bread, other than white	38.92	29.98	77
Cookies and crackers	67.33	48.10	71
Cookies	44.90	36.07	80
Crackers	22.43	12.03	54
Frozen and refrigerated bakery products	21.92	17.94	82
Other bakery products	110.95	72.18	65
Biscuits and rolls	38.49	21.22	55
Cakes and cupcakes	34.63	26.79	77
Bread and cracker products	4.23	3.23	76
Sweetrolls, coffee cakes, doughnuts	20.80	12.16	58
Pies, tarts, turnovers	12.80	8.79	69
Meats, poultry, fish, and eggs	**752.43**	**833.07**	**111**
Beef	227.60	207.47	91
Ground beef	84.47	78.79	93
Roast	40.09	36.56	91
Chuck roast	12.63	12.74	101
Round roast	13.18	13.15	100
Other roast	14.28	10.67	75
Steak	86.84	79.89	92
Round steak	18.82	16.14	86

(continued)

(continued from previous page)

	average spending of total consumer units	black consumer units	
		average spending	indexed spending*
Sirloin steak	$23.42	$19.05	81
Other steak	44.61	44.69	100
Other beef	16.19	12.23	76
Pork	156.00	212.35	136
Bacon	20.32	36.21	178
Pork chops	39.69	51.47	130
Ham	37.06	40.78	110
Ham, not canned	34.76	38.60	111
Canned ham	2.31	2.18	94
Sausage	22.12	34.88	158
Other pork	36.79	49.01	133
Other meats	103.63	101.91	98
Frankfurters	22.13	26.55	120
Lunch meats (cold cuts)	69.66	59.24	85
Bologna, liverwurst, salami	25.45	28.27	111
Other lunchmeats	44.22	30.97	70
Lamb, organ meats and others	11.84	16.12	136
Lamb and organ meats	9.31	13.10	141
Mutton, goat and game	2.54	3.02	119
Poultry	137.65	162.65	118
Fresh and frozen chickens	105.14	124.13	118
Fresh and frozen whole chicken	28.21	33.74	120
Fresh and frozen chicken parts	76.93	90.40	118
Other poultry	32.51	38.52	118
Fish and seafood	97.33	114.88	118
Canned fish and seafood	17.11	11.08	65
Fresh fish and shellfish	52.43	64.61	123
Frozen fish and shellfish	27.79	39.19	141
Eggs	30.23	33.81	112
Dairy products	**296.61**	**200.19**	**67**
Fresh milk and cream	123.00	86.16	70
Fresh milk, all types	113.81	80.12	70
Cream	9.19	6.04	66
Other dairy products	173.60	114.03	66
Butter	12.31	9.19	75
Cheese	88.00	50.75	58
Ice cream and related products	51.24	37.79	74
Miscellaneous dairy products	22.05	16.29	74
Fruits and vegetables	**456.67**	**376.99**	**83**
Fresh fruits	144.14	112.16	78
Apples	29.15	22.47	77
Bananas	30.26	25.46	84

(continued)

(continued from previous page)

	average spending of total consumer units	black consumer units	
		average spending	indexed spending*
Oranges	$16.27	$18.14	111
Citrus fruits, excl. oranges	12.03	7.25	60
Other fresh fruits	56.43	38.84	69
Fresh vegetables	137.31	107.05	78
Potatoes	28.50	24.92	87
Lettuce	18.22	13.03	72
Tomatoes	21.64	16.23	75
Other fresh vegetables	68.95	52.87	77
Processed fruits	95.70	89.43	93
Frozen fruits and fruit juices	17.00	10.77	63
Frozen orange juice	8.66	4.25	49
Frozen fruits	1.81	1.12	62
Frozen fruit juices	6.53	5.40	83
Canned fruits	13.88	10.20	73
Dried fruit	5.86	3.17	54
Fresh fruit juice	17.55	20.84	119
Canned and bottled fruit juice	41.40	44.45	107
Processed vegetables	79.52	68.37	86
Frozen vegetables	28.07	21.59	77
Canned and dried vegetables and juices	51.44	46.78	91
Canned beans	11.26	9.93	88
Canned corn	6.91	7.55	109
Frozen vegetable juices	0.31	0.10	32
Fresh and canned vegetable juices	6.87	6.42	93
Other food at home	**856.08**	**595.93**	**70**
Sugar and other sweets	112.08	89.91	80
Candy and chewing gum	67.43	45.02	67
Sugar	17.44	24.29	139
Artificial sweeteners	4.51	4.49	100
Jams, preserves, other sweets	22.70	16.11	71
Fats and oils	82.22	73.25	89
Margarine	12.74	10.71	84
Fats and oils	24.60	27.58	112
Salad dressings	26.16	23.92	91
Nondairy cream and imitation milk	7.15	3.62	51
Peanut butter	11.58	7.43	64
Miscellaneous foods	376.59	243.15	65
Frozen prepared foods	66.03	41.13	62
Frozen meals	19.87	13.52	68
Other frozen prepared foods	46.16	27.60	60
Canned and packaged soups	31.25	22.83	73
Potato chips, nuts, and other snacks	80.50	53.14	66

(continued)

(continued from previous page)

	average spending of total consumer units	black consumer units	
		average spending	indexed spending*
Potato chips and other snacks	$62.33	$45.05	72
Nuts	18.17	8.09	45
Condiments and seasonings	86.51	61.98	72
Salt, spices, and other seasonings	20.29	22.03	109
Olives, pickles, relishes	10.14	6.05	60
Sauces and gravies	39.88	25.69	64
Baking needs and miscellaneous products	16.20	8.21	51
Other canned/packaged prepared foods	112.30	64.08	57
Prepared salads	13.51	7.82	58
Prepared desserts	8.99	4.27	47
Baby food	25.02	12.55	50
Misc. prepared foods	64.79	39.43	61
Nonalcoholic beverages	240.27	176.98	74
Cola	89.20	66.01	74
Other carbonated drinks	42.50	33.16	78
Coffee	46.33	22.66	49
Roasted coffee	30.90	14.55	47
Instant and freeze-dried coffee	15.43	8.11	53
Noncarbonated fruit-flavored drinks, including nonfrozen lemonade	24.83	26.28	106
Tea	15.64	11.81	76
Nonalcoholic beer	1.01	2.11	209
Other nonalcoholic beverages and ice	20.75	14.95	72
Food prepared by consumer unit on out-of-town trips	44.91	12.64	28
FOOD AWAY FROM HOME	**1,702.43**	**954.21**	**56**
Meals at restaurants, carry-outs, other	**1,331.44**	**781.36**	**59**
Lunch	464.83	294.63	63
Dinner	653.29	362.25	55
Snacks and nonalcoholic beverages	111.73	50.92	46
Breakfast and brunch	101.59	73.55	72
Board (including at school)	**54.60**	**20.33**	**37**
Catered affairs	**43.89**	**32.70**	**75**
Food on out-of-town trips	**196.85**	**66.43**	**34**
School lunches	**49.41**	**40.71**	**82**
Meals as pay	**26.23**	**12.69**	**48**
ALCOHOLIC BEVERAGES	**$277.28**	**$137.77**	**50**
At home	**165.34**	**106.06**	**64**
Beer and ale	87.91	57.42	65
Whiskey	13.37	7.76	58
Wine	48.68	27.31	56
Other alcoholic beverages	15.39	13.57	88

(continued)

(continued from previous page)

	average spending of total consumer units	black consumer units	
		average spending	indexed spending*
Away from home	$111.94	$31.71	28
Beer and ale	33.45	9.75	29
Wine	20.29	5.80	29
Other alcoholic beverages	29.77	7.82	26
Alcoholic beverages purchased on trips	28.43	8.34	29
HOUSING	**$10,464.95**	**$7,930.59**	**76**
SHELTER	**$5,931.76**	**4,318.07**	**73**
Owned dwellings**	**3,754.44**	**1,773.34**	**47**
Mortgage interest and charges	2,106.99	963.85	46
Mortgage interest	1,991.49	928.03	47
Interest paid, home equity loan	53.32	22.74	43
Interest paid, home equity line of credit	61.81	13.09	21
Prepayment penalty charges	0.37	–	–
Property taxes	931.76	419.83	45
Maintenance, repairs, insurance, other expenses	715.68	389.65	54
Homeowner's and related insurance	225.32	133.79	59
Fire and extended coverage	6.69	4.48	67
Homeowner's insurance	218.63	129.31	59
Ground rent	31.63	4.83	15
Maintenance and repair services	365.24	222.67	61
Painting and papering	41.18	20.17	49
Plumbing and water heating	33.28	13.69	41
Heat, air conditioning, electrical work	72.49	36.11	50
Roofing and gutters	65.15	47.88	73
Other repair and maintenance services	130.33	93.33	72
Repair and replacement of hard-surface flooring	21.23	10.31	49
Repair of built-in appliances	1.59	1.18	74
Maintenance and repair materials	71.32	26.65	37
Paints, wallpaper, and supplies	19.60	9.32	48
Tools and equipment for painting, wallpapering	2.11	1.00	47
Plumbing supplies and equipment	7.26	1.09	15
Electrical supplies, heating and cooling equipment	5.22	0.53	10
Hard-surface flooring, repair and replacement	3.51	4.29	122
Roofing and gutters	4.30	2.19	51
Plaster, paneling, siding, windows, doors, screens, awnings	11.53	2.03	18
Patio, walk, fence, driveway, masonry, brick, and stucco work	0.88	0.02	2
Landscape maintenance	1.78	0.43	24
Miscellaneous supplies and equipment	15.13	5.76	38
Insulation, other maintenance and repair	11.41	4.16	36

(continued)

(continued from previous page)

	average spending of total consumer units	black consumer units	
		average spending	indexed spending*
Finish basement, remodel rooms, or			
build patios, walks, etc.	$3.72	$1.60	43
Property management and security	22.17	1.71	8
Property management	16.64	1.66	10
Management and upkeep services for security	5.53	0.05	1
Rented dwellings	**1,785.64**	**2,395.67**	**134**
Rent	1,716.25	2,321.13	135
Rent as pay	48.68	52.71	108
Maintenance, insurance, and other expenses	20.71	21.82	105
Tenant's insurance	7.35	8.44	115
Maintenance and repair services	5.32	6.05	114
Repair or maintenance services	4.93	3.68	75
Repair and replacement of hard-surface flooring	0.32	2.37	741
Repair of built-in appliances	0.07	–	–
Maintenance and repair materials	8.04	7.33	91
Paint, wallpaper, and supplies	1.48	2.16	146
Painting and wallpapering	0.16	0.23	144
Plastering, panels, roofing, gutters, etc.	0.71	0.88	124
Patio, walk, fence, driveway, masonry,			
brick, and stucco work	0.03	–	–
Plumbing supplies and equipment	1.14	0.62	54
Electrical supplies, heating and cooling equipment	0.31	0.29	94
Miscellaneous supplies and equipment	3.53	2.48	70
Insulation, other maintenance and repair	1.43	2.19	153
Materials for additions, finishing			
basements, remodeling rooms	2.07	0.28	14
Construction materials for jobs not started	0.04	–	–
Hard-surface flooring	0.22	0.68	309
Landscape maintenance	0.46	–	–
Other lodging	**391.68**	**149.07**	**38**
Owned vacation homes	127.18	41.67	33
Mortgage interest and charges	48.74	31.24	64
Mortgage interest	47.03	31.24	66
Interest paid, home equity loan	0.12	–	–
Interest paid, home equity line of credit	1.59	–	–
Property taxes	54.14	9.46	17
Maintenance, insurance, and other expenses	24.29	0.97	4
Homeowner's and related insurance	6.10	0.67	11
Homeowner's insurance	5.90	0.67	11
Fire and extended coverage	0.20	–	–

(continued)

(continued from previous page)

	average spending of total consumer units	black consumer units average spending	black consumer units indexed spending*
Ground rent	$2.33	–	–
Maintenance and repair services	10.56	$0.06	1
Maintenance and repair materials	2.00	–	–
Property management and security	2.64	0.24	9
Property management	1.88	0.24	13
Management and upkeep services for security	0.75	–	–
Parking	0.67	–	–
Housing while attending school	54.91	18.24	33
Lodging on out-of-town trips	209.59	89.16	43
UTILITIES, FUELS, PUBLIC SERVICES	**2,192.58**	**2,215.05**	**101**
Natural gas	**268.26**	**324.64**	**121**
Electricity	**869.67**	**850.72**	**98**
Fuel oil and other fuels	**86.66**	**41.92**	**48**
Fuel oil	50.69	23.72	47
Coal	2.13	–	–
Bottled and tank gas	28.02	12.81	46
Wood and other fuels	$5.83	5.39	92
Telephone services	**708.40**	**770.23**	**109**
Telephone services in home city, excluding mobile car phones	682.65	745.99	109
Telephone services for mobile car phones	25.75	24.24	94
Water and other public services	**259.59**	**227.54**	**88**
Water and sewerage maintenance	187.25	176.37	94
Trash and garbage collection	**70.49**	**50.37**	**71**
Septic tank cleaning	**1.84**	**0.80**	**43**
HOUSEHOLD SERVICES	**508.34**	**298.32**	**59**
Personal services	**258.04**	**205.81**	**80**
Babysitting and child care in your own home	39.63	17.71	45
Babysitting and child care in someone else's home	36.48	32.61	89
Care for elderly, invalids, handicapped, etc.	35.33	13.17	37
Adult day care centers	1.05	–	–
Day care centers, nurseries, and preschools	145.55	142.33	98
Other household services	**250.30**	**92.52**	**37**
Housekeeping services	85.16	12.09	14
Gardening, lawn care service	63.96	28.31	44
Water softening service	2.90	0.70	24
Nonclothing laundry and dry cleaning, sent out	1.69	1.28	76
Nonclothing laundry and dry cleaning, coin-operated	4.83	6.98	145
Termite and other pest control services	11.70	3.47	30

(continued)

(continued from previous page)

	average spending of total consumer units	black consumer units	
		average spending	indexed spending*
Other home services	$16.60	$10.55	64
Termite and other pest control products	0.16	0.03	19
Moving, storage, and freight express	27.71	12.18	44
Appliance repair, including service center	14.07	8.24	59
Reupholstering and furniture repair	10.80	1.19	11
Repairs and rental of equipment and power tools	5.79	2.49	43
Appliance rental	1.67	3.01	180
Rental of office equipment for nonbusiness use	0.29	0.80	276
Repair of misc. household equipment and furnishings	1.75	–	–
Repair of computer systems for nonbusiness use	0.82	0.20	24
Computer information services	0.39	0.99	254
HOUSEKEEPING SUPPLIES	**429.59**	**235.77**	**55**
Laundry and cleaning supplies	**110.26**	**97.72**	**89**
Soaps and detergents	63.62	61.87	97
Other laundry cleaning products	46.64	35.85	77
Other household products	**193.90**	**93.75**	**48**
Cleansing and toilet tissue, paper towels, and napkins	60.03	47.06	78
Miscellaneous household products	71.57	28.58	40
Lawn and garden supplies	62.29	18.11	29
Postage and stationery	**125.43**	**44.29**	**35**
Stationery, stationery supplies, giftwrap	61.49	19.54	32
Postage	62.40	24.00	38
Delivery services	1.54	0.75	49
HOUSEHOLD FURNISHINGS & EQUIPMENT	**1,402.69**	**863.39**	**62**
Household textiles	**100.47**	**46.92**	**47**
Bathroom linens	15.50	11.47	74
Bedroom linens	45.50	19.50	43
Kitchen and dining room linens	9.26	4.66	50
Curtains and draperies	17.36	5.93	34
Slipcovers and decorative pillows	1.74	0.26	15
Sewing materials for household items	10.01	4.65	46
Other linens	1.09	0.44	40
Furniture	**327.49**	**339.05**	**104**
Mattresses and springs	41.36	53.06	128
Other bedroom furniture	51.66	69.62	135
Sofas	77.20	77.40	100
Living room chairs	39.35	33.75	86
Living room tables	16.51	18.81	114
Kitchen and dining room furniture	46.95	38.60	82
Infants' furniture	6.74	9.13	135

(continued)

(continued from previous page)

	average spending of total consumer units	black consumer units	
		average spending	indexed spending*
Outdoor furniture	$10.77	$6.24	58
Wall units, cabinets, and other furniture	36.95	32.43	88
Floor coverings	**177.25**	**35.58**	**20**
Major appliances	**154.88**	**170.08**	**110**
Dishwashers (built-in), garbage disposals, range hoods (renter)	0.95	1.89	199
Dishwashers (built-in), garbage disposals, range hoods (owner)	10.23	5.95	58
Refrigerators and freezers (renter)	6.69	13.60	203
Refrigerators and freezers (owner)	42.27	45.76	108
Washing machines (renter)	5.26	11.87	226
Washing machines (owner)	14.58	10.39	71
Clothes dryers (renter)	3.25	4.72	145
Clothes dryers (owner)	10.62	6.60	62
Cooking stoves, ovens (renter)	2.57	6.71	261
Cooking stoves, ovens (owner)	18.72	22.52	120
Microwave ovens (renter)	2.87	6.77	236
Microwave ovens (owner)	6.01	4.43	74
Portable dishwasher (renter)	0.17	–	–
Portable dishwasher (owner)	0.52	0.58	112
Window air conditioners (renter)	2.75	4.25	155
Window air conditioners (owner)	8.64	13.79	160
Electric floor-cleaning equipment	12.94	6.88	53
Sewing machines	4.81	1.83	38
Miscelaneous household appliances	1.03	1.56	151
Small appliances and miscellaneous housewares	**85.16**	**40.51**	**48**
Housewares	62.80	25.73	41
Plastic dinnerware	1.48	0.81	55
China and other dinnerware	11.29	3.66	32
Flatware	4.01	1.48	37
Glassware	6.91	3.23	47
Silver serving pieces	2.03	0.32	16
Other serving pieces	1.28	1.08	84
Nonelectric cookware	16.04	5.85	36
Tableware, nonelectric kitchenware	19.77	9.29	47
Small appliances	22.36	14.78	66
Small electric kitchen appliances	15.65	7.57	48
Portable heating and cooling equipment	6.70	7.21	108
Miscellaneous household equipment	**557.43**	**234.25**	**42**
Window coverings	10.64	4.71	44
Infants' equipment	8.02	0.96	12

(continued)

(continued from previous page)

	average spending of total consumer units	black consumer units	
		average spending	indexed spending*
Laundry and cleaning equipment	$11.33	$6.14	54
Outdoor equipment	4.08	0.69	17
Clocks	3.37	0.72	21
Lamps and lighting fixtures	29.77	0.97	3
Other household decorative items	137.82	75.28	55
Telephones and accessories	14.44	7.51	52
Lawn and garden equipment	42.14	14.57	35
Power tools	15.61	3.90	25
Small miscellaneous furnishings	2.02	10.91	540
Hand tools	10.16	0.73	7
Indoor plants and fresh flowers	46.82	15.28	33
Closet and storage items	6.93	4.30	62
Rental of furniture	3.24	7.93	245
Luggage	9.25	6.41	69
Computers and computer hardware, nonbusiness use	135.02	37.77	28
Computer software and accessories, nonbusiness use	18.23	6.71	37
Telephone answering devices	3.58	2.25	63
Calculators	1.88	1.42	76
Business equipment for home use	4.11	2.66	65
Other hardware	13.63	2.28	17
Smoke alarms (owner)	1.21	0.51	42
Smoke alarms (renter)	0.17	0.11	65
Other household appliances (owner)	4.71	2.77	59
Other household appliances (renter)	1.04	1.34	129
Miscellaneous household equipment and parts	18.22	6.71	37
APPAREL AND SERVICES	**$1,703.63**	**$1,859.71**	**109**
MEN AND BOYS	**425.33**	**373.28**	**88**
Men, aged 16 or older	**329.46**	**225.76**	**69**
Suits	33.42	36.43	109
Sportcoats and tailored jackets	13.23	10.46	79
Coats and jackets	30.16	17.42	58
Underwear	17.80	13.26	74
Hosiery	12.85	6.87	53
Sleepwear	3.50	5.63	161
Accessories	34.98	27.09	77
Sweaters and vests	12.43	9.65	78
Active sportswear	10.14	4.22	42
Shirts	76.52	40.55	53
Pants	63.37	42.18	67
Shorts and shorts sets	16.23	6.96	43

(continued)

(continued from previous page)

	average spending of total consumer units	black consumer units	
		average spending	indexed spending*
Uniforms	$3.67	$4.45	121
Costumes	1.17	0.61	52
Boys, aged 2 to 15	**95.86**	**147.52**	**154**
Coats and jackets	9.27	10.39	112
Sweaters	1.92	2.90	151
Shirts	20.82	20.57	99
Underwear	5.76	3.32	58
Sleepwear	1.12	2.10	188
Hosiery	4.01	3.45	86
Accessories	6.66	6.10	92
Suits, sportcoats, and vests	3.59	–	–
Pants	24.03	51.94	216
Shorts and shorts sets	11.44	36.26	317
Uniforms	4.06	4.31	106
Costumes	0.93	1.01	109
WOMEN AND GIRLS	**660.49**	**706.35**	**107**
Women, aged 16 or older	**559.19**	**589.32**	**105**
Coats and jackets	41.43	53.69	130
Dresses	83.48	85.30	102
Sportcoats and tailored jackets	4.29	–	–
Sweaters and vests	28.51	14.85	52
Shirts, blouses, and tops	100.86	74.09	73
Skirts	20.49	17.45	85
Pants	70.73	120.57	170
Shorts and shorts sets	26.72	25.04	94
Active sportswear	27.19	12.74	47
Sleepwear	23.65	15.21	64
Undergarments	30.37	52.14	172
Hosiery	20.88	29.11	139
Suits	32.66	37.04	113
Accessories	43.56	47.76	110
Uniforms	2.42	2.65	110
Costumes	1.93	1.69	88
Girls, aged 2 to 15	**101.30**	**117.03**	**116**
Coats and jackets	6.86	9.38	137
Dresses and suits	13.17	21.76	165
Shirts, blouses, and sweaters	20.67	15.41	75
Skirts and pants	18.18	30.33	167
Shorts and shorts sets	9.89	10.84	110
Active sportswear	11.39	2.54	22
Underwear and sleepwear	7.47	10.92	146

(continued)

(continued from previous page)

	average spending of total consumer units	black consumer units	
		average spending	indexed spending*
Hosiery	$4.78	$7.72	162
Accessories	4.51	4.37	97
Uniforms	1.92	2.44	127
Costumes	2.47	1.34	54
Children under age 2	**80.61**	**86.93**	**108**
Coats, jackets, and snowsuits	3.10	4.71	152
Outerwear including dresses	22.66	26.40	117
Underwear	46.09	45.93	100
Sleepwear and loungewear	3.76	4.49	119
Accessories	4.99	5.41	108
FOOTWEAR	**278.36**	**443.12**	**159**
Men's	94.82	99.48	105
Boys'	30.48	47.71	157
Women's	117.81	198.05	168
Girls'	35.24	97.87	278
OTHER APPAREL PRODUCTS, SERVICES	**258.84**	**250.03**	**97**
Material for making clothes	4.95	3.14	63
Sewing patterns and notions	1.92	0.69	36
Watches	19.16	26.40	138
Jewelry	104.17	56.50	54
Shoe repair and other shoe services	2.66	1.79	67
Coin-operated apparel laundry and dry cleaning	39.46	62.52	158
Apparel alteration, repair, and tailoring services	5.82	4.74	81
Clothing rental	3.48	3.56	102
Watch and jewelry repair	5.07	2.14	42
Professional laundry, dry cleaning	71.68	88.19	123
Clothing storage	0.47	0.36	77
TRANSPORTATION	**$6,015.97**	**$4,504.93**	**75**
VEHICLE PURCHASES	**2,639.33**	**2,128.53**	**81**
Cars and trucks, new	**1,194.00**	**999.47**	**84**
New cars	670.88	763.22	114
New trucks	523.11	236.25	45
Cars and trucks, used	**1,410.96**	**1,083.65**	**77**
Used cars	916.45	900.17	98
Used trucks	494.51	183.49	37
Other vehicles	**34.38**	**45.40**	**132**
GASOLINE AND MOTOR OIL	**1,006.05**	**706.32**	**70**
Gasoline	901.97	665.59	74
Diesel fuel	10.15	3.00	30

(continued)

(continued from previous page)

	average spending of total consumer units	black consumer units	
		average spending	indexed spending*
Gasoline on out-of-town trips	$81.98	$30.84	38
Motor oil	11.13	6.58	59
Motor oil on out-of-town trips	0.83	0.31	37
OTHER VEHICLE EXPENSES	**2,015.78**	**1,435.49**	**71**
Vehicle finance charges	**260.57**	**252.87**	**97**
Automobile finance charges	148.57	191.54	129
Truck finance charges	99.53	55.94	56
Motorcycle and plane finance charges	1.26	0.40	32
Other vehicle finance charges	11.22	5.00	45
Maintenance and repairs	**652.77**	**500.89**	**77**
Coolant, additives, brake, and transmission fluids	5.63	3.52	63
Tires	87.06	58.88	68
Parts, equipment, and accessories	60.29	23.72	39
Vehicle audio equipment	10.31	–	–
Vehicle products	3.37	2.16	64
Miscellaneous auto repair, servicing	33.68	14.54	43
Body work and painting	29.52	31.92	108
Clutch, transmission repair	45.69	37.50	82
Drive shaft and rear-end repair	6.14	11.81	192
Brake work	39.22	32.81	84
Repair to steering or front-end	20.68	17.12	83
Repair to engine cooling system	23.28	21.28	91
Motor tune-up	42.61	28.81	68
Lube, oil change, and oil filters	42.90	26.92	63
Front-end alignment, wheel balance, rotation	11.11	8.78	79
Shock absorber replacement	7.35	7.22	98
Brake adjustment	3.18	2.86	90
Gas tank repair, replacement	1.54	0.38	25
Tire repair and other repair work	33.28	36.05	108
Vehicle air conditioning repair	14.28	13.62	95
Exhaust system repair	20.87	13.67	66
Electrical system repair	29.58	23.65	80
Motor repair, replacement	67.64	74.55	110
Auto repair service policy	5.94	5.53	93
Vehicle insurance	**712.81**	**495.60**	**70**
Vehicle rental, leases, licenses, other charges	**389.63**	**186.13**	**48**
Leased and rented vehicles	235.64	96.60	41
Rented vehicles	37.70	17.37	46
Auto rental	7.09	4.64	65
Auto rental, out-of-town trips	25.95	9.16	35

(continued)

(continued from previous page)

	average spending of total consumer units	black consumer units	
		average spending	indexed spending*
Truck rental	$1.19	$0.33	28
Truck rental, out-of-town trips	3.26	3.25	100
Leased vehicles	197.94	79.22	40
Car lease payments	128.53	58.69	46
Cash down payment (car lease)	13.44	3.24	24
Termination fee (car lease)	0.41	–	–
Truck lease payments	52.98	17.30	33
Cash down payment (truck lease)	2.33	–	–
Termination fee (truck lease)	0.26	–	–
State and local registration	84.53	44.39	53
Driver's license	6.92	4.26	62
Vehicle inspection	8.76	5.27	60
Parking fees	25.38	22.99	91
Parking fees in home city, excluding residence	21.97	21.49	98
Parking fees, out-of-town trips	3.41	1.51	44
Tolls	11.19	3.34	30
Tolls on out-of-town trips	4.53	1.74	38
Towing charges	4.86	4.56	94
Automobile service club fees	7.83	2.99	38
PUBLIC TRANSPORTATION	**354.81**	**234.59**	**66**
Airline fares	225.58	83.98	37
Intercity bus fares	14.09	8.60	61
Intracity mass transit fares	48.51	104.49	215
Local transportation on out-of-town trips	8.46	3.65	43
Taxi fares on trips	4.97	2.14	43
Taxi fares	6.95	14.38	207
Intercity train fares	18.41	6.73	37
Ship fares	27.31	9.82	36
School bus	0.53	0.79	149
HEALTH CARE	**$1,732.33**	**$1,056.61**	**61**
Health insurance	**860.45**	**571.53**	**66**
Commercial health insurance	241.22	181.91	75
Blue Cross, Blue Shield	171.78	104.60	61
Health maintenance plans (HMOs)	146.87	122.08	83
Medicare payments	172.13	127.61	74
Commercial Medicare supplements and other health insurance	128.44	35.33	28
Medical services	**511.47**	**223.32**	**44**
Physician's services	146.97	73.68	50
Dental services	186.29	48.73	26

(continued)

(continued from previous page)

	average spending of total consumer units	black consumer units	
		average spending	indexed spending*
Eye care services	$28.83	$16.92	59
Service by professionals other than physician	38.24	4.05	11
Lab tests, X-rays	21.92	13.28	61
Hospital room	33.04	24.15	73
Hospital services other than room	37.16	25.13	68
Care in convalescent or nursing home	7.90	5.96	75
Repair of medical equipment	1.11	–	–
Other medical services	10.01	11.42	114
Drugs	**279.96**	**216.76**	**77**
Nonprescription drugs	79.03	58.65	74
Prescription drugs	200.94	158.11	79
Medical supplies	**80.45**	**45.00**	**56**
Eyeglasses and contact lenses	52.06	28.94	56
Topicals and dressings	20.73	11.17	54
Medical equipment for general use	2.53	1.80	71
Supportive and convalescent medical equipment	3.83	2.23	58
Rental of medical equipment	0.34	0.05	15
Rental of supportive, convalescent medical equipment	0.96	0.81	84
ENTERTAINMENT	**$1,612.09**	**$935.38**	**58**
FEES AND ADMISSIONS	**432.91**	**146.75**	**34**
Recreation expenses, out-of-town trips	21.21	10.79	51
Social, recreation, civic club membership fees	80.67	20.96	26
Fees for participant sports	66.55	16.01	24
Participant sports, out-of-town trips	29.25	4.16	14
Movie, theater, opera, ballet admissions	73.42	38.63	53
Movie, other admissions, out-of-town trips	40.50	13.86	34
Admissions to sporting events	28.71	13.01	45
Admissions to sports events, out-of-town trips	13.50	4.62	34
Fees for recreational lessons	57.91	13.92	24
Other entertainment services, out-of-town trips	21.21	10.79	51
TELEVISION, RADIO, AND SOUND EQUIPMENT	**541.77**	**515.72**	**95**
Televisions	**370.32**	**372.17**	**100**
Community antenna or cable TV	219.69	232.45	106
Black-and-white TV sets	1.89	–	–
Color TV, console	29.53	43.48	147
Color TV, portable, table model	44.90	44.54	99
VCRs and video disc players	27.33	18.59	68
Video cassettes, tapes, and discs	24.05	15.72	65
Video game hardware and software	14.68	11.91	81

(continued)

(continued from previous page)

	average spending of total consumer units	black consumer units	
		average spending	indexed spending*
Repair of TV, radio, and sound equipment	$7.19	$3.03	42
Rental of televisions	1.06	2.44	230
Radios and sound equipment	**171.45**	**143.55**	**84**
Radios	10.61	3.82	36
Tape recorders and players	11.26	43.37	385
Sound components and component systems	32.12	21.40	67
Miscellaneous sound equipment	0.48	–	–
Sound equipment accessories	4.46	1.02	23
Compact disc, tape, record, video mail order clubs	11.99	5.56	46
Records, CDs, audio tapes, needles	38.49	26.36	68
Rental of VCR, radio, sound equipment	0.27	0.49	181
Musical instruments and accessories	17.75	11.87	67
Rental and repair of musical instruments	1.65	0.17	10
Rental of video cassettes, tapes, discs, films	42.38	29.49	70
PETS, TOYS, PLAYGROUND EQUIPMENT	**322.19**	**119.28**	**37**
Pets	**199.89**	**37.33**	**19**
Pet food	79.56	19.92	25
Pet purchase, supplies, and medicines	47.03	6.28	13
Pet services	18.78	1.76	9
Veterinary services	54.52	9.38	17
Toys, games, hobbies, and tricycles	**120.29**	**81.41**	**68**
Playground equipment	**2.00**	**0.53**	**27**
OTHER ENTERTAINMENT EQUIPMENT, SUPPLIES, AND SERVICES	315.22	153.63	49
Unmotored recreational vehicles	**28.10**	–	–
Boat without motor and boat trailers	3.69	–	–
Trailer and other attachable campers	24.41	–	–
Motorized recreational vehicles	**77.41**	**93.23**	**120**
Motorized camper	21.18	50.91	240
Other vehicle	11.89	–	–
Motor boats	44.34	43.32	98
Rental of recreational vehicles	**3.42**	**0.44**	**13**
Outboard motors	**0.36**	–	–
Docking and landing fees	**4.49**	**3.35**	**75**
Sports, recreation, exercise equipment	**110.81**	**25.20**	**23**
Athletic gear, game tables, exercise equipment	50.33	14.66	29
Bicycles	12.59	7.69	61
Camping equipment	6.51	0.89	14
Hunting and fishing equipment	17.00	0.27	2

(continued)

(continued from previous page)

	average spending of total consumer units	black consumer units	
		average spending	indexed spending*
Winter sports equipment	$3.78	$0.06	2
Water sports equipment	9.47	0.18	2
Other sports equipment	9.50	1.40	15
Rental and repair of miscellaneous sports equipment	1.64	0.05	3
Photographic equipment and supplies	**81.18**	**26.19**	**32**
Film	20.27	9.32	46
Other photographic supplies	1.12	–	–
Film processing	28.56	10.08	35
Repair and rental of photographic equipment	0.29	0.27	93
Photographic equipment	12.56	5.39	43
Photographer fees	18.39	1.15	6
Fireworks	**2.03**	**1.47**	**72**
Souvenirs	**0.14**	**0.35**	**250**
Visual goods	**1.51**	**–**	**–**
Pinball, electronic video games	**5.78**	**3.39**	**59**

PERSONAL CARE PRODUCTS AND SERVICES

PERSONAL CARE PRODUCTS AND SERVICES	**$403.47**	**$372.27**	**92**
Personal care products	**213.44**	**190.20**	**89**
Hair care products	38.65	34.04	88
Nonelectric articles for the hair	4.43	6.06	137
Wigs and hairpieces	0.95	2.14	225
Oral hygiene products	22.19	18.59	84
Shaving products	11.91	3.16	27
Cosmetics, perfume, and bath products	105.36	98.27	93
Deodorants, feminine hygiene, misc. products	26.10	25.60	98
Electric personal care appliances	3.85	2.35	61
Personal care services	**190.03**	**182.07**	**96**
Personal care services for females	97.61	79.99	82
Personal care services for males	92.19	102.07	111
Repair of personal care appliances	0.24	–	–

READING

READING	**$162.57**	**$72.89**	**45**
Newspaper subscriptions	51.79	23.45	45
Newspaper, nonsubscriptions	17.40	16.06	92
Magazine subscriptions	24.74	9.19	37
Magazines, nonsubscriptions	11.00	5.02	46
Newsletters	0.28	–	–
Books purchased through book clubs	9.33	1.63	17
Books not purchased through book clubs	46.51	17.53	38
Encyclopedia and other reference book sets	1.52	0.02	1

(continued)

(continued from previous page)

	average spending of total consumer units	black consumer units	
		average spending	indexed spending*
EDUCATION	**$471.47**	**$214.56**	**46**
College tuition	265.22	91.85	35
Elementary and high school tuition	81.97	54.31	66
Other schools tuition	14.06	7.30	52
Other school expenses including rentals	17.30	9.93	57
Books, supplies for college	36.06	24.83	69
Books, supplies for elementary, high school	8.56	5.34	62
Books, supplies for day care, nursery school	2.09	2.75	132
Miscellaneous school expenses and supplies	46.21	18.25	39
TOBACCO PRODUCTS AND SMOKING SUPPLIES	**$268.82**	**$177.15**	**66**
Cigarettes	243.09	162.37	67
Other tobacco products	24.30	14.29	59
Smoking accessories	1.43	0.48	34
MISCELLANEOUS EXPENSES	**$766.23**	**$450.15**	**59**
Miscellaneous fees, gambling losses	54.70	25.93	47
Legal fees	98.35	21.32	22
Funeral expenses	86.83	89.22	103
Safe deposit box rental	5.51	1.50	27
Checking accounts, other bank service charges	25.62	22.10	86
Cemetery lots, vaults, and maintenance fees	15.50	8.46	55
Accounting fees	40.94	18.15	44
Miscellaneous personal services	21.64	9.95	46
Finance charges, except mortgage and vehicles	229.82	176.74	77
Occupational expenses, union and professional fees	97.90	46.29	47
Expenses for other properties	85.37	28.41	33
Interest paid, home equity line of credit (other property)	0.12	–	–
Credit card membership fees	3.92	2.08	53
CASH CONTRIBUTIONS	**$925.39**	**$593.13**	**64**
Cash contributions to non-consumer unit members, including students, alimony, child support	233.28	177.37	76
Gifts of cash, stocks, bonds to non-c.u. member	174.20	41.73	24
Contributions to charities	85.58	23.21	27
Contributions to church	385.94	344.99	89
Contributions to educational organizations	35.65	1.74	5
Political contributions	3.39	0.66	19
Other contributions	7.35	3.41	46

(continued)

(continued from previous page)

	average spending of total consumer units	black consumer units	
		average spending	indexed spending*
PERSONAL INSURANCE AND PENSIONS	**$2,967.05**	**$1815.26**	**61**
Life and other personal insurance except health	**374.03**	**345.86**	**92**
Life, endowment, annuity, other personal insurance	361.44	343.94	95
Other nonhealth insurance	12.59	1.92	15
Pensions and Social Security	**2,593.02**	**1469.40**	**57**
Deductions for government retirement	66.21	48.28	73
Deductions for railroad retirement	5.28	–	–
Deductions for private pensions	325.82	104.37	32
Non-payroll deposit to retirement plans	312.41	83.08	27
Deductions for Social Security	1,883.30	1233.67	66
GIFTS*	**$986.63**	**$596.33**	**60**
FOOD	**87.72**	**41.53**	**47**
Cakes and cupcakes	1.97	1.00	51
Candy and chewing gum	12.79	5.07	40
Potato chips and other snacks	1.30	1.24	95
Board (including at school)	32.09	10.04	31
Catered affairs	16.33	17.04	104
HOUSING	**249.80**	**114.53**	**46**
Housekeeping supplies	**37.72**	**12.85**	**34**
Other household products	9.11	3.12	34
Miscellaneous household products	4.39	1.58	36
Lawn and garden supplies	3.51	0.09	3
Stationery, stationery supplies, giftwraps	22.53	7.43	33
Postage	4.17	1.51	36
Household textiles	**10.20**	**5.96**	**58**
Bathroom linens	2.75	2.66	97
Bedroom linens	4.44	3.29	74
Appliances and miscellaneous housewares	**27.44**	**11.25**	**41**
Major appliances	4.79	4.44	93
Small appliances and miscellaneous housewares	22.65	6.80	30
China and other dinnerware	2.91	0.50	17
Glassware	3.60	1.57	44
Nonelectric cookware	3.98	–	–
Tableware, nonelectric kitchenware	4.98	2.64	53
Small electric kitchen appliances	3.64	1.77	49
Miscellaneous household equipment	**65.94**	**16.09**	**24**
Lamps and lighting fixtures	3.33	3.60	108
Other household decorative items	21.54	2.61	12

(continued)

(continued from previous page)

	average spending of total consumer units	black consumer units	
		average spending	indexed spending*
Lawn and garden equipment	$0.96	$0.11	11
Indoor plants, fresh flowers	20.72	2.21	11
Computers and hardware, nonbusiness use	4.01	–	–
Other housing	**108.51**	**68.38**	**63**
Repair or maintenance services	1.03	0.73	71
Housing while attending school	34.67	12.60	36
Lodging on out-of-town trips	2.10	1.69	80
Electricity (renter)	10.47	17.24	165
Telephone services in home city, excluding mobile car phone	12.23	11.28	92
Day-care centers, nurseries, and preschools	15.05	7.19	48
Housekeeping services	3.90	0.20	5
Gardening, lawn care service	2.74	1.28	47
Moving, storage, freight express	1.50	0.33	22
Sofas	0.93	–	–
Kitchen, dining room furniture	0.50	–	–
Infants' furniture	1.64	2.60	159
APPAREL AND SERVICES	**258.22**	**242.60**	**94**
Males, aged 2 or older	**69.77**	**55.60**	**80**
Men's coats and jackets	4.70	–	–
Men's accessories	6.98	11.38	163
Men's sweaters and vests	3.46	1.37	40
Men's active sportswear	1.42	0.37	26
Men's shirts	17.03	12.82	75
Men's pants	9.29	10.30	111
Boys' shirts	4.31	0.97	23
Boys' accessories	1.19	0.31	26
Boys' pants	2.31	0.84	36
Boys' shorts and short sets	0.92	1.35	147
Females, aged 2 or older	**93.61**	**83.89**	**90**
Women's coats and jackets	5.41	10.88	201
Women's dresses	5.36	9.96	186
Women's vests and sweaters	8.05	1.61	20
Women's shirts, tops, blouses	14.11	20.23	143
Women's pants	9.09	11.21	123
Women's active sportswear	6.11	–	–
Women's sleepwear	7.35	3.50	48
Women's undergarments	2.44	3.05	125
Women's suits	1.62	3.54	219
Women's accessories	9.16	8.22	90

(continued)

(continued from previous page)

	average spending of total consumer units	black consumer units	
		average spending	indexed spending*
Girls' dresses and suits	$2.61	$3.78	145
Girls' shirts, blouses, sweaters	4.16	1.14	27
Girls' skirts and pants	1.83	0.86	47
Children under age 2	**39.47**	**35.29**	**89**
Infant dresses, outerwear	13.60	11.57	85
Infant underwear	19.47	18.94	97
Infant nightwear, loungewear	2.25	1.71	76
Infant accessories	2.55	1.75	69
Other apparel products and services	**55.37**	**67.82**	**122**
Jewelry and watches	26.56	5.56	21
Watches	2.66	1.51	57
Jewelry	23.90	4.05	17
All other apparel products and services	28.81	62.26	216
Men's footwear	7.15	6.20	87
Boys' footwear	1.95	4.47	229
Women's footwear	10.36	19.50	188
Girls' footwear	7.76	31.91	411
TRANSPORTATION	**47.84**	**19.75**	**41**
New cars	1.90	–	–
Used cars	3.19	–	–
Gasoline on out-of-town trips	13.01	4.00	31
Airline fares	10.75	6.91	64
Ship fares	3.10	1.69	55
HEALTH CARE	**22.21**	**11.47**	**52**
Physicians services	2.69	0.65	24
Dental services	4.70	0.28	6
Hospital room	0.31	0.12	39
Hospital service other than room	0.88	0.08	9
Care in convalescent or nursing home	4.50	5.96	132
Prescription drugs	1.38	0.91	66
ENTERTAINMENT	**86.44**	**31.63**	**37**
Toys, games, hobbies, tricycles	**29.34**	**14.54**	**50**
Other entertainment	**57.10**	**17.10**	**30**
Movie, other admissions, out-of-town trips	7.07	2.16	31
Admission to sports events, out-of-town trips	2.36	0.72	31
Fees for recreational lessons	2.93	0.53	18
Community antenna or cable TV	2.54	2.02	80
Color TV, portable, table model	3.47	1.02	29
VCRs, video disc players	2.04	1.66	81
Video game hardware and software	2.9	1.17	40

(continued)

(continued from previous page)

	average spending of total consumer units	black consumer units	
		average spending	indexed spending*
Radios	$2.67	$0.33	12
Sound components and component systems	2.62	3.41	130
Veterinary services	3.05	0.76	25
Athletic gear, game tables, and exercise equipment	2.40	0.19	8
EDUCATION	**120.19**	**58.97**	**49**
College tuition	96.63	47.17	49
Elementary, high school tuition	8.17	0.45	6
Other school tuition	1.07	1.21	113
Other school expenses including rentals	1.86	3.50	188
School books, supplies, equipment for college	6.55	5.90	90
School supplies, etc., unspecified	5.29	0.15	3
ALL OTHER GIFTS	**114.22**	**75.86**	**66**

* The index compares the spending of the average black consumer unit with the spending of the average consumer unit by dividing black spending by average spending in each category and multiplying by 100. An index of 100 means black spending in the category equals average spending. An index of 132 means black spending is 32 percent above average, while an index of 75 means black spending is 25 percent below average.
** This figure does not include the amount paid for mortgage principal, which is considered an asset.
*** Expenditures on gifts are also included in the preceding product and service categories. Food spending, for example, includes the amount spent on gifts of food.
Note: In this table blacks are defined as non-Hispanic African American consumer units. The Bureau of Labor Statistics uses consumer units rather than households as the sampling unit in the Consumer Expenditure Survey. For the definition of a consumer unit, see the Glossary. Expenditures for gifts may not add to the total for gifts category because the listing is incomplete. (–) means not applicable or the sample is too small to make a reliable estimate.
Source: Bureau of Labor Statistics, unpublished tables from the 1995 Consumer Expenditure Survey; calculations by New Strategist

Blacks: Wealth

Although blacks have been gaining in income, they have little wealth.

The median net worth (assets minus debts) of nonwhite and Hispanic households amounted to just $16,500 in 1995, far below the $56,400 net worth of the average American household. Nonwhite and Hispanic net worth declined 2.4 percent between 1992 and 1995, after adjusting for inflation. (Note: The Federal Reserve collects wealth data for only two racial and ethnic categories: non-Hispanic whites, and nonwhites and Hispanics. The nonwhite and Hispanic category includes Asians, blacks, Hispanics, and Native Americans.)

The net worth of nonwhite and Hispanic households is below average in large part because blacks and Hispanics are less likely to own a home than the average householder. Home equity accounts for the largest share of Americans' net worth. Only 48 percent of nonwhite and Hispanic householders own a home, according to the Federal Reserve Board's 1995 Survey of Consumer Finances. Nonwhite and Hispanic householders have only $5,200 in financial assets, with transaction accounts (such as checking accounts) owned by the largest share (69 percent). Most nonwhite and Hispanic householders are in debt, owing a median of $12,200 in 1995.

■ The net worth of nonwhites/Hispanics will not increase much without a substantial rise in minority homeownership. Because so many black households are female-headed families with low incomes, black homeownership is likely to remain well below average.

Net worth of nonwhite and Hispanic households is well below average

(median net worth of nonwhite and Hispanic and total households, 1995)

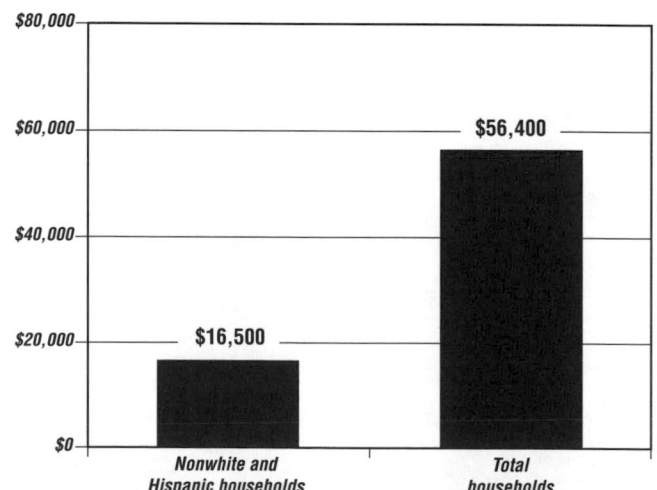

Net Worth, Assets, and Debts of
Nonwhite and Hispanic Households, 1992 and 1995

(median net worth of nonwhite and Hispanic households, and median value of assets and debts, 1992 and 1995; percent change 1992—95; in 1995 dollars)

	1995	1992	percent change 1992–1995
Median net worth	$16,500	$16,900	–2.4%
Median value of nonfinancial assets	42,100	40,400	4.2
Median value of financial assets	5,200	3,400	52.9
Median value of debts	12,200	9,700	25.8

Source: Federal Reserve Board, Family Finances in the U.S.: Recent Evidence from the Survey of Consumer Finances, *Federal Reserve Bulletin, January 1997; calculations by New Strategist*

Nonfinancial Assets of Nonwhite and Hispanic Households, 1992 and 1995

(percent of nonwhite and Hispanic households owning nonfinancial assets, and median value of assets for owners, 1992 and 1995; percentage point change in households with asset and percent change in value of asset, 1992–95; in 1995 dollars)

	1995	1992	percentage point change, 1992–95
Percent owning asset			
Any nonfinancial asset	78.1%	79.7%	–1.6
Vehicles	71.1	72.7	–1.6
Primary residence	48.2	48.8	–0.6
Investment real estate	10.2	11.2	–1.0
Business	5.4	7.1	–1.7
Other nonfinancial	3.5	4.2	–0.7

	1995	1992	percent change 1992–95
Median value of asset for owners			
Any nonfinancial asset	$42,100	$40,400	4.2%
Vehicles	7,700	5,300	45.3
Primary residence	70,000	54,200	29.2
Investment real estate	33,500	48,800	–31.4
Business	26,300	48,800	–46.1
Other nonfinancial	8,000	9,200	–13.0

Source: Federal Reserve Board, Family Finances in the U.S.: Recent Evidence from the Survey of Consumer Finances, *Federal Reserve Bulletin, January 1997; calculations by New Strategist*

Financial Assets of Nonwhite and Hispanic Households, 1992 and 1995

(percent of nonwhite and Hispanic households owning financial assets, and median value of assets for owners, 1992 and 1995; percentage point change in households with asset and percent change in value of asset, 1992–95; in 1995 dollars)

	1995	1992	percentage point change, 1992–95
Percent owning asset			
Any financial asset	77.4%	74.8%	2.6
Transaction accounts	69.1	69.1	0.0
Certificates of deposit	5.9	7.8	−1.9
Savings bonds	11.3	11.7	−0.4
Bonds	0.6	1.3	−0.7
Stocks	5.5	6.3	−0.8
Mutual funds	3.5	3.4	0.1
Retirement accounts	29.2	21.6	7.6
Life insurance	24.4	24.3	0.1
Other managed assets	1.0	1.2	−0.2
Other financial assets	8.5	7.8	0.7

	1995	1992	percent change 1992–95
Median value of asset for owners			
Any financial asset	$5,200	$3,400	52.9%
Transaction accounts	1,500	1,100	36.4
Certificates of deposit	10,000	8,700	14.9
Savings bonds	500	600	−16.7
Bonds	27,000	32,000	−15.6
Stocks	5,000	6,500	−23.1
Mutual funds	7,800	18,400	−57.6
Retirement accounts	9,600	10,900	−11.9
Life insurance	5,000	3,500	42.9
Other managed assets	1,800	9,800	−81.6
Other financial assets	1,500	1,400	7.1

Source: Federal Reserve Board, Family Finances in the U.S.: Recent Evidence from the Survey of Consumer Finances, *Federal Reserve Bulletin, January 1997; calculations by New Strategist*

Nonwhite and Hispanic Households with Debt, 1992 and 1995

(percent of nonwhite and Hispanic households with debt, and median value of debt for those with debts, 1992 and 1995; percentage point change in households with debt and percent change in amount of debt, 1992–95; in 1995 dollars)

	1995	1992	*percentage point change, 1992–95*
Percent with debt			
Any debt	73.1%	71.4%	1.7
Mortgage and home equity	32.7	30.6	2.1
Installment	46.9	45.5	1.4
Other lines of credit	1.3	1.6	–0.3
Credit card	48.8	42.9	5.9
Investment real estate	4.4	4.3	0.1
Other debt	8.5	9.8	–1.3

	1995	1992	*percent change 1992–95*
Median value of debt for debtors			
Any debt	$12,200	$9,700	25.8%
Mortgage and home equity	36,500	33,800	8.0
Installment	5,000	3,500	42.9
Other lines of credit	800	2,400	–66.7
Credit card	1,200	900	33.3
Investment real estate	25,000	19,500	28.2
Other debt	1,500	2,200	–31.8

Source: Federal Reserve Board, Family Finances in the U.S.: Recent Evidence from the Survey of Consumer Finances, *Federal Reserve Bulletin, January 1997; calculations by New Strategist*

Hispanics

■ The Hispanic population is projected to grow from 30 million in 1998 to more than 52 million by 2020. Hispanics will become the largest minority in 2009, when they will outnumber blacks.

■ Hispanics lag far behind the total population in educational attainment because many are immigrants who came to the United States as adults with little schooling.

■ Hispanics are more likely to be without health insurance than any other racial or ethnic group. In 1996, 34 percent did not have health insurance.

■ Over half of Hispanic households are headed by married couples. Sixty-four percent of Hispanic couples have children under age 18 at home.

■ Seventeen percent of Hispanic households do not have a telephone. Among Puerto Ricans, 22 percent do not have a telephone.

■ The median income of Hispanic households fell 7 percent between 1990 and 1996, the sharpest decline among all racial and ethnic groups.

■ Hispanic women are less likely to be in the labor force than black, white, and Asian women. Consequently, only 48 percent of Hispanic couples are dual earners.

■ The net worth of Hispanic and nonwhite households stood a median of $16,500 in 1995, well below the $56,400 median for all households.

■ Note: Hispanics may be of any race. There are Asian, black, Native American, and white Hispanics. See the table on page 3 for the racial composition of Hispanics.

Hispanics are 11 percent of the U.S. population

(percent distribution of total persons by race and ethnicity, 1998)

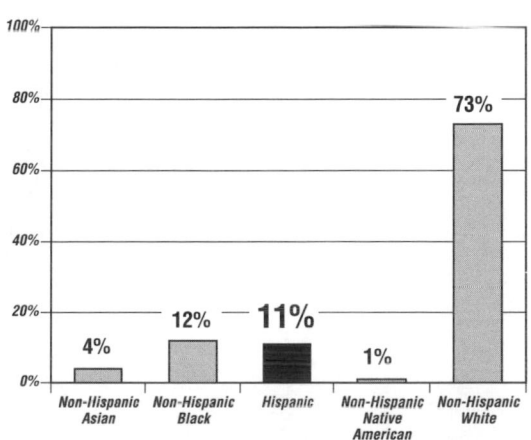

Hispanics: Education

Hispanics' educational attainment lags behind that of whites, blacks, and Asians.

Hispanics are much less educated than the average American because many are immigrants who came to the United States as adults with few years of schooling. Overall, only 53 percent of Hispanics had a high school diploma in 1996, versus 82 percent of the total population. The proportion of Hispanics with a high school diploma ranges from 47 percent of Mexican Americans to 66 percent of "other" Hispanics.

Only 9 percent of Hispanics have a college degree, versus 24 percent of the total population. More than 1 million Hispanics were enrolled in college in 1995, 36 percent of them full-time students at four-year schools.

Hispanics earned over 54,000 bachelor's degrees in 1994–95, or about 5 percent of all bachelor's degrees awarded that year. Hispanics earned 14 percent of the bachelor's degrees awarded in foreign languages and literature. At the first-professional degree level, Hispanics were awarded 6 percent of the degrees in dentistry and podiatry.

■ With so many Hispanic immigrants coming to the U.S. from countries where adults have little schooling, such as Mexico, the educational attainment of Hispanics as a whole will remain well below average.

Hispanics are much less educated than the average American

(percent of Hispanic and total persons aged 25 or older who are high school or college graduates, 1996)

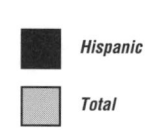

Hispanic

Total

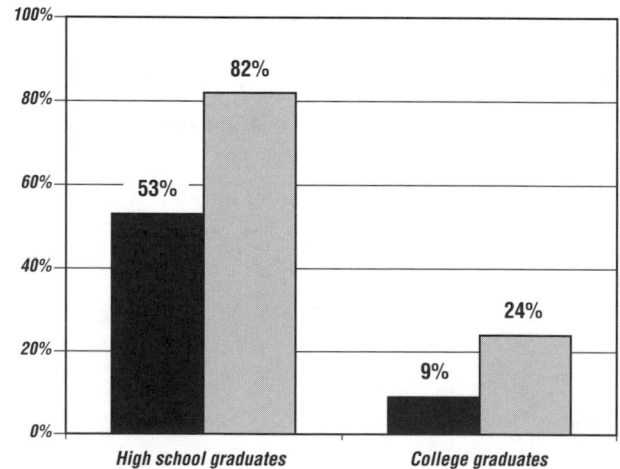

Educational Attainment of Hispanics by Sex, 1996

(number and percent distribution of Hispanics aged 25 or older by educational attainment and sex, 1996; numbers in thousands)

	total		men		women	
	number	*percent*	*number*	*percent*	*number*	*percent*
Total, aged 25 or older	**14,541**	**100.0%**	**7,229**	**100.0%**	**7,311**	**100.0%**
Not a high school graduate	6,842	47.1	3,398	47.0	3,416	46.7
High school graduate or more	7,726	53.1	3,832	53.0	3,895	53.3
High school graduate only	3,780	26.0	1,878	26.0	1,902	26.0
Some college or associate's degree	2,596	17.9	1,211	16.8	1,384	18.9
Bachelor's degree or more	1,350	9.3	743	10.3	609	8.3
Bachelor's degree only	967	6.7	503	7.0	465	6.4
Master's degree	258	1.8	159	2.2	98	1.3
Professional degree	71	0.5	43	0.6	29	0.4
Doctoral degree	54	0.4	38	0.5	17	0.2

Source: Bureau of the Census, Educational Attainment in the United States: March 1996, *Current Population Reports, P20-493, 1997; calculations by New Strategist*

Educational Attainment of Hispanics by Ethnicity, 1996

(number and percent distribution of Hispanics aged 25 or older by educational attainment and ethnicity, 1996; numbers in thousands)

	total	Mexican	Puerto Rican	Cuban	Central & South Amer.	other Hispanic
Number						
Total, aged 25 or older	**14,541**	**8,691**	**1,592**	**821**	**2,272**	**1,165**
Not a high school graduate	6,815	4,616	630	297	880	392
High school graduate or more	7,726	4,075	962	524	1,392	773
High school graduate only	3,780	2,181	450	197	599	354
Some college or assoc. degree	2,596	1,332	336	173	486	268
Bachelor's degree or more	1,350	562	176	154	307	151
Bachelor's degree only	967	415	121	93	228	109
Graduate degree	383	147	55	61	79	42
Percent distribution						
Total, aged 25 or older	**100.0%**	**100.0%**	**100.0%**	**100.0%**	**100.0%**	**100.0%**
Not a high school graduate	46.9	53.1	39.6	36.2	38.7	33.6
High school graduate or more	53.1	46.9	60.4	63.8	61.3	66.4
High school graduate only	26.0	25.1	28.3	24.0	26.4	30.4
Some college or associate's degree	17.9	15.3	21.1	21.1	21.4	23.0
Bachelor's degree or more	9.3	6.5	11.1	18.8	13.5	13.0
Bachelor's degree only	6.7	4.8	7.6	11.3	10.0	9.4
Graduate degree	2.6	1.7	3.5	7.4	3.5	3.6

Source: Bureau of the Census, Internet web site http://www.census.gov; *calculations by New Strategist*

Hispanic High School and College Graduates by Sex, 1980 to 1996

(percent of Hispanics aged 25 or older who are high school or college graduates, by sex, selected years 1980–96)

	total	men	women
High school graduates			
1996	53.1%	53.0%	53.3%
1990	50.8	50.3	51.3
1985	47.9	48.5	47.4
1980	45.3	46.4	44.1
College graduates			
1996	9.3	10.6	8.3
1990	9.2	9.8	8.7
1985	8.5	9.7	7.3
1980	7.9	9.7	6.2

Source: Bureau of the Census, Statistical Abstract of the United States: 1997 *(117th edition.) Washington, DC, 1997; and Internet web site,* http://www.census.gov

Hispanic High School and College Graduates by Age and Sex, 1996

(percent of Hispanics aged 25 or older who are high school or college graduates by age and sex, 1996)

	total	men	women
High school graduates			
Total, aged 25 or older	**53.1%**	**53.0%**	**53.3%**
Aged 25 to 29	61.1	59.7	62.9
Aged 30 to 34	60.9	57.6	64.7
Aged 35 to 39	56.2	56.4	56.0
Aged 40 to 44	56.2	55.6	56.7
Aged 45 to 49	55.6	55.0	56.2
Aged 50 to 54	47.5	46.2	48.6
Aged 55 to 59	41.7	39.1	43.8
Aged 60 to 64	38.9	42.3	36.0
Aged 65 or older	30.4	32.8	28.6
College graduates			
Total, aged 25 or older	**9.3**	**10.3**	**8.3**
Aged 25 to 29	10.0	10.2	9.8
Aged 30 to 34	10.5	9.5	11.5
Aged 35 to 39	9.9	10.0	9.8
Aged 40 to 44	10.9	11.9	9.8
Aged 45 to 49	9.5	11.7	7.5
Aged 50 to 54	7.0	8.9	5.5
Aged 55 to 59	7.5	11.0	4.6
Aged 60 to 64	7.6	11.7	4.0
Aged 65 or older	6.0	8.7	4.0

Source: Bureau of the Census, Educational Attainment in the United States: March 1996, *Current Population Reports, P20-493, 1997*

Hispanic High School and College Graduates
by Age and Region, 1996

(percent of Hispanics aged 25 or older who are high school or college graduates, by age and region, 1996)

	Northeast	*Midwest*	*South*	*West*
High school graduates				
Total, aged 25 or older	**55.9%**	**54.3%**	**55.0%**	**50.4%**
Aged 25 to 34	65.3	62.1	66.1	56.3
Aged 35 to 44	61.4	54.0	59.6	52.1
Aged 45 to 54	53.6	50.9	54.2	49.4
Aged 55 to 64	39.3	51.2	38.8	41.1
Aged 65 or older	32.3	29.1	31.3	28.8
College graduates				
Total, aged 25 or older	**10.0**	**10.2**	**10.7**	**7.8**
Aged 25 to 34	11.5	12.9	11.4	8.8
Aged 35 to 44	12.7	8.8	12.8	7.8
Aged 45 to 54	8.0	6.9	10.0	7.3
Aged 55 to 64	6.5	15.1	7.7	6.7
Aged 65 or older	4.5	4.2	7.9	4.8

Source: Bureau of the Census, Educational Attainment in the United States: March 1996, *Current Population Reports, P20-493, 1997*

Hispanic High School and College Graduates by State, 1990

(percent of Hispanics aged 25 or older who are high school or college graduates, by state, 1990)

	high school graduate or more	college graduate		high school graduate or more	college graduate
United States	**49.8%**	**9.2%**	Missouri	71.0%	18.0%
Alabama	73.8	20.1	Montana	66.4	10.9
Alaska	80.4	14.6	Nebraska	60.0	9.4
Arizona	51.7	6.9	Nevada	53.7	7.0
Arkansas	59.1	11.1	New Hampshire	78.2	25.5
California	45.0	7.1	New Jersey	53.9	10.8
Colorado	58.3	8.6	New Mexico	59.6	8.7
Connecticut	53.5	12.1	New York	50.4	9.3
Delaware	60.1	16.5	North Carolina	71.0	17.9
District of Columbia	52.6	24.0	North Dakota	75.2	15.9
Florida	57.2	14.2	Ohio	63.3	14.2
Georgia	66.2	20.5	Oklahoma	55.9	10.5
Hawaii	73.9	10.3	Oregon	53.0	10.1
Idaho	43.4	6.6	Pennsylvania	52.2	11.8
Illinois	45.0	8.0	Rhode Island	46.8	8.9
Indiana	62.6	10.8	South Carolina	71.8	19.8
Iowa	64.2	13.7	South Dakota	71.3	13.4
Kansas	58.1	10.1	Tennessee	71.5	21.9
Kentucky	74.0	18.9	Texas	44.6	7.3
Louisiana	67.6	16.6	Utah	61.0	9.1
Maine	83.8	23.6	Vermont	84.7	28.2
Maryland	70.3	25.2	Virginia	70.5	22.4
Massachusetts	52.0	13.6	Washington	56.7	11.0
Michigan	60.9	11.6	West Virginia	70.3	17.6
Minnesota	71.1	17.2	Wisconsin	54.1	10.0
Mississippi	67.7	17.1	Wyoming	59.3	4.8

Source: National Center for Education Statistics, Digest of Education Statistics 1993, *NCES 93-292, 1993*

School Enrollment of Total and Mexican Hispanics by Age and Sex, 1995

(number and percent of Hispanics and Mexican Hispanics aged 3 or older enrolled in school, by age and sex, October 1995; numbers in thousands)

	total		male		female	
	number	percent	number	percent	number	percent
Total Hispanics						
Total, aged 3 or older	**8,563**	**32.9%**	**4,343**	**33.1%**	**4,220**	**32.7%**
Aged 3 and 4	503	36.9	286	40.8	217	32.7
Aged 5 and 6	1,159	93.9	597	93.6	582	94.3
Aged 7 to 9	1,560	98.5	751	98.8	809	98.2
Aged 10 o 13	2,060	99.2	1,091	98.8	969	99.6
Aged 14 and 15	977	98.9	506	98.4	469	99.4
Aged 16 and 17	778	88.2	381	88.4	397	88.0
Aged 18 and 19	467	46.1	253	47.4	214	44.8
Aged 20 and 21	268	27.1	120	24.8	147	29.2
Aged 22 to 24	250	15.6	131	14.8	118	16.6
Aged 25 to 29	172	7.1	71	5.6	101	8.7
Aged 30 to 34	120	4.7	60	4.5	60	4.9
Aged 35 to 44	187	4.6	63	3.1	124	6.1
Aged 45 to 54	53	2.4	29	2.6	24	2.1
Aged 55 or older	10	0.3	1	0.1	9	0.5
Mexican Hispanics						
Total, aged 3 or older	**5,782**	**33.8**	**2,984**	**33.7**	**2,799**	**33.8**
Aged 3 and 4	360	35.4	205	40.1	155	30.7
Aged 5 and 6	810	93.9	411	93.9	399	93.8
Aged 7 to 9	1,085	98.8	531	99.4	554	98.2
Aged 10 o 13	1,426	99.0	770	98.7	656	99.3
Aged 14 and 15	682	99.2	366	99.2	315	99.2
Aged 16 and 17	531	86.0	253	88.1	277	87.8
Aged 18 and 19	279	42.1	164	44.7	115	38.9
Aged 20 and 21	154	22.7	66	20.6	87	24.7
Aged 22 to 24	148	13.0	92	13.6	56	12.1
Aged 25 to 29	102	6.1	45	5.0	57	7.3
Aged 30 to 34	62	3.8	27	3.2	35	4.6
Aged 35 to 44	118	4.4	41	2.9	77	6.0
Aged 45 to 54	22	1.6	12	1.7	10	1.5
Aged 55 or older	5	0.3	1	0.1	5	0.5

Source: Bureau of the Census, School Enrollment—Social and Economic Characteristics of Students: October 1995, *Current Population Reports, P20-492, 1997*

Hispanic Families with Children in College, 1995

(total number of Hispanic families, number with children aged 18 to 24, and number and percent with children aged 18 to 24 attending college full-time as of October 1995, by household income in 1994; numbers in thousands)

	total	with children aged 18–24	with one or more children attending college full-time		
			number	percent of total families	percent of families with children 18–24
Total families	**6,572**	**1,370**	**349**	**5.3%**	**25.5%**
Under $20,000	2,979	522	97	3.3	18.6
$20,000 to $29,999	1,104	280	74	6.7	26.4
$30,000 to $39,999	686	134	38	5.5	28.4
$40,000 to $49,999	416	106	37	8.9	34.9
$50,000 to $74,999	493	98	28	5.7	28.6
$75,000 or more	276	61	28	10.1	45.9

Source: Bureau of the Census, School Enrollment—Social and Economic Characteristics of Students: October 1995, *Current Population Reports, P20-492, 1997; calculations by New Strategist*

College Enrollment of Hispanics by Age, 1995

(number and percent distribution of Hispanics aged 15 or older enrolled in college by age, type of school, and attendance status, October 1995; numbers in thousands)

	total	total	undergraduate two-year college			undergraduate four-year college			graduate		
			total	full-time	part-time	total	full-time	part-time	total	full-time	part-time
Total enrolled	1,207	1,096	464	221	243	632	437	195	111	51	60
Aged 15 to 17	20	19	6	4	2	13	13	–	–	–	–
Aged 18 and 19	264	261	105	87	15	156	133	23	5	5	–
Aged 20 and 21	245	240	88	39	49	152	128	23	5	5	–
Aged 22 to 24	236	214	93	44	48	121	85	36	23	12	11
Aged 25 to 29	153	122	51	7	44	71	39	32	31	16	15
Aged 30 to 34	97	83	42	20	22	41	19	23	13	8	6
Aged 35 to 39	67	58	29	6	23	29	13	16	10	2	8
Aged 40 to 44	81	69	40	9	31	29	6	23	13	1	12
Aged 45 to 49	24	21	9	5	4	12	1	11	3	–	3
Aged 50 to 54	10	8	–	–	–	8	–	8	3	3	–
Aged 55 or older	9	4	4	–	4	–	–	–	5	–	5

(continued)

(continued from previous page)

Percent distribution by age	total	undergraduate							graduate		
		total	two-year college			four-year college			total	full-time	part-time
			total	full-time	part-time	total	full-time	part-time			
Total enrolled	100.0%	100.0%	100.0%	100.0%	100.0%	100.0%	100.0%	100.0%	100.0%	100.0%	100.0%
Aged 15 to 17	1.7	1.7	1.3	1.8	0.8	2.1	3.0	–	–	–	–
Aged 18 and 19	21.9	23.8	22.6	39.4	6.2	24.7	30.4	11.8	4.5	9.8	–
Aged 20 and 21	20.3	21.9	19.0	17.6	20.2	24.1	29.3	11.8	4.5	9.8	–
Aged 22 to 24	19.6	19.5	20.0	19.9	19.8	19.1	19.5	18.5	20.7	23.5	18.3
Aged 25 to 29	12.7	11.1	11.0	3.2	18.1	11.2	8.9	16.4	27.9	31.4	25.0
Aged 30 to 34	8.0	7.6	9.1	9.0	9.1	6.5	4.3	11.8	11.7	15.7	10.0
Aged 35 to 39	5.6	5.3	6.3	2.7	9.5	4.6	3.0	8.2	9.0	3.9	13.3
Aged 40 to 44	6.7	6.3	8.6	4.1	12.8	4.6	1.4	11.8	11.7	2.0	20.0
Aged 45 to 49	2.0	1.9	1.9	2.3	1.6	1.9	0.2	5.6	2.7	–	5.0
Aged 50 to 54	0.8	0.7	–	–	–	1.3	–	4.1	2.7	5.9	–
Aged 55 or older	0.7	0.4	0.9	–	1.6	–	–	–	4.5	–	8.3

(continued)

(continued from previous page)

Percent distribution by type of school and attendance status

	total	undergraduate		two-year college			four-year college			graduate		
		total	total	full-time	part-time	total	full-time	part-time	total	full-time	part-time
Total enrolled	**100.0%**	**90.8%**	**38.4%**	**18.3%**	**20.1%**	**52.4%**	**36.2%**	**16.2%**	**9.2%**	**4.2%**	**5.0%**
Aged 15 to 17	100.0	95.0	30.0	20.0	10.0	65.0	65.0	–	–	–	–
Aged 18 and 19	100.0	98.9	39.8	33.0	5.7	59.1	50.4	8.7	1.9	1.9	–
Aged 20 and 21	100.0	98.0	35.9	15.9	20.0	62.0	52.2	9.4	2.0	2.0	–
Aged 22 to 24	100.0	90.7	39.4	18.6	20.3	51.3	36.0	15.3	9.7	5.1	4.7
Aged 25 to 29	100.0	79.7	33.3	4.6	28.8	46.4	25.5	20.9	20.3	10.5	9.8
Aged 30 to 34	100.0	85.6	43.3	20.6	22.7	42.3	19.6	23.7	13.4	8.2	6.2
Aged 35 to 39	100.0	86.6	43.3	9.0	34.3	43.3	19.4	23.9	14.9	3.0	11.9
Aged 40 to 44	100.0	85.2	49.4	11.1	38.3	35.8	7.4	28.4	16.0	1.2	14.8
Aged 45 to 49	100.0	87.5	37.5	20.8	16.7	50.0	4.2	45.8	12.5	–	12.5
Aged 50 to 54	100.0	80.0	–	–	–	80.0	–	80.0	30.0	30.0	–
Aged 55 or older	100.0	44.4	44.4	–	44.4	–	–	–	55.6	55.6	55.6

Note: (–) means sample is too small to make a reliable estimate.
Source: Bureau of the Census, School Enrollment—Social and Economic Characteristics of Students: October 1995, Current Population Reports, P20-492, 1997; calculations by New Strategist

Bachelor's, Master's, and Doctoral Degrees
Earned by Hispanics by Field of Study, 1994–95

(number and percent of bachelor's, master's, and doctoral degrees earned by Hispanics, by field of study, 1994–95)

	bachelor's		master's		doctoral	
	number	percent	number	percent	number	percent
Total degrees	**54,201**	**4.7%**	**12,907**	**3.3%**	**984**	**2.2%**
Agriculture and natural resources	460	2.3	98	2.3	19	1.5
Architecture and related programs	544	6.2	155	4.0	6	4.3
Area, ethnic, and cultural studies	519	9.1	93	5.7	6	3.2
Biological and life sciences	2,331	4.2	154	2.9	98	2.1
Business, management, and admin. services	10,753	4.6	2,590	2.8	16	1.1
Communications	2,014	4.2	131	2.5	6	1.9
Communications technologies	14	2.0	12	2.6	–	–
Computer and information sciences	1,077	4.4	207	2.0	6	0.7
Construction trades	–	–	1	14.3	–	–
Education	3,430	3.2	4,048	4.0	252	3.6
Engineering	2,724	4.4	688	2.4	60	1.0
Engineering-related technologies	688	4.4	31	2.8	–	–
English language and literature	2,101	4.0	198	2.5	26	1.7
Foreign languages and literature	1,903	13.8	288	9.2	71	7.8
Health professions and related sciences	2,601	3.3	849	2.7	38	1.8
Home economics	395	2.6	92	3.2	7	1.8
Law and legal studies	88	4.3	65	2.6	–	–
Liberal arts and sciences	2,413	7.2	70	2.7	–	–
Library science	–	–	114	2.3	2	3.6
Mathematics	520	3.8	72	1.7	14	1.1
Mechanics and repairers	–	–	–	–	–	–
Multi- and interdisciplinary studies	2,088	8.0	65	2.6	8	3.4
Parks, recreation, leisure, and fitness	499	3.9	33	1.9	7	4.7
Philosophy and religion	315	4.3	51	3.7	9	1.8
Physical sciences	507	2.6	119	2.1	62	1.4
Precision production trades	11	3.1	–	–	–	–
Protective services	1,701	7.0	54	3.2	–	–
Psychology	4,149	5.8	579	4.2	129	3.4
Public administration and services	1,170	6.3	1,128	4.8	13	2.3
R.O.T.C. and military sciences	–	–	4	3.2	–	–
Social sciences and history	7,002	5.5	483	3.3	86	2.3
Theological studies and religious vocations	136	2.4	120	2.3	30	1.9
Transportation and material moving	120	3.2	19	2.3	–	–
Visual and performing arts	1,928	4.0	296	2.9	13	1.2

Note: (–) means no degrees were awarded.
Source: National Center for Education Statistics, Digest of Education Statistics 1997, *NCES 98-015, 1997; calculations by New Strategist*

First-Professional Degrees Earned
by Hispanics by Field of Study, 1994–95

(number and percent of first-professional degrees earned by Hispanics by field of study, 1994–95)

	number	percent
Total degrees	**3,231**	**4.3%**
Dentistry (D.D.S. or D.M.D.)	233	6.0
Medicine (M.D.)	648	4.2
Optometry (O.D.)	36	3.0
Osteopathic medicine (D.O.)	67	3.6
Pharmacy (Pharm. D.)	50	2.2
Podiatry (Pod. D., D.P., or D.P.M.)	32	5.9
Veterinary medicine (D.V.M.)	53	2.5
Chiropractic medicine (D.C. or D.C.M.)	81	2.7
Law (LL.B. or J.D.)	1,897	4.8
Theology (M.Div., M.H.L., B.D., or Ord.)	132	2.2
Other	2	2.7

Source: National Center for Education Statistics, Digest of Education Statistics 1997, *NCES 98-015, 1997; calculations by New Strategist*

Hispanics: Health

Among all Americans, Hispanics are most likely to be without health insurance.

Hispanics fare better than the total population on some health measures and worse on others. Hispanics are less likely to die of cancer and heart disease than the average American, but their homicide rate is 59 percent above average. Infant mortality is below average, but the incidence of AIDS and tuberculosis is above average.

Nearly 700,000 babies were born to Hispanic women in 1996, or 18 percent of all children born that year. This proportion should rise to 24 percent by 2020. Hispanics accounted for 47 percent of all births in California in 1996 and for 43 percent of births in Texas. Eighty-six percent of Hispanic births in California and 89 percent of those in Texas were to Mexican-American women.

Twenty-one percent of Hispanics had a disability in 1994–95. This is a slightly smaller proportion than that for Americans as a whole because Hispanics are younger than average. Hispanics are more likely to be without health insurance than any other racial or ethnic group. In 1996, 34 percent did not have health insurance, more than double the 16 percent of the total population that lacks health insurance.

Hispanics' life expectancy exceeds that of the average American. At birth, Hispanic males can expect to live to age 75, or two years longer than the average American male. Hispanic females can expect to live to age 83, or three years longer than the average female.

■ The health status of Hispanics is greatly influenced by immigration. Not only do immigrants boost the Hispanic birth rate, but they also are less likely to be covered by health insurance than the average American.

Hispanic share of births is rising

(births to Hispanic women as a percent of total births, 1996 and 2020)

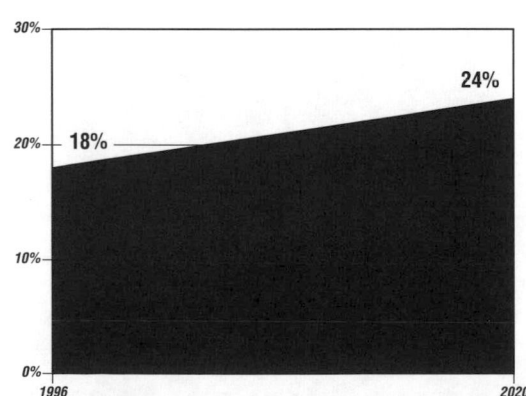

Health Indicators for Hispanics, 1993 and 1994

(selected indicators of total population and Hispanic health status, and index of Hispanic health indicators to total, 1993 and 1994)

	total population indicator	Hispanic indicator	index
Infant mortality rate (deaths before age 1 per 1,000 live births), 1993	8.4	7.1	85
Total deaths per 100,000 population, 1993	513.3	385.2	75
Motor vehicle crash deaths per 100,000 population, 1993	16.0	16.8	105
Work-related injury deaths per 100,000 people aged 16 or older, 1994	3.3	3.5	106
Suicides per 100,000 population, 1993	11.3	7.3	65
Homicides per 100,000 population, 1993	10.7	17.0	159
Lung cancer deaths per 100,000 population, 1993	39.3	14.5	37
Female breast cancer deaths per 100,000 population, 1993	21.5	12.4	58
Cardiovascular disease deaths per 100,000 population, 1993	181.8	120.4	66
Heart disease deaths per 100,000 population, 1993	145.3	94.8	65
Stroke deaths per 100,000 population, 1993	26.5	19.5	74
Reported incidence of AIDS per 100,000 population, 1994	26.9	44.9	167
Reported incidence of tuberculosis per 100,000 population, 1994	9.4	19.5	207
Reported incidence of syphilis per 100,000 population, 1994	8.1	3.5	43
Prevalence of low birth weight, as percent of total live births, 1994	7.3	6.2	85
Births to girls aged 10 to 17, as percent of total live births, 1994	5.3	7.6	143
Percent of mothers without care, first trimester of pregnancy, 1994	19.8	31.1	157
Percent under age 18 living in poverty, 1994	21.8	41.5	190
Percent living in counties exceeding U.S. air quality standards, 1994	24.9	45.2	182

Note: The index for each indicator is calculated by dividing the Hispanic figure by the total population figure and multiplying by 100. For example, the index of 85 in the first row indicates that Hispanic infant mortality is 15 percent below the rate for all infants.
Source: National Center for Health Statistics, Health Status Indicators by Race and Hispanic Origin, Healthy People 2000 Review, 1995–96; calculations by New Strategist

Births to Hispanic Women by Age, 1996

(number and percent distribution of births to Hispanic women, by age, 1996)

	number	percent
Total births	**697,829**	**100.0%**
Under age 15	3,084	0.4
Aged 15 to 19	118,612	17.0
Aged 20 to 24	213,685	30.6
Aged 25 to 29	184,368	26.4
Aged 30 to 34	118,677	17.0
Aged 35 to 39	49,280	7.1
Aged 40 or older	10,123	1.5

Source: National Center for Health Statistics, Births and Deaths: United States, 1996, *Monthly Vital Statistics Report, Vol. 46, No. 1, Supplement 2, 1997; calculations by New Strategist*

Births to Unmarried Hispanic Women by Age, 1995

(number and percent of births to unmarried Hispanic women, by age; 1995)

	number	percent of total Hispanic births
Births to unmarried Hispanics	**277,602**	**40.8%**
Under age 15	2,741	86.0
Aged 15 to 19	79,669	67.3
Aged 20 to 24	93,742	45.0
Aged 25 to 29	55,431	31.1
Aged 30 to 34	30,375	26.4
Aged 35 to 39	12,845	27.4
Aged 40 or older	2,799	29.0

Source: National Center for Health Statistics, Advance Report of Final Natality Statistics, 1995, *Monthly Vital Statistics Report, Vol. 45, No. 11 Supplement, 1997; calculations by New Strategist*

Births to Hispanic Women by Age and Ethnicity, 1995

(number and percent distribution of births to Hispanic women by age and ethnicity, 1995)

	total	*Mexican*	*Puerto Rican*	*Cuban*	*Central & Sout h Amer.*	*other Hispanic*
Total births	**679,768**	**469,615**	**54,824**	**12,473**	**94,996**	**47,860**
Under age 15	3,187	2,319	371	11	188	298
Aged 15 to 19	118,449	85,781	12,522	954	9,874	9,318
Aged 20 to 24	208,211	151,485	16,848	2,400	23,554	13,924
Aged 25 to 29	178,258	122,606	12,990	3,642	27,361	11,659
Aged 30 to 34	115,063	72,487	8,172	3,873	22,029	8,502
Aged 35 to 39	49,964	28,937	3,305	1,346	9,881	3,495
Aged 40 or older	9,636	6,000	616	247	2,109	664
Percent distribution by ethnicity						
Total births	**100.0%**	**69.1%**	**8.1%**	**1.8%**	**14.0%**	**7.0%**
Under age 15	100.0	72.8	11.6	0.3	5.9	9.4
Aged 15 to 19	100.0	72.4	10.6	0.8	8.3	7.9
Aged 20 to 24	100.0	72.8	8.1	1.2	11.3	6.7
Aged 25 to 29	100.0	68.8	7.3	2.0	15.3	6.5
Aged 30 to 34	100.0	63.0	7.1	3.4	19.1	7.4
Aged 35 to 39	100.0	57.9	6.6	2.7	19.8	7.0
Aged 40 or older	100.0	62.3	6.4	2.6	21.9	6.9
Percent distribution by age						
Total births	**100.0%**	**100.0%**	**100.0%**	**100.0%**	**100.0%**	**100.0%**
Under age 15	0.5	0.5	0.7	0.1	0.2	0.6
Aged 15 to 19	17.4	18.3	22.8	7.6	10.4	19.5
Aged 20 to 24	30.6	32.3	30.7	19.2	24.8	29.1
Aged 25 to 29	26.2	26.1	23.7	29.2	28.8	24.4
Aged 30 to 34	16.9	15.4	14.9	31.1	23.2	17.8
Aged 35 to 39	7.4	6.2	6.0	10.8	10.4	7.3
Aged 40 or older	1.4	1.3	1.1	2.0	2.2	1.4

Source: National Center for Health Statistics, Advance Report of Final Natality Statistics, 1995, *Monthly Vital Statistics Report, Vol. 45, No. 11 Supplement, 1997; calculations by New Strategist*

Births to Hispanic Women by State and Ethnicity, 1995

(number of births to Hispanic women by state and ethnicity, 1995)

	total	Mexican	Puerto Rican	Cuban	Central & South Amer.	other Hispanic
United States	**679,768**	**469,615**	**54,824**	**12,473**	**94,996**	**47,860**
Alabama	758	483	92	20	107	56
Alaska	574	236	56	4	54	224
Arizona	25,504	24,538	193	41	429	303
Arkansas	1,004	837	23	7	100	37
California	254,001	218,238	2,006	828	27,207	5,720
Colorado	11,523	7,291	185	29	249	3,769
Connecticut	5,505	294	3,839	80	1,000	292
Delaware	585	232	237	2	102	12
District of Columbia	685	30	16	4	564	71
Florida	34,509	6,584	5,860	8,517	11,433	2,115
Georgia	5,067	3,697	368	79	665	258
Hawaii	2,029	407	608	9	58	947
Idaho	2,040	1,791	12	4	50	183
Illinois	32,166	26,168	3,075	196	898	1,829
Indiana	2,546	1,921	271	20	131	203
Iowa	1,279	1,009	35	8	106	119
Kansas	2,828	2,370	71	14	140	233
Kentucky	493	260	74	28	70	61
Louisiana	1,158	405	172	54	280	247
Maine	112	25	12	1	15	59
Maryland	3,155	509	245	51	1,747	603
Massachusetts	8,109	321	4,077	92	3,195	424
Michigan	4,781	3,196	425	68	236	856
Minnesota	1,915	1,439	68	10	194	204
Mississippi	220	110	16	10	18	66
Missouri	1,288	942	73	16	131	126
Montana	282	175	6	–	7	94
Nebraska	1,615	1,259	18	7	150	181
Nevada	6,124	4,969	122	117	646	250
New Hampshire	214	48	65	4	17	80
New Jersey	18,835	2,105	7,225	890	8,235	380
New Mexico	12,900	4,351	36	53	74	8,386
New York	54,193	6,161	16,127	499	24,269	7,137
North Carolina	4,244	2,935	413	60	592	244
North Dakota	147	83	11	1	15	37
Ohio	2,801	1,277	1,147	42	162	173

(continued)

(continued from previous page)

	total	Mexican	Puerto Rican	Cuban	Central & South Amer.	other Hispanic
Oklahoma	2,358	1,704	90	6	94	462
Oregon	5,002	4,639	42	14	215	92
Pennsylvania	6,572	764	4,432	97	664	615
Rhode Island	1,554	80	482	12	863	117
South Carolina	763	427	107	16	115	96
South Dakota	116	79	8	–	15	14
Tennessee	1,111	629	128	44	104	206
Texas	137,131	121,720	882	264	6,396	7,867
Utah	3,110	2,327	59	18	326	380
Vermont	27	7	8	2	5	5
Virginia	4,841	932	493	85	2,459	872
Washington	8,502	7,119	196	32	221	932
West Virginia	90	33	11	1	9	36
Wisconsin	2,858	2,002	595	17	140	102
Wyoming	548	437	8	–	20	83

Note: (–) means no births.
Source: National Center for Health Statistics, Advance Report of Final Natality Statistics, 1995, *Monthly Vital Statistics Report, Vol. 45, No. 11 Supplement, 1997; calculations by New Strategist*

Distribution of Births to Hispanic Women by State and Ethnicity, 1995

(percent distribution of births to Hispanic women, by state and ethnicity, 1995)

	total	Mexican	Puerto Rican	Cuban	Central & South Amer.	other Hispanic
United States	100.0%	100.0%	100.0%	100.0%	100.0%	100.0%
Alabama	0.1	0.1	0.2	0.2	0.1	0.1
Alaska	0.1	0.1	0.1	0.0	0.1	0.5
Arizona	3.8	5.2	0.4	0.3	0.5	0.6
Arkansas	0.1	0.2	0.0	0.1	0.1	0.1
California	37.4	46.5	3.7	6.6	28.6	12.0
Colorado	1.7	1.6	0.3	0.2	0.3	7.9
Connecticut	0.8	0.1	7.0	0.6	1.1	0.6
Delaware	0.1	0.0	0.4	0.0	0.1	0.0
District of Columbia	0.1	0.0	0.0	0.0	0.6	0.1
Florida	5.1	1.4	10.7	68.3	12.0	4.4
Georgia	0.7	0.8	0.7	0.6	0.7	0.5
Hawaii	0.3	0.1	1.1	0.1	0.1	2.0
Idaho	0.3	0.4	0.0	0.0	0.1	0.4
Illinois	4.7	5.6	5.6	1.6	0.9	3.8
Indiana	0.4	0.4	0.5	0.2	0.1	0.4
Iowa	0.2	0.2	0.1	0.1	0.1	0.2
Kansas	0.4	0.5	0.1	0.1	0.1	0.5
Kentucky	0.1	0.1	0.1	0.2	0.1	0.1
Louisiana	0.2	0.1	0.3	0.4	0.3	0.5
Maine	0.0	0.0	0.0	0.0	0.0	0.1
Maryland	0.5	0.1	0.4	0.4	1.8	1.3
Massachusetts	1.2	0.1	7.4	0.7	3.4	0.9
Michigan	0.7	0.7	0.8	0.5	0.2	1.8
Minnesota	0.3	0.3	0.1	0.1	0.2	0.4
Mississippi	0.0	0.0	0.0	0.1	0.0	0.1
Missouri	0.2	0.2	0.1	0.1	0.1	0.3
Montana	0.0	0.0	0.0	–	0.0	0.2
Nebraska	0.2	0.3	0.0	0.1	0.2	0.4
Nevada	0.9	1.1	0.2	0.9	0.7	0.5
New Hampshire	0.0	0.0	0.1	0.0	0.0	0.2
New Jersey	2.8	0.4	13.2	7.1	8.7	0.8
New Mexico	1.9	0.9	0.1	0.4	0.1	17.5
New York	8.0	1.3	29.4	4.0	25.5	14.9
North Carolina	0.6	0.6	0.8	0.5	0.6	0.5
North Dakota	0.0	0.0	0.0	0.0	0.0	0.1
Ohio	0.4	0.3	2.1	0.3	0.2	0.4

(continued)

(continued from previous page)

	total	Mexican	Puerto Rican	Cuban	Central & South Amer.	other Hispanic
Oklahoma	0.3%	0.4%	0.2%	0.0%	0.1%	1.0%
Oregon	0.7	1.0	0.1	0.1	0.2	0.2
Pennsylvania	1.0	0.2	8.1	0.8	0.7	1.3
Rhode Island	0.2	0.0	0.9	0.1	0.9	0.2
South Carolina	0.1	0.1	0.2	0.1	0.1	0.2
South Dakota	0.0	0.0	0.0	–	0.0	0.0
Tennessee	0.2	0.1	0.2	0.4	0.1	0.4
Texas	20.2	25.9	1.6	2.1	6.7	16.4
Utah	0.5	0.5	0.1	0.1	0.3	0.8
Vermont	0.0	0.0	0.0	0.0	0.0	0.0
Virginia	0.7	0.2	0.9	0.7	2.6	1.8
Washington	1.3	1.5	0.4	0.3	0.2	1.9
West Virginia	0.0	0.0	0.0	0.0	0.0	0.1
Wisconsin	0.4	0.4	1.1	0.1	0.1	0.2
Wyoming	0.1	0.1	0.0	–	0.0	0.2

Note: (–) means no births.
Source: Calculations by New Strategist based on National Center for Health Statistics data in Advance Report of Final Natality Statistics, 1995, *Monthly Vital Statistics Report, Vol. 45, No. 11 Supplement, 1997*

Ethnic Share of Hispanic Births by State, 1995

(births to Hispanic ethnic groups as a percent of total Hispanic births, by state, 1995)

	total	Mexican	Puerto Rican	Cuban	Central & South Amer.	other Hispanic
United States	**100.0%**	**69.1%**	**8.1%**	**1.8%**	**14.0%**	**7.0%**
Alabama	100.0	63.7	12.1	2.6	14.1	7.4
Alaska	100.0	41.1	9.8	0.7	9.4	39.0
Arizona	100.0	96.2	0.8	0.2	1.7	1.2
Arkansas	100.0	83.4	2.3	0.7	10.0	3.7
California	100.0	85.9	0.8	0.3	10.7	2.3
Colorado	100.0	63.3	1.6	0.3	2.2	32.7
Connecticut	100.0	5.3	69.7	1.5	18.2	5.3
Delaware	100.0	39.7	40.5	0.3	17.4	2.1
District of Columbia	100.0	4.4	2.3	0.6	82.3	10.4
Florida	100.0	19.1	17.0	24.7	33.1	6.1
Georgia	100.0	73.0	7.3	1.6	13.1	5.1
Hawaii	100.0	20.1	30.0	0.4	2.9	46.7
Idaho	100.0	87.8	0.6	0.2	2.5	9.0
Illinois	100.0	81.4	9.6	0.6	2.8	5.7
Indiana	100.0	75.5	10.6	0.8	5.1	8.0
Iowa	100.0	78.9	2.7	0.6	8.3	9.3
Kansas	100.0	83.8	2.5	0.5	5.0	8.2
Kentucky	100.0	52.7	15.0	5.7	14.2	12.4
Louisiana	100.0	35.0	14.9	4.7	24.2	21.3
Maine	100.0	22.3	10.7	0.9	13.4	52.7
Maryland	100.0	16.1	7.8	1.6	55.4	19.1
Massachusetts	100.0	4.0	50.3	1.1	39.4	5.2
Michigan	100.0	66.8	8.9	1.4	4.9	17.9
Minnesota	100.0	75.1	3.6	0.5	10.1	10.7
Mississippi	100.0	50.0	7.3	4.5	8.2	30.0
Missouri	100.0	73.1	5.7	1.2	10.2	9.8
Montana	100.0	62.1	2.1	–	2.5	33.3
Nebraska	100.0	78.0	1.1	0.4	9.3	11.2
Nevada	100.0	81.1	2.0	1.9	10.5	4.1
New Hampshire	100.0	22.4	30.4	1.9	7.9	37.4
New Jersey	100.0	11.2	38.4	4.7	43.7	2.0
New Mexico	100.0	33.7	0.3	0.4	0.6	65.0
New York	100.0	11.4	29.8	0.9	44.8	13.2
North Carolina	100.0	69.2	9.7	1.4	13.9	5.7
North Dakota	100.0	56.5	7.5	0.7	10.2	25.2
Ohio	100.0	45.6	40.9	1.5	5.8	6.2

(continued)

(continued from previous page)

	total	Mexican	Puerto Rican	Cuban	Central & South Amer.	other Hispanic
Oklahoma	100.0%	72.3%	3.8%	0.3%	4.0%	19.6%
Oregon	100.0	92.7	0.8	0.3	4.3	1.8
Pennsylvania	100.0	11.6	67.4	1.5	10.1	9.4
Rhode Island	100.0	5.1	31.0	0.8	55.5	7.5
South Carolina	100.0	56.0	14.0	2.1	15.1	12.6
South Dakota	100.0	68.1	6.9	–	12.9	12.1
Tennessee	100.0	56.6	11.5	4.0	9.4	18.5
Texas	100.0	88.8	0.6	0.2	4.7	5.7
Utah	100.0	74.8	1.9	0.6	10.5	12.2
Vermont	100.0	25.9	29.6	7.4	18.5	18.5
Virginia	100.0	19.3	10.2	1.8	50.8	18.0
Washington	100.0	83.7	2.3	0.4	2.6	11.0
West Virginia	100.0	36.7	12.2	1.1	10.0	40.0
Wisconsin	100.0	70.0	20.8	0.6	4.9	3.6
Wyoming	100.0	79.7	1.5	–	3.6	15.1

Note: (–) means no births.
Source: Calculations by New Strategist based on National Center for Health Statistics data in Advance Report of Final Natality Statistics, 1995, *Monthly Vital Statistics Report, Vol. 45, No. 11 Supplement, 1997*

Births to Hispanic Women by State, 1996

(number and percent distribution of births to Hispanic women by state, and Hispanic births as a percent of total births by state, 1996)

	number	percent	Hispanic share of total births
United States	**697,829**	**100.0%**	**17.8%**
Alabama	937	0.1	1.5
Alaska	673	0.1	6.6
Arizona	29,217	4.2	36.7
Arkansas	1,315	0.2	3.6
California	251,123	36.0	46.5
Colorado	12,380	1.8	22.2
Connecticut	5,614	0.8	12.7
Delaware	666	0.1	6.5
District of Columbia	772	0.1	9.3
Florida	35,708	5.1	18.8
Georgia	6,312	0.9	5.5
Hawaii	2,151	0.3	11.7
Idaho	2,220	0.3	11.6
Illinois	33,040	4.7	17.9
Indiana	3,036	0.4	3.6
Iowa	1,481	0.2	4.0
Kansas	3,504	0.5	8.8
Kentucky	558	0.1	1.1
Louisiana	1,288	0.2	1.9
Maine	115	0.0	0.8
Maryland	3,146	0.5	4.5
Massachusetts	7,737	1.1	9.6
Michigan	5,197	0.7	3.8
Minnesota	2,287	0.3	3.6
Mississippi	283	0.0	0.7
Missouri	1,516	0.2	2.1
Montana	299	0.0	2.8
Nebraska	1,866	0.3	8.0
Nevada	6,946	1.0	26.7
New Hampshire	232	0.0	1.6
New Jersey	19,458	2.8	17.1
New Mexico	13,250	1.9	48.7
New York	53,024	7.6	19.5
North Carolina	5,500	0.8	5.2
North Dakota	137	0.0	1.6
Ohio	2,992	0.4	2.0

(continued)

(continued from previous page)

	number	percent	Hispanic share of total births
Oklahoma	2,882	0.4%	6.2%
Oregon	5,464	0.8	12.5
Pennsylvania	6,811	1.0	4.5
Rhode Island	1,633	0.2	13.0
South Carolina	960	0.1	1.9
South Dakota	146	0.0	1.4
Tennessee	1,425	0.2	1.9
Texas	140,539	20.1	43.0
Utah	3,865	0.6	9.3
Vermont	39	0.0	0.6
Virginia	5,158	0.7	5.6
Washington	9,183	1.3	11.5
West Virginia	122	0.0	0.6
Wisconsin	3,099	0.4	4.6
Wyoming	523	0.1	8.3

Source: National Center for Health Statistics, Births and Deaths: United States, 1996; Monthly Vital Statistics Report, Vol. 46, No.1, Supplement 2, 1997; calculations by New Strategist

Projections of Births to Hispanic Women, 1998 to 2020

(number of births to Hispanic women, and Hispanic births as a percent of total births, 1998–2020; numbers in thousands)

	number	*Hispanic share of total births*
1998	654	16.8%
1999	668	17.1
2000	683	17.5
2001	699	17.9
2002	715	18.2
2003	732	18.6
2004	750	18.9
2005	769	19.2
2006	790	19.5
2007	813	19.9
2008	837	20.2
2009	863	20.6
2010	888	20.9
2011	913	21.3
2012	936	21.6
2013	959	21.9
2014	980	22.2
2015	1,001	22.5
2016	1,021	22.8
2017	1,041	23.1
2018	1,060	23.4
2019	1,079	23.7
2020	1,099	24.0

Source: Bureau of the Census, Population Projections of the United States, by Age, Sex, Race, and Hispanic Origin: 1995 to 2050, *Current Population Reports, P25-1130, 1996; calculations by New Strategist*

Hispanics with Disabilities by Type of Disability and Age, 1994–95

(total number of Hispanics aged 15 or older, and percent with a disability by type of disability and age, 1994–95; numbers in thousands)

	15 or older	15 to 21	22 to 44	45 to 54	55 to 64	65 to 79	80 or older
Total persons	**18,815**	**3,539**	**10,176**	**2,263**	**1,390**	**1,197**	**251**
With any disability	**20.6%**	**9.3%**	**14.4%**	**28.1%**	**42.9%**	**55.3%**	**76.8%**
Severe	10.9	2.3	6.7	15.7	27.7	33.1	62.1
Not severe	9.7	7.0	7.7	12.4	15.2	22.2	14.7
With a mental disability	3.7	3.5	2.7	5.6	4.0	6.2	27.2
Uses wheelchair	0.6	0.4	0.2	0.4	0.7	3.1	11.1
Used cane/crutch/walker for six or more months	1.6	–	0.5	1.5	3.6	8.2	23.6
Difficulty with or unable to perform one or more functional activities	**13.7**	**0.9**	**8.0**	**18.9**	**30.6**	**48.9**	**75.5**
Seeing words and letters	3.1	0.7	1.5	5.7	6.9	14.3	17.7
Hearing normal conversation	2.6	0.7	1.3	3.0	6.2	10.3	31.4
Having speech understood	0.7	1.3	0.4	0.4	0.8	2.2	3.0
Lifting, carrying 10 pounds	6.8	1.2	4.0	10.5	15.9	25.9	48.3
Climbing stairs without resting	7.6	1.0	3.7	11.4	21.9	31.8	56.7
Walking three city blocks	6.9	1.5	3.5	10.2	17.2	28.6	62.4
Difficulty with or unable to perform one or more ADLs	**2.8**	**0.7**	**1.3**	**3.8**	**5.2**	**11.4**	**32.4**
Getting around inside the home	1.1	0.4	0.4	1.2	0.9	6.4	17.7
Getting in/out of bed or chair	1.8	0.4	0.8	2.7	4.2	7.2	25.3
Bathing	1.4	0.5	0.4	2.2	2.7	6.4	24.5
Dressing	1.3	0.6	0.6	1.8	2.2	5.3	18.1
Eating	0.4	0.3	0.2	0.3	0.5	1.8	6.2
Getting to/using toilet	0.6	0.3	0.2	0.8	1.6	1.9	14.9
Difficulty with or unable to perform one or more IADLs	**4.7**	**1.6**	**2.2**	**6.3**	**9.1**	**17.5**	**51.4**
Going outside alone	2.7	0.8	1.0	4.0	4.6	12.6	43.6
Keeping track of money/bills	1.2	1.1	0.4	2.0	1.1	3.9	21.6
Preparing meals	1.2	1.0	0.4	1.4	1.5	5.3	21.1
Doing light housework	2.8	0.8	1.3	3.7	6.2	11.7	33.4
Taking prescribed medicines	1.0	1.1	0.4	1.1	0.7	4.0	17.9
Using the telephone	0.7	0.6	0.2	0.2	1.4	3.8	12.4
Needs personal assistance with an ADL or an IADL	**3.5**	**1.3**	**1.5**	**4.4**	**5.2**	**14.3**	**46.7**

Note: (–) means sample is too small to make a reliable estimate. An ADL is an activity of daily living; an IADL is an instrumental activity of daily living.
Source: Bureau of the Census, Internet web site, http://www.census.gov

Health Insurance Coverage of Hispanics by Age, 1996

(number and percent distribution of Hispanics by age and health insurance coverage status, 1996; numbers in thousands)

| | | | covered by private or government health insurance | | | | | | |
| | | | private health insurance | | government health insurance | | | | |
	total	total	total	group health	total	Medicaid	Medicare	Champus	not covered
Number									
Total persons	**29,614**	**19,689**	**13,136**	**18,044**	**8,510**	**6,230**	**1,806**	**474**	**9,924**
Under age 18	10,511	7,498	4,188	4,014	3,795	3,563	94	138	3,014
Aged 18 to 24	3,626	1,870	1,302	1,726	679	610	9	60	1,756
Aged 25 to 34	5,494	3,245	2,652	4,410	731	596	47	88	2,249
Aged 35 to 44	4,387	2,854	2,313	3,802	666	545	53	68	1,533
Aged 45 to 54	2,461	1,696	1,439	2,403	356	231	83	42	764
Aged 55 to 64	1,619	1,104	797	1,220	426	238	155	33	515
Aged 65 or older	1,516	1,424	444	470	1,859	448	1,365	46	92
Percent distribution by									
health insurance coverage status									
Total persons	**100.0%**	**66.5%**	**44.4%**	**60.9%**	**28.7%**	**21.0%**	**6.1%**	**1.6%**	**33.5%**
Under age 18	100.0	71.3	39.8	38.2	36.1	33.9	0.9	1.3	28.7
Aged 18 to 24	100.0	51.6	35.9	47.6	18.7	16.8	0.2	1.7	48.4
Aged 25 to 34	100.0	59.1	48.3	80.3	13.3	10.8	0.9	1.6	40.9
Aged 35 to 44	100.0	65.1	52.7	86.7	15.2	12.4	1.2	1.6	34.9
Aged 45 to 54	100.0	68.9	58.5	97.6	14.5	9.4	3.4	1.7	31.0
Aged 55 to 64	100.0	68.2	49.2	75.4	26.3	14.7	9.6	2.0	31.8
Aged 65 or older	100.0	93.9	29.3	31.0	122.6	29.6	90.0	3.0	6.1
Percent distribution by age									
Total persons	**100.0%**	**100.0%**	**100.0%**	**100.0%**	**100.0%**	**100.0%**	**100.0%**	**100.0%**	**100.0%**
Under age 18	35.5	38.1	31.9	22.2	44.6	57.2	5.2	29.1	30.4
Aged 18 to 24	12.2	9.5	9.9	9.6	8.0	9.8	0.5	12.7	17.7
Aged 25 to 34	18.6	16.5	20.2	24.4	8.6	9.6	2.6	18.6	22.7
Aged 35 to 44	14.8	14.5	17.6	21.1	7.8	8.7	2.9	14.3	15.4
Aged 45 to 54	8.3	8.6	11.0	13.3	4.2	3.7	4.6	8.9	7.7
Aged 55 to 64	5.5	5.6	6.1	6.8	5.0	3.8	8.6	7.0	5.2
Aged 65 or older	5.1	7.2	3.4	2.6	21.8	7.2	75.6	9.7	0.9

Note: Numbers will not add to total because some persons have more than one type of health insurance.
Source: Bureau of the Census, unpublished tables from the 1997 Current Population Survey; calculations by New Strategist

Leading Causes of Death among Hispanics, 1995

(total number of deaths among Hispanics, and number and percent accounted for by ten leading causes of death, 1995)

	number	percent
All causes	**94,776**	**100.0%**
1. Diseases of heart	22,403	23.6
2. Malignant neoplasms	17,419	18.4
3. Unintentional injuries	7,784	8.2
4. Human immunodeficiency virus infections	6,110	6.4
5. Cerebrovascular diseases	4,992	5.3
6. Diabetes mellitus	4,194	4.4
7. Homicide and legal intervention	4,009	4.2
8. Pneumonia and influenza	2,694	2.8
9. Chronic liver diseases and cirrhosis	2,684	2.8
10. Chronic obstructive pulmonary diseases	2,329	2.5
All other causes	20,158	21.3

Source: National Center for Health Statistics, Health, United States, 1996–97; *calculations by New Strategist*

Life Expectancy of Hispanics at Birth and Age 65, 1998 to 2020

(average number of years of life remaining at birth and at age 65 for Hispanics by sex, selected years 1998–2020; difference between Hispanic and total life expectancy at birth and at age 65, by sex, 1998 and 2020)

	life expectancy (years)	
	males	females
AT BIRTH		
1998	75.1	82.6
2000	75.2	82.8
2005	75.5	83.3
2010	76.4	84.0
2015	77.4	84.7
2020	78.3	85.4
Life expectancy of Hispanics minus life expectancy of total Americans		
1998	2.3	3.0
2020	2.8	3.9
AT AGE 65		
1998	18.9	22.2
2000	19.1	22.4
2005	19.8	23.0
2010	20.4	23.5
2015	21.0	24.0
2020	21.6	24.5
Life expectancy of Hispanics minus life expectancy of total Americans		
1998	3.2	2.9
2020	4.0	3.9

Source: Bureau of the Census, Population Projections of the United States, by Age, Sex, Race, and Hispanic Origin: 1995 to 2050, *Current Population Reports, P25-1130, 1996; calculations by New Strategist*

Hispanics: Households

Most Hispanic couples have children under age 18 at home.

Largely because of immigration, Hispanic householders are much younger than house-holders in the nation as a whole. Only 11 percent of Hispanic householders are aged 65 or older, versus 22 percent of total householders; 37 percent are under age 35, versus 25 percent of total householders.

Married couples account for 54 percent of Hispanic households, a share that is equal to that of total households. But Hispanic couples are much more likely to be raising children—68 percent have children under age 18 at home as compared with only 47 percent of all married couples. Sixty-six percent of Hispanic children live with both parents, slightly less than the 72 percent of all children who live with both parents.

The marital status of Hispanic men and women is similar to that of the population as a whole. Fifty-four percent of Hispanic men and 57 percent of Hispanic women are currently married. The majority of men aged 30 or older and women aged 25 to 64 are currently married.

■ Nuclear families (married couples with children) are a bigger share of Hispanic households than of both black and white households. This is because many are immigrants from countries where traditional family life is common.

Hispanic households are more traditional than average

(percent distribution of Hispanic and total married couples by presence of children under age 18, 1996)

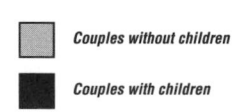

Couples without children

Couples with children

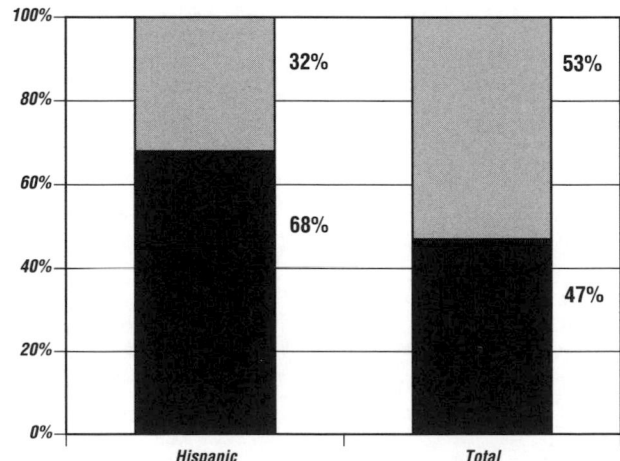

Hispanic Households by Age of Householder, 1996

(number and percent distribution of Hispanic households by age of householder, 1996; numbers in thousands)

	number	percent
Total households	**7,939**	**100.0%**
Under age 25	749	9.4
Aged 25 to 29	964	12.1
Aged 30 to 34	1,231	15.5
Aged 35 to 39	1,154	14.5
Aged 40 to 44	954	12.0
Aged 45 to 54	1,181	14.9
Aged 55 to 64	808	10.2
Aged 65 to 74	609	7.7
Aged 75 or older	288	3.7

Source: Bureau of the Census, Household and Family Characteristics: March 1996, *Current Population Reports, P20-495(U), 1997; calculations by New Strategist*

Hispanic Households by Household Type, 1996

(number and percent distribution of Hispanic households by type, 1996; numbers in thousands)

	number	percent
Total households	**7,939**	**100.0%**
Family households	**6,287**	**79.2**
Married couple families	4,247	53.5
With children under age 18	2,902	36.6
Without children under age 18	1,345	16.9
Female householder, no spouse present	1,604	20.2
With children under age 18	1,283	16.2
Without children under age 18	322	4.1
Male householder, no spouse present	436	5.5
Nonfamily households	**1,652**	**20.8**
Female householder	787	9.9
Living alone	667	8.4
Male householder	865	10.9
Living alone	602	7.6

Source: Bureau of the Census, Household and Family Characteristics: March 1996, *Current Population Reports, P20-495 (Update), 1997; calculations by New Strategist*

Hispanic Households by Age of Householder and Household Type, 1996

(number and percent distribution of Hispanic households by age of householder and household type, 1996; numbers in thousands)

| | total | family households | | | | nonfamily households | |
		total	married couples	female householder no spouse present	male householder no spouse present	female householder	male householder
Total households, number	**7,939**	**6,287**	**4,247**	**1,604**	**436**	**787**	**865**
Under age 20	110	87	28	30	29	15	9
Aged 20 to 24	639	496	266	163	66	69	75
Aged 25 to 29	964	779	526	202	51	56	129
Aged 30 to 34	1,231	1,068	760	233	75	42	122
Aged 35 to 39	1,154	981	654	278	49	41	132
Aged 40 to 44	954	808	534	231	43	45	101
Aged 45 to 49	670	540	377	132	31	60	70
Aged 50 to 54	511	415	285	101	28	54	43
Aged 55 to 59	425	327	236	59	32	57	42
Aged 60 to 64	383	269	205	54	10	66	47
Aged 65 to 74	609	382	283	86	13	171	56
Aged 75 to 84	220	105	73	27	5	83	32
Aged 85 or older	68	32	20	9	3	29	7
Total households, percent	**100.0%**	**79.2%**	**53.5%**	**20.2%**	**5.5%**	**9.9%**	**10.9%**
Under age 20	100.0	79.1	25.5	27.3	26.4	13.6	8.2
Aged 20 to 24	100.0	77.6	41.6	25.5	10.3	10.8	11.7
Aged 25 to 29	100.0	80.8	54.6	21.0	5.3	5.8	13.4
Aged 30 to 34	100.0	86.8	61.7	18.9	6.1	3.4	9.9
Aged 35 to 39	100.0	85.0	56.7	24.1	4.2	3.6	11.4
Aged 40 to 44	100.0	84.7	56.0	24.2	4.5	4.7	10.6
Aged 45 to 49	100.0	80.6	56.3	19.7	4.6	9.0	10.4
Aged 50 to 54	100.0	81.2	55.8	19.8	5.5	10.6	8.4
Aged 55 to 59	100.0	76.9	55.5	13.9	7.5	13.4	9.9
Aged 60 to 64	100.0	70.2	53.5	14.1	2.6	17.2	12.3
Aged 65 to 74	100.0	62.7	46.5	14.1	2.1	28.1	9.2
Aged 75 to 84	100.0	47.7	33.2	12.3	2.3	37.7	14.5
Aged 85 or older	100.0	47.1	29.4	13.2	4.4	42.6	10.3

Source: Bureau of the Census, Household and Family Characteristics: March 1996, *Current Population Reports, P20-495(Update), 1997; calculations by New Strategist*

Hispanic Households by Size, 1996

(number and percent distribution of Hispanic households by size, 1996; numbers in thousands)

	number	percent
Total households	**7,939**	**100.0%**
One person	1,260	15.9
Two persons	1,788	22.5
Three persons	1,528	19.2
Four persons	1,508	19.0
Five persons	964	12.1
Six persons	523	6.6
Seven or more persons	368	4.6

Source: Bureau of the Census, Household and Family Characteristics: March 1996, *Current Population Reports, P20-495(Update), 1997; calculations by New Strategist*

Hispanic Married Couples by Presence of Children and Age of Householder, 1996

(number and percent distribution of Hispanic married couples by presence and number of own children under age 18 at home and by age of householder, 1996; numbers in thousands)

	total	< age 20	20–24	25–29	30–34	35–39	40–44	45–54	55–64	65+
					age of householder					
Married couples, number	**4,247**	**28**	**266**	**526**	**760**	**654**	**534**	**662**	**441**	**376**
Without children <18	1,515	14	79	136	124	69	77	285	366	365
With children <18	2,731	13	187	390	636	585	457	377	75	11
One	896	9	99	150	164	99	129	189	51	6
Two	998	4	67	159	230	213	182	125	13	5
Three or more	837	–	21	82	243	274	145	62	10	–
Married couples, percent	**100.0%**	**100.0%**	**100.0%**	**100.0%**	**100.0%**	**100.0%**	**100.0%**	**100.0%**	**100.0%**	**100.0%**
Without children <18	35.7	50.0	29.7	25.9	16.3	10.6	14.4	43.1	83.0	97.1
With children <18	64.3	46.4	70.3	74.1	83.7	89.4	85.6	56.9	17.0	2.9
One	21.1	32.1	37.2	28.5	21.6	15.1	24.2	28.5	11.6	1.6
Two	23.5	14.3	25.2	30.2	30.3	32.6	34.1	18.9	2.9	1.3
Three or more	19.7	–	7.9	15.6	32.0	41.9	27.2	9.4	2.3	–

Note: (–) means sample is too small to make a reliable estimate.
Source: Bureau of the Census, Household and Family Characteristics: March 1996, *Current Population Reports, P20-495(Update), 1997; calculations by New Strategist*

Hispanic Female-Headed Families by Presence of Children and Age of Householder, 1996

(number and percent distribution of Hispanic female-headed families by presence and number of own children under age 18 at home and by age of householder, 1996; numbers in thousands)

	total	< age 20	20–24	25–29	30–34	35–39	40–44	45–54	55–64	65+
						age of householder				
Female-headed families, number	**1,604**	**30**	**163**	**202**	**233**	**278**	**231**	**233**	**113**	**122**
Without children <18	466	9	23	22	13	19	52	117	95	117
With children <18	1,138	21	140	180	220	259	179	116	18	5
One	462	6	58	57	63	95	85	84	12	3
Two	389	15	52	65	73	87	69	22	6	–
Three or more	288	–	30	58	84	78	26	10	–	2
Female-headed families, percent	**100.0%**	**100.0%**	**100.0%**	**100.0%**	**100.0%**	**100.0%**	**100.0%**	**100.0%**	**100.0%**	**100.0%**
Without children <18	29.1	30.0	14.1	10.9	5.6	6.8	22.5	50.2	84.1	95.9
With children <18	70.9	70.0	85.9	89.1	94.4	93.2	77.5	49.8	15.9	4.1
One	28.8	20.0	35.6	28.2	27.0	34.2	36.8	36.1	10.6	2.5
Two	24.3	50.0	31.9	32.2	31.3	31.3	29.9	9.4	5.3	–
Three or more	18.0	–	18.4	28.7	36.1	28.1	11.3	4.3	–	1.6

Note: (–) means sample is too small to make a reliable estimate.
Source: Bureau of the Census, Household and Family Characteristics: March 1996, *Current Population Reports, P20-495(Update), 1997; calculations by New Strategist*

Hispanic Single-Person Households by Age of Householder, 1996

(number and percent distribution of Hispanic single-person households and single-person households as a percent of total Hispanic households, by age of householder, 1996; numbers in thousands)

	number	*percent*	*percent of total Hispanic households*
Total households	**1,260**	**100.0%**	**15.9%**
Under age 25	79	6.3	10.5
Aged 25 to 29	100	7.9	10.4
Aged 30 to 34	105	8.3	8.5
Aged 35 to 39	124	9.8	10.7
Aged 40 to 44	112	8.9	11.7
Aged 45 to 54	191	15.2	16.2
Aged 55 to 64	181	14.4	22.4
Aged 65 to 74	222	17.6	36.5
Aged 75 or older	146	11.6	50.7
Median age (years)	50.3		

Source: Bureau of the Census, Household and Family Characteristics: March 1996, *Current Population Reports, P20-495(Update), 1997; calculations by New Strategist*

Living Arrangements of Hispanic Children by Age, 1995

(number and percent distribution of Hispanic children by living arrangement, marital status of parent, and age of child, 1995; numbers in thousands)

	total	under age 6	aged 6 to 11	aged 12 to 17
Number with one or both parents	**9,405**	**3,767**	**2,996**	**2,643**
Living with both parents	6,191	2,450	2,038	1,703
Living with mother only	2,798	1,157	825	816
Never married	1,017	622	255	140
Divorced	766	184	280	302
Married, spouse absent	889	328	253	308
Widowed	126	23	36	67
Living with father only	417	159	133	124
Never married	183	127	47	9
Divorced	135	16	55	65
Married, spouse absent	79	12	26	41
Widowed	20	5	6	9
Percent with one or both parents	**100.0%**	**100.0%**	**100.0%**	**100.0%**
Living with both parents	65.8	65.0	68.0	64.4
Living with mother only	29.8	30.7	27.5	30.9
Never married	10.8	16.5	8.5	5.3
Divorced	8.1	4.9	9.3	11.4
Married, spouse absent	9.5	8.7	8.4	11.7
Widowed	1.3	0.6	1.2	2.5
Living with father only	4.4	4.2	4.4	4.7
Never married	1.9	3.4	1.6	0.3
Divorced	1.4	0.4	1.8	2.5
Married, spouse absent	0.8	0.3	0.9	1.6
Widowed	0.2	–	0.2	0.3

Note: (–) means sample is too small to make a reliable estimate.
Source: Bureau of the Census, Marital Status and Living Arrangements: March 1995, *Current Population Reports, P20-491, 1996; calculations by New Strategist*

Living Arrangements of Hispanic Men by Age, 1995

(number and percent distribution of Hispanic men aged 18 or older by living arrangement and age, 1995; numbers in thousands)

	total	18 to 19	20 to 24	25 to 29	30 to 34	35 to 39	40 to 44	45 to 54	55 to 64	65 to 74	75 or older
Hispanic men, number	**8,821**	**475**	**1,344**	**1,357**	**1,415**	**1,097**	**803**	**1,093**	**603**	**446**	**188**
Family householder or spouse	4,692	27	307	594	814	694	566	820	456	307	107
Child of householder	1,363	287	523	213	136	100	43	52	7	2	–
Other member of family household	1,090	76	213	210	180	102	69	73	66	62	39
Nonfamily householder	782	12	62	139	131	112	70	87	59	71	39
Other member of nonfamily household	868	69	231	191	150	89	55	61	15	4	3
Group quarters*	26	4	8	10	4	–	–	–	–	–	–
Hispanic men, percent	**100.0%**	**100.0%**	**100.0%**	**100.0%**	**100.0%**	**100.0%**	**100.0%**	**100.0%**	**100.0%**	**100.0%**	**100.0%**
Family householder or spouse	53.2	5.7	22.8	43.8	57.5	63.3	70.5	75.0	75.6	68.8	56.9
Child of householder	15.5	60.4	38.9	15.7	9.6	9.1	5.4	4.8	1.2	0.4	–
Other member of family household	12.4	16.0	15.8	15.5	12.7	9.3	8.6	6.7	10.9	13.9	20.7
Nonfamily householder	8.9	2.5	4.6	10.2	9.3	10.2	8.7	8.0	9.8	15.9	20.7
Other member of nonfamily household	9.8	14.5	17.2	14.1	10.6	8.1	6.8	5.6	2.5	0.9	1.6
Group quarters*	0.3	0.8	0.6	0.7	0.3	–	–	–	–	–	–

* The Current Population Survey does not include people living in institutions such as prisons, the military, or college dormitories. It defines people living in group quarters as those in noninstitutional living arrangements that are not conventional housing units, such as rooming houses, staff quarters at a hospital, and halfway houses.
Note: (–) means sample is too small to make a reliable estimate.
Source: Bureau of the Census, Marital Status and Living Arrangements: March 1995, Current Population Reports, P20-491, 1996; calculations by New Strategist

Living Arrangements of Hispanic Women by Age, 1995

(number and percent distribution of Hispanic women aged 18 or older by living arrangement and age, 1995; numbers in thousands)

	total	18 to 19	20 to 24	25 to 29	30 to 34	35 to 39	40 to 44	45 to 54	55 to 64	65 to 74	75 or older
Hispanic women, number	**8,797**	**494**	**1,135**	**1,243**	**1,201**	**1,071**	**890**	**1,178**	**791**	**513**	**281**
Family householder or spouse	5,886	71	503	837	983	877	748	941	564	270	92
Child of householder	958	316	342	128	64	38	30	21	16	2	1
Other member of family household	875	72	152	125	67	70	49	90	102	67	81
Nonfamily householder	747	10	59	75	48	40	47	95	99	171	103
Other member of nonfamily household	328	25	77	77	39	46	16	31	10	3	4
Group quarters*	3	–	2	1	–	–	–	–	–	–	–
Hispanic women, percent	**100.0%**	**100.0%**	**100.0%**	**100.0%**	**100.0%**	**100.0%**	**100.0%**	**100.0%**	**100.0%**	**100.0%**	**100.0%**
Family householder or spouse	66.9	14.4	44.3	67.3	81.8	81.9	84.0	79.9	71.3	52.6	32.7
Child of householder	10.9	64.0	30.1	10.3	5.3	3.5	3.4	1.8	2.0	0.4	0.4
Other member of family household	9.9	14.6	13.4	10.1	5.6	6.5	5.5	7.6	12.9	13.1	28.8
Nonfamily householder	8.5	2.0	5.2	6.0	4.0	3.7	5.3	8.1	12.5	33.3	36.7
Other member of nonfamily household	3.7	5.1	6.8	6.2	3.2	4.3	1.8	2.6	1.3	0.6	1.4
Group quarters*	0.0	–	0.2	0.1	–	–	–	–	–	–	–

* The Current Population Survey does not include people living in institutions such as prisons, the military, or college dormitories. It defines people living in group quarters as those in noninstitutional living arrangements that are not conventional housing units, such as rooming houses, staff quarters at a hospital, and halfway houses.

Note: (–) means sample is too small to make a reliable estimate.

Source: Bureau of the Census, Marital Status and Living Arrangements: March 1995, Current Population Reports, P20-491, 1996; calculations by New Strategist

Marital Status of Hispanic Men by Age, 1995

(number and percent distribution of Hispanic men aged 15 or older by age and marital status, 1995; numbers in thousands)

	total	never married	married	divorced	widowed
Total men, number	**9,555**	**3,703**	**5,115**	**581**	**157**
Aged 15 to 19	1,208	1,182	25	1	–
Aged 20 to 24	1,344	976	360	8	–
Aged 25 to 29	1,357	645	650	62	–
Aged 30 to 34	1,415	409	903	100	3
Aged 35 to 39	1,097	250	748	93	5
Aged 40 to 44	803	95	617	90	1
Aged 45 to 54	1,093	96	865	117	14
Aged 55 to 64	603	31	500	54	18
Aged 65 to 74	446	10	333	39	64
Aged 75 to 84	144	7	91	15	32
Aged 85 or older	44	2	22	2	18
Total men, percent	**100.0%**	**38.8%**	**53.5%**	**6.1%**	**1.6%**
Aged 15 to 19	100.0	97.8	2.1	0.1	–
Aged 20 to 24	100.0	72.6	26.8	0.6	–
Aged 25 to 29	100.0	47.5	47.9	4.6	–
Aged 30 to 34	100.0	28.9	63.8	7.1	0.2
Aged 35 to 39	100.0	22.8	68.2	8.5	0.5
Aged 40 to 44	100.0	11.8	76.8	11.2	0.1
Aged 45 to 54	100.0	8.8	79.1	10.7	1.3
Aged 55 to 64	100.0	5.1	82.9	9.0	3.0
Aged 65 to 74	100.0	2.2	74.7	8.7	14.3
Aged 75 to 84	100.0	4.9	63.2	10.4	22.2
Aged 85 or older	100.0	4.5	50.0	4.5	40.9

Note: (–) means sample is too small to make a reliable estimate.
Source: Bureau of the Census, Marital Status and Living Arrangements: March 1995, *Current Population Reports, P20-491, 1996*

Marital Status of Hispanic Women by Age, 1995

(number and percent distribution of Hispanic women aged 15 or older by age and marital status, 1995; numbers in thousands)

	total	never married	married	divorced	widowed
Total women, number	**9,433**	**2,681**	**5,360**	**809**	**582**
Aged 15 to 19	1,129	1,030	95	2	2
Aged 20 to 24	1,135	588	510	35	3
Aged 25 to 29	1,243	385	795	61	2
Aged 30 to 34	1,201	229	863	100	10
Aged 35 to 39	1,071	144	752	156	19
Aged 40 to 44	890	97	642	131	20
Aged 45 to 54	1,178	95	868	154	61
Aged 55 to 64	791	52	525	99	115
Aged 65 to 74	513	45	245	60	163
Aged 75 to 84	215	13	56	11	134
Aged 85 or older	66	2	11	1	52
Total women, percent	**100.0%**	**28.4%**	**56.8%**	**8.6%**	**6.2%**
Aged 15 to 19	100.0	91.2	8.4	0.2	0.2
Aged 20 to 24	100.0	51.8	44.9	3.1	0.3
Aged 25 to 29	100.0	31.0	64.0	4.9	0.2
Aged 30 to 34	100.0	19.1	71.9	8.3	0.8
Aged 35 to 39	100.0	13.4	70.2	14.6	1.8
Aged 40 to 44	100.0	10.9	72.1	14.7	2.2
Aged 45 to 54	100.0	8.1	73.7	13.1	5.2
Aged 55 to 64	100.0	6.6	66.4	12.5	14.5
Aged 65 to 74	100.0	8.8	47.8	11.7	31.8
Aged 75 to 84	100.0	6.0	26.0	5.1	62.3
Aged 85 or older	100.0	3.0	16.7	1.5	78.8

Source: Bureau of the Census, Marital Status and Living Arrangements: March 1995, *Current Population Reports, P20-491, 1996*

Hispanics: Housing

Hispanics are much less likely to own a home than the average American.

Forty-two percent of the nation's 7.8 million Hispanic householders own their home. This compares with a homeownership rate of 65 percent for all Americans. Hispanic homeowners valued their homes at a median of $89,851 in 1995. Most bought their homes using savings for the down payment.

Regardless of homeownership status, most Hispanics are satisfied with their homes. On a scale of 1 to 10, with 1 being the worst and 10 the best, 67 percent rate their homes an eight or higher. Most Hispanics are also satisfied with their neighborhoods. Only 11 percent say their neighborhood has a crime problem.

Hispanic householders are much more likely to be without a telephone than the average American—17 versus 6 percent. Among Puerto Ricans, 22 percent have no phone available.

Twenty-one percent of Hispanics moved between March 1995 and March 1996. This mobility rate is higher than that of the total population because Hispanics are younger than average and because so many are renters, who have higher mobility rates than homeowners.

■ Hispanic homeownership will continue to lag behind that of the average American because so many Hispanics are immigrants with low incomes.

Most Hispanic households are in the South or West

(percent distribution of Hispanic households by region, 1995)

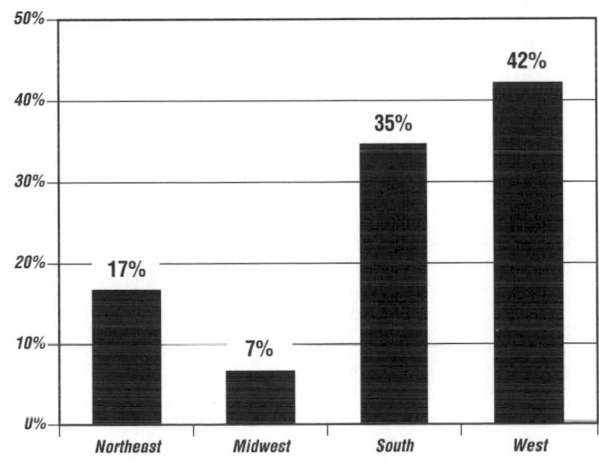

Region of Residence and Metropolitan Status
of Housing Units Occupied by Hispanics, 1995

(number, percent distribution, and percent of housing units occupied by Hispanics, by regional, metropolitan, and homeownership status, 1995; numbers in thousands)

	total		owner			renter		
	number	percent distrib.	number	percent distrib.	percent of total	number	percent distrib.	percent of total
Total occupied housing units	**7,757**	**100.0%**	**3,245**	**100.0%**	**41.8%**	**4,512**	**100.0%**	**58.2%**
Northeast	1,294	16.7	298	9.1	22.9	996	22.1	77.0
Midwest	510	6.6	262	8.1	51.4	248	5.5	48.6
South	2,686	34.6	1,392	42.9	51.8	1,294	28.7	48.2
West	3,267	42.1	1,293	39.8	39.6	1,973	43.7	60.4
In metropolitan areas	7,037	90.7	2,842	87.6	40.4	4,195	93.0	59.6
In central cities	3,803	49.0	1,228	37.8	32.3	2,576	57.1	67.7
In suburbs	3,234	41.7	1,614	49.7	49.9	1,619	35.9	50.1
Outside metropolitan areas	720	9.3	403	12.4	56.0	317	7.0	44.0

Source: Bureau of the Census, American Housing Survey for the United States in 1995, *Current Housing Reports, H150/95, 1997; calculations by New Strategist*

Characteristics of Housing Units Occupied by Hispanics, 1995

(number and percent distribution of housing units occupied by Hispanics, by selected housing characteristics and homeownership status, 1995; numbers in thousands)

	total		owner-occupied		renter-occupied	
	number	*percent*	*number*	*percent*	*number*	*percent*
Total occupied housing units	**7,757**	**100.0%**	**3,245**	**100.0%**	**4,512**	**100.0%**
Units in structure						
One, detached	3,699	47.7	2,677	82.5	1,021	22.6
One, attached	393	5.1	129	4.0	264	5.9
Two to four	1,170	15.1	133	4.1	1,037	23.0
Five to nine	687	8.9	29	0.9	658	14.6
10 to 19	561	7.2	19	0.6	542	12.0
20 to 49	568	7.3	26	0.8	541	12.0
50 or more	387	5.0	30	0.9	358	7.9
Mobile home or trailer	292	3.8	201	6.2	91	2.0
Median number of rooms in unit	**5**	**–**	**6**	**–**	**4**	**–**
Median square footage of unit	**1,377**	**–**	**1,468**	**–**	**1,118**	**–**
Number of bathrooms						
None	52	0.7	7	0.2	45	1.0
One	4,646	59.9	1,172	36.1	3,475	77.0
One and one-half	787	10.1	443	13.7	344	7.6
Two or more	2,272	29.3	1,623	50.0	648	14.4
Primary heating fuel						
Housing units with heating fuel	7,423	95.7	3,146	96.9	4,277	94.8
Electricity	2,198	28.3	908	28.0	1,290	28.6
Piped gas	4,009	51.7	1,846	56.9	2,163	47.9
Bottled gas	122	1.6	81	2.5	41	0.9
Fuel oil	752	9.7	149	4.6	603	13.4
Kerosene or other liquid fuel	32	0.4	18	0.6	14	0.3
Coal or coke	7	0.1	2	0.1	4	–
Wood	250	3.2	122	3.8	128	2.8
Solar energy	–	–	–	–	–	–
Other	52	0.7	18	0.6	34	0.8

(continued)

(continued from previous page)

Selected equipment	total		owner-occupied		renter-occupied	
	number	*percent*	*number*	*percent*	*number*	*percent*
Dishwasher	2,717	35.0%	1,468	45.2%	1,249	27.7%
Washing machine	4,581	59.1	2,941	90.6	1,640	36.3
Clothes dryer	3,497	45.1	2,423	74.7	1,074	23.8
Disposal in kitchen sink	3,213	41.4	1,411	43.5	1,802	39.9
Air conditioning	2,878	37.1	1,515	46.7	1,363	30.2
Porch, deck, balcony, or patio	5,005	64.5	2,597	80.0	2,408	53.4
Telephone	6,725	86.7	3,058	94.2	3,667	81.3
Usable fireplace	1,422	18.3	992	30.6	430	9.5
Garage or carport	3,689	47.6	2,326	71.7	1,363	30.2
Cars and trucks available						
No cars, trucks, or vans	1,327	17.1	125	3.9	1,202	26.6
One car, with or without						
trucks or vans	3,564	45.9	1,464	45.1	2,100	46.5
Two or more cars	2,164	27.9	1,310	40.4	854	18.9
Overall opinion of housing unit						
1 (worst)	96	1.2	11	0.3	85	1.9
2	49	0.6	8	0.2	41	0.9
3	97	1.3	12	0.4	86	1.9
4	126	1.6	26	0.8	100	2.2
5	721	9.3	146	4.5	576	12.8
6	433	5.6	148	4.6	284	6.3
7	932	12.0	295	9.1	638	14.1
8	1,884	24.3	769	23.7	1,115	24.7
9	1,091	14.1	568	17.5	523	11.6
10 (best)	2,224	28.7	1,254	38.6	970	21.5

Note: (–) means not applicable or sample is too small to make a reliable estimate.
Source: Bureau of the Census, American Housing Survey for the United States in 1995, Current Housing Reports, H150/95, 1997; calculations by New Strategist

Telephone Availability for Hispanic Households by Ethnicity, 1996

(number and percent distribution of total and Hispanic households by telephone availability and ethnicity, 1996; numbers in thousands)

	total households	total Hispanic	Mexican	Puerto Rican	Cuban	Central & S. Amer.	other Hispanic
Total households	**99,627**	**7,939**	**4,660**	**1,029**	**444**	**1,138**	**667**
Telephone in household	91,705	6,328	3,676	770	376	948	558
Telephone available to household	1,777	245	143	35	16	29	23
Telephone not available	6,146	1,366	842	224	53	161	86
Total households	**100.0%**	**100.0%**	**100.0%**	**100.0%**	**100.0%**	**100.0%**	**100.0%**
Telephone in household	92.0	79.7	78.9	74.9	84.6	83.3	83.6
Telephone available to household	1.8	3.1	3.1	3.4	3.5	2.5	3.5
Telephone not available	6.2	17.2	18.1	21.8	11.9	14.1	12.9

Source: Bureau of the Census, Internet web site http://www.census.gov

Neighborhood Characteristics of Housing Units Occupied by Hispanics, 1995

(number and percent distribution of housing units occupied by Hispanics, by selected neighborhood characteristics and homeownership status, 1995; numbers in thousands)

	total		owner-occupied		renter-occupied	
	number	*percent*	*number*	*percent*	*number*	*percent*
Total occupied housing units	**7,757**	**100.0%**	**3,245**	**100.0%**	**4,512**	**100.0%**
Overall opinion of neighborhood						
1 (worst)	216	2.8	24	0.7	192	4.3
2	81	1.0	22	0.7	59	1.3
3	159	2.0	34	1.0	125	2.8
4	211	2.7	63	1.9	148	3.3
5	793	10.2	254	7.8	539	11.9
6	504	6.5	149	4.6	355	7.9
7	764	9.8	324	10.0	440	9.8
8	1,606	20.7	673	20.7	933	20.7
9	972	12.5	480	14.8	492	10.9
10 (best)	2,264	29.2	1,185	36.5	1,079	23.9
Neighborhood problems						
No problems	4,657	60.0	2,053	63.3	2,604	57.7
With problems*	2,892	37.3	1,149	35.4	1,743	38.6
Crime	871	11.2	243	7.5	627	13.9
Noise	751	9.7	191	5.9	560	12.4
Traffic	484	6.2	200	6.2	284	6.3
Litter or housing deterioration	398	9.0	166	5.1	232	5.1
Poor city or county services	128	1.7	65	2.0	63	1.4
Undesirable commerical, institutional, industrial	89	1.1	40	1.2	49	1.1
People	1,146	14.8	373	11.5	773	17.1
Other	623	8.0	321	9.9	302	6.7
Not reported	47	0.6	22	0.7	25	0.6

* Numbers will not add to total because more than one problem could be cited.
Source: Bureau of the Census, American Housing Survey for the United States in 1995, Current Housing Reports, H150/95, 1997; calculations by New Strategist

Housing Value and Purchase Price
for Hispanic Homeowners, 1995

(number and percent distribution of Hispanic homeowners by value of home, purchase price, and major source of down payment, 1995; numbers in thousands)

	number	percent
Total homeowners	**3,245**	**100.0%**
Value of home		
Under $50,000	810	25.0
$50,000 to $79,999	618	19.0
$80,000 to $99,999	396	12.2
$100,000 to $149,999	646	19.9
$150,000 to $199,999	401	12.4
$200,000 to $299,999	270	8.3
$300,000 or more	105	3.2
Median	$89,851	
Purchase price*		
Home purchased or built	3,162	97.4
Under $50,000	1,332	41.0
$50,000 to $79,999	512	15.8
$80,000 to $99,999	257	7.9
$100,000 to $149,999	335	10.3
$150,000 to $199,999	208	6.4
$200,000 to $299,999	91	2.8
$300,000 or more	29	0.9
Received as inheritance or gift	65	2.0
Median purchase price	$52,708	
Major source of down payment*		
Sale of previous home	548	16.9
Savings or cash on hand	1,830	56.4
Sale of other investment	15	0.5
Borrowing, other than mortgage on this property	100	3.1
Inheritance or gift	85	2.6
Land where building built used for financing	15	0.5
Other	187	5.8
No down payment	205	6.3

* Numbers may not add to total because "not reported" is not shown.
Source: Bureau of the Census, American Housing Survey for the United States in 1995, *Current Housing Reports, H150/95RV, 1997; calculations by New Strategist*

Geographical Mobility of the Hispanic Population by Age, 1995–96

(total number of Hispanics aged 1 or older, and number and percent of those who moved between March 1995 and March 1996, by age of person and type of move; numbers in thousands)

			different house in the U.S.							
					different county					
							different state			
	total	same house (non-movers)	total	same county	total	same state	total	same region	different region	moved from abroad
Number										
Total, aged 1 or older	**27,729**	**21,340**	**5,878**	**4,713**	**1,165**	**594**	**571**	**266**	**305**	**511**
Aged 1 to 4	2,685	1,855	786	671	115	65	50	20	30	44
Aged 5 to 9	2,915	2,250	621	512	109	47	62	22	40	44
Aged 10 to 14	2,549	2,088	430	336	94	39	55	26	29	32
Aged 15 to 19	2,433	1,890	493	386	107	51	56	37	20	51
Aged 15 to 17	1,449	1,174	249	196	53	28	25	12	13	26
Aged 18 and 19	984	715	244	189	54	23	31	24	7	25
Aged 20 to 24	2,606	1,657	851	691	160	105	55	26	29	98
Aged 25 to 29	2,612	1,707	832	666	167	77	90	52	37	73
Aged 30 to 34	2,743	2,030	631	502	129	64	64	28	36	83
Aged 35 to 39	2,343	1,874	424	326	98	60	38	14	25	45
Aged 40 to 44	1,722	1,412	293	218	76	28	48	12	36	17
Aged 45 to 49	1,194	1,025	160	122	38	17	21	10	11	9
Aged 50 to 54	977	852	119	90	29	13	17	10	6	6
Aged 55 to 59	806	729	72	56	15	13	2	2	–	5
Aged 60 to 64	686	628	55	42	13	5	8	5	2	3
Aged 60 and 61	300	268	29	23	7	4	3	1	1	3
Aged 62 to 64	386	361	25	19	6	1	5	4	1	–
Aged 65 to 69	591	545	46	39	7	2	4	–	4	–
Aged 70 to 74	392	368	23	21	3	1	1	1	–	–
Aged 75 to 79	235	218	15	11	3	3	–	–	–	2
Aged 80 to 84	121	114	7	7	–	–	–	–	–	–
Aged 85 or older	119	98	21	17	5	5	–	–	–	–
Median age	26.3	27.7	23.6	23.3	25.0	24.6	25.4	25.2	25.7	24.3

(continued)

(continued from previous page)

Percent	total	same house (non- movers)	total	same county	total	same state	total	same region	different region	moved from abroad
					different house in the U.S.					
							different county			
								different state		
Total, aged 1 or older	**100.0%**	**77.0%**	**21.2%**	**17.0%**	**4.2%**	**2.1%**	**2.1%**	**1.0%**	**1.1%**	**1.8%**
Aged 1 to 4	100.0	69.1	29.3	25.0	4.3	2.4	1.9	0.7	1.1	1.6
Aged 5 to 9	100.0	77.2	21.3	17.6	3.7	1.6	2.1	0.8	1.4	1.5
Aged 10 to 14	100.0	81.9	16.9	13.2	3.7	1.5	2.2	1.0	1.1	1.3
Aged 15 to 19	100.0	77.7	20.3	15.9	4.4	2.1	2.3	1.5	0.8	2.1
Aged 15 to 17	100.0	81.0	17.2	13.5	3.7	1.9	1.7	0.8	0.9	1.8
Aged 18 and 19	100.0	72.7	24.8	19.2	5.5	2.3	3.2	2.4	0.7	2.5
Aged 20 to 24	100.0	63.6	32.7	26.5	6.1	4.0	2.1	1.0	1.1	3.8
Aged 25 to 29	100.0	65.4	31.9	25.5	6.4	2.9	3.4	2.0	1.4	2.8
Aged 30 to 34	100.0	74.0	23.0	18.3	4.7	2.3	2.3	1.0	1.3	3.0
Aged 35 to 39	100.0	80.0	18.1	13.9	4.2	2.6	1.6	0.6	1.1	1.9
Aged 40 to 44	100.0	82.0	17.0	12.7	4.4	1.6	2.8	0.7	2.1	1.0
Aged 45 to 49	100.0	85.8	13.4	10.2	3.2	1.4	1.8	0.8	0.9	0.8
Aged 50 to 54	100.0	87.2	12.2	9.2	3.0	1.3	1.7	1.0	0.6	0.6
Aged 55 to 59	100.0	90.4	8.9	6.9	1.9	1.6	0.2	0.2	–	0.6
Aged 60 to 64	100.0	91.5	8.0	6.1	1.9	0.7	1.2	0.7	0.3	0.4
Aged 60 and 61	100.0	89.3	9.7	7.7	2.3	1.3	1.0	0.3	0.3	1.0
Aged 62 to 64	100.0	93.5	6.5	4.9	1.6	0.3	1.3	1.0	0.3	–
Aged 65 to 69	100.0	92.2	7.8	6.6	1.2	0.3	0.7	–	0.7	–
Aged 70 to 74	100.0	93.9	5.9	5.4	0.8	0.3	0.3	0.3	–	–
Aged 75 to 79	100.0	92.8	6.4	4.7	1.3	1.3	–	–	–	0.9
Aged 80 to 84	100.0	94.2	5.8	5.8	–	–	–	–	–	–
Aged 85 or older	100.0	82.4	17.6	14.3	4.2	4.2	–	–	–	–

Note: (–) means sample is too small to make a reliable estimate.
Source: Bureau of the Census, Geographical Mobility: March 1995 to March 1996, *Current Population Reports, P20-497(Update), 1997; calculations by New Strategist*

Reasons for Moving among Hispanic Households by Homeownership Status, 1995

(number and percent distribution of Hispanic households that moved in the past 12 months by reason for move and for choosing new neighborhood and house, and by comparison with previous home and neighborhood, by homeownership status, 1995; numbers in thousands)

	total		owner-occupied		renter-occupied	
	number	*percent*	*number*	*percent*	*number*	*percent*
Total movers	**2,041**	**100.0%**	**332**	**100.0%**	**1,709**	**100.0%**
Reasons for leaving previous unit*						
Private displacement	117	5.7	19	5.7	98	5.7
Government displacement	24	1.2	1	–	23	1.3
Disaster loss	5	0.2	–	–	5	0.3
New job or job transfer	138	6.8	10	3.0	128	7.5
To be closer to work, school, other	225	11.0	22	6.6	203	11.9
Other, financial or employment-related	106	5.2	6	1.8	100	5.9
To establish own household	367	18.0	58	17.5	308	18.0
Needed larger house or apartment	326	16.0	62	18.7	264	15.4
Married	45	2.2	13	3.9	31	1.8
Widowed, divorced, or separated	59	2.9	12	3.6	47	2.8
Other, family or person-related	190	9.3	25	7.5	165	9.7
Wanted better home	285	14.0	50	15.1	235	13.8
Change from owner to renter	20	1.0	–	–	20	1.2
Change from renter to owner	112	5.5	112	33.7	–	–
Wanted lower rent or maintenance	134	6.6	7	2.1	127	7.4
Choice of present neighborhood*						
Convenient to job	450	22.0	36	10.8	414	24.2
Convenient to friends or relatives	419	20.5	52	15.7	367	21.5
Convenient to leisure activities	48	2.4	9	2.7	39	2.3
Convenient to public transportation	102	5.0	7	2.1	95	5.6
Good schools	207	10.1	44	13.3	163	9.5
Other public services	51	2.5	16	4.8	35	2.0
Looks or design of neighborhood	310	15.2	70	21.1	239	14.0
House was most important consideration	479	23.5	128	38.6	351	20.5
Neighborhood search						
Looked at just this neighborhood	944	46.3	82	24.7	862	50.4
Looked at other neighborhoods	1,014	49.7	233	70.2	781	45.7

(continued)

(continued from previous page)

Choice of present home*	total		owner-occupied		renter-occupied	
	number	percent	number	percent	number	percent
Financial reasons	891	43.7%	173	52.1%	718	42.0%
Room layout or design	338	16.6	90	27.1	248	14.5
Kitchen	26	1.3	14	0.0	12	0.7
Size	355	17.4	65	19.6	290	17.0
Exterior appearance	116	5.7	31	9.3	86	5.0
Yard, trees, view	106	5.2	37	11.1	70	4.1
Quality of construction	46	2.3	19	5.7	27	1.6
Only one available	262	12.8	21	6.3	241	14.1
Other reasons	532	26.1	77	23.2	454	26.6
Comparison to previous home						
Better home	1,125	55.1	231	69.6	894	52.3
Worse home	305	14.9	23	6.9	282	16.5
About the same	525	25.7	59	17.8	466	27.3
Comparison to previous neighborhood						
Better neighborhood	821	40.2	180	54.2	641	37.5
Worse neighborhood	293	14.4	22	6.6	270	15.8
About the same	692	33.9	94	28.3	598	35.0
Same neighborhood	155	7.6	18	5.4	137	8.0

* Numbers may not add to total because more than one category may apply and unreported reasons are not shown.
Note: (–) means not applicable or sample is too small to make a reliable estimate.
Source: Bureau of the Census, American Housing Survey for the United States in 1995, *Current Housing Reports, H150/95RV, 1997; calculations by New Strategist*

Hispanic Homeownership in the 50 Metropolitan Areas with the Most Hispanic Households, 1990

(number of Hispanic households, percent of total households that are Hispanic, percent of Hispanic households that are owner occupied, and median value of Hispanic owner-occupied houses, in the U.S. and in the 50 metropolitan areas with the most Hispanic households, ranked alphabetically, 1990; numbers in thousands)

	number	Hispanic share of total households	owner-occupied percent	owner-occupied median value
Total Hispanic households	**6,002**	**6.5%**	**42.4%**	**$77,200**
Albuquerque, NM	58	31.1	59.7	69,500
Anaheim–Santa Ana, CA	121	14.7	39.2	201,200
Austin, TX	47	15.6	39.6	56,300
Bakersfield, CA	36	19.6	43.9	64,600
Bergen–Passaic, NJ	41	8.9	31.5	195,500
Boston, MA	37	3.4	19.1	176,100
Brownsville–Harlingen, TX	53	71.7	60.9	33,500
Chicago, IL	189	8.5	36.7	84,500
Corpus Christi, TX	51	43.4	57.2	40,500
Dallas, TX	95	9.9	38.2	58,100
Denver, CO	66	10.1	47.6	70,500
Detroit, MI	25	1.6	58.8	52,300
El Paso, TX	108	60.3	58.2	50,500
Fort Lauderdale–Hollywood–Pompano Beach, FL	35	6.7	54.2	85,000
Fort Worth-Arlington, TX	40	8.1	45.6	50,100
Fresno, CA	59	26.8	40.8	64,900
Houston, TX	187	15.7	39.3	44,200
Jersey City, NJ	60	28.7	20.0	164,500
Laredo, TX	31	90.9	61.3	47,800
Las Cruces, NM	21	47.2	66.0	52,200
Las Vegas, NV	24	8.4	39.0	81,700
Los Angeles–Long Beach, CA	784	26.2	35.1	172,800
McAllen–Edinburg–Mission, TX	79	76.3	68.1	31,200
Miami-Hialeah, FL	320	46.2	48.2	86,700
Middlesex–Somerset–Hunterdon, NJ	20	5.4	40.5	162,100
Modesto, CA	19	15.5	49.0	104,000
Nassau–Suffolk, NY	40	4.7	56.4	164,400
New Orleans, LA	18	3.9	50.9	67,800
New York, NY	584	17.9	12.1	183,300

(continued)

(continued from previous page)

	number	Hispanic share of total households	owner-occupied percent	owner-occupied median value
Newark, NJ	55	8.5%	30.2%	$165,400
Oakland, CA	76	9.8	48.9	183,700
Orlando, FL	29	7.3	51.4	79,300
Oxnard–Ventura, CA	39	17.8	47.4	203,100
Philadelphia, PA-NJ	48	2.7	47.1	43,300
Phoenix, AZ	90	11.2	49.1	62,100
Riverside–San Bernardino, CA	164	18.9	55.0	117,800
Sacramento, CA	49	8.8	47.5	110,300
Salinas–Seaside–Monterey, CA	26	23.0	35.9	140,500
Salt Lake City–Ogden, UT	17	5.0	49.7	57,300
San Antonio, TX	178	39.6	56.5	42,200
San Diego, CA	125	14.0	37.9	148,500
San Francisco, CA	65	10.0	34.1	277,300
San Jose, CA	78	14.9	45.1	226,300
Santa Barbara–Santa Maria–Lompoc, CA	23	18.1	38.6	170,000
Stockton, CA	28	17.7	44.5	93,800
Tampa–St. Petersburg–Clearwater, FL	47	5.4	59.8	66,200
Tucson, AZ	47	18.0	55.7	58,600
Visalia–Tulare–Porterville, CA	28	28.5	46.1	58,400
Washington, DC-MD-VA	62	4.2	37.5	159,100
West Palm Beach-Boca Raton–Delray Beach, FL	20	5.4	52.8	80,900

Source: Bureau of the Census, Housing in Metropolitan Areas—Hispanic Households, *Statistical Brief, SB/95-4, 1995; calculations by New Strategist*

Hispanics: Income

The incomes of Hispanics are falling because so many are immigrants with little earning power.

The median income of Hispanic households fell 7 percent between 1990 and 1996, to $24,906 after adjusting for inflation. This was the sharpest income decline among all racial and ethnic groups. Consequently, Hispanic median household income fell relative to the median of total households, from 75 to 70 percent.

Hispanic household income peaks in the 45-to-54 age group, with a median of $30,709 in 1996. By household type, median income is greatest for married couples, at $32,379.

Hispanic men who worked full-time had a median income of $21,265 in 1996, while women who worked full-time had a median income of $19,272. Between 1990 and 1996, the median income of Hispanic men who worked full-time fell 8.5 percent after adjusting for inflation, while the median income of Hispanic women who worked full-time fell 1.6 percent. Hispanics earn less than the average worker because so many are recent immigrants. By ethnicity, earnings are greatest for Cuban men. Seventeen percent of Cuban men who work full-time earned more than $50,000 in 1995.

More than one in four Hispanic families is poor, including 18 percent of couples and 51 percent of female-headed families. Since 1980, the number of Hispanic families in poverty has grown 33 percent.

■ The arrival of Hispanic immigrants with little education from relatively poor countries such as Mexico lowers the incomes of Hispanics overall. The economic status of Hispanics will remain below that of the average American as long as immigrants account for such a large share of the population.

Hispanic household income peaks among 45-to-54-year-olds

(median income of Hispanic households by age, 1996)

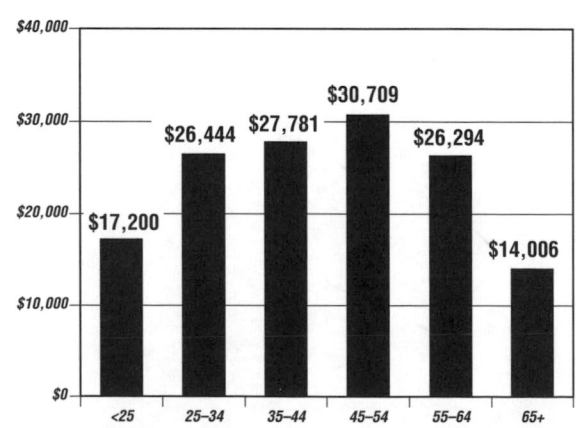

Median Income of Hispanic Households, 1980 to 1996

(median income of Hispanic households, and ratio of Hispanic to total households' median income, 1980–96; percent change in income and ratio, selected years; in 1996 dollars)

	median income	ratio Hispanic/total
1996	$24,906	.70
1995	23,535	.67
1994	24,796	.73
1993	24,850	.73
1992	25,271	.74
1991	26,140	.75
1990	26,806	.75
1989	27,737	.76
1988	27,002	.75
1987	26,706	.74
1986	26,272	.74
1985	25,467	.74
1984	25,660	.76
1983	25,057	.76
1982	24,910	.75
1981	26,643	.80
1980	26,025	.77
Percent change		
1990–1996	−7.1%	−5.9%
1980–1996	−4.3	−9.0

Note: Ratios are calculated by dividing median income of Hispanic households by median of total households.
Source: U.S. Bureau of the Census, unpublished tables from the 1997 Current Population Survey; calculations by New Strategist

Income Distribution of Hispanic Households by Age of Householder, 1996

(number and percent distribution of Hispanic households by household income and age of house-holder, 1996; households in thousands as of 1997)

	total	< age 25	25–34	35–44	45–54	55–64	65+
Total households, number	**8,225**	**687**	**2,263**	**2,229**	**1,296**	**854**	**895**
Under $10,000	1,415	169	287	290	165	172	332
$10,000 to $19,999	1,894	231	522	480	249	175	237
$20,000 to $29,999	1,475	125	460	425	221	126	119
$30,000 to $39,999	1,019	56	352	318	134	84	78
$40,000 to $49,999	783	47	233	226	153	74	50
$50,000 to $59,999	519	24	154	148	106	62	26
$60,000 to $69,999	352	18	83	113	76	45	17
$70,000 to $79,999	250	7	65	65	55	45	12
$80,000 to $89,999	146	3	33	58	20	24	9
$90,000 to $99,999	85	2	16	17	29	11	7
$100,000 or more	286	5	60	86	87	38	10
Median income	$24,906	$17,200	$26,444	$27,781	$30,709	$26,294	$14,006
Total households, percent	**100.0%**	**100.0%**	**100.0%**	**100.0%**	**100.0%**	**100.0%**	**100.0%**
Under $10,000	17.2	24.6	12.7	13.0	12.7	20.1	37.1
$10,000 to $19,999	23.0	33.6	23.1	21.5	19.2	20.5	26.5
$20,000 to $29,999	17.9	18.2	20.3	19.1	17.1	14.8	13.3
$30,000 to $39,999	12.4	8.2	15.6	14.3	10.3	9.8	8.7
$40,000 to $49,999	9.5	6.8	10.3	10.1	11.8	8.7	5.6
$50,000 to $59,999	6.3	3.5	6.8	6.6	8.2	7.3	2.9
$60,000 to $69,999	4.3	2.6	3.7	5.1	5.9	5.3	1.9
$70,000 to $79,999	3.0	1.0	2.9	2.9	4.2	5.3	1.3
$80,000 to $89,999	1.8	0.4	1.5	2.6	1.5	2.8	1.0
$90,000 to $99,999	1.0	0.3	0.7	0.8	2.2	1.3	0.8
$100,000 or more	3.5	0.7	2.7	3.9	6.7	4.4	1.1

Source: Bureau of the Census, unpublished tables from the 1997 Current Population Survey; calculations by New Strategist

Income Distribution of Hispanic Households by Household Type, 1996

(number and percent distribution of Hispanic households by household income and household type, 1996; households in thousands as of 1997)

| | | family households | | | | nonfamily households | | | | |
| | | | | | | | female hh | | male hh | |
	total households	total	married couples	female hh, no spouse present	male hh, no spouse present	total	total	living alone	total	living alone
Total households, number	**8,225**	**6,631**	**4,520**	**1,617**	**494**	**1,593**	**740**	**621**	**854**	**575**
Under $10,000	1,415	870	274	550	44	545	329	321	218	196
$10,000 to $19,999	1,894	1,503	919	474	110	393	172	145	221	160
$20,000 to $29,999	1,475	1,235	862	261	111	240	102	72	138	80
$30,000 to $39,999	1,019	881	649	144	87	139	53	34	86	62
$40,000 to $49,999	783	674	544	78	52	110	40	25	70	31
$50,000 to $59,999	519	453	371	45	35	66	24	15	44	19
$60,000 to $69,999	352	315	278	20	17	37	9	2	29	10
$70,000 to $79,999	250	226	189	25	12	23	4	4	20	8
$80,000 to $89,999	146	136	124	7	7	10	3	2	8	3
$90,000 to $99,999	85	82	66	9	6	3	–	–	3	–
$100,000 or more	286	260	245	6	9	26	5	0	21	4
Median income	$24,906	$27,152	$32,379	$14,535	$28,322	$15,705	$11,770	$9,746	$19,323	$14,506
Total households, percent	**100.0%**	**100.0%**	**100.0%**	**100.0%**	**100.0%**	**100.0%**	**100.0%**	**100.0%**	**100.0%**	**100.0%**
Under $10,000	17.2	13.1	6.1	34.0	8.9	34.2	44.5	51.7	25.5	34.1
$10,000 to $19,999	23.0	22.7	20.3	29.3	22.3	24.7	23.2	23.3	25.9	27.8
$20,000 to $29,999	17.9	18.6	19.1	16.1	22.5	15.1	13.8	11.6	16.2	13.9
$30,000 to $39,999	12.4	13.3	14.4	8.9	17.6	8.7	7.2	5.5	10.1	10.8
$40,000 to $49,999	9.5	10.2	12.0	4.8	10.5	6.9	5.4	4.0	8.2	5.4
$50,000 to $59,999	6.3	6.8	8.2	2.8	7.1	4.1	3.2	2.4	5.2	3.3
$60,000 to $69,999	4.3	4.8	6.2	1.2	3.4	2.3	1.2	0.3	3.4	1.7
$70,000 to $79,999	3.0	3.4	4.2	1.5	2.4	1.4	0.5	0.6	2.3	1.4
$80,000 to $89,999	1.8	2.1	2.7	0.4	1.4	0.6	0.4	0.3	0.9	0.5
$90,000 to $99,999	1.0	1.2	1.5	0.6	1.2	0.2	–	–	0.4	–
$100,000 or more	3.5	3.9	5.4	0.4	1.8	1.6	0.7	–	2.5	0.7

Note: (–) means sample is too small to make a reliable estimate.
Source: Bureau of the Census, unpublished tables from the 1997 Current Population Survey; calculations by New Strategist

Income Distribution of Hispanic Men by Age, 1996

(number and percent distribution of Hispanic men aged 15 or older by income and age, 1996; men in thousands as of 1997)

	total	< age 25	25–34	35–44	45–54	55–64	65+
Total men, number	**10,627**	**2,872**	**2,904**	**2,253**	**1,218**	**741**	**640**
Without income	1,322	943	150	109	39	43	38
With income	9,305	1,929	2,754	2,144	1,179	698	602
Under $10,000	2,731	1,093	525	404	226	196	291
$10,000 to $19,999	3,076	648	1,034	635	348	219	194
$20,000 to $29,999	1,608	118	621	458	245	115	52
$30,000 to $39,999	883	53	316	273	136	65	37
$40,000 to $49,999	433	9	129	163	87	35	9
$50,000 to $74,999	407	9	94	150	94	44	15
$75,000 to $99,999	87	–	20	33	26	7	1
$100,000 or more	78	–	15	28	17	16	3
Median income of men with income	$15,437	$8,325	$17,293	$20,562	$20,418	$15,997	$10,332
Total men, percent	**100.0%**	**100.0%**	**100.0%**	**100.0%**	**100.0%**	**100.0%**	**100.0%**
Without income	12.4	32.8	5.2	4.8	3.2	5.8	5.9
With income	87.6	67.2	94.8	95.2	96.8	94.2	94.1
Under $10,000	25.7	38.1	18.1	17.9	18.6	26.5	45.5
$10,000 to $19,999	28.9	22.6	35.6	28.2	28.6	29.6	30.3
$20,000 to $29,999	15.1	4.1	21.4	20.3	20.1	15.5	8.1
$30,000 to $39,999	8.3	1.8	10.9	12.1	11.2	8.8	5.8
$40,000 to $49,999	4.1	0.3	4.4	7.2	7.1	4.7	1.4
$50,000 to $74,999	3.8	0.3	3.2	6.7	7.7	5.9	2.3
$75,000 to $99,999	0.8	–	0.7	1.5	2.1	0.9	0.2
$100,000 or more	0.7	–	0.5	1.2	1.4	2.2	0.5

Note: (–) means sample is too small to make a reliable estimate.
Source: Bureau of the Census, unpublished tables from the 1997 Current Population Survey; calculations by New Strategist

Income Distribution of Hispanic Women by Age, 1996

(number and percent distribution of Hispanic women aged 15 or older by income and age, 1996; women in thousands as of 1997)

	total	< age 25	25–34	35–44	45–54	55-64	aged 65+
Total women, number	**10,073**	**2,351**	**2,591**	**2,135**	**1,242**	**877**	**876**
Without income	2,329	944	527	357	227	176	98
With income	7,744	1,407	2,064	1,778	1,015	701	779
Under $10,000	4,039	1,005	912	725	422	373	601
$10,000 to $19,999	1,995	309	590	523	299	160	116
$20,000 to $29,999	975	76	364	277	152	81	26
$30,000 to $39,999	382	12	107	138	60	45	19
$40,000 to $49,999	165	–	42	52	42	21	8
$50,000 to $74,999	147	3	44	46	30	15	5
$75,000 to $99,999	17	–	3	4	6	2	2
$100,000 or more	21	–	3	11	5	3	–
Median income of women with income	$9,484	$5,640	$11,455	$11,856	$12,167	$9,039	$6,928
Total women, percent	**100.0%**	**100.0%**	**100.0%**	**100.0%**	**100.0%**	**100.0%**	**100.0%**
Without income	23.1	40.2	20.3	16.7	18.3	20.1	11.2
With income	76.9	59.8	79.7	83.3	81.7	79.9	88.9
Under $10,000	40.1	42.7	35.2	34.0	34.0	42.5	68.6
$10,000 to $19,999	19.8	13.1	22.8	24.5	24.1	18.2	13.2
$20,000 to $29,999	9.7	3.2	14.0	13.0	12.2	9.2	3.0
$30,000 to $39,999	3.8	0.5	4.1	6.5	4.8	5.1	2.2
$40,000 to $49,999	1.6	–	1.6	2.4	3.4	2.4	0.9
$50,000 to $74,999	1.5	0.1	1.7	2.2	2.4	1.7	0.6
$75,000 to $99,999	0.2	–	0.1	0.2	0.5	0.2	0.2
$100,000 or more	0.2	–	0.1	0.5	0.4	0.3	–

Note: (–) means sample is too small to make a reliable estimate.
Source: U.S. Bureau of the Census, unpublished tables from the 1997 Current Population Survey; calculations by New Strategist

Median Earnings of Hispanics Who Work Full-Time by Sex, 1980 to 1996

(median earnings of Hispanics who work year-round, full-time by sex; ratio of Hispanic to total population median earnings, and Hispanic female earnings as a percent of Hispanic male earnings, 1980–96; percent change in earnings and ratios for selected years; in 1996 dollars)

| | Hispanic men | | Hispanic women | | Hispanic women's earnings as a |
	median earnings	ratio Hispanic/total	median earnings	ratio Hispanic/total	percent of Hisp. men's earnings
1996	$21,265	.63	$19,272	.77	90.6%
1995	21,160	.64	18,382	.75	86.9
1994	21,730	.65	19,499	.79	89.7
1993	22,176	.66	18,580	.76	83.8
1992	22,204	.64	19,765	.80	89.0
1991	23,071	.66	19,063	.78	82.6
1990	23,238	.67	19,425	.79	83.6
1989	23,473	.65	20,253	.82	86.3
1988	24,125	.67	20,161	.82	83.6
1987	24,419	.66	20,444	.84	83.7
1986	24,348	.66	20,315	.84	83.4
1985	25,291	.69	19,717	.83	78.0
1984	25,935	.72	19,672	.84	75.9
1983	25,818	.73	18,705	.82	72.4
1982	25,585	.72	18,649	.83	72.9
1981	26,088	.72	19,011	.88	72.9
1980	26,290	.72	18,849	.85	71.7
Percent change					
1990–1996	−8.5%	−5.1%	−0.8%	−1.6%	8.4%
1980–1996	−19.1	−11.8	2.2	−9.4	26.4

Note: Hispanic/total ratios are calculated by dividing median earnings of Hispanic men and women by median for total men and women.
Source: Bureau of the Census, unpublished tables from the 1997 Current Population Survey; calculations by New Strategist

Median Earnings of Hispanics Who Work Full-Time by Education and Sex, 1996

(median earnings of Hispanics aged 25 or older who work year-round, full-time, by educational attainment and sex, 1996)

	men	women	Hispanic women's earnings as a percent of Hispanic men's earnings
Total persons	**$19,217**	**$13,695**	**71.3%**
Less than 9th grade	13,485	9,392	69.6
9th to 12th grade, no diploma	15,850	10,360	65.4
High school graduate	21,234	14,146	66.6
Some college, no degree	23,711	16,386	69.1
Associate's degree	26,864	20,515	76.4
Bachelor's degree or more	33,669	27,045	80.3
Bachelor's degree	32,259	26,454	82.0
Master's degree	30,093	31,860	105.9
Professional degree	45,250	38,602	85.3
Doctoral degree	52,263	21,706	41.5

Source: U.S. Bureau of the Census, unpublished tables from the 1997 Current Population Survey; calculations by New Strategist

Earnings of Hispanic Men by Ethnicity, 1995

(number and percent distribution of Hispanic men aged 15 or older by work status, earnings, and ethnicity, 1995; men in thousands as of 1996)

	total	Mexican	Puerto Rican	Cuban	Central & South Amer.	other Hispanic
TOTAL MEN						
Total number	**7,472**	**4,845**	**638**	**331**	**1,126**	**532**
Loss or under $10,000	2,168	1,485	145	64	312	161
$10,000 to $24,999	3,282	2,191	265	129	514	184
$25,000 to $49,999	1,605	969	176	93	239	128
$50,000 or more	417	201	52	45	61	59
Total percent	**100.0%**	**100.0%**	**100.0%**	**100.0%**	**100.0%**	**100.0%**
Loss or under $10,000	29.0	30.7	22.7	19.3	27.7	30.3
$10,000 to $24,999	43.9	45.2	41.5	39.0	45.6	34.6
$25,000 to $49,999	21.5	20.0	27.6	28.1	21.2	24.1
$50,000 or more	5.6	4.1	8.2	13.6	5.4	11.1
YEAR-ROUND, FULL-TIME WORKERS						
Total number	**4,960**	**3,136**	**450**	**246**	**780**	**347**
Loss or under $10,000	501	353	23	16	73	36
$10,000 to $24,999	2,619	1,730	217	95	433	144
$25,000 to $49,999	1,468	878	163	92	217	118
$50,000 or more	372	176	47	42	56	50
Total percent	**100.0%**	**100.0%**	**100.0%**	**100.0%**	**100.0%**	**100.0%**
Loss or under $10,000	10.1	11.3	5.1	6.5	9.4	10.4
$10,000 to $24,999	52.8	55.2	48.2	38.6	55.5	41.5
$25,000 to $49,999	29.6	28.0	36.2	37.4	27.8	34.0
$50,000 or more	7.5	5.6	10.4	17.1	7.2	14.4

Source: Bureau of the Census, Internet web site, http://www.census.gov

Earnings of Hispanic Women by Ethnicity, 1995

(number and percent distribution of Hispanic women aged 15 or older by work status, earnings, and ethnicity, 1995; women in thousands as of 1996)

	total	Mexican	Puerto Rican	Cuban	Central & South Amer.	other Hispanic
TOTAL WOMEN						
Total number	**5,215**	**3,070**	**546**	**249**	**906**	**443**
Loss or under $10,000	2,270	1,454	188	78	378	173
$10,000 to $24,999	2,086	1,208	226	100	373	178
$25,000 to $49,999	754	373	103	61	139	78
$50,000 or more	105	34	30	10	17	15
Total percent	**100.0%**	**100.0%**	**100.0%**	**100.0%**	**100.0%**	**100.0%**
Loss or under $10,000	43.5	47.4	34.4	31.3	41.7	39.1
$10,000 to $24,999	40.0	39.3	41.4	40.2	41.2	40.2
$25,000 to $49,999	14.5	12.1	18.9	24.5	15.3	17.6
$50,000 or more	2.0	1.1	5.5	4.0	1.9	3.4
YEAR-ROUND, FULL-TIME WORKERS						
Total number	**2,771**	**1,550**	**303**	**153**	**523**	**241**
Loss or under $10,000	432	274	26	11	95	26
$10,000 to $24,999	1,601	932	168	76	291	134
$25,000 to $49,999	651	315	87	56	122	71
$50,000 or more	87	29	22	10	16	11
Total percent	**100.0%**	**100.0%**	**100.0%**	**100.0%**	**100.0%**	**100.0%**
Loss or under $10,000	15.6	17.7	8.6	7.2	18.2	10.8
$10,000 to $24,999	57.8	60.1	55.4	49.7	55.6	55.6
$25,000 to $49,999	23.5	20.3	28.7	36.6	23.3	29.5
$50,000 or more	3.1	1.9	7.3	6.5	3.1	4.6

Source: Bureau of the Census, Internet web site, http://www.census.gov

Hispanic Families below the Poverty Level, 1980 to 1996

(total number of Hispanic families, and number and percent below poverty level by type of family and presence of children under age 18 at home, 1980–96; percent change in numbers and rates for selected years; families in thousands as of March the following year)

	total families			married couples			female hh, no spouse present		
		in poverty			in poverty			in poverty	
	total	*number*	*percent*	*total*	*number*	*percent*	*total*	*number*	*percent*
With and without children under age 18									
1996	6,631	1,748	26.4%	4,520	815	18.0%	1,617	823	50.9%
1995	6,287	1,695	27.0	4,247	803	18.9	1,604	792	49.4
1994	6,202	1,724	27.8	4,236	827	19.5	1,485	773	52.1
1993	5,946	1,625	27.3	4,038	770	19.1	1,498	772	51.6
1992	5,733	1,529	26.7	3,940	743	18.8	1,348	664	49.3
1991	5,177	1,372	26.5	3,532	674	19.1	1,261	627	49.7
1990	4,981	1,244	25.0	3,454	605	17.5	1,186	573	48.3
1989	4,840	1,133	23.4	3,395	549	16.2	1,116	530	47.5
1988	4,823	1,141	23.7	3,398	547	16.1	1,112	546	49.1
1987	4,576	1,168	25.5	3,196	556	17.4	1,082	565	52.2
1986	4,403	1,085	24.7	3,118	518	16.6	1,032	528	51.2
1985	4,206	1,074	25.5	2,962	505	17.0	980	521	53.1
1984	3,939	991	25.2	2,824	469	16.6	905	483	53.4
1983	3,788	981	25.9	2,752	437	17.7	860	454	52.8
1982	3,369	916	27.2	2,448	465	19.0	767	425	55.4
1981	3,305	792	24.0	2,414	366	15.1	750	399	53.2
1980	3,235	751	23.2	2,365	363	15.3	706	362	51.3
Percent change									
1990–1996	33.1%	40.5%	5.6%	30.9%	34.7%	2.9%	36.3%	43.6%	5.4%
1980–1996	105.0	132.8	13.8	91.1	124.5	17.6	129.0	127.3	–0.8

(continued)

(continued from previous page)

	total families			married couples			female hh, no spouse present		
		in poverty			in poverty			in poverty	
	total	number	percent	total	number	percent	total	number	percent
With children									
under age 18									
1996	4,689	1,549	33.0%	3,124	687	22.0%	1,274	760	59.7%
1995	4,422	1,470	33.2	2,902	657	22.6	1,283	735	57.3
1994	4,377	1,497	34.2	2,923	698	23.9	1,182	700	59.2
1993	4,153	1,424	34.3	2,747	652	23.7	1,167	706	60.5
1992	3,962	1,302	32.9	2,692	615	22.9	1,037	598	57.7
1991	3,621	1,219	33.7	2,445	575	23.5	972	584	60.1
1990	3,497	1,085	31.0	2,405	501	20.8	921	536	58.2
1989	3,314	986	29.8	2,309	453	19.6	848	491	57.9
1988	3,325	988	29.7	2,339	445	19.0	861	510	59.2
1987	3,201	1,022	31.9	2,197	460	20.9	865	527	60.9
1986	3,080	949	30.8	–	–	–	822	489	59.5
1985	2,973	955	32.1	–	–	–	771	493	64.0
1984	2,789	872	31.3	–	–	–	711	447	62.8
1983	2,697	867	21.1	–	–	–	660	418	63.4
1982	2,458	802	32.6	–	–	–	613	391	63.8
1981	2,428	692	28.5	–	–	–	622	374	60.0
1980	2,409	655	27.2	–	–	–	–	–	–
Percent change									
1990–1996	34.1%	45.4%	6.5%	29.9%	37.1%	5.8%	38.3%	41.8%	2.6%
1980–1996	94.6	136.5	21.3	–	–	–	–	–	–

Note: (–) means data not available.
Source: Bureau of the Census, unpublished tables from the 1997 Current Population Survey; calculations by New Strategist

Hispanics in Poverty by Sex and Age, 1996

(total number of Hispanics, and number and percent below poverty level by sex and age, 1996; persons in thousands as of 1997)

	total	in poverty number	in poverty percent
Total persons	**29,614**	**8,697**	**29.4%**
Under age 18	10,511	4,237	40.3
Aged 18 to 24	3,626	1,051	29.0
Aged 25 to 34	5,494	1,259	22.9
Aged 35 to 44	4,387	1,032	23.5
Aged 45 to 54	2,461	416	16.9
Aged 55 to 59	937	180	19.2
Aged 60 to 64	682	151	22.2
Aged 65 to 74	992	231	23.3
Aged 75 or older	524	140	26.6
Females, total	**14,417**	**4,618**	**32.0**
Under age 18	5,055	2,078	41.1
Aged 18 to 24	1,640	537	32.8
Aged 25 to 34	2,591	735	28.4
Aged 35 to 44	2,135	567	26.5
Aged 45 to 54	1,242	242	19.5
Aged 55 to 59	518	121	23.4
Aged 60 to 64	359	95	26.4
Aged 65 to 74	559	157	28.0
Aged 75 or older	317	87	27.3
Males, total	**15,197**	**4,079**	**26.8**
Under age 18	5,456	2,159	39.6
Aged 18 to 24	1,986	514	25.9
Aged 25 to 34	2,904	524	18.1
Aged 35 to 44	2,253	466	20.7
Aged 45 to 54	1,218	174	14.3
Aged 55 to 59	418	59	14.0
Aged 60 to 64	323	56	17.5
Aged 65 to 74	432	74	17.2
Aged 75 or older	207	53	25.6

Source: Bureau of the Census, unpublished tables from the 1997 Current Population Survey

Hispanics: Labor Force

Hispanic women are less likely to be in the labor force than the average woman.

The labor force participation rate of Hispanic men, at 80 percent, is significantly higher than the 75 percent of all men. In contrast, Hispanic women are much less likely to work than the average woman, 55 versus 60 percent. Among Hispanic women, those of Puerto Rican origin are least likely to work, with a labor force participation rate of just 49 percent.

Only 15 percent of Hispanic workers are in managerial or professional specialty jobs, accounting for only 5 percent of the employed in those occupations. The occupational distribution of Hispanics varies by ethnicity. While 22 percent of Cubans are employed in managerial or professional specialty occupations, the figure is just 12 percent among Mexicans.

Forty-eight percent of Hispanic households have two or more earners, a slightly greater share than the 45 percent of all households with two earners. Nevertheless, among Hispanic married couples, only 48 percent are dual earners—less than the 56 percent national average. For 36 percent of Hispanic couples, the husband is the only worker.

Between 1996 and 2006, the number of Hispanic workers will grow 36 percent. Hispanics will account for 12 percent of the labor force in 2006.

■ Hispanics are far less likely to be employed in professional or managerial occupations than whites, blacks, and Asians. The explanation for this gap lies in the large share of Hispanics who are poorly educated immigrants, many of whom work on farms or in private households.

Hispanic women are less likely to work than black or white women

(percent of women aged 16 or older in the labor force by race and ethnicity, 1997)

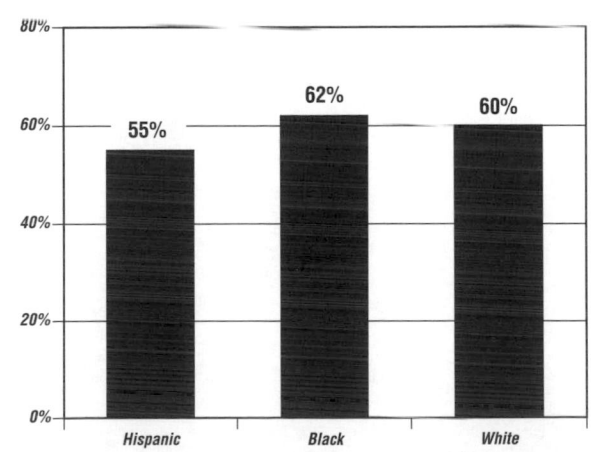

Employment Status of Hispanics by Sex and Age, 1997

(employment status of the civilian noninstitutionalized Hispanic population aged 16 or older, by sex and age, 1997; numbers in thousands)

				civilian labor force				not in labor force	
	total	percent of population	employed	percent of labor force	unemployed	percent of labor force		total	percent of population
Total persons	**13,796**	**67.9%**	**12,726**	**92.2%**	**1,069**	**7.7%**		**6,526**	**32.1%**
Aged 16 to 19	911	43.0	714	78.4	197	21.6		1,210	57.0
Aged 20 to 24	2,004	76.4	1,798	89.7	206	10.3		618	23.6
Aged 25 to 34	4,298	79.5	4,029	93.7	269	6.3		1,107	20.5
Aged 35 to 44	3,601	80.9	3,371	93.6	229	6.4		852	19.1
Aged 45 to 54	1,945	75.4	1,846	94.9	99	5.1		636	24.6
Aged 55 to 64	850	53.8	794	93.4	56	6.6		730	46.2
Aged 65 or older	186	11.9	173	93.0	13	7.0		1,372	88.1
Total men	**8,309**	**80.1**	**7,728**	**93.0**	**582**	**7.0**		**2,059**	**19.9**
Aged 16 to 19	531	47.4	420	79.1	110	20.7		588	52.6
Aged 20 to 24	1,267	88.1	1,142	90.1	125	9.9		172	11.9
Aged 25 to 34	2,684	93.5	2,547	94.9	137	5.1		188	6.5
Aged 35 to 44	2,091	91.9	1,978	94.6	113	5.4		184	8.1
Aged 45 to 54	1,112	87.8	1,059	95.2	54	4.9		154	12.2
Aged 55 to 64	511	68.4	477	93.3	35	6.8		236	31.6
Aged 65 or older	113	17.3	105	92.9	8	7.1		538	82.7
Total women	**5,486**	**55.1**	**4,999**	**91.1**	**488**	**8.9**		**4,466**	**44.9**
Aged 16 to 19	381	38.0	294	77.2	87	22.8		622	62.0
Aged 20 to 24	737	62.3	656	89.0	81	11.0		447	37.7
Aged 25 to 34	1,614	63.7	1,482	91.8	132	8.2		919	36.3
Aged 35 to 44	1,510	69.3	1,393	92.3	117	7.7		668	30.7
Aged 45 to 54	833	63.3	787	94.5	46	5.5		482	36.7
Aged 55 to 64	338	40.6	318	94.1	21	6.2		494	59.4
Aged 65 or older	73	8.1	69	94.5	4	5.5		834	91.9

Note: The civilian labor force equals the number of employed plus the number of unemployed persons. The civilian population equals the number of persons in the labor force plus the number of those not in the labor force.
Source: Bureau of Labor Statistics, Employment and Earnings, January 1998; calculations by New Strategist

Employment Status of Hispanics by Ethnicity, 1996

(employment status of the civilian noninstitutionalized Hispanic population aged 16 or older, by ethnicity, 1996; numbers in thousands)

			civilian labor force				not in labor force	
	total	percent of population	employed	percent of labor force	unemployed	percent of labor force	total	percent of population
Total Hispanics	**12,410**	**65.0%**	**11,191**	**90.2%**	**1,219**	**9.8%**	**6,672**	**35.0%**
Mexican	7,723	66.2	6,958	90.1	765	9.9	3,935	33.8
Puerto Rican	1,164	56.8	1,039	89.3	125	10.7	886	43.2
Cuban	576	61.2	540	93.8	36	6.3	365	38.8
Central and South American	2,012	68.6	1,832	91.1	180	8.9	921	31.4
Other Hispanic	935	62.3	822	87.9	113	12.1	566	37.7
Total Hispanic men	**7,404**	**77.4**	**6,685**	**90.3**	**719**	**9.7**	**2,164**	**22.6**
Mexican	4,825	79.8	4,360	90.4	465	9.6	1,225	20.2
Puerto Rican	613	66.5	551	89.9	62	10.1	309	33.5
Cuban	329	69.4	307	93.3	22	6.7	145	30.6
Central and South American	1,107	79.4	1,021	92.2	86	7.8	288	20.6
Other Hispanic	530	72.9	446	84.2	84	15.8	197	27.1
Total Hispanic women	**5,005**	**52.6**	**4,506**	**90.0**	**499**	**10.0**	**4,507**	**47.4**
Mexican	2,898	51.7	2,598	89.6	300	10.4	2,710	48.3
Puerto Rican	551	48.9	488	88.6	63	11.4	576	51.1
Cuban	247	52.9	233	94.3	14	5.7	220	47.1
Central and South American	904	58.8	811	89.7	93	10.3	632	41.2
Other Hispanic	405	52.3	376	92.8	29	7.2	369	47.7

Note: The civilian labor force equals the number of employed plus the number of unemployed persons. The civilian population equals the number of persons in the labor force plus the number of those not in the labor force.
Source: Bureau of the Census, Internet web site, http://www.census.gov; calculations by New Strategist

Hispanic Workers by Occupation, 1997

(total number of employed persons aged 16 or older in the civilian labor force; number and percent distribution of employed Hispanics, and Hispanic share of total employed, by occupation, 1997; numbers in thousands)

	total	Hispanic number	Hispanic percent	Hispanic share of total employed
Total employed, number	**129,558**	**12,726**	**100.0%**	**9.8%**
Managerial and professional specialty	**37,686**	**1,867**	**14.7**	**5.0**
Executive, administrative, and managerial	18,440	1,001	7.9	5.4
Professional specialty	19,245	866	6.8	4.5
Technical, sales, and administrative support	**38,309**	**3,026**	**23.8**	**7.9**
Technicians and related support	4,214	256	2.0	6.1
Sales occupations	15,734	1,198	9.4	7.6
Administrative support, including clerical	18,361	1,572	12.4	8.6
Service occupations	**17,537**	**2,560**	**20.1**	**14.6**
Private household	795	212	1.7	26.7
Protective service	2,300	202	1.6	8.8
Service, except private household and protective	14,442	2,146	16.9	14.9
Precision production, craft, and repair	**14,124**	**1,714**	**13.5**	**12.1**
Mechanics and repairers	4,675	479	3.8	10.2
Construction trades	5,378	736	5.8	13.7
Other precision production, craft, and repair	4,071	499	3.9	12.3
Operators, fabricators, and laborers	**18,399**	**2,839**	**22.3**	**15.4**
Machine operators, assemblers, and inspectors	7,962	1,426	11.2	17.9
Transportation and material moving occupations	5,389	592	4.7	11.0
Handlers, equipment cleaners, helpers, and laborers	5,048	821	6.5	16.3
Farming, forestry, and fishing	**3,503**	**721**	**5.7**	**20.6**

Source: Bureau of Labor Statistics, Employment and Earnings, *January 1998; calculations by New Strategist*

Hispanic Workers by Occupation and Ethnicity, 1996

(number and percent distribution of employed Hispanics aged 16 or older in the civilian labor force, by ethnicity, 1996; numbers in thousands)

	total	Mexican	Puerto Rican	Cuban	Central & South Amer.	other Hispanic
Total employed, number	**11,191**	**6,958**	**1,039**	**540**	**1,832**	**822**
Managerial and professional specialty	1,547	838	197	119	224	170
Technical, sales, administrative support	2,792	1,569	319	185	461	257
Service occupations	2,361	1,405	213	82	502	160
Precision production, craft, and repair	1,359	927	87	60	209	76
Operators, fabricators, and laborers	2,538	1,701	217	85	396	139
Farming, forestry, and fishing	594	519	6	10	40	20
Total employed, percent	**100.0%**	**100.0%**	**100.0%**	**100.0%**	**100.0%**	**100.0%**
Managerial and professional specialty	13.8	12.0	19.0	22.0	12.2	20.7
Technical, sales, and administrative support	24.9	22.5	30.7	34.3	25.2	31.3
Service occupations	21.1	20.2	20.5	15.2	27.4	19.5
Precision production, craft, and repair	12.1	13.3	8.4	11.1	11.4	9.2
Operators, fabricators, and laborers	22.7	24.4	20.9	15.7	21.6	16.9
Farming, forestry, and fishing	5.3	7.5	0.6	1.9	2.2	2.4

Source: Bureau of the Census, Internet web site; http://www.census.gov; *calculations by New Strategist*

Hispanic Worker Share by Detailed Occupation, 1997

(total number of employed persons aged 16 or older in the civilian labor force; and Hispanic share of total employed, by selected occupation, 1997; numbers in thousands)

	total	percent Hispanic
Total employed	**129,558**	**9.8%**
Managerial and professional specialty	**37,686**	**5.0**
Executive, administrative, and managerial	18,440	5.4
Officials and administrators, public administrators	606	5.6
Financial managers	688	5.1
Personnel and labor relations managers	108	2.9
Purchasing managers	114	4.6
Managers, marketing, advertising, and public relations	711	4.8
Administrators, education and related fields	733	5.8
Managers, medicine and health	701	4.3
Managers, food serving and lodging establishments	1,408	9.1
Managers, property and real estate	535	10.3
Professional specialty	19,245	4.5
Architects	169	5.1
Engineers	2,036	3.8
Mathematical and computer scientists	1,494	3.1
Natural scientists	529	2.2
Physicians	724	4.8
Dentists	138	1.1
Registered nurses	2,065	2.9
Pharmacists	200	2.6
Dietitians	101	6.0
Therapists	455	4.0
Teachers, college and university	869	3.4
Teachers, except college and university	4,798	5.4
Librarians, archivists, and curators	217	4.7
Economists	135	3.7
Psychologists	256	4.5
Social, recreation, and religious workers	1,357	6.9
Lawyers and judges	925	3.8
Writers, artists, entertainers, and athletes	2,234	5.8
Technical, sales, and administrative support	**38,309**	**7.9**
Technicians and related support	4,214	6.1
Health technologists and technicians	1,693	6.3
Engineering and related technologists and technicians	960	6.7
Science technicians	287	8.3

(continued)

(continued from previous page)

	total	percent Hispanic
Technicians, except health, engineering, and science	1,275	4.8%
Airplane pilots and navigators	120	2.4
Computer programmers	626	4.5
Legal assistants	346	5.8
Sales occupations	15,734	7.6
Supervisors and proprietors	4,635	6.8
Sales representatives, finance and business services	2,613	4.5
Sales representatives, commodities, except retail	1,507	5.0
Sales workers, retail and personal services	6,887	10.0
Administrative support, including clerical	18,361	8.6
Supervisors	685	6.1
Computer equipment operators	392	7.0
Secretaries, stenographers, and typists	3,692	6.9
Information clerks	1,993	9.5
Records processing occupations, except financial	935	9.5
Financial records processing	2,196	6.4
Service occupations	**17,537**	**14.6**
Private household	795	26.6
Protective	2,300	8.8
Firefighting and fire prevention	233	5.7
Police and detectives	1,005	7.6
Guards	881	11.0
Service occupations, ex. private hh and protective services	14,442	14.9
Food preparation and service occupations	5,999	16.4
Health service occupations	2,447	9.2
Cleaning and building service occupations	3,108	21.3
Personal service occupations	2,888	9.6
Precision production, craft, and repair	**14,124**	**12.1**
Mechanics and repairers	4,675	10.2
Construction trades	5,378	13.7
Extractive occupations	145	14.2
Precision production occupations	3,926	12.2
Operators, fabricators, and laborers	**18,399**	**15.4**
Machine operators, assemblers, and inspectors	7,962	17.9
Transportation and material moving occupations	5,389	11.0
Motor vehicle operators	4,089	10.9
Truck drivers	95	11.1
Bus drivers	472	7.9
Taxicab drivers and chauffers	248	14.7
Material moving equipment operators	1,125	12.7
Handlers, equipment cleaners, helpers, and laborers	5,048	16.3
Farming, forestry, and fishing	**3,503**	**20.6**

Source: Bureau of Labor Statistics, Employment and Earnings, *January 1998*

Hispanic Workers by Industry, 1997

(total number of employed persons aged 16 or older in the civilian labor force; number and percent distribution of employed Hispanics, and Hispanic share of total employed, by industry, 1997; numbers in thousands)

		Hispanic		Hispanic share of
	total	number	percent	total employed
Total employed	**129,558**	**12,726**	**100.0%**	**9.8%**
Agriculture	3,399	659	5.2	19.4
Mining	634	60	0.5	9.4
Construction	8,302	980	7.7	11.8
Manufacturing	20,835	2,334	18.3	11.2
Durable goods	12,437	1,231	9.7	9.9
Nondurable goods	8,399	1,109	8.7	13.2
Transportation, communications, and other public utilities	9,182	790	6.2	8.6
Wholesale and retail trade	26,777	2,972	23.4	11.1
Wholesale trade	4,907	525	4.1	10.7
Retail trade	21,869	2,449	19.2	11.2
Finance, insurance, and real estate	8,297	597	4.7	7.2
Services	46,393	3,943	31.0	8.5
Private households	921	236	1.9	25.6
Other service industries	45,472	3,729	29.3	8.2
Professional and related services	30,935	2,042	16.0	6.6
Public administration	5,738	373	2.9	6.5

Note: Numbers may not add to total due to rounding.
Source: Bureau of Labor Statistics, Employment and Earnings, *January 1998; calculations by New Strategist*

Hispanic Households by Number of Earners, 1996

(number and percent distribution of Hispanic households by number of earners, 1996; numbers in thousands)

	number	percent
Total households	**8,225**	**100.0%**
No earners	1,281	15.6
One earner	2,959	36.0
Two or more earners	3,984	48.4
Two earners	2,863	34.8
Three earners	787	9.6
Four or more earners	334	4.1

Source: Bureau of the Census, Income, Poverty, and Valuation of Noncash Benefits: 1996, *Current Population Reports, P60-197, 1997; calculations by New Strategist*

Labor Force Status of Hispanic Married Couples, 1996

(number and percent distribution of Hispanic married couples by age of householder and labor force status of husband and wife, 1996; numbers in thousands)

	total married couples	husband and/or wife in labor force			neither husband nor wife in labor force
		husband and wife	*husband only*	*wife only*	
Total couples, number	**4,247**	**2,037**	**1,529**	**204**	**477**
Under age 20	28	10	15	–	2
Aged 20 to 24	266	115	134	4	14
Aged 25 to 29	526	266	240	12	8
Aged 30 to 34	760	412	312	17	18
Aged 35 to 39	654	377	241	13	23
Aged 40 to 44	534	319	177	25	13
Aged 45 to 49	377	211	127	19	20
Aged 50 to 54	285	156	88	17	24
Aged 55 to 59	236	102	90	12	32
Aged 60 to 64	205	43	59	38	64
Aged 65 to 74	283	23	44	41	175
Aged 75 to 84	73	1	1	4	67
Aged 85 or older	20	2	–	2	16
Total couples, percent	**100.0%**	**48.0%**	**36.0%**	**4.8%**	**11.2%**
Under age 20	100.0	35.7	53.6	–	7.1
Aged 20 to 24	100.0	43.2	50.4	1.5	5.3
Aged 25 to 29	100.0	50.6	45.6	2.3	1.5
Aged 30 to 34	100.0	54.2	41.1	2.2	2.4
Aged 35 to 39	100.0	57.6	36.9	2.0	3.5
Aged 40 to 44	100.0	59.7	33.1	4.7	2.4
Aged 45 to 49	100.0	56.0	33.7	5.0	5.3
Aged 50 to 54	100.0	54.7	30.9	6.0	8.4
Aged 55 to 59	100.0	43.2	38.1	5.1	13.6
Aged 60 to 64	100.0	21.0	28.8	18.5	31.2
Aged 65 to 74	100.0	8.1	15.5	14.5	61.8
Aged 75 to 84	100.0	1.4	1.4	5.5	91.8
Aged 85 or older	100.0	10.0	–	10.0	80.0

Note: (–) means sample is too small to make a reliable estimate.
Source: Bureau of the Census, Household and Family Characteristics: March 1996, *Current Population Reports, P20-495(Update), 1997; calculations by New Strategist*

Union Membership of Hispanics, 1997

(number of employed Hispanic wage and salary workers aged 16 or older, number and percent who are represented by unions or are union members, and median weekly earnings by union membership status; by sex, 1997; numbers in thousands)

	total	*men*	*women*
Total employed	**11,881**	**7,153**	**4,728**
Represented by unions*	1,602	1,023	579
Percent of employed	13.5%	14.3%	12.2%
Members of unions**	1,407	904	503
Percent of employed	11.8%	12.6%	10.6%
Median weekly earnings, total***	$351	$371	$318
Represented by unions*	501	526	430
Members of unions**	506	538	440
Non-union	331	348	309

* Members of a labor union or an employee association similar to a union as well as workers who report no union affiliation but whose jobs are covered by a union or an employee association contract.
** Members of a labor union or an employee association similar to a union.
*** Full-time wage and salary workers.
Source: Bureau of Labor Statistics, Employment and Earnings, *January 1998*

Projections of the Hispanic Labor Force by Sex, 1996 to 2006

(number of Hispanics in the civilian labor force in 1996 and 2006, and percent change in number; labor force participation rate of Hispanics in 1996 and 2006, and Hispanic share of total labor force in 1996 and 2006; by sex; numbers in thousands)

| | number in labor force | | percent change |
	1996	2006	1996–2006
Total	**12,774**	**17,401**	**36.2%**
Men	7,646	10,235	33.9
Women	5,128	7,166	39.7

| | labor force participation rate | | percentage point change |
	1996	2006	1996–2006
Total	**66.5%**	**65.7%**	**–0.8**
Men	79.6	77.1	–2.5
Women	53.4	57.2	3.8

| | percent of total labor force | | percentage point change |
	1996	2006	1996–2006
Total	**9.5%**	**11.7%**	**2.2**
Men	10.6	13.1	2.5
Women	8.3	10.1	1.9

Source: Bureau of Labor Statistics, Monthly Labor Review, *November 1997; calculations by New Strategist*

Hispanics: Population

Hispanics will become the largest minority group in the U.S. in 2009.

The Hispanic population is projected to grow from nearly 30 million in 1998 to more than 52 million by 2020, when Hispanics will account for 16 percent of the U.S. population. Although the Hispanic population is growing faster than the black population, the number of Hispanics will not surpass the number of blacks in the U.S. until 2009.

A much larger share of children and young adults are Hispanic than of older Americans. Sixteen percent of children under age 5 are Hispanic, versus only 4 percent of people aged 85 or older. Behind this difference is the higher fertility of Hispanic women compared to other racial and ethnic groups. Among Hispanics, the three largest ethnic groups are Mexican (63 percent), Puerto Rican (11 percent) and Cuban (4 percent).

Hispanics are most likely to live in the West (45 percent) and South (31 percent). Fifty-eight percent of Mexican Americans live in the West, while 69 percent of Puerto Ricans live in the Northeast, and 71 percent of Cubans live in the South. Hispanics account for 26 percent of California's population, and Los Angeles is home to more Hispanics than any other metropolitan area in the U.S.

■ The importance of the Hispanic market varies by geography. Hispanics are a powerful segment of the population in some of the nation's most populous states such as California and Texas. But in many states and regions, they are only a tiny share of the population.

The Hispanic population will top 50 million by 2020

(number of Hispanics in the U.S. population, 1988 to 2020)

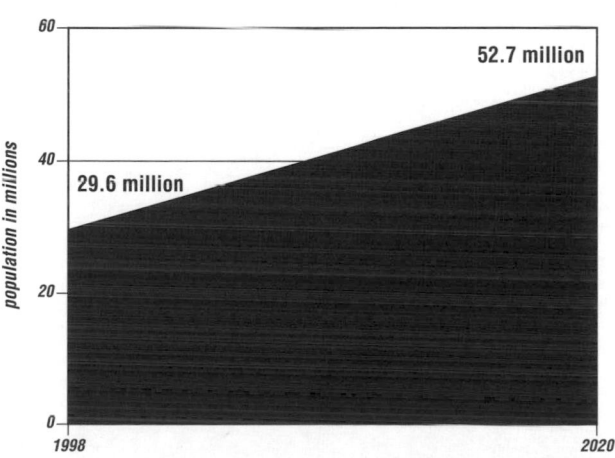

Hispanics by Age, 1995 to 2020

(number of Hispanics by age, selected years 1995–2020; percent change 1995–2000 and 2000–2010; numbers in thousands)

	1995	1998	2000	2010	2020	percent change 1995–2000	percent change 2000–2010
Total persons	**26,936**	**29,566**	**31,366**	**41,139**	**52,652**	**16.4%**	**31.2%**
Under age 5	3,136	3,133	3,203	4,080	5,185	2.1	27.4
Aged 5 to 9	2,658	3,127	3,298	3,742	4,839	24.1	13.5
Aged 10 to 14	2,426	2,663	2,906	3,627	4,529	19.8	24.8
Aged 15 to 19	2,285	2,576	2,732	3,893	4,362	19.6	42.5
Aged 20 to 24	2,336	2,415	2,574	3,499	4,231	10.2	35.9
Aged 25 to 29	2,498	2,525	2,510	3,154	4,250	0.5	25.7
Aged 30 to 34	2,533	2,643	2,671	2,905	3,796	5.4	8.8
Aged 35 to 39	2,159	2,453	2,618	2,760	3,411	21.3	5.4
Aged 40 to 44	1,727	2,024	2,218	2,802	3,044	28.4	26.3
Aged 45 to 49	1,313	1,550	1,727	2,640	2,787	31.5	52.9
Aged 50 to 54	962	1,164	1,322	2,193	2,762	37.4	65.9
Aged 55 to 59	762	872	962	1,709	2,599	26.2	77.7
Aged 60 to 64	635	701	755	1,288	2,123	18.9	70.6
Aged 65 to 69	543	589	618	922	1,629	13.8	49.2
Aged 70 to 74	405	462	502	684	1,175	24.0	36.3
Aged 75 to 79	256	320	362	521	795	41.4	43.9
Aged 80 to 84	170	186	206	374	531	21.2	81.6
Aged 85 or older	131	161	183	345	605	39.7	88.5
Aged 18 to 24	3,245	3,432	3,678	5,101	5,981	13.3	38.7
Aged 18 or older	17,340	19,084	20,332	27,398	35,488	17.3	34.8
Aged 65 or older	1,505	1,719	1,872	2,847	4,735	24.4	52.1

Source: Bureau of the Census, Population Projections of the United States, by Age, Sex, Race, and Hispanic Origin: 1995 to 2050, *Current Population Reports, P25-1130, 1996; calculations by New Strategist*

Hispanic Share of the Total Population by Age, 1995 to 2020

(Hispanics as a percent of the total population by age, selected years 1995–2020)

	1995	1998	2000	2010	2020
Total persons	**10.2%**	**11.0%**	**11.4%**	**13.8%**	**16.3%**
Under age 5	16.0	16.4	16.9	20.4	23.6
Aged 5 to 9	13.8	15.6	16.6	19.2	22.5
Aged 10 to 14	12.8	13.7	14.5	17.9	21.2
Aged 15 to 19	12.6	13.3	13.8	17.9	20.4
Aged 20 to 24	13.1	13.8	14.1	16.6	19.9
Aged 25 to 29	13.2	13.6	14.2	16.0	19.7
Aged 30 to 34	11.6	13.1	13.7	15.6	17.8
Aged 35 to 39	9.7	10.9	11.8	14.9	16.6
Aged 40 to 44	8.5	9.3	9.9	14.0	16.0
Aged 45 to 49	7.5	8.2	8.7	12.1	15.2
Aged 50 to 54	7.1	7.4	7.7	10.1	14.3
Aged 55 to 59	6.9	7.0	7.2	9.0	12.3
Aged 60 to 64	6.3	6.8	7.1	7.9	10.3
Aged 65 to 69	5.5	6.2	6.6	7.6	9.3
Aged 70 to 74	4.6	5.3	5.8	7.6	8.5
Aged 75 to 79	3.8	4.4	4.9	7.3	8.4
Aged 80 to 84	3.8	3.9	4.2	6.7	8.9
Aged 85 or older	3.6	4.0	4.3	6.1	9.4
Aged 18 to 24	13.0	13.6	14.0	16.9	20.0
Aged 18 or older	8.9	9.6	10.0	12.2	14.5
Aged 65 or older	4.5	5.0	5.4	7.2	8.9

Source: Calculations by New Strategist based on Census Bureau data in Population Projections of the United States, by Age, Sex, Race, and Hispanic Origin: 1995 to 2050, *Current Population Reports, P25-1130, 1996*

Hispanics by Age and Sex, 1998

(number of Hispanics by age and sex, and sex ratio by age, 1998; numbers in thousands)

	total	male	female	sex ratio*
Total persons	**29,566**	**14,922**	**14,644**	**102**
Under age 5	3,133	1,601	1,532	105
Aged 5 to 9	3,127	1,599	1,528	105
Aged 10 to 14	2,663	1,362	1,302	105
Aged 15 to 19	2,576	1,321	1,255	105
Aged 20 to 24	2,415	1,242	1,173	106
Aged 25 to 29	2,525	1,334	1,192	112
Aged 30 to 34	2,643	1,394	1,249	112
Aged 35 to 39	2,453	1,270	1,182	107
Aged 40 to 44	2,024	1,023	1,001	102
Aged 45 to 49	1,550	764	786	97
Aged 50 to 54	1,164	560	604	93
Aged 55 to 59	872	411	461	89
Aged 60 to 64	701	324	377	86
Aged 65 to 69	589	264	325	81
Aged 70 to 74	462	200	262	76
Aged 75 to 79	320	133	187	71
Aged 80 to 84	186	68	118	58
Aged 85 or older	161	51	111	46
Aged 18 to 24	3,432	1,764	1,669	106
Aged 18 or older	19,084	9,561	9,523	100
Aged 65 or older	1,719	717	1,002	72

* The sex ratio is the number of males per 100 females.
Source: Bureau of the Census, Population Projections of the United States, by Age, Sex, Race, and Hispanic Origin: 1995 to 2050, *Current Population Reports, P25-1130, 1996; calculations by New Strategist*

Hispanics by Ethnicity, Age, and Ability to Speak English, 1990

(number and percent of Hispanics aged 5 or older who do not speak English "very well" by ethnicity and age, for the three largest Hispanic ethnic groups and other Hispanics, 1990; numbers in thousands)

	total	5 to 17	18 to 64	65 to 74	75 or older
Total aged 5 or older, number	**7,717**	**1,450**	**5,645**	378	243
Mexican	4,605	988	3,325	179	113
Puerto Rican	794	169	554	47	24
Cuban	484	25	321	79	58
Other Hispanic	1,833	267	1,446	73	47
Total aged 5 or older, percent	**39.4%**	**27.3%**	**42.7%**	**56.4%**	**63.0%**
Mexican	38.9	28.1	42.7	52.7	61.3
Puerto Rican	33.5	25.5	34.8	62.3	63.7
Cuban	48.6	19.0	46.2	81.1	85.0
Other Hispanic	41.9	27.0	46.1	46.2	50.0

Source: Bureau of the Census, Persons of Hispanic Origin in the United States, *1990 Census of Population, CP-3-3, 1990; calculations by New Strategist*

Hispanics by Age and Ethnicity, 1996

(number and percent distribution of Hispanics by age and ethnicity, 1996; numbers in thousands)

	total	Mexican	Puerto Rican	Cuban	Central & South Amer.	other Hispanic
Total, number	**28,438**	**18,039**	**3,123**	**1,127**	**4,060**	**2,089**
Under age 5	3,394	2,405	321	56	409	202
Aged 5 to 9	2,915	1,959	352	69	338	198
Aged 10 to 14	2,549	1,702	333	51	306	157
Aged 15 to 19	2,433	1,542	289	57	356	189
Aged 20 to 24	2,606	1,739	237	72	379	179
Aged 25 to 29	2,612	1,740	225	84	389	174
Aged 30 to 34	2,743	1,715	287	107	464	171
Aged 35 to 39	2,343	1,407	277	104	393	163
Aged 40 to 44	1,722	1,007	203	69	284	159
Aged 45 to 49	1,194	681	137	67	196	113
Aged 50 to 54	977	543	141	45	163	86
Aged 55 to 59	806	422	115	75	122	72
Aged 60 to 64	686	399	78	59	85	65
Aged 65 to 69	591	317	52	72	95	56
Aged 70 to 74	392	209	37	58	40	49
Aged 75 to 79	235	119	22	42	17	36
Aged 80 to 84	121	65	8	20	15	13
Aged 85 or older	119	68	11	20	10	10
Total, percent	**100.0%**	**63.4%**	**11.0%**	**4.0%**	**14.3%**	**7.3%**
Under age 5	100.0	70.9	9.5	1.6	12.1	6.0
Aged 5 to 9	100.0	67.2	12.1	2.4	11.6	6.8
Aged 10 to 14	100.0	66.8	13.1	2.0	12.0	6.2
Aged 15 to 19	100.0	63.4	11.9	2.3	14.6	7.8
Aged 20 to 24	100.0	66.7	9.1	2.8	14.5	6.9
Aged 25 to 29	100.0	66.6	8.6	3.2	14.9	6.7
Aged 30 to 34	100.0	62.5	10.5	3.9	16.9	6.2
Aged 35 to 39	100.0	60.1	11.8	4.4	16.8	7.0
Aged 40 to 44	100.0	58.5	11.8	4.0	16.5	9.2
Aged 45 to 49	100.0	57.0	11.5	5.6	16.4	9.5
Aged 50 to 54	100.0	55.6	14.4	4.6	16.7	8.8
Aged 55 to 59	100.0	52.4	14.3	9.3	15.1	8.9
Aged 60 to 64	100.0	58.2	11.4	8.6	12.4	9.5
Aged 65 to 69	100.0	53.6	8.8	12.2	16.1	9.5
Aged 70 to 74	100.0	53.3	9.4	14.8	10.2	12.5
Aged 75 to 79	100.0	50.6	9.4	17.9	7.2	15.3
Aged 80 to 84	100.0	53.7	6.6	16.5	12.4	10.7
Aged 85 or older	100.0	57.1	9.2	16.8	8.4	8.4

Source: Bureau of the Census, Internet web site, http://www.census.gov

Characteristics of Hispanic Immigrants from Mexico and Cuba, 1996

(number and percent distribution of Hispanic immigrants born in Mexico and Cuba by age, sex, income, and education, 1996; numbers in thousands)

	Mexico		Cuba	
	number	percent	number	percent
Total foreign born	**6,679**	**100.0%**	**772**	**100.0%**
Age				
Under age 5	85	1.3	2	0.3
Aged 5 to 15	684	10.2	17	2.2
Aged 16 or 17	151	2.3	8	1.0
Aged 18 to 24	1,116	16.7	36	4.7
Aged 25 to 29	1,017	15.2	35	4.5
Aged 30 to 34	944	14.1	88	11.4
Aged 35 to 44	1,314	19.7	146	18.9
Aged 45 to 64	1,024	15.3	239	31.0
Aged 65 or older	343	5.1	200	25.9
Sex				
Male	3,650	54.6	375	48.6
Female	3,029	45.4	398	51.6
Income in 1995				
Total with income	**4,694**	**100.0**	**665**	**100.0**
Under $10,000	2,047	43.6	268	40.3
$10,000 to $19,999	1,711	36.5	177	26.6
$20,000 to $34,999	696	14.8	115	17.3
$35,000 to $49,999	176	3.7	53	8.0
$50,000 or more	64	1.4	52	7.8
Education				
Total aged 25 or older	4,643	100.0	709	100.0
Not a high school graduate	3,262	70.3	279	39.4
High school graduate or some college	1,232	26.5	303	42.7
Bachelor's degree	120	2.6	73	10.3
Graduate/professional degree	29	0.6	54	7.6

Source: Bureau of the Census, Internet web site, http://www.census.gov; *calculations by New Strategist*

Hispanic Immigrants by Country of Birth, 1996

(total number of immigrants, number of Hispanic immigrants, Hispanic share of total, and share of Hispanic immigrants, by country of birth, 1996; ranked by number of immigrants within regions)

	number	share of total immigrants	share of Hispanic immigrants
TOTAL IMMIGRANTS	915,900	100.0%	–
Total Hispanic immigrants	386,431	42.2	100.0
Mexico	163,572	17.9	42.3
Caribbean, total	116,801	12.8	30.2
Dominican Republic	39,604	4.3	10.2
Cuba	26,466	2.9	6.8
Jamaica	19,089	2.1	4.9
Haiti	18,386	2.0	4.8
Trinidad and Tobago	7,344	0.8	1.9
Barbados	1,043	0.1	0.3
Dominica	797	0.1	0.2
Grenada	787	0.1	0.2
Other Caribbean nations	3,285	0.4	0.9
Central America, total	44,289	4.8	11.5
El Salvador	17,903	2.0	4.6
Guatemala	8,763	1.0	2.3
Nicaragua	6,903	0.8	1.8
Honduras	5,870	0.6	1.5
Panama	2,560	0.3	0.7
Costa Rica	1,504	0.2	0.4
Belize	786	0.1	0.2
Other Central American nations	53	–	–
South America, total	61,769	6.7	16.0
Columbia	14,283	1.6	3.7
Peru	12,871	1.4	3.3
Guyana	9,489	1.0	2.5
Ecuador	8,321	0.9	2.2
Brazil	5,891	0.6	1.5
Venezuela	3,468	0.4	0.9
Argentina	2,456	0.3	0.6
Bolivia	1,913	0.2	0.5
Chile	1,706	0.2	0.4
Other South American nations	1,371	0.1	0.4

Note: (–) means not applicable or less than 0.05 percent.
Source: U.S. Immigration and Naturalization Service, 1996 Statistical Yearbook of the Immigration and Naturalization Service, 1997; calculations by New Strategist

Hispanics by Region, Division, and Ethnicity, 1990

(number and percent distribution of Hispanics by region, division, and ethnicity, 1990; numbers in thousands)

	total Hispanic	Mexican	Puerto Rican	Cuban	other Hispanic
Number					
UNITED STATES	**22,354**	**13,496**	**2,728**	**1,044**	**5,086**
Northeast	**3,754**	**175**	**1,872**	**184**	**1,524**
New England	568	29	316	16	207
Middle Atlantic	3,186	146	1,556	167	1,317
Midwest	**1,727**	**1,153**	**258**	**37**	**279**
East North Central	1,438	944	244	30	220
West North Central	289	209	14	6	60
South	**6,767**	**4,344**	**406**	**735**	**1,282**
South Atlantic	2,133	315	338	702	778
East South Central	95	39	13	5	39
West South Central	4,539	3,990	55	28	466
West	**10,106**	**7,824**	**192**	**88**	**2,002**
Mountain	1,992	1,440	26	12	514
Pacific	8,114	6,384	166	76	1,488
Percent distribution by region and division					
UNITED STATES	**100.0%**	**100.0%**	**100.0%**	**100.0%**	**100.0%**
Northeast	**16.8**	**1.3**	**68.6**	**17.6**	**30.0**
New England	2.5	0.2	11.6	1.6	4.1
Middle Atlantic	14.3	1.1	57.0	16.0	25.9
Midwest	**7.7**	**8.5**	**9.4**	**3.5**	**5.5**
East North Central	6.4	7.0	8.9	2.9	4.3
West North Central	1.3	1.5	0.5	0.6	1.2
South	**30.3**	**32.2**	**14.9**	**70.5**	**25.2**
South Atlantic	9.5	2.3	12.4	67.3	15.3
East South Central	0.4	0.3	0.5	0.5	0.8
West South Central	20.3	29.6	2.0	2.7	9.2
West	**45.2**	**58.0**	**7.0**	**8.5**	**39.4**
Mountain	8.9	10.7	1.0	1.1	10.1
Pacific	36.3	47.3	6.1	7.3	29.2

(continued)

(continued from previous page)

	total Hispanic	Mexican	Puerto Rican	Cuban	other Hispanic
Percent distribution by ethnicity					
UNITED STATES	**100.0%**	**60.4%**	**12.2%**	**4.7%**	**22.8%**
Northeast	**100.0**	**4.7**	**49.9**	**4.9**	**40.6**
New England	100.0	5.1	55.7	2.9	36.4
Middle Atlantic	100.0	4.6	48.8	5.2	41.3
Midwest	**100.0**	**66.8**	**14.9**	**2.1**	**16.2**
East North Central	100.0	65.7	16.9	2.1	15.3
West North Central	100.0	72.4	4.9	2.1	20.6
South	**100.0**	**64.2**	**6.0**	**10.9**	**18.9**
South Atlantic	100.0	14.8	15.9	32.9	36.5
East South Central	100.0	40.7	13.5	5.3	40.5
West South Central	100.0	87.9	1.2	0.6	10.3
West	**100.0**	**77.4**	**1.9**	**0.9**	**19.8**
Mountain	100.0	72.3	1.3	0.6	25.8
Pacific	100.0	78.7	2.0	0.9	18.3

Source: Bureau of the Census, General Population Characteristics, 1990 Census of Population, CP-1-1, 1992; calculations by New Strategist

Hispanics by Region and Division, 1995 to 2020

(number and percent distribution of Hispanics and Hispanic share of the total population by region and division, selected years 1995–2020; percent change in number and percentage point change in distribution and share, 1995–2000 and 2000–2010; numbers in thousands)

	1995	2000	2010	2020	percent change 1995–2000	percent change 2000–2010
Number						
UNITED STATES	**26,932**	**31,366**	**41,138**	**52,652**	**16.5%**	**31.2%**
Northeast	**4,406**	**5,016**	**6,314**	**7,785**	**13.8**	**25.9**
New England	686	833	1,164	1,548	21.4	39.7
Middle Atlantic	3,719	4,185	5,151	6,237	12.5	23.1
Midwest	**2,089**	**2,438**	**3,155**	**3,950**	**16.7**	**29.4**
East North Central	1,719	1,987	2,543	3,165	15.6	28.0
West North Central	371	452	614	787	21.8	35.8
South	**8,224**	**9,610**	**12,547**	**15,905**	**16.9**	**30.6**
South Atlantic	2,689	3,306	4,564	5,955	22.9	38.1
East South Central	124	149	192	235	20.2	28.9
West South Central	5,410	6,152	7,792	9,713	13.7	26.7
West	**12,212**	**14,300**	**19,123**	**25,014**	**17.1**	**33.7**
Mountain	2,450	2,965	3,935	4,963	21.0	32.7
Pacific	9,762	11,337	15,187	20,050	16.1	34.0

	1995	2000	2010	2020	percentage point change 1995–2000	percentage point change 2000–2010
Percent distribution						
UNITED STATES	**100.0%**	**100.0%**	**100.0%**	**100.0%**	**–**	**–**
Northeast	**16.4**	**16.0**	**15.3**	**14.8**	**–0.4**	**–0.7**
New England	2.5	2.7	2.8	2.9	0.2	0.1
Middle Atlantic	13.8	13.3	12.5	11.8	–0.5	–0.8
Midwest	**7.8**	**7.8**	**7.7**	**7.5**	**0.0**	**–0.1**
East North Central	6.4	6.3	6.2	6.0	–0.1	–0.1
West North Central	1.4	1.4	1.5	1.5	0.0	0.1
South	**30.5**	**30.6**	**30.5**	**30.2**	**0.1**	**–0.1**
South Atlantic	10.0	10.5	11.1	11.3	0.5	0.6
East South Central	0.5	0.5	0.5	0.4	0.0	–0.0
West South Central	20.1	19.6	18.9	18.4	–0.5	–0.7
West	**45.3**	**45.6**	**46.5**	**47.5**	**0.3**	**0.9**
Mountain	9.1	9.5	9.6	9.4	0.4	0.1
Pacific	36.2	36.1	36.9	38.1	–0.1	0.8

(continued)

(continued from previous page)

Percent share	1995	2000	2010	2020	percentage point change 1995–2000	2000–2010
UNITED STATES	**10.3%**	**11.4%**	**13.8%**	**16.3%**	**1.2**	**2.4**
Northeast	**8.6**	**9.6**	**11.8**	**13.9**	**1.0**	**2.2**
New England	5.2	6.1	8.2	10.4	0.9	2.1
Middle Atlantic	9.7	10.9	13.0	15.2	1.2	2.1
Midwest	**3.4**	**3.8**	**4.8**	**5.8**	**0.4**	**1.0**
East North Central	4.0	4.5	5.6	6.7	0.5	1.1
West North Central	2.0	2.4	3.0	3.7	0.4	0.6
South	**9.0**	**9.8**	**11.7**	**13.6**	**0.8**	**1.9**
South Atlantic	5.7	6.6	8.2	9.9	0.9	1.6
East South Central	0.8	0.9	1.1	1.2	0.1	0.2
West South Central	18.8	20.1	22.9	25.8	1.3	2.8
West	**21.2**	**23.3**	**27.1**	**30.7**	**2.1**	**3.8**
Mountain	15.7	16.7	19.5	22.5	1.0	2.8
Pacific	23.3	26.0	30.2	33.7	2.7	4.2

Note: (–) means not applicable.
Source: Bureau of the Census, Population Projecctions for States, by Age, Sex, Race, and Hispanic Origin: 1995 to 2025, *Current Population Reports, PPL-47, 1996; calculations by New Strategist*

Hispanics by State and Ethnicity, 1990

(number of Hispanics, by state and ethnicity, 1990; numbers in thousands)

	total	Mexican	Puerto Rican	Cuban	other Hispanic
United States	**22,354**	**13,496**	**2,728**	**1,044**	**5,086**
Alabama	25	10	4	1	10
Alaska	18	9	2	–	6
Arizona	688	616	8	2	62
Arkansas	20	12	1	–	6
California	7,688	6,119	126	72	1,371
Colorado	424	282	7	2	133
Connecticut	213	8	147	6	51
Delaware	16	3	8	1	4
District of Columbia	33	3	2	1	26
Florida	1,574	161	247	674	492
Georgia	109	49	17	8	34
Hawaii	81	14	26	1	41
Idaho	53	43	1	–	9
Illinois	904	624	146	18	116
Indiana	99	67	14	2	16
Iowa	33	24	1	–	7
Kansas	94	76	4	1	13
Kentucky	22	9	4	1	9
Louisiana	93	23	6	9	55
Maine	7	2	1	–	3
Maryland	125	18	18	6	83
Massachusetts	288	13	151	8	116
Michigan	202	138	19	5	40
Minnesota	54	35	3	2	14
Mississippi	16	7	1	–	7
Missouri	62	38	4	2	17
Montana	12	8	–	–	3
Nebraska	37	30	1	–	6
Nevada	124	85	4	6	29
New Hampshire	11	2	3	1	5
New Jersey	740	29	320	85	306
New Mexico	579	329	3	1	247
New York	2,214	93	1,087	74	960

(continued)

(continued from previous page)

	total	Mexican	Puerto Rican	Cuban	other Hispanic
North Carolina	77	33	15	4	26
North Dakota	5	3	–	–	1
Ohio	140	58	46	4	32
Oklahoma	86	63	5	1	17
Oregon	113	86	3	1	23
Pennsylvania	232	24	149	7	52
Rhode Island	46	2	13	1	29
South Carolina	31	11	6	2	11
South Dakota	5	3	–	–	1
Tennessee	33	14	4	2	13
Texas	4,340	3,891	43	18	388
Utah	85	57	2	–	25
Vermont	4	1	1	–	2
Virginia	160	33	24	6	97
Washington	215	156	9	2	47
West Virginia	8	3	1	–	5
Wisconsin	93	58	19	2	15
Wyoming	26	19	–	–	7

Note: (–) means less than 500.
Source: Bureau of the Census, Internet web site, http://www.census.gov

Distribution of Hispanics by State and Ethnicity, 1990

(percent distribution of Hispanics by state and ethnicity, 1990)

	total	Mexican	Puerto Rican	Cuban	other Hispanic
United States	**100.0%**	**100.0%**	**100.0%**	**100.0%**	**100.0%**
Alabama	0.1	0.1	0.1	0.1	0.2
Alaska	0.1	0.1	0.1	0.0	0.1
Arizona	3.1	4.6	0.3	0.2	1.2
Arkansas	0.1	0.1	0.0	0.0	0.1
California	34.4	45.3	4.6	6.9	26.9
Colorado	1.9	2.1	0.3	0.2	2.6
Connecticut	1.0	0.1	5.4	0.6	1.0
Delaware	0.1	0.0	0.3	0.1	0.1
District of Columbia	0.1	0.0	0.1	0.1	0.5
Florida	7.0	1.2	9.1	64.6	9.7
Georgia	0.5	0.4	0.6	0.7	0.7
Hawaii	0.4	0.1	0.9	0.1	0.8
Idaho	0.2	0.3	0.0	0.0	0.2
Illinois	4.0	4.6	5.4	1.7	2.3
Indiana	0.4	0.5	0.5	0.2	0.3
Iowa	0.1	0.2	0.0	0.0	0.1
Kansas	0.4	0.6	0.1	0.1	0.3
Kentucky	0.1	0.1	0.1	0.1	0.2
Louisiana	0.4	0.2	0.2	0.8	1.1
Maine	0.0	0.0	0.0	0.0	0.1
Maryland	0.6	0.1	0.6	0.6	1.6
Massachusetts	1.3	0.1	5.5	0.8	2.3
Michigan	0.9	1.0	0.7	0.5	0.8
Minnesota	0.2	0.3	0.1	0.1	0.3
Mississippi	0.1	0.0	0.0	0.0	0.1
Missouri	0.3	0.3	0.1	0.2	0.3
Montana	0.1	0.1	0.0	0.0	0.1
Nebraska	0.2	0.2	0.0	0.0	0.1
Nevada	0.6	0.6	0.2	0.6	0.6
New Hampshire	0.1	0.0	0.1	0.1	0.1
New Jersey	3.3	0.2	11.7	8.2	6.0
New Mexico	2.6	2.4	0.1	0.1	4.9
New York	9.9	0.7	39.8	7.1	18.9

(continued)

(continued from previous page)

	total	Mexican	Puerto Rican	Cuban	other Hispanic
North Carolina	0.3%	0.2%	0.5%	0.4%	0.5%
North Dakota	0.0	0.0	0.0	0.0	0.0
Ohio	0.6	0.4	1.7	0.3	0.6
Oklahoma	0.4	0.5	0.2	0.1	0.3
Oregon	0.5	0.6	0.1	0.1	0.5
Pennsylvania	1.0	0.2	5.5	0.7	1.0
Rhode Island	0.2	0.0	0.5	0.1	0.6
South Carolina	0.1	0.1	0.2	0.2	0.2
South Dakota	0.0	0.0	0.0	0.0	0.0
Tennessee	0.1	0.1	0.2	0.2	0.2
Texas	19.4	28.8	1.6	1.7	7.6
Utah	0.4	0.4	0.1	0.0	0.5
Vermont	0.0	0.0	0.0	0.0	0.0
Virginia	0.7	0.2	0.9	0.6	1.9
Washington	1.0	1.2	0.3	0.2	0.9
West Virginia	0.0	0.0	0.0	0.0	0.1
Wisconsin	0.4	0.4	0.7	0.2	0.3
Wyoming	0.1	0.1	0.0	0.0	0.1

Source: Calculations by New Strategist based on Census Bureau data from the 1990 Census at Internet web site, http://www.census.gov

Ethnic Share of Hispanic Population by State, 1990

(Hispanic ethnic groups as a percent of total Hispanic population, by state, 1990)

	total Hispanics	Mexican	Puerto Rican	Cuban	other
United States	**100.0%**	**60.4%**	**12.2%**	**4.7%**	**22.8%**
Alabama	100.0	38.6	14.4	5.9	41.0
Alaska	100.0	52.4	10.9	1.6	35.2
Arizona	100.0	89.5	1.2	0.3	9.0
Arkansas	100.0	62.9	5.9	2.5	28.7
California	100.0	79.6	1.6	0.9	17.8
Colorado	100.0	66.6	1.7	0.5	31.2
Connecticut	100.0	3.9	68.9	3.0	24.2
Delaware	100.0	19.5	52.2	4.6	23.7
District of Columbia	100.0	9.1	6.7	3.8	80.4
Florida	100.0	10.3	15.7	42.8	31.2
Georgia	100.0	45.2	16.0	7.2	31.7
Hawaii	100.0	17.7	31.7	0.7	50.0
Idaho	100.0	81.6	1.3	0.3	16.8
Illinois	100.0	69.0	16.1	2.0	12.9
Indiana	100.0	67.6	14.2	1.9	16.4
Iowa	100.0	74.7	3.9	1.5	19.9
Kansas	100.0	80.9	3.8	1.5	13.8
Kentucky	100.0	39.5	16.7	4.9	38.8
Louisiana	100.0	25.2	6.6	9.2	58.9
Maine	100.0	31.5	18.3	5.1	45.0
Maryland	100.0	14.7	14.0	5.1	66.2
Massachusetts	100.0	4.4	52.6	2.8	40.2
Michigan	100.0	68.6	9.2	2.6	19.6
Minnesota	100.0	64.4	6.1	2.9	26.7
Mississippi	100.0	42.2	8.2	3.1	46.5
Missouri	100.0	62.0	6.4	3.4	28.1
Montana	100.0	68.7	3.6	1.0	26.7
Nebraska	100.0	80.2	3.1	1.3	15.3
Nevada	100.0	68.5	3.4	4.8	23.2
New Hampshire	100.0	20.8	29.1	5.1	44.9
New Jersey	100.0	3.9	43.3	11.5	41.3
New Mexico	100.0	56.8	0.5	0.2	42.6
New York	100.0	4.2	49.1	3.4	43.4

(continued)

(continued from previous page)

	total Hispanics	Mexican	Puerto Rican	Cuban	other
North Carolina	100.0%	42.6%	19.1%	4.9%	33.5%
North Dakota	100.0	61.7	8.3	1.4	28.7
Ohio	100.0	41.4	32.8	2.5	23.2
Oklahoma	100.0	73.4	5.4	1.2	20.0
Oregon	100.0	76.0	2.5	1.2	20.4
Pennsylvania	100.0	10.4	64.1	3.2	22.2
Rhode Island	100.0	5.3	28.4	1.8	64.4
South Carolina	100.0	36.1	21.0	5.4	37.5
South Dakota	100.0	65.5	7.2	0.8	26.5
Tennessee	100.0	42.4	13.1	6.1	38.4
Texas	100.0	89.7	1.0	0.4	8.9
Utah	100.0	67.2	2.6	0.5	29.7
Vermont	100.0	19.8	18.0	4.6	57.6
Virginia	100.0	20.6	14.8	3.9	60.7
Washington	100.0	72.6	4.4	1.1	21.9
West Virginia	100.0	33.1	10.6	3.1	53.3
Wisconsin	100.0	61.8	20.5	1.8	15.9
Wyoming	100.0	72.7	1.3	0.2	25.8

Source: Calculations by New Strategist based on Census Bureau data from the 1990 census at Internet web site, http://www.census.gov

Hispanics by State, 1995 to 2020

(number of Hispanics by state, selected years 1995–2020; percent change 1995–2000 and 2000–2010; numbers in thousands)

	1995	2000	2010	2020	percent change 1995–2000	percent change 2000–2010
United States	26,932	31,366	41,138	52,652	16.5%	31.2%
Alabama	32	37	47	57	15.6	27.0
Alaska	25	31	41	54	24.0	32.3
Arizona	868	1,071	1,450	1,846	23.4	35.4
Arkansas	27	33	46	60	22.2	39.4
California	9,206	10,647	14,214	18,757	15.7	33.5
Colorado	507	594	770	959	17.2	29.6
Connecticut	248	288	386	509	16.1	34.0
Delaware	19	25	33	43	31.6	32.0
District of Columbia	37	40	55	70	8.1	37.5
Florida	1,955	2,390	3,319	4,372	22.3	38.9
Georgia	150	189	252	311	26.0	33.3
Hawaii	100	107	132	166	7.0	23.4
Idaho	72	96	140	181	33.3	45.8
Illinois	1,090	1,267	1,637	2,051	16.2	29.2
Indiana	119	140	179	219	17.6	27.9
Iowa	46	54	71	86	17.4	31.5
Kansas	114	138	191	250	21.1	38.4
Kentucky	27	32	42	51	18.5	31.3
Louisiana	105	119	156	201	13.3	31.1
Maine	6	8	14	18	33.3	75.0
Maryland	172	214	300	389	24.4	40.2
Massachusetts	355	437	619	824	23.1	41.6
Michigan	233	261	319	390	12.0	22.2
Minnesota	73	95	132	171	30.1	38.9
Mississippi	19	21	27	33	10.5	28.6
Missouri	74	90	121	155	21.6	34.4
Montana	16	20	28	34	25.0	40.0
Nebraska	50	61	80	100	22.0	31.1
Nevada	192	277	403	519	44.3	45.5
New Hampshire	13	17	22	31	30.8	29.4
New Jersey	896	1,044	1,348	1,682	16.5	29.1
New Mexico	657	736	912	1,121	12.0	23.9
New York	2,541	2,805	3,357	3,982	10.4	19.7
North Carolina	100	121	154	188	21.0	27.3
North Dakota	4	6	10	12	50.0	66.7

(continued)

(continued from previous page)

	1995	2000	2010	2020	percent change 1995–2000	2000–2010
Ohio	162	183	230	288	13.0%	25.7%
Oklahoma	104	124	167	220	19.2	34.7
Oregon	150	195	278	374	30.0	42.6
Pennsylvania	279	334	448	570	19.7	34.1
Rhode Island	60	76	112	154	26.7	47.4
South Carolina	36	42	58	73	16.7	38.1
South Dakota	7	8	10	12	14.3	25.0
Tennessee	45	57	75	92	26.7	31.6
Texas	5,173	5,875	7,421	9,233	13.6	26.3
Utah	110	138	185	237	25.5	34.1
Vermont	4	6	8	12	50.0	33.3
Virginia	209	269	376	482	28.7	39.8
Washington	284	360	519	700	26.8	44.2
West Virginia	9	11	17	22	22.2	54.5
Wisconsin	114	136	173	213	19.3	27.2
Wyoming	27	35	48	64	29.6	37.1

Note: Numbers may not add to total due to rounding.
Source: Bureau of the Census, Population Projections for States, by Age, Sex, Race, and Hispanic Origin: 1995 to 2025, *Current Population Reports, PPL-47, 1996; calculations by New Strategist*

Distribution of Hispanics by State, 1995 to 2020

(percent distribution of Hispanics by state, selected years 1995–2020)

	1995	*2000*	*2010*	*2020*
United States	**100.0%**	**100.0%**	**100.0%**	**100.0%**
Alabama	0.1	0.1	0.1	0.1
Alaska	0.1	0.1	0.1	0.1
Arizona	3.2	3.4	3.5	3.5
Arkansas	0.1	0.1	0.1	0.1
California	34.2	33.9	34.6	35.6
Colorado	1.9	1.9	1.9	1.8
Connecticut	0.9	0.9	0.9	1.0
Delaware	0.1	0.1	0.1	0.1
District of Columbia	0.1	0.1	0.1	0.1
Florida	7.3	7.6	8.1	8.3
Georgia	0.6	0.6	0.6	0.6
Hawaii	0.4	0.3	0.3	0.3
Idaho	0.3	0.3	0.3	0.3
Illinois	4.0	4.0	4.0	3.9
Indiana	0.4	0.4	0.4	0.4
Iowa	0.2	0.2	0.2	0.2
Kansas	0.4	0.4	0.5	0.5
Kentucky	0.1	0.1	0.1	0.1
Louisiana	0.4	0.4	0.4	0.4
Maine	0.0	0.0	0.0	0.0
Maryland	0.6	0.7	0.7	0.7
Massachusetts	1.3	1.4	1.5	1.6
Michigan	0.9	0.8	0.8	0.7
Minnesota	0.3	0.3	0.3	0.3
Mississippi	0.1	0.1	0.1	0.1
Missouri	0.3	0.3	0.3	0.3
Montana	0.1	0.1	0.1	0.1
Nebraska	0.2	0.2	0.2	0.2
Nevada	0.7	0.9	1.0	1.0
New Hampshire	0.0	0.1	0.1	0.1
New Jersey	3.3	3.3	3.3	3.2
New Mexico	2.4	2.3	2.2	2.1
New York	9.4	8.9	8.2	7.6
North Carolina	0.4	0.4	0.4	0.4
North Dakota	0.0	0.0	0.0	0.0
Ohio	0.6	0.6	0.6	0.5

(continued)

(continued from previous page)

	1995	2000	2010	2020
Oklahoma	0.4%	0.4%	0.4%	0.4%
Oregon	0.6	0.6	0.7	0.7
Pennsylvania	1.0	1.1	1.1	1.1
Rhode Island	0.2	0.2	0.3	0.3
South Carolina	0.1	0.1	0.1	0.1
South Dakota	0.0	0.0	0.0	0.0
Tennessee	0.2	0.2	0.2	0.2
Texas	19.2	18.7	18.0	17.5
Utah	0.4	0.4	0.4	0.5
Vermont	0.0	0.0	0.0	0.0
Virginia	0.8	0.9	0.9	0.9
Washington	1.1	1.1	1.3	1.3
West Virginia	0.0	0.0	0.0	0.0
Wisconsin	0.4	0.4	0.4	0.4
Wyoming	0.1	0.1	0.1	0.1

Source: Calculations by New Strategist based on Census Bureau data in Population Projections for States, by Age, Sex, Race, and Hispanic Origin: 1995 to 2025, *Current Population Reports, PPL-47, 1996*

Hispanic Share of State Populations, 1995 to 2020

(Hispanics as a percent of state populations, selected years 1995 to 2020; percentage point change in share, 1995–2020)

	1995	2000	2010	2020	percentage point change 1995–2020
United States	**10.2%**	**11.4%**	**13.8%**	**16.3%**	**6.1**
Alabama	0.8	0.8	1.0	1.1	0.4
Alaska	4.1	4.7	5.5	6.4	2.3
Arizona	20.6	22.3	26.3	30.2	9.6
Arkansas	1.1	1.3	1.6	2.0	0.9
California	29.1	32.7	37.8	41.4	12.3
Colorado	13.5	14.3	16.5	19.1	5.6
Connecticut	7.6	8.8	11.4	14.1	6.5
Delaware	2.6	3.3	4.0	5.1	2.4
District of Columbia	6.7	7.6	9.8	11.2	4.5
Florida	13.8	15.7	19.1	22.3	8.5
Georgia	2.1	2.4	2.9	3.3	1.2
Hawaii	8.4	8.5	9.2	9.9	1.5
Idaho	6.2	7.1	9.0	10.8	4.6
Illinois	9.2	10.5	13.1	15.6	6.4
Indiana	2.1	2.3	2.8	3.4	1.3
Iowa	1.6	1.9	2.4	2.8	1.2
Kansas	4.4	5.2	6.7	8.3	3.8
Kentucky	0.7	0.8	1.0	1.2	0.5
Louisiana	2.4	2.7	3.3	4.0	1.6
Maine	0.5	0.6	1.1	1.3	0.8
Maryland	3.4	4.1	5.3	6.4	3.0
Massachusetts	5.8	7.0	9.6	12.2	6.4
Michigan	2.4	2.7	3.2	3.9	1.5
Minnesota	1.6	2.0	2.6	3.2	1.6
Mississippi	0.7	0.7	0.9	1.1	0.4
Missouri	1.4	1.6	2.1	2.5	1.1
Montana	1.8	2.1	2.7	3.1	1.3
Nebraska	3.1	3.6	4.4	5.3	2.2
Nevada	12.5	14.8	18.9	23.2	10.6
New Hampshire	1.1	1.4	1.7	2.2	1.1
New Jersey	11.3	12.8	15.6	18.2	6.9
New Mexico	39.0	39.6	42.3	45.7	6.7
New York	14.0	15.5	18.1	20.6	6.6
North Carolina	1.4	1.6	1.8	2.1	0.7
North Dakota	0.6	0.9	1.4	1.7	1.0

(continued)

(continued from previous page)

	1995	2000	2010	2020	percentage point change 1995–2020
Ohio	1.5%	1.6%	2.0%	2.5%	1.0
Oklahoma	3.2	3.7	4.6	5.6	2.4
Oregon	4.8	5.7	7.3	9.0	4.2
Pennsylvania	2.3	2.7	3.6	4.5	2.2
Rhode Island	6.1	7.6	10.8	13.9	7.9
South Carolina	1.0	1.1	1.4	1.6	0.6
South Dakota	1.0	1.0	1.2	1.4	0.4
Tennessee	0.9	1.0	1.2	1.4	0.6
Texas	27.6	29.2	32.5	35.9	8.3
Utah	5.6	6.3	7.3	8.5	2.9
Vermont	0.7	1.0	1.2	1.8	1.1
Virginia	3.2	3.8	4.9	5.9	2.7
Washington	5.2	6.1	7.8	9.4	4.2
West Virginia	0.5	0.6	0.9	1.2	0.7
Wisconsin	2.2	2.6	3.1	3.7	1.5
Wyoming	5.6	6.7	7.9	9.6	3.9

Source: Calculations by New Strategist based on Census Bureau data in Population Projections for States, by Age, Sex, Race, and Hispanic Origin: 1995 to 2025, *Current Population Reports, PPL-47, 1996*

Metropolitan Areas with the Most Hispanics, 1990

(metropolitan areas with at least 100,000 Hispanics ranked by size of Hispanic population; number of Hispanics and Hispanic share of total metropolitan population, 1990; numbers in thousands)

		number	percent
1.	Los Angeles–Riverside–Orange County, CA	4,779	32.9%
2.	New York–Northern New Jersey–Long Island, NY-NJ-CT-PA	2,843	14.7
3.	Miami-Fort Lauderdale, FL	1,062	33.3
4.	San Francisco–Oakland–San Jose, CA	970	15.5
5.	Chicago–Gary–Kenosha, IL-IN-WI	898	10.9
6.	Houston–Galveston–Brazoria, TX	773	20.7
7.	San Antonio, TX	628	47.4
8.	Dallas–Fort Worth, TX	526	13.0
9.	San Diego, CA	511	20.4
10.	El Paso, TX	412	69.6
11.	Phoenix–Mesa, AZ	380	17.0
12.	McAllen–Edinburg–Mission, TX	327	85.2
13.	Fresno, CA	267	35.3
14.	Washington–Baltimore, DC-MD-VA-WV	259	3.9
15.	Denver–Boulder–Greeley, CO	254	12.8
16.	Boston–Brockton–Nashua, MA-NH-ME-CT	239	4.4
17.	Philadelphia–Wilmington–Atlantic City, PA-NJ-DE-MD	224	3.8
18.	Albuquerque, NM	218	37.1
19.	Brownsville–Harlingen–San Benito, TX	213	81.9
20.	Corpus Christi, TX	182	52.0
21.	Austin–San Marcos, TX	177	20.9
22.	Sacramento–Yolo, CA	172	11.6
23.	Tucson, AZ	163	24.5
24.	Bakersfield, CA	152	28.0
25.	Tampa–St. Petersburg–Clearwater, FL	139	6.7
26.	Laredo, TX	125	93.9
27.	Visalia–Tulare–Porterville, CA	121	38.8
28.	Salinas, CA	120	33.6
29.	Stockton–Lodi, CA	113	23.4
30.	Detroit–Ann Arbor–Flint, MI	105	2.0
31.	Orlando, FL	101	8.2

Source: Bureau of the Census, Statistical Abstract of the United States 1993; *calculations by New Strategist*

Hispanics: Spending

Hispanic spending is focused on the home.

The nation's 8 million Hispanic consumer units spent an average of $26,794 in 1995, according to the Consumer Expenditure Survey. With a spending index of 83, Hispanics spend 17 percent less than the average consumer unit.

While Hispanic spending is below average in many categories, it is above average on a wide variety of items. Because of their larger families, Hispanics spend 20 percent more than the average consumer unit on food at home. Hispanics spend more than the average consumer unit on items such as rice; white bread; meats, poultry, fish, and eggs; dairy products; fruits and vegetables; beer and ale; telephone services; laundry and cleaning supplies; infants' furniture; children's clothes; used trucks; and video rentals.

■ Hispanic spending is greatly influenced by immigration. Because many Hispanics come from Mexico and other countries with traditional, family-oriented cultures, their spending on items for the home—such as food, cleaning supplies, video rentals, and so on—is much higher than average.

Hispanics spend 17 percent less than the average consumer unit

(average annual spending of consumer units by race and Hispanic origin of householder, 1995)

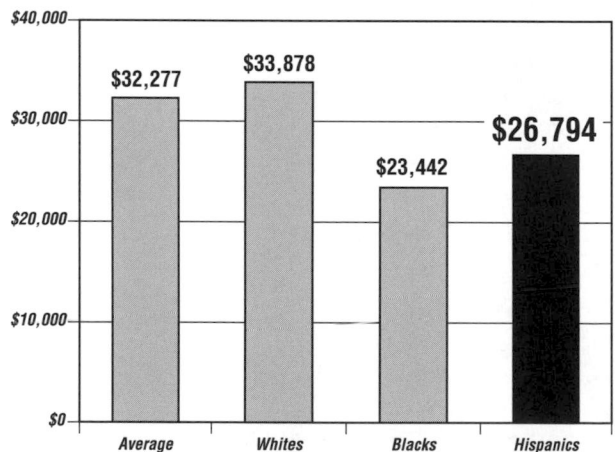

Average and Indexed Spending of Hispanic Households, 1995

(average annual expenditures of total and Hispanic consumer units, and indexed expenditures of Hispanic consumer units, 1995)

	average spending of total consumer units	Hispanic consumer units	
		average spending	indexed spending*
Number of consumer units	103,024,000	8,006,000	–
Average before-tax income of consumer unit	$36,948.00	$27,242.00	74
Average spending of consumer unit, total	32,276.59	26,793.76	83
FOOD	**$4,505.34**	**$4,678.46**	**104**
FOOD AT HOME	2,802.91	3,369.67	120
Cereals and bakery products	**441.13**	**454.03**	**103**
Cereals and cereal products	165.23	202.90	123
Flour	8.42	18.78	223
Prepared flour mixes	12.80	9.92	78
Ready-to-eat and cooked cereal	97.00	105.01	108
Rice	20.17	38.61	191
Pasta, cornmeal, and other cereal products	26.84	30.57	114
Bakery products	275.90	251.14	91
Bread	75.70	81.47	108
White bread	36.77	45.52	124
Bread, other than white	38.92	35.94	92
Cookies and crackers	67.33	59.19	88
Cookies	44.90	43.20	96
Crackers	22.43	16.00	71
Frozen and refrigerated bakery products	21.92	17.01	78
Other bakery products	110.95	93.46	84
Biscuits and rolls	38.49	24.48	64
Cakes and cupcakes	34.63	32.21	93
Bread and cracker products	4.23	1.74	41
Sweetrolls, coffee cakes, doughnuts	20.80	23.62	114
Pies, tarts, turnovers	12.80	11.41	89
Meats, poultry, fish, and eggs	**752.43**	**1,096.56**	**146**
Beef	227.60	331.37	146
Ground beef	84.47	120.56	143
Roast	40.09	47.70	119
Chuck roast	12.63	14.71	116
Round roast	13.18	9.28	70
Other roast	14.28	23.70	166
Steak	86.84	136.73	157
Round steak	18.82	32.93	175

(continued)

	average spending of total consumer units	Hispanic consumer units	
		average spending	indexed spending*
Sirloin steak	$23.42	$37.14	159
Other steak	44.61	66.67	149
Other beef	16.19	26.38	163
Pork	156.00	229.30	147
Bacon	20.32	25.58	126
Pork chops	39.69	63.84	161
Ham	37.06	51.52	139
Ham, not canned	34.76	48.54	140
Canned ham	2.31	2.98	129
Sausage	22.12	28.85	130
Other pork	36.79	59.51	162
Other meats	103.63	120.91	117
Frankfurters	22.13	23.52	106
Lunch meats (cold cuts)	69.66	72.32	104
Bologna, liverwurst, salami	25.45	31.03	122
Other lunchmeats	44.22	41.29	93
Lamb, organ meats, and others	11.84	25.07	212
Lamb and organ meats	9.31	17.78	191
Mutton, goat and game	2.54	7.29	287
Poultry	137.65	204.51	149
Fresh and frozen chickens	105.14	155.94	148
Fresh and frozen whole chicken	28.21	54.56	193
Fresh and frozen chicken parts	76.93	101.39	132
Other poultry	32.51	48.57	149
Fish and seafood	97.33	148.05	152
Canned fish and seafood	17.11	15.90	93
Fresh fish and shellfish	52.43	94.58	180
Frozen fish and shellfish	27.79	37.57	135
Eggs	30.23	62.41	206
Dairy products	**296.61**	**346.71**	**117**
Fresh milk and cream	123.00	178.86	145
Fresh milk, all types	113.81	168.19	148
Cream	9.19	10.67	116
Other dairy products	173.60	167.85	97
Butter	12.31	14.30	116
Cheese	88.00	89.48	102
Ice cream and related products	51.24	45.25	88
Miscellaneous dairy products	22.05	18.82	85
Fruits and vegetables	**456.67**	**593.50**	**130**
Fresh fruits	144.14	202.41	140
Apples	29.15	38.75	133
Bananas	30.26	44.87	148

(continued)

(continued from previous page)

	average spending of total consumer units	Hispanic consumer units	
		average spending	indexed spending*
Oranges	$16.27	$26.12	161
Citrus fruits, excl. oranges	12.03	20.83	173
Other fresh fruits	56.43	71.83	127
Fresh vegetables	137.31	184.71	135
Potatoes	28.50	28.63	100
Lettuce	18.22	22.43	123
Tomatoes	21.64	44.15	204
Other fresh vegetables	68.95	89.49	130
Processed fruits	95.70	117.33	123
Frozen fruits and fruit juices	17.00	20.45	120
Frozen orange juice	8.66	10.12	117
Frozen fruits	1.81	1.24	69
Frozen fruit juices	6.53	9.09	139
Canned fruits	13.88	10.77	78
Dried fruit	5.86	5.40	92
Fresh fruit juice	17.55	23.31	133
Canned and bottled fruit juice	41.40	57.40	139
Processed vegetables	79.52	89.05	112
Frozen vegetables	28.07	21.61	77
Canned and dried vegetables and juices	51.44	67.44	131
Canned beans	11.26	12.43	110
Canned corn	6.91	10.09	146
Frozen vegetable juices	0.31	0.88	284
Fresh and canned vegetable juices	6.87	9.08	132
Other food at home	**856.08**	**878.87**	**103**
Sugar and other sweets	112.08	95.55	85
Candy and chewing gum	67.43	42.47	63
Sugar	17.44	30.71	176
Artificial sweeteners	4.51	5.07	112
Jams, preserves, other sweets	22.70	17.30	76
Fats and oils	82.22	112.73	137
Margarine	12.74	12.40	97
Fats and oils	24.60	55.07	224
Salad dressings	26.16	29.72	114
Nondairy cream and imitation milk	7.15	4.00	56
Peanut butter	11.58	11.55	100
Miscellaneous foods	376.59	385.80	102
Frozen prepared foods	66.03	50.54	77
Frozen meals	19.87	14.54	73
Other frozen prepared foods	46.16	36.00	78
Canned and packaged soups	31.25	31.03	99
Potato chips, nuts, and other snacks	80.50	63.81	79

(continued)

(continued from previous page)

	average spending of total consumer units	Hispanic consumer units	
		average spending	indexed spending*
Potato chips and other snacks	$62.33	$48.51	78
Nuts	18.17	15.30	84
Condiments and seasonings	86.51	76.88	89
Salt, spices, and other seasonings	20.29	23.96	118
Olives, pickles, relishes	10.14	8.14	80
Sauces and gravies	39.88	35.02	88
Baking needs and miscellaneous products	16.20	9.77	60
Other canned/packaged prepared foods	112.30	163.53	146
Prepared salads	13.51	8.58	64
Prepared desserts	8.99	8.17	91
Baby food	25.02	63.94	256
Miscellaneous prepared foods	64.79	82.83	128
Nonalcoholic beverages	240.27	257.62	107
Cola	89.20	100.36	113
Other carbonated drinks	42.50	37.39	88
Coffee	46.33	47.66	103
Roasted coffee	30.90	24.66	80
Instant and freeze-dried coffee	15.43	23.01	149
Noncarbonated fruit-flavored drinks, including nonfrozen lemonade	24.83	34.05	137
Tea	15.64	11.68	75
Nonalcoholic beer	1.01	–	–
Other nonalcoholic beverages and ice	20.75	26.48	128
Food prepared by consumer unit on out-of-town trips	44.91	27.17	60
FOOD AWAY FROM HOME	**1,702.43**	**1,308.79**	**77**
Meals at restaurants, carry-outs, other	**1,331.44**	**1,085.57**	**82**
Lunch	464.83	431.03	93
Dinner	653.29	487.80	75
Snacks and nonalcoholic beverages	111.73	72.62	65
Breakfast and brunch	101.59	94.12	93
Board (including at school)	**54.60**	**18.42**	**34**
Catered affairs	**43.89**	**10.18**	**23**
Food on out-of-town trips	**196.85**	**98.53**	**50**
School lunches	**49.41**	**39.27**	**79**
Meals as pay	**26.23**	**56.81**	**217**
ALCOHOLIC BEVERAGES	**$277.28**	**$196.84**	**71**
At home	**165.34**	**147.98**	**90**
Beer and ale	87.91	117.60	134
Whiskey	13.37	7.34	55
Wine	48.68	14.06	29
Other alcoholic beverages	15.39	8.98	58

(continued)

(continued from previous page)

	average spending of total consumer units	Hispanic consumer units	
		average spending	indexed spending*
Away from home	**$111.94**	**$48.86**	**44**
Beer and ale	33.45	14.32	43
Wine	20.29	8.46	42
Other alcoholic beverages	29.77	14.05	47
Alcoholic beverages purchased on trips	28.43	12.04	42
HOUSING	**$10,464.95**	**$9,223.26**	**88**
SHELTER	**5,931.76**	**5,571.89**	**94**
Owned dwellings**	**3,754.44**	**2,354.23**	**63**
Mortgage interest and charges	2,106.99	1,521.14	72
Mortgage interest	1,991.49	1,474.09	74
Interest paid, home equity loan	53.32	35.92	67
Interest paid, home equity line of credit	61.81	11.13	18
Prepayment penalty charges	0.37	–	–
Property taxes	931.76	466.32	50
Maintenance, repairs, insurance, other expenses	715.68	366.77	51
Homeowner's and related insurance	225.32	131.86	59
Fire and extended coverage	6.69	5.94	89
Homeowner's insurance	218.63	125.91	58
Ground rent	31.63	32.37	102
Maintenance and repair services	365.24	154.03	42
Painting and papering	41.18	4.97	12
Plumbing and water heating	33.28	15.84	48
Heat, air conditioning, electrical work	72.49	19.82	27
Roofing and gutters	65.15	74.94	115
Other repair and maintenance services	130.33	37.38	29
Repair and replacement of hard-surface flooring	21.23	0.80	4
Repair of built-in appliances	1.59	0.29	18
Maintenance and repair materials	71.32	41.99	59
Paints, wallpaper, and supplies	19.60	6.68	34
Tools and equipment for painting, wallpapering	2.11	0.72	34
Plumbing supplies and equipment	7.26	2.95	41
Electrical supplies, heating and cooling equipment	5.22	1.50	29
Hard-surface flooring, repair and replacement	3.51	2.97	85
Roofing and gutters	4.30	3.95	92
Plaster, paneling, siding, windows, doors, screens, awnings	11.53	7.09	61
Patio, walk, fence, driveway, masonry, brick, and stucco work	0.88	0.27	31
Landscape maintenance	1.78	2.20	124
Miscellaneous supplies and equipment	15.13	13.67	90
Insulation, other maintenance and repair	11.41	7.02	62

(continued)

(continued from previous page)

	average spending of total consumer units	Hispanic consumer units	
		average spending	indexed spending*
Finish basement, remodel rooms, or build patios, walks, etc.	$3.72	$6.65	179
Property management and security	22.17	6.52	29
Property management	16.64	3.91	23
Management and upkeep services for security	5.53	2.62	47
Rented dwellings	**1,785.64**	**3,102.39**	**174**
Rent	1,716.25	2,990.76	174
Rent as pay	48.68	97.17	200
Maintenance, insurance, and other expenses	20.71	14.45	70
Tenant's insurance	7.35	2.82	38
Maintenance and repair services	5.32	7.72	145
Repair or maintenance services	4.93	7.10	144
Repair and replacement of hard-surface flooring	0.32	0.62	194
Repair of built-in appliances	0.07	–	–
Maintenance and repair materials	8.04	3.91	49
Paint, wallpaper, and supplies	1.48	1.60	108
Painting and wallpapering	0.16	0.17	106
Plastering, panels, roofing, gutters, etc.	0.71	0.68	96
Patio, walk, fence, driveway, masonry, brick, and stucco work	0.03	–	–
Plumbing supplies and equipment	1.14	0.06	5
Electrical supplies, heating and cooling equipment	0.31	0.05	16
Miscellaneous supplies and equipment	3.53	0.35	10
Insulation, other maintenance and repair	1.43	0.11	8
Materials for additions, finishing basements, remodeling rooms	2.07	–	–
Construction materials for jobs not started	0.04	0.24	600
Hard-surface flooring	0.22	1.00	455
Landscape maintenance	0.46	–	–
Other lodging	**391.68**	**115.26**	**29**
Owned vacation homes	127.18	36.06	28
Mortgage interest and charges	48.74	14.78	30
Mortgage interest	47.03	13.26	28
Interest paid, home equity loan	0.12	1.52	1,267
Interest paid, home equity line of credit	1.59	–	–
Property taxes	54.14	17.00	31
Maintenance, insurance, and other expenses	24.29	4.29	18
Homeowner's and related insurance	6.10	3.19	52
Homeowner's insurance	5.90	3.19	54
Fire and extended coverage	0.20	–	–

(continued)

(continued from previous page)

	average spending of total consumer units	Hispanic consumer units	
		average spending	indexed spending*
Ground rent	$2.33	–	–
Maintenance and repair services	10.56	$0.54	5
Maintenance and repair materials	2.00	–	–
Property management and security	2.64	0.57	22
Property management	1.88	0.46	24
Management and upkeep services for security	0.75	0.10	13
Parking	0.67	–	–
Housing while attending school	54.91	2.67	5
Lodging on out-of-town trips	209.59	76.53	37
UTILITIES, FUELS, PUBLIC SERVICES	**2,192.58**	**1,957.91**	**89**
Natural gas	**268.26**	**223.23**	**83**
Electricity	**869.67**	**693.30**	**80**
Fuel oil and other fuels	**86.66**	**19.47**	**22**
Fuel oil	50.69	11.08	22
Coal	2.13	0.36	17
Bottled and tank gas	28.02	6.85	24
Wood and other fuels	5.83	1.18	20
Telephone services	**708.40**	**796.24**	**112**
Telephone services in home city, excluding mobile car phones	682.65	784.25	115
Telephone services for mobile car phones	25.75	11.99	47
Water and other public services	**259.59**	**225.66**	**87**
Water and sewerage maintenance	187.25	165.50	88
Trash and garbage collection	**70.49**	**59.04**	**84**
Septic tank cleaning	**1.84**	**1.13**	**61**
HOUSEHOLD SERVICES	**508.34**	**315.83**	**62**
Personal services	**258.04**	**211.48**	**82**
Babysitting and child care in your own home	39.63	49.10	124
Babysitting and child care in someone else's home	36.48	74.71	205
Care for elderly, invalids, handicapped, etc.	35.33	0.22	1
Adult day care centers	1.05	–	–
Day care centers, nurseries, and preschools	145.55	87.46	60
Other household services	**250.30**	**104.35**	**42**
Housekeeping services	85.16	23.06	27
Gardening, lawn care service	63.96	25.21	39
Water softening service	2.90	2.52	87
Nonclothing laundry and dry cleaning, sent out	1.69	0.69	41
Nonclothing laundry and dry cleaning, coin-operated	4.83	12.88	267
Termite and other pest control services	11.70	4.97	42

(continued)

(continued from previous page)

	average spending of total consumer units	Hispanic consumer units	
		average spending	indexed spending*
Other home services	$16.60	$5.70	34
Termite and other pest control products	0.16	0.12	75
Moving, storage, and freight express	27.71	10.67	39
Appliance repair, including service center	14.07	8.84	63
Reupholstering and furniture repair	10.80	5.93	55
Repairs and rental of equipment and power tools	5.79	0.95	16
Appliance rental	1.67	2.58	154
Rental of office equipment for nonbusiness use	0.29	0.23	79
Repair of misc. household equipment and furnishings	1.75	–	–
Repair of computer systems for nonbusiness use	0.82	–	–
Computer information services	0.39	–	–
HOUSEKEEPING SUPPLIES	**429.59**	**387.11**	**90**
Laundry and cleaning supplies	**110.26**	**159.56**	**145**
Soaps and detergents	63.62	98.45	155
Other laundry cleaning products	46.64	61.11	131
Other household products	**193.90**	**157.65**	**81**
Cleansing and toilet tissue, paper towels, and napkins	60.03	71.11	118
Miscellaneous household products	71.57	53.02	74
Lawn and garden supplies	62.29	33.51	54
Postage and stationery	**125.43**	**69.91**	**56**
Stationery, stationery supplies, giftwrap	61.49	36.34	59
Postage	62.40	33.57	54
Delivery services	1.54	–	–
HOUSEHOLD FURNISHINGS & EQUIPMENT	**1,402.69**	**990.52**	**71**
Household textiles	**100.47**	**59.05**	**59**
Bathroom linens	15.50	7.69	50
Bedroom linens	45.50	27.50	60
Kitchen and dining room linens	9.26	8.01	87
Curtains and draperies	17.36	10.76	62
Slipcovers and decorative pillows	1.74	0.52	30
Sewing materials for household items	10.01	3.88	39
Other linens	1.09	0.67	61
Furniture	**327.49**	**278.12**	**85**
Mattresses and springs	41.36	32.11	78
Other bedroom furniture	51.66	62.48	121
Sofas	77.20	73.41	95
Living room chairs	39.35	18.51	47
Living room tables	16.51	10.69	65
Kitchen and dining room furniture	46.95	39.55	84
Infants' furniture	6.74	7.34	109

(continued)

(continued from previous page)

	average spending of total consumer units	Hispanic consumer units	
		average spending	indexed spending*
Outdoor furniture	$10.77	$6.19	57
Wall units, cabinets, and other furniture	36.95	37.84	102
Floor coverings	**177.25**	**122.11**	**69**
Major appliances	**154.88**	**117.57**	**76**
Dishwashers (built-in), garbage disposals, range hoods (renter)	0.95	0.24	25
Dishwashers (built-in), garbage disposals, range hoods (owner)	10.23	4.20	41
Refrigerators and freezers (renter)	6.69	6.18	92
Refrigerators and freezers (owner)	42.27	28.75	68
Washing machines (renter)	5.26	5.00	95
Washing machines (owner)	14.58	11.46	79
Clothes dryers (renter)	3.25	4.87	150
Clothes dryers (owner)	10.62	8.02	76
Cooking stoves, ovens (renter)	2.57	1.84	72
Cooking stoves, ovens (owner)	18.72	18.04	96
Microwave ovens (renter)	2.87	6.73	234
Microwave ovens (owner)	6.01	2.20	37
Portable dishwasher (renter)	0.17	–	–
Portable dishwasher (owner)	0.52	–	–
Window air conditioners (renter)	2.75	5.05	184
Window air conditioners (owner)	8.64	4.87	56
Electric floor-cleaning equipment	12.94	6.28	49
Sewing machines	4.81	2.75	57
Miscellaneous household appliances	1.03	1.09	106
Small appliances and miscellaneous housewares	**85.16**	**49.82**	**59**
Housewares	62.80	33.36	53
Plastic dinnerware	1.48	0.94	64
China and other dinnerware	11.29	7.49	66
Flatware	4.01	2.29	57
Glassware	6.91	1.06	15
Silver serving pieces	2.03	0.97	48
Other serving pieces	1.28	0.45	35
Nonelectric cookware	16.04	13.82	86
Tableware, nonelectric kitchenware	19.77	6.35	32
Small appliances	22.36	16.46	74
Small electric kitchen appliances	15.65	12.08	77
Portable heating and cooling equipment	6.70	4.39	66
Miscellaneous household equipment	**557.43**	**363.85**	**65**
Window coverings	10.64	5.16	48
Infants' equipment	8.02	38.79	484

(continued)

(continued from previous page)

	average spending of total consumer units	Hispanic consumer units	
		average spending	indexed spending*
Laundry and cleaning equipment	$11.33	$19.85	175
Outdoor equipment	4.08	1.26	31
Clocks	3.37	2.33	69
Lamps and lighting fixtures	29.77	34.44	116
Other household decorative items	137.82	56.13	41
Telephones and accessories	14.44	23.86	165
Lawn and garden equipment	42.14	21.99	52
Power tools	15.61	5.55	36
Small miscellaneous furnishings	2.02	0.17	8
Hand tools	10.16	29.65	292
Indoor plants and fresh flowers	46.82	19.94	43
Closet and storage items	6.93	2.65	38
Rental of furniture	3.24	3.41	105
Luggage	9.25	6.10	66
Computers and computer hardware, nonbusiness use	135.02	54.45	40
Computer software and accessories, nonbusiness use	18.23	11.02	60
Telephone answering devices	3.58	1.68	47
Calculators	1.88	1.60	85
Business equipment for home use	4.11	3.23	79
Other hardware	13.63	6.43	47
Smoke alarms (owner)	1.21	1.38	114
Smoke alarms (renter)	0.17	0.15	88
Other household appliances (owner)	4.71	6.53	139
Other household appliances (renter)	1.04	1.18	113
Miscellaneous household equipment and parts	18.22	4.90	27
APPAREL AND SERVICES	**$1,703.63**	**$1,719.04**	**101**
MEN AND BOYS	**425.33**	**421.95**	**99**
Men, aged 16 or older	**329.46**	**308.91**	**94**
Suits	33.42	18.04	54
Sportcoats and tailored jackets	13.23	6.36	48
Coats and jackets	30.16	21.55	71
Underwear	17.80	21.72	122
Hosiery	12.85	10.22	80
Sleepwear	3.50	1.28	37
Accessories	34.98	27.94	80
Sweaters and vests	12.43	7.81	63
Active sportswear	10.14	6.18	61
Shirts	76.52	79.45	104
Pants	63.37	93.25	147
Shorts and shorts sets	16.23	9.99	62

(continued)

(continued from previous page)

	average spending of total consumer units	Hispanic consumer units	
		average spending	indexed spending*
Uniforms	$3.67	$4.65	127
Costumes	1.17	0.47	40
Boys, aged 2 to 15	**95.86**	**113.04**	**118**
Coats and jackets	9.27	1.49	16
Sweaters	1.92	2.23	116
Shirts	20.82	37.53	180
Underwear	5.76	8.13	141
Sleepwear	1.12	–	
Hosiery	4.01	2.22	55
Accessories	6.66	9.98	150
Suits, sportcoats, and vests	3.59	2.80	78
Pants	24.03	24.61	102
Shorts and shorts sets	11.44	14.83	130
Uniforms	4.06	3.41	84
Costumes	0.93	1.02	110
WOMEN AND GIRLS	**660.49**	**506.91**	**77**
Women, aged 16 or older	**559.19**	**398.36**	**71**
Coats and jackets	41.43	24.68	60
Dresses	83.48	78.93	95
Sportcoats and tailored jackets	4.29	3.10	72
Sweaters and vests	28.51	14.91	52
Shirts, blouses, and tops	100.86	74.12	73
Skirts	20.49	13.49	66
Pants	70.73	45.93	65
Shorts and shorts sets	26.72	16.07	60
Active sportswear	27.19	13.47	50
Sleepwear	23.65	19.89	84
Undergarments	30.37	16.36	54
Hosiery	20.88	17.51	84
Suits	32.66	18.00	55
Accessories	43.56	38.55	88
Uniforms	2.42	1.33	55
Costumes	1.93	2.03	105
Girls, aged 2 to 15	**101.30**	**108.55**	**107**
Coats and jackets	6.86	8.40	122
Dresses and suits	13.17	15.46	117
Shirts, blouses, and sweaters	20.67	20.26	98
Skirts and pants	18.18	19.90	109
Shorts and shorts sets	9.89	12.68	128
Active sportswear	11.39	7.07	62
Underwear and sleepwear	7.47	7.12	95

(continued)

(continued from previous page)

	average spending of total consumer units	Hispanic consumer units	
		average spending	indexed spending*
Hosiery	$4.78	$5.51	115
Accessories	4.51	4.73	105
Uniforms	1.92	3.00	156
Costumes	2.47	4.41	179
Children under age 2	**80.61**	**158.31**	**196**
Coats, jackets, and snowsuits	3.10	4.09	132
Outerwear including dresses	22.66	27.73	122
Underwear	46.09	114.08	248
Sleepwear and loungewear	3.76	4.89	130
Accessories	4.99	7.52	151
FOOTWEAR	**278.36**	**334.11**	**120**
Men's	94.82	114.70	121
Boys'	30.48	37.69	124
Women's	117.81	135.20	115
Girls'	35.24	46.52	132
OTHER APPAREL PRODUCTS, SERVICES	**258.84**	**297.76**	**115**
Material for making clothes	4.95	4.52	91
Sewing patterns and notions	1.92	1.28	67
Watches	19.16	18.80	98
Jewelry	104.17	89.52	86
Shoe repair and other shoe services	2.66	0.92	35
Coin-operated apparel laundry and dry cleaning	39.46	120.41	305
Apparel alteration, repair, and tailoring services	5.82	2.03	35
Clothing rental	3.48	2.71	78
Watch and jewelry repair	5.07	2.36	47
Professional laundry, dry cleaning	71.68	55.19	77
Clothing storage	0.47	–	–
TRANSPORTATION	**$6,015.97**	**$5,144.63**	**86**
VEHICLE PURCHASES	**2,639.33**	**2,497.01**	**95**
Cars and trucks, new	**1,194.00**	**860.75**	**72**
New cars	670.88	568.78	85
New trucks	523.11	291.97	56
Cars and trucks, used	**1,410.96**	**1,636.27**	**116**
Used cars	916.45	770.04	84
Used trucks	494.51	866.23	175
Other vehicles	**34.38**	**–**	**–**
GASOLINE AND MOTOR OIL	**1,006.05**	**891.11**	**89**
Gasoline	901.97	815.40	90
Diesel fuel	10.15	14.00	138

(continued)

(continued from previous page)

	average spending of total consumer units	Hispanic consumer units	
		average spending	indexed spending*
Gasoline on out-of-town trips	$81.98	$48.19	59
Motor oil	11.13	13.04	117
Motor oil on out-of-town trips	0.83	0.49	59
OTHER VEHICLE EXPENSES	**2,015.78**	**1,437.63**	**71**
Vehicle finance charges	**260.57**	**172.29**	**66**
Automobile finance charges	148.57	103.82	70
Truck finance charges	99.53	58.35	59
Motorcycle and plane finance charges	1.26	0.39	31
Other vehicle finance charges	11.22	9.73	87
Maintenance and repairs	**652.77**	**476.52**	**73**
Coolant, additives, brake, and transmission fluids	5.63	6.04	107
Tires	87.06	57.86	66
Parts, equipment, and accessories	60.29	54.63	91
Vehicle audio equipment	10.31	–	–
Vehicle products	3.37	2.15	64
Miscellaneous auto repair, servicing	33.68	12.18	36
Body work and painting	29.52	29.18	99
Clutch, transmission repair	45.69	41.72	91
Drive shaft and rear-end repair	6.14	4.25	69
Brake work	39.22	29.86	76
Repair to steering or front-end	20.68	20.44	99
Repair to engine cooling system	23.28	13.39	58
Motor tune-up	42.61	35.26	83
Lube, oil change, and oil filters	42.90	25.76	60
Front-end alignment, wheel balance, rotation	11.11	5.52	50
Shock absorber replacement	7.35	3.81	52
Brake adjustment	3.18	2.73	86
Gas tank repair, replacement	1.54	0.86	56
Tire repair and other repair work	33.28	22.39	67
Vehicle air conditioning repair	14.28	9.80	69
Exhaust system repair	20.87	15.61	75
Electrical system repair	29.58	17.51	59
Motor repair, replacement	67.64	53.27	79
Auto repair service policy	5.94	2.72	46
Vehicle insurance	**712.81**	**527.91**	**74**
Vehicle rental, leases, licenses, other charges	**389.63**	**260.90**	**67**
Leased and rented vehicles	235.64	133.89	57
Rented vehicles	37.70	26.80	71
Auto rental	7.09	12.29	173
Auto rental, out-of-town trips	25.95	13.94	54

(continued)

(continued from previous page)

	average spending of total consumer units	Hispanic consumer units	
		average spending	indexed spending*
Truck rental	$1.19	$0.30	25
Truck rental, out-of-town trips	3.26	0.27	8
Leased vehicles	197.94	107.09	54
Car lease payments	128.53	48.85	38
Cash down payment (car lease)	13.44	–	–
Termination fee (car lease)	0.41	–	–
Truck lease payments	52.98	51.49	97
Cash down payment (truck lease)	2.33	3.68	158
Termination fee (truck lease)	0.26	3.07	1,181
State and local registration	84.53	70.65	84
Driver's license	6.92	5.51	80
Vehicle inspection	8.76	11.84	135
Parking fees	25.38	14.52	57
Parking fees in home city, excluding residence	21.97	12.48	57
Parking fees, out-of-town trips	3.41	2.04	60
Tolls	11.19	12.85	115
Tolls on out-of-town trips	4.53	3.18	70
Towing charges	4.86	5.07	104
Automobile service club fees	7.83	3.40	43
PUBLIC TRANSPORTATION	**354.81**	**318.88**	**90**
Airline fares	225.58	169.50	75
Intercity bus fares	14.09	8.67	62
Intracity mass transit fares	48.51	110.96	229
Local transportation on out-of-town trips	8.46	5.32	63
Taxi fares on trips	4.97	3.13	63
Taxi fares	6.95	6.69	96
Intercity train fares	18.41	9.90	54
Ship fares	27.31	3.59	13
School bus	0.53	1.12	211
HEALTH CARE	**$1,732.33**	**$1,054.82**	**61**
Health insurance	**860.45**	**476.76**	**55**
Commercial health insurance	241.22	85.51	35
Blue Cross, Blue Shield	171.78	82.03	48
Health maintenance plans (HMOs)	146.87	128.31	87
Medicare payments	172.13	81.77	48
Commercial Medicare supplements and other health insurance	128.44	99.14	77
Medical services	**511.47**	**393.90**	**77**
Physician's services	146.97	100.79	69
Dental services	186.29	135.96	73

(continued)

(continued from previous page)

	average spending of total consumer units	Hispanic consumer units	
		average spending	indexed spending*
Eye care services	$28.83	$15.57	54
Service by professionals other than physicians	38.24	23.76	62
Lab tests, X-rays	21.92	16.99	78
Hospital room	33.04	12.39	38
Hospital services other than room	37.16	86.03	232
Care in convalescent or nursing home	7.90	0.02	0
Repair of medical equipment	1.11	–	–
Other medical services	10.01	2.40	24
Drugs	**279.96**	**138.97**	**50**
Nonprescription drugs	79.03	61.01	77
Prescription drugs	200.94	77.95	39
Medical supplies	**80.45**	**45.19**	**56**
Eyeglasses and contact lenses	52.06	30.24	58
Topicals and dressings	20.73	13.85	67
Medical equipment for general use	2.53	0.58	23
Supportive and convalescent medical equipment	3.83	0.08	2
Rental of medical equipment	0.34	–	–
Rental of supportive, convalescent medical equipment	0.96	0.43	45
ENTERTAINMENT	**$1,612.09**	**$1,059.90**	**66**
FEES AND ADMISSIONS	**432.91**	**231.36**	**53**
Recreation expenses, out-of-town trips	21.21	10.05	47
Social, recreation, civic club membership fees	80.67	32.50	40
Fees for participant sports	66.55	28.63	43
Participant sports, out-of-town trips	29.25	7.53	26
Movie, theater, opera, ballet admissions	73.42	68.28	93
Movie, other admissions, out-of-town trips	40.50	23.79	59
Admissions to sporting events	28.71	9.02	31
Admissions to sports events, out-of-town trips	13.50	7.93	59
Fees for recreational lessons	57.91	33.59	58
Other entertainment services, out-of-town trips	21.21	10.05	47
TELEVISION, RADIO, AND SOUND EQUIPMENT	**541.77**	**459.48**	**85**
Televisions	**370.32**	**303.44**	**82**
Community antenna or cable TV	219.69	163.41	74
Black-and-white TV set	1.89	–	–
Color TV, console	29.53	30.34	103
Color TV, portable, table model	44.90	38.36	85
VCRs and video disc players	27.33	27.89	102
Video cassettes, tapes, and discs	24.05	17.93	75
Video game hardware and software	14.68	14.24	97

(continued)

(continued from previous page)

	average spending of total consumer units	Hispanic consumer units	
		average spending	indexed spending*
Repair of TV, radio, and sound equipment	$7.19	$4.09	57
Rental of television sets	1.06	7.19	678
Radios and sound equipment	**171.45**	**156.04**	**91**
Radios	10.61	7.85	74
Tape recorders and players	11.26	–	–
Sound components and component systems	32.12	26.52	83
Miscellaneous sound equipment	0.48	–	–
Sound equipment accessories	4.46	9.10	204
Compact disc, tape, record, video mail order clubs	11.99	5.33	44
Records, CDs, audio tapes, needles	38.49	34.16	89
Rental of VCR, radio, sound equipment	0.27	1.51	559
Musical instruments and accessories	17.75	20.14	113
Rental and repair of musical instruments	1.65	1.54	93
Rental of video cassettes, tapes, discs, films	42.38	49.88	118
PETS, TOYS, PLAYGROUND EQUIPMENT	**322.19**	**173.60**	**54**
Pets	**199.89**	**72.84**	**36**
Pet food	79.56	46.64	59
Pet purchase, supplies, and medicines	47.03	6.95	15
Pet services	18.78	3.76	20
Veterinary services	54.52	15.49	28
Toys, games, hobbies, and tricycles	**120.29**	**100.42**	**83**
Playground equipment	**2.00**	**0.33**	**17**
OTHER ENTERTAINMENT EQUIPMENT, SUPPLIES, AND SERVICES	315.22	195.45	62
Unmotored recreational vehicles	**28.10**	**4.35**	**15**
Boats without motor and boat trailers	3.69	2.52	68
Trailers and other attachable campers	24.41	1.83	7
Motorized recreational vehicles	**77.41**	**60.11**	**78**
Motorized campers	21.18	–	–
Other vehicles	11.89	4.73	40
Motorboats	44.34	55.38	125
Rental of recreational vehicles	**3.42**	**2.52**	**74**
Outboard motors	**0.36**	**–**	**–**
Docking and landing fees	**4.49**	**0.13**	**3**
Sports, recreation, exercise equipment	**110.81**	**50.67**	**46**
Athletic gear, game tables, exercise equipment	50.33	23.35	46
Bicycles	12.59	11.75	93
Camping equipment	6.51	2.95	45
Hunting and fishing equipment	17.00	5.17	30

(continued)

(continued from previous page)

	average spending of total consumer units	Hispanic consumer units	
		average spending	indexed spending*
Winter sports equipment	$3.78	–	–
Water sports equipment	9.47	$3.55	37
Other sports equipment	9.50	3.90	41
Rental and repair of miscellaneous sports equipment	1.64	–	–
Photographic equipment and supplies	**81.18**	**72.35**	**89**
Film	20.27	15.22	75
Other photographic supplies	1.12	–	–
Film processing	28.56	17.83	62
Repair and rental of photographic equipment	0.29	–	–
Photographic equipment	12.56	9.97	79
Photographer fees	18.39	29.33	159
Fireworks	**2.03**	**3.83**	**189**
Souvenirs	**0.14**	–	–
Visual goods	**1.51**	**0.04**	**3**
Pinball, electronic video games	**5.78**	**1.46**	**25**
PERSONAL CARE PRODUCTS AND SERVICES	**$403.47**	**$369.27**	**92**
Personal care products	**213.44**	**215.45**	**101**
Hair care products	38.65	49.71	129
Nonelectric articles for the hair	4.43	6.30	142
Wigs and hairpieces	0.95	0.14	15
Oral hygiene products	22.19	27.02	122
Shaving products	11.91	9.19	77
Cosmetics, perfume, and bath products	105.36	88.61	84
Deodorants, feminine hygiene, miscellaneous products	26.10	31.32	120
Electric personal care appliances	3.85	3.18	83
Personal care services	**190.03**	**153.82**	**81**
Personal care services for females	97.61	47.19	48
Personal care services for males	92.19	106.55	116
Repair of personal care appliances	0.24	0.08	33
READING	**$162.57**	**$74.15**	**46**
Newspaper subscriptions	51.79	21.13	41
Newspaper, nonsubscriptions	17.40	11.64	67
Magazine subscriptions	24.74	8.84	36
Magazines, nonsubscriptions	11.00	6.83	62
Newsletters	0.28	–	–
Books purchased through book clubs	9.33	5.70	61
Books not purchased through book clubs	46.51	18.78	40
Encyclopedia and other reference book sets	1.52	1.24	82

(continued)

(continued from previous page)

	average spending of total consumer units	Hispanic consumer units	
		average spending	indexed spending*
EDUCATION	**$471.47**	**$293.14**	**62**
College tuition	265.22	139.28	53
Elementary and high school tuition	81.97	66.44	81
Other schools tuition	14.06	8.45	60
Other school expenses including rentals	17.30	12.79	74
Books, supplies for college	36.06	28.71	80
Books, supplies for elementary, high school	8.56	9.13	107
Books, supplies for day care, nursery school	2.09	2.79	133
Miscellaneous school expenses and supplies	46.21	25.55	55
TOBACCO PRODUCTS AND SMOKING SUPPLIES	**$268.82**	**$141.51**	**53**
Cigarettes	243.09	136.84	56
Other tobacco products	24.30	3.65	15
Smoking accessories	1.43	1.02	71
MISCELLANEOUS EXPENSES	**$766.23**	**$525.60**	**69**
Miscellaneous fees, gambling losses	54.70	30.15	55
Legal fees	98.35	56.97	58
Funeral expenses	86.83	53.60	62
Safe deposit box rental	5.51	0.82	15
Checking accounts, other bank service charges	25.62	21.98	86
Cemetery lots, vaults, and maintenance fees	15.50	15.26	98
Accounting fees	40.94	19.20	47
Miscellaneous personal services	21.64	14.08	65
Finance charges, except mortgage and vehicles	229.82	197.12	86
Occupational expenses, union and professional fees	97.90	34.00	35
Expenses for other properties	85.37	79.18	93
Interest paid, home equity line of credit (other property)	0.12	–	–
Credit card membership fees	3.92	3.24	83
CASH CONTRIBUTIONS	**$925.39**	**$377.53**	**41**
Cash contributions to non–consumer unit members, including students, alimony, child support	233.28	148.79	64
Gifts of cash, stocks, bonds to non–c.u. member	174.20	84.32	48
Contributions to charities	85.58	17.58	21
Contributions to church	385.94	118.22	31
Contributions to educational organizations	35.65	4.69	13
Political contributions	3.39	0.37	11
Other contributions	7.35	3.55	48

(continued)

(continued from previous page)

	average spending of total consumer units	Hispanic consumer units average spending	Hispanic consumer units indexed spending*
PERSONAL INSURANCE AND PENSIONS	**$2,967.05**	**$1,935.62**	**65**
Life and other personal insurance except health	**374.03**	**189.61**	**51**
Life, endowment, annuity, other personal insurance	361.44	184.89	51
Other nonhealth insurance	12.59	4.72	37
Pensions and Social Security	**2,593.02**	**1,746.01**	**67**
Deductions for government retirement	66.21	25.80	39
Deductions for railroad retirement	5.28	–	–
Deductions for private pensions	325.82	84.30	26
Non-payroll deposit to retirement plans	312.41	79.59	25
Deductions for Social Security	1,883.30	1,556.32	83
GIFTS*	**$986.63**	**$492.84**	**50**
FOOD	**87.72**	**27.87**	**32**
Cakes and cupcakes	1.97	–	–
Candy and chewing gum	12.79	4.08	32
Potato chips and other snacks	1.30	0.73	56
Board (including at school)	32.09	6.07	19
Catered affairs	16.33	0.50	3
HOUSING	**249.80**	**88.46**	**35**
Housekeeping supplies	**37.72**	**17.63**	**47**
Other household products	9.11	3.76	41
Miscellaneous household products	4.39	3.00	68
Lawn and garden supplies	3.51	0.54	15
Stationery, stationery supplies, giftwraps	22.53	9.15	41
Postage	4.17	2.82	68
Household textiles	**10.20**	**5.99**	**59**
Bathroom linens	2.75	–	–
Bedroom linens	4.44	5.61	126
Appliances and miscellaneous housewares	**27.44**	**5.58**	**20**
Major appliances	4.79	1.15	24
Small appliances and miscellaneous housewares	22.65	4.43	20
China and other dinnerware	2.91	1.50	52
Glassware	3.60	–	–
Nonelectric cookware	3.98	–	–
Tableware, nonelectric kitchenware	4.98	1.33	27
Small electric kitchen appliances	3.64	1.49	41
Miscellaneous household equipment	**65.94**	**20.77**	**31**
Lamps and lighting fixtures	3.33	–	–
Other household decorative items	21.54	4.04	19

(continued)

(continued from previous page)

	average spending of total consumer units	Hispanic consumer units	
		average spending	indexed spending*
Lawn and garden equipment	$0.96	–	–
Indoor plants, fresh flowers	20.72	$8.52	41
Computers and hardware, nonbusiness use	4.01	0.09	2
Other housing	**108.51**	**38.48**	**35**
Repair and maintenance services	1.03	–	–
Housing while attending school	34.67	–	–
Lodging on out-of-town trips	2.10	0.58	28
Electricity (renter)	10.47	4.10	39
Telephone services in home city, excluding mobile car phone	12.23	11.23	92
Day-care centers, nurseries, and preschools	15.05	5.06	34
Housekeeping services	3.90	–	–
Gardening, lawn care service	2.74	4.09	149
Moving, storage, freight express	1.50	0.05	3
Sofas	0.93	–	–
Kitchen, dining room furniture	0.50	–	–
Infants' furniture	1.64	0.15	9
APPAREL AND SERVICES	**258.22**	**246.19**	**95**
Males, aged 2 or older	**69.77**	**41.25**	**59**
Men's coats and jackets	4.70	2.46	52
Men's accessories	6.98	5.05	72
Men's sweaters and vests	3.46	1.84	53
Men's active sportswear	1.42	0.58	41
Men's shirts	17.03	9.05	53
Men's pants	9.29	9.88	106
Boys' shirts	4.31	2.03	47
Boys' accessories	1.19	0.33	28
Boys' pants	2.31	–	–
Boys' shorts and short sets	0.92	0.27	29
Females, aged 2 or older	**93.61**	**86.29**	**92**
Women's coats and jackets	5.41	4.54	84
Women's dresses	5.36	6.65	124
Women's vests and sweaters	8.05	7.52	93
Women's shirts, tops, blouses	14.11	20.01	142
Women's pants	9.09	2.72	30
Women's active sportswear	6.11	3.27	54
Women's sleepwear	7.35	1.32	18
Women's undergarments	2.44	0.36	15
Women's suits	1.62	0.03	2
Women's accessories	9.16	15.23	166

(continued)

(continued from previous page)

	average spending of total consumer units	Hispanic consumer units	
		average spending	indexed spending*
Girls' dresses and suits	$2.61	$0.48	18
Girls' shirts, blouses, sweaters	4.16	5.29	127
Girls' skirts and pants	1.83	0.59	32
Children under age 2	**39.47**	**76.09**	**193**
Infant dresses, outerwear	13.60	9.43	69
Infant underwear	19.47	61.17	314
Infant nightwear, loungewear	2.25	1.64	73
Infanct accessories	2.55	2.32	91
Other apparel products and services	**55.37**	**42.56**	**77**
Jewelry and watches	26.56	8.30	31
Watches	2.66	0.75	28
Jewelry	23.90	7.55	32
All other apparel products and services	28.81	34.26	119
Men's footwear	7.15	7.82	109
Boys' footwear	1.95	0.84	43
Women's footwear	10.36	11.93	115
Girls' footwear	7.76	13.53	174
TRANSPORTATION	**47.84**	**22.92**	**48**
New cars	1.90	–	–
Used cars	3.19	–	–
Gasoline on out-of-town trips	13.01	6.99	54
Airline fares	10.75	6.55	61
Ship fares	3.10	2.30	74
HEALTH CARE	**22.21**	**3.11**	**14**
Physicians' services	2.69	0.26	10
Dental services	4.70	0.27	6
Hospital room	0.31	–	–
Hospital service other than room	0.88	–	–
Care in convalescent or nursing home	4.50	–	–
Prescription drugs	1.38	1.05	76
ENTERTAINMENT	**86.44**	**37.30**	**43**
Toys, games, hobbies, tricycles	**29.34**	**21.91**	**75**
Other entertainment	**57.10**	**15.39**	**27**
Movie, other admissions, out-of-town trips	7.07	3.97	56
Admissions to sports events, out-of-town trips	2.36	1.32	56
Fees for recreational lessons	2.93	0.56	19
Community antenna or cable TV	2.54	1.91	75
Color TV, portable, table model	3.47	–	–
VCRs, video disc players	2.04	0.40	20
Video game hardware and software	2.90	0.24	8

(continued)

(continued from previous page)

	average spending of total consumer units	Hispanic consumer units	
		average spending	indexed spending*
Radios	$2.67	–	–
Sound components and component systems	2.62	$0.61	23
Veterinary services	3.05	0.81	27
Athletic gear, game tables, and exercise equipment	2.40	4.32	180
EDUCATION	**120.19**	**15.34**	**13**
College tuition	96.63	8.76	9
Elementary, high school tuition	8.17	2.42	30
Other school tuition	1.07	–	–
Other school expenses including rentals	1.86	0.36	19
School books, supplies, equipment for college	6.55	2.67	41
School supplies, etc., unspecified	5.29	0.58	11
ALL OTHER GIFTS	**114.22**	**51.67**	**45**

* The index compares the spending of the average Hispanic consumer unit with the spending of the average consumer unit by dividing Hispanic spending by average spending in each category and multiplying by 100. An index of 100 means Hispanic spending in the category equals average spending. An index of 132 means Hispanic spending is 32 percent above average, while an index of 75 means Hispanic spending is 25 percent below average.
** This figure does not include the amount paid for mortgage principal, which is considered an asset.
*** Expenditures on gifts are also included in the preceding product and service categories. Food spending, for example, includes the amount spent on gifts of food.
Note: The Bureau of Labor Statistics uses consumer units rather than households as the sampling unit in the Consumer Expenditure Survey. For the definition of a consumer unit, see the Glossary. Expenditures for gifts may not add to the total for gifts because the listing is incomplete. (–) means not applicable or the sample is too small to make a reliable estimate.
Source: Bureau of Labor Statistics, unpublished tables from the 1995 Consumer Expenditure Survey; calculations by New Strategist

Hispanics: Wealth

Hispanics have little wealth because most do not own a home.

The median net worth (assets minus debts) of Hispanic and nonwhite households amounted to just $16,500 in 1995, far below the $56,400 net worth of the average American household. Between 1992 and 1995, Hispanic and nonwhite net worth declined 2.4 percent after adjusting for inflation. (Note: The Federal Reserve collects wealth data for only two racial and ethnic categories: non-Hispanic whites, and nonwhites and Hispanics. The nonwhite and Hispanic category includes Asians, blacks, Hispanics, and Native Americans.)

The net worth of Hispanic and nonwhite households is below average because Hispanics and blacks are less likely to own a home than the average householder. Home equity accounts for the largest share of Americans' net worth. Only 48 percent of Hispanic and nonwhite householders own a home, according to the Federal Reserve Board's 1995 Survey of Consumer Finances. The nonfinancial asset held by the largest share of Hispanics/nonwhites is a vehicle, owned by 71 percent.

Hispanic and nonwhite householders have only $5,200 in financial assets, with transaction accounts (such as checking accounts) owned by the largest share (69 percent). Most Hispanic and nonwhite householders are in debt, owing a median of $12,200 in 1995.

■ The net worth of Hispanics/nonwhites is influenced by immigration. Until immigrants become a smaller share of the Hispanic population, Hispanic wealth is likely to remain well below average.

The net worth of Hispanic and nonwhite households is well below average

(median net worth of Hispanic and nonwhite and total households, 1995)

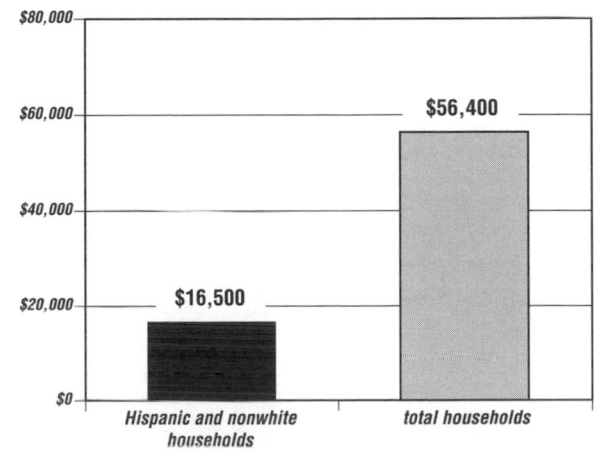

Net Worth, Assets, and Debts of
Hispanic and Nonwhite Households, 1992 and 1995

*(median net worth of Hispanic and nonwhite households, and median value of assets and debts, 1992
and 1995; percent change 1992–95; in 1995 dollars)*

	1995	1992	percent change 1992–1995
Median net worth	$16,500	$16,900	−2.4%
Median value of nonfinancial assets	42,100	40,400	4.2
Median value of financial assets	5,200	3,400	52.9
Median value of debts	12,200	9,700	25.8

Source: Federal Reserve Board, Family Finances in the U.S.: Recent Evidence from the Survey of Consumer
Finances, *Federal Reserve Bulletin, January 1997; calculations by New Strategist*

Nonfinancial Assets of Hispanic and Nonwhite Households, 1992 and 1995

(percent of Hispanic and nonwhite households owning nonfinancial assets, and median value of assets for owners, 1992 and 1995; percentage point change in households with asset and percent change in value of asset, 1992–95; in 1995 dollars)

	1995	1992	percentage point change, 1992–95
Percent owning asset			
Any nonfinancial asset	78.1%	79.7%	−1.6
Vehicles	71.1	72.7	−1.6
Primary residence	48.2	48.8	−0.6
Investment real estate	10.2	11.2	−1.0
Business	5.4	7.1	−1.7
Other nonfinancial	3.5	4.2	−0.7

	1995	1992	percent change 1992–95
Median value of asset for owners			
Any nonfinancial asset	$42,100	$40,400	4.2%
Vehicles	7,700	5,300	45.3
Primary residence	70,000	54,200	29.2
Investment real estate	33,500	48,800	−31.4
Business	26,300	48,800	−46.1
Other nonfinancial	8,000	9,200	−13.0

Source: Federal Reserve Board, Family Finances in the U.S.: Recent Evidence from the Survey of Consumer Finances, *Federal Reserve Bulletin, January 1997; calculations by New Strategist*

Financial Assets of Hispanic and Nonwhite Households, 1992 and 1995

(percent of Hispanic and nonwhite households owning financial assets, and median value of assets for owners, 1992 and 1995; percentage point change in households with asset and percent change in value of asset, 1992–95; in 1995 dollars)

	1995	1992	percentage point change, 1992–95
Percent owning asset			
Any financial asset	77.4%	74.8%	2.6
Transaction accounts	69.1	69.1	0.0
Certificates of deposit	5.9	7.8	–1.9
Savings bonds	11.3	11.7	–0.4
Bonds	0.6	1.3	–0.7
Stocks	5.5	6.3	–0.8
Mutual funds	3.5	3.4	0.1
Retirement accounts	29.2	21.6	7.6
Life insurance	24.4	24.3	0.1
Other managed assets	1.0	1.2	–0.2
Other financial assets	8.5	7.8	0.7

	1995	1992	percent change 1992–95
Median value of asset for owners			
Any financial asset	$5,200	$3,400	52.9%
Transaction accounts	1,500	1,100	36.4
Certificates of deposit	10,000	8,700	14.9
Savings bonds	500	600	–16.7
Bonds	27,000	32,000	–15.6
Stocks	5,000	6,500	–23.1
Mutual funds	7,800	18,400	–57.6
Retirement accounts	9,600	10,900	–11.9
Life insurance	5,000	3,500	42.9
Other managed assets	1,800	9,800	–81.6
Other financial assets	1,500	1,400	7.1

Source: Federal Reserve Board, Family Finances in the U.S.: Recent Evidence from the Survey of Consumer Finances, *Federal Reserve Bulletin, January 1997; calculations by New Strategist*

Hispanic and Nonwhite Households with Debt, 1992 and 1995

(percent of Hispanic and nonwhite households with debt, and median value of debt for those with debts, 1992 and 1995; percentage point change in households with debt and percent change in amount of debt, 1992–95; in 1995 dollars)

	1995	1992	percentage point change, 1992–95
Percent with debt			
Any debt	73.1%	71.4%	1.7
Mortgage and home equity	32.7	30.6	2.1
Installment	46.9	45.5	1.4
Other lines of credit	1.3	1.6	–0.3
Credit card	48.8	42.9	5.9
Investment real estate	4.4	4.3	0.1
Other debt	8.5	9.8	–1.3

	1995	1992	percent change 1992–95
Median value of debt for debtors			
Any debt	$12,200	$9,700	25.8%
Mortgage and home equity	36,500	33,800	8.0
Installment	5,000	3,500	42.9
Other lines of credit	800	2,400	–66.7
Credit card	1,200	900	33.3
Investment real estate	25,000	19,500	28.2
Other debt	1,500	2,200	31.8

Source: Federal Reserve Board, Family Finances in the U.S.: Recent Evidence from the Survey of Consumer Finances, Federal Reserve Bulletin, January 1997; calculations by New Strategist

Native Americans

■ Numbering 2.3 million, Native Americans are the smallest racial minority in the U.S., accounting for just 0.9 percent of all Americans. The largest tribe is the Cherokee, which accounts for 19 percent of all Native Americans.

■ While most Native Americans are high school graduates, their educational attainment, which varies greatly by tribe, is far below that of the average American.

■ On many measures, the health of Native Americans is better than that of the average American. They are less likely to die from lung cancer, breast cancer, and cardiovascular diseases, and AIDS is relatively rare among this population segment.

■ Native American households are far more likely than American households overall to include children. Consequently, household size is larger for Native American households than for the average household.

■ Fully 30 percent of Native Americans are poor, and poverty is greatest among those under age 18. Poverty rates vary greatly by tribe, however.

■ More than 40 percent of Native American workers can be found in three occupations: precision production, craft and repair; administrative support; and service occupations.

■ Note: There are no spending or wealth data for Native Americans.

Native Americans account for less than 1 percent of the U.S. population

(percent distribution of total persons by race and ethnicity, 1998)

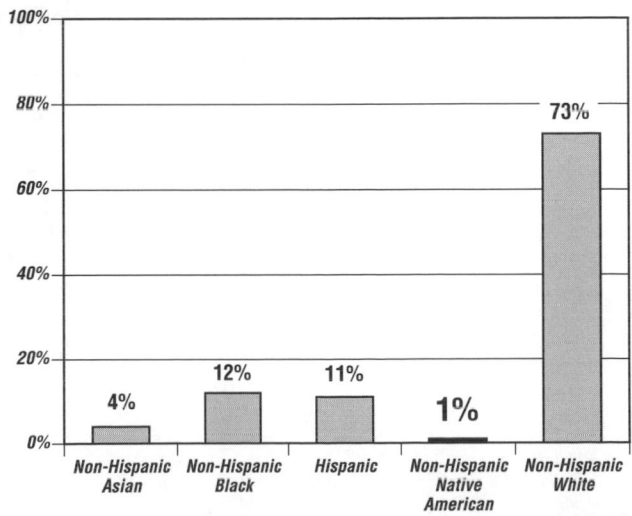

Native Americans: Education

Native Americans are much less educated than the average American, but educational attainment varies greatly by tribe.

While most Native Americans are high school graduates, their educational attainment is far below that of the average American. In 1990, 66 percent of Native Americans were high school graduates, versus 78 percent of the total population. Only 9 percent were college graduates, less than half that share of all Americans. But the educational attainment of Native Americans varies greatly by tribe. The Osage, for example, are more likely to be high school graduates than the average American.

Over 130,000 Native Americans were enrolled in college in 1995, accounting for just under 1 percent of total college enrollment. Among Native Americans in college, women greatly outnumber men. Native Americans earned over 6,600 bachelor's degrees in 1994–95, just 0.6 percent of all bachelor's degrees awarded that year.

■ Widespread poverty among Native Americans makes it difficult for them to afford a college education. Until their economic status improves, the educational attainment of Native Americans will remain below average.

Native American educational attainment is below average

(percent of Native American and total persons aged 25 or older who are high school or college graduates, 1990)

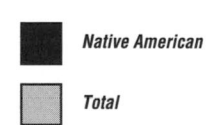

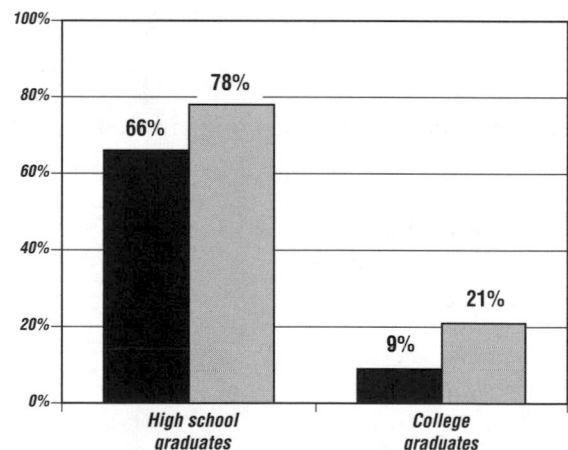

Educational Attainment of Native Americans by Sex, 1990

(number and percent distribution of Native Americans aged 25 or older by educational attainment and sex, 1990; numbers in thousands)

	total		men		women	
	number	*percent*	*number*	*percent*	*number*	*percent*
Total, aged 25 or older	**1,041**	**100.0%**	**498**	**100.0%**	**543**	**100.0%**
Not a high school graduate	358	34.4	170	34.2	188	34.6
High school graduate or more	683	65.6	328	65.8	356	65.4
Some college or assoc. degree	284	27.3	134	26.9	151	27.7
Bachelor's degree or more	97	9.4	50	10.1	47	8.7

Source: Bureau of the Census, Characteristics of American Indians by Tribe and Language, *1990 Census of Population, CP-3-7, 1994; calculations by New Strategist*

Educational Attainment of Native Americans by Tribe, 1990

(percent of Native Americans aged 25 or older who are high school or college graduates, by tribe, 1990; ranked alphabetically)

	high school graduates	college graduates
Total, aged 25 or older	**65.6%**	**9.4%**
Alaskan Athabaskans	65.1	5.1
Apache	63.8	6.9
Blackfoot	71.4	9.5
Canadian and Latin American	59.0	10.5
Cherokee	68.2	11.1
Cheyenne	69.5	6.9
Chickasaw	74.2	14.6
Chippewa	69.7	8.2
Choctaw	70.3	13.3
Comanche	74.2	14.2
Creek	73.2	12.7
Iroquois	71.9	11.3
Lumbee	51.6	9.4
Navajo	51.0	4.5
Osage	86.7	22.1
Paiute	66.2	5.4
Pima	47.5	2.8
Potawatomi	76.5	14.4
Pueblo	71.5	7.3
Puget Sound Salish	69.1	7.7
Seminole	70.5	11.1
Sioux	69.7	8.9
Tlingit	73.3	6.7
Tohono O'Odham	53.4	1.2
Yaqui	48.5	4.3

Source: Bureau of the Census, Characteristics of American Indians by Tribe and Language, *1990 Census of Population, CP-3-7, 1994*

Native American High School and College Graduates by State, 1990

(percent of Native Americans aged 25 or older who are high school or college graduates, by state, 1990)

	high school graduates	college graduates		high school graduates	college graduates
United States	**65.5%**	**9.3%**	Missouri	65.1%	11.0%
Alabama	64.9	11.6	Montana	68.1	7.9
Alaska	63.1	4.1	Nebraska	69.0	8.8
Arizona	52.1	4.6	Nevada	69.8	8.0
Arkansas	65.4	9.8	New Hampshire	65.9	16.0
California	71.4	11.1	New Jersey	66.9	14.8
Colorado	73.9	12.1	New Mexico	58.2	5.8
Connecticut	68.9	12.5	New York	65.2	13.4
Delaware	62.0	10.2	North Carolina	51.5	7.9
District of Columbia	66.3	17.7	North Dakota	64.3	8.3
Florida	68.2	11.5	Ohio	65.3	8.3
Georgia	71.6	12.5	Oklahoma	68.1	10.8
Hawaii	84.4	17.7	Oregon	71.0	8.3
Idaho	68.1	7.2	Pennsylvania	67.8	12.0
Illinois	71.4	13.4	Rhode Island	64.5	8.3
Indiana	65.0	8.4	South Carolina	62.5	10.9
Iowa	67.6	9.7	South Dakota	62.5	6.8
Kansas	75.4	10.8	Tennessee	63.1	10.5
Kentucky	59.8	8.0	Texas	70.9	13.9
Louisiana	49.1	5.5	Utah	59.3	6.4
Maine	69.9	7.7	Vermont	66.8	11.1
Maryland	73.4	19.7	Virginia	70.7	14.7
Massachusetts	71.1	14.9	Washington	72.3	9.1
Michigan	67.8	7.6	West Virginia	57.9	6.5
Minnesota	68.2	7.7	Wisconsin	66.8	5.5
Mississippi	57.4	8.1	Wyoming	68.2	6.2

Source: National Center for Education Statistics, Digest of Education Statistics 1993, NCES 93-292, 1993; calculations by New Strategist

School Enrollment of Native Americans by Age, 1990

(number and percent of Native Americans aged 3 or older enrolled in school by age, April 1990; numbers in thousands)

	number	*percent*
Total, aged 3 or older	**612**	**33.5%**
Aged 3 and 4	18	24.6
Aged 5 to 14	343	92.6
Aged 15 to 19	130	75.1
Aged 20 to 24	38	23.1
Aged 25 to 34	42	12.0
Aged 35 or older	39	5.7

Source: U.S. Bureau of the Census, Characteristics of American Indians by Tribe and Language, *1990 Census of Population, 1990 CP-3-7, 1994; calculations by New Strategist*

College Enrollment of Native Americans by Sex, 1995

(number of Native Americans enrolled in institutions of higher education by level of study and sex, and Native American enrollment as a percent of total enrollment, fall 1995; numbers in thousands)

	total		*men*		*women*	
	number	*percent of total enrollment*	*number*	*percent of total men enrolled*	*number*	*percent of total women enrolled*
Total	**131**	**0.9%**	**55**	**0.9%**	**77**	**0.0%**
Undergraduate	121	1.0	50	0.9	71	1.0
Graduate	9	0.5	3	0.4	5	0.5
First-professional	2	0.7	1	0.7	1	0.7

Source: National Center for Education Statistics, Digest of Education Statistics 1997, *NCES 98-015, 1997; calculations by New Strategist*

Bachelor's, Master's, and Doctoral Degrees Earned by Native Americans by Field of Study, 1994–95

(number and percent of bachelor's, master's, and doctoral degrees earned by Native Americans, by field of study, 1994–95)

	bachelor's		master's		doctoral	
	number	percent	number	percent	number	percent
Total degrees	**6,606**	**0.6%**	**1,621**	**0.4%**	**130**	**0.3%**
Agriculture and natural resources	163	0.8	15	0.4	2	0.2
Architecture and related programs	28	0.3	9	0.2	–	–
Area, ethnic, and cultural studies	47	0.8	12	0.7	4	2.2
Biological and life sciences	291	0.5	21	0.4	4	0.1
Business, management, and administrative services	999	0.4	311	0.3	5	0.4
Communications	204	0.4	21	0.4	–	–
Communications technologies	2	0.3	–	–	–	–
Computer and information sciences	113	0.5	17	0.2	–	–
Construction trades	1	0.9	–	–	–	–
Education	846	0.8	514	0.5	40	0.6
Engineering	226	0.4	45	0.2	5	0.1
Engineering-related technologies	115	0.7	6	0.5	1	5.6
English language and literature	288	0.6	38	0.5	7	0.4
Foreign languages and literature	55	0.4	5	0.2	3	0.3
Health professions and related sciences	467	0.6	131	0.4	9	0.4
Home economics	93	0.6	12	0.4	–	–
Law and legal studies	14	0.7	6	0.2	–	–
Liberal arts and sciences	298	0.9	14	0.5	–	–
Library science	1	2.0	12	0.2	–	–
Mathematics	59	0.4	11	0.3	1	0.1
Mechanics and repairers	–	–	–	–	–	–
Multi- and interdisciplinary studies	147	0.6	13	0.5	2	0.8
Parks, recreation, leisure, and fitness	74	0.6	7	0.4	–	–
Philosophy and religion	42	0.6	9	0.7	2	0.4
Physical sciences	102	0.5	23	0.4	9	0.2
Precision production trades	1	0.3	–	–	–	–
Protective services	203	0.8	3	0.2	–	–
Psychology	417	0.6	88	0.6	18	0.5
Public administration and services	205	1.1	137	0.6	2	0.4
R.O.T.C. and military sciences	–	–	1	0.8	–	–
Social sciences and history	798	0.6	87	0.6	10	0.3
Theological studies and religious vocations	24	0.4	4	0.1	4	0.3
Transportation and material moving	24	0.6	6	0.7	–	–
Visual and performing arts	259	0.5	43	0.4	2	0.2

Note: (–) means no degrees were awarded.
Source: National Center for Education Statistics, Digest of Education Statistics 1997, NCES 98-015, 1997; calculations by New Strategist

First-Professional Degrees Earned
by Native Americans by Field of Study, 1994–95

(number and percent of first-professional degrees earned by Native Americans, by field of study, 1994–95)

	number	percent
Total degrees	**412**	**0.5%**
Dentistry (D.D.S. or D.M.D.)	12	0.3
Medicine (M.D.)	65	0.4
Optometry (O.D.)	5	0.4
Osteopathic medicine (D.O.)	9	0.5
Pharmacy (Pharm. D.)	7	0.3
Podiatry (Pod. D., D.P., or D.P.M.)	1	0.2
Veterinary medicine (D.V.M.)	12	0.6
Chiropractic medicine (D.C. or D.C.M.)	14	0.5
Law (LL.B. or J.D.)	272	0.7
Theology (M.Div., M.H.L., B.D., or Ord.)	15	0.3
Other	–	–

Note: (–) means no degrees were awarded.
Source: National Center for Education Statistics, Digest of Education Statistics 1997, *NCES 98-015, 1997; calculations by New Strategist*

Native Americans: Health

On many measures, the health of Native Americans is better than average.

Native Americans are less likely to die from lung cancer, breast cancer, and cardiovascular disease than the average American, and AIDS is relatively rare in this segment of the population. But Native Americans are twice as likely to die in motor vehicle accidents. Teen births are common among Native Americans, with 9 percent of all births occurring to girls aged 10 to 17—64 percent higher than the proportion for the total population. Because many Native Americans are nonmetropolitan residents, only 20 percent live in counties with polluted air.

The nearly 39,000 births to Native American women in 1996 accounted for only 1 percent of all U.S. births, but births to Native Americans were 24 percent of births in Alaska, 11 percent in Montana, 12 percent in New Mexico, and 16 percent in South Dakota.

Native Americans are more likely to be disabled than the average American. They have a disability rate of 30 percent versus 24 percent nationally.

Because cancer and heart disease are less common among Native Americans than among the total population, their life expectancy at age 65 exceeds that of the average American. Native American men aged 65 can expect to live 18 more years, two years longer than the average 65-year-old man. Native American women aged 65 can expect to live 23 more years, three years longer than the average woman.

■ Many of the health problems of Native Americans are common in populations where poverty is widespread. These include tuberculosis, disability, and teen pregnancy.

Life expectancy of Native Americans aged 65 is above average

(number of years of life remaining for Native American and total persons at age 65, by sex, 1998)

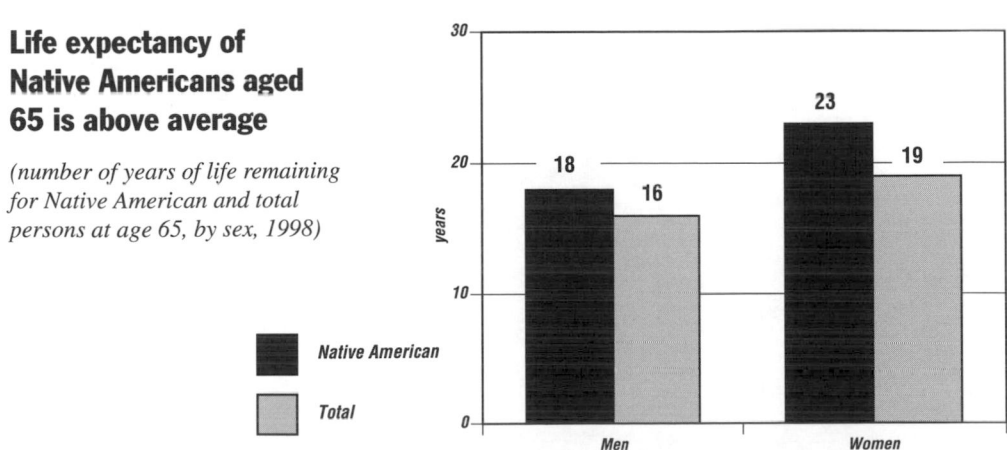

Health Indicators for Native Americans, 1993 and 1994

(selected indicators of total population and Native American health status, and index of Native American health indicators to total, 1993 and 1994)

	total population indicator	Native American indicator	index
Infant mortality rate (deaths before age 1 per 1,000 live births), 1993	8.4	11.3	135
Total deaths per 100,000 population, 1993	513.3	468.9	91
Motor vehicle crash deaths per 100,000 population, 1993	16.0	32.3	202
Work-related injury deaths per 100,000 people aged 16 or older, 1994	3.3	3.2	97
Suicides per 100,000 population, 1993	11.3	12.1	107
Homicides per 100,000 population, 1993	10.7	11.0	103
Lung cancer deaths per 100,000 population, 1993	39.3	22.0	56
Female breast cancer deaths per 100,000 population, 1993	21.5	9.4	44
Cardiovascular disease deaths per 100,000 population, 1993	181.8	136.0	75
Heart disease deaths per 100,000 population, 1993	145.3	108.9	75
Stroke deaths per 100,000 population, 1993	26.5	20.7	78
Reported incidence of AIDS per 100,000 population, 1994*	26.9	12.1	45
Reported incidence of tuberculosis per 100,000 population, 1994*	9.4	17.4	185
Reported incidence of syphilis per 100,000 population, 1994*	8.1	2.0	25
Prevalence of low birth weight, as percent of total live births, 1994	7.3	6.4	88
Births to girls aged 10 to 17, as percent of total live births, 1994	5.3	8.7	164
Percent of mothers without care, first trimester of pregnancy, 1994	19.8	34.8	176
Percent under age 18 living in poverty, 1994	21.8	–	–
Percent living in counties exceeding U.S. air quality standards, 1994	24.9	20.0	80

* Data are for the non-Hispanic Native American population.
Note: (–) means data are not available. The index for each indicator is calculated by dividing the Native American figure by the total population figure and multiplying by 100. For example, the index of 135 in the first row indicates that Native American infant mortality is 35 percent above the rate for all infants.
Source: National Center for Health Statistics, Health Status Indicators by Race and Hispanic Origin, *Healthy People 2000 Review, 1995–96; calculations by New Strategist*

Births to Native Americans by Age, 1996

(number and percent distribution of births to Native American women, by age, 1996)

	number	percent
Total births	**38,456**	**100.0%**
Under age 15	208	0.5
Aged 15 to 19	7,851	20.4
Aged 20 to 24	12,334	32.1
Aged 25 to 29	9,026	23.5
Aged 30 to 34	5,867	15.3
Aged 35 to 39	2,630	6.8
Aged 40 or older	541	1.4

Source: National Center for Health Statistics, Births and Deaths: United States, 1996, *Monthly Vital Statistics Report, Vol. 46, No. 1, Supplement 2, 1997; calculations by New Strategist*

Births to Native American Women by State, 1996

(number and percent distribution of Native American births by state, and Native American births as a percent of total births by state, 1996)

	number	percent	Native American share of total births
United States	**38,546**	**100.0%**	**1.0%**
Alabama	124	0.3	0.2
Alaska	2,405	6.2	23.7
Arizona	5,770	15.0	7.2
Arkansas	244	0.6	0.7
California	3,462	9.0	0.6
Colorado	587	1.5	1.1
Connecticut	106	0.3	0.2
Delaware	17	0.0	0.2
District of Columbia	4	0.0	0.0
Florida	631	1.6	0.3
Georgia	195	0.5	0.2
Hawaii	183	0.5	1.0
Idaho	290	0.8	1.5
Illinois	225	0.6	0.1
Indiana	122	0.3	0.1
Iowa	200	0.5	0.5
Kansas	315	0.8	0.8
Kentucky	77	0.2	0.1
Louisiana	253	0.7	0.4
Maine	84	0.2	0.6
Maryland	167	0.4	0.2
Massachusetts	162	0.4	0.2
Michigan	837	2.2	0.6
Minnesota	1,065	2.8	1.7
Mississippi	197	0.5	0.5
Missouri	270	0.7	0.4
Montana	1,173	3.0	11.0
Nebraska	331	0.9	1.4
Nevada	419	1.1	1.6
New Hampshire	23	0.1	0.2
New Jersey	228	0.6	0.2
New Mexico	3,184	8.3	11.7
New York	632	1.6	0.2
North Carolina	1,571	4.1	1.5
North Dakota	752	2.0	9.0

(continued)

(continued from previous page)

	number	percent	Native American share of total births
Ohio	260	0.7%	0.2%
Oklahoma	4,303	11.2	9.3
Oregon	673	1.7	1.5
Pennsylvania	222	0.6	0.1
Rhode Island	137	0.4	1.1
South Carolina	114	0.3	0.2
South Dakota	1,635	4.2	15.6
Tennessee	191	0.5	0.3
Texas	823	2.1	0.3
Utah	626	1.6	1.5
Vermont	9	0.0	0.1
Virginia	172	0.4	0.2
Washington	1,913	5.0	2.4
West Virginia	10	0.0	0.0
Wisconsin	846	2.2	1.3
Wyoming	218	0.6	3.5

Source: National Center for Health Statistics, Births and Deaths: United States, 1996, *Monthly Vital Statistics Report , Vol. 46, No. 1, Supplement 2, 1997; calculations by New Strategist*

Projections of Births to Native American Women, 1998 to 2020

(number of births to Native American women, and Native American births as a percent of total births, 1998–2020; numbers in thousands)

	number	*Native American share of total births*
1998	34	0.9
1999	35	0.9
2000	35	0.9
2001	36	0.9
2002	36	0.9
2003	37	0.9
2004	38	1.0
2005	38	0.9
2006	39	1.0
2007	39	1.0
2008	40	1.0
2009	41	1.0
2010	41	1.0
2011	41	1.0
2012	42	1.0
2013	42	1.0
2014	42	1.0
2015	42	0.9
2016	43	1.0
2017	43	1.0
2018	43	0.9
2019	44	1.0
2020	44	1.0

Source: Bureau of the Census, Population Projections of the United States, by Age, Sex, Race, and Hispanic Origin: 1995 to 2050, Current Population Reports, P25-1130, 1996; calculations by New Strategist

Native Americans with Disabilities by Type of Disability, 1994–95

(number and percent distribution of Native Americans with a disability by type of disability, 1994–95; numbers in thousands)

	number	percent
Total Native Americans	**1,350**	**100.0%**
With any disability	402	29.7
Severe	191	14.1
Not severe	211	15.6
Uses wheelchair	2	0.2
Used cane/crutch/walker for six or more months	32	2.4
Difficulty with or unable to perform one or more functional activities	251	18.6
Difficulty with or unable to perform one or more ADLs	62	4.6
Difficulty with or unable to perform one or more IADLs	86	6.4
Needs personal assistance with an ADL or an IADL	61	4.5

Note: Functional activities are seeing, hearing, speaking, lifting, climbing stairs, and walking. An ADL is an activity of daily living and includes getting around inside the house, getting in and out of bed or chair, bathing, dressing, eating, and using the toilet. An IADL is an instrumental activity of daily living and includes going outside alone, keeping track of money and bills, preparing meals, doing light housework, taking prescribed medicines, and using the telephone.
Source: Bureau of the Census, Internet web site, http://www.census.gov

Life Expectancy of Native Americans at Birth and Age 65, 1998 to 2020

(average number of years of life remaining at birth and at age 65 for Native Americans by sex, selected years 1998–2020; difference between Native American and total life expectancy at birth and at age 65 by sex, 1998 and 2020)

	life expectancy (years)	
	males	*females*
AT BIRTH		
1998	72.4	80.7
2000	72.6	80.9
2005	73.1	81.4
2010	73.8	81.9
2015	74.4	82.3
2020	75.1	82.8
Life expectancy of Native Americans minus		
life expectancy of total Americans		
1998	–0.4	1.1
2020	–0.4	1.3
AT AGE 65		
1998	18.1	22.6
2000	18.2	22.7
2005	18.6	23.0
2010	18.9	23.2
2015	19.3	23.5
2020	19.7	23.8
Life expectancy of Native Americans minus		
life expectancy of total Americans		
1998	2.4	3.3
2020	2.1	3.2

Source: Bureau of the Census, Population Projections of the United States, by Age, Sex, Race, and Hispanic Origin: 1995 to 2050, *Current Population Reports, P25-1130, 1996; calculations by New Strategist*

Native Americans: Households

Native American households are larger than average and more likely to include children.

Native American married couples are much more likely to have children under age 18 in their home than all married couples. Among Native American couples, a 58 percent majority have children at home. This compares with fewer than half of couples nationally.

Married couples are a smaller share of Native American households (49 percent) than of all households, while female-headed families are a larger share. In 1990, female-headed families accounted for 20 percent of all Native American households. Fewer than half of Native American men and women are currently married.

Native American households are larger than the average household. Fifty-five percent of Native American households are home to three or more people, versus the minority of total households.

■ The large share of families headed by women without a spouse contributes to the high poverty rate among Native Americans.

Female-headed families account for a large share of Native American households

(percent of Native American and total households headed by married couples and female-headed families, 1990)

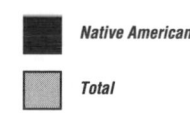
Native American

Total

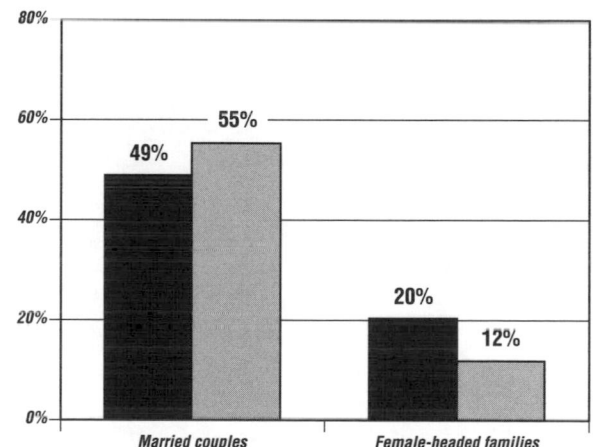

Native American Households by Household Type, 1990

(number and percent distribution of Native American households by type, 1990; numbers in thousands)

	number	percent
Total households	**605**	**100.0%**
Family households	**449**	**74.3**
Married couples	296	48.9
With children under age 18	172	28.5
Without children under age 18	123	20.4
Female householder, no spouse present	118	19.5
With children under age 18	78	13.0
Without children under age 18	39	6.5
Male householder, no spouse present	36	5.9
Nonfamily households	**156**	**25.7**
Living alone	122	20.1

Source: Bureau of the Census, Characteristics of American Indians by Tribe and Language, *1990 Census of Population, CP-3-7, 1994; calculations by New Strategist*

Native American Households by Size, 1990

(number and percent distribution of Native American households by size, 1990; numbers in thousands)

	number	*percent*
Total households	**605**	**100.0%**
One person	122	20.1
Two persons	153	25.2
Three persons	113	18.7
Four persons	101	16.7
Five persons	61	10.1
Six persons	30	4.9
Seven or more persons	25	4.2

Source: Bureau of the Census, Characteristics of American Indians by Tribe and Language, *1990 Census of Population, CP-3-7, 1994; calculations by New Strategist*

Marital Status of Native Americans by Sex, 1990

(number and percent distribution of Native Americans aged 15 or older by sex and marital status, 1990; numbers in thousands)

	number	percent
Men, aged 15 or older	**672**	**100.0%**
Never married	248	37.0
Married	318	47.3
Separated	20	2.9
Divorced	71	10.6
Widowed	15	2.3
Women, aged 15 or older	**706**	**100.0**
Never married	199	28.2
Married	325	46.0
Separated	29	4.1
Divorced	93	13.1
Widowed	61	8.6

Source: Bureau of the Census, Characteristics of American Indians by Tribe and Language, *1990 Census of Population, CP-3-7, 1994; calculations by New Strategist*

Native Americans: Housing

Most Native Americans do not own a home, but the majority of those living in the Northeast and South are homeowners.

Only 48 percent of Native Americans owned their home in 1995, a much smaller share than the 65 percent homeownership rate among all Americans. The homeownership rate reaches 60 percent for Native Americans in the Northeast, however, and stands at 54 percent for those in the South.

While utility gas is the most common house heating fuel among both homeowners and renters, 19 percent of Native American homeowners use wood—the largest share among all racial and ethnic groups.

Most Native Americans have at least one vehicle available to them, and most homeowners have at least two. But one in four Native American renters does not have use of a car, truck, or other vehicle.

■ Native Americans are more likely to live in nonmetropolitan areas than any other racial or ethnic group. Because homes are less expensive in nonmetropolitan areas, the Native American homeownership rate is higher than that of both blacks and Hispanics.

Many Native Americans live in nonmetropolitan areas

(percent distribution of Native American households by metropolitan status, 1995)

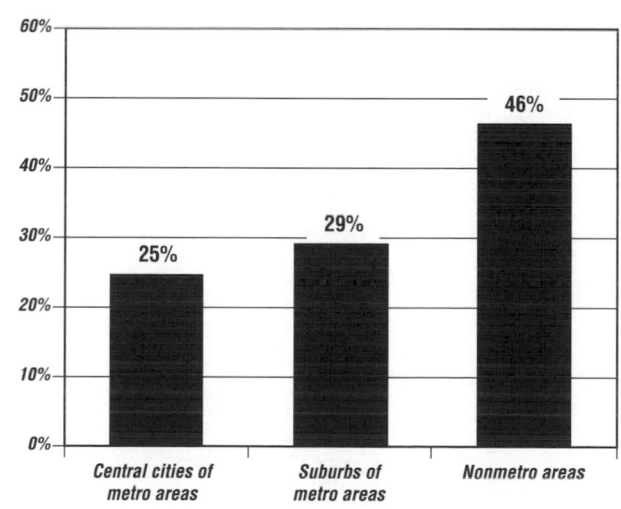

Region of Residence and Metropolitan Status of Housing Units Occupied by Native Americans, 1995

(number, percent distribution, and percent of housing units occupied by Native Americans, by regional, metropolitan, and homeownership status, 1995; numbers in thousands)

	total		owner			renter		
	number	percent distrib.	number	percent distrib.	percent of total	number	percent distrib.	percent of total
Total occupied housing units	**601**	**100.0%**	**287**	**100.0%**	**47.8%**	**314**	**100.0%**	**52.2%**
Northeast	48	8.0	29	10.1	60.4	19	6.1	39.6
Midwest	115	19.1	40	13.9	34.8	75	23.9	65.2
South	112	18.6	60	20.9	53.6	51	16.2	45.5
West	327	54.4	158	55.1	48.3	169	53.8	51.7
In metropolitan areas	323	53.7	131	45.6	40.6	192	61.1	59.4
In central cities	148	24.6	45	15.7	30.4	103	32.8	69.6
In suburbs	175	29.1	86	30.0	49.1	89	28.3	50.9
Outside metropolitan areas	278	46.3	156	54.4	56.1	122	38.9	43.9

Source: Bureau of the Census, American Housing Survey for the United States in 1995, *Current Housing Reports, H150/95, 1997; calculations by New Strategist*

Characteristics of Housing Units
Occupied by Native Americans, 1990

(number and percent distribution of housing units occupied by Native Americans, by selected housing characteristics and homeownership status, 1990; numbers in thousands)

	total		owner-occupied		renter-occupied	
	number	*percent*	*number*	*percent*	*number*	*percent*
Total occupied housing units	**599**	**100.0%**	**317**	**100.0%**	**282**	**100.0%**
Median number of persons in unit	2.77	–	2.91	–	2.61	–
Median number of rooms in unit	4.7	–	5.2	–	4.1	–
Plumbing facilities						
Complete plumbing	567	94.7	292	92.1	275	97.5
Lacks complete plumbing	32	5.3	25	7.9	7	2.5
Primary heating fuel						
Utility gas	258	43.1	125	39.4	132	46.8
Electricity	145	24.2	58	18.3	87	30.9
Wood	75	12.5	59	18.6	16	5.7
Bottled tank or LP gas	69	11.5	46	14.5	23	8.2
Fuel oil, kerosene, etc.	41	6.8	23	7.3	18	6.4
Other	11	1.8	6	1.9	6	2.1
Vehicles available						
None	97	16.2	30	9.5	67	23.8
One	222	37.1	94	29.7	128	45.4
Two	187	31.2	120	37.9	67	23.8
Three or more	94	15.7	73	23.0	20	7.1

Source: Bureau of the Census, Characteristics of American Indians by Tribe and Language, *1990 Census of Population, CP 3 7, 1994; calculations by New Strategist*

Native Americans: Income

Native Americans are less well off than the average American, but income varies greatly by tribe.

The median income of Native American households is far below the national median, at $19,900 in 1989 versus $30,056 nationally. Only 1 percent of Native American households had a median income of $100,000 or more. Median household income varies by tribe, however, ranging from $29,211 for the Osage to just $11,402 for the Tohono O'Odham.

The large share of female-headed families among Native American households accounts for the low incomes of this minority group. Nearly half the Native American female-headed families had incomes below $10,000 in 1989. In contrast, most Native American married couples had incomes of $25,000 or more.

Fully 30 percent of Native Americans are poor, and poverty is greatest among children. Overall, 51 percent of female-headed Native American families are poor, versus just 17 percent of married couples. Poverty rates vary greatly by tribe, however. More than 50 percent of the Tohono O'Odham and Pima are poor, versus only 15 percent of the Tlingit.

■ Two factors explain the low incomes and high poverty rate among Native Americans: low levels of educational attainment and large numbers of female-headed families. Until these factors change, the economic status of Native Americans will remain below average.

Many Native American households have low incomes

(percent distribution of Native American households by household income, 1989)

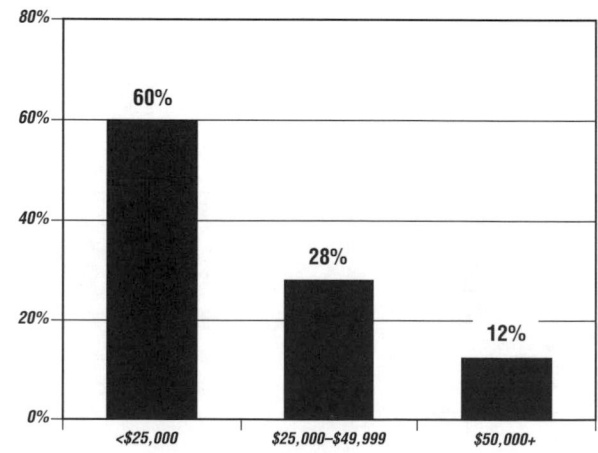

Income Distribution of Native American Households, 1989

(number and percent distribution of Native American households by household income, 1989; households in thousands as of 1990)

	number	percent
Total households	**605**	**100.0%**
Under $10,000	165	27.4
$10,000 to $14,999	73	12.1
$15,000 to $24,999	123	20.3
$25,000 to $34,999	88	14.6
$35,000 to $49,999	81	13.4
$50,000 to $74,999	52	8.7
$75,000 to $99,999	14	2.3
$100,000 or more	8	1.4
Median income	$19,900	–

Source: Bureau of the Census, Characteristics of American Indians by Tribe and Language, *1990 Census of Population, CP-3-7, 1994; calculations by New Strategist*

Household Income of Native Americans by Tribe, 1989

(median household income of the 25 largest Native American tribes, ranked by income, 1989)

	median household income
Osage	$29,211
Tlingit	28,703
Canadian and Latin American	24,502
Potawatomi	23,722
Iroquois	23,460
Chickasaw	23,325
Comanche	22,958
Cherokee	21,922
Creek	21,913
Lumbee	21,708
Choctaw	21,640
Seminole	21,633
Blackfoot	20,860
Puget Sound Salish	19,191
Paiute	19,154
Pueblo	19,097
Chippewa	18,801
Yaqui	18,667
Apache	18,484
Alaskan Athabaskans	17,348
Cheyenne	16,371
Sioux	15,611
Navajo	12,817
Pima	12,063
Tohono O'Odham	11,402

Source: Bureau of the Census, Characteristics of American Indians by Tribe and Language, *1990 Census of Population, CP-3-7, 1994; calculations by New Strategist*

Income Distribution of Native American Families by Family Type, 1989

(number and percent distribution of Native American families by family income and family type, 1989; families in thousands as of 1990)

	number	percent
Total families	**449**	**100.0%**
Under $10,000	107	23.8
$10,000 to $14,999	53	11.9
$15,000 to $24,999	92	20.4
$25,000 to $34,999	69	15.3
$35,000 to $49,999	66	14.7
$50,000 to $74,999	44	9.8
$75,000 to $99,999	12	2.6
$100,000 or more	7	1.5
Median family income	$21,619	–
Married couples	**296**	**100.0**
Under $15,000	69	23.4
$15,000 to $24,999	61	20.6
$25,000 to $34,999	53	18.0
$35,000 to $49,999	56	18.9
$50,000 to $74,999	40	13.4
$75,000 or more	17	5.7
Female householders, no spouse present	**118**	**100.0**
Under $10,000	56	47.7
$10,000 to $14,999	18	15.3
$15,000 to $24,999	23	19.2
$25,000 to $49,999	17	14.8
$50,000 or more	3	3.0

Source: Bureau of the Census, Characteristics of American Indians by Tribe and Language, 1990 Census of Population, CP-3-7, 1994; calculations by New Strategist

Incomes of Native Americans by Sex, 1989

(number and median income of Native Americans aged 15 or older with income, percent who are full-time workers, and median income of full-time workers, by sex, 1989; persons in thousands as of 1990)

	men	women
Total persons with income, aged 15 or older	**581**	**564**
Median income	$12,226	$7,327
Percent year-round, full-time workers	41.5%	30.1%
Median income of year-round, full-time workers	$22,005	$16,613

Source: Bureau of the Census, Characteristics of American Indians by Tribe and Language, *1990 Census of Population, CP-3-7, 1994*

Native Americans below the Poverty Level, 1989

(number of Native American families and persons, and number and percent below poverty level by type of family and age of person, 1989; families and persons in thousands as of 1990)

	total	in poverty number	in poverty percent
Total families	**449**	**122**	**27.2%**
Married couples	296	50	17.0
Female householders, no spouse present	118	60	50.8
Total persons	**1,937**	**585**	**30.2**
Under age 18	662	253	38.2
Aged 65 or older	114	33	28.5

Source: Bureau of the Census, Characteristics of American Indians by Tribe and Language, *1990 Census of Population, CP-3-7, 1994; calculations by New Strategist*

Native Americans below the Poverty Level by Tribe, 1989

(number and percent of Native American persons and families below poverty level, for the 25 largest tribes, 1989; ranked by percent of persons in poverty; persons and families in thousands as of 1990)

	persons		families	
	number	percent	number	percent
Total in poverty	**585**	**31.2%**	**122**	**27.2%**
Tohono O'Odham	9	55.8	2	54.1
Pima	8	53.3	2	53.6
Navajo	108	48.8	21	47.3
Sioux	46	44.4	9	39.4
Cheyenne	5	42.3	1	35.8
Yaqui	4	40.9	1	37.0
Apache	19	37.5	4	31.8
Chippewa	35	34.3	8	31.2
Pueblo	18	33.2	4	31.2
Blackfoot	11	30.9	3	27.6
Puget Sound Salish	3	30.0	1	28.8
Paiute	3	28.9	1	27.2
Alaskan Athabaskans	4	28.1	1	28.6
Seminole	4	27.6	1	22.6
Comanche	3	27.5	1	20.9
Creek	11	23.4	2	19.0
Canadian and Latin American	6	23.1	1	19.9
Choctaw	19	23.0	4	19.9
Lumbee	11	22.1	3	20.2
Cherokee	79	22.0	19	19.4
Chickasaw	5	21.4	1	17.0
Potawatomi	3	21.1	1	17.3
Iroquois	10	20.1	2	17.3
Osage	2	15.9	–	16.4
Tlingit	2	15.8	–	14.9

Note: (–) means less than 500.
Source: Bureau of the Census, Characteristics of American Indians by Tribe and Language, 1990 Census of Population, CP-3-7, 1994; calculations by New Strategist

Native Americans: Labor Force

Most Native American couples are dual earners.

Nearly two-thirds of Native American households headed by married couples have two or more workers. Among the many Native American female-headed families, however, 27 percent have no earners and 48 percent have only one earner—which explains their low incomes.

More than 40 percent of Native American workers can be found in three occupations: precision production, craft, and repair (14 percent); administrative support (15 percent); and service occupations (16 percent). Just 9 percent of Native Americans are executives, administrators, or managers. By industry, Native Americans are most heavily represented in mining and public administration. They account for more than 1 percent of the employed in each of these industries.

■ Native Americans are underrepresented in executive and managerial occupations because they are much less educated than the average American.

Most households headed by Native American couples have at least two workers

(percent distribution of Native American married couples by number of earners, 1990)

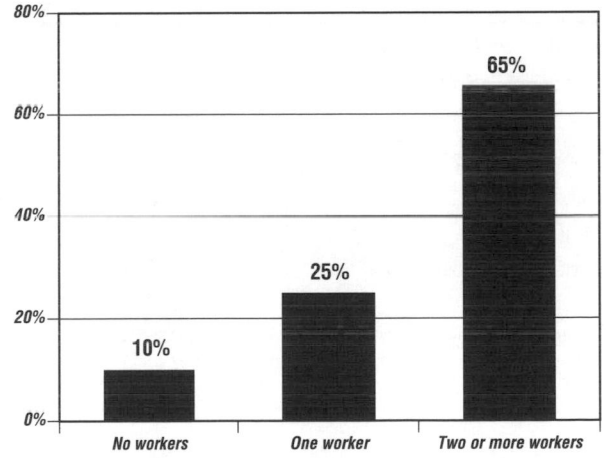

Native American Families by Number of Workers, 1990

(number and percent distribution of Native American families by number of workers and type of family, 1990; numbers in thousands)

	total		married couples		female householders, no spouse present	
	number	percent	number	percent	number	percent
Total families	**449**	**100.0%**	**296**	**100.0%**	**118**	**100.0%**
No workers	66	14.6	29	9.8	31	26.6
One worker	149	33.2	73	24.8	56	47.9
Two or more workers	234	52.2	193	65.4	30	25.5

Source: Bureau of the Census, Characteristics of American Indians by Tribe and Language, *1990 Census of Population, CP-3-7, 1994; calculations by New Strategist*

Labor Force Status of Native American Husbands and Wives, 1990

(number and percent distribution of Native American married couples by labor force status of husbands and wives, 1990; numbers in thousands)

	total		wife in labor force		wife not in labor force	
	number	percent	number	percent	number	percent
Total married couples	**296**	**100.0%**	**175**	**59.4%**	**120**	**40.6%**
Husband in labor force	233	78.8	155	52.5	78	26.3
Husband not in labor force	63	21.2	20	6.9	42	14.3

Source: Bureau of the Census, Characteristics of American Indians by Tribe and Language, *1990 Census of Population, CP-3-7, 1994; calculations by New Strategist*

Native Americans by Occupation, 1990

(number and percent distribution of employed Native Americans aged 16 or older by occupation, and Native Americans as a percent of total employed workers by occupation, 1990; numbers in thousands)

	number	*percent*	*share of total workers*
Total employed, aged 16 or older	**706**	**100.0%**	**0.6%**
Executive, administrative, and managerial	61	8.6	0.4
Professional specialty	68	9.7	0.4
Technicians and related support	23	3.2	0.5
Sales	61	8.7	0.4
Administrative support, including clerical	104	14.8	0.6
Private household	4	0.5	0.6
Protective service	17	2.4	0.9
Service occupations, except protective and household	109	15.5	0.9
Farming, forestry, and fishing	24	3.4	0.8
Precision production, craft, and repair	97	13.8	0.7
Machine operators, assemblers, and inspectors	59	8.4	0.7
Transportation and material moving	38	5.4	0.8
Handlers, equipment cleaners, helpers, and laborers	40	5.7	0.9

Source: Bureau of the Census, Characteristics of American Indians by Tribe and Language, *1990 Census of Population, CP-3-7, 1994; calculations by New Strategist*

Native Americans by Industry, 1990

(total number and percent distribution of employed Native Americans aged 16 or older by industry, and Native Americans as a percent of total employed workers by industry, 1990; numbers in thousands)

	number	percent	share of total workers
Total employed, aged 16 or older	**706**	**100.0%**	**0.6%**
Agriculture, forestry, and fisheries	25	3.5	0.8
Mining	8	1.1	1.1
Construction	60	8.5	0.8
Manufacturing	115	16.3	0.6
Durable goods	44	6.2	0.4
Nondurable goods	71	10.1	0.9
Transportation	30	4.3	0.6
Communication and other public utilities	19	2.6	0.6
Wholesale trade	23	3.2	0.5
Retail trade	115	16.3	0.6
Finance, insurance, and real estate	28	4.0	0.4
Business and repair services	33	4.6	0.6
Personal, entertainment, and recreation services	39	5.5	0.7
Professional and related services	156	22.0	0.6
Health services	57	8.0	0.6
Educational services	56	8.0	0.6
Public administration	56	7.9	1.0

Source: Bureau of the Census, Characteristics of American Indians by Tribe and Language, *1990 Census of Population, CP-3-7, 1994; calculations by New Strategist*

Native Americans: Population

Native Americans are the smallest minority group in the U.S., but their number is growing faster than average.

Numbering 2.3 million, Native Americans are the smallest minority group in the U.S. and account for just 0.9 percent of all Americans. The number of Native Americans is expected to rise to 3.1 million by 2020, while their share of the population will inch up to 1.0 percent. The largest tribe is the Cherokee, accounting for 19 percent of all Native Americans.

While only 9 percent of Native Americans aged 5 or older do not speak English "very well," this figure rises to 33 percent among the Navajo and 31 percent among the Yaqui.

Nearly half of Native Americans live in the West, and another 30 percent in the South. Each of three states was home to more than 10 percent of the nation's Native Americans in 1995: Arizona (10.9 percent), California (13.4 percent), and Oklahoma (11.8 percent). Native Americans account for 15 percent of Alaska's population, the largest share among the 50 states.

Native Americans accounted for 7 percent of the population of Tulsa, Oklahoma, in 1990, and for 5 percent of the populations of Oklahoma City and Albuquerque, New Mexico.

■ Although the Native American population is growing faster than the total population, the Native American share of the population is not projected to rise much because they number so few.

The Native American population will top 3 million by 2020

(number of Native Americans, 1998 and 2020)

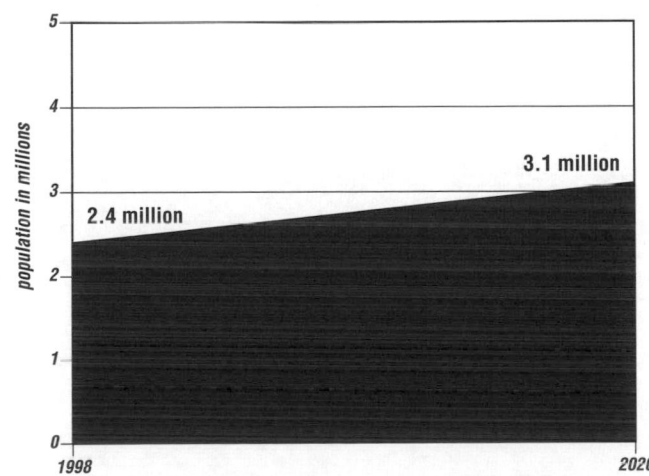

Native Americans by Age, 1995 to 2020

(number of Native Americans by age, selected years 1995–2020; percent change 1995–2000 and 2000–2010; numbers in thousands)

	1995	1998	2000	2010	2020	percent change 1995–2000	percent change 2000–2010
Total persons	**2,241**	**2,337**	**2,402**	**2,754**	**3,129**	**7.2%**	**14.7%**
Under age 5	207	207	210	245	266	1.4	16.7
Aged 5 to 9	228	224	215	235	269	–5.7	9.3
Aged 10 to 14	233	242	253	244	285	8.6	–3.6
Aged 15 to 19	200	225	235	242	265	17.5	3.0
Aged 20 to 24	184	182	194	248	240	5.4	27.8
Aged 25 to 29	179	187	184	228	236	2.8	23.9
Aged 30 to 34	185	177	177	192	246	–4.3	8.5
Aged 35 to 39	177	182	181	178	221	2.3	–1.7
Aged 40 to 44	156	167	173	171	186	10.9	–1.2
Aged 45 to 49	125	137	146	168	166	16.8	15.1
Aged 50 to 54	94	108	117	154	152	24.5	31.6
Aged 55 to 59	72	80	86	126	146	19.4	46.5
Aged 60 to 64	58	63	66	99	131	13.8	50.0
Aged 65 to 69	47	50	52	70	104	10.6	34.6
Aged 70 to 74	38	40	41	52	78	7.9	26.8
Aged 75 to 79	25	29	32	38	53	28.0	18.8
Aged 80 to 84	16	18	19	27	35	18.8	42.1
Aged 85 or older	16	20	22	36	51	37.5	63.6
Aged 18 to 24	257	264	282	343	340	9.7	21.6
Aged 18 or older	1,445	1,521	1,578	1,882	2,145	9.2	19.3
Aged 65 or older	142	156	165	223	321	16.2	35.2

Source: Bureau of the Census, Population Projections of the United States, by Age, Sex, Race, and Hispanic Origin: 1995 to 2050, *Current Population Reports, P25-1130, 1996; calculations by New Strategist*

Native American Share of the Total Population by Age, 1995 to 2020

(Native Americans as a percent of the total population by age, selected years 1995–2020)

	1995	*1998*	*2000*	*2010*	*2020*
Total persons	**0.9%**	**0.9%**	**0.9%**	**0.9%**	**1.0%**
Under age 5	1.1	1.1	1.1	1.2	1.2
Aged 5 to 9	1.2	1.1	1.1	1.2	1.2
Aged 10 to 14	1.2	1.2	1.3	1.2	1.3
Aged 15 to 19	1.1	1.2	1.2	1.1	1.2
Aged 20 to 24	1.0	1.0	1.1	1.2	1.1
Aged 25 to 29	0.9	1.0	1.0	1.2	1.1
Aged 30 to 34	0.8	0.9	0.9	1.0	1.2
Aged 35 to 39	0.8	0.8	0.8	1.0	1.1
Aged 40 to 44	0.8	0.8	0.8	0.9	1.0
Aged 45 to 49	0.7	0.7	0.7	0.8	0.9
Aged 50 to 54	0.7	0.7	0.7	0.7	0.8
Aged 55 to 59	0.6	0.6	0.6	0.7	0.7
Aged 60 to 64	0.6	0.6	0.6	0.6	0.6
Aged 65 to 69	0.5	0.5	0.6	0.6	0.6
Aged 70 to 74	0.4	0.5	0.5	0.6	0.6
Aged 75 to 79	0.4	0.4	0.4	0.5	0.6
Aged 80 to 84	0.4	0.4	0.4	0.5	0.6
Aged 85 or older	0.4	0.5	0.5	0.6	0.8
Aged 18 to 24	1.0	1.0	1.1	1.1	1.1
Aged 18 or older	0.7	0.8	0.8	0.8	0.9
Aged 65 or older	0.4	0.5	0.5	0.6	0.6

Source: Calculations by New Strategist based on Census Bureau data in Population Projections of the United States, by Age, Sex, Race, and Hispanic Origin: 1995 to 2050, *Current Population Reports, P25-1130, 1996*

Non-Hispanic Native Americans by Age, 1995 to 2020

(number of non-Hispanic Native Americans by age, selected years 1995–2020; percent change 1995–2000 and 2000–2010; numbers in thousands)

						percent change	
	1995	*1998*	*2000*	*2010*	*2020*	*1995–2000*	*2000–2010*
Total persons	**1,931**	**2,005**	**2,054**	**2,320**	**2,601**	**6.4%**	**13.0%**
Under age 5	176	177	180	206	222	2.3	14.4
Aged 5 to 9	191	189	182	199	224	–4.7	9.3
Aged 10 to 14	198	204	212	207	236	7.1	–2.4
Aged 15 to 19	171	190	197	202	221	15.2	2.5
Aged 20 to 24	157	155	164	204	200	4.5	24.4
Aged 25 to 29	150	157	156	189	194	4.0	21.2
Aged 30 to 34	157	148	147	160	199	–6.4	8.8
Aged 35 to 39	152	155	152	149	181	0.0	–2.0
Aged 40 to 44	136	144	149	141	154	9.6	–5.4
Aged 45 to 49	111	120	127	141	138	14.4	11.0
Aged 50 to 54	84	96	104	131	125	23.8	26.0
Aged 55 to 59	65	72	77	109	122	18.5	41.6
Aged 60 to 64	53	56	59	86	110	11.3	45.8
Aged 65 to 69	42	44	46	61	89	9.5	32.6
Aged 70 to 74	34	35	36	45	67	5.9	25.0
Aged 75 to 79	23	27	28	33	45	21.7	17.9
Aged 80 to 84	15	17	18	23	30	20.0	27.8
Aged 85 or older	13	18	21	34	45	61.5	61.9
Aged 18 to 24	219	225	238	282	282	8.7	18.5
Aged 18 or older	1,257	1,315	1,358	1,584	1,781	8.0	16.6
Aged 65 or older	129	141	149	197	275	15.5	32.2

Source: Bureau of the Census, Population Projections of the United States, by Age, Sex, Race, and Hispanic Origin: 1995 to 2050, *Current Population Reports, P25-1130, 1996; calculations by New Strategist*

Native Americans by Age and Sex, 1998

(number of Native Americans by age and sex, and sex ratio by age, 1998; numbers in thousands)

	total	male	female	sex ratio*
Total persons	**2,337**	**1,154**	**1,183**	**98**
Under age 5	207	105	102	103
Aged 5 to 9	224	114	110	104
Aged 10 to 14	242	123	119	103
Aged 15 to 19	225	113	112	101
Aged 20 to 24	182	91	91	100
Aged 25 to 29	187	96	90	107
Aged 30 to 34	177	90	87	103
Aged 35 to 39	182	91	91	100
Aged 40 to 44	167	82	86	95
Aged 45 to 49	137	67	71	94
Aged 50 to 54	108	52	56	93
Aged 55 to 59	80	37	42	88
Aged 60 to 64	63	29	34	85
Aged 65 to 69	50	22	28	79
Aged 70 to 74	40	17	22	77
Aged 75 to 79	29	12	17	71
Aged 80 to 84	18	7	11	64
Aged 85 or older	20	6	13	46
Aged 18 to 24	264	132	133	99
Aged 18 or older	1,521	741	781	95
Aged 65 or older	156	64	91	70

* The sex ratio is the number of males per 100 females.
Source: Bureau of the Census, Population Projections of the United States, by Age, Sex, Race, and Hispanic Origin: 1995 to 2050, Current Population Reports, P25-1130, 1996; calculations by New Strategist

Native Americans by Tribe, 1980 and 1990

(number and percent distribution of Native Americans by tribe for 25 largest tribes, 1980 and 1990; change in number and percent change 1980–90; ranked by size of tribe in 1990; numbers in thousands)

	1990		1980		change, 1980–90	
	number	*percent*	*number*	*percent*	*number*	*percent*
Total persons	**1,937**	**100.0%**	**1,479**	**100.0%**	**459**	**31.0%**
Cherokee	369	19.0	232	15.7	137	59.0
Navajo	225	11.6	159	10.7	67	42.0
Sioux	107	5.5	79	5.3	29	36.5
Chippewa	106	5.5	74	5.0	32	44.0
Choctaw	86	4.5	50	3.4	36	71.7
Pueblo	55	2.9	43	2.9	13	30.0
Apache	53	2.8	36	2.4	17	48.7
Iroquois	53	2.7	38	2.6	14	37.5
Lumbee	51	2.6	29	1.9	22	77.7
Creek	46	2.4	28	1.9	18	62.2
Blackfoot	38	2.0	22	1.5	16	73.0
Canadian and Latin American	27	1.4	8	0.5	19	248.3
Chickasaw	22	1.1	10	0.7	11	108.6
Tohono O'Odham	17	0.9	13	0.9	4	26.9
Potawatomi	17	0.9	10	0.7	7	72.1
Seminole	16	0.8	10	0.7	5	50.2
Pima	15	0.8	12	0.8	3	28.6
Tlingit	14	0.7	10	0.6	5	51.6
Alaskan Athabaskans	14	0.7	10	0.7	4	40.1
Cheyenne	12	0.6	10	0.7	2	19.1
Comanche	11	0.6	9	0.6	2	26.6
Paiute	11	0.6	10	0.6	2	19.4
Osage	10	0.5	7	0.5	4	51.5
Puget Sound Salish	10	0.5	7	0.4	4	57.5
Yaqui	10	0.5	5	0.4	5	89.3

Note: Total excludes Eskimos and Aleuts. Numbers by tribe will not sum to total because not all tribes are shown.
Source: U.S. Bureau of the Census, Internet web site, http://www.census.gov; *calculations by New Strategist*

Native Americans by Tribe and Ability to Speak English, 1990

(number of Native Americans aged 5 or older and percent who do not speak English "very well," for 25 largest tribes ranked by size of tribe, 1990; numbers in thousands)

	number	percent who do not speak English "very well"
Total persons, aged 5 or older	**1,750**	**8.9%**
Cherokee	346	1.9
Navajo	195	33.4
Sioux	94	4.6
Chippewa	95	1.6
Choctaw	79	5.1
Pueblo	50	23.0
Apache	48	15.6
Iroquois	48	2.2
Lumbee	47	1.2
Creek	42	3.1
Blackfoot	35	1.7
Canadian and Latin American	25	23.8
Chickasaw	20	1.5
Tohono O'Odham	15	26.1
Potawatomi	15	1.0
Seminole	14	6.3
Pima	13	11.8
Tlingit	13	2.4
Alaskan Athabaskans	13	5.8
Cheyenne	10	6.2
Comanche	10	2.2
Paiute	10	4.9
Osage	9	0.9
Puget Sound Salish	9	0.8
Yaqui	9	30.6

Note: Numbers by tribe will not sum to total because not all tribes are shown.
Source: Bureau of the Census, Characteristics of American Indians by Tribe and Language, *1990 Census of Population, CP-3-7, 1994; calculations by New Strategist*

Native Americans by Region and Tribe, 1990

(number and percent distribution of Native Americans by 25 largest tribes and region, 1990, ranked by size of tribe in 1990; numbers in thousands)

| | number | percent | | | | |
		total	Northeast	Midwest	South	West
Total persons	**1,937**	**100.0%**	**6.3%**	**17.9%**	**30.2%**	**45.6%**
Cherokee	369	100.0	4.8	15.5	55.0	24.8
Navajo	225	100.0	0.5	1.2	2.2	96.1
Sioux	107	100.0	2.3	64.7	7.3	25.6
Chippewa	106	100.0	1.4	77.5	4.7	16.4
Choctaw	86	100.0	0.9	4.7	76.1	18.4
Pueblo	55	100.0	1.1	1.7	4.6	92.5
Apache	53	100.0	3.0	7.1	15.2	74.7
Iroquois	53	100.0	44.8	25.4	16.3	13.6
Lumbee	51	100.0	1.0	2.7	94.7	1.6
Creek	46	100.0	1.4	5.1	80.6	12.9
Blackfoot	38	100.0	11.2	16.5	15.0	57.3
Canadian and Latin American	27	100.0	15.8	14.3	18.9	51.0
Chickasaw	22	100.0	0.7	3.7	75.1	20.4
Tohono O'Odham	17	100.0	0.4	1.1	1.1	97.4
Potawatomi	17	100.0	1.5	39.7	37.6	21.2
Seminole	16	100.0	6.3	7.0	69.2	17.5
Pima	15	100.0	0.3	1.0	2.0	96.7
Tlingit	14	100.0	1.0	1.9	2.0	95.2
Alaskan Athabaskans	14	100.0	1.3	2.5	2.6	93.6
Cheyenne	12	100.0	2.2	10.1	29.3	58.5
Comanche	11	100.0	2.3	8.2	66.1	23.3
Paiute	11	100.0	0.5	1.9	2.4	95.2
Osage	10	100.0	1.0	10.6	62.5	25.9
Puget Sound Salish	10	100.0	0.7	1.7	2.8	94.7
Yaqui	10	100.0	0.2	1.3	2.4	96.1

Note: Total excludes Eskimos and Aleuts. Numbers by tribe will not sum to total because not all tribes are shown.
Source: Bureau of the Census, Characteristics of American Indians by Tribe and Language, 1990 Census of Population, CP-3-7, 1994; calculations by New Strategist

Native Americans by Region and Division, 1995 to 2020

(number and percent distribution of Native Americans and Native American share of the total population by region and division, selected years 1995–2020; percent change in number and percentage point change in distribution and share, 1995–2000 and 2000–2010; numbers in thousands)

	1995	2000	2010	2020	percent change 1995–2000	percent change 2000–2010
Number						
UNITED STATES	**2,239**	**2,402**	**2,754**	**3,130**	**7.3%**	**14.7%**
Northeast	**141**	**149**	**168**	**190**	**5.7**	**12.8**
New England	36	37	43	48	2.8	16.2
Middle Atlantic	105	111	126	141	5.7	13.5
Midwest	**369**	**405**	**474**	**545**	**9.8**	**17.0**
East North Central	164	174	193	212	6.1	10.9
West North Central	205	231	282	332	12.7	22.1
South	**622**	**669**	**765**	**859**	**7.6**	**14.3**
South Atlantic	197	212	238	264	7.6	12.3
East South Central	43	46	52	55	7.0	13.0
West South Central	382	411	475	540	7.6	15.6
West	**1,107**	**1,179**	**1,347**	**1,536**	**6.5**	**14.2**
Mountain	565	632	745	855	11.9	17.9
Pacific	542	547	602	681	0.9	10.1

	1995	2000	2010	2020	percentage point change 1995–2000	percentage point change 2000–2010
Percent distribution						
UNITED STATES	**100.0%**	**100.0%**	**100.0%**	**100.0%**	**–**	**–**
Northeast	**6.3**	**6.2**	**6.1**	**6.1**	**–0.1**	**–0.1**
New England	1.6	1.5	1.6	1.5	–0.1	0.1
Middle Atlantic	4.7	4.6	4.6	4.5	–0.1	–0.0
Midwest	**16.5**	**16.9**	**17.2**	**17.4**	**0.4**	**0.3**
East North Central	7.3	7.2	7.0	6.8	–0.1	–0.2
West North Central	9.2	9.6	10.2	10.6	0.4	0.6
South	**27.8**	**27.9**	**27.8**	**27.4**	**0.1**	**–0.1**
South Atlantic	8.8	8.8	8.6	8.4	0.0	–0.2
East South Central	1.9	1.9	1.9	1.8	0.0	0.0
West South Central	17.1	17.1	17.2	17.3	0.0	0.1
West	**49.4**	**49.1**	**48.9**	**49.1**	**–0.3**	**–0.2**
Mountain	25.2	26.3	27.1	27.3	1.1	0.8
Pacific	24.2	22.8	21.9	21.8	–1.4	–0.9

(continued)

(continued from previous page)

Percent share	1995	2000	2010	2020	percentage point change 1995–2000	2000–2010
UNITED STATES	**0.9%**	**0.9%**	**0.9%**	**1.0%**	**0.0%**	**0.0%**
Northeast	**0.3**	**0.3**	**0.3**	**0.3**	**0.0**	**0.0**
New England	0.3	0.3	0.3	0.3	0.0	0.0
Middle Atlantic	0.3	0.3	0.3	0.3	0.0	0.0
Midwest	**0.6**	**0.6**	**0.7**	**0.8**	**0.0**	**0.1**
East North Central	0.4	0.4	0.4	0.5	0.0	0.0
West North Central	1.1	1.2	1.4	1.6	0.1	0.2
South	**0.7**	**0.7**	**0.7**	**0.7**	**0.0**	**0.0**
South Atlantic	0.4	0.4	0.4	0.4	0.0	0.0
East South Central	0.3	0.3	0.3	0.3	0.0	0.0
West South Central	1.3	1.3	1.4	1.4	0.0	0.1
West	**1.9**	**1.9**	**1.9**	**1.9**	**0.0**	**0.0**
Mountain	3.6	3.6	3.7	3.9	0.0	0.1
Pacific	1.3	1.3	1.2	1.1	0.0	–0.1

Note: (–) means not applicable.
Source: Bureau of the Census, Population Projections for States, by Age, Sex, Race, and Hispanic Origin: 1995 to 2025, Current Population Reports, PPL-47, 1996; calculations by New Strategist

Native Americans by State, 1995 to 2020

(number of Native Americans by state, selected years 1995–2020; percent change 1995–2000 and 2000–2010; numbers in thousands)

	1995	2000	2010	2020	percent change 1995–2000	percent change 2000–2010
United States	**2,239**	**2,402**	**2,754**	**3,130**	**7.3%**	**14.7%**
Alabama	16	18	20	22	12.5	11.1
Alaska	92	93	91	94	1.1	−2.2
Arizona	244	262	290	318	7.4	10.7
Arkansas	14	15	18	18	7.1	20.0
California	299	292	318	367	−2.3	8.9
Colorado	35	41	51	56	17.1	24.4
Connecticut	8	8	8	10	0.0	0.0
Delaware	2	2	2	2	0.0	0.0
District of Columbia	1	–	–	–	–	–
Florida	45	51	64	77	13.3	25.5
Georgia	16	17	18	21	6.3	5.9
Hawaii	6	6	7	8	0.0	16.7
Idaho	16	21	27	30	31.3	28.6
Illinois	25	26	31	36	4.0	19.2
Indiana	14	16	17	18	14.3	6.3
Iowa	8	9	12	14	12.5	33.3
Kansas	23	27	30	34	17.4	11.1
Kentucky	6	6	8	8	0.0	33.3
Louisiana	20	20	22	24	0.0	10.0
Maine	6	6	6	6	0.0	0.0
Maryland	14	16	16	19	14.3	0.0
Massachusetts	14	14	15	16	0.0	7.1
Michigan	59	61	65	70	3.4	6.6
Minnesota	56	64	80	96	14.3	25.0
Mississippi	8	8	8	8	0.0	0.0
Missouri	22	24	28	30	9.1	16.7
Montana	53	61	72	85	15.1	18.0
Nebraska	14	16	20	23	14.3	25.0
Nevada	26	31	32	33	19.2	3.2
New Hampshire	2	2	2	4	0.0	0.0
New Jersey	20	20	23	27	0.0	15.0
New Mexico	150	169	209	253	12.7	23.7
New York	69	73	79	87	5.8	8.2
North Carolina	89	94	101	106	5.6	7.4
North Dakota	28	32	43	53	14.3	34.4

(continued)

(continued from previous page)

	1995	2000	2010	2020	percent change 1995-2000	percent change 2000-2010
Ohio	22	22	24	29	0.0%	9.1%
Oklahoma	265	281	315	351	6.0	12.1
Oregon	45	51	59	68	13.3	15.7
Pennsylvania	16	18	22	26	12.5	22.2
Rhode Island	4	4	8	9	0.0	100.0
South Carolina	8	8	9	10	0.0	12.5
South Dakota	54	60	72	84	11.1	20.0
Tennessee	10	12	14	17	20.0	16.7
Texas	84	95	120	146	13.1	26.3
Utah	30	37	47	55	23.3	27.0
Vermont	2	2	2	2	0.0	0.0
Virginia	18	19	21	24	5.6	10.5
Washington	100	107	126	143	7.0	17.8
West Virginia	2	2	2	2	0.0	0.0
Wisconsin	45	49	55	61	8.9	12.2
Wyoming	11	13	19	24	18.2	46.2

Note: Numbers may not add to total due to rounding. (–) means number is less than 500.
Source: Bureau of the Census, Population Projections for States, by Age, Sex, Race, and Hispanic Origin: 1995 to 2025, Current Population Reports, PPL-47, 1996; calculations by New Strategist

Distribution of Native Americans by State, 1995 to 2020

(percent distribution of Native Americans by state, selected years 1995–2020)

	1995	*2000*	*2010*	*2020*
United States	**100.0%**	**100.0%**	**100.0%**	**100.0%**
Alabama	0.7	0.7	0.7	0.7
Alaska	4.1	3.9	3.3	3.0
Arizona	10.9	10.9	10.5	10.2
Arkansas	0.6	0.6	0.7	0.6
California	13.4	12.2	11.5	11.7
Colorado	1.6	1.7	1.9	1.8
Connecticut	0.4	0.3	0.3	0.3
Delaware	0.1	0.1	0.1	0.1
District of Columbia	0.0	0.0	0.0	0.0
Florida	2.0	2.1	2.3	2.5
Georgia	0.7	0.7	0.7	0.7
Hawaii	0.3	0.2	0.3	0.3
Idaho	0.7	0.9	1.0	1.0
Illinois	1.1	1.1	1.1	1.2
Indiana	0.6	0.7	0.6	0.6
Iowa	0.4	0.4	0.4	0.4
Kansas	1.0	1.1	1.1	1.1
Kentucky	0.3	0.2	0.3	0.3
Louisiana	0.9	0.8	0.8	0.8
Maine	0.3	0.2	0.2	0.2
Maryland	0.6	0.7	0.6	0.6
Massachusetts	0.6	0.6	0.5	0.5
Michigan	2.6	2.5	2.4	2.2
Minnesota	2.5	2.7	2.9	3.1
Mississippi	0.4	0.3	0.3	0.3
Missouri	1.0	1.0	1.0	1.0
Montana	2.4	2.5	2.6	2.7
Nebraska	0.6	0.7	0.7	0.7
Nevada	1.2	1.3	1.2	1.1
New Hampshire	0.1	0.1	0.1	0.1
New Jersey	0.9	0.8	0.8	0.9
New Mexico	6.7	7.0	7.6	8.1
New York	3.1	3.0	2.9	2.8
North Carolina	4.0	3.9	3.7	3.4
North Dakota	1.3	1.3	1.6	1.7

(continued)

(continued from previous page)

	1995	2000	2010	2020
Ohio	1.0%	0.9%	0.9%	0.9%
Oklahoma	11.8	11.7	11.4	11.2
Oregon	2.0	2.1	2.1	2.2
Pennsylvania	0.7	0.7	0.8	0.8
Rhode Island	0.2	0.2	0.3	0.3
South Carolina	0.4	0.3	0.3	0.3
South Dakota	2.4	2.5	2.6	2.7
Tennessee	0.4	0.5	0.5	0.5
Texas	3.8	4.0	4.4	4.7
Utah	1.3	1.5	1.7	1.8
Vermont	0.1	0.1	0.1	0.1
Virginia	0.8	0.8	0.8	0.8
Washington	4.5	4.5	4.6	4.6
West Virginia	0.1	0.1	0.1	0.1
Wisconsin	2.0	2.0	2.0	1.9
Wyoming	0.5	0.5	0.7	0.8

Source: Calculations by New Strategist based on Census Bureau data in Population Projections for States, by Age, Sex, Race, and Hispanic Origin: 1993 to 2020, *Current Population Reports, PPL-47, 1996*

Native American Share of State Populations, 1995 to 2020

(Native Americans as a percent of state populations, selected years 1995–2020; percentage point change, 1995–2020)

	1995	2000	2010	2020	percentage point change 1995–2020
United States	**0.9%**	**0.9%**	**1.0%**	**1.1%**	**0.2%**
Alabama	0.4	0.4	0.4	0.5	0.1
Alaska	15.2	14.7	13.9	12.6	−2.6
Arizona	5.8	5.7	6.0	5.8	0.0
Arkansas	0.6	0.6	0.7	0.6	0.1
California	0.9	0.9	1.0	1.0	0.0
Colorado	0.9	1.0	1.2	1.2	0.3
Connecticut	0.2	0.2	0.2	0.3	0.0
Delaware	0.3	0.3	0.3	0.2	−0.1
District of Columbia	0.2	–	–	–	–
Florida	0.3	0.3	0.4	0.4	0.1
Georgia	0.2	0.2	0.2	0.2	0.0
Hawaii	0.5	0.5	0.6	0.6	0.1
Idaho	1.4	1.6	2.0	1.9	0.6
Illinois	0.2	0.2	0.3	0.3	0.1
Indiana	0.2	0.3	0.3	0.3	0.0
Iowa	0.3	0.3	0.4	0.5	0.2
Kansas	0.9	1.0	1.1	1.2	0.3
Kentucky	0.2	0.2	0.2	0.2	0.0
Louisiana	0.5	0.5	0.5	0.5	0.1
Maine	0.5	0.5	0.5	0.5	0.0
Maryland	0.3	0.3	0.3	0.3	0.1
Massachusetts	0.2	0.2	0.2	0.2	0.0
Michigan	0.6	0.6	0.7	0.7	0.1
Minnesota	1.2	1.3	1.7	1.9	0.7
Mississippi	0.3	0.3	0.3	0.3	0.0
Missouri	0.4	0.4	0.5	0.5	0.1
Montana	6.1	6.6	7.6	8.2	2.1
Nebraska	0.9	1.0	1.2	1.3	0.4
Nevada	1.7	1.8	1.7	1.5	−0.2
New Hampshire	0.2	0.2	0.2	0.3	0.1
New Jersey	0.3	0.2	0.3	0.3	0.1
New Mexico	8.9	9.4	11.2	11.7	2.8
New York	0.4	0.4	0.4	0.5	0.1
North Carolina	1.2	1.2	1.3	1.2	0.0
North Dakota	4.4	4.9	6.5	7.7	3.3

(continued)

(continued from previous page)

	1995	2000	2010	2020	percentage point change 1995–2020
Ohio	0.2%	0.2%	0.2%	0.3%	0.1%
Oklahoma	8.1	8.4	9.3	9.6	1.6
Oregon	1.4	1.5	1.7	1.8	0.4
Pennsylvania	0.1	0.1	0.2	0.2	0.1
Rhode Island	0.4	0.4	0.8	0.9	0.5
South Carolina	0.2	0.2	0.2	0.2	0.0
South Dakota	7.4	7.9	9.3	10.2	2.8
Tennessee	0.2	0.2	0.2	0.3	0.1
Texas	0.4	0.5	0.6	0.6	0.2
Utah	1.5	1.8	2.1	2.2	0.6
Vermont	0.3	0.3	0.3	0.3	0.0
Virginia	0.3	0.3	0.3	0.3	0.0
Washington	1.8	1.9	2.2	2.1	0.3
West Virginia	0.1	0.1	0.1	0.1	0.0
Wisconsin	0.9	0.9	1.0	1.1	0.2
Wyoming	2.3	2.6	3.6	4.0	1.7

Note: (–) means less than 0.05.
Source: Calculations by New Strategist based on Census Bureau data in Population Projections for States, by Age, Sex, Race, and Hispanic Origin: 1995 to 2025, *Current Population Reports, PPL-47, 1996*

Metropolitan Areas with the Most Native Americans, 1990

(ten metropolitan areas with the most Native Americans ranked by size of Native American population; number of Native Americans and Native American share of total metropolitan population, 1990; numbers in thousands)

		number	percent
1.	Los Angeles–Riverside–Orange County, CA	87	0.6%
2.	Phoenix–Mesa, AZ	49	2.2
3.	New York–Northern New Jersey–Long Island, NY-NJ-CT-PA	48	0.2
4.	Tulsa, OK	48	6.8
5.	Oklahoma City, OK	46	4.8
6.	San Francisco–Oakland–San Jose, CA	41	0.7
7.	Seattle–Tacoma–Bremerton, WA	38	1.3
8.	Albuquerque, NM	30	5.1
9.	Minneapolis–St. Paul, MN	24	1.0
10.	Detroit–Ann Arbor–Flint, MI	21	0.4

Source: Bureau of the Census, Statistical Abstract of the United States 1993; calculations by New Strategist

5

Whites

■ The white population is projected to grow from 223 million in 1998 to 255 million by 2020, when whites will account for 79 percent of the total U.S. population. Only 64 percent of the population will be non-Hispanic white in 2020.

■ Eighty-three percent of whites are high school graduates and 24 percent have graduated from college.

■ Two in three whites report being in excellent or very good health, while just 10 percent say their health is only fair or poor.

■ Fifty-seven percent of white households are married couples and 27 percent are nuclear families, about the same shares as for households in the nation as a whole. Female-headed families with children account for just 7 percent of white households.

■ Among white households, median income peaks at $52,750 for householders aged 45 to 54. By household type, white married couples have the highest incomes—$50,302 in 1996.

■ The nation's non-Hispanic white households spent an average of $33,878 in 1995 and their net worth was $73,900.

**Non-Hispanic whites
are 73 percent of
the U.S. population**

*(percent distribution of
total persons by race and
ethnicity, 1998)*

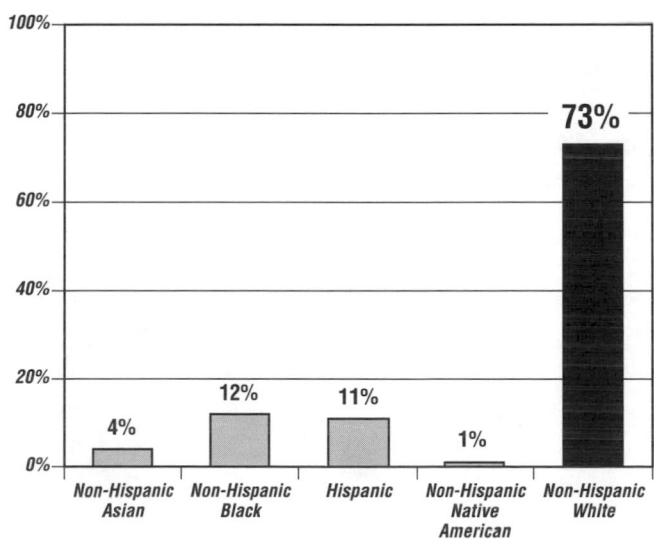

Whites: Education

Whites' educational attainment has grown sharply over the past few decades.

Educational attainment among whites closely matches that of the total population since the great majority of Americans are white. Overall, 83 percent of whites are high school graduates and 24 percent have graduated from college. Since 1980, the proportion of whites with a high school diploma has climbed 12 percentage points as the well-educated baby-boom generation matured and boosted overall educational attainment.

Among white families with children aged 18 to 24, 42 percent have at least one child in college full-time—a far higher proportion than that of black or Hispanic families. Among white families with dependents in the 18-to-24 age group and incomes of $75,000 or more, 66 percent have a child in college full-time.

Non-Hispanic whites earned 79 percent of all bachelor's degrees awarded in 1994–95, 74 percent of all master's degrees, and 63 percent of all doctorates. Of the first-professional degrees awarded in 1994–95, the largest share accounted for by non-Hispanic whites was in veterinary medicine (92 percent). The smallest share was in pharmacy (64 percent).

■ The non-Hispanic white share of college degrees awarded each year is shrinking as minorities make up a larger proportion of college students. Nevertheless, non-Hispanic whites still account for the great majority of college degrees—and will for years to come.

One in four whites has a college degree

(percent of whites aged 25 or older who are high school or college graduates, 1980 and 1996)

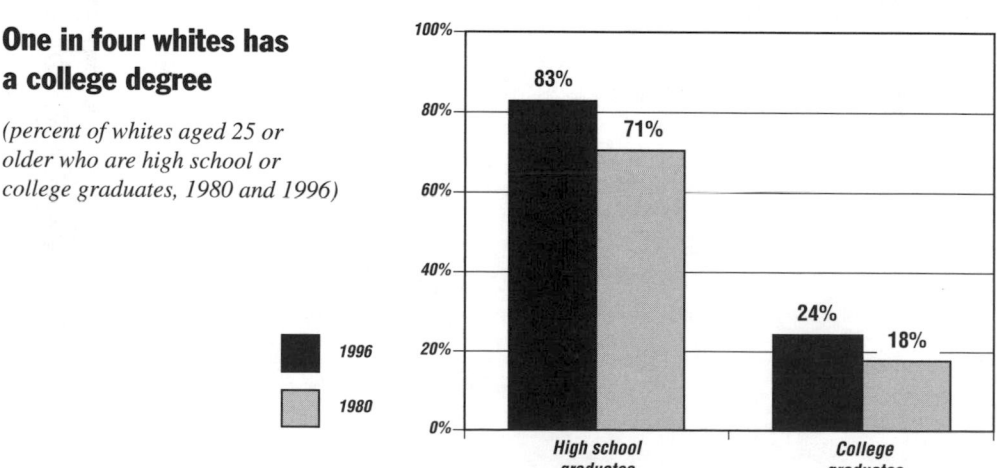

Educational Attainment of Whites by Sex, 1996

(number and percent distribution of whites aged 25 or older by educational attainment and sex, 1996; numbers in thousands)

	total		men		women	
	number	*percent*	*number*	*percent*	*number*	*percent*
Total, aged 25 or older	**142,733**	**100.0%**	**68,795**	**100.0%**	**73,939**	**100.0%**
Not a high school graduate	24,601	17.2	11,884	17.3	12,719	17.2
High school graduate or more	118,130	82.8	56,910	82.7	61,221	82.8
High school graduate only	48,356	33.9	21,818	31.7	26,538	35.9
Some college/assoc. degree	35,160	24.6	16,599	24.1	18,561	25.1
Bachelor's degree or more	34,614	24.3	18,493	26.9	16,122	21.8
Bachelor's degree only	23,044	16.1	11,715	17.0	11,329	15.3
Master's degree	8,009	5.6	4,276	6.2	3,733	5.0
Professional degree	2,183	1.5	1,534	2.2	650	0.9
Doctoral degree	1,378	1.0	968	1.4	410	0.6

Source: Bureau of the Census, Educational Attainment in the United States: March 1996, *Current Population Reports, P20-493, 1997; calculations by New Strategist*

White High School and College Graduates by Sex, 1980 to 1996

(percent of whites aged 25 or older who are high school or college graduates, by sex, selected years 1980–96)

	total	men	women
High school graduates			
1996	82.8%	82.7%	82.8%
1990	79.1	79.1	79.0
1985	75.5	76.0	75.1
1980	70.5	71.0	70.1
College graduates			
1996	24.3	26.9	21.8
1990	22.0	25.3	19.0
1985	20.0	24.0	16.3
1980	17.8	22.1	14.0

Source: Bureau of the Census, Educational Attainment in the United States: March 1996, *Current Population Reports, P20-493, 1997; and Internet web site,* http://www.census.gov

White High School and College Graduates by Age and Sex, 1996

(percent of whites aged 25 or older who are high school or college graduates by age and sex, 1996)

	total	men	women
High school graduates			
Total, aged 25 or older	**82.8%**	**82.7%**	**82.8%**
Aged 25 to 29	87.5	86.3	88.8
Aged 30 to 34	86.9	85.4	88.4
Aged 35 to 39	87.8	87.1	88.5
Aged 40 to 44	89.4	88.2	90.6
Aged 45 to 49	90.2	90.2	90.3
Aged 50 to 54	85.7	86.1	85.3
Aged 55 to 59	81.3	80.9	81.7
Aged 60 to 64	77.7	78.0	77.5
Aged 65 to 69	72.4	71.6	73.2
Aged 70 to 74	70.9	70.3	71.4
Aged 75 or older	60.8	61.2	60.6
College graduates			
Total, aged 25 or older	**24.3**	**26.9**	**21.8**
Aged 25 to 29	28.1	27.2	29.1
Aged 30 to 34	27.0	26.7	27.2
Aged 35 to 39	26.4	26.4	26.4
Aged 40 to 44	27.8	27.9	27.8
Aged 45 to 49	31.3	35.7	26.9
Aged 50 to 54	26.3	30.8	22.3
Aged 55 to 59	21.2	26.0	16.6
Aged 60 to 64	20.3	26.6	14.6
Aged 65 to 69	15.9	21.1	11.3
Aged 70 to 74	14.6	21.9	8.9
Aged 75 or older	13.2	16.6	11.2

Source: Bureau of the Census, Educational Attainment in the United States: March 1996, *Current Population Reports, P20-493, 1997*

White High School and College Graduates by Age and Region, 1996

(percent of whites aged 25 or older who are high school or college graduates, by age and region, 1996)

	Northeast	Midwest	South	West
High school graduates				
Total, aged 25 or older	**84.0%**	**85.7%**	**79.5%**	**83.3%**
Aged 25 to 34	90.8	92.1	85.4	81.7
Aged 35 to 44	90.6	92.0	86.3	86.0
Aged 45 to 54	89.3	91.5	84.9	88.9
Aged 55 to 64	80.7	82.8	74.7	83.6
Aged 65 or older	66.3	66.7	63.3	75.2
College graduates				
Total, aged 25 or older	**27.3**	**23.2**	**22.7**	**24.9**
Aged 25 to 34	32.7	29.8	25.4	24.0
Aged 35 to 44	32.2	25.3	26.2	25.7
Aged 45 to 54	32.6	26.8	27.7	30.8
Aged 55 to 64	22.5	18.7	18.1	26.7
Aged 65 or older	14.2	12.8	13.9	17.7

Source: Bureau of the Census, Educational Attainment in the United States: March 1996, *Current Population Reports, P20-493, 1997*

White High School and College Graduates by State, 1990

(percent of whites aged 25 or older who are high school or college graduates, by state, 1990)

	high school graduate or more	college graduate		high school graduate or more	college graduate
United States	**77.9%**	**21.5%**	Missouri	74.9%	18.3%
Alabama	70.3	17.3	Montana	81.7	20.3
Alaska	91.1	26.8	Nebraska	82.4	19.2
Arizona	82.4	22.2	Nevada	80.9	15.9
Arkansas	68.6	14.1	New Hampshire	82.2	24.2
California	81.1	25.4	New Jersey	78.6	25.8
Colorado	86.1	28.3	New Mexico	78.6	23.4
Connecticut	80.9	28.5	New York	78.5	25.3
Delaware	80.3	23.0	North Carolina	73.1	19.3
District of Columbia	93.1	69.0	North Dakota	76.9	18.3
Florida	77.0	19.3	Ohio	76.9	17.6
Georgia	74.9	21.8	Oklahoma	75.7	18.7
Hawaii	89.3	30.2	Oregon	82.3	20.8
Idaho	80.9	18.0	Pennsylvania	75.9	18.5
Illinois	79.1	22.4	Rhode Island	73.0	21.8
Indiana	76.5	17.6	South Carolina	73.6	19.8
Iowa	80.3	16.7	South Dakota	77.8	17.6
Kansas	82.4	21.7	Tennessee	68.2	16.7
Kentucky	64.7	13.9	Texas	76.2	22.6
Louisiana	74.2	18.7	Utah	86.2	22.7
Maine	78.9	18.8	Vermont	80.8	24.2
Maryland	80.8	28.9	Virginia	78.3	27.0
Massachusetts	81.2	27.7	Washington	85.0	23.3
Michigan	78.6	18.1	West Virginia	66.0	12.2
Minnesota	82.8	21.9	Wisconsin	79.6	18.1
Mississippi	71.7	17.2	Wyoming	83.9	19.3

Source: National Center for Education Statistics, Digest of Education Statistics 1993, *NCES 93-292, 1993*

School Enrollment of Whites by Age and Sex, 1995

(number and percent of whites aged 3 or older enrolled in school by age and sex, October 1995; numbers in thousands)

	total		male		female	
	number	*percent*	*number*	*percent*	*number*	*percent*
Total, aged 3 or older	**55,186**	**26.6%**	**27,765**	**27.3%**	**27,421**	**25.8%**
Aged 3 and 4	3,205	49.6	1,642	49.6	1,563	49.6
Aged 5 and 6	6,211	96.2	3,162	95.5	3,048	96.9
Aged 7 to 9	9,088	98.9	4,667	99.0	4,421	98.8
Aged 10 o 13	12,208	99.0	6,261	99.0	5,947	99.1
Aged 14 and 15	6,008	98.8	3,084	98.8	2,924	96.8
Aged 16 and 17	5,484	93.7	2,833	94.2	2,651	93.3
Aged 18 and 19	3,379	59.3	1,714	59.4	1,665	59.2
Aged 20 and 21	2,483	46.2	1,225	46.3	1,258	46.0
Aged 22 to 24	2,033	23.1	1,008	22.7	1,025	23.6
Aged 25 to 29	1,783	11.5	873	11.3	911	11.7
Aged 30 to 34	979	5.5	446	5.0	534	6.0
Aged 35 to 44	1,499	4.2	586	3.3	913	5.1
Aged 45 to 54	655	2.5	209	1.6	448	3.3
Aged 55 or older	170	0.4	55	0.3	115	0.5

Source: Bureau of the Census, School Enrollment—Social and Economic Characteristics of Students: October 1995, *Current Population Reports, P20-492, 1997*

White Families with Children in College, 1995

(total number of white families, number with children aged 18 to 24, and number and percent with children aged 18 to 24 attending college full-time, as of October 1995, by household income in 1994; numbers in thousands)

	total	with children aged 18–24	with one or more children attending college full-time		
			number	percent of total families	percent of families with children 18–24
Total families	**59,078**	**7,928**	**3,338**	**5.7%**	**42.1%**
Under $20,000	11,632	1,237	261	2.2	21.1
$20,000 to $29,999	8,436	917	319	3.8	34.8
$30,000 to $39,999	7,918	926	329	4.2	35.5
$40,000 to $49,999	6,110	794	298	4.9	37.5
$50,000 to $74,999	10,081	1,647	791	7.8	48.0
$75,000 or more	8,199	1,505	994	12.1	66.0

Source: Bureau of the Census, School Enrollment   Social and Economic Characteristics of Students: October 1995, Current Population Reports, P20-492, 1997; calculations by New Strategist

College Enrollment of Whites by Age, 1995

(number and percent distribution of whites aged 15 or older enrolled in college by age, type of school, and attendance status, October 1995; numbers in thousands)

	total enrolled	undergraduate total	two-year college			four-year college			graduate		
			total	full-time	part-time	total	full-time	part-time	total	full-time	part-time
Total enrolled	**12,021**	**9,791**	**3,067**	**1,574**	**1,492**	**6,724**	**5,252**	**1,472**	**2,231**	**947**	**1,285**
Aged 15 to 17	116	115	38	27	11	77	74	4	1	1	0
Aged 18 and 19	2,577	2,572	794	624	170	1,778	1,675	103	5	5	0
Aged 20 and 21	2,437	2,393	464	307	157	1,929	1,746	183	44	32	13
Aged 22 to 24	1,997	1,622	460	227	233	1,162	924	238	375	282	93
Aged 25 to 29	1,745	1,092	420	136	285	672	381	291	652	324	329
Aged 30 to 34	941	623	261	101	159	362	159	203	318	121	196
Aged 35 to 39	829	539	236	68	168	303	135	168	290	96	193
Aged 40 to 44	605	410	182	39	143	228	76	152	195	35	159
Aged 45 to 49	420	227	107	25	82	120	50	70	194	31	163
Aged 50 to 54	198	115	39	15	24	76	28	48	82	17	66
Aged 55 or older	156	81	65	6	59	16	4	12	76	2	74

(continued)

(continued from previous page)

Percent distribution by age	Total enrolled total	undergraduate total	two-year college total	full-time	part-time	four-year college total	full-time	part-time	graduate total	full-time	part-time
Total enrolled	100.0%	100.0%	100.0%	100.0%	100.0%	100.0%	100.0%	100.0%	100.0%	100.0%	100.0%
Aged 15 to 17	1.0	1.2	1.2	1.7	0.7	1.1	1.4	0.3	0.0	0.1	–
Aged 18 and 19	21.4	26.3	25.9	39.6	11.4	26.4	31.9	7.0	0.2	0.5	–
Aged 20 and 21	20.3	24.4	15.1	19.5	10.5	28.7	33.2	12.4	2.0	3.4	1.0
Aged 22 to 24	16.6	16.6	15.0	14.4	15.6	17.3	17.6	16.2	16.8	29.8	7.2
Aged 25 to 29	14.5	11.2	13.7	8.6	19.1	10.0	7.3	19.8	29.2	34.2	25.6
Aged 30 to 34	7.8	5.4	8.5	6.4	10.7	5.4	3.0	13.8	14.3	12.8	15.3
Aged 35 to 39	6.9	5.5	7.7	4.3	11.3	4.5	2.6	11.4	13.0	10.1	15.0
Aged 40 to 44	5.0	4.2	5.9	2.5	9.6	3.4	1.4	10.3	8.7	3.7	12.4
Aged 45 to 49	3.5	2.3	3.5	1.6	5.5	1.8	1.0	4.8	8.7	3.3	12.7
Aged 50 to 54	1.6	1.2	1.3	1.0	1.6	1.1	0.5	3.3	3.7	1.8	5.1
Aged 55 or older	1.3	0.8	2.1	0.4	4.0	0.2	0.1	0.8	3.4	0.2	5.8

(continued)

(continued from previous page)

Percent distribution by attendance status

| | total | undergraduate | | | | | | four-year college | | | graduate | | |
| | | total | two-year college | | | total | full-time | part-time | total | full-time | part-time |
			total	full-time	part-time							
Total enrolled	**100.0%**	**81.4%**	**25.5%**	**13.1%**	**12.4%**	**55.9%**	**43.7%**	**12.2%**	**18.6%**	**7.9%**	**10.7%**
Aged 15 to 17	100.0	99.1	32.8	23.3	9.5	66.4	63.8	3.4	0.9	0.9	–
Aged 18 and 19	100.0	99.8	30.8	24.2	6.6	69.0	65.0	4.0	0.2	0.2	–
Aged 20 and 21	100.0	98.2	19.0	12.6	6.4	79.2	71.6	7.5	1.8	1.3	0.5
Aged 22 to 24	100.0	81.2	23.0	11.4	11.7	58.2	46.3	11.9	18.8	14.1	4.7
Aged 25 to 29	100.0	62.6	24.1	7.8	16.3	38.5	21.8	16.7	37.4	18.6	18.9
Aged 30 to 34	100.0	66.2	27.7	10.7	16.9	38.5	16.9	21.6	33.8	12.9	20.8
Aged 35 to 39	100.0	65.0	28.5	8.2	20.3	36.6	16.3	20.3	35.0	11.6	23.3
Aged 40 to 44	100.0	67.8	30.1	6.4	23.6	37.7	12.6	25.1	32.2	5.8	26.3
Aged 45 to 49	100.0	54.0	25.5	6.0	19.5	28.6	11.9	16.7	46.2	7.4	38.8
Aged 50 to 54	100.0	58.1	19.7	7.6	12.1	38.4	14.1	24.2	41.4	8.6	33.3
Aged 55 or older	100.0	51.9	41.7	3.8	37.8	10.3	2.6	7.7	48.7	1.3	47.4

Note: (–) means sample is too small to make a reliable estimate.
Source: Bureau of the Census, School Enrollment—Social and Economic Characteristics of Students: October 1995, Current Population Reports, P20-492, 1997; calculations by New Strategist

Bachelor's, Master's, and Doctoral Degrees
Earned by Non-Hispanic Whites by Field of Study, 1994–95

(number and percent of bachelor's, master's, and doctoral degrees earned by non-Hispanic whites, by field of study, 1994–95)

	bachelor's		master's		doctoral	
	number	percent	number	percent	number	percent
Total degrees	**913,377**	**78.8%**	**292,784**	**73.7%**	**27,826**	**62.6%**
Agriculture and natural resources	17,986	90.7	3,007	70.7	601	47.5
Architecture and related programs	6,716	76.7	2,628	67.0	69	48.9
Area, ethnic, and cultural studies	3,704	64.9	1,138	69.4	121	65.1
Biological and life sciences	41,573	74.3	3,741	69.4	2,883	62.1
Business, management, and admin. services	176,471	75.3	66,553	70.9	848	60.8
Communications	39,240	81.6	3,597	70.0	234	73.1
Communications technologies	553	79.1	259	55.5	1	100.0
Computer and information sciences	15,932	65.3	4,521	43.8	401	45.4
Construction trades	95	84.1	–	–	–	–
Education	93,033	87.7	83,646	82.6	5,205	75.4
Engineering	44,735	71.8	14,686	51.4	2,333	38.2
Engineering-related technologies	12,332	78.9	808	72.8	7	38.9
English language and literature	43,881	84.5	6,758	86.1	1,268	81.2
Foreign languages and literature	10,251	74.4	2,071	66.0	536	59.2
Health professions and related sciences	66,402	83.2	25,244	80.8	1,311	63.4
Home economics	13,103	85.4	2,176	76.0	279	71.9
Law and legal studies	1,646	81.0	1,228	48.9	32	36.4
Liberal arts and sciences	25,842	77.5	2,114	82.4	71	78.9
Library science	46	92.0	4,384	86.7	29	52.7
Mathematics	10,559	76.9	2,523	60.3	562	45.8
Mechanics and repairers	57	86.4	–	–	–	–
Multi- and interdisciplinary studies	20,006	76.8	2,001	81.4	155	65.1
Parks, recreation, leisure, and fitness	11,245	87.2	1,519	86.6	110	73.8
Philosophy and religion	6,102	83.9	1,128	81.7	401	79.1
Physical sciences	15,398	80.3	3,385	58.8	2,455	54.8
Precision production trades	281	79.6	5	100.0	–	–
Protective services	17,980	74.4	1,321	77.4	17	65.4
Psychology	57,297	79.5	11,562	83.1	3,231	84.5
Public administration and services	13,533	72.8	18,056	76.8	381	68.5
R.O.T.C. and military sciences	26	96.3	105	84.7	–	–
Social sciences and history	99,544	77.7	10,299	69.4	2,360	63.4
Theological studies and religious vocations	4,830	86.6	3,949	75.4	1,108	69.6
Transportation and material moving	3,213	86.9	741	90.0	–	–
Visual and performing arts	39,765	81.7	7,631	74.3	817	75.6

Note: (–) means no degrees were awarded.
Source: National Center for Education Statistics, Digest of Education Statistics 1997, NCES 98-015, 1997; calculations by New Strategist

First-Professional Degrees Earned
by Non-Hispanic Whites by Field of Study, 1994–95

(number and percent of first-professional degrees earned by non-Hispanic whites by field of study, 1994–95)

	number	percent
Total degrees	**59,402**	**78.4%**
Dentistry (D.D.S. or D.M.D.)	2,616	67.1
Medicine (M.D.)	11,215	72.2
Optometry (O.D.)	899	75.9
Osteopathic medicine (D.O.)	1,524	82.2
Pharmacy (Pharm. D.)	1,444	63.8
Podiatry (Pod. D., D.P., or D.P.M.)	416	76.3
Veterinary medicine (D.V.M.)	1,983	92.3
Chiropractic medicine (D.C. or D.C.M.)	2,477	83.5
Law (LL.B. or J.D.)	32,126	81.6
Theology (M.Div., M.H.L., B.D., or Ord.)	4,641	77.6
Other	61	81.3

Source: National Center for Education Statistics, Digest of Education Statistics 1997, *NCES 98-015, 1997; calculations by New Strategist*

Whites: Health

Most whites say their health is excellent or good, but 24 percent of those aged 15 or older are disabled.

Two in three whites report being in excellent or very good health, while just 10 percent say their health is only fair or poor. Because whites comprise the majority of Americans, these proportions closely match those of the total population.

Health indicators for whites are close to the average on most measures, with a few exceptions. The incidence of AIDS, tuberculosis, and syphilis is much lower among whites than among the total population. The suicide rate among whites is slightly higher than average.

While 80 percent of all births in 1996 were to white women, many white women are Hispanic. Thus, only about 62 percent of the nation's births are to non-Hispanic white women.

Twenty-four percent of whites aged 15 or older are disabled, the same rate as for the population as a whole. Among all racial and ethnic groups, whites are least likely to be without health insurance. In 1996, only 14 percent did not have health insurance coverage. Among whites under age 18, however, 27 percent did not have health insurance.

White life expectancy is slightly above average. At birth, non-Hispanic white males can expect to live 1.2 years longer than the average American male, while non-Hispanic white females can expect to live 0.7 years longer than average.

■ As the white population ages, the percentage of Americans with disabilities will rise.

Disability rates rise with age

(percent of whites aged 15 or older who are disabled, 1994–95)

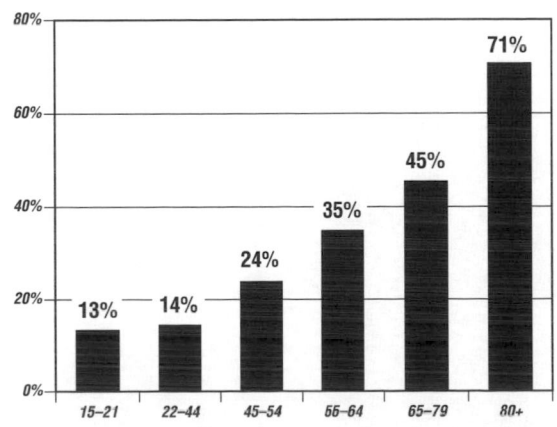

Health Status of Whites by Age, 1994

(percent distribution of self-assessed or parent-assessed health status of whites, by age, 1994)

	total	excellent	very good	good	fair	poor
Total persons	**100.0%**	**39.0%**	**29.0%**	**22.5%**	**6.8%**	**2.7%**
Under age 5	100.0	55.0	27.6	14.9	2.2	0.3
Aged 5 to 17	100.0	53.4	27.6	16.4	2.3	0.4
Aged 18 to 24	100.0	44.6	31.9	19.7	3.3	0.5
Aged 25 to 44	100.0	40.2	31.9	21.4	4.9	1.6
Aged 45 to 64	100.0	30.1	28.5	26.5	10.3	4.6
Aged 65 or older	100.0	16.2	23.7	33.6	17.6	9.0

Source: National Center for Health Statistics, Current Estimates from the National Health Interview Survey, 1994, *Series 10, No. 193, 1995*

Health Indicators for Whites, 1993 and 1994

(selected indicators of total population and white health status, and index of white health indicators to total, 1993 and 1994)

	total population indicator	white indicator	index
Infant mortality rate (deaths before age 1 per 1,000 live births), 1993	8.4	6.8	81
Total deaths per 100,000 population, 1993	513.3	485.1	95
Motor vehicle crash deaths per 100,000 population, 1993	16.0	16.1	101
Work-related injury deaths per 100,000 people aged 16 or older, 1994	3.3	3.2	97
Suicides per 100,000 population, 1993	11.3	12.0	106
Homicides per 100,000 population, 1993	10.7	6.0	56
Lung cancer deaths per 100,000 population, 1993	39.3	38.9	99
Female breast cancer deaths per 100,000 population, 1993	21.5	21.2	99
Cardiovascular disease deaths per 100,000 population, 1993	181.8	173.9	96
Heart disease deaths per 100,000 population, 1993	145.3	139.9	96
Stroke deaths per 100,000 population, 1993	26.5	24.5	92
Reported incidence of AIDS per 100,000 population, 1994*	26.9	14.8	55
Reported incidence of tuberculosis per 100,000 population, 1994*	9.4	3.4	36
Reported incidence of syphilis per 100,000 population, 1994*	8.1	1.0	12
Prevalence of low birth weight, as percent of total live births, 1994	7.3	6.1	84
Births to girls aged 10 to 17, as percent of total live births, 1994	5.3	4.2	79
Percent of mothers without care, first trimester of pregnancy, 1994	19.8	17.2	87
Percent under age 18 living in poverty, 1994	21.8	16.9	78
Percent living in counties exceeding U.S. air quality standards, 1994	24.9	23.6	95

* Data are for the non-Hispanic white population.
Note: The index for each indicator is calculated by dividing the white figure by the total population figure and multiplying by 100. For example, the index of 81 in the first row indicates that white infant mortality is 19 percent below the rate for all infants.
Source: National Center for Health Statistics, Health Status Indicators by Race and Hispanic Origin, *Healthy People 2000 Review, 1995–96; calculations by New Strategist*

Births to White Women by Age, 1996

(number and percent distribution of births to white women, by age, 1996)

	number	percent
Total births	**3,113,014**	**100.0%**
Under age 15	5,570	0.2
Aged 15 to 19	346,509	11.1
Aged 20 to 24	731,148	23.5
Aged 25 to 29	884,787	28.4
Aged 30 to 34	753,589	24.2
Aged 35 to 39	331,044	10.6
Aged 40 or older	60,368	1.9

Source: National Center for Health Statistics, Births and Deaths: United States, 1996, *Monthly Vital Statistics Report, Vol. 46, No. 1, Supplement 2, 1997; calculations by New Strategist*

Births to Unmarried White Women by Age, 1995

(number and percent of births to unmarried white women, by age; 1995)

	number	percent of total white births
Total births to unmarried whites	**784,992**	**25.3%**
Under age 15	5,196	88.8
Aged 15 to 19	236,546	67.7
Aged 20 to 24	271,466	36.5
Aged 25 to 29	143,006	16.4
Aged 30 to 34	82,392	10.9
Aged 35 to 39	37,931	12.0
Aged 40 or older	8,455	15.0

Source: National Center for Health Statistics, Advance Report of Final Natality Statistics: 1995, *Monthly Vital Statistics Report, Vol. 45, No. 11(S), 1997; calculations by New Strategist*

Births to White Women by State, 1996

(number and percent distribution of births to white women by state, and white births as a percent of total births by state, 1996)

	number	percent	white share of total births
United States	**3,113,014**	**100.0%**	**79.5%**
Alabama	40,943	1.3	66.6
Alaska	6,930	0.2	68.2
Arizona	69,869	2.2	87.8
Arkansas	27,915	0.9	76.7
California	440,213	14.1	81.6
Colorado	51,100	1.6	91.5
Connecticut	37,755	1.2	85.2
Delaware	7,620	0.2	74.4
District of Columbia	2,062	0.1	24.7
Florida	142,670	4.6	75.3
Georgia	73,762	2.4	64.2
Hawaii	4,790	0.2	26.1
Idaho	18,446	0.6	96.8
Illinois	141,603	4.5	76.8
Indiana	73,237	2.4	87.9
Iowa	35,125	1.1	94.6
Kansas	35,518	1.1	89.4
Kentucky	47,243	1.5	89.8
Louisiana	37,983	1.2	57.4
Maine	13,461	0.4	97.7
Maryland	44,763	1.4	64.2
Massachusetts	69,418	2.2	86.3
Michigan	109,200	3.5	79.4
Minnesota	57,003	1.8	89.4
Mississippi	21,801	0.7	52.3
Missouri	61,277	2.0	83.1
Montana	9,390	0.3	87.7
Nebraska	21,373	0.7	91.6
Nevada	22,262	0.7	85.5
New Hampshire	14,252	0.5	98.0
New Jersey	86,407	2.8	75.9
New Mexico	23,193	0.7	85.2
New York	197,275	6.3	72.7
North Carolina	74,710	2.4	70.7
North Dakota	7,416	0.2	88.7
Ohio	128,739	4.1	84.3

(continued)

(continued from previous page)

	number	percent	white share of total births
Oklahoma	36,642	1.2%	79.3%
Oregon	40,456	1.3	92.6
Pennsylvania	125,639	4.0	83.8
Rhode Island	11,049	0.4	88.3
South Carolina	32,197	1.0	63.4
South Dakota	8,662	0.3	82.7
Tennessee	56,539	1.8	76.6
Texas	278,760	9.0	85.2
Utah	39,291	1.3	94.9
Vermont	6,666	0.2	98.8
Virginia	67,359	2.2	72.9
Washington	69,329	2.2	86.7
West Virginia	19,808	0.6	95.7
Wisconsin	57,936	1.9	86.4
Wyoming	5,956	0.2	94.8

Source: National Center for Health Statistics, Births and Deaths: United States, 1996, *Monthly Vital Statistics Report, Vol. 46, No. 1, Supplement 2, 1997; calculations by New Strategist*

Projections of Births to White and Non-Hispanic White Women, 1998 to 2020

(number of births to white and non-Hispanic white women, and white and non-Hispanic white births as a percent of total births, 1998–2020; numbers in thousands)

	white		non-Hispanic white	
	number	share of total births	number	share of total births
1998	3,005	77.1%	2,410	61.8%
1999	2,993	76.8	2,385	61.2
2000	2,986	76.6	2,365	60.7
2001	2,983	76.4	2,348	60.1
2002	2,985	76.1	2,336	59.6
2003	2,993	76.0	2,329	59.1
2004	3,006	75.8	2,326	58.6
2005	3,025	75.6	2,328	58.2
2006	3,050	75.5	2,334	57.7
2007	3,080	75.3	2,344	57.3
2008	3,114	75.2	2,356	56.9
2009	3,149	75.1	2,368	56.5
2010	3,184	75.0	2,380	56.1
2011	3,217	75.0	2,391	55.7
2012	3,247	74.9	2,400	55.4
2013	3,274	74.8	2,406	55.0
2014	3,299	74.7	2,411	54.6
2015	3,320	74.6	2,414	54.2
2016	3,338	74.5	2,414	53.9
2017	3,353	74.4	2,411	53.5
2018	3,365	74.2	2,407	53.1
2019	3,376	74.1	2,400	52.7
2020	3,384	73.9	2,391	52.2

Source: Bureau of the Census, Population Projections of the United States, by Age, Sex, Race, and Hispanic Origin: 1995 to 2050, *Current Population Reports, P25-1130, 1996; calculations by New Strategist*

Acute Health Conditions among Whites by Age, 1994

(number of acute conditions and rate per 100 whites, by type of acute condition and age, 1994; numbers in thousands)

	total conditions		under age 18		aged 18 to 44		aged 45 or older	
	number	rate	number	rate	number	rate	number	rate
Total acute conditions	**376,062**	**175.3**	**154,351**	**279.4**	**143,214**	**162.1**	**78,497**	**110.7**
Infective/parasitic diseases	**46,374**	**21.6**	**27,530**	**49.8**	**14,059**	**15.9**	**4,785**	**6.7**
Common childhood diseases	3,054	1.4	2,629	4.8	425	0.5	–	–
Intestinal virus	9,926	4.6	5,414	9.8	3,589	4.1	923	1.3
Viral infections	14,285	6.7	8,466	15.3	3,681	4.2	2,138	3.0
Other	19,108	8.9	11,021	20.0	6,364	7.2	1,724	2.4
Respiratory conditions	**176,767**	**82.4**	**69,663**	**126.1**	**71,913**	**81.4**	**35,191**	**49.6**
Common cold	52,150	24.3	21,870	39.6	20,100	22.8	10,181	14.4
Other acute upper respiratory infections	27,431	12.8	13,977	25.3	9,474	10.7	3,981	5.6
Influenza	78,327	36.5	26,767	48.5	35,587	40.3	15,973	22.5
Acute bronchitis	10,916	5.1	3,949	7.1	4,098	4.6	2,869	4.0
Pneumonia	3,535	1.6	1,423	2.6	972	1.1	1,140	1.6
Other respiratory conditions	4,407	2.1	1,678	3.0	1,682	1.9	1,047	1.5
Digestive system conditions	**12,149**	**5.7**	**4,892**	**8.9**	**3,937**	**4.5**	**3,319**	**4.7**
Dental conditions	1,922	0.9	544	1.0	905	1.0	472	0.7
Indigestion, nausea, vomiting	6,327	2.9	3,352	6.1	1,940	2.2	1,036	1.5
Other digestive conditions	3,900	1.8	996	1.8	1,092	1.2	1,811	2.6
Injuries	**53,108**	**24.8**	**15,489**	**28.0**	**24,527**	**27.8**	**13,092**	**18.5**
Fractures and dislocations	6,998	3.3	2,320	4.2	2,669	3.0	2,009	2.8
Sprains and strains	12,450	5.8	2,415	4.4	7,146	8.1	2,890	4.1
Open wounds and lacerations	9,322	4.3	3,329	6.0	4,555	5.2	1,439	2.0
Contusions/superficial injuries	9,879	4.6	3,009	5.4	3,884	4.4	2,986	4.2
Other current injuries	14,458	6.7	4,417	8.0	6,273	7.1	3,769	5.3

(continued)

(continued from previous page)

	total conditions		under age 18		aged 18 to 44		aged 45 or older	
	number	*rate*	*number*	*rate*	*number*	*rate*	*number*	*rate*
Selected other acute conditions	**60,758**	**28.3**	**28,748**	**52.0**	**19,363**	**21.9**	**12,647**	**17.8**
Eye conditions	2,680	1.2	824	1.5	858	1.0	998	1.4
Acute ear infections	21,298	9.9	17,085	30.9	2,697	3.1	1,517	2.1
Other ear conditions	3,293	1.5	1,775	3.2	662	0.7	855	1.2
Acute urinary conditions	7,320	3.4	1,115	2.0	3,499	4.0	2,617	3.7
Disorders of menstruation	885	0.4	317	0.6	522	0.6	45	0.1
Other disorders of female genital tract	2,152	1.0	117	0.2	1,705	1.9	330	0.5
Delivery and other conditions of pregnancy	2,932	1.4	54	0.1	2,878	3.3	–	–
Skin conditions	5,161	2.4	2,092	3.8	1,477	1.7	1,592	2.2
Acute musculoskeletal conditions	7,791	3.6	877	1.6	3,157	3.6	3,758	5.3
Headache, excl. migraine	3,069	1.4	965	1.7	1,549	1.8	555	0.8
Fever, unspecified	4,268	2.0	3,529	6.4	359	0.4	379	0.5
All other acute conditions	**26,907**	**12.5**	**8,029**	**14.5**	**9,415**	**10.7**	**9,463**	**13.3**

Note: The acute conditions shown here are those that caused people to restrict their activity for at least half a day, or that caused people to contact a physician about the illness or injury. (–) means not applicable or sample is too small to make a reliable estimate.
Source: National Center for Health Statistics, Current Estimates from the National Health Interview Survey, 1994, Series 10, No. 193, 1995

Chronic Health Conditions among Whites by Age, 1994

(number of chronic conditions and rate per 1,000 whites, by type of chronic condition and age, 1994; numbers in thousands)

	under age 45		aged 45 to 64		aged 65 to 74		aged 75 or older	
	number	rate	number	rate	number	rate	number	rate
Selected skin and musculoskeletal conditions								
Arthritis	4,852	33.8	10,355	239.8	7,798	481.8	6,122	529.4
Gout, including gouty arthritis	288	2.0	775	17.9	545	33.7	426	36.8
Intervertebral disc disorders	2,279	15.9	2,335	54.1	570	35.2	312	27.0
Bone spur or tendinitis, unspecified	925	6.4	1,112	25.8	399	24.7	138	11.9
Disorders of bone or cartilage	470	3.3	430	10.0	306	18.9	268	23.2
Trouble with bunions	881	6.1	952	22.0	473	29.2	595	51.4
Bursitis, unclassified	1,652	11.5	1,699	39.3	796	49.2	428	37.0
Sebaceous skin cyst	655	4.6	233	5.4	161	9.9	75	6.5
Trouble with acne	4,046	28.2	209	4.8	68	4.2	16	1.4
Psoriasis	1,207	8.4	802	18.6	266	16.4	139	12.0
Dermatitis	5,589	38.9	1,478	34.2	576	35.6	387	33.5
Trouble with dry skin, unclassified	2,782	19.4	1,420	32.9	519	32.1	540	46.7
Trouble with ingrown nails	2,579	18.0	1,386	32.1	753	46.5	629	54.4
Trouble with corns/calluses	1,357	9.5	1,204	27.9	521	32.2	491	42.5
Impairments								
Visual impairment	3,004	20.9	1,898	44.0	1,054	65.1	1,219	105.4
Color blindness	1,398	9.7	869	20.1	380	23.5	126	10.9
Cataracts	401	2.8	739	17.1	1,839	113.6	2,751	237.9
Glaucoma	242	1.7	467	10.8	468	28.9	871	75.3
Hearing impairment	5,470	38.1	6,305	146.0	4,050	250.2	4,357	376.7
Tinnitus	1,539	10.7	2,063	47.8	1,592	98.4	1,065	92.1
Speech impairment	1,765	12.3	317	7.3	167	10.3	55	4.8
Absence of extremities	414	2.9	323	7.5	216	13.3	224	19.4
Paralysis of extremities, complete or partial	363	2.5	348	8.1	178	11.0	222	19.2
Deformity or orthopedic impairment	14,789	103.0	7,317	169.4	2,605	161.0	2,075	179.4
Back	9,756	68.0	4,559	105.6	1,522	94.0	974	84.2
Upper extremities	1,658	11.5	1,079	25.0	343	21.2	460	39.8
Lower extremities	5,331	37.1	2,904	67.3	1,126	69.6	1,050	90.8

(continued)

(continued from previous page)

	under age 45		aged 45 to 64		aged 65 to 74		aged 75 or older	
	number	*rate*	*number*	*rate*	*number*	*rate*	*number*	*rate*
Selected digestive conditions								
Ulcer	1,711	11.9	981	22.7	484	29.9	308	26.6
Hernia of abdominal cavity	988	6.9	1,512	35.0	1,052	65.0	825	71.3
Gastritis or duodenitis	1418	9.9	856	19.8	472	29.2	330	28.5
Frequent indigestion	3172	22.1	1,873	43.4	718	44.4	590	51.0
Enteritis or colitis	776	5.4	649	15.0	228	14.1	204	17.6
Spastic colon	828	5.8	610	14.1	262	16.2	205	17.7
Diverticula of intestines	240	1.7	849	19.7	557	34.4	446	38.6
Frequent constipation	1278	8.9	493	11.4	504	31.1	964	83.4
Selected conditions of the genitourinary, nervous, endocrine, metabolic, and blood and blood-forming systems								
Goiter/other thyroid disorders	1,315	9.2	1,315	30.5	796	49.2	600	51.9
Diabetes	1,086	7.6	2,314	53.6	1,572	97.1	1,053	91.1
Anemias	1,935	13.5	710	16.4	274	16.9	320	27.7
Epilepsy	786	5.5	193	4.5	106	6.5	36	3.1
Migraine headache	6,719	46.8	2,222	51.5	415	25.6	212	18.3
Neuralgia/neuritis, unspecified	142	1.0	162	3.8	97	6.0	95	8.2
Kidney trouble	1,716	12.0	753	17.4	264	16.3	342	29.6
Bladder trouble	1,235	8.6	765	17.7	630	38.9	440	38.0
Diseases of prostate	274	1.9	584	13.5	751	46.4	739	63.9
Diseases of female genital organs	2,925	20.4	1,149	26.6	166	10.3	66	5.7
Selected circulatory conditions								
Rheumatic fever with or without heart disease	801	5.6	516	11.9	333	20.6	130	11.2
Heart disease	4,432	30.9	5,977	138.4	4,880	301.5	4,534	392.0
Ischemic heart disease	347	2.4	2,538	58.8	2,352	145.3	2,127	183.9
Heart rhythm disorders	3,130	21.8	2,091	48.4	1,314	81.2	1,309	113.2
Tachycardia or rapid heart	637	4.4	689	16.0	499	30.8	509	44.0
Heart murmurs	2,151	15.0	983	22.8	339	20.9	275	23.8
Other and unspecified heart rhythm disorders	342	2.4	419	9.7	475	29.3	525	45.4
Other selected diseases of heart, excl. hypertension	955	6.7	1,348	31.2	1,214	75.0	1,099	95.0
High blood pressure (hypertension)	4,312	30.0	8,987	208.1	5,482	338.7	4,359	376.9
Cerebrovascular disease	149	1.0	763	17.7	656	40.5	920	79.6
Hardening of the arteries	39	0.3	483	11.2	647	40.0	907	78.4
Varicose veins of lower extremities	2,170	15.1	2,247	52.0	1,303	80.5	910	78.7
Hemorrhoids	3,752	26.1	2,803	64.9	1,084	67.0	752	65.0

(continued)

(continued from previous page)

	under age 45		aged 45 to 64		aged 65 to 74		aged 75 or older	
	number	*rate*	*number*	*rate*	*number*	*rate*	*number*	*rate*
Selected respiratory conditions								
Chronic bronchitis	7,800	54.3	3,077	71.3	1,023	63.2	667	57.7
Asthma	8,353	58.2	2,258	52.3	878	54.3	563	48.7
Hay fever or allergic rhinitis								
without asthma	14,931	104.0	5,424	125.6	1,331	82.2	835	72.2
Chronic sinusitis	17,545	122.2	7,913	183.2	2,539	156.9	1,851	160.1
Deviated nasal septum	917	6.4	644	14.9	296	18.3	64	5.5
Chronic disease of tonsils								
or adenoids	2,238	15.6	96	2.2	12	0.7	–	–
Emphysema	104	0.7	464	10.7	802	49.6	548	47.4

Note: Chronic conditions are those that last longer than three months or belong to a group of conditions that are considered chronic regardless of when they began. (–) means not applicable or sample is too small to make a reliable estimate.
Source: National Center for Health Statistics, Current Estimates from the National Health Interview Survey, 1994, *Series 10, No. 193, 1995*

Non-Hispanic Whites with Disabilities by Type of Disability and Age, 1994–95

(total number of non-Hispanic whites aged 15 or older, and percent with a disability by type of disability and age, 1994–95; numbers in thousands)

	15 or older	15 to 21	22 to 44	45 to 54	55 to 64	65 to 79	80 or older
Total persons	**154,813**	**16,822**	**70,242**	**24,082**	**16,788**	**20,918**	**5,962**
With any disability	**24.3%**	**13.3%**	**14.4%**	**23.8%**	**34.8%**	**45.4%**	**70.6%**
Severe	12.2	3.3	5.6	10.5	20.0	25.8	52.4
Not severe	12.1	10.0	8.9	13.3	14.8	19.6	18.2
With a mental disability	4.8	5.6	3.7	4.1	4.3	4.9	18.1
Uses wheelchair	0.9	0.2	0.3	0.4	1.2	1.9	6.5
Used cane/crutch/walker for six or more months	2.6	0.2	0.4	1.3	2.9	7.0	23.9
Difficulty with or unable to perform one or more functional activities	**16.8**	**3.8**	**7.5**	**15.4**	**25.1**	**39.3**	**67.1**
Seeing words and letters	4.2	0.8	1.5	3.6	5.4	8.8	25.2
Hearing normal conversation	5.5	1.2	2.3	4.4	6.8	12.7	28.1
Having speech understood	1.0	0.9	0.5	0.7	1.3	1.9	4.6
Lifting, carrying 10 pounds	8.0	1.0	3.0	6.7	11.5	19.2	38.9
Climbing stairs without resting	9.0	1.1	2.7	7.0	13.8	23.1	43.8
Walking three city blocks	9.4	1.1	2.9	7.1	14.7	23.6	47.4
Difficulty with or unable to perform one or more ADLs	**4.1**	**0.6**	**1.4**	**3.0**	**5.5**	**9.6**	**26.6**
Getting around inside the home	1.7	0.2	0.5	0.9	2.1	3.8	13.8
Getting in/out of bed or chair	2.8	0.3	1.0	2.1	3.7	6.4	17.2
Bathing	2.2	0.3	0.6	1.1	2.7	5.1	18.7
Dressing	1.6	0.3	0.5	0.9	2.1	3.4	11.6
Eating	0.5	0.2	0.2	0.3	0.7	1.2	3.2
Getting to/using toilet	1.0	0.3	0.3	0.4	1.1	2.2	8.0
Difficulty with or unable to perform one or more IADLs	**6.1**	**1.6**	**2.3**	**4.1**	**7.2**	**14.1**	**39.4**
Going outside alone	4.1	0.7	1.2	2.4	4.9	9.7	30.3
Keeping track of money/bills	1.9	0.9	0.8	1.1	1.5	3.3	15.4
Preparing meals	2.1	0.6	0.8	1.0	2.0	4.3	17.1
Doing light housework	3.3	0.6	1.2	2.1	4.2	7.5	22.3
Taking prescribed medicines	1.5	0.7	0.6	0.8	1.1	2.9	12.2
Using the telephone	1.5	0.5	0.4	0.6	1.2	3.5	13.1
Needs personal assistance with an ADL or an IADL	**4.7**	**1.4**	**1.8**	**3.0**	**5.7**	**10.5**	**33.1**

Note: An ADL is an activity of daily living; an IADL is an instrumental activity of daily living.
Source: Bureau of the Census, Internet web site, http://www.census.gov

Health Insurance Coverage of Whites by Age, 1996

(number and percent distribution of whites by age and health insurance coverage status, 1996; numbers in thousands)

| | | covered by private or government health insurance | | | | | | | |
| | | | private health insurance | | | government health insurance | | | not |
	total	total	total	group health	total	Medicaid	Medicare	Champus	covered
Number									
Total persons	**219,656**	**188,098**	**161,676**	**139,788**	**58,604**	**20,710**	**30,913**	**6,981**	**31,558**
Under age 18	55,606	47,962	39,573	36,894	11,722	9,728	260	1,734	7,644
Aged 18 to 24	19,992	14,507	12,745	10,516	2,669	1,909	109	651	5,485
Aged 25 to 34	32,638	25,752	23,471	22,014	3,321	2,158	308	855	6,886
Aged 35 to 44	36,438	30,978	28,740	26,769	3,538	2,100	567	871	5,460
Aged 45 to 54	28,071	24,566	22,951	21,192	3,089	1,286	742	1,061	3,505
Aged 55 to 64	18,447	16,101	14,417	12,401	3,440	1,078	1,434	928	2,346
Aged 65 or older	28,464	28,232	19,779	10,003	30,825	2,450	27,493	882	232
Percent distribution by									
health insurance coverage status									
Total persons	**100.0%**	**85.6%**	**73.6%**	**63.6%**	**26.7%**	**9.4%**	**14.1%**	**3.2%**	**14.4%**
Under age 18	100.0	86.3	71.2	66.3	21.1	17.5	0.5	3.1	13.7
Aged 18 to 24	100.0	72.6	63.8	52.6	13.4	9.5	0.5	3.3	27.4
Aged 25 to 34	100.0	78.9	71.9	67.4	10.2	6.6	0.9	2.6	21.1
Aged 35 to 44	100.0	85.0	78.9	73.5	9.7	5.8	1.6	2.4	15.0
Aged 45 to 54	100.0	87.5	81.8	75.5	11.0	4.6	2.6	3.8	12.5
Aged 55 to 64	100.0	87.3	78.2	67.2	18.6	5.8	7.8	5.0	12.7
Aged 65 or older	100.0	99.2	69.5	35.1	108.3	8.6	96.6	3.1	0.8
Percent distribution by age									
Total persons	**100.0%**	**100.0%**	**100.0%**	**100.0%**	**100.0%**	**100.0%**	**100.0%**	**100.0%**	**100.0%**
Under age 18	25.3	25.5	24.5	26.4	20.0	47.0	0.8	24.8	24.2
Aged 18 to 24	9.1	7.7	7.9	7.5	4.6	9.2	0.4	9.3	17.4
Aged 25 to 34	14.9	13.7	14.5	15.7	5.7	10.4	1.0	12.2	21.8
Aged 35 to 44	16.6	16.5	17.8	19.1	6.0	10.1	1.8	12.5	17.3
Aged 45 to 54	12.8	13.1	14.2	15.2	5.3	6.2	2.4	15.2	11.1
Aged 55 to 64	8.4	8.6	8.9	8.9	5.9	5.2	4.6	13.3	7.4
Aged 65 or older	13.0	15.0	12.2	7.2	52.6	11.8	88.9	12.6	0.7

Note: Numbers may not add to total because some people have more than one type of health insurance.
Source: Bureau of the Census, unpublished tables from the 1997 Current Population Survey; calculations by New Strategist

Physician Contacts by Whites, 1994

(total number of physician contacts by whites and number per person per year, by age and type of contact, 1994)

	total	telephone	office	hospital	other
Total contacts	**1,349,712**	**178,178**	**768,003**	**163,355**	**230,703**
Under age 18	259,274	38,081	157,015	31,947	30,393
Aged 18 to 44	457,689	63,758	263,260	57,163	70,363
Aged 45 to 64	318,523	47,642	177,681	44,167	46,081
Aged 65 or older	314,225	28,697	170,047	30,079	83,866
Contacts per person	**6.3**	**0.8**	**3.6**	**0.8**	**1.1**
Under age 18	4.7	0.7	2.8	0.6	0.6
Aged 18 to 44	5.2	0.7	3.0	0.6	0.8
Aged 45 to 64	7.4	1.1	4.1	1.0	1.1
Aged 65 or older	11.3	1.0	6.1	1.1	3.0

Source: National Center for Health Statistics, Current Estimates from the National Health Interview Survey, 1994, Series 10, No. 193, 1995

Leading Causes of Death among Whites, 1995

(number of deaths among whites, and number and percent accounted for by ten leading causes of death, 1995)

		number	percent
	All causes	**1,987,437**	**100.0%**
1.	Diseases of heart	649,089	32.7
2.	Malignant neoplasms	468,897	23.6
3.	Cerebrovascular diseases	136,481	6.9
4.	Chronic obstructive pulmonary diseases	95,077	4.8
5.	Unintentional injuries	77,748	3.9
6.	Pneumonia and influenza	73,641	3.7
7.	Diabetes mellitus	47,475	2.4
8.	Suicides	28,187	1.4
9.	Human immunodeficiency virus infections	25,509	1.3
10.	Chronic liver diseases and cirrhosis	21,432	1.1
	All other causes	363,901	80.7

Source: National Center for Health Statistics, Health, United States, 1996–97; *calculations by New Strategist*

Life Expectancy of Whites at Birth and Age 65, 1998 to 2020

(average number of years of life remaining at birth and at age 65 for whites by ethnicity and sex, selected years 1998–2020; difference between white and total life expectancy at birth and at age 65 by ethnicity and sex, 1998 and 2020)

| | life expectancy (years) | | | |
| | white | | non-Hispanic white | |
	males	*females*	*males*	*females*
AT BIRTH				
1998	73.9	80.3	74.0	80.3
2000	74.2	80.5	74.3	80.5
2005	74.7	81.0	74.9	81.0
2010	75.5	81.6	75.7	81.5
2015	76.3	82.1	76.4	81.9
2020	77.1	82.6	77.2	82.4
Life expectancy of whites/non-Hispanic whites				
minus life expectancy of total Americans				
1998	1.1	0.7	1.2	0.7
2020	1.6	1.1	1.7	0.9
AT AGE 65				
1998	16.0	19.6	15.9	19.5
2000	16.2	19.7	16.1	19.6
2005	16.8	20.0	16.7	19.9
2010	17.3	20.4	17.1	20.2
2015	17.8	20.8	17.5	20.5
2020	18.3	21.1	18.0	20.8
Life expectancy of whites/non-Hispanic whites				
minus life expectancy of total Americans				
1998	0.3	0.3	0.2	0.2
2020	0.7	0.5	0.4	0.2

Source: Bureau of the Census, Population Projections of the United States, by Age, Sex, Race, and Hispanic Origin: 1995 to 2050, *Current Population Reports, P25-1130, 1996; calculations by New Strategist*

Whites: Households

Most white households are headed by married couples, but only 27 percent have children under age 18 at home.

Because whites make up the majority of the American population, the household composition and living arrangements of whites mirror those of the total population. Twenty-three percent of white householders are aged 65 or older, versus 22 percent of the total. Twenty-four percent of white householder are under age 35, versus 25 percent of total householders.

Fifty-seven percent of white households are married couples, and 27 percent are nuclear families—meaning a husband, wife, and children under age 18. These figures are about the same as for households in the nation as a whole. Female-headed families with children account for just 7 percent of white households.

Seventy-nine percent of white children live with both parents, while 18 percent live with their mother only. Nearly half of white men aged 20 to 24 still live with their parents, as does one in five men aged 25 to 29.

Among white men aged 15 or older, 61 percent are currently married. The proportion is somewhat smaller among women, at 59 percent. The majority of white men aged 30 or older are married, as are most white women between the ages of 25 and 74.

■ Despite all the changes in family life over the past few decades, female-headed families remain uncommon among households headed by whites.

Most white households are headed by married couples

(percent distribution of white households by type, 1996)

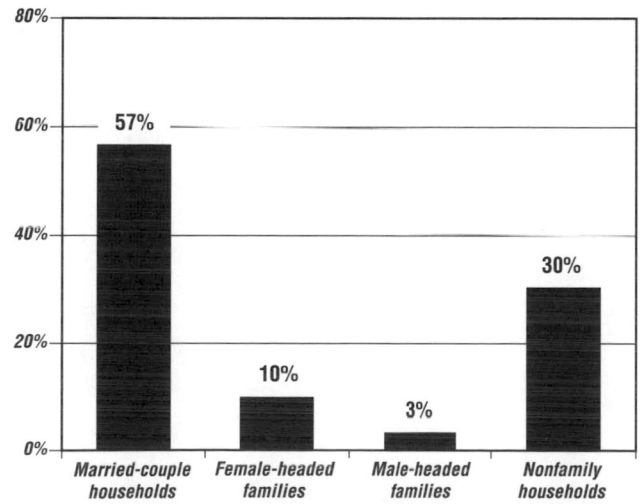

White Households by Age of Householder, 1996

(number and percent distribution of white households by age of householder, 1996; numbers in thousands)

	number	percent
Total households	**84,511**	**100.0%**
Under age 25	4,254	5.0
Aged 25 to 29	6,778	8.0
Aged 30 to 34	8,952	10.6
Aged 35 to 39	9,755	11.5
Aged 40 to 44	9,618	11.4
Aged 45 to 54	15,214	18.0
Aged 55 to 64	10,614	12.6
Aged 65 to 74	10,583	12.5
Aged 75 or older	8,743	10.4

Source: Bureau of the Census, Household and Family Characteristics: March 1996, *Current Population Reports, P20-495(Update), 1997; calculations by New Strategist*

White Households by Household Type, 1996

(number and percent distribution of white households by type, 1996; numbers in thousands)

	number	percent
Total households	**84,511**	**100.0%**
Family households	**58,869**	**69.7**
Married-couple families	47,873	56.6
With children under age 18	22,660	26.8
Without children under age 18	25,214	29.8
Female householder, no spouse present	8,284	9.8
With children under age 18	5,554	6.6
Without children under age 18	2,730	3.2
Male householder, no spouse present	2,712	3.2
Nonfamily households	**25,642**	**30.3**
Female householder	14,275	16.9
Living alone	12,460	14.7
Male householder	11,367	13.5
Living alone	8,728	10.3

Source: Bureau of the Census, Household and Family Characteristics: March 1996, *Current Population Reports, P20-495(Update), 1997; calculations by New Strategist*

White Households by Age of Householder and Household Type, 1996

(number and percent distribution of white households by age of householder and household type, 1996; numbers in thousands)

	total	family households total	married couples	female householder no spouse present	male householder no spouse present	nonfamily households female householder	male householder
Total households, number	**84,511**	**58,869**	**47,873**	**8,284**	**2,712**	**14,275**	**11,367**
Under age 20	451	226	65	102	59	138	88
Aged 20 to 24	3,803	2,107	1,314	560	233	793	903
Aged 25 to 29	6,778	4,465	3,465	717	283	910	1,403
Aged 30 to 34	8,952	6,744	5,394	1,010	341	801	1,407
Aged 35 to 39	9,755	7,655	6,069	1,221	365	714	1,386
Aged 40 to 44	9,618	7,753	6,169	1,224	360	693	1,172
Aged 45 to 49	8,801	6,905	5,665	911	329	836	1,060
Aged 50 to 54	6,414	4,927	4,156	571	200	804	683
Aged 55 to 59	5,602	4,233	3,776	328	129	784	585
Aged 60 to 64	5,012	3,680	3,167	402	111	833	500
Aged 65 to 74	10,583	6,574	5,720	666	188	2,860	1,149
Aged 75 to 84	6,892	3,120	2,590	440	90	3,035	737
Aged 85 or older	1,851	481	325	130	27	1,074	295
Total households, percent	**100.0%**	**69.7%**	**56.6%**	**9.8%**	**3.2%**	**16.9%**	**13.5%**
Under age 20	100.0	50.1	14.4	22.6	13.1	30.6	19.5
Aged 20 to 24	100.0	55.4	34.6	14.7	6.1	20.9	23.7
Aged 25 to 29	100.0	65.9	51.1	10.6	4.2	13.4	20.7
Aged 30 to 34	100.0	75.3	60.3	11.3	3.8	8.9	15.7
Aged 35 to 39	100.0	78.5	62.2	12.5	3.7	7.3	14.2
Aged 40 to 44	100.0	80.6	64.1	12.7	3.7	7.2	12.2
Aged 45 to 49	100.0	78.5	64.4	10.4	3.7	9.5	12.0
Aged 50 to 54	100.0	76.8	64.8	8.9	3.1	12.5	10.6
Aged 55 to 59	100.0	75.6	67.4	5.9	2.3	14.0	10.4
Aged 60 to 64	100.0	73.4	63.2	8.0	2.2	16.6	10.0
Aged 65 to 74	100.0	62.1	54.0	6.3	1.8	27.0	10.9
Aged 75 to 84	100.0	45.3	37.6	6.4	1.3	44.0	10.7
Aged 85 or older	100.0	26.0	17.6	7.0	1.5	58.0	15.9

Source: Bureau of the Census, Household and Family Characteristics: March 1996, *Current Population Reports, P20-495(Update), 1997; calculations by New Strategist*

White Households by Size, 1996

(number and percent distribution of white households by size, 1996; numbers in thousands)

	number	percent
Total households	**84,511**	**100.0%**
One person	21,194	25.1
Two persons	28,615	33.9
Three persons	13,873	16.4
Four persons	12,659	15.o
Five persons	5,350	6.3
Six persons	1,856	2.2
Seven or more persons	965	1.1

Source: Bureau of the Census, Household and Family Characteristics: March 1996, *Current Population Reports, P20-495(Update), 1997; calculations by New Strategist*

White Married Couples by Presence of Children and Age of Householder, 1996

(number and percent distribution of white married couples by presence and number of own children under age 18 at home and age of householder, 1996; numbers in thousands)

	total	< age 20	20–24	25–29	30–34	35–39	40–44	45–54	55–64	65+
						age of householder				
Married couples, number	**47,873**	**65**	**1314**	**3,465**	**5,394**	**6,069**	**6,169**	**9,820**	**6,943**	**8,635**
Without children <18	26,038	32	542	1,358	1,131	975	1,309	5,727	6,411	8,553
With children <18	21,835	33	772	2,106	4,262	5,094	4,860	4,093	532	82
One	8,132	27	483	987	1,355	1,169	1,495	2,180	378	58
Two	9,080	6	236	820	1,871	2,311	2,271	1,420	121	24
Three or more	4,624	–	53	300	1,037	1,614	1,093	494	33	1
Married couples, percent	**100.0%**	**100.0%**	**100.0%**	**100.0%**	**100.0%**	**100.0%**	**100.0%**	**100.0%**	**100.0%**	**100.0%**
Without children <18	54.4	49.2	41.2	39.2	21.0	16.1	21.2	58.3	92.3	99.1
With children <18	45.6	50.8	58.8	60.8	79.0	83.9	78.8	41.7	7.7	0.9
One	17.0	41.5	36.8	28.5	25.1	19.3	24.2	22.2	5.4	0.7
Two	19.0	9.2	18.0	23.7	34.7	38.1	36.8	14.5	1.7	0.3
Three or more	9.7	–	4.0	8.7	19.2	26.6	17.7	5.0	0.5	0.0

Note: (–) means sample is too small to make a reliable estimate.
Source: Bureau of the Census, Household and Family Characteristics: March 1996, *Current Population Reports, P20-495(Update), 1997; calculations by New Strategist*

White Female-Headed Families by Presence of Children and Age of Householder, 1996

(number and percent distribution of white female-headed families by presence and number of own children under age 18 at home and age of householder, 1996; numbers in thousands)

	total	< age 20	20–24	25–29	30–34	35–39	40–44	45–54	55–64	65+
					age of householder					
Female-headed families, number	**8,284**	**102**	**560**	**717**	**1,010**	**1,221**	**1,224**	**1,483**	**730**	**1,236**
Without children <18	3,309	50	73	90	53	104	237	808	678	1,218
With children <18	4,975	52	486	628	957	1,118	987	675	52	19
One	2,537	33	297	271	361	467	559	488	44	16
Two	1,649	19	128	226	374	424	322	147	8	1
Three or more	789	–	62	131	224	227	105	41	–	2
Female-headed families, percent	**100.0%**	**100.0%**	**100.0%**	**100.0%**	**100.0%**	**100.0%**	**100.0%**	**100.0%**	**100.0%**	**100.0%**
Without children <18	39.9	49.0	13.0	12.6	5.2	8.5	19.4	54.5	92.9	98.5
With children <18	60.1	51.0	86.8	87.6	94.8	91.6	80.6	45.5	7.1	1.5
One	30.6	32.4	53.0	37.8	35.7	38.2	45.7	32.9	6.0	1.3
Two	19.9	18.6	22.9	31.5	37.0	34.7	26.3	9.9	1.1	0.1
Three or more	9.5	–	11.1	18.3	22.2	18.6	8.6	2.8	–	0.2

Note: (–) means sample is too small to make a reliable estimate.
Source: Bureau of the Census, Household and Family Characteristics: March 1996, Current Population Reports, P20-495(Update), 1997; calculations by New Strategist

White Single-Person Households by Age of Householder, 1996

(number and percent distribution of white single-person households and single-person households as a percent of total white households, by age of householder, 1996; numbers in thousands)

	number	percent	percent of total white households
Total households	**21,194**	**100.0%**	**25.1%**
Under age 25	888	4.2	20.9
Aged 25 to 29	1,395	6.6	20.6
Aged 30 to 34	1,596	7.5	17.8
Aged 35 to 39	1,613	7.6	16.5
Aged 40 to 44	1,536	7.2	16.0
Aged 45 to 54	2,877	13.6	18.9
Aged 55 to 64	2,434	11.5	22.9
Aged 65 to 74	3,844	18.1	36.3
Aged 75 or older	5,011	23.6	72.7
Median age (years)	57.9	–	–

Source: Bureau of the Census, Household and Family Characteristics: March 1996, *Current Population Reports, P20-495(Update), 1997; calculations by New Strategist*

Living Arrangements of White Children by Age, 1995

(number and percent distribution of white children by living arrangement, marital status of parent, and age of child, 1995; numbers in thousands)

	total	under age 6	aged 6 to 11	aged 12 to 17
Number with one or both parents	**53,665**	**18,613**	**17,929**	**17,123**
Living with both parents	41,946	14,666	14,117	13,164
Living with mother only	9,827	3,337	3,241	3,248
Never married	2,317	1,493	564	261
Divorced	4,587	927	1,703	1,957
Married, spouse absent	2,491	861	857	774
Widowed	432	57	118	257
Living with father only	1,892	610	571	711
Never married	443	338	88	17
Divorced	1,044	180	371	494
Married, spouse absent	306	80	87	140
Widowed	98	13	25	61
Percent with one or both parents	**100.0%**	**100.0%**	**100.0%**	**100.0%**
Living with both parents	78.2	78.8	78.7	76.9
Living with mother only	18.3	17.9	18.1	19.0
Never married	4.3	8.0	3.1	1.5
Divorced	8.5	5.0	9.5	11.4
Married, spouse absent	4.6	4.6	4.8	4.5
Widowed	0.8	0.3	0.7	1.5
Living with father only	3.5	3.3	3.2	4.2
Never married	0.8	1.8	0.5	0.1
Divorced	1.9	1.0	2.1	2.9
Married, spouse absent	0.6	0.4	0.5	0.8
Widowed	0.2	0.1	0.1	0.4

Source: Bureau of the Census, Marital Status and Living Arrangements: March 1995, *Current Population Reports, P20-491, 1996; calculations by New Strategist*

Living Arrangements of White Men by Age, 1995

(number and percent distribution of white men aged 18 or older by living arrangement and age, 1995; numbers in thousands)

	total	18 to 19	20 to 24	25 to 29	30 to 34	35 to 39	40 to 44	45 to 54	55 to 64	65 to 74	75 or older
White men, number	**78,054**	**2,840**	**7,329**	**7,881**	**9,071**	**9,232**	**8,398**	**12,908**	**8,712**	**7,248**	**4,435**
Family householder or spouse	50,326	77	1,395	3,597	5,842	6,437	6,295	10,362	7,201	5,939	3,181
Child of householder	9,863	2,310	3,501	1,507	832	733	488	389	86	6	11
Other member of family household	2,672	159	504	439	379	256	197	220	181	169	168
Nonfamily householder	11,083	92	975	1,426	1,378	1,322	1,073	1,587	1,117	1,063	1,050
Other member of nonfamily household	4,054	194	940	895	633	482	343	348	125	71	23
Group quarters*	56	8	14	17	7	2	2	2	2	–	2
White men, percent	**100.0%**	**100.0%**	**100.0%**	**100.0%**	**100.0%**	**100.0%**	**100.0%**	**100.0%**	**100.0%**	**100.0%**	**100.0%**
Family householder or spouse	64.5	2.7	19.0	45.6	64.4	69.7	75.0	80.3	82.7	81.9	71.7
Child of householder	12.6	81.3	47.8	19.1	9.2	7.9	5.8	3.0	1.0	0.1	0.2
Other member of family household	3.4	5.6	6.9	5.6	4.2	2.8	2.3	1.7	2.1	2.3	3.8
Nonfamily householder	14.2	3.2	13.3	18.1	15.2	14.3	12.8	12.3	12.8	14.7	23.7
Other member of nonfamily household	5.2	6.8	12.8	11.4	7.0	5.2	4.1	2.7	1.4	1.0	0.5
Group quarters*	0.1	0.3	0.2	0.2	0.1	0.0	0.0	0.0	0.0	–	0.0

* The Current Population Survey does not include people living in institutions such as prisons, the military, or college dormitories. It defines people living in group quarters as those in noninstitutional living arrangements that are not conventional housing units, such as rooming houses, staff quarters at a hospital, and halfway houses.

Note: (–) means sample is too small to make a reliable estimate.

Source: Bureau of the Census, Marital Status and Living Arrangements: March 1995, Current Population Reports, P20-491, 1996; calculations by New Strategist

Living Arrangements of White Women by Age, 1995

(number and percent distribution of white women aged 18 or older by living arrangement and age, 1995; numbers in thousands)

	total	18 to 19	20 to 24	25 to 29	30 to 34	35 to 39	40 to 44	45 to 54	55 to 64	65 to 74	75 or older
White women, number	**83,219**	**2,764**	**7,228**	**7,770**	**9,017**	**9,155**	**8,414**	**13,246**	**9,323**	**8,953**	**7,349**
Family householder or spouse	55,866	281	2,543	5,035	7,189	7,696	7,151	10,928	7,067	5,549	2,427
Child of householder	6,790	2,031	2,596	826	425	299	216	243	91	48	15
Other member of family household	3,337	193	390	357	264	209	181	265	366	354	758
Nonfamily householder	14,204	90	834	904	774	701	675	1,549	1,670	2,935	4,072
Other member of nonfamily household	2,963	159	839	638	365	248	191	260	125	60	68
Group quarters*	59	–	26	10	–	2	–	1	4	7	9
White women, percent	**100.0%**	**100.0%**	**100.0%**	**100.0%**	**100.0%**	**100.0%**	**100.0%**	**100.0%**	**100.0%**	**100.0%**	**100.0%**
Family householder or spouse	67.1	10.2	35.2	64.8	79.7	84.1	85.0	82.5	75.8	62.0	33.0
Child of householder	8.2	73.5	35.9	10.6	4.7	3.3	2.6	1.8	1.0	0.5	0.2
Other member of family household	4.0	7.0	5.4	4.6	2.9	2.3	2.2	2.0	3.9	4.0	10.3
Nonfamily householder	17.1	3.3	11.5	11.6	8.6	7.7	8.0	11.7	17.9	32.8	55.4
Other member of nonfamily household	3.6	6.1	11.6	8.2	4.0	2.7	2.3	2.0	1.3	0.7	0.9
Group quarters*	0.1	–	0.4	0.1	–	0.0	–	0.0	0.0	0.1	0.1

* The Current Population Survey does not include people living in institutions such as prisons, the military, or college dormitories. It defines people living in group quarters as those in noninstitutional living arrangements that are not conventional housing units, such as rooming houses, staff quarters at a hospital, and halfway houses.

Note: (–) means sample is too small to make a reliable estimate.

Source: Bureau of the Census, Marital Status and Living Arrangements: March 1995, Current Population Reports, P20-491, 1996; calculations by New Strategist

Marital Status of White Men by Age, 1995

(number and percent distribution of white men aged 15 or older by age and marital status, 1995; numbers in thousands)

	total	never married	married	divorced	widowed
Total men, number	**82,566**	**23,667**	**50,658**	**6,321**	**1,921**
Aged 15 to 19	7,352	7,255	88	7	2
Aged 20 to 24	7,329	5,798	1,441	90	–
Aged 25 to 29	7,881	3,827	3,695	354	6
Aged 30 to 34	9,071	2,301	5,943	817	10
Aged 35 to 39	9,232	1,683	6,489	1,030	30
Aged 40 to 44	8,398	1,047	6,309	1,007	35
Aged 45 to 54	12,908	921	10,308	1,551	128
Aged 55 to 64	8,712	374	7,251	872	214
Aged 65 to 74	7,248	300	5,943	441	564
Aged 75 to 84	3,673	128	2,800	127	618
Aged 85 or older	762	32	392	24	314
Total men, percent	**100.0%**	**28.7%**	**61.4%**	**7.7%**	**2.3%**
Aged 15 to 19	100.0	98.7	1.2	0.1	0.0
Aged 20 to 24	100.0	79.1	19.7	1.2	–
Aged 25 to 29	100.0	48.6	46.9	4.5	0.1
Aged 30 to 34	100.0	25.4	65.5	9.0	0.1
Aged 35 to 39	100.0	18.2	70.3	11.2	0.3
Aged 40 to 44	100.0	12.5	75.1	12.0	0.4
Aged 45 to 54	100.0	7.1	79.9	12.0	1.0
Aged 55 to 64	100.0	4.3	83.2	10.0	2.5
Aged 65 to 74	100.0	4.1	82.0	6.1	7.8
Aged 75 to 84	100.0	3.5	76.2	3.5	16.8
Aged 85 or older	100.0	4.2	51.4	3.1	41.2

Note: (–) means sample is too small to make a reliable estimate.
Source: Bureau of the Census, Marital Status and Living Arrangements: March 1995, *Current Population Reports, P20-491, 1996*

Marital Status of White Women by Age, 1995

(number and percent distribution of white women aged 15 or older by age and marital status, 1995; numbers in thousands)

	total	never married	married	divorced	widowed
Total women, number	**87,484**	**18,250**	**51,390**	**8,445**	**9,399**
Aged 15 to 19	7,029	6,718	2,216	15	–
Aged 20 to 24	7,228	4,603	2,394	218	14
Aged 25 to 29	7,770	2,395	4,777	581	17
Aged 30 to 34	9,017	1,412	6,617	944	44
Aged 35 to 39	9,155	891	6,911	1,262	91
Aged 40 to 44	8,414	562	6,483	1,265	104
Aged 45 to 54	13,246	672	10,119	1,985	469
Aged 55 to 64	9,323	351	6,666	1,240	1,066
Aged 65 to 74	8,953	331	5,078	662	2,882
Aged 75 to 84	5,538	220	1,831	237	3,251
Aged 85 or older	1,811	95	218	35	1,462
Total women, percent	**100.0%**	**20.9%**	**58.7%**	**9.7%**	**10.7%**
Aged 15 to 19	100.0	95.6	31.5	0.2	–
Aged 20 to 24	100.0	63.7	33.1	3.0	0.2
Aged 25 to 29	100.0	30.8	61.5	7.5	0.2
Aged 30 to 34	100.0	15.7	73.4	10.5	0.5
Aged 35 to 39	100.0	9.7	75.5	13.8	1.0
Aged 40 to 44	100.0	6.7	77.1	15.0	1.2
Aged 45 to 54	100.0	5.1	76.4	15.0	3.5
Aged 55 to 64	100.0	3.8	71.5	13.3	11.4
Aged 65 to 74	100.0	3.7	56.7	7.4	32.2
Aged 75 to 84	100.0	4.0	33.1	4.3	58.7
Aged 85 or older	100.0	5.2	12.0	1.9	80.7

Note: (–) means sample is too small to make a reliable esitmate.
Source: Bureau of the Census, Marital Status and Living Arrangements: March 1995, *Current Population Reports, P20-491, 1996*

Whites: Housing

More than two-thirds of white householders own their home.

Sixty-nine percent of the nation's white householders own their homes. Homeowner-ship among whites ranges from a high of 74 percent in the Midwest to a low of 62 percent in the West.

Only 15 percent of whites moved between 1995 and 1996, a smaller share than those of blacks and Hispanics. Behind the low mobility of whites is their high home-ownership rate, since homeowners are much less likely to move than renters. Whites in their 20s are most likely to move, with about one in three having moved between 1995 and 1996. The whites least likely to move are those aged 70 or older.

Among the 50 metropolitan areas with the most non-Hispanic white households in 1990, non-Hispanic whites accounted for the largest share of households (94 per-cent) in Albany-Schenectady-Troy, New York, and Minneapolis, Minnesota. Non-His-panic whites accounted for the smallest share of households in Los Angeles (53 per-cent) and New York (56 percent).

■ Homeownership among whites is likely to climb in the future as the baby-boom generation enters the ages at which homeownership peaks.

The suburbs are home to the largest share of white households

(percent distribution of white households by metropolitan status, 1995)

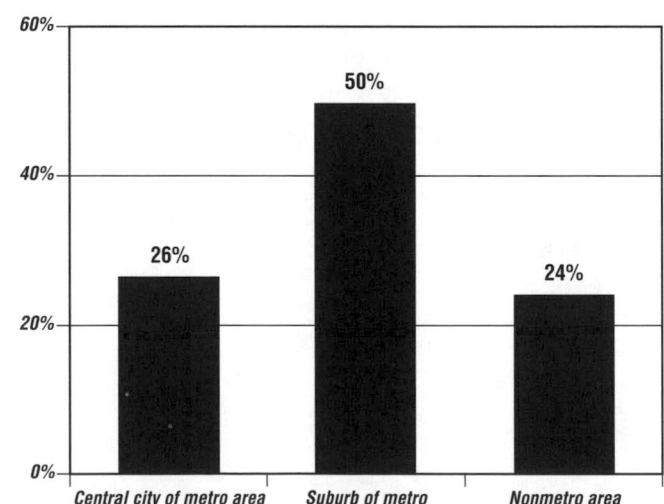

Region of Residence and Metropolitan Status of Housing Units Occupied by Whites, 1995

(number, percent distribution, and percent of housing units occupied by whites, by regional, metropolitan, and homeownership status, 1995; numbers in thousands)

	total		owner			renter		
	number	*percent distrib.*	*number*	*percent distrib.*	*percent of total*	*number*	*percent distrib.*	*percent of total*
Total occupied housing units	**81,611**	**100.0%**	**56,507**	**100.0%**	**69.2%**	**25,104**	**100.0%**	**30.8%**
Northeast	16,062	19.7	10,882	19.3	67.7	5,200	20.7	32.4
Midwest	20,948	25.7	15,441	27.3	73.7	5,507	21.9	26.3
South	27,091	33.2	19,422	34.4	71.7	7,669	30.5	28.3
West	17,490	21.4	10,763	19.0	61.5	6,727	26.8	38.5
In metropolitan areas	62,036	76.0	41,801	74.0	67.4	20,235	80.6	32.6
In central cities	21,519	26.4	11,764	20.8	54.7	9,755	38.9	45.3
In suburbs	40,517	49.6	30,037	53.2	74.1	10,480	41.7	25.9
Outside metropolitan areas	19,574	24.0	14,705	26.0	75.1	4,869	19.4	24.9

Source: Bureau of the Census, American Housing Survey for the United States in 1995, *Current Housing Reports, H150/95, 1997; calculations by New Strategist*

Telephone Availability in
Non-Hispanic White Households, 1996

(number and percent distribution of total and non-Hispanic white households by telephone availability, 1996; numbers in thousands)

	total	non-Hispanic white
Total households	**99,627**	**76,932**
Telephone in household	91,705	72,696
Telephone available to household	1,777	1,101
Telephone not available	6,146	3,135
Total households	**100.0%**	**100.0%**
Telephone in household	92.0	94.5
Telephone available to household	1.8	1.4
Telephone not available	6.2	4.1

Source: Bureau of the Census, Internet web site http://www.census.gov

Geographical Mobility of the White Population by Age, 1995–96

(total number of whites aged 1 or older, and number and percent of those who moved between March 1995 and March 1996, by age of person and type of move; numbers in thousands)

			different house in the U.S.							moved from abroad
					different county					
							different state			
		same house (non-movers)		same county		same state		same region	different region	
Number	total		total		total		total			
Total, aged 1 or older	215,344	181,477	32,906	20,775	12,131	6,615	5,516	2,692	2,825	960
Aged 1 to 4	12,637	9,638	2,900	1,956	944	511	433	187	246	99
Aged 5 to 9	15,734	12,965	2,681	1,747	934	483	451	191	259	88
Aged 10 to 14	15,376	13,292	2,032	1,336	696	344	352	197	155	52
Aged 15 to 19	14,769	12,517	2,179	1,433	746	441	305	178	127	74
Aged 15 to 17	9,013	7,895	1,085	727	358	207	151	87	65	33
Aged 18 and 19	5,756	4,622	1,093	706	388	234	154	91	63	41
Aged 20 to 24	14,094	9,161	4,770	3,059	1,711	956	756	362	394	163
Aged 25 to 29	15,808	10,516	5,145	3,169	1,976	1,083	893	428	465	147
Aged 30 to 34	17,679	13,991	3,537	2,167	1,370	700	670	321	349	151
Aged 35 to 39	18,587	15,768	2,728	1,766	962	553	409	180	229	92
Aged 40 to 44	17,207	15,241	1,923	1,253	670	384	286	134	152	43
Aged 45 to 49	15,356	13,747	1,590	978	612	312	300	178	122	19
Aged 50 to 54	11,464	10,462	991	564	427	248	179	112	67	10
Aged 55 to 59	9,705	9,052	646	357	289	164	125	61	63	8
Aged 60 to 64	8,491	7,970	513	260	253	155	98	42	56	7
Aged 60 and 61	3,512	3,292	215	121	94	63	31	14	17	5
Aged 62 to 64	4,979	4,678	298	138	160	93	67	28	39	2
Aged 65 to 69	8,651	8,214	435	256	179	100	79	36	43	2
Aged 70 to 74	7,656	7,355	301	178	123	61	62	30	32	–
Aged 75 to 79	5,893	5,640	249	134	115	56	59	26	33	4
Aged 80 to 84	3,698	3,554	141	85	56	25	31	12	19	2
Aged 85 or older	2,538	2,393	145	78	67	40	28	17	11	–
Median age	35.4	37.8	26.8	26.4	27.6	27.6	27.6	27.7	27.5	25.2

(continued)

(continued from previous page)

Percent	total	same house (non-movers)	different house in the U.S.		different county				different state		moved from abroad
			total	same county	total	same state	total	same region	different region	
Total, aged 1 or older	**100.0%**	**84.3%**	**15.3%**	**9.6%**	**5.6%**	**3.1%**	**2.6%**	**1.3%**	**1.3%**	**0.4%**
Aged 1 to 4	100.0	76.3	22.9	15.5	7.5	4.0	3.4	1.5	1.9	0.8
Aged 5 to 9	100.0	82.4	17.0	11.1	5.9	3.1	2.9	1.2	1.6	0.6
Aged 10 to 14	100.0	86.4	13.2	8.7	4.5	2.2	2.3	1.3	1.0	0.3
Aged 15 to 19	100.0	84.8	14.8	9.7	5.1	3.0	2.1	1.2	0.9	0.5
Aged 15 to 17	100.0	87.6	12.0	8.1	4.0	2.3	1.7	1.0	0.7	0.4
Aged 18 and 19	100.0	80.3	19.0	12.3	6.7	4.1	2.7	1.6	1.1	0.7
Aged 20 to 24	100.0	65.0	33.8	21.7	12.1	6.8	5.4	2.6	2.8	1.2
Aged 25 to 29	100.0	66.5	32.5	20.0	12.5	6.9	5.6	2.7	2.9	0.9
Aged 30 to 34	100.0	79.1	20.0	12.3	7.7	4.0	3.8	1.8	2.0	0.9
Aged 35 to 39	100.0	84.8	14.7	9.5	5.2	3.0	2.2	1.0	1.2	0.5
Aged 40 to 44	100.0	88.6	11.2	7.3	3.9	2.2	1.7	0.8	0.9	0.2
Aged 45 to 49	100.0	89.5	10.4	6.4	4.0	2.0	2.0	1.2	0.8	0.1
Aged 50 to 54	100.0	91.3	8.6	4.9	3.7	2.2	1.6	1.0	0.6	0.1
Aged 55 to 59	100.0	93.3	6.7	3.7	3.0	1.7	1.3	0.6	0.6	0.1
Aged 60 to 64	100.0	93.9	6.0	3.1	3.0	1.8	1.2	0.5	0.7	0.1
Aged 60 and 61	100.0	93.7	6.1	3.4	2.7	1.8	0.9	0.4	0.5	0.1
Aged 62 to 64	100.0	94.0	6.0	2.8	3.2	1.9	1.3	0.6	0.8	0.0
Aged 65 to 69	100.0	94.9	5.0	3.0	2.1	1.2	0.9	0.4	0.5	0.0
Aged 70 to 74	100.0	96.1	3.9	2.3	1.6	0.8	0.8	0.4	0.4	–
Aged 75 to 79	100.0	95.7	4.2	2.3	2.0	1.0	1.0	0.4	0.6	0.1
Aged 80 to 84	100.0	96.1	3.8	2.3	1.5	0.7	0.8	0.3	0.5	0.1
Aged 85 or older	100.0	94.3	5.7	3.1	2.6	1.6	1.1	0.7	0.4	–

Note: (–) means sample is too small to make a reliable estimate.
Source: Bureau of the Census, Geographical Mobility: March 1995 to March 1996, *Current Population Reports, P20-497(Update), 1997; calculations by New Strategist*

White Homeownership in the 50 Metropolitan Areas with the Most White Households, 1990

(number of white households, percent of total households that are white, percent of white households that are owner occupied, and median value of white owner-occupied houses, in the U.S. and in the 50 metropolitan areas with the most white households, ranked alphabetically, 1990; numbers in thousands)

	number	white share of total households	owner-occupied percent	owner-occupied median value
Total white households	**76,880**	**83.6%**	**68.2%**	**$80,200**
Anaheim–Santa Ana, CA	700	84.6	62.4	255,700
Atlanta, GA	781	73.9	70.0	94,000
Baltimore, MD	657	74.6	71.6	109,900
Bergen–Passaic, NJ	397	85.5	68.5	215,400
Boston, MA	965	89.3	59.4	186,600
Buffalo, NY	326	86.6	68.3	75,200
Charlotte–Gastonia–Rock Hill, NC-SC	358	81.2	72.1	76,100
Chicago, IL	1,614	72.7	66.3	118,900
Cincinnati, OH	472	86.1	67.8	72,000
Cleveland, OH	568	79.8	71.3	77,500
Columbus, OH	458	87.3	63.2	73,700
Dallas, TX	739	77.4	60.1	86,700
Denver, CO	570	87.7	64.3	88,100
Detroit, MI	1,259	77.8	75.7	74,200
Fort Lauderdale–Hollywood–Pompano Beach, FL	459	86.8	71.4	94,400
Fort Worth-Arlington, TX	414	83.7	63.6	74,500
Houston, TX	844	71.2	59.9	70,100
Indianapolis, IN	413	86.1	67.2	69,300
Kansas City, MO-KS	518	86.1	68.3	68,700
Los Angeles–Long Beach, CA	1,941	64.9	53.7	246,600
Louisville, KY-IN	320	86.9	71.2	58,300
Miami–Hialeah, FL	534	77.1	57.5	91,900
Middlesex–Somerset–Hunterdon, NJ	321	88.0	73.8	173,500
Milwaukee, WI	462	86.0	64.1	78,400
Minneapolis–St. Paul, MN-WI	880	94.1	70.8	87,600
Monmouth–Ocean, NJ	339	92.7	79.5	151,300
Nashville, TN	318	84.6	67.1	78,200
Nassau–Suffolk, NY	779	91.0	82.1	188,800
New York, NY	2,053	63.1	41.1	222,400

(continued)

(continued from previous page)

	number	white share of total households	owner-occupied percent	owner-occupied median value
Newark, NJ	478	73.3%	68.9%	$196,400
Norfolk–Virginia Beach–Newport News, VA	349	70.8	65.3	90,600
Oakland, CA	554	71.1	64.0	234,400
Orlando, FL	346	86.1	64.3	85,300
Philadelphia, PA-NJ	1,405	79.0	73.6	112,400
Phoenix, AZ	716	88.7	65.7	86,000
Pittsburgh, PA	750	91.5	72.1	55,700
Portland, OR	452	92.8	62.1	72,700
Riverside–San Bernardino, CA	696	80.2	68.5	135,400
Rochester, NY	335	89.3	71.4	86,500
Sacramento, CA	463	83.1	61.8	139,600
Salt Lake City–Ogden, UT	327	94.1	68.8	71,300
San Antonio, TX	354	78.4	61.9	61,500
San Diego, CA	725	81.7	57.4	192,900
San Francisco, CA	477	74.2	50.4	348,200
San Jose, CA	395	76.0	61.8	297,100
Seattle, WA	703	89.3	62.2	138,000
St. Louis, MO-IL	770	83.3	73.1	72,600
Tampa–St. Petersburg–Clearwater, FL	790	90.9	71.6	72,700
West Palm Beach–Boca Raton–Delray Beach, FL	1,006	68.9	68.5	180,500
Washington, DC-MD-VA	326	89.2	75.5	103,200

Source: Bureau of the Census, unpublished tables from the 1990 census; calculations by New Strategist

Non-Hispanic White Homeownership in the 50 Metropolitan Areas with the Most Non-Hispanic White Households, 1990

(number of non-Hispanic white households, percent of total households that are non-Hispanic white, percent of non-Hispanic white households that are owner occupied, and median value of non-Hispanic white owner-occupied houses, in the U.S. and in the 50 metropolitan areas with the most non-Hispanic white households, ranked alphabetically, 1990; numbers in thousands)

	number	non-Hispanic white share of *total households*	owner-occupied *percent*	owner-occupied *median value*
Total non-Hispanic white households	**73,634**	**80.0%**	**69.1%**	**$80,300**
Albany–Schenectady–Troy, NY	314	93.6	66.3	99,300
Anaheim–Santa Ana, CA	627	75.8	64.8	260,100
Atlanta, GA	771	73.0	70.3	94,000
Baltimore, MD	651	74.0	71.7	109,900
Bergen-Passaic, NJ	374	80.6	70.3	215,800
Boston, MA	947	87.6	60.0	186,600
Buffalo, NY	323	85.7	68.6	75,200
Charlotte–Gastonia–Rock Hill, NC-SC	356	80.7	72.2	76,100
Chicago, IL	1,529	68.8	67.6	119,700
Cincinnati, OH	471	85.8	67.8	72,000
Cleveland, OH	563	79.1	71.4	77,600
Columbus, OH	456	86.9	63.2	73,700
Dallas, TX	698	73.1	61.2	87,700
Dayton–Springfield, OH	313	85.9	68.6	66,700
Denver, CO	533	82.1	65.1	89,000
Detroit, MI	1,245	76.9	75.8	74,300
Fort Lauderdale–Hollywood–Pompano Beach, FL	431	81.5	72.3	95,100
Fort Worth–Arlington, TX	396	80.0	64.2	75,100
Houston, TX	755	63.6	62.0	72,300
Indianapolis, IN	411	85.6	67.2	69,300
Kansas City, MO-KS	512	84.9	68.4	68,800
Los Angeles–Long Beach, CA	1,585	53.0	56.6	262,400
Louisville, KY-IN	318	86.5	71.2	58,200
Miami–Hialeah, FL	309	84.8	74.8	98,100
Milwaukee, WI	456	84.7	64.4	78,600
Minneapolis–St. Paul, MN-WI	874	93.5	70.9	87,700
Monmouth–Ocean, NJ	332	90.9	79.9	151,300
Nashville, TN	316	84.2	67.2	78,200

(continued)

(continued from previous page)

	number	non-Hispanic white share of total households	owner-occupied	
			percent	median value
Nassau–Suffolk, NY	750	87.6%	82.9%	$189,400
New York, NY	1,813	55.7	44.2	223,700
Newark, NJ	445	68.2	71.3	197,100
Norfolk–Virginia Beach–Newport News, VA	345	69.8	65.5	90,600
Oakland, CA	515	66.0	64.6	237,400
Orlando, FL	325	81.0	64.9	85,600
Philadelphia, PA-NJ	1,387	78.0	73.8	112,700
Phoenix, AZ	673	83.4	66.5	87,000
Pittsburgh, PA	747	91.1	72.1	55,700
Portland, OR	446	91.5	62.4	72,800
Riverside–San Bernardino, CA	619	71.4	69.7	137,000
Rochester, NY	331	88.3	71.7	86,500
Sacramento, CA	438	78.7	62.3	140,500
Salt Lake City–Ogden, UT	318	91.6	69.2	71,600
San Diego, CA	664	74.8	58.7	195,300
San Francisco, CA	438	68.2	51.5	353,100
San Jose, CA	354	68.1	63.3	304,400
Seattle, WA	694	88.2	62.4	138,000
St. Louis, MO-IL	764	82.6	73.2	72,600
Tampa–St. Petersburg–Clearwater, FL	753	86.6	72.0	73,000
Washington, DC-MD-VA	972	66.6	69.3	180,700
West Palm Beach–Boca Raton–Delray Beach, FL	311	85.2	76.4	104,700

Source: Bureau of the Census, unpublished tables from the 1990 census; calculations by New Strategist

Whites: Income

The median income of white householders aged 45 to 54 stood at $52,750 in 1996.

The median income of white households fell 0.9 percent between 1990 and 1996, to $37,161 after adjusting for inflation. This decline can be accounted for entirely by the steep drop in the income of Hispanic households during those years, since most Hispanics are white. The median household income of non-Hispanic whites rose 1 percent between 1990 and 1996.

Among white households, median income peaks at $52,750 for householders aged 45 to 54. By household type, white married couples have the highest incomes—$50,302 in 1996.

White men who work full-time earned a median of $34,741 in 1996, 4 percent less than they did in 1990 after adjusting for inflation. The median earnings of white women who work full-time rose 1 percent during those years to $25,358, after adjusting for inflation. Since 1980, the median income of white women has grown from 59 to 73 percent of the median income of white men.

The white poverty rate was higher in 1996 than in 1990. But only 9 percent of all white families are poor. The figure falls to 5 percent among white married couples. Overall, about 11 percent of whites are poor, including 16 percent of children under age 18.

■ White households have much higher incomes than black and Hispanic households. Behind the income gap is the large proportion of white households headed by dual-income married couples.

Household income peaks in the 45-to-54 age group

(median income of white households by age, 1996)

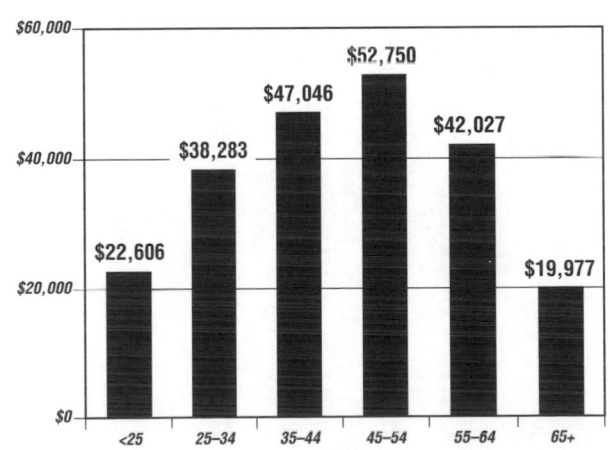

Median Income of White and Non-Hispanic White Households, 1980 to 1996

(median income of white and non-Hispanic white households, ratio of white and non-Hispanic white to total households median income, and ratio of non-Hispanic white to white median income; percent change in incomes and ratios, selected years; in 1996 dollars)

| | white | | non-Hispanic white | | |
	median income	ratio white/total	median income	ratio non-Hispanic white/total	ratio non-Hispanic white/white
1996	$37,161	1.05	$38,787	1.09	1.04
1995	36,822	1.05	38,276	1.09	1.04
1994	36,026	1.05	37,188	1.09	1.03
1993	35,788	1.06	37,105	1.09	1.04
1992	36,020	1.05	37,229	1.09	1.03
1991	36,367	1.05	37,236	1.07	1.02
1990	37,492	1.04	38,349	1.07	1.02
1989	38,473	1.05	39,301	1.07	1.02
1988	38,172	1.06	39,224	1.09	1.03
1987	37,924	1.05	38,967	1.08	1.03
1986	37,471	1.05	38,323	1.08	1.02
1985	36,320	1.05	37,137	1.08	1.02
1984	35,709	1.05	36,451	1.08	1.02
1983	34,502	1.05	–	–	–
1982	34,657	1.05	35,238	1.06	1.02
1981	35,094	1.06	35,601	1.07	1.01
1980	35,620	1.06	36,251	1.07	1.02
Percent change					
1990–1996	–0.9%	0.4%	1.1%	2.4%	2.0%
1980–1996	4.3	–0.8	7.0	1.8	2.6

Note: White and non-Hispanic white/total population ratios are calculated by dividing median income of white and non-Hispanic white households by median of total households. Non-Hispanic white/white ratio is calculated by dividing median income of non-Hispanic white households by median of white households. (–) means data are not available.
Source: U.S. Bureau of the Census, unpublished tables from the 1997 Current Population Survey; calculations by New Strategist

Income Distribution of White Households
by Age of Householder, 1996

(number and percent distribution of white households by household income and age of householder, 1996; households in thousands as of 1997)

	total	< age 25	25–34	35–44	45–54	55–64	65+
Total households, number	**85,059**	**4,040**	**15,661**	**19,642**	**15,936**	**10,598**	**19,182**
Under $10,000	8,575	726	1,085	1,121	896	1,029	3,717
$10,000 to $19,999	13,493	1,012	1,961	1,856	1,377	1,403	5,886
$20,000 to $29,999	12,483	859	2,626	2,443	1,595	1,426	3,532
$30,000 to $39,999	10,515	580	2,528	2,548	1,663	1,168	2,029
$40,000 to $49,999	9,186	363	2,059	2,463	1,924	1,112	1,266
$50,000 to $59,999	7,672	217	1,763	2,223	1,601	1,086	782
$60,000 to $69,999	5,912	99	1,241	1,933	1,385	769	486
$70,000 to $79,999	4,528	73	827	1,405	1,233	605	387
$80,000 to $89,999	3,030	30	458	928	932	447	237
$90,000 to $99,999	2,107	21	285	614	697	295	193
$100,000 or more	7,558	61	829	2,109	2,635	1,257	667
Median income	$37,161	$22,606	$38,283	$47,046	$52,750	$42,027	$19,977
Total households, percent	**100.0%**	**100.0%**	**100.0%**	**100.0%**	**100.0%**	**100.0%**	**100.0%**
Under $10,000	10.1	18.0	6.9	5.7	5.6	9.7	19.4
$10,000 to $19,999	15.9	25.0	12.5	9.4	8.6	13.2	30.7
$20,000 to $29,999	14.7	21.3	16.8	12.4	10.0	13.5	18.4
$30,000 to $39,999	12.4	14.4	16.1	13.0	10.4	11.0	10.6
$40,000 to $49,999	10.8	9.0	13.1	12.5	12.1	10.5	6.6
$50,000 to $59,999	9.0	5.4	11.3	11.3	10.0	10.2	4.1
$60,000 to $69,999	7.0	2.5	7.9	9.8	8.7	7.3	2.5
$70,000 to $79,999	5.3	1.8	5.3	7.2	7.7	5.7	2.0
$80,000 to $89,999	3.6	0.7	2.9	4.7	5.8	4.2	1.2
$90,000 to $99,999	2.5	0.5	1.8	3.1	4.4	2.8	1.0
$100,000 or more	8.9	1.5	5.3	10.7	16.5	11.9	3.5

Source: Bureau of the Census, unpublished tables from the 1997 Current Population Survey; calculations by New Strategist

Income Distribution of White Households by Household Type, 1996

(number and percent distribution of white households and percent distribution by household income and household type, 1996; households in thousands as of 1997)

	total households	family households				nonfamily households				
				female hh, no spouse present	*male hh, no spouse present*		*female hh*		*male hh*	
	total households	*total*	*married couples*	*spouse present*	*spouse present*	*total*	*total*	*living alone*	*total*	*living alone*
Total households, number	**85,059**	**58,934**	**47,650**	**8,339**	**2,944**	**26,125**	**14,644**	**12,783**	**11,481**	**8,730**
Under $10,000	8,575	3,106	1,350	1,557	199	5,469	3,968	3,894	1,500	1,400
$10,000 to $19,999	13,493	6,733	4,389	1,888	456	6,760	4,405	4,158	2,354	2,038
$20,000 to $29,999	12,483	8,013	5,926	1,562	526	4,467	2,338	1,999	2,131	1,731
$30,000 to $39,999	10,515	7,544	5,977	1,133	430	2,972	1,312	1,110	1,660	1,248
$40,000 to $49,999	9,186	7,155	5,985	773	399	2,031	863	634	1,167	804
$50,000 to $59,999	7,672	6,268	5,434	513	321	1,404	597	381	809	520
$60,000 to $69,999	5,912	5,023	4,530	303	190	889	367	198	524	283
$70,000 to $79,999	4,528	3,947	3,592	214	141	581	210	117	371	181
$80,000 to $89,999	3,030	2,595	2,400	119	75	435	173	84	263	135
$90,000 to $99,999	2,107	1,852	1,711	85	56	254	100	47	155	72
$100,000 or more	7,558	6,697	6,356	190	151	861	311	164	550	318
Median income	$37,161	$45,382	$50,302	$24,375	$36,938	$21,536	$16,765	$14,890	$28,520	$25,098
Total households, percent	**100.0%**	**100.0%**	**100.0%**	**100.0%**	**100.0%**	**100.0%**	**100.0%**	**100.0%**	**100.0%**	**100.0%**
Under $10,000	10.1	5.3	2.8	18.7	6.8	20.9	27.1	30.5	13.1	16.0
$10,000 to $19,999	15.9	11.4	9.2	22.6	15.5	25.9	30.1	32.5	20.5	23.3
$20,000 to $29,999	14.7	13.6	12.4	18.7	17.9	17.1	16.0	15.6	18.6	19.8
$30,000 to $39,999	12.4	12.8	12.5	13.6	14.6	11.4	9.0	8.7	14.5	14.3
$40,000 to $49,999	10.8	12.1	12.6	9.3	13.6	7.8	5.9	5.0	10.2	9.2
$50,000 to $59,999	9.0	10.6	11.4	6.2	10.9	5.4	4.1	3.0	7.0	6.0
$60,000 to $69,999	7.0	8.5	9.5	3.6	6.5	3.4	2.5	1.5	4.6	3.2
$70,000 to $79,999	5.3	6.7	7.5	2.6	4.8	2.2	1.4	0.9	3.2	2.1
$80,000 to $89,999	3.6	4.4	5.0	1.4	2.5	1.7	1.2	0.7	2.3	1.5
$90,000 to $99,999	2.5	3.1	3.6	1.0	1.9	1.0	0.7	0.4	1.4	0.8
$100,000 or more	8.9	11.4	13.3	2.3	5.1	3.3	2.1	1.3	4.8	3.6

Source: Bureau of the Census, unpublished tables from the 1997 Current Population Survey; calculations by New Strategist

Income Distribution of White Men by Age, 1996

(number and percent distribution of white men aged 15 or older by income and age, 1996; men in thousands as of 1997)

	total	< age 25	25–34	35–44	45–54	55–64	65+
Total men, number	**84,540**	**14,969**	**16,449**	**18,314**	**13,882**	**8,904**	**12,022**
Without income	4,499	3,184	363	365	239	196	151
With income	80,041	11,785	16,086	17,949	13,642	8,708	11,872
Under $10,000	15,403	7,035	1,863	1,634	1,275	1,195	2,404
$10,000 to $19,999	16,935	2,901	3,644	2,684	1,762	1,498	4,444
$20,000 to $29,999	14,506	1,221	4,043	3,247	2,114	1,531	2,350
$30,000 to $39,999	10,898	415	2,927	3,208	2,077	1,269	1,001
$40,000 to $49,999	7,280	123	1,618	2,342	1,793	899	507
$50,000 to $74,999	9,011	68	1,465	2,951	2,660	1,210	654
$75,000 to $99,999	2,937	11	261	913	980	525	248
$100,000 or more	3,075	12	263	972	981	583	265
Median income of men with income	$24,949	$7,240	$25,726	$34,026	$37,278	$30,841	$17,268
Total men, percent	**100.0%**	**100.0%**	**100.0%**	**100.0%**	**100.0%**	**100.0%**	**100.0%**
Without income	5.3	21.3	2.2	2.0	1.7	2.2	1.3
With income	94.7	78.7	97.8	98.0	98.3	97.8	98.8
Under $10,000	18.2	47.0	11.3	8.9	9.2	13.4	20.0
$10,000 to $19,999	20.0	19.4	22.2	14.7	12.7	16.8	37.0
$20,000 to $29,999	17.2	8.2	24.6	17.7	15.2	17.2	19.5
$30,000 to $39,999	12.9	2.8	17.8	17.5	15.0	14.3	8.3
$40,000 to $49,999	8.6	0.8	9.8	12.8	12.9	10.1	4.2
$50,000 to $74,999	10.7	0.5	8.9	16.1	19.2	13.6	5.4
$75,000 to $99,999	3.5	0.1	1.6	5.0	7.1	5.9	2.1
$100,000 or more	3.6	0.1	1.6	5.3	7.1	6.5	2.2

Source: U.S. Bureau of the Census, unpublished tables from the 1997 Current Population Survey; calculations by New Strategist

Income Distribution of White Women by Age, 1996

(number and percent distribution of white women aged 15 or older by income and age, 1996; women in thousands as of 1997)

	total	< age 25	25–34	35–44	45–54	55–64	aged 65+
Total women, number	**88,756**	**14,269**	**16,189**	**18,124**	**14,189**	**9,543**	**16,442**
Without income	8,015	3,392	1,376	1,198	952	763	334
With income	80,741	10,877	14,813	16,927	13,237	8,780	16,108
Under $10,000	32,493	7,404	4,736	5,064	3,715	3,431	8,145
$10,000 to $19,999	20,566	2,471	3,675	3,807	3,151	2,237	5,226
$20,000 to $29,999	12,606	735	3,359	3,353	2,387	1,315	1,457
$30,000 to $39,999	6,865	178	1,686	2,087	1,603	720	591
$40,000 to $49,999	3,647	45	671	1,161	1,078	418	275
$50,000 to $74,999	3,176	26	515	965	954	470	244
$75,000 to $99,999	754	11	101	273	192	99	76
$100,000 or more	636	7	69	220	160	89	92
Median income of women with income	$12,961	$5,904	$17,035	$18,617	$19,159	$13,589	$9,919
Total women, percent	**100.0%**	**100.0%**	**100.0%**	**100.0%**	**100.0%**	**100.0%**	**100.0%**
Without income	9.0	23.8	8.5	6.6	6.7	8.0	2.0
With income	91.0	76.2	91.5	93.4	93.3	92.0	98.0
Under $10,000	36.6	51.9	29.3	27.9	26.2	36.0	49.5
$10,000 to $19,999	23.2	17.3	22.7	21.0	22.2	23.4	31.8
$20,000 to $29,999	14.2	5.2	20.7	18.5	16.8	13.8	8.9
$30,000 to $39,999	7.7	1.2	10.4	11.5	11.3	7.5	3.6
$40,000 to $49,999	4.1	0.3	4.1	6.4	7.6	4.4	1.7
$50,000 to $74,999	3.6	0.2	3.2	5.3	6.7	4.9	1.5
$75,000 to $99,999	0.8	0.1	0.6	1.5	1.4	1.0	0.5
$100,000 or more	0.7	0.0	0.4	1.2	1.1	0.9	0.6

Source: U.S. Bureau of the Census, unpublished tables from the 1997 Current Population Survey; calculations by New Strategist

Median Earnings of Whites Who Work Full-Time by Sex, 1980 to 1996

(median earnings of whites who work year-round, full-time by sex; ratio of white to total population median earnings, and white female earnings as a percent of white male earnings, 1980–96; percent change in earnings and ratios for selected years; in 1996 dollars)

	white men		white women		white women's earnings as a percent of white men's earnings
	median earnings	ratio white/total	median earnings	ratio white/total	
1996	$34,741	1.04	$25,358	1.02	73.0%
1995	34,505	1.04	24,980	1.02	72.4
1994	34,344	1.03	25,297	1.03	73.7
1993	34,564	1.02	24,951	1.02	72.2
1992	35,300	1.02	24,993	1.01	70.8
1991	35,657	1.02	24,831	1.01	69.6
1990	36,111	1.04	25,016	1.01	69.3
1989	37,545	1.04	25,143	1.01	67.0
1988	37,484	1.03	24,965	1.02	66.6
1987	37,710	1.02	24,708	1.02	65.5
1986	38,104	1.03	24,481	1.02	64.2
1985	37,465	1.03	24,034	1.01	64.2
1984	37,490	1.03	23,520	1.01	62.7
1983	36,412	1.03	23,121	1.01	63.5
1982	36,487	1.03	22,726	1.01	62.3
1981	36,879	1.02	22,055	1.02	59.8
1980	37,595	1.03	22,311	1.01	59.3
Percent change					
1990–1996	–3.8%	–0.2%	1.4%	0.5%	5.4%
1980–1996	–7.6	0.7	13.7	0.7	23.0

Note: White/total ratios are calculated by dividing median earnings of white men and women by median of total men and women.
Source: Bureau of the Census, unpublished tables from the 1997 Current Population Survey; calculations by New Strategist

Median Earnings of Whites Who Work Full-Time by Education and Sex, 1996

(median earnings of whites aged 25 or older who work year-round, full-time, by educational attainment and sex, 1996)

	men	women	white women's earnings as a percent of white men's earnings
Total persons	**$35,424**	**$25,187**	**71.1%**
Less than 9th grade	17,349	13,032	75.1
9th to 12th grade, no diploma	22,476	16,135	71.8
High school graduate	30,572	20,792	68.0
Some college, no degree	34,779	24,088	69.3
Associate's degree	36,524	27,017	74.0
Bachelor's degree or more	50,651	35,468	70.0
Bachelor's degree	45,150	32,150	71.2
Master's degree	56,957	40,476	71.1
Professional degree	80,239	59,566	74.2
Doctoral degree	66,844	55,174	82.5

Source: U.S. Bureau of the Census, unpublished tables from the 1997 Current Population Survey; calculations by New Strategist

White Families below the Poverty Level, 1980 to 1996

(total number of white families, and number and percent below poverty level, by presence of children under age 18 at home and type of family, 1980–96; percent change in numbers and rates for selected years; families in thousands as of March the following year)

	total families			married couples			female hh, no spouse present		
		in poverty			in poverty			in poverty	
	total	number	percent	total	number	percent	total	number	percent
With and without children under age 18									
1996	58,934	5,059	8.6%	47,650	2,416	5.1%	8,339	2,276	27.3%
1995	58,872	4,994	8.5	47,877	2,443	5.1	8,284	2,200	26.6
1994	58,444	5,312	9.1	47,905	2,629	5.5	8,031	2,329	29.0
1993	57,881	5,452	9.4	47,452	2,757	5.8	8,131	2,376	29.2
1992	57,669	5,255	9.1	47,383	2,677	5.7	7,868	2,245	28.5
1991	57,224	5,022	8.8	47,124	2,573	5.5	7,726	2,192	28.4
1990	56,803	4,622	8.1	47,014	2,386	5.1	7,512	2,010	26.8
1989	56,590	4,409	7.8	46,981	2,329	5.0	7,306	1,858	25.4
1988	56,492	4,471	7.9	46,877	2,294	4.9	7,342	1,945	26.5
1987	56,086	4,567	8.1	46,510	2,382	5.1	7,297	1,961	26.9
1986	55,676	4,811	8.6	46,410	2,591	5.6	7,227	2,041	28.2
1985	54,991	4,963	9.1	45,924	2,815	6.1	7,111	1,950	27.4
1984	54,400	4,925	9.1	45,643	2,858	6.3	6,941	1,878	27.1
1983	53,890	5,220	9.7	45,470	3,125	6.9	6,796	1,926	28.3
1982	53,407	5,118	9.6	42,252	3,104	6.9	6,507	1,813	27.9
1981	53,269	4,670	8.8	45,007	2,712	6.0	6,620	1,814	27.4
1980	52,710	4,195	8.0	44,860	2,437	5.4	6,266	1,609	25.7
Percent change									
1990–1996	3.8%	9.5%	6.2%	1.4%	1.3%	0.0%	11.0%	13.2%	1.9%
1980–1996	11.8	20.6	7.5	6.2	–0.9	–5.6	33.1	41.5	6.2

(continued)

(continued from previous page)

	total families			married couples			female hh, no spouse present		
		in poverty			*in poverty*			*in poverty*	
	total	*number*	*percent*	*total*	*number*	*percent*	*total*	*number*	*percent*
With children									
under age 18									
1996	29,826	3,863	13.0%	22,757	1,548	6.8%	5,501	2,032	36.9%
1995	29,713	3,839	12.9	22,663	1,583	7.0	5,554	1,980	35.6
1994	29,548	4,025	13.6	22,839	1,706	7.5	5,390	2,064	38.3
1993	29,234	4,226	14.5	22,670	1,868	8.2	5,361	2,123	39.6
1992	28,790	4,020	14.0	22,440	1,753	7.8	5,099	2,021	39.6
1991	28,368	3,880	13.7	22,213	1,715	7.7	4,967	1,969	39.6
1990	28,117	3,553	12.6	22,289	1,572	7.1	4,786	1,814	37.9
1989	27,977	3,290	11.8	22,271	1,457	6.5	4,627	1,671	36.1
1988	27,999	3,321	11.9	22,435	1,434	6.4	4,553	1,740	38.2
1987	27,930	3,433	12.3	22,336	1,538	6.9	4,548	1,742	38.3
1986	27,929	3,637	13.0	22,466	1,692	7.5	4,552	1,812	39.8
1985	27,795	3,695	13.3	22,399	1,827	8.2	4,470	1,730	38.7
1984	27,380	3,679	13.4	22,181	1,879	8.5	4,337	1,682	38.8
1983	27,303	3,859	14.1	22,361	2,060	9.2	4,210	1,676	39.8
1982	27,118	3,709	13.7	22,390	2,005	9.0	4,037	1,584	39.3
1981	27,223	3,362	12.4	22,334	1,723	7.7	4,237	1,564	36.9
1980	27,416	3,078	11.2	22,793	1,544	6.8	3,995	1,433	35.9
Percent change									
1990–1996	6.1%	8.7%	3.2%	2.1%	−1.5%	−4.2%	14.9%	12.0%	−2.6%
1980–1996	8.8	25.5	16.1	−0.2	0.3	0.0	37.7	41.8	2.8

Source: Bureau of the Census, unpublished tables from the 1997 Current Population Survey

Whites in Poverty by Sex and Age, 1996

(total number of whites, and number and percent below poverty level by sex and age, 1996; persons in thousands as of 1997)

| | | in poverty | |
	total	number	percent
Total persons	**219,656**	**24,650**	**11.2%**
Under age 18	55,606	9,044	16.3
Aged 18 to 24	19,992	3,123	15.6
Aged 25 to 34	32,638	3,487	10.7
Aged 35 to 44	36,438	2,976	8.2
Aged 45 to 54	28,071	1,764	6.3
Aged 55 to 59	9,935	770	7.7
Aged 60 to 64	8,512	820	9.6
Aged 65 to 74	15,983	1,170	7.3
Aged 75 or older	12,481	1,497	12.0
Females, total	**111,318**	**14,012**	**12.6**
Under age 18	27,033	4,451	16.5
Aged 18 to 24	9,798	1,834	18.7
Aged 25 to 34	16,189	2,116	13.1
Aged 35 to 44	18,124	1,678	9.3
Aged 45 to 54	14,189	999	7.0
Aged 55 to 59	5,104	455	8.9
Aged 60 to 64	4,439	495	11.1
Aged 65 to 74	8,765	828	9.5
Aged 75 or older	7,677	1,157	15.1
Males, total	**108,338**	**10,638**	**9.8**
Under age 18	28,573	4,593	16.1
Aged 18 to 24	10,194	1,289	12.6
Aged 25 to 34	16,449	1,371	8.3
Aged 35 to 44	18,314	1,298	7.1
Aged 45 to 54	13,882	765	5.5
Aged 55 to 59	4,831	315	6.5
Aged 60 to 64	4,073	326	8.0
Aged 65 to 74	7,218	342	4.7
Aged 75 or older	4,804	340	7.1

Source: Bureau of the Census, unpublished tables from the 1997 Current Population Survey

Whites: Labor Force

Three in ten white workers are employed in managerial or professional specialty occupations.

Seventy-six percent of white men and 60 percent of white women were in the labor force in 1997. Because whites comprise the great majority of the population, their labor force participation rate closely matches that of the total population.

Thirty percent of whites are employed in managerial or professional specialty occupations. Another 30 percent are in technical, sales, or administrative support work. Only 15 percent of white workers are union members, including 17 percent of male and 13 percent of female workers.

Forty-six percent of white households have two or more earners. Among white couples, a 56 percent majority are dual earners. Only 22 percent are traditional, that is, only the husband works.

Between 1996 and 2006, the number of white workers will grow 9 percent, while the number of non-Hispanic white workers will increase just 7 percent. In the year 2006, non-Hispanic whites will account for 73 percent of all workers, down from 75 percent in 1996.

■ White households have much higher incomes than black and Hispanic households because so many are headed by dual-earner married couples. Until the dual-earner share of black and Hispanic households matches that of whites, the income gap will remain.

Most white couples are dual earners

(percent distribution of married couples by labor force status of husband and wife, 1996)

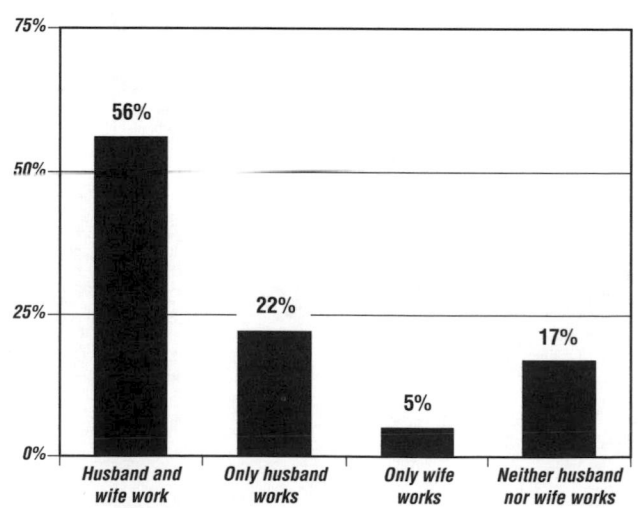

Employment Status of Whites by Sex and Age, 1997

(employment status of the civilian noninstitutionalized white population aged 16 or older, by sex and age, 1997; numbers in thousands)

				civilian labor force				not in labor force	
	total	percent of population	employed	percent of labor force	unemployed	percent of labor force		total	percent of population
Total persons	**114,693**	**67.5%**	**109,856**	**95.8%**	**4,836**	**4.2%**		**55,301**	**32.5%**
Aged 16 to 19	6,720	55.2	5,807	86.4	912	13.6		5,462	44.8
Aged 20 to 24	11,127	79.6	10,362	93.1	765	6.9		2,855	20.4
Aged 25 to 34	27,362	85.3	26,294	96.1	1,068	3.9		4,729	14.7
Aged 35 to 44	31,171	85.8	30,137	96.7	1,035	3.3		5,154	14.2
Aged 45 to 54	23,709	83.5	23,061	97.3	648	2.7		4,678	16.5
Aged 55 to 64	11,066	59.9	10,785	97.5	302	2.7		7,425	40.1
Aged 65 or older	3,517	12.3	3,411	97.0	106	3.0		24,998	87.7
Total men	**62,639**	**75.9**	**59,996**	**95.8**	**2,641**	**4.2**		**19,938**	**24.1**
Aged 16 to 19	3,513	56.1	3,011	85.7	502	14.3		2,744	43.9
Aged 20 to 24	6,029	85.1	5,590	92.7	439	7.3		1,058	14.9
Aged 25 to 34	15,120	94.2	14,567	96.3	553	3.7		923	5.8
Aged 35 to 44	17,019	93.7	16,470	96.8	549	3.2		1,144	6.3
Aged 45 to 54	12,710	90.6	12,352	97.2	358	2.8		1,320	9.4
Aged 55 to 64	6,154	68.9	5,972	97.0	182	3.0		2,775	31.1
Aged 65 or older	2,094	17.4	2,037	97.3	58	2.8		9,973	82.6
Total women	**52,054**	**59.5**	**49,859**	**95.8**	**2,195**	**4.2**		**35,363**	**40.5**
Aged 16 to 19	3,207	54.1	2,796	87.2	411	12.8		2,718	45.9
Aged 20 to 24	5,099	73.9	4,773	93.6	326	6.4		1,797	26.1
Aged 25 to 34	12,242	76.3	11,727	95.8	515	4.2		3,805	23.7
Aged 35 to 44	14,153	77.9	13,667	96.6	486	3.4		4,009	22.1
Aged 45 to 54	10,999	76.6	10,709	97.4	290	2.6		3,359	23.4
Aged 55 to 64	4,932	51.5	4,813	97.6	119	2.4		4,650	48.5
Aged 65 or older	1,422	8.6	1,374	96.6	49	3.4		15,025	91.4

Note: The civilian labor force equals the number of employed plus the number of unemployed persons. The civilian population equals the number of persons in the labor force plus the number of those not in the labor force.
Source: Bureau of Labor Statistics, Employment and Earnings, *January 1998; calculations by New Strategist*

White Workers by Occupation, 1997

(total number of employed persons aged 16 or older in the civilian labor force; number and percent distribution of employed whites, and white share of total employed, by occupation, 1997; numbers in thousands)

	total	white number	white percent	white share of total employed
Total employed	**129,558**	**109,856**	**100.0%**	**84.8%**
Managerial and professional specialty	**37,686**	**33,089**	**30.1**	**87.8**
Executive, administrative, and managerial	18,440	16,420	14.9	89.0
Professional specialty	19,245	16,669	15.2	86.6
Technical, sales, and administrative support	**38,309**	**32,624**	**29.7**	**85.2**
Technicians and related support	4,214	3,571	3.3	84.7
Sales occupations	15,734	13,730	12.5	87.3
Administrative support, including clerical	18,361	15,323	13.9	83.5
Service occupations	**17,537**	**13,604**	**12.4**	**77.6**
Private household	795	642	0.6	80.8
Protective service	2,300	1,800	1.6	78.3
Service, except private household and protective	14,442	11,162	10.2	77.3
Precision production, craft, and repair	**14,124**	**12,472**	**11.4**	**88.3**
Mechanics and repairers	4,675	4,146	3.8	88.7
Construction trades	5,378	4,859	4.4	90.3
Other precision production, craft, and repair	4,071	3,467	3.2	85.2
Operators, fabricators, and laborers	**18,399**	**14,813**	**13.5**	**80.5**
Machine operators, assemblers, and inspectors	7,962	6,322	5.8	79.4
Transportation and material moving occupations	5,389	4,435	4.0	82.3
Handlers, equipment cleaners, helpers, and laborers	5,048	4,057	3.7	80.4
Farming, forestry, and fishing	**3,503**	**3,254**	**3.0**	**92.9**

Source: Bureau of Labor Statistics, Employment and Earnings, *January 1998; calculations by New Strategist*

White Workers by Industry, 1997

(total number of employed persons aged 16 or older in the civilian labor force; number and percent distribution of employed whites, and white share of total employed, by industry, 1997; numbers in thousands)

	total	white		white share of total employed
		number	*percent*	
Total employed	**129,558**	**109,856**	**100.0%**	**84.8%**
Agriculture	3,399	3,208	2.9	94.4
Mining	634	599	0.5	94.5
Construction	8,302	7,538	6.9	90.8
Manufacturing	20,835	17,601	16.0	84.5
Durable goods	12,437	10,694	9.7	86.0
Nondurable goods	8,399	6,907	6.3	82.2
Transportation, communications, and other public utilities	9,182	7,462	6.8	81.3
Wholesale and retail trade	26,777	23,047	21.0	86.1
Wholesale trade	4,907	4,407	4.0	89.8
Retail trade	21,869	18,639	17.0	85.2
Finance, insurance, and real estate	8,297	7,163	6.5	86.3
Services	46,393	38,692	35.2	83.4
Private households	921	728	0.7	79.0
Other service industries	45,472	37,963	34.6	83.5
Professional and related services	30,935	25,831	23.5	83.5
Public administration	5,738	4,547	4.1	79.2

Source: Bureau of Labor Statistics, Employment and Earnings, *January 1998; calculations by New Strategist*

White Households by Number of Earners, 1996

(number and percent distribution of white households by number of earners, 1996; numbers in thousands)

	number	percent
Total households	**85,059**	**100.0%**
No earners	17,815	20.9
One earner	27,854	32.7
Two or more earners	39,391	46.3
Two earners	30,828	36.2
Three earners	6,356	7.5
Four or more earners	2,207	2.6

Source: Bureau of the Census, Money Income: 1996, *Current Population Reports, P60-197, 1997; calculations by New Strategist*

Labor Force Status of White Married Couples, 1996

(number and percent distribution of white married couples by age of householder and labor force status of husband and wife,1996; numbers in thousands)

	total married couples	husband and/or wife in labor force			neither husband nor wife in labor force
		husband and wife	*husband only*	*wife only*	
Total couples, number	**47,873**	**26,699**	**10,462**	**2,403**	**8,309**
Under age 20	65	28	29	3	5
Aged 20 to 24	1,314	848	402	34	30
Aged 25 to 29	3,465	2,458	911	67	29
Aged 30 to 34	5,394	3,726	1,518	91	58
Aged 35 to 39	6,069	4,274	1,602	104	89
Aged 40 to 44	6,169	4,516	1,331	213	109
Aged 45 to 49	5,665	4,157	1,175	207	125
Aged 50 to 54	4,156	2,816	943	226	171
Aged 55 to 59	3,776	2,083	980	348	365
Aged 60 to 64	3,167	1,040	686	472	969
Aged 65 to 74	5,720	686	727	533	3,773
Aged 75 to 84	2,590	62	151	98	2,279
Aged 85 or older	325	4	6	7	308
Total couples, percent	**100.0%**	**55.8%**	**21.9%**	**5.0%**	**17.4%**
Under age 20	100.0	43.1	44.6	4.6	7.7
Aged 20 to 24	100.0	64.5	30.6	2.6	2.3
Aged 25 to 29	100.0	70.9	26.3	1.9	0.8
Aged 30 to 34	100.0	69.1	28.1	1.7	1.1
Aged 35 to 39	100.0	70.4	26.4	1.7	1.5
Aged 40 to 44	100.0	73.2	21.6	3.5	1.8
Aged 45 to 49	100.0	73.4	20.7	3.7	2.2
Aged 50 to 54	100.0	67.8	22.7	5.4	4.1
Aged 55 to 59	100.0	55.2	26.0	9.2	9.7
Aged 60 to 64	100.0	32.8	21.7	14.9	30.6
Aged 65 to 74	100.0	12.0	12.7	9.3	66.0
Aged 75 to 84	100.0	2.4	5.8	3.8	88.0
Aged 85 or older	100.0	1.2	1.8	2.2	94.8

Source: Bureau of the Census, Household and Family Characteristics: March 1996, *Current Population Reports, P20-495(Update), 1997; calculations by New Strategist*

Union Membership of Whites, 1997

(number of employed white wage and salary workers aged 16 or older, number and percent of those who are represented by unions or are union members, and median weekly earnings by union membership status; by sex, 1997; numbers in thousands)

	total	*men*	*women*
Total employed	**96,104**	**50,941**	**45,163**
Represented by unions*	14,538	8,859	5,679
Percent of employed	15.1%	17.4%	12.6%
Members of unions**	13,088	8,171	4,917
Percent of employed	13.6%	16.0%	10.9%
Median weekly earnings, total***	$519	$595	$444
Represented by unions*	654	695	587
Members of unions**	663	699	595
Non-union	494	569	421

* Members of a labor union or an employee association similar to a union as well as workers who report no union affiliation but whose jobs are covered by a union or an employee association contract.
** Members of a labor union or an employee association similar to a union.
*** Full-time wage and salary workers.
Source: Bureau of Labor Statistics, Employment and Earnings, *January 1998*

Projections of the White and Non-Hispanic White Labor Force by Sex, 1996 to 2006

(number of whites and non-Hispanic whites in the civilian labor force in 1996 and 2006, and percent change in number; labor force participation rate of whites and non-Hispanic whites in 1996 and 2006, and white and non-Hispanic white share of total labor force in 1996 and 2006; by sex; numbers in thousands)

	WHITE			NON-HISPANIC WHITE		
	number in labor force		*percent change*	*number in labor force*		*percent change*
	1996	*2006*	*1996–2006*	*1996*	*2006*	*1996–2006*
Total	**113,108**	**123,581**	**9.3%**	**100,915**	**108,166**	**7.2%**
Men	61,783	66,008	6.8	54,451	56,856	4.4
Women	51,325	57,572	12.2	46,464	51,310	10.4

	labor force participation rate		*percentage point change*	*labor force participation rate*		*percentage point change*
	1996	*2006*	*1996–2006*	*1996*	*2006*	*1996–2006*
Total	**67.2%**	**68.1%**	**0.9**	**67.3%**	**68.7%**	**1.4**
Men	75.8	74.3	−1.5	75.3	74.1	−1.2
Women	59.1	62.0	2.9	59.8	63.7	3.9

	percent of total labor force		*percentage point change*	*percent of total labor force*		*percentage point change*
	1996	*2006*	*1996–2006*	*1996*	*2006*	*1996–2006*
Total	**84.4%**	**83.0%**	**−1.4**	**75.3%**	**72.7%**	**−2.7**
Men	85.7	84.4	−1.3	75.5	72.7	−2.9
Women	83.0	81.5	−1.4	75.1	72.7	−2.5

Source: Bureau of Labor Statistics, Monthly Labor Review, November 1997 *and Internet,* http://www.census.gov; *calculations by New Strategist*

Whites: Population

The non-Hispanic white population should grow just 2 percent between 1995 and 2000.

The white population is projected to grow from 223 million in 1998 to nearly 255 million by 2020, when whites will account for 79 percent of the total U.S. population. A growing share of the white population is Hispanic, and the non-Hispanic white population is growing more slowly than the white population as a whole. Consequently, the non-Hispanic white share of the population is shrinking. By 2020, non-Hispanic whites will account for just 64 percent of the total population, down from 73 percent in 1998.

Non-Hispanic whites account for a smaller share of children and young adults than of older Americans because Hispanics are a growing proportion of the younger age groups. Just 63 percent of all Americans under age 5 are non-Hispanic whites, versus 87 percent of those aged 85 or older. While there are 96 non-Hispanic whites for every 100 whites among people aged 80 or older, the ratio falls to 81 among children under age 5.

Because whites comprise the great majority of the American population, the regional distribution of whites is similar to that of the population as a whole. Eleven percent of whites live in California, the most populous state. The white share of the population is smallest in Hawaii, at 34 percent, because the majority of Hawaii's population is Asian. The white share of the population is greatest in Maine, at 98.5 percent in 1995.

■ In many states, non-Hispanic whites are already a minority among children. In the years ahead, a growing number of states will join this "minority majority" club.

Non-Hispanic whites are a shrinking share of the population

(percent of total persons who are non-Hispanic white, 1998 and 2020)

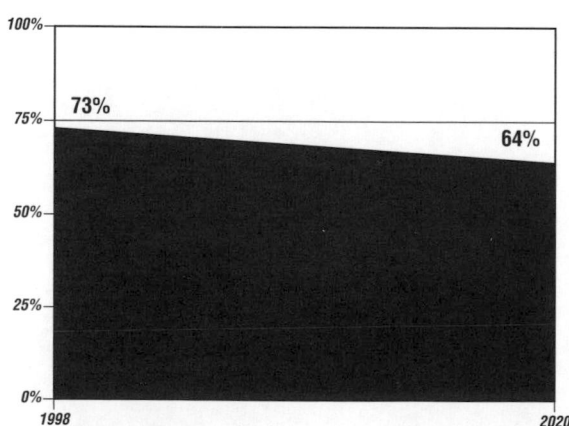

Whites by Age, 1995 to 2020

(number of whites by age, selected years 1995–2020; percent change 1995–2000 and 2000–2010; numbers in thousands)

	1995	1998	2000	2010	2020	percent change 1995–2000	percent change 2000–2010
Total persons	**218,078**	**222,648**	**225,532**	**239,588**	**254,887**	**3.4%**	**6.2%**
Under age 5	15,442	14,928	14,724	15,142	16,419	–4.6	2.8
Aged 5 to 9	15,235	15,768	15,622	14,813	16,122	2.5	–5.2
Aged 10 to 14	15,040	15,292	15,728	15,416	15,848	4.6	–2.0
Aged 15 to 19	14,365	15,373	15,658	16,799	15,958	9.0	7.3
Aged 20 to 24	14,310	13,920	14,511	16,499	16,186	1.4	13.7
Aged 25 to 29	15,393	14,889	14,092	15,488	16,576	–8.5	9.9
Aged 30 to 34	17,988	16,382	15,745	14,611	16,542	–12.5	–7.2
Aged 35 to 39	18,464	18,595	18,156	14,605	16,016	–1.7	–19.6
Aged 40 to 44	16,933	18,128	18,606	16,041	14,921	9.9	–13.8
Aged 45 to 49	14,858	15,807	16,574	17,916	14,479	11.5	8.1
Aged 50 to 54	11,728	13,471	14,674	17,995	15,591	25.1	22.6
Aged 55 to 59	9,542	10,677	11,449	16,013	17,411	20.0	39.9
Aged 60 to 64	8,722	8,849	9,151	13,833	17,107	4.9	51.2
Aged 65 to 69	8,719	8,324	8,135	10,385	14,711	–6.7	27.7
Aged 70 to 74	7,919	7,821	7,711	7,716	11,906	–2.6	0.1
Aged 75 to 79	6,040	6,488	6,670	6,232	8,210	10.4	–6.6
Aged 80 to 84	4,070	4,306	4,461	4,975	5,209	9.6	11.5
Aged 85 or older	3,308	3,630	3,866	5,108	5,677	16.9	32.1
Aged 18 to 24	19,936	20,029	20,853	23,489	22,667	4.6	12.6
Aged 18 or older	163,321	167,398	170,142	184,407	197,021	4.2	8.4
Aged 65 or older	30,057	30,569	30,843	34,416	45,712	2.6	11.6

Source: Bureau of the Census, Population Projections of the United States, by Age, Sex, Race, and Hispanic Origin: 1995 to 2050, *Current Population Reports, P25-1130, 1996; calculations by New Strategist*

White Share of the Total Population by Age, 1995 to 2020

(whites as a percent of the total population by age, selected years 1995–2020)

	1995	1998	2000	2010	2020
Total persons	**83.0%**	**82.5%**	**82.1%**	**80.5%**	**79.0%**
Under age 5	78.8	78.1	77.5	75.7	74.7
Aged 5 to 9	79.3	78.7	78.4	76.0	74.8
Aged 10 to 14	79.5	78.9	78.4	76.2	74.3
Aged 15 to 19	79.5	79.1	79.0	77.1	74.7
Aged 20 to 24	80.1	79.8	79.5	78.1	76.0
Aged 25 to 29	81.1	80.2	79.5	78.6	76.9
Aged 30 to 34	82.2	81.1	80.7	78.6	77.4
Aged 35 to 39	82.9	82.4	81.9	78.8	78.0
Aged 40 to 44	83.7	83.1	82.8	80.3	78.2
Aged 45 to 49	85.1	84.0	83.7	81.9	78.8
Aged 50 to 54	86.0	85.8	85.2	83.0	80.5
Aged 55 to 59	86.0	86.1	86.0	84.0	82.3
Aged 60 to 64	86.8	86.2	85.9	85.3	83.2
Aged 65 to 69	87.9	87.0	86.5	85.7	83.9
Aged 70 to 74	89.6	88.9	88.4	86.3	85.9
Aged 75 to 79	90.4	90.1	90.0	87.5	87.0
Aged 80 to 84	91.1	91.2	91.0	89.5	87.7
Aged 85 or older	91.0	90.9	90.8	90.1	87.9
Aged 18 to 24	80.0	79.6	79.4	77.9	75.8
Aged 18 or older	84.2	83.8	83.5	81.9	80.4
Aged 65 or older	89.6	89.2	88.9	87.3	85.9

Source: Calculations by New Strategist based on Census Bureau data in Population Projections of the United States, by Age, Sex, Race, and Hispanic Origin: 1995 to 2050, *Current Population Reports, P25-1130, 1996*

Non-Hispanic Whites by Age, 1995 to 2020

(number of non–Hispanic whites by age, selected years 1995–2020; percent change 1995–2000 and 2000–2010; numbers in thousands)

	1995	1998	2000	2010	2020	percent change 1995–2000	percent change 2000–2010
Total persons	**193,566**	**195,786**	**197,061**	**202,390**	**207,393**	**1.8%**	**2.7%**
Under age 5	12,577	12,071	11,807	11,445	11,724	–6.1	–3.1
Aged 5 to 9	12,828	12,923	12,615	11,422	11,748	–1.7	–9.5
Aged 10 to 14	12,840	12,886	13,109	12,135	11,770	2.1	–7.4
Aged 15 to 19	12,286	13,037	13,184	13,270	12,026	7.3	0.7
Aged 20 to 24	12,181	11,720	12,171	13,345	12,360	–0.1	9.6
Aged 25 to 29	13,127	12,601	11,816	12,643	12,734	–10.0	7.0
Aged 30 to 34	15,686	13,985	13,328	11,988	13,134	–15.0	–10.1
Aged 35 to 39	16,508	16,371	15,783	12,114	12,949	–4.4	–23.2
Aged 40 to 44	15,369	16,297	16,599	13,514	12,181	8.0	–18.6
Aged 45 to 49	13,665	14,402	15,012	15,528	11,967	9.9	3.4
Aged 50 to 54	10,850	12,412	13,473	16,013	13,102	24.2	18.9
Aged 55 to 59	8,845	9,882	10,574	14,469	15,060	19.5	36.8
Aged 60 to 64	8,141	8,209	8,465	12,668	15,192	4.0	49.7
Aged 65 to 69	8,221	7,787	7,574	9,554	13,249	–7.9	26.1
Aged 70 to 74	7,544	7,397	7,251	7,099	10,849	–3.9	–2.1
Aged 75 to 79	5,803	6,193	6,336	5,761	7,495	9.2	–9.1
Aged 80 to 84	3,912	4,134	4,271	4,633	4,729	9.2	8.5
Aged 85 or older	3,184	3,478	3,694	4,788	5,123	16.0	29.6
Aged 18 to 24	16,977	16,905	17,510	18,879	17,261	3.1	7.8
Aged 18 or older	147,833	150,054	151,685	159,652	165,025	2.6	5.3
Aged 65 or older	28,665	28,988	29,126	31,835	41,445	1.6	9.3

Source: Bureau of the Census, Population Projections of the United States, by Age, Sex, Race, and Hispanic Origin: 1995 to 2050, Current Population Reports, P25-1130, 1996; calculations by New Strategist

Non-Hispanic White Share of the Total Population by Age, 1995 to 2020

(non-Hispanic whites as a percent of the total population by age, selected years 1995–2020)

	1995	1998	2000	2010	2020
Total persons	**73.6%**	**72.5%**	**71.8%**	**68.0%**	**64.3%**
Under age 5	64.2	63.1	62.2	57.2	53.3
Aged 5 to 9	66.8	64.5	63.3	58.6	54.5
Aged 10 to 14	67.9	66.5	65.4	60.0	55.2
Aged 15 to 19	68.0	67.1	66.5	60.9	56.3
Aged 20 to 24	68.1	67.2	66.7	63.1	58.0
Aged 25 to 29	69.2	67.9	66.7	64.1	59.0
Aged 30 to 34	71.7	69.3	68.3	64.5	61.5
Aged 35 to 39	74.1	72.5	71.2	65.4	63.1
Aged 40 to 44	76.0	74.7	73.8	67.6	63.8
Aged 45 to 49	78.3	76.6	75.8	71.0	65.1
Aged 50 to 54	79.6	79.0	78.2	73.9	67.7
Aged 55 to 59	79.8	79.7	79.5	75.9	71.2
Aged 60 to 64	81.0	80.0	79.5	78.1	73.9
Aged 65 to 69	82.8	81.4	80.5	78.9	75.6
Aged 70 to 74	85.4	84.1	83.1	79.4	78.3
Aged 75 to 79	86.8	86.0	85.4	80.9	79.4
Aged 80 to 84	87.6	87.6	87.2	83.4	79.6
Aged 85 or older	87.6	87.1	86.7	84.4	79.3
Aged 18 to 24	68.1	67.2	66.7	62.6	57.7
Aged 18 or older	76.2	75.1	74.4	70.9	67.3
Aged 65 or older	85.5	84.5	83.9	80.8	77.9

Source: Calculations by New Strategist based on Census Bureau data in Population Projections of the United States, by Age, Sex, Race, and Hispanic Origin: 1995 to 2050, *Current Population Reports, P25-1130, 1996*

Whites and Non-Hispanic Whites by Age, 1998

(number of whites and non-Hispanic whites, and ratio of non-Hispanic whites to whites, by age, 1998; numbers in thousands)

	whites	non-Hispanic whites	ratio of non-Hispanic whites to total whites*
Total persons	**222,648**	**195,786**	**88**
Under age 5	14,928	12,071	81
Aged 5 to 9	15,768	12,923	82
Aged 10 to 14	15,292	12,886	84
Aged 15 to 19	15,373	13,037	85
Aged 20 to 24	13,920	11,720	84
Aged 25 to 29	14,889	12,601	85
Aged 30 to 34	16,382	13,985	85
Aged 35 to 39	18,595	16,371	88
Aged 40 to 44	18,128	16,297	90
Aged 45 to 49	15,807	14,402	91
Aged 50 to 54	13,471	12,412	92
Aged 55 to 59	10,677	9,882	93
Aged 60 to 64	8,849	8,209	93
Aged 65 to 69	8,324	7,787	94
Aged 70 to 74	7,821	7,397	95
Aged 75 to 79	6,488	6,193	95
Aged 80 to 84	4,306	4,134	96
Aged 85 or older	3,630	3,478	96
Aged 18 to 24	20,029	16,905	84
Aged 18 or older	167,398	150,054	90
Aged 65 or older	30,569	28,988	95

* The ratio is the number of non-Hispanic whites per 100 whites.
Source: Bureau of the Census, Population Projections of the United States, by Age, Sex, Race, and Hispanic Origin: 1995 to 2050, Current Population Reports, P25-1130, 1996; calculations by New Strategist

Whites by Age and Sex, 1998

(number of whites by age and sex, and sex ratio by age, 1998; numbers in thousands)

	total	male	female	sex ratio*
Total persons	**222,648**	**109,316**	**113,332**	**96**
Under age 5	14,928	7,653	7,275	105
Aged 5 to 9	15,768	8,086	7,682	105
Aged 10 to 14	15,292	7,848	7,444	105
Aged 15 to 19	15,373	7,903	7,470	106
Aged 20 to 24	13,920	7,115	6,806	105
Aged 25 to 29	14,889	7,515	7,374	102
Aged 30 to 34	16,382	8,247	8,135	101
Aged 35 to 39	18,595	9,362	9,234	101
Aged 40 to 44	18,128	9,073	9,055	100
Aged 45 to 49	15,807	7,846	7,961	99
Aged 50 to 54	13,471	6,623	6,848	97
Aged 55 to 59	10,677	5,188	5,488	95
Aged 60 to 64	8,849	4,233	4,615	92
Aged 65 to 69	8,324	3,847	4,477	86
Aged 70 to 74	7,821	3,449	4,373	79
Aged 75 to 79	6,488	2,702	3,786	71
Aged 80 to 84	4,306	1,600	2,706	59
Aged 85 or older	3,630	1,026	2,604	39
Aged 18 to 24	20,029	10,246	9,784	105
Aged 18 or older	167,398	80,958	86,439	94
Aged 65 or older	30,569	12,624	17,945	70

* The sex ratio is the number of males per 100 females.
Source: Bureau of the Census, Population Projections of the United States, by Age, Sex, Race, and Hispanic Origin: 1995 to 2050, Current Population Reports, P25-1130, 1996; calculations by New Strategist

Non-Hispanic Whites by Age and Sex, 1998

(number of non-Hispanic whites by age and sex, and sex ratio by age, 1998; numbers in thousands)

	total	male	female	sex ratio*
Total persons	**195,786**	**95,741**	**100,045**	**96**
Under age 5	12,071	6,193	5,878	105
Aged 5 to 9	12,923	6,631	6,291	105
Aged 10 to 14	12,886	6,618	6,268	106
Aged 15 to 19	13,037	6,705	6,332	106
Aged 20 to 24	11,720	5,981	5,739	104
Aged 25 to 29	12,601	6,303	6,298	100
Aged 30 to 34	13,985	6,980	7,005	100
Aged 35 to 39	16,371	8,208	8,163	101
Aged 40 to 44	16,297	8,147	8,150	100
Aged 45 to 49	14,402	7,153	7,250	99
Aged 50 to 54	12,412	6,112	6,300	97
Aged 55 to 59	9,882	4,813	5,069	95
Aged 60 to 64	8,209	3,936	4,273	92
Aged 65 to 69	7,787	3,605	4,182	86
Aged 70 to 74	7,397	3,263	4,134	79
Aged 75 to 79	6,193	2,579	3,615	71
Aged 80 to 84	4,134	1,536	2,597	59
Aged 85 or older	3,478	978	2,500	39
Aged 18 to 24	16,905	8,638	8,267	104
Aged 18 or older	150,054	72,251	77,803	93
Aged 65 or older	28,988	11,960	17,028	70

* The sex ratio is the number of males per 100 females.
Source: Bureau of the Census, Population Projections of the United States, by Age, Sex, Race, and Hispanic Origin: *1995 to 2050,* Current Population Reports, P25-1130, 1996; calculations by New Strategist

Whites by Region and Division, 1995 to 2020

(number and percent distribution of whites and white share of the total population by region and division, selected years 1995–2020; percent change in number and percentage point change in distribution and share, 1995–2000 and 2000–2010; numbers in thousands)

	1995	2000	2010	2020	percent change 1995–2000	percent change 2000–2010
Number						
UNITED STATES	**218,034**	**225,533**	**239,588**	**254,887**	**3.4%**	**6.2%**
Northeast	**43,359**	**43,279**	**43,330**	**44,072**	**–0.2**	**0.1**
New England	12,242	12,348	12,590	12,979	0.9	2.0
Middle Atlantic	31,117	30,931	30,740	31,093	–0.6	–0.6
Midwest	**54,251**	**55,327**	**56,628**	**57,724**	**2.0**	**2.4**
East North Central	37,371	37,910	38,487	39,009	1.4	1.5
West North Central	16,880	17,418	18,142	18,715	3.2	4.2
South	**72,228**	**76,059**	**82,498**	**88,432**	**5.3**	**8.5**
South Atlantic	35,943	37,933	41,099	43,942	5.5	8.3
East South Central	12,727	13,365	14,221	14,779	5.0	6.4
West South Central	23,557	24,758	27,176	29,709	5.1	9.8
West	**48,195**	**50,868**	**57,134**	**64,662**	**5.5**	**12.3**
Mountain	14,278	16,074	18,153	19,616	12.6	12.9
Pacific	33,917	34,794	38,979	45,045	2.6	12.0

	1995	2000	2010	2020	percentage point change 1995–2000	percentage point change 2000–2010
Percent distribution						
UNITED STATES	**100.0%**	**100.0%**	**100.0%**	**100.0%**	**–**	**–**
Northeast	**19.9**	**19.2**	**18.1**	**17.3**	**–0.7%**	**–1.1%**
New England	5.6	5.5	5.3	5.1	–0.1	–0.2
Middle Atlantic	14.3	13.7	12.8	12.2	–0.6	–0.9
Midwest	**24.9**	**24.5**	**23.6**	**22.6**	**–0.4**	**–0.9**
East North Central	17.1	16.8	16.1	15.3	–0.3	–0.7
West North Central	7.7	7.7	7.6	7.3	0.0	–0.1
South	**33.1**	**33.7**	**34.4**	**34.7**	**0.6**	**0.7**
South Atlantic	16.5	16.8	17.2	17.2	0.3	0.4
East South Central	5.8	5.9	5.9	5.8	0.1	0.0
West South Central	10.8	11.0	11.3	11.7	0.2	0.3
West	**22.1**	**22.6**	**23.8**	**25.4**	**0.5**	**1.2**
Mountain	6.5	7.1	7.6	7.7	0.6	0.5
Pacific	15.6	15.4	16.3	17.7	–0.2	0.9

(continued)

(continued from previous page)

Percent share	1995	2000	2010	2020	percentage point change 1995–2000	2000–2010
UNITED STATES	**83.0%**	**82.1%**	**80.5%**	**79.0%**	**–0.9**	**–1.6**
Northeast	**84.2**	**83.1**	**80.7**	**78.6**	**–1.1**	**–2.4**
New England	92.0	90.9	88.8	86.9	–1.1	–2.1
Middle Atlantic	81.6	80.3	77.8	75.5	–1.3	–2.5
Midwest	**87.8**	**87.1**	**85.9**	**84.7**	**–0.7**	**–1.2**
East North Central	86.0	85.3	84.1	82.9	–0.7	–1.2
West North Central	92.0	91.3	90.0	88.9	–0.7	–1.3
South	**78.6**	**77.9**	**76.7**	**75.5**	**–0.7**	**–1.2**
South Atlantic	76.5	75.6	74.1	72.7	–0.9	–1.5
East South Central	79.2	79.0	78.5	77.8	–0.2	–0.5
West South Central	81.7	81.1	79.9	78.9	–0.6	–1.2
West	**83.7**	**82.8**	**81.0**	**79.4**	**–0.9**	**–1.8**
Mountain	91.3	90.7	89.8	89.0	–0.6	–0.9
Pacific	80.8	79.6	77.5	75.8	–1.2	–2.1

Note: (–) means not applicable.
Source: Bureau of the Census, Population Projecctions for States, by Age, Sex, Race, and Hispanic Origin: 1995 to 2025, *Current Population Reports, PPL-47, 1996; calculations by New Strategist*

Whites by State, 1995 to 2020

(number of whites by state, selected years 1995–2020, and percent change 1995–2000 and 2000–2010; numbers in thousands)

| | *1995* | *2000* | *2010* | *2020* | percent change | |
					1995–2000	*2000–2010*
UNITED STATES	**218,034**	**225,533**	**239,588**	**254,887**	**3.4%**	**6.2%**
Alabama	3,121	3,262	3,509	3,706	4.5	7.6
Alaska	460	486	524	550	5.7	7.8
Arizona	3,748	4,252	4,867	5,352	13.4	14.5
Arkansas	2,061	2,186	2,363	2,491	6.1	8.1
California	25,249	25,517	28,655	33,734	1.1	12.3
Colorado	3,465	3,823	4,216	4,488	10.3	10.3
Connecticut	2,902	2,873	2,893	3,004	−1.0	0.7
Delaware	570	603	626	631	5.8	3.8
District of Columbia	183	184	209	230	0.5	13.6
Florida	11,823	12,588	14,113	15,766	6.5	12.1
Georgia	5,055	5,436	5,893	6,177	7.5	8.4
Hawaii	398	423	478	538	6.3	13.0
Idaho	1,129	1,300	1,497	1,610	15.1	15.2
Illinois	9,635	9,736	9,968	10,319	1.0	2.4
Indiana	5,270	5,466	5,671	5,776	3.7	3.8
Iowa	2,745	2,786	2,825	2,850	1.5	1.4
Kansas	2,344	2,419	2,550	2,682	3.2	5.4
Kentucky	3,555	3,671	3,817	3,898	3.3	4.0
Louisiana	2,889	2,895	2,979	3,097	0.2	2.9
Maine	1,222	1,238	1,296	1,364	1.3	4.7
Maryland	3,496	3,546	3,621	3,725	1.4	2.1
Massachusetts	5,498	5,523	5,549	5,635	0.5	0.5
Michigan	7,981	8,021	8,016	8,018	0.5	−0.1
Minnesota	4,318	4,469	4,662	4,806	3.5	4.3
Mississippi	1,703	1,774	1,861	1,918	4.2	4.9
Missouri	4,659	4,825	5,061	5,248	3.6	4.9
Montana	810	879	952	992	8.5	8.3
Nebraska	1,542	1,595	1,668	1,727	3.4	4.6
Nevada	1,334	1,619	1,817	1,887	21.4	12.2
New Hampshire	1,127	1,199	1,293	1,365	6.4	7.8
New Jersey	6,402	6,442	6,512	6,701	0.6	1.1
New Mexico	1,472	1,615	1,843	2,071	9.7	14.1
New York	14,006	13,747	13,529	13,683	−1.8	−1.6
North Carolina	5,434	5,851	6,367	6,696	7.7	8.8
North Dakota	603	617	635	648	2.3	2.9
Ohio	9,766	9,835	9,842	9,824	0.7	0.1

(continued)

(continued from previous page)

	1995	2000	2010	2020	percent change 1995–2000	percent change 2000–2010
Oklahoma	2,712	2,759	2,917	3,095	1.7%	5.7%
Oregon	2,947	3,167	3,508	3,821	7.5	10.8
Pennsylvania	10,709	10,741	10,700	10,707	0.3	–0.4
Rhode Island	916	911	922	957	–0.5	1.2
South Carolina	2,533	2,660	2,898	3,100	5.0	8.9
South Dakota	668	706	739	754	5.7	4.7
Tennessee	4,347	4,658	5,036	5,257	7.2	8.1
Texas	15,894	16,920	18,917	21,026	6.5	11.8
Utah	1,859	2,087	2,390	2,587	12.3	14.5
Vermont	576	606	638	655	5.2	5.3
Virginia	5,090	5,295	5,599	5,850	4.0	5.7
Washington	4,864	5,200	5,811	6,403	6.9	11.8
West Virginia	1,759	1,769	1,772	1,765	0.6	0.2
Wisconsin	4,720	4,853	4,968	5,070	2.8	2.4
Wyoming	462	501	573	626	8.4	14.4

Note: Numbers may not add to total due to rounding.
Source: Bureau of the Census, Population Projections for States, by Age, Sex, Race, and Hispanic Origin: 1995 to 2025, PPL-47, 1996; calculations by New Strategist

Distribution of Whites by State, 1995 to 2020

(percent distribution of whites by state, selected years 1995–2020)

	1995	2000	2010	2020
United States	100.0%	100.0%	100.0%	100.0%
Alabama	1.4	1.4	1.5	1.5
Alaska	0.2	0.2	0.2	0.2
Arizona	1.7	1.9	2.0	2.1
Arkansas	0.9	1.0	1.0	1.0
California	11.6	11.3	12.0	13.2
Colorado	1.6	1.7	1.8	1.8
Connecticut	1.3	1.3	1.2	1.2
Delaware	0.3	0.3	0.3	0.2
District of Columbia	0.1	0.1	0.1	0.1
Florida	5.4	5.6	5.9	6.2
Georgia	2.3	2.4	2.5	2.4
Hawaii	0.2	0.2	0.2	0.2
Idaho	0.5	0.6	0.6	0.6
Illinois	4.4	4.3	4.2	4.0
Indiana	2.4	2.4	2.4	2.3
Iowa	1.3	1.2	1.2	1.1
Kansas	1.1	1.1	1.1	1.1
Kentucky	1.6	1.6	1.6	1.5
Louisiana	1.3	1.3	1.2	1.2
Maine	0.6	0.5	0.5%	0.5
Maryland	1.6	1.6	1.5	1.5
Massachusetts	2.5	2.4	2.3	2.2
Michigan	3.7	3.6	3.3	3.1
Minnesota	2.0	2.0	1.9	1.9
Mississippi	0.8	0.8	0.8	0.8
Missouri	2.1	2.1	2.1	2.1
Montana	0.4	0.4	0.4	0.4
Nebraska	0.7	0.7	0.7	0.7
Nevada	0.6	0.7	0.8	0.7
New Hampshire	0.5	0.5	0.5	0.5
New Jersey	2.9	2.9	2.7	2.6
New Mexico	0.7	0.7	0.8	0.8
New York	6.4	6.1	5.6	5.4
North Carolina	2.5	2.6	2.7	2.6
North Dakota	0.3	0.3	0.3	0.3
Ohio	4.5	4.4	4.1	3.9

(continued)

(continued from previous page)

	1995	*2000*	*2010*	*2020*
Oklahoma	1.2%	1.2%	1.2%	1.2%
Oregon	1.4	1.4	1.5	1.5
Pennsylvania	4.9	4.8	4.5	4.2
Rhode Island	0.4	0.4	0.4	0.4
South Carolina	1.2	1.2	1.2	1.2
South Dakota	0.3	0.3	0.3	0.3
Tennessee	2.0	2.1	2.1	2.1
Texas	7.3	7.5	7.9	8.2
Utah	0.9	0.9	1.0	1.0
Vermont	0.3	0.3	0.3	0.3
Virginia	2.3	2.3	2.3	2.3
Washington	2.2	2.3	2.4	2.5
West Virginia	0.8	0.8	0.7	0.7
Wisconsin	2.2	2.2	2.1	2.0
Wyoming	0.2	0.2	0.2	0.2

Source: Calculations by New Strategist based on Census Bureau data in Population Projections for States, by Age, Sex, Race, and Hispanic Origin: 1995 to 2025, *PPL-47, 1996*

White Share of State Populations, 1995 to 2020

(whites as a percent of state populations, selected years 1995–2020; percentage point change 1995–2020)

	1995	2000	2010	2020	percentage point change 1995–2020
United States	**83.0%**	**82.1%**	**80.5%**	**79.0%**	**–4.0**
Alabama	73.4	73.3	73.1	72.7	–0.7
Alaska	76.2	74.4	70.3	65.6	–10.5
Arizona	88.9	88.6	88.1	87.6	–1.3
Arkansas	83.0	83.1	83.2	83.1	0.1
California	79.9	78.5	76.1	74.5	–5.4
Colorado	92.5	91.7	90.5	89.5	–2.9
Connecticut	88.6	87.5	85.1	83.0	–5.7
Delaware	79.5	78.5	76.6	74.5	–5.0
District of Columbia	33.0	35.2	37.3	36.8	3.8
Florida	83.5	82.6	81.3	80.3	–3.2
Georgia	70.2	69.0	66.8	64.7	–5.5
Hawaii	33.5	33.7	33.2	32.1	–1.4
Idaho	97.1	96.5	96.1	95.7	–1.4
Illinois	81.4	80.8	79.6	78.6	–2.8
Indiana	90.8	90.4	89.8	89.1	–1.7
Iowa	96.6	96.1	95.2	94.4	–2.2
Kansas	91.4	90.7	89.5	88.6	–2.8
Kentucky	92.1	91.9	91.5	91.1	–1.0
Louisiana	66.5	65.4	63.6	62.1	–4.5
Maine	98.5	98.3	98.0	97.7	–0.8
Maryland	69.3	67.2	64.0	61.4	–8.0
Massachusetts	90.5	89.1	86.3	83.7	–6.8
Michigan	83.6	82.9	81.5	80.2	–3.4
Minnesota	93.7	92.5	90.6	88.9	–4.8
Mississippi	63.1	63.0	62.6	62.0	–1.1
Missouri	87.5	87.1	86.3	85.5	–2.0
Montana	93.1	92.5	91.5	90.4	–2.7
Nebraska	94.2	93.5	92.4	91.3	–2.9
Nevada	87.2	86.5	85.3	84.2	–3.0
New Hampshire	98.2	98.0	97.3	96.8	–1.4
New Jersey	80.6	78.8	75.4	72.5	–8.0
New Mexico	87.4	86.8	85.5	84.4	–3.0
New York	77.2	75.8	73.0	70.7	–6.5
North Carolina	75.5	75.2	74.5	73.5	–2.0
North Dakota	94.1	93.2	92.0	90.4	–3.7
Ohio	87.6	86.9	85.5	84.2	–3.4

(continued)

(continued from previous page)

	1995	2000	2010	2020	percentage point change 1995–2020
Oklahoma	82.7%	81.8%	80.2%	78.8%	−4.0
Oregon	93.8	93.2	92.2	91.5	−2.3
Pennsylvania	88.7	88.0	86.6	85.2	−3.5
Rhode Island	92.5	91.3	88.8	86.6	−5.9
South Carolina	69.0	68.9	68.9	68.6	−0.3
South Dakota	91.6	90.9	89.5	88.4	−3.2
Tennessee	82.7	82.3	81.5	80.5	−2.2
Texas	84.9	84.1	82.8	81.7	−3.2
Utah	95.3	94.6	93.7	93.0	−2.3
Vermont	98.5	98.2	98.0	97.6	−0.8
Virginia	76.9	75.7	73.4	71.3	−5.6
Washington	89.6	88.8	87.3	86.0	3.6
West Virginia	96.2	96.1	95.7	95.4	−0.8
Wisconsin	92.1	91.1	88.9	87.6	−4.5
Wyoming	96.3	95.4	94.4	93.4	−2.8

Source: Calculations by New Strategist based on Census Bureau data in Population Projections for States, by Age, Sex, Race, and Hispanic Origin: 1995 to 2025, *PPL–47, 1996*

Whites: Spending

The spending of whites is close to the average on most items.

The nation's 85 million white consumer units spent an average of $33,878 in 1995, according to the Consumer Expenditure Survey—5 percent more than the average consumer unit. The income of white consumer units is 6 percent above average.

There are a few items on which whites spend significantly less than the average consumer unit. These include lamb and organ meats; sugar; fats and oils; rented dwellings; infants' equipment; coin-operated laundries; and intracity mass transit fares.

Whites spend significantly more than the average consumer unit on items such as alcoholic beverages consumed away from home; owned dwellings; lodging while on out-of-town trips; housekeeping services; new trucks; airline and ship fares; fees and admissions to entertainment events; pets; and reading material.

■ White spending is higher on many items typically purchased by more affluent and better-educated consumers. As blacks and Hispanics gain in education and income, their spending will more closely match that of whites.

Whites spend 5 percent more than the average consumer unit

(average annual spending of consumer units by race and Hispanic origin of householder, 1995)

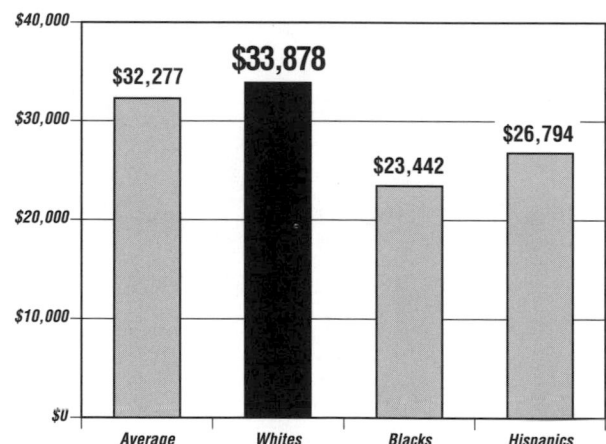

Average and Indexed Spending of White Households, 1995

(average annual expenditures of total and white consumer units, and indexed expenditures of white consumer units, 1995)

	average spending of total consumer units	white consumer units	
		average spending	indexed spending*
Number of consumer units	103,024,000	84,772,000	–
Average before-tax income of consumer unit	$36,948.00	$39,226.00	106
Average spending of consumer unit, total	32,276.59	33,878.41	105
FOOD	**$4,505.34**	**$4,638.50**	**103**
FOOD AT HOME	2,802.91	2,802.62	100
Cereals and bakery products	**441.13**	**450.19**	**102**
Cereals and cereal products	165.23	162.48	98
Flour	8.42	7.31	87
Prepared flour mixes	12.80	13.22	103
Ready-to-eat and cooked cereal	97.00	97.68	101
Rice	20.17	17.14	85
Pasta, cornmeal, and other cereal products	26.84	27.12	101
Bakery products	275.90	287.71	104
Bread	75.70	76.46	101
White bread	36.77	36.09	98
Bread, other than white	38.92	40.37	104
Cookies and crackers	67.33	70.62	105
Cookies	44.90	46.21	103
Crackers	22.43	24.41	109
Frozen and refrigerated bakery products	21.92	22.92	105
Other bakery products	110.95	117.70	106
Biscuits and rolls	38.49	42.12	109
Cakes and cupcakes	34.63	35.89	104
Bread and cracker products	4.23	4.61	109
Sweetrolls, coffee cakes, doughnuts	20.80	21.64	104
Pies, tarts, turnovers	12.80	13.46	105
Meats, poultry, fish, and eggs	**752.43**	**707.85**	**94**
Beef	227.60	219.90	97
Ground beef	84.47	81.62	97
Roast	40.09	39.80	99
Chuck roast	12.63	12.40	98
Round roast	13.18	13.57	103
Other roast	14.28	13.82	97
Steak	86.84	82.79	95
Round steak	18.82	17.76	94

(continued)

	average spending of total consumer units	white consumer units	
		average spending	indexed spending*
Sirloin steak	$23.42	$22.62	97
Other steak	44.61	42.41	95
Other beef	16.19	15.69	97
Pork	156.00	141.43	91
Bacon	20.32	17.75	87
Pork chops	39.69	35.77	90
Ham	37.06	35.15	95
Ham, not canned	34.76	32.89	95
Canned ham	2.31	2.26	98
Sausage	22.12	19.81	90
Other pork	36.79	32.96	90
Other meats	103.63	102.14	99
Frankfurters	22.13	21.41	97
Lunch meats (cold cuts)	69.66	70.75	102
Bologna, liverwurst, salami	25.45	24.53	96
Other lunchmeats	44.22	46.22	105
Lamb, organ meats, and others	11.84	9.98	84
Lamb and organ meats	9.31	7.97	86
Mutton, goat and game	2.54	2.00	79
Poultry	137.65	127.78	93
Fresh and frozen chickens	105.14	97.64	93
Fresh and frozen whole chicken	28.21	24.88	88
Fresh and frozen chicken parts	76.93	72.76	95
Other poultry	32.51	30.14	93
Fish and seafood	97.33	90.02	92
Canned fish and seafood	17.11	18.01	105
Fresh fish and shellfish	52.43	46.67	89
Frozen fish and shellfish	27.79	25.34	91
Eggs	30.23	26.58	88
Dairy products	**296.61**	**304.10**	**103**
Fresh milk and cream	123.00	122.22	99
Fresh milk, all types	113.81	112.77	99
Cream	9.19	9.45	103
Other dairy products	173.60	181.88	105
Butter	12.31	12.52	102
Cheese	88.00	92.67	105
Ice cream and related products	51.24	53.58	105
Miscellaneous dairy products	22.05	23.12	105
Fruits and vegetables	**456.67**	**453.39**	**99**
Fresh fruits	144.14	142.50	99
Apples	29.15	29.06	100
Bananas	30.26	29.43	97

(continued)

(continued from previous page)

	average spending of total consumer units	white consumer units	
		average spending	indexed spending*
Oranges	$16.27	$15.05	93
Citrus fruits, excl. oranges	12.03	11.78	98
Other fresh fruits	56.43	57.17	101
Fresh vegetables	137.31	136.52	99
Potatoes	28.50	28.95	102
Lettuce	18.22	18.47	101
Tomatoes	21.64	20.10	93
Other fresh vegetables	68.95	68.99	100
Processed fruits	95.70	94.36	99
Frozen fruits and fruit juices	17.00	17.47	103
Frozen orange juice	8.66	9.09	105
Frozen fruits	1.81	1.96	108
Frozen fruit juices	6.53	6.42	98
Canned fruits	13.88	14.67	106
Dried fruits	5.86	6.25	107
Fresh fruit juice	17.55	16.55	94
Canned and bottled fruit juice	41.40	39.42	95
Processed vegetables	79.52	80.01	101
Frozen vegetables	28.07	29.55	105
Canned and dried vegetables and juices	51.44	50.46	98
Canned beans	11.26	11.32	101
Canned corn	6.91	6.51	94
Frozen vegetable juices	0.31	0.28	90
Fresh and canned vegetable juices	6.87	6.71	98
Other food at home	**856.08**	**887.10**	**104**
Sugar and other sweets	112.08	116.59	104
Candy and chewing gum	67.43	72.81	108
Sugar	17.44	15.23	87
Artificial sweeteners	4.51	4.46	99
Jams, preserves, other sweets	22.70	24.09	106
Fats and oils	82.22	80.35	98
Margarine	12.74	13.03	102
Fats and oils	24.60	21.20	86
Salad dressings	26.16	26.09	100
Nondairy cream and imitation milk	7.15	7.91	111
Peanut butter	11.58	12.12	105
Miscellaneous foods	376.59	392.94	104
Frozen prepared foods	66.03	70.79	107
Frozen meals	19.87	21.22	107
Other frozen prepared foods	46.16	49.57	107
Canned and packaged soups	31.25	32.36	104
Potato chips, nuts, and other snacks	80.50	85.69	106

(continued)

(continued from previous page)

	average spending of total consumer units	white consumer units	
		average spending	indexed spending*
Potato chips and other snacks	$62.33	$65.93	106
Nuts	18.17	19.76	109
Condiments and seasonings	86.51	90.64	105
Salt, spices, and other seasonings	20.29	19.70	97
Olives, pickles, relishes	10.14	10.87	107
Sauces and gravies	39.88	42.19	106
Baking needs and miscellaneous products	16.20	17.87	110
Other canned/packaged prepared foods	112.30	113.46	101
Prepared salads	13.51	14.73	109
Prepared desserts	8.99	9.68	108
Baby food	25.02	22.77	91
Misc. prepared foods	64.79	66.27	102
Nonalcoholic beverages	240.27	246.73	103
Cola	89.20	91.09	102
Other carbonated drinks	42.50	44.21	104
Coffee	46.33	49.26	106
Roasted coffee	30.90	33.64	109
Instant and freeze-dried coffee	15.43	15.62	101
Noncarbonated fruit-flavored drinks, including nonfrozen lemonade	24.83	23.73	96
Tea	15.64	16.53	106
Nonalcoholic beer	1.01	0.97	96
Other nonalcoholic beverages and ice	20.75	20.94	101
Food prepared by consumer unit on out-of-town trips	44.91	50.49	112
FOOD AWAY FROM HOME	**1,702.43**	**1,835.88**	**108**
Meals at restaurants, carry-outs, other	**1,331.44**	**1,426.99**	**107**
Lunch	464.83	490.20	105
Dinner	653.29	707.35	108
Snacks and nonalcoholic beverages	111.73	123.48	111
Breakfast and brunch	101.59	105.96	104
Board (including at school)	**54.60**	**62.16**	**114**
Catered affairs	**43.89**	**48.42**	**110**
Food on out-of-town trips	**196.85**	**221.90**	**113**
School lunches	**49.41**	**51.42**	**104**
Meals as pay	**26.23**	**24.98**	**95**
ALCOHOLIC BEVERAGES	**$277.28**	**$303.06**	**109**
At home	**165.34**	**174.73**	**106**
Beer and ale	87.91	88.90	101
Whiskey	13.37	14.69	110
Wine	48.68	54.88	113
Other alcoholic beverages	15.39	16.26	106

(continued)

(continued from previous page)

	average spending of total consumer units	white consumer units	
		average spending	indexed spending*
Away from home	$111.94	$128.33	115
Beer and ale	33.45	38.42	115
Wine	20.29	23.34	115
Other alcoholic beverages	29.77	34.17	115
Alcoholic beverages purchased on trips	28.43	32.40	114
HOUSING	**$10,464.95**	**$10,894.16**	**104**
SHELTER	**5,931.76**	**6,160.78**	**104**
Owned dwellings**	**3,754.44**	**4,126.12**	**110**
Mortgage interest and charges	2,106.99	2,300.49	109
Mortgage interest	1,991.49	2,168.89	109
Interest paid, home equity loan	53.32	58.65	110
Interest paid, home equity line of credit	61.81	72.49	117
Prepayment penalty charges	0.37	0.46	124
Property taxes	931.76	1,037.60	111
Maintenance, repairs, insurance, other expenses	715.68	788.04	110
Homeowner's and related insurance	225.32	245.21	109
Fire and extended coverage	6.69	7.03	105
Homeowner's insurance	218.63	238.18	109
Ground rent	31.63	34.80	110
Maintenance and repair services	365.24	402.42	110
Painting and papering	41.18	47.14	114
Plumbing and water heating	33.28	37.29	112
Heat, air conditioning, electrical work	72.49	81.86	113
Roofing and gutters	65.15	66.32	102
Other repair and maintenance services	130.33	143.58	110
Repair and replacement of hard-surface flooring	21.23	24.48	115
Repair of built-in appliances	1.59	1.76	111
Maintenance and repair materials	71.32	79.48	111
Paints, wallpaper, and supplies	19.60	22.07	113
Tools and equipment for painting, wallpapering	2.11	2.37	112
Plumbing supplies and equipment	7.26	8.41	116
Electrical supplies, heating and cooling equipment	5.22	6.14	118
Hard-surface flooring, repair and replacement	3.51	3.46	99
Roofing and gutters	4.30	4.59	107
Plaster, paneling, siding, windows, doors, screens, awnings	11.53	13.09	114
Patio, walk, fence, driveway, masonry, brick, and stucco work	0.88	1.04	118
Landscape maintenance	1.78	1.90	107
Miscellaneous supplies and equipment	15.13	16.40	108
Insulation, other maintenance and repair	11.41	12.70	111

(continued)

(continued from previous page)

	average spending of total consumer units	white consumer units	
		average spending	indexed spending*
Finish basement, remodel rooms, or build patios, walks, etc.	$3.72	$3.70	99
Property management and security	22.17	26.12	118
Property management	16.64	19.65	118
Management and upkeep services for security	5.53	6.47	117
Rented dwellings	**1,785.64**	**1,587.56**	**89**
Rent	1,716.25	1,522.77	89
Rent as pay	48.68	43.62	90
Maintenance, insurance, and other expenses	20.71	21.17	102
Tenant's insurance	7.35	7.64	104
Maintenance and repair services	5.32	5.00	94
Repair or maintenance services	4.93	4.87	99
Repair and replacement of hard-surface flooring	0.32	0.04	13
Repair of built-in appliances	0.07	0.09	129
Maintenance and repair materials	8.04	8.52	106
Paint, wallpaper, and supplies	1.48	1.38	93
Painting and wallpapering	0.16	0.15	94
Plastering, panels, roofing, gutters, etc.	0.71	0.69	97
Patio, walk, fence, driveway, masonry, brick, and stucco work	0.03	0.04	133
Plumbing supplies and equipment	1.14	1.30	114
Electrical supplies, heating and cooling equipment	0.31	0.34	110
Miscellaneous supplies and equipment	3.53	3.96	112
Insulation, other maintenance and repair	1.43	1.46	102
Materials for additions, finishing basements, remodeling rooms	2.07	2.48	120
Construction materials for jobs not started	0.04	0.02	50
Hard surface flooring	0.22	0.90	409
Landscape maintenance	0.46	0.56	122
Other lodging	**391.68**	**447.10**	**114**
Owned vacation homes	127.18	146.11	115
Mortgage interest and charges	48.74	54.06	111
Mortgage interest	47.03	52.12	111
Interest paid, home equity loan	0.12	–	–
Interest paid, home equity line of credit	1.59	1.93	121
Property taxes	54.14	63.05	116
Maintenance, insurance, and other expenses	24.29	29.00	119
Homeowner's and related insurance	6.10	7.03	115
Homeowner's insurance	5.90	6.78	115
Fire and extended coverage	0.20	0.25	125

(continued)

(continued from previous page)

	average spending of total consumer units	white consumer units	
		average spending	indexed spending*
Ground rent	$2.33	$2.83	121
Maintenance and repair services	10.56	12.77	121
Maintenance and repair materials	2.00	2.43	122
Property management and security	2.64	3.12	118
Property management	1.88	2.22	118
Management and upkeep services for security	0.75	0.91	121
Parking	0.67	0.81	121
Housing while attending school	54.91	64.28	117
Lodging on out-of-town trips	209.59	236.71	113
UTILITIES, FUELS, PUBLIC SERVICES	**2,192.58**	**2,212.02**	**101**
Natural gas	**268.26**	**265.70**	**99**
Electricity	**869.67**	**888.62**	**102**
Fuel oil and other fuels	**86.66**	**98.41**	**114**
Fuel oil	50.69	57.69	114
Coal	2.13	2.55	120
Bottled and tank gas	28.02	31.86	114
Wood and other fuels	5.83	6.32	108
Telephone services	**708.40**	**692.63**	**98**
Telephone services in home city, excluding mobile car phones	682.65	665.40	97
Telephone services for mobile car phones	25.75	27.23	106
Water and other public services	**259.59**	**266.67**	**103**
Water and sewerage maintenance	187.25	190.62	102
Trash and garbage collection	**70.49**	**74.01**	**105**
Septic tank cleaning	**1.84**	**2.04**	**111**
HOUSEHOLD SERVICES	**508.34**	**551.93**	**109**
Personal services	**258.04**	**268.75**	**104**
Babysitting and child care in your own home	39.63	41.38	104
Babysitting and child care in someone else's home	36.48	33.34	91
Care for elderly, invalids, handicapped, etc.	35.33	41.33	117
Adult day care centers	1.05	1.28	122
Day care centers, nurseries, and preschools	145.55	151.42	104
Other household services	**250.30**	**283.18**	**113**
Housekeeping services	85.16	99.85	117
Gardening, lawn care service	63.96	71.93	112
Water softening service	2.90	3.20	110
Nonclothing laundry and dry cleaning, sent out	1.69	1.84	109
Nonclothing laundry and dry cleaning, coin-operated	4.83	3.81	79
Termite and other pest control services	11.70	13.33	114

(continued)

(continued from previous page)

	average spending of total consumer units	white consumer units	
		average spending	indexed spending*
Other home services	$16.60	$18.36	111
Termite and other pest control products	0.16	0.18	113
Moving, storage, and freight express	27.71	31.20	113
Appliance repair, including service center	14.07	15.27	109
Reupholstering and furniture repair	10.80	12.42	115
Repairs and rental of equipment and power tools	5.79	6.65	115
Appliance rental	1.67	1.43	86
Rental of office equipment for nonbusiness use	0.29	0.23	79
Repair of miscellaneous household equip. and furnishings	1.75	2.15	123
Repair of computer systems for nonbusiness use	0.82	0.97	118
Computer information services	0.39	0.35	90
HOUSEKEEPING SUPPLIES	**429.59**	**458.87**	**107**
Laundry and cleaning supplies	**110.26**	**106.99**	**97**
Soaps and detergents	63.62	60.39	95
Other laundry cleaning products	46.64	46.59	100
Other household products	**193.90**	**210.45**	**109**
Cleansing and toilet tissue, paper towels, and napkins	60.03	60.61	101
Miscellaneous household products	71.57	78.97	110
Lawn and garden supplies	62.29	70.86	114
Postage and stationery	**125.43**	**141.43**	**113**
Stationery, stationery supplies, giftwrap	61.49	69.41	113
Postage	62.40	70.23	113
Delivery services	1.54	1.79	116
HOUSEHOLD FURNISHINGS & EQUIPMENT	**1,402.69**	**1,510.56**	**108**
Household textiles	**100.47**	**111.35**	**111**
Bathroom linens	15.50	16.80	108
Bedroom linens	45.50	50.65	111
Kitchen and dining room linens	9.26	9.98	108
Curtains and draperies	17.36	19.37	112
Slipcovers and decorative pillows	1.74	2.03	117
Sewing materials for household items	10.01	11.32	113
Other linens	1.09	1.21	111
Furniture	**327.49**	**330.76**	**101**
Mattresses and springs	41.36	40.82	99
Other bedroom furniture	51.66	48.47	94
Sofas	77.20	77.54	100
Living room chairs	39.35	41.99	107
Living room tables	16.51	16.78	102
Kitchen and dining room furniture	46.95	48.66	104
Infants' furniture	6.74	6.40	95

(continued)

(continued from previous page)

	average spending of total consumer units	white consumer units	
		average spending	indexed spending*
Outdoor furniture	$10.77	$11.75	109
Wall units, cabinets, and other furniture	36.95	38.36	104
Floor coverings	**177.25**	**201.24**	**114**
Major appliances	**154.88**	**156.57**	**101**
Dishwashers (built-in), garbage disposals, range hoods (renter)	0.95	0.91	96
Dishwashers (built-in), garbage disposals, range hoods (owner)	10.23	11.31	111
Refrigerators and freezers (renter)	6.69	5.90	88
Refrigerators and freezers (owner)	42.27	43.13	102
Washing machines (renter)	5.26	4.49	85
Washing machines (owner)	14.58	15.38	105
Clothes dryers (renter)	3.25	2.92	90
Clothes dryers (owner)	10.62	11.35	107
Cooking stoves, ovens (renter)	2.57	2.14	83
Cooking stoves, ovens (owner)	18.72	18.32	98
Microwave ovens (renter)	2.87	2.04	71
Microwave ovens (owner)	6.01	6.56	109
Portable dishwasher (renter)	0.17	0.20	118
Portable dishwasher (owner)	0.52	0.57	110
Window air conditioners (renter)	2.75	2.35	85
Window air conditioners (owner)	8.64	8.37	97
Electric floor-cleaning equipment	12.94	14.30	111
Sewing machines	4.81	5.37	112
Miscellaneous household appliances	1.03	0.96	93
Small appliances and miscellaneous housewares	**85.16**	**94.22**	**111**
Housewares	62.80	70.39	112
Plastic dinnerware	1.48	1.61	109
China and other dinnerware	11.29	12.57	111
Flatware	4.01	4.48	112
Glassware	6.91	7.97	115
Silver serving pieces	2.03	2.35	116
Other serving pieces	1.28	1.38	108
Nonelectric cookware	16.04	17.58	110
Tableware, nonelectric kitchenware	19.77	22.46	114
Small appliances	22.36	23.83	107
Small electric kitchen appliances	15.65	16.97	108
Portable heating and cooling equipment	6.70	6.86	102
Miscellaneous household equipment	**557.43**	**616.43**	**111**
Window coverings	10.64	11.88	112
Infants' equipment	8.02	5.88	73

(continued)

(continued from previous page)

	average spending of total consumer units	white consumer units	
		average spending	*indexed spending**
Laundry and cleaning equipment	$11.33	$11.16	98
Outdoor equipment	4.08	4.76	117
Clocks	3.37	3.78	112
Lamps and lighting fixtures	29.77	31.91	107
Other household decorative items	137.82	154.02	112
Telephones and accessories	14.44	14.40	100
Lawn and garden equipment	42.14	47.38	112
Power tools	15.61	17.98	115
Small miscellaneous furnishings	2.02	1.05	52
Hand tools	10.16	9.44	93
Indoor plants and fresh flowers	46.82	53.56	114
Closet and storage items	6.93	7.70	111
Rental of furniture	3.24	2.65	82
Luggage	9.25	9.89	107
Computers and computer hardware, nonbusiness use	135.02	154.38	114
Computer software and accessories, nonbusiness use	18.23	20.30	111
Telephone answering devices	3.58	3.92	109
Calculators	1.88	1.96	104
Business equipment for home use	4.11	4.37	106
Other hardware	13.63	15.81	116
Smoke alarms (owner)	1.21	1.28	106
Smoke alarms (renter)	0.17	0.18	106
Other household appliances (owner)	4.71	4.77	101
Other household appliances (renter)	1.04	0.99	95
Miscellaneous household equipment and parts	18.22	21.02	115
APPAREL AND SERVICES	**$1,703.63**	**$1,682.25**	**99**
MEN AND BOYS	**425.33**	**432.22**	**102**
Men, aged 16 or older	**329.46**	**344.70**	**105**
Suits	33.42	34.51	103
Sportcoats and tailored jackets	13.23	14.22	107
Coats and jackets	30.16	32.67	108
Underwear	17.80	18.00	101
Hosiery	12.85	13.88	108
Sleepwear	3.50	3.44	98
Accessories	34.98	36.70	105
Sweaters and vests	12.43	13.20	106
Active sportswear	10.14	11.23	111
Shirts	76.52	80.88	106
Pants	63.37	63.14	100
Shorts and shorts sets	16.23	18.05	111

(continued)

(continued from previous page)

	average spending of total consumer units	white consumer units	
		average spending	indexed spending*
Uniforms	$3.67	$3.48	95
Costumes	1.17	1.30	111
Boys, aged 2 to 15	**95.86**	**87.52**	**91**
Coats and jackets	9.27	9.89	107
Sweaters	1.92	1.78	93
Shirts	20.82	19.20	92
Underwear	5.76	5.84	101
Sleepwear	1.12	1.11	99
Hosiery	4.01	4.26	106
Accessories	6.66	6.40	96
Suits, sportcoats, and vests	3.59	4.14	115
Pants	24.03	20.36	85
Shorts and shorts sets	11.44	7.89	69
Uniforms	4.06	4.09	101
Costumes	0.93	0.91	98
WOMEN AND GIRLS	**660.49**	**670.11**	**101**
Women, aged 16 or older	**559.19**	**571.28**	**102**
Coats and jackets	41.43	41.51	100
Dresses	83.48	83.69	100
Sportcoats and tailored jackets	4.29	4.96	116
Sweaters and vests	28.51	31.63	111
Shirts, blouses, and tops	100.86	106.98	106
Skirts	20.49	21.57	105
Pants	70.73	66.74	94
Shorts and shorts sets	26.72	28.00	105
Active sportswear	27.19	30.43	112
Sleepwear	23.65	25.12	106
Undergarments	30.37	28.95	95
Hosiery	20.88	20.21	97
Suits	32.66	33.52	103
Accessories	43.56	43.52	100
Uniforms	2.42	2.50	103
Costumes	1.93	1.95	101
Girls, aged 2 to 15	**101.30**	**98.83**	**98**
Coats and jackets	6.86	6.41	93
Dresses and suits	13.17	11.91	90
Shirts, blouses, and sweaters	20.67	21.39	103
Skirts and pants	18.18	16.55	91
Shorts and shorts sets	9.89	9.51	96
Active sportswear	11.39	12.97	114
Underwear and sleepwear	7.47	7.08	95

(continued)

(continued from previous page)

	average spending of total consumer units	white consumer units	
		average spending	indexed spending*
Hosiery	$4.78	$4.33	91
Accessories	4.51	4.50	100
Uniforms	1.92	1.75	91
Costumes	2.47	2.42	98
Children under age 2	**80.61**	**72.18**	**90**
Coats, jackets, and snowsuits	3.10	2.81	91
Outerwear including dresses	22.66	21.73	96
Underwear	46.09	39.37	85
Sleepwear and loungewear	3.76	3.57	95
Accessories	4.99	4.71	94
FOOTWEAR	**278.36**	**251.51**	**90**
Men's	94.82	92.24	97
Boys'	30.48	27.54	90
Women's	117.81	105.71	90
Girls'	35.24	26.02	74
OTHER APPAREL PRODUCTS, SERVICES	**258.84**	**256.23**	**99**
Material for making clothes	4.95	5.21	105
Sewing patterns and notions	1.92	2.13	111
Watches	19.16	18.32	96
Jewelry	104.17	111.31	107
Shoe repair and other shoe services	2.66	2.93	110
Coin-operated apparel laundry and dry cleaning	39.46	29.03	74
Apparel alteration, repair, and tailoring services	5.82	6.31	108
Clothing rental	3.48	3.54	102
Watch and jewelry repair	5.07	5.68	112
Professional laundry, dry cleaning	71.68	71.24	99
Clothing storage	0.47	0.53	113
TRANSPORTATION	**$6,015.97**	**$6,281.72**	**104**
VEHICLE PURCHASES	**2,639.33**	**2,714.51**	**103**
Cars and trucks, new	**1,194.00**	**1,248.98**	**105**
New cars	670.88	669.37	100
New trucks	523.11	579.62	111
Cars and trucks, used	**1,410.96**	**1,429.24**	**101**
Used cars	916.45	932.25	102
Used trucks	494.51	496.99	101
Other vehicles	**34.38**	**36.30**	**106**
GASOLINE AND MOTOR OIL	**1,006.05**	**1,053.13**	**105**
Gasoline	901.97	938.72	104
Diesel fuel	10.15	10.65	105

(continued)

(continued from previous page)

	average spending of total consumer units	white consumer units	
		average spending	indexed spending*
Gasoline on out-of-town trips	$81.98	$91.35	111
Motor oil	11.13	11.50	103
Motor oil on out-of-town trips	0.83	0.92	111
OTHER VEHICLE EXPENSES	**2,015.78**	**2,141.34**	**106**
Vehicle finance charges	**260.57**	**269.84**	**104**
Automobile finance charges	148.57	147.60	99
Truck finance charges	99.53	108.69	109
Motorcycle and plane finance charges	1.26	1.44	114
Other vehicle finance charges	11.22	12.11	108
Maintenance and repairs	**652.77**	**688.54**	**105**
Coolant, additives, brake, and transmission fluids	5.63	5.85	104
Tires	87.06	93.22	107
Parts, equipment, and accessories	60.29	65.59	109
Vehicle audio equipment	10.31	12.67	123
Vehicle products	3.37	3.65	108
Miscellaneous auto repair, servicing	33.68	38.28	114
Body work and painting	29.52	29.26	99
Clutch, transmission repair	45.69	47.06	103
Drive shaft and rear-end repair	6.14	5.63	92
Brake work	39.22	40.88	104
Repair to steering or front-end	20.68	21.13	102
Repair to engine cooling system	23.28	24.46	105
Motor tune-up	42.61	44.97	106
Lube, oil change, and oil filters	42.90	46.45	108
Front-end alignment, wheel balance, rotation	11.11	11.92	107
Shock absorber replacement	7.35	7.70	105
Brake adjustment	3.18	3.26	103
Gas tank repair, replacement	1.54	1.76	114
Tire repair and other repair work	33.28	33.97	102
Vehicle air conditioning repair	14.28	14.78	104
Exhaust system repair	20.87	22.24	107
Electrical system repair	29.58	31.44	106
Motor repair, replacement	67.64	68.16	101
Auto repair service policy	5.94	6.29	106
Vehicle insurance	**712.81**	**756.52**	**106**
Vehicle rental, leases, licenses, other charges	**389.63**	**426.44**	**109**
Leased and rented vehicles	235.64	262.05	111
Rented vehicles	37.70	41.18	109
Auto rental	7.09	6.89	97
Auto rental, out-of-town trips	25.95	29.11	112

(continued)

(continued from previous page)

	average spending of total consumer units	white consumer units	
		average spending	*indexed spending**
Truck rental	$1.19	$1.38	116
Truck rental, out-of-town trips	3.26	3.54	109
Leased vehicles	197.94	220.87	112
Car lease payments	128.53	144.50	112
Cash down payment (car lease)	13.44	15.95	119
Termination fee (car lease)	0.41	0.50	122
Truck lease payments	52.98	57.43	108
Cash down payment (truck lease)	2.33	2.48	106
Termination fee (truck lease)	0.26	0.02	8
State and local registration	84.53	90.69	107
Driver's license	6.92	7.37	107
Vehicle inspection	8.76	8.89	101
Parking fees	25.38	26.69	105
Parking fees in home city, excluding residence	21.97	22.92	104
Parking fees, out-of-town trips	3.41	3.77	111
Tolls	11.19	12.04	108
Tolls on out-of-town trips	4.53	4.99	110
Towing charges	4.86	4.88	100
Automobile service club fees	7.83	8.83	113
PUBLIC TRANSPORTATION	**354.81**	**372.73**	**105**
Airline fares	225.58	247.99	110
Intercity bus fares	14.09	15.26	108
Intracity mass transit fares	48.51	35.84	74
Local transportation on out-of-town trips	8.46	9.34	110
Taxi fares on trips	4.97	5.48	110
Taxi fares	6.95	6.07	87
Intercity train fares	18.41	20.63	112
Ship fares	27.31	31.66	116
School bus	0.53	0.45	85
HEALTH CARE	**$1,732.33**	**$1,878.38**	**108**
Health insurance	**860.45**	**931.60**	**108**
Commercial health insurance	241.22	263.10	109
Blue Cross, Blue Shield	171.78	188.37	110
Health maintenance plans (HMOs)	146.87	151.62	103
Medicare payments	172.13	186.05	108
Commercial Medicare supplements and other health insurance	128.44	142.46	111
Medical services	**511.47**	**557.42**	**109**
Physician's services	146.97	160.18	109
Dental services	186.29	207.67	111

(continued)

(continued from previous page)

	average spending of total consumer units	white consumer units	
		average spending	indexed spending [*]
Eye care services	$28.83	$31.52	109
Service by professionals other than physicians	38.24	43.74	114
Lab tests, X-rays	21.92	23.43	107
Hospital room	33.04	36.07	109
Hospital services other than room	37.16	34.00	91
Care in convalescent or nursing home	7.90	8.88	112
Repair of medical equipment	1.11	1.36	123
Other medical services	10.01	10.55	105
Drugs	**279.96**	**301.18**	**108**
Nonprescription drugs	79.03	83.45	106
Prescription drugs	200.94	217.73	108
Medical supplies	**80.45**	**88.18**	**110**
Eyeglasses and contact lenses	52.06	56.92	109
Topicals and dressings	20.73	22.65	109
Medical equipment for general use	2.53	2.80	111
Supportive and convalescent medical equipment	3.83	4.38	114
Rental of medical equipment	0.34	0.41	121
Rental of supportive, convalescent medical equipment	0.96	1.02	106
ENTERTAINMENT	**$1,612.09**	**$1,747.29**	**108**
FEES AND ADMISSIONS	**432.91**	**486.54**	**112**
Recreation expenses, out-of-town trips	21.21	23.52	111
Social, recreation, civic club membership fees	80.67	92.44	115
Fees for participant sports	66.55	76.24	115
Participant sports, out-of-town trips	29.25	34.33	117
Movie, theater, opera, ballet admissions	73.42	78.11	106
Movie, other admissions, out-of-town trips	40.50	45.30	112
Admissions to sporting events	28.71	32.46	113
Admissions to sports events, out-of-town trips	13.50	15.10	112
Fees for recreational lessons	57.91	65.52	113
Other entertainment services, out-of-town trips	21.21	23.52	111
TELEVISION, RADIO, AND SOUND EQUIPMENT	**541.77**	**552.59**	**102**
Televisions	**370.32**	**376.44**	**102**
Community antenna or cable TV	219.69	223.47	102
Black-and-white TV sets	1.89	2.32	123
Color TV, console	29.53	27.76	94
Color TV, portable, table model	44.90	45.56	101
VCRs and video disc players	27.33	28.33	104
Video cassettes, tapes, and discs	24.05	25.64	107
Video game hardware and software	14.68	15.05	103

(continued)

(continued from previous page)

	average spending of total consumer units	white consumer units	
		average spending	indexed spending*
Repair of TV, radio, and sound equipment	$7.19	$7.98	111
Rental of television sets	1.06	0.32	30
Radios and sound equipment	**171.45**	**176.14**	**103**
Radios	10.61	11.77	111
Tape recorders and players	11.26	8.22	73
Sound components and component systems	32.12	33.94	106
Miscellaneous sound equipment	0.48	0.60	125
Sound equipment accessories	4.46	4.44	100
Compact disc, tape, record, video mail order clubs	11.99	13.40	112
Records, CDs, audio tapes, needles	38.49	40.37	105
Rental of VCR, radio, sound equipment	0.27	0.12	44
Musical instruments and accessories	17.75	18.23	103
Rental and repair of musical instruments	1.65	1.84	112
Rental of video cassettes, tapes, discs, films	42.38	43.23	102
PETS, TOYS, PLAYGROUND EQUIPMENT	**322.19**	**361.94**	**112**
Pets	**199.89**	**232.74**	**116**
Pet food	79.56	90.54	114
Pet purchase, supplies, and medicines	47.03	56.28	120
Pet services	18.78	22.25	118
Veterinary services	54.52	63.66	117
Toys, games, hobbies, and tricycles	**120.29**	**126.87**	**105**
Playground equipment	**2.00**	**2.34**	**117**
OTHER ENTERTAINMENT EQUIPMENT, SUPPLIES, AND SERVICES	315.22	346.22	110
Unmotored recreational vehicles	**28.10**	**33.74**	**120**
Boats without motor and boat trailers	3.69	4.24	115
Trailers and other attachable campers	24.41	29.49	121
Motorized recreational vehicles	**77.41**	**77.13**	**100**
Motorized campers	21.18	19.58	92
Other vehicles	11.89	14.01	118
Motorboats	44.34	43.54	98
Rental of recreational vehicles	**3.42**	**3.86**	**113**
Outboard motors	**0.36**	**0.43**	**119**
Docking and landing fees	**4.49**	**5.04**	**112**
Sports, recreation, exercise equipment	**110.81**	**126.84**	**114**
Athletic gear, game tables, exercise equipment	50.33	57.19	114
Bicycles	12.59	13.26	105
Camping equipment	6.51	7.53	116
Hunting and fishing equipment	17.00	20.14	118

(continued)

(continued from previous page)

	average spending of total consumer units	white consumer units	
		average spending	indexed spending*
Winter sports equipment	$3.78	$4.58	121
Water sports equipment	9.47	11.15	118
Other sports equipment	9.50	11.01	116
Rental and repair of miscellaneous sports equipment	1.64	1.98	121
Photographic equipment and supplies	**81.18**	**88.77**	**109**
Film	20.27	22.07	109
Other photographic supplies	1.12	1.37	122
Film processing	28.56	31.80	111
Repair and rental of photographic equiment.	0.29	0.32	110
Photographic equipment	12.56	13.67	109
Photographer fees	18.39	19.53	106
Fireworks	**2.03**	**1.92**	**95**
Souvenirs	**0.14**	**0.12**	**86**
Visual goods	**1.51**	**1.85**	**123**
Pinball, electronic video games	**5.78**	**6.52**	**113**

PERSONAL CARE PRODUCTS AND SERVICES	**$403.47**	**$411.04**	**102**
Personal care products	**213.44**	**216.23**	**101**
Hair care products	38.65	38.14	99
Nonelectric articles for the hair	4.43	4.03	91
Wigs and hairpieces	0.95	0.88	93
Oral hygiene products	22.19	22.17	100
Shaving products	11.91	13.32	112
Cosmetics, perfume, and bath products	105.36	107.94	102
Deodorants, feminine hygiene, miscellaneous products	26.10	25.65	98
Electric personal care appliances	3.85	4.10	106
Personal care services	**190.03**	**194.81**	**103**
Personal care services for females	97.61	104.89	107
Personal care services for males	92.19	89.64	97
Repair of personal care appliances	0.24	0.28	117

READING	**$162.57**	**$181.77**	**112**
Newspaper subscriptions	51.79	58.11	112
Newspaper, nonsubscriptions	17.40	18.11	104
Magazine subscriptions	24.74	28.12	114
Magazines, nonsubscriptions	11.00	12.12	110
Newsletters	0.28	0.34	121
Books purchased through book clubs	9.33	10.61	114
Books not purchased through book clubs	46.51	52.64	113
Encyclopedia and other reference book sets	1.52	1.73	114

(continued)

	average spending of total consumer units	white consumer units	
		average spending	indexed spending*
EDUCATION	**$471.47**	**$519.69**	**110**
College tuition	265.22	298.07	112
Elementary and high school tuition	81.97	86.78	106
Other schools tuition	14.06	15.40	110
Other school expenses including rentals	17.30	18.62	108
Books, supplies for college	36.06	38.11	106
Books, supplies for elementary, high school	8.56	8.89	104
Books, supplies for day care, nursery school	2.09	1.94	93
Miscellaneous school expenses and supplies	46.21	51.88	112
TOBACCO PRODUCTS AND SMOKING SUPPLIES	**$268.82**	**$291.93**	**109**
Cigarettes	243.09	262.88	108
Other tobacco products	24.30	27.46	113
Smoking accessories	1.43	1.59	111
MISCELLANEOUS EXPENSES	**$766.23**	**$827.66**	**108**
Miscellaneous fees, gambling losses	54.70	60.86	111
Legal fees	98.35	111.57	113
Funeral expenses	86.83	89.68	103
Safe deposit box rental	5.51	6.43	117
Checking accounts, other bank service charges	25.62	26.39	103
Cemetery lots, vaults, and maintenance fees	15.50	16.37	106
Accounting fees	40.94	45.75	112
Miscellaneous personal services	21.64	23.90	110
Finance charges, except mortgage and vehicles	229.82	239.33	104
Occupational expenses, union and professional fees	97.90	110.17	113
Expenses for other properties	85.37	92.84	109
Interest paid, home equity line of credit (other property)	0.12	0.15	125
Credit card membership fees	3.92	4.21	107
CASH CONTRIBUTIONS	**$925.39**	**$1,017.30**	**110**
Cash contributions to non-c.u. members, including students, alimony, child support	233.28	248.02	106
Gifts of cash, stocks, bonds to non-c.u. member	174.20	198.69	114
Contributions to charities	85.58	99.54	116
Contributions to church	385.94	416.17	108
Contributions to educational organizations	35.65	42.68	120
Political contributions	3.39	4.01	118
Other contributions	7.35	8.19	111

(continued)

(continued from previous page)

	average spending of total consumer units	white consumer units	
		average spending	indexed spending*
PERSONAL INSURANCE AND PENSIONS	**$2,967.05**	**$3,203.67**	**108**
Life and other personal insurance except health	**374.03**	**394.85**	**106**
Life, endowment, annuity, other personal insurance	361.44	380.23	105
Other nonhealth insurance	12.59	14.62	116
Pensions and Social Security	**2,593.02**	**2,808.82**	**108**
Deductions for government retirement	66.21	72.19	109
Deductions for railroad retirement	5.28	6.42	122
Deductions for private pensions	325.82	375.40	115
Non-payroll deposit to retirement plans	312.41	362.12	116
Deductions for Social Security	1,883.30	1,992.69	106
GIFTS*	**$986.63**	**$1,082.11**	**110**
FOOD	**87.72**	**99.25**	**113**
Cakes and cupcakes	1.97	2.30	117
Candy and chewing gum	12.79	14.65	115
Potato chips and other snacks	1.30	1.36	105
Board (including at school)	32.09	37.22	116
Catered affairs	16.33	17.74	109
HOUSING	**249.80**	**282.43**	**113**
Housekeeping supplies	**37.72**	**42.93**	**114**
Other household products	9.11	10.42	114
Miscellaneous household products	4.39	4.89	111
Lawn and garden supplies	3.51	4.25	121
Stationery, stationery supplies, giftwraps	22.53	25.81	115
Postage	4.17	4.64	111
Household textiles	**10.20**	**11.16**	**109**
Bathroom linens	2.75	3.03	110
Bedroom linens	4.44	4.47	101
Appliances and miscellaneous housewares	**27.44**	**31.60**	**115**
Major appliances	4.79	5.18	108
Small appliances and miscellaneous housewares	22.65	26.42	117
China and other dinnerware	2.91	3.33	114
Glassware	3.60	4.23	118
Nonelectric cookware	3.98	4.90	123
Tableware, nonelectric kitchenware	4.98	5.65	113
Small electric kitchen appliances	3.64	4.07	112
Miscellaneous household equipment	**65.94**	**76.76**	**116**
Lamps and lighting fixtures	3.33	3.63	109
Other household decorative items	21.54	25.73	119

(continued)

	average spending of total consumer units	white consumer units	
		average spending	indexed spending*
Lawn and garden equipment	$0.96	$1.15	120
Indoor plants, fresh flowers	20.72	24.33	117
Computers and hardware, nonbusiness use	4.01	4.86	121
Other housing	**108.51**	**119.98**	**111**
Repair or maintenance services	1.03	1.17	114
Housing while attending school	34.67	40.61	117
Lodging on out-of-town trips	2.10	2.29	109
Electricity (renter)	10.47	110.26	1,053
Telephone services in home city, excluding mobile car phone	12.23	12.44	102
Day-care centers, nurseries, and preschools	15.05	16.95	113
Housekeeping services	3.90	4.72	121
Gardening, lawn care services	2.74	2.80	102
Moving, storage, freight express	1.50	1.77	118
Sofas	0.93	1.13	122
Kitchen, dining room furniture	0.50	0.61	122
Infants' furniture	1.64	1.67	102
APPAREL AND SERVICES	**258.22**	**261.03**	**101**
Males, aged 2 or older	**69.77**	**74.40**	**107**
Men's coats and jackets	4.70	5.53	118
Men's accessories	6.98	6.60	95
Men's sweaters and vests	3.46	3.87	112
Men's active sportswear	1.42	1.62	114
Men's shirts	17.03	18.36	108
Men's pants	9.29	9.10	98
Boys' shirts	4.31	4.97	115
Boys' accessories	1.19	1.38	116
Boys' pants	2.31	2.73	118
Boys' shorts and short sets	0.92	0.93	101
Females, aged 2 or older	**93.61**	**95.57**	**102**
Women's coats and jackets	5.41	4.79	89
Women's dresses	5.36	4.63	86
Women's vests and sweaters	8.05	8.94	111
Women's shirts, tops, blouses	14.11	12.73	90
Women's pants	9.09	9.44	104
Women's active sportswear	6.11	7.18	118
Women's sleepwear	7.35	8.45	115
Women's undergarments	2.44	2.57	105
Women's suits	1.62	1.54	95
Women's accessories	9.16	8.68	95

(continued)

(continued from previous page)

	average spending of total consumer units	white consumer units	
		average spending	indexed spending*
Girls' dresses and suits	$2.61	$2.67	102
Girls' shirts, blouses, sweaters	4.16	4.44	107
Girls' skirts and pants	1.83	2.06	113
Children under age 2	**39.47**	**36.32**	**92**
Infant dresses, outerwear	13.60	14.24	105
Infant underwear	19.47	15.40	79
Infant nightwear, loungewear	2.25	2.37	105
Infant accessories	2.55	2.67	105
Other apparel products and services	**55.37**	**54.74**	**99**
Jewelry and watches	26.56	30.82	116
Watches	2.66	2.98	112
Jewelry	23.90	27.84	116
All other apparel products and services	28.81	23.92	83
Men's footwear	7.15	7.21	101
Boys' footwear	1.95	1.74	89
Women's footwear	10.36	9.02	87
Girls' footwear	7.76	4.06	52
TRANSPORTATION	**47.84**	**53.65**	**112**
New cars	1.90	2.31	122
Used cars	3.19	3.88	122
Gasoline on out-of-town trips	13.01	14.67	113
Airline fares	10.75	11.61	108
Ship fares	3.10	3.35	108
HEALTH CARE	**22.21**	**25.34**	**114**
Physicians' services	2.69	3.16	117
Dental services	4.70	5.65	120
Hospital room	0.31	0.36	116
Hospital service other than room	0.88	1.06	120
Care in convalescent or nursing home	4.50	4.75	106
Prescription drugs	1.38	1.47	107
ENTERTAINMENT	**86.44**	**97.89**	**113**
Toys, games, hobbies, tricycles	**29.34**	**31.83**	**108**
Other entertainment	**57.10**	**66.06**	**116**
Movie, other admissions, out-of-town trips	7.07	7.96	113
Admissions to sports events, out-of-town trips	2.36	2.65	112
Fees for recreational lessons	2.93	3.45	118
Community antenna or cable TV	2.54	2.67	105
Color TV, portable, table model	3.47	4.09	118
VCRs, video disc players	2.04	2.24	110
Video game hardware and software	2.90	3.36	116

(continued)

(continued from previous page)

	average spending of total consumer units	white consumer units	
		average spending	indexed spending*
Radios	$2.67	$3.24	121
Sound components and component systems	2.62	2.71	103
Veterinary services	3.05	3.54	116
Athletic gear, game tables, and exercise equipment	2.40	2.48	103
EDUCATION	**120.19**	**137.55**	**114**
College tuition	96.63	110.91	115
Elementary, high school tuition	8.17	9.64	118
Other school tuition	1.07	1.16	108
Other school expenses including rentals	1.86	1.81	97
School books, supplies, equipment for college	6.55	7.00	107
School supplies, etc., unspecified	5.29	6.42	121
ALL OTHER GIFTS	**114.22**	**124.98**	**109**

* The index compares the spending of the average white consumer unit with the spending of the average consumer unit by dividing white spending by average spending in each category and multiplying by 100. An index of 100 means white spending in the category equals average spending. An index of 132 means white spending is 32 percent above average, while an index of 75 means white spending is 25 percent below average.
** This figure does not include the amount paid for mortgage principal, which is considered an asset.
*** Expenditures on gifts are also included in the preceding product and service categories. Food spending, for example, includes the amount spent on gifts of food.
Note: In this table, whites are defined as non-Hispanic, non-African American consumer units and they include a small number of Asian and Native American consumer units. The Bureau of Labor Statistics uses consumer units rather than households as the sampling unit in the Consumer Expenditure Survey. For the definition of a consumer unit, see the Glossary. Expenditures for gifts may not add to the total for gifts because the listing is incomplete. (–) means not applicable or the sample is too small to make a reliable estimate.
Source: Bureau of Labor Statistics, unpublished tables from the 1995 Consumer Expenditure Survey; calculations by New Strategist

Whites: Wealth

Whites are the only population segment with significant wealth.

The median net worth (assets minus debts) of non-Hispanic white households stood at $73,900 in 1995, far above the $56,400 net worth of the average American household. Between 1992 and 1995, the median net worth of non-Hispanic whites rose 3 percent, after adjusting for inflation.

The net worth of non-Hispanic white households is above average because non-Hispanic whites are much more likely to own a home than other segments of the population. Home equity accounts for the largest share of Americans' net worth. Fully 69 percent of non-Hispanic white householders owned their home in 1995, according to the Federal Reserve Board's Survey of Consumer Finances. The nonfinancial asset held by the largest share of non-Hispanic whites is a vehicle, owned by 88 percent.

Non-Hispanic white householders have only $16,900 in financial assets, with transaction accounts (such as checking accounts) owned by the largest share (92 percent). Forty-seven percent have retirement accounts and 34 percent have life insurance.

Most non-Hispanic white householders are in debt, owing a median of $27,200. The debt of these households rose 14 percent between 1992 and 1995 as homeownership increased.

■ The wealth of non-Hispanic white householders should rise in the future because baby boomers are entering the age range in which homeownership and saving for retirement peak.

The net worth of non-Hispanic whites is well above average

(median net worth of non-Hispanic white and total households, 1995)

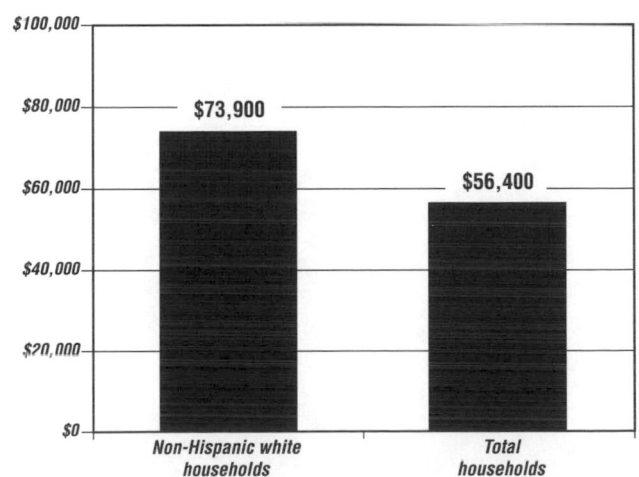

Net Worth, Assets, and Debts of Non-Hispanic White Households, 1992 and 1995

(median net worth of non-Hispanic white households, and median value of assets and debts, 1992 and 1995; percent change 1992–1995; in 1995 dollars)

	1995	1992	percent change 1992–1995
Median net worth	$73,900	$71,700	3.1%
Median value of nonfinancial assets	93,000	85,500	8.8
Median value of financial assets	16,900	16,300	3.7
Median value of debts	27,200	23,900	13.8

Source: Federal Reserve Board, Family Finances in the U.S.: Recent Evidence from the Survey of Consumer Finances, *Federal Reserve Bulletin, January 1997; calculations by New Strategist*

Nonfinancial Assets of Non-Hispanic White Households, 1992 and 1995

(percent of non-Hispanic white households owning nonfinancial assets, and median value of assets for owners, 1992 and 1995; percentage point change in households with asset and percent change in value of asset, 1992–95; in 1995 dollars)

	1995	1992	percentage point change, 1992–95
Percent owning asset			
Any nonfinancial asset	94.9%	94.8%	0.1
Vehicles	88.1	90.7	−2.6
Primary residence	69.4	68.9	0.5
Investment real estate	19.7	21.9	−2.2
Business	12.6	13.5	−0.9
Other nonfinancial	10.5	9.7	0.8

	1995	1992	percent change 1992–95
Median value of asset for owners			
Any nonfinancial asset	$93,000	$85,500	8.8%
Vehicles	10,800	7,800	38.5
Primary residence	92,000	92,200	−0.2
Investment real estate	50,000	48,800	2.5
Business	45,000	70,500	−36.2
Other nonfinancial	10,000	7,600	31.6

Source: Federal Reserve Board, Family Finances in the U.S.: Recent Evidence from the Survey of Consumer Finances, *Federal Reserve Bulletin, January 1997; calculations by New Strategist*

Financial Assets of Non-Hispanic White Households, 1992 and 1995

(percent of non-Hispanic white households owning financial assets, and median value of assets for owners, 1992 and 1995; percentage point change in households with asset and percent change in value of asset, 1992–95; in 1995 dollars)

	1995	1992	percentage point change, 1992–95
Percent owning asset			
Any financial asset	94.7%	95.4%	–0.7
Transaction accounts	92.4	92.9	–0.5
Certificates of deposit	16.5	19.6	–3.1
Savings bonds	26.2	25.8	0.4
Bonds	3.7	5.2	–1.5
Stocks	18.2	20.4	–2.2
Mutual funds	14.5	12.7	1.8
Retirement accounts	47.0	43.3	3.7
Life insurance	33.5	38.3	–4.8
Other managed assets	4.7	4.9	–0.2
Other financial assets	11.7	11.8	–0.1

	1995	1992	percent change 1992–95
Median value of asset for owners			
Any financial asset	$16,900	$16,300	3.7%
Transaction accounts	2,500	3,000	–16.7
Certificates of deposit	10,000	11,900	–16.0
Savings bonds	1,000	700	42.9
Bonds	26,200	32,600	–19.6
Stocks	8,600	8,700	–1.1
Mutual funds	20,000	17,400	14.9
Retirement accounts	17,500	16,300	7.4
Life insurance	5,000	3,300	51.5
Other managed assets	30,000	24,100	24.5
Other financial assets	4,000	3,100	29.0

Source: Federal Reserve Board, Family Finances in the U.S.: Recent Evidence from the Survey of Consumer Finances, Federal Reserve Bulletin, January 1997; calculations by New Strategist

Non-Hispanic White Households with Debt, 1992 and 1995

(percent of non-Hispanic white households with debt, and median value of debt for those with debts, 1992 and 1995; percentage point change in households with debt and percent change in amount of debt, 1992–95; in 1995 dollars)

	1995	1992	percentage point change, 1992–95
Percent with debt			
Any debt	75.8%	74.4%	1.4
Mortgage and home equity	43.5	41.9	1.6
Installment	46.4	46.4	0.0
Other lines of credit	2.1	2.7	–0.6
Credit card	47.5	44.1	3.4
Investment real estate	6.9	8.9	–2.0
Other debt	9.1	8.4	0.7

	1995	1992	percent change 1992–95
Median value of debt for debtors			
Any debt	$27,200	$23,900	13.8%
Mortgage and home equity	54,000	48,800	10.7
Installment	6,400	5,500	16.4
Other lines of credit	3,500	2,200	59.1
Credit card	1,500	1,100	36.4
Investment real estate	29,000	26,600	9.0
Other debt	2,000	3,300	–39.4

Source: Federal Reserve Board, Family Finances in the U.S.: Recent Evidence from the Survey of Consumer Finances, *Federal Reserve Bulletin, January 1997; calculations by New Strategist*

Total Population

■ Between 1998 and 2020, the non-Hispanic white share of the population will fall from 73 to 64 percent.

■ Eighty-two percent of Americans had a high school diploma in 1996, up from 69 percent in 1980.

■ At birth, the average American male can expect to live to age 73, while the average female can expect to live to age 80.

■ Seventy-two percent of American children live with both parents, while 25 percent live with their mother only.

■ The median income of American households fell 1 percent between 1990 and 1996, to $35,492, after adjusting for inflation. Despite this decline, median household income in 1996 was 5 percent higher than in 1980.

■ The U.S. received over 915,000 immigrants in 1996. Thirty-four percent were from Asia and 18 percent from Mexico, the single largest country of origin.

More than one in four Americans is a member of a minority group

(percent distribution of total persons by race and ethnicity, 1998)

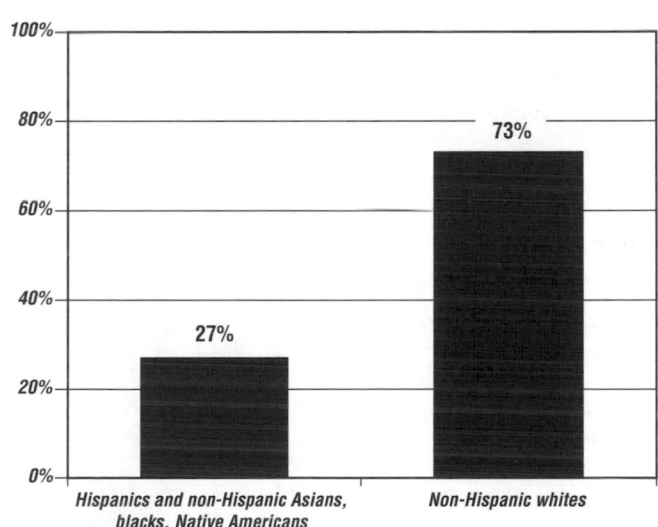

Total Population: Education

The educational attainment of Americans has soared over the past few decades.

Overall, 82 percent of Americans had a high school diploma in 1996, up from 69 percent in 1980. The proportion of Americans with a high school diploma did not top 50 percent until the late 1960s, then rose rapidly as the well-educated baby-boom generation entered adulthood.

Twenty-four percent of Americans have a college degree, including 26 percent of men and 21 percent of women. Fully 34 percent of men aged 45 to 49 in 1996 had a college degree, the most educated group of all Americans. Among the 50 states, the proportion of the population with a college degree is highest (27 percent) in Massachusetts, and lowest (12 percent) in West Virginia.

Among all families with children aged 18 to 24, 40 percent have a child in college full-time. The proportion of families with a child in college rises steadily with income, to 65 percent among families with incomes of $75,000 or more.

More than 1.1 million bachelor's degrees were awarded in 1994–95, over 397,000 master's degrees, and over 44,000 doctorates. At 75,800, the number of people earning first-professional degrees is far greater than the number of those earning doctorates. The most popular first-professional degree field is law, and 39,349 people earned law degrees in 1994–95.

■ The educational attainment of Americans will continue to rise as well-educated younger generations replace less-educated older Americans.

The educational attainment of Americans has increased sharply since 1980

(percent of persons aged 25 or older who are high school or college graduates, 1980 and 1996)

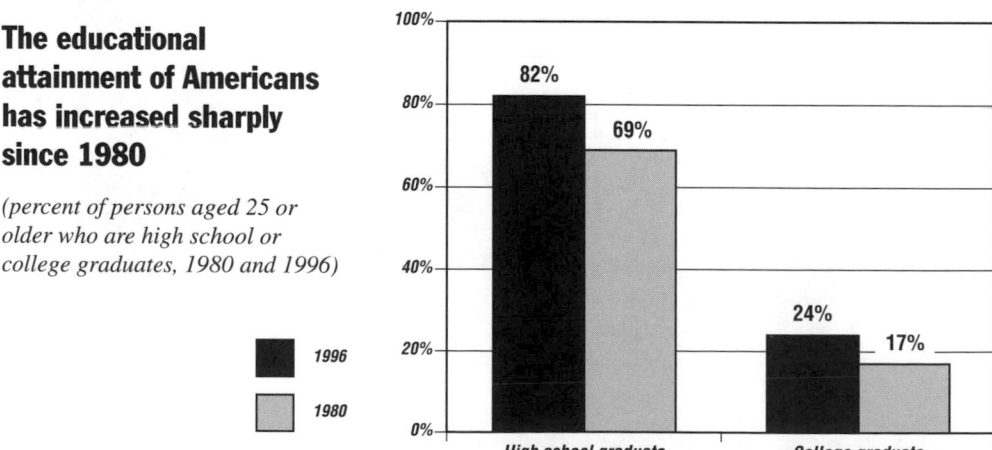

■ 1996
■ 1980

Educational Attainment of the Total Population by Sex, 1996

(number and percent distribution of total persons aged 25 or older by educational attainment and sex, 1996; numbers in thousands)

	total		men		women	
	number	*percent*	*number*	*percent*	*number*	*percent*
Total, aged 25 or older	**168,323**	**100.0%**	**80,339**	**100.0%**	**87,984**	**100.0%**
Not a high school graduate	30,724	18.3	14,534	18.1	16,190	18.4
High school graduate or more	137,599	81.7	65,804	81.9	71,795	81.6
High school graduate only	56,559	33.6	25,649	31.9	30,911	35.1
Some college or assoc. degree	41,372	24.6	19,301	24.0	22,071	25.1
Bachelor's degree or more	39,668	23.6	20,854	26.0	18,813	21.4
Bachelor's degree only	26,540	15.8	13,219	16.5	13,321	15.1
Master's degree	9,101	5.4	4,812	6.0	4,288	4.9
Professional degree	2,416	1.4	1,671	2.1	745	0.8
Doctoral degree	1,611	1.0	1,152	1.4	459	0.5

Source: Bureau of the Census, Educational Attainment in the United States: March 1996, *Current Population Reports, P20-493, 1997; calculations by New Strategist*

Total High School and College Graduates by Sex, 1980 to 1996

(percent of total persons aged 25 or older who are high school or college graduates, by sex, selected years 1980–96)

	total	men	women
High school graduates			
1996	81.7%	81.9%	81.6%
1990	77.6	77.7	77.5
1985	73.9	74.4	73.5
1980	68.6	69.2	68.1
College graduates			
1996	23.6	26.0	21.4
1990	21.3	24.4	18.4
1985	19.4	23.1	16
1980	17.0	20.9	13.6

Source: Bureau of the Census, Educational Attainment in the United States: March 1996, *Current Population Reports, P20-493, 1997; and Internet web site,* http://www.census.gov

Total High School and College Graduates by Age and Sex, 1996

(percent of total persons aged 25 or older who are high school or college graduates by age and sex, 1996)

	total	*men*	*women*
High school graduates			
Total, aged 25 or older	**81.7%**	**81.9%**	**81.6%**
Aged 25 to 29	87.3	86.5	88.1
Aged 30 to 34	86.5	85.3	87.7
Aged 35 to 39	87.6	86.9	88.2
Aged 40 to 44	88.3	87.0	89.5
Aged 45 to 49	88.3	88.6	88.1
Aged 50 to 54	83.9	84.2	83.7
Aged 55 to 59	79.2	78.8	79.5
Aged 60 to 64	75.5	76.2	74.9
Aged 65 to 69	70.1	69.9	70.2
Aged 70 to 74	68.5	68.6	68.4
Aged 75 or older	58.7	59.1	58.6
College graduates			
Total, aged 25 or older	**23.6**	**26.0**	**21.4**
Aged 25 to 29	27.1	26.1	28.2
Aged 30 to 34	25.9	25.7	26.2
Aged 35 to 39	25.7	25.7	25.8
Aged 40 to 44	26.9	27.0	26.7
Aged 45 to 49	29.9	34.1	25.8
Aged 50 to 54	25.3	29.4	21.6
Aged 55 to 59	20.7	25.0	16.6
Aged 60 to 64	19.6	25.5	14.5
Aged 65 to 69	15.5	20.7	11.0
Aged 70 to 74	14.1	21.0	8.8
Aged 75 or older	12.7	15.7	10.8

Source: Bureau of the Census, Educational Attainment in the United States: March 1996, *Current Population Reports, P20-493, 1997*

Total High School and College Graduates by Age and Region, 1996

(percent of the total persons aged 25 or older who are high school or college graduates, by age and region, 1996)

	Northeast	Midwest	South	West
High school graduates				
Total, aged 25 or older	**82.9%**	**85.0%**	**78.2%**	**83.0%**
Aged 25 to 34	89.6	91.3	85.2	83.0
Aged 35 to 44	89.7	91.4	85.8	85.9
Aged 45 to 54	87.5	90.1	82.6	87.7
Aged 55 to 64	78.6	81.9	71.2	82.7
Aged 65 or older	65.0	65.7	59.6	73.4
College graduates				
Total, aged 25 or older	**26.4**	**22.7**	**21.3**	**25.5**
Aged 25 to 34	31.0	28.8	23.5	25
Aged 35 to 44	31.1	24.4	24.6	26.6
Aged 45 to 54	30.9	25.7	25.7	31.5
Aged 55 to 64	21.8	18.8	17.0	26.3
Aged 65 or older	13.9	12.6	13.0	17.5

Source: Bureau of the Census, Educational Attainment in the United States: March 1996, *Current Population Reports, P20-493, 1997*

Total High School and College Graduates by State, 1990

(percent of total persons aged 25 or older who are high school or college graduates, by state, 1990)

	high school graduate or more	college graduate		high school graduate or more	college graduate
United States	**75.2%**	**20.3%**	Missouri	73.9%	17.8%
Alabama	66.9	15.7	Montana	81.0	19.8
Alaska	86.6	23.0	Nebraska	81.8	18.9
Arizona	78.7	20.3	Nevada	78.8	15.3
Arkansas	66.3	13.3	New Hampshire	82.2	24.4
California	76.2	23.4	New Jersey	76.7	24.9
Colorado	84.4	27.0	New Mexico	75.1	20.4
Connecticut	79.2	27.2	New York	76.7	23.1
Delaware	77.5	21.4	North Carolina	70.0	17.4
District of Columbia	73.1	33.3	North Dakota	76.7	18.1
Florida	74.4	18.3	Ohio	75.7	17.0
Georgia	70.9	19.3	Oklahoma	74.6	17.8
Hawaii	80.1	22.9	Oregon	81.5	20.6
Idaho	79.7	17.7	Pennsylvania	74.7	17.9
Illinois	76.2	21.0	Rhode Island	72.0	21.3
Indiana	75.6	15.6	South Carolina	68.3	16.6
Iowa	80.1	16.9	South Dakota	77.1	17.2
Kansas	81.3	21.1	Tennessee	67.1	16.0
Kentucky	64.6	13.6	Texas	72.1	20.3
Louisiana	68.3	16.1	Utah	85.1	22.3
Maine	78.8	18.8	Vermont	80.8	24.3
Maryland	78.4	26.5	Virginia	75.2	24.5
Massachusetts	80.0	27.2	Washington	83.8	22.9
Michigan	76.8	17.4	West Virginia	66.0	12.3
Minnesota	82.4	21.8	Wisconsin	78.6	17.7
Mississippi	64.3	14.7	Wyoming	83.0	18.8

Source: National Center for Education Statistics, Digest of Education Statistics 1993, NCES 93-292, 1993

School Enrollment of the Total Population by Age and Sex, 1995

(number and percent of total persons aged 3 or older enrolled in school by age and sex, October 1995; numbers in thousands)

	total		male		female	
	number	*percent*	*number*	*percent*	*number*	*percent*
Total, aged 3 or older	**69,769**	**27.8%**	**34,998**	**28.7%**	**34,770**	**27.0%**
Aged 3 and 4	4,042	48.7	2,078	49.4	1,965	48.1
Aged 5 and 6	7,901	96.0	4,041	95.3	3,860	96.8
Aged 7 to 9	11,555	98.7	5,890	98.9	5,665	98.5
Aged 10 to 13	15,448	99.1	7,910	99.1	7,538	99.1
Aged 14 and 15	7,651	98.9	3,911	99.0	3,739	98.8
Aged 16 and 17	6,997	93.6	3,643	94.5	3,354	92.6
Aged 18 and 19	4,274	59.4	2,150	59.5	2,124	59.2
Aged 20 and 21	3,025	44.9	1,467	44.7	1,558	45.1
Aged 22 to 24	2,545	23.2	1,244	22.8	1,301	23.6
Aged 25 to 29	2,216	11.6	1,031	11.0	1,185	12.2
Aged 30 to 34	1,284	6.0	577	5.4	707	6.5
Aged 35 to 44	1,832	4.3	733	3.5	1,099	5.1
Aged 45 to 54	781	2.5	252	1.7	529	3.3
Aged 55 or older	217	0.4	70	0.3	146	0.5

Source: Bureau of the Census, School Enrollment—Social and Economic Characteristics of Students: October 1995, *Current Population Reports, P20-492, 1997*

Total Families with Children in College, 1995

(total number of families, number with children aged 18 to 24, and number and percent with children aged 18 to 24 attending college full-time, as of October 1995, by household income in 1994; numbers in thousands)

	total	with children aged 18–24	with one or more children attending college full-time		
			number	percent of total families	percent of families with children 18–24
Total families	**70,339**	**9,997**	**3,987**	**5.7%**	**39.9%**
Under $20,000	16,034	1,947	404	2.5	20.7
$20,000 to $29,999	10,079	1,238	424	4.2	34.2
$30,000 to $39,999	9,144	1,146	410	4.5	35.8
$40,000 to $49,999	6,859	927	350	5.1	37.8
$50,000 to $74,999	11,259	1,879	886	7.9	47.2
$75,000 or more	8,875	1,679	1,090	12.3	64.9

Source: Bureau of the Census, School Enrollment—Social and Economic Characteristics of Students: October 1995, *Current Population Reports, P20-492, 1997; calculations by New Strategist*

College Enrollment of the Total Population by Age, 1995

(number and percent distribution of total persons aged 15 or older enrolled in college by age, type of school, and attendance status, October 1995; numbers in thousands)

	total	undergraduate total	two-year college			four-year college			graduate		
			total	full-time	part-time	total	full-time	part-time	total	full-time	part-time
Total enrolled	14,715	11,966	3,882	2,022	1,860	8,084	6,322	1,762	2,749	1,199	1,550
Aged 15 to 17	158	155	49	38	11	106	102	4	3	3	–
Aged 18 and 19	3,101	3,096	979	773	206	2,117	1,989	128	5	5	–
Aged 20 and 21	2,940	2,881	608	397	211	2,273	2,065	208	60	43	17
Aged 22 to 24	2,498	2,033	593	298	295	1,440	1,145	294	465	352	112
Aged 25 to 29	2,143	1,353	529	185	344	824	484	340	789	406	383
Aged 30 to 34	1,206	797	363	136	228	434	199	235	409	165	244
Aged 35 to 39	1,009	649	285	97	188	364	159	205	360	119	242
Aged 40 to 44	733	495	221	46	175	274	90	184	238	42	196
Aged 45 to 49	502	277	140	29	111	137	54	82	225	40	185
Aged 50 to 54	227	127	44	15	29	83	28	55	100	20	80
Aged 55 or older	197	102	70	8	62	32	6	25	94	5	90

(continued)

(continued from previous page)

| | | undergraduate | | | | | | | graduate | | |
| | | | two-year college | | | four-year college | | | | | |
Percent distribution by age	total	total	total	full-time	part-time	total	full-time	part-time	total	full-time	part-time
Total enrolled	100.0%	100.0%	100.0%	100.0%	100.0%	100.0%	100.0%	100.0%	100.0%	100.0%	100.0%
Aged 15 to 17	1.1	1.3	1.3	1.9	0.6	1.3	1.6	0.2	0.1	0.3	–
Aged 18 and 19	21.1	25.9	25.2	38.2	11.1	26.2	31.5	7.3	0.2	0.4	–
Aged 20 and 21	20.0	24.1	15.7	19.6	11.3	28.1	32.7	11.8	2.2	3.6	1.1
Aged 22 to 24	17.0	17.0	15.3	14.7	15.9	17.8	18.1	16.7	16.9	29.4	7.2
Aged 25 to 29	14.6	11.3	13.6	9.1	18.5	10.2	7.7	19.3	28.7	33.9	24.7
Aged 30 to 34	8.2	6.7	9.4	6.7	12.3	5.4	3.1	13.3	14.9	13.8	15.7
Aged 35 to 39	6.9	5.4	7.3	4.8	10.1	4.5	2.5	11.6	13.1	9.9	15.6
Aged 40 to 44	5.0	4.1	5.7	2.3	9.4	3.4	1.4	10.4	8.7	3.5	12.6
Aged 45 to 49	3.4	2.3	3.6	1.4	6.0	1.7	0.9	4.7	8.2	3.3	11.9
Aged 50 to 54	1.5	1.1	1.1	0.7	1.6	1.0	0.4	3.1	3.6	1.7	5.2
Aged 55 or older	1.3	0.9	1.8	0.4	3.3	0.4	0.1	1.4	3.4	0.4	5.8

(continued)

(continued from previous page)

Percent distribution by type of school and attendance status

	total	undergraduate							graduate		
		total	two-year college			four-year college			total	full-time	part-time
			total	full-time	part-time	total	full-time	part-time			
Total enrolled	**100.0%**	**81.3%**	**26.4%**	**13.7%**	**12.6%**	**54.9%**	**43.0%**	**12.0%**	**18.7%**	**8.1%**	**10.5%**
Aged 15 to 17	100.0	98.1	31.0	24.1	7.0	67.1	64.6	2.5	1.9	1.9	–
Aged 18 and 19	100.0	99.8	31.6	24.9	6.6	68.3	64.1	4.1	0.2	0.2	–
Aged 20 and 21	100.0	98.0	20.7	13.5	7.2	77.3	70.2	7.1	2.0	1.5	0.6
Aged 22 to 24	100.0	81.4	23.7	11.9	11.8	57.6	45.8	11.8	18.6	14.1	4.5
Aged 25 to 29	100.0	63.1	24.7	8.6	16.1	38.5	22.6	15.9	36.8	18.9	17.9
Aged 30 to 34	100.0	66.1	30.1	11.3	18.9	36.0	16.5	19.5	33.9	13.7	20.2
Aged 35 to 39	100.0	64.3	28.2	9.6	18.6	36.1	15.8	20.3	35.7	11.8	24.0
Aged 40 to 44	100.0	67.5	30.2	6.3	23.9	37.4	12.3	25.1	32.5	5.7	26.7
Aged 45 to 49	100.0	55.2	27.9	5.8	22.1	27.3	10.8	16.3	44.8	8.0	36.9
Aged 50 to 54	100.0	55.9	19.4	6.6	12.8	36.6	12.3	24.2	44.1	8.8	35.2
Aged 55 or older	100.0	51.8	35.5	4.1	31.5	16.2	3.0	12.7	47.7	2.5	45.7

Note: (–) means sample is too small to make a reliable estimate.
Source: Bureau of the Census, School Enrollment—Social and Economic Characteristics of Students: October 1995, Current Population Reports, P20-492, 1997; calculations by New Strategist

Bachelor's, Master's, and Doctoral Degrees
Earned by the Total Population by Field of Study, 1994–95

(number of bachelor's, master's, and doctoral degrees earned by total persons, by field of study, 1994–95)

	bachelor's	master's	doctoral
Total degrees	**1,158,788**	**397,052**	**44,427**
Agriculture and natural resources	19,841	4,252	1,264
Architecture and related programs	8,756	3,923	141
Area, ethnic, and cultural studies	5,706	1,639	186
Biological and life sciences	55,984	5,393	4,645
Business, management, and admin. services	234,323	93,809	1,394
Communications	48,104	5,142	320
Communications technologies	699	467	1
Computer and information sciences	24,404	10,326	884
Construction trades	113	7	–
Education	106,079	101,242	6,905
Engineering	62,342	28,553	6,110
Engineering-related technologies	15,633	1,110	18
English language and literature	51,901	7,845	1,561
Foreign languages and literature	13,775	3,136	905
Health professions and related sciences	79,855	31,243	2,069
Home economics	15,345	2,864	388
Law and legal studies	2,032	2,511	88
Liberal arts and sciences	33,356	2,565	90
Library science	50	5,057	55
Mathematics	13,723	4,181	1,226
Mechanics and repairers	66	–	–
Multi- and interdisciplinary studies	26,033	2,457	238
Parks, recreation, leisure, and fitness	12,889	1,755	149
Philosophy and religion	7,276	1,380	507
Physical sciences	19,177	5,753	4,483
Precision production trades	353	5	–
Protective services	24,157	1,706	26
Psychology	72,083	13,921	3,822
Public administration and services	18,586	23,501	556
R.O.T.C. and military sciences	27	124	–
Social sciences and history	128,154	14,845	3,725
Theological studies and religious vocations	5,578	5,240	1,591
Transportation and material moving	3,698	823	–
Visual and performing arts	48690	10,277	1,080

Note: (–) means no degrees were awarded.
Source: National Center for Education Statistics, Digest of Education Statistics 1997, *NCES 98–015, 1997*

Total First-Professional Degrees Earned by Field of Study, 1994–95

(number of first-professional degrees earned by total persons, by field of study, 1994–95)

	number
Total degrees	**75,800**
Dentistry (D.D.S. or D.M.D.)	3,897
Medicine (M.D.)	15,537
Optometry (O.D.)	1,185
Osteopathic medicine (D.O.)	1,854
Pharmacy (Pharm. D.)	2,264
Podiatry (Pod. D., D.P., or D.P.M.)	545
Veterinary medicine (D.V.M.)	2,148
Chiropractic medicine (D.C. or D.C.M.)	2,968
Law (LL.B. or J.D.)	39,349
Theology (M.Div., M.H.L., B.D., or Ord.)	5,978
Other	75

Source: National Center for Education Statistics, Digest of Education Statistics 1997, *NCES 98-015, 1997*

Total Population: Health

Most Americans feel good, although one in four is disabled.

Sixty-seven percent of Americans say their health is excellent or good, while only 10 percent rate their health as fair or poor. But a surprisingly large number of Americans report being disabled—24 percent of people aged 15 or older. The most common disabilities are incapacity to walk three city blocks, to climb stairs, and to carry 10 pounds.

Nearly 4 million babies were born to American women in 1996, most to women in their 20s. One-third of all births were to unmarried women. The annual number of births is projected to rise above 4 million again early in the next century.

Overall, Americans report an average of two acute illnesses per year. The rate of acute illness is highest in the youngest age group. Chronic conditions are most common in the oldest age group, with arthritis affecting over half of people aged 75 or older. The average American contacts a physician six times per year.

Sixteen percent of the total population is without health insurance, but this proportion is a much higher 29 percent among 18-to-24-year-olds.

Heart disease and cancer are the leading causes of death among Americans, while AIDS ranks eighth. At birth, the average American male can expect to live to age 73, the average female to age 80. At age 65, men can expect 16 more years of life, women 19.

■ With the aging of the population, the proportion of Americans with disabilities is certain to rise. As the disabled become an ever-larger minority, they will become more vocal in demanding improved handicapped access to stores, restaurants, and places of employment.

Most Americans feel excellent or very good

(percent distribution of total persons by self-assessed health status, 1994)

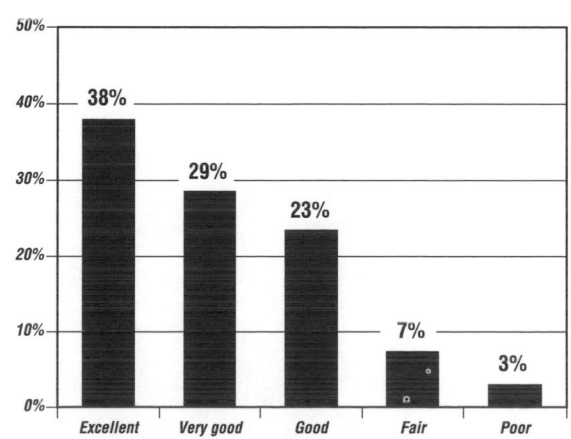

Health Status of the Total Population by Age, 1994

(percent distribution of self-assessed or parent-assessed health status of total persons, by age, 1994)

	total	excellent	very good	good	fair	poor
Total persons	**100.0%**	**37.9%**	**28.5%**	**23.4%**	**7.3%**	**2.9%**
Under age 5	100.0	53.4	27.3	16.4	2.5	0.4
Aged 5 to 17	100.0	51.2	27.3	18.4	2.6	0.4
Aged 18 to 24	100.0	43.0	31.5	21.1	3.7	0.6
Aged 25 to 44	100.0	38.8	31.1	22.6	5.7	1.8
Aged 45 to 64	100.0	28.4	27.7	27.3	11.4	5.2
Aged 65 or older	100.0	15.7	23.0	33.4	18.4	9.6

Source: National Center for Health Statistics, Current Estimates from the National Health Interview Survey, 1994, *Series 10, No. 193, 1995*

Births to Total Women by Age, 1996

(number and percent distribution of births to women, by age, 1996)

	number	percent
Total births	**3,914,953**	**100.0%**
Under age 15	11,242	0.3
Aged 15 to 19	494,272	12.6
Aged 20 to 24	951,247	24.3
Aged 25 to 29	1,078,411	27.5
Aged 30 to 34	904,810	23.1
Aged 35 to 39	400,810	10.2
Aged 40 or older	74,643	1.9

Source: National Center for Health Statistics, Births and Deaths: United States, 1996, Monthly Vital Statistics Report; Vol. 46, No.1, Supplement 2, 1997; calculations by New Strategist

Births to Total Unmarried Women by Age, 1995

(number and percent of births to unmarried women, by age; 1995)

	number	percent of total births in age group
Total births to unmarried women	**1,253,976**	**32.2%**
Under age 15	11,441	93.5
Aged 15 to 19	375,738	75.2
Aged 20 to 24	432,003	44.7
Aged 25 to 29	228,614	21.5
Aged 30 to 34	133,282	14.7
Aged 35 to 39	60,234	15.7
Aged 40 or older	12,664	18.1

Source: National Center for Health Statistics, Advance Report of Final Natality Statistics: 1995, *Monthly Vital Statistics Report, Vol. 45, No. 11(S), 1997*

Births to Total Women by State, 1996

(number and percent distribution of total births by state, 1996)

	number	*percent*
United States	**3,914,953**	**100.0%**
Alabama	61,477	1.6
Alaska	10,161	0.3
Arizona	79,590	2.0
Arkansas	36,418	0.9
California	539,789	13.8
Colorado	55,840	1.4
Connecticut	44,312	1.1
Delaware	10,243	0.3
District of Columbia	8,336	0.2
Florida	189,458	4.8
Georgia	114,848	2.9
Hawaii	18,334	0.5
Idaho	19,059	0.5
Illinois	184,369	4.7
Indiana	83,303	2.1
Iowa	37,120	0.9
Kansas	39,734	1.0
Kentucky	52,632	1.3
Louisiana	66,178	1.7
Maine	13,775	0.4
Maryland	69,696	1.8
Massachusetts	80,457	2.1
Michigan	137,471	3.5
Minnesota	63,779	1.6
Mississippi	41,662	1.1
Missouri	73,782	1.9
Montana	10,707	0.3
Nebraska	23,321	0.6
Nevada	26,034	0.7
New Hampshire	14,548	0.4
New Jersey	113,902	2.9
New Mexico	27,235	0.7
New York	271,458	6.9
North Carolina	105,741	2.7
North Dakota	8,358	0.2
Ohio	152,664	3.9

(continued)

(continued from previous page)

	number	percent
Oklahoma	46,209	1.2%
Oregon	43,677	1.1
Pennsylvania	149,962	3.8
Rhode Island	12,514	0.3
South Carolina	50,807	1.3
South Dakota	10,475	0.3
Tennessee	73,779	1.9
Texas	327,163	8.4
Utah	41,388	1.1
Vermont	6,745	0.2
Virginia	92,400	2.4
Washington	79,959	2.0
West Virginia	20,704	0.5
Wisconsin	67,094	1.7
Wyoming	6,285	0.2

Source: National Center for Health Statistics, Births and Deaths: United States, 1996, *Monthly Vital Statistics Report, Vol. 46, No. 1, Supplement 2, 1997; calculations by New Strategist*

Projections of Total Births, 1998 to 2020

(total number of births, 1998 to 2020, numbers in thousands)

	number of births
1998	3,899
1999	3,896
2000	3,899
2001	3,907
2002	3,920
2003	3,940
2004	3,967
2005	4,001
2006	4,042
2007	4,089
2008	4,140
2009	4,192
2010	4,243
2011	4,291
2012	4,336
2013	4,378
2014	4,415
2015	4,450
2016	4,481
2017	4,509
2018	4,534
2019	4,557
2020	4,579

Source: Bureau of the Census, Population Projections of the United States, by Age, Sex, Race, and Hispanic Origin: 1995 to 2050, *Current Population Reports, P25-1130, 1996; calculations by New Strategist*

Acute Health Conditions among the Total Population by Age, 1994

(number of acute conditions and rate per 100 persons, by type of acute condition and age, 1994; numbers in thousands)

	total conditions		under age 5		aged 5–17		aged 18–24		aged 25–44		aged 45 or older	
	number	rate	number	rate	number	rate	number	rate	number	rate	number	rate
Total acute conditions	445,169	171.5	73,473	358.8	109,073	220.1	44,403	175.6	127,222	153.5	90,998	111.7
Infective/parasitic diseases	**54,201**	**20.9**	**11,210**	**54.7**	**20,778**	**41.9**	**4,668**	**18.5**	**12,066**	**14.6**	**5,478**	**6.7**
Common childhood diseases	3,798	1.5	1,757	8.6	1,424	2.9	237	0.9	380	0.5	0	–
Intestinal virus	11,902	4.6	1,706	8.3	4,706	9.5	1,233	4.9	3,124	3.8	1,133	1.4
Viral infections	17,257	6.6	4,238	20.7	5,807	11.7	1,415	5.6	3,457	4.2	2,341	2.9
Other	21,244	8.2	3,508	17.1	8,842	17.8	1,784	7.1	5,106	6.2	2,004	2.5
Respiratory conditions	**208,930**	**80.5**	**31,499**	**153.8**	**51,209**	**103.4**	**20,831**	**82.4**	**63,925**	**77.1**	**41,467**	**50.9**
Common cold	65,968	25.4	14,020	68.5	14,574	29.4	6,590	26.1	18,591	22.4	12,194	15.0
Other acute upper respiratory infections	30,866	11.9	5,141	25.1	10,074	20.3	2,491	9.9	8,333	10.1	4,827	5.9
Influenza	90,447	34.8	7,645	37.3	22,921	46.3	9,783	38.7	31,351	37.8	18,746	23.0
Acute bronchitis	12,149	4.7	2,304	11.3	2,115	4.3	868	3.4	3,624	4.4	3,238	4.0
Pneumonia	4,220	1.6	1,150	5.6	551	1.1	441	1.7	761	0.9	1,317	1.6
Other respiratory conditions	5,280	2.0	1,239	6.0	973	2.0	659	2.6	1,265	1.5	1,145	1.4
Digestive system conditions	**15,863**	**6.1**	**2,155**	**10.5**	**4,110**	**8.3**	**1,866**	**7.4**	**3,918**	**4.7**	**3,813**	**4.7**
Dental conditions	2,891	1.1	691	3.4	355	0.7	463	1.8	771	0.9	611	0.8
Indigestion, nausea, vomiting	8,323	3.2	830	4.1	2,992	6.0	1,135	4.5	2,114	2.6	1,252	1.5
Other digestive conditions	4,649	1.8	634	3.1	763	1.5	268	1.1	1,033	1.2	1,951	2.4

(continued)

(continued from previous page)

	total conditions		under age 5		aged 5–17		aged 18–24		aged 25–44		aged 45 or older	
	number	rate	number	rate	number	rate	number	rate	number	rate	number	rate
Injuries	**61,887**	**23.8**	**5,246**	**25.6**	**12,904**	**26.0**	**8,267**	**32.7**	**20,726**	**25.0**	**14,744**	**18.1**
Fractures and dislocations	7,893	3.0	392	1.9	2,289	4.6	840	3.3	2,100	2.5	2,272	2.8
Sprains and strains	14,195	5.5	174	0.8	2,408	4.9	2,639	10.4	5,740	6.9	3,235	4.0
Open wounds/lacerations	10,874	4.2	1,200	5.9	2,846	5.7	1,486	5.9	3,796	4.6	1,545	1.9
Contusions and superficial injuries	12,117	4.7	1,064	5.2	2,747	5.5	1,234	4.9	3,421	4.1	3,652	4.5
Other current injuries	16,807	6.5	2,416	11.8	2,614	5.3	2,067	8.2	5,670	6.8	4,041	5.0
Selected other acute conditions	**71,337**	**27.5**	**18,502**	**90.3**	**15,022**	**30.3**	**6,347**	**25.1**	**16,900**	**20.4**	**14,565**	**17.9**
Eye conditions	3,160	1.2	535	2.6	403	0.8	200	0.8	774	0.9	1,247	1.5
Acute ear infections	24,123	9.3	12,839	62.7	6,751	13.6	611	2.4	2,344	2.8	1,578	1.9
Other ear conditions	3,781	1.5	1,032	5.0	1,000	2.0	85	0.3	808	1.0	855	1.0
Acute urinary conditions	8,140	3.1	570	2.8	599	1.2	1,412	5.6	2,729	3.3	2,831	3.5
Disorders of menstruation	1,146	0.4	–	–	480	1.0	185	0.7	436	0.5	45	0.1
Other disorders of female genital tract	2,652	1.0	–	–	117	0.2	587	2.3	1,476	1.8	473	0.6
Delivery and other conditions of pregnancy	3,707	1.4	–	–	91	0.2	1,219	4.8	2,397	2.9	–	–
Skin conditions	6,165	2.4	1,205	5.9	1,332	2.7	552	2.2	1,161	1.4	1,914	2.4
Acute musculoskeletal conditions	9,078	3.5	153	0.8	759	1.5	697	2.8	3,083	3.7	4,376	5.4
Headache, excl. migraine	3,975	1.5	–	–	1,189	2.4	556	2.2	1,363	1.6	866	1.1
Fever, unspecified	5,410	2.1	2,158	10.5	2,301	4.6	243	1.0	329	0.4	379	0.5
All other acute conditions	**32,952**	**12.7**	**4,861**	**23.7**	**5,050**	**10.2**	**2,424**	**9.6**	**9,686**	**11.7**	**10,930**	**13.4**

Note: The acute conditions shown here are those that caused people to restrict their activity for at least half a day, or that caused people to contact a physician about the illness or injury. (–) means not applicable or sample is too small to make a reliable estimate.
Source: National Center for Health Statistics, Current Estimates from the National Health Interview Survey, 1994, Series 10, No. 193, 1995

Chronic Health Conditions among the Total Population by Age, 1994

(number of chronic conditions and rate per 1,000 persons, by type of chronic condition and age, 1994; numbers in thousands)

	total		under age 18		aged 18 to 44		aged 45 to 64		aged 65 to 74		aged 75 or older	
	number	rate	number	rate	number	rate	number	rate	number	rate	number	rate
Selected skin and musculoskeletal conditions												
Arthritis	33,446	128.8	187	2.7	5,656	52.3	12,045	239.0	8,704	476.9	6,854	536.6
Gout, incl. gouty arthritis	2,485	9.6	–	–	375	3.5	963	19.1	599	32.8	549	43.0
Intervertebral disc disorders	5,994	23.1	17	0.2	2,435	22.5	2,558	50.7	672	36.8	312	24.4
Bone spur or tendinitis, unspecified	2,717	10.5	75	1.1	890	8.2	1,207	23.9	399	21.9	146	11.4
Disorders of bone/cartilage	1,520	5.9	78	1.1	438	4.0	430	8.5	306	16.8	268	21.0
Trouble with bunions	3,296	12.7	78	1.1	1,031	9.5	1,078	21.4	496	27.2	613	48.0
Bursitis, unclassified	5,279	20.3	48	0.7	1,700	15.7	2,119	42.0	927	50.8	485	38.0
Sebaceous skin cyst	1,239	4.8	42	0.6	704	6.5	238	4.7	181	9.9	75	5.9
Trouble with acne	5,250	20.2	2,059	29.4	2,856	26.4	251	5.0	68	3.7	16	1.3
Psoriasis	2,571	9.9	283	4.0	979	9.0	859	17.0	278	15.2	171	13.4
Dermatitis	9,192	35.4	2,631	37.6	3,867	35.7	1,693	33.6	596	32.7	405	31.7
Trouble with dry skin, unclassified	6,166	23.7	846	12.1	2,503	23.1	1,660	32.9	610	33.4	546	42.7
Trouble with ingrown nails	5,987	23.1	705	10.1	2,182	20.2	1,556	30.9	869	47.6	675	52.8
Trouble with corns/calluses	4,356	16.8	59	0.8	1,645	15.2	1,462	29.0	642	35.2	549	43.0

(continued)

(continued from previous page)

	total		under age 18		aged 18 to 44		aged 45 to 64		aged 65 to 74		aged 75 or older	
	number	rate	number	rate	number	rate	number	rate	number	rate	number	rate
Impairments												
Visual impairment	8,601	33.1	609	8.7	3,168	29.3	2,273	45.1	1,122	61.5	1,428	111.8
Color blindness	3,183	12.3	296	4.2	1,367	12.6	1,009	20.0	385	21.1	126	9.9
Cataracts	6,473	24.9	96	1.4	347	3.2	872	17.3	2,062	113.0	3,096	242.4
Glaucoma	2,603	10.0	22	0.3	315	2.9	593	11.8	614	33.6	1,059	82.9
Hearing impairment	22,400	86.3	1,224	17.5	5,339	49.4	6,952	137.9	4,282	234.6	4,603	360.4
Tinnitus	7,033	27.1	149	2.1	1,756	16.2	2,334	46.3	1,645	90.1	1,149	90.0
Speech impairment	3,179	12.2	1,461	20.9	988	9.1	451	8.9	202	11.1	76	6.0
Absence of extremities	1,404	5.4	23	0.3	437	4.0	392	7.8	310	17.0	243	19.0
Paralysis of extremities, complete or partial	1,416	5.5	154	2.2	339	3.1	457	9.1	211	11.6	254	19.9
Deformity or orthopedic impairment	31,068	119.7	1,961	28.0	15,400	142.4	8,570	170.0	2,812	154.1	2,326	182.1
Back	19,208	74.0	786	11.2	10,504	97.1	5,157	102.3	1,641	89.9	1,120	87.7
Upper extremities	3,991	15.4	85	1.2	1,779	16.4	1,284	25.5	347	19.0	496	38.8
Lower extremities	12,490	48.1	1,153	16.5	5,401	49.9	3,527	70.0	1,213	66.5	1,197	93.7
Selected digestive conditions												
Ulcer	4,447	17.1	90	1.3	2,105	19.5	1,272	25.2	653	35.8	326	25.5
Hernia of abdominal cavity	4,778	18.4	91	1.3	1,116	10.3	1,574	31.2	1,154	63.2	843	66.0
Gastritis or duodenitis	3,410	13.1	193	2.8	1,451	13.4	888	17.6	509	27.9	370	29.0
Frequent indigestion	6,957	26.8	139	2.0	3,372	31.2	2,060	40.9	778	42.6	607	47.5
Enteritis or colitis	2,014	7.8	68	1.0	855	7.9	659	13.1	228	12.5	204	16.0
Spastic colon	2,063	7.9	13	0.2	923	8.5	633	12.6	289	15.8	205	16.1
Diverticula of intestines	2,150	8.3	–	–	249	2.3	882	17.5	573	31.4	446	34.9
Frequent constipation	4,040	15.6	348	5.0	1,378	12.7	619	12.3	592	32.4	1,102	86.3

(continued)

(continued from previous page)

Selected conditions of the genitourinary, nervous, endocrine, metabolic, and blood and blood-forming systems

	total		under age 18		aged 18 to 44		aged 45 to 64		aged 65 to 74		aged 75 or older	
	number	rate	number	rate	number	rate	number	rate	number	rate	number	rate
Goiter or other disorders of the thyroid	4,509	17.4	14	0.2	1,498	13.8	1,506	29.9	865	47.4	626	49.0
Diabetes	7,766	29.9	97	1.4	1,346	12.4	3,182	63.1	1,855	101.6	1,287	100.8
Anemias	4,664	18.0	854	12.2	2,288	21.2	889	17.6	305	16.7	328	25.7
Epilepsy	1,396	5.4	331	4.7	652	6.0	236	4.7	108	5.9	69	5.4
Migraine headache	11,256	43.4	1,127	16.1	6,807	62.9	2,647	52.5	442	24.2	233	18.2
Neuralgia/neuritis, unspecified	566	2.2	–	–	162	1.5	189	3.7	108	5.9	107	8.4
Kidney trouble	3,512	13.5	238	3.4	1,712	15.8	867	17.2	268	14.7	428	33.5
Bladder trouble	3,747	14.4	311	4.4	1,353	12.5	852	16.9	660	36.2	571	44.7
Diseases of prostate	2,641	10.2	–	–	316	2.9	689	13.7	858	47.0	777	60.8
Diseases of female genital organs	5,052	19.5	249	3.6	3,231	29.9	1,332	26.4	166	9.1	73	5.7
Selected circulatory conditions												
Rheumatic fever with or without heart disease	2,066	8.0	95	1.4	849	7.8	623	12.4	340	18.6	159	12.4
Heart disease	22,279	85.8	1,265	18.1	4,097	37.9	6,838	135.7	5,133	281.2	4,946	387.3
Ischemic heart disease	8,004	30.8	10	0.1	440	4.1	2,842	56.4	2,446	134.0	2,265	177.3
Heart rhythm disorders	8,934	34.4	976	13.9	2,798	25.9	2,401	47.6	1,359	74.5	1,399	109.5
Tachycardia/rapid heart	2,529	9.7	95	1.4	603	5.6	776	15.4	514	28.2	541	42.4
Heart murmurs	4,472	17.2	844	12.1	1,832	16.9	1,142	22.7	345	18.9	309	24.2
Other and unspecified heart rhythm disorders	1,933	7.4	37	0.5	363	3.4	483	9.6	501	27.4	549	43.0
Other selected diseases of heart, excl. hypertension	5,342	20.6	279	4.0	859	7.9	1,595	31.6	1,328	72.8	1,282	100.4

(continued)

(continued from previous page)

	total		under age 18		aged 18 to 44		aged 45 to 64		aged 65 to 74		aged 75 or older	
	number	rate	number	rate	number	rate	number	rate	number	rate	number	rate
High blood pressure (hypertension)	28,236	108.8	189	2.7	5,549	51.3	11,206	222.3	6,338	347.2	4,955	388.0
Cerebrovascular disease	2,978	11.5	60	0.9	219	2.0	919	18.2	743	40.7	1,037	81.2
Hardening of the arteries	2,239	8.6	–	–	39	0.4	559	11.1	694	38.0	947	74.1
Varicose veins of lower extremities	7,260	28.0	–	–	2,398	22.2	2,545	50.5	1,369	75.0	948	74.2
Hemorrhoids	9,321	35.9	25	0.4	4,255	39.3	3,128	62.1	1,126	61.7	787	61.6
Selected respiratory conditions												
Chronic bronchitis	14,021	54.0	3,873	55.3	5,047	46.7	3,223	63.9	1,138	62.3	739	57.9
Asthma	14,562	56.1	4,837	69.1	5,598	51.7	2,561	50.8	956	52.4	610	47.8
Hay fever or allergic rhinitis without asthma	26,146	100.7	4,236	60.5	13,339	123.3	6,089	120.8	1,581	86.6	900	70.5
Chronic sinusitis	34,902	134.4	4,552	65.1	16,586	153.3	9,067	179.9	2,739	150.1	1,948	152.5
Deviated nasal septum	2,028	7.8	56	0.8	938	8.7	674	13.4	296	16.2	64	5.0
Chronic disease of tonsils or adenoids	2,925	11.3	1,615	23.1	1,148	10.6	150	3.0	12	0.7	–	–
Emphysema	2,028	7.8	–	–	117	1.1	497	9.9	859	47.1	554	43.4

Note: Chronic conditions are those that last longer than three months or belong to a group of conditions that are considered chronic regardless of when they began. (–) means not applicable or sample is too small to make a reliable estimate.
Source: National Center for Health Statistics, Current Estimates from the National Health Interview Survey, 1994, Series 10, No. 193, 1995

Total Persons with Disabilities by Type of Disability and Age, 1994–95

(total number of persons aged 15 or older, and percent with a disability by type of disability and age, 1994–95; numbers in thousands)

	15 or older	15 to 21	22 to 44	45 to 54	55 to 64	65 to 79	80 or older
Total persons	202,368	25,146	95,002	30,316	20,647	24,471	6,785
With any disability	**24.0%**	**12.1%**	**14.9%**	**24.5%**	**36.3%**	**47.3%**	**71.5%**
Severe	12.5	3.2	6.4	11.5	21.9	27.8	53.5
Not severe	11.5	8.9	8.5	13.0	14.4	19.5	18.1
With a mental disability	4.8	4.9	3.8	4.4	4.5	5.7	18.8
Uses wheelchair	0.9	0.3	0.3	0.4	1.3	2.1	6.9
Used cane/crutch/walker for six or more months	2.6	0.2	0.5	1.4	3.3	7.8	24.3
Difficulty with or unable to perform one or more functional activities	**16.4**	**3.7**	**7.8**	**16.1**	**26.2**	**41.2**	**67.8**
Seeing words and letters	5.8	0.7	1.6	4.2	6.0	10.0	74.8
Hearing normal conversation	6.2	1.0	2.0	4.1	6.5	12.5	71.8
Having speech understood	1.0	1.0	0.6	0.7	1.3	2.0	4.5
Lifting, carrying 10 pounds	7.9	1.1	3.2	7.4	12.9	20.9	39.6
Climbing stairs without resting	8.9	1.2	3.1	7.8	15.3	25.2	45.3
Walking three city blocks	9.1	1.3	3.3	7.7	15.5	25.2	48.5
Difficulty with or unable to perform one or more ADLs	**4.0**	**0.6**	**1.5**	**3.1**	**6.0**	**10.5**	**27.5**
Getting around inside the home	1.7	0.3	0.5	1.0	2.3	4.6	14.7
Getting in/out of bed or chair	2.7	0.4	1.0	2.2	4.1	6.9	18.0
Bathing	2.2	0.3	0.7	1.3	3.0	5.8	19.4
Dressing	1.6	0.3	0.6	1.0	2.4	3.8	12.2
Eating	0.5	0.2	0.2	0.3	0.8	1.4	3.4
Getting to/using toilet	0.9	0.3	0.3	0.5	1.3	2.5	8.9
Difficulty with or unable to perform one or more IADLs	**6.1**	**1.5**	**2.5**	**4.5**	**8.1**	**15.3**	**40.4**
Going outside alone	4.0	0.7	1.2	2.6	5.5	10.8	31.4
Keeping track of money/bills	1.9	0.9	0.9	1.3	1.7	3.8	15.8
Preparing meals	2.1	0.6	0.8	1.1	2.2	5.0	17.8
Doing light housework	3.4	0.6	1.3	2.3	4.7	8.6	23.7
Taking prescribed medicines	1.5	0.8	0.6	1.0	1.3	3.4	12.8
Using the telephone	1.3	0.5	0.4	0.6	1.3	3.6	13.3
Needs personal assistance with an ADL or an IADL	**4.7**	**1.3**	**1.9**	**3.3**	**6.1**	**11.5**	**34.1**

Note: An ADL is an activity of daily living; an IADL is an instrumental activity of daily living.
Source: Bureau of the Census, Internet web site, http://www.census.gov

Health Insurance Coverage of the Total Population by Age, 1996

(number and percent distribution of persons by age and health insurance coverage status, 1996; numbers in thousands)

| | | | covered by private or government health insurance | | | | | | |
| | | | private health insurance | | government health insurance | | | | |
	total	*total*	*total*	*group health*	*total*	*Medicaid*	*Medicare*	*Champus*	*not covered*
Number									
Total persons	**266,218**	**224,744**	**187,250**	**163,082**	**75,157**	**31,236**	**35,209**	**8,712**	**41,474**
Under age 18	70,650	60,337	47,074	43,915	18,044	15,287	466	2,291	10,313
Aged 18 to 24	24,987	17,770	15,066	12,423	3,894	2,909	156	829	7,217
Aged 25 to 34	40,256	31,283	27,915	26,205	4,783	3,264	433	1,086	8,974
Aged 35 to 44	43,960	36,809	33,448	31,231	5,049	3,109	767	1,173	7,152
Aged 45 to 54	33,013	28,504	26,266	24,329	4,105	1,875	948	1,282	4,509
Aged 55 to 64	21,475	18,501	16,258	14,031	4,451	1,577	1,822	1,052	2,974
Aged 65 or older	31,877	31,541	21,224	10,948	34,829	3,215	30,616	998	336
Percent									
Total persons	**100.0%**	**84.4%**	**70.3%**	**61.3%**	**28.2%**	**11.7%**	**13.2%**	**3.3%**	**15.6%**
Under age 18	100.0	85.4	66.6	62.2	25.5	21.6	0.7	3.2	14.6
Aged 18 to 24	100.0	71.1	60.3	49.7	15.6	11.6	0.6	3.3	28.9
Aged 25 to 34	100.0	77.7	69.3	65.1	11.9	8.1	1.1	2.7	22.3
Aged 35 to 44	100.0	83.7	76.1	71.0	11.5	7.1	1.7	2.7	16.3
Aged 45 to 54	100.0	86.3	79.6	73.7	12.4	5.7	2.9	3.9	13.7
Aged 55 to 64	100.0	86.2	75.7	65.3	20.7	7.3	8.5	4.9	13.8
Aged 65 or older	100.0	98.9	66.6	34.3	109.3	10.1	96.0	3.1	1.1

Note: Numbers may not add to total because some people have more than one type of health insurance.
Source: Bureau of the Census, unpublished tables from the 1997 Current Population Survey; calculations by New Strategist

Physician Contacts by the Total Population, 1994

(number of physician contacts by total persons and number per person per year, by age and type of contact, 1994)

	total	telephone	office	hospital	other
Total contacts	**1,581,640**	**197,524**	**877,815**	**208,060**	**286,851**
Under age 5	138,403	21,162	81,292	17,465	17,420
Aged 5 to 17	172,037	21,730	101,475	25,437	22,247
Aged 18 to 24	98,390	9,866	52,873	14,830	20,207
Aged 25 to 44	451,816	62,661	253,672	60,129	71,993
Aged 45 to 64	370,426	52,001	202,280	55,080	57,916
Aged 65 to 74	188,340	17,573	103,724	22,307	43,566
Aged 75 or older	162,227	12,531	82,499	12,811	53,503
Contacts per person	**6.1**	**0.8**	**3.4**	**0.8**	**1.1**
Under age 5	6.8	1.0	4.0	0.9	0.9
Aged 5 to 17	3.5	0.4	2.0	0.5	0.4
Aged 18 to 24	3.9	0.4	2.1	0.6	0.8
Aged 25 to 44	5.5	0.8	3.1	0.7	0.9
Aged 45 to 64	7.3	1.0	4.0	1.1	1.1
Aged 65 to 74	10.3	1.0	5.7	1.2	2.4
Aged 75 or older	12.7	1.0	6.5	1.0	4.2

Source: National Center for Health Statistics, Current Estimates from the National Health Interview Survey, 1994, *Series 10, No. 193, 1995*

Leading Causes of Death among the Total Population, 1995

(total number of deaths, and number and percent accounted for by ten leading causes of death, 1995)

		number	*percent*
	All causes	**2,312,132**	**100.0%**
1.	Diseases of heart	737,563	31.9
2.	Malignant neoplasms	538,455	23.3
3.	Cerebrovascular diseases	157,991	6.8
4.	Chronic obstructive pulmonary diseases and allied conditions	102,899	4.5
5.	Accidents and adverse effects	93,320	4.0
6.	Pneumonia and influenza	82,923	3.6
7.	Diabetes mellitus	59,254	2.6
8.	Human immunodeficiency virus infections	43,115	1.9
9.	Suicides	31,284	1.4
10.	Chronic liver diseases and cirrhosis	25,222	1.1
	All other causes	440,106	19.0

Source: National Center for Health Statistics, Report of Final Mortality Statistics, 1995, *Monthly Vital Statistics Report, 1997, Vol. 46, No. 1, Supplement 2, 1997; calculations by New Strategist*

Life Expectancy of the Total Population at Birth and Age 65, 1998 to 2020

(average number of years of life remaining at birth and at age 65 for total males and females, selected years 1998–2020)

	life expectancy (years)	
	males	*females*
At birth		
1998	72.8	79.6
2000	73.0	79.7
2005	73.5	80.2
2010	74.1	80.6
2015	74.8	81.1
2020	75.5	81.5
At age 65		
1998	15.7	19.3
2000	15.9	19.5
2005	16.4	19.7
2010	16.8	20.0
2015	17.2	20.3
2020	17.6	20.6

Source: Bureau of the Census, Population Projections of the United States, by Age, Sex, Race, and Hispanic Origin: 1995 to 2050, *Current Population Reports, P25–1130, 1996*

Total Population: Households

One in four of the nation's householders is a person who lives alone.

The age distribution of American households is bulging around middle age. People aged 35 to 54 head 41 percent of all households. Another 25 percent are headed by people under age 35, and a nearly equal proportion (22 percent) are headed by people aged 65 or older.

Married couples head slightly more than half of all households (54 percent). Couples without children under age 18 at home are a larger share of households (29 percent) than those with children at home (25 percent). Female-headed families account for another 13 percent of households. One in four householders is a person who lives alone.

Seventy-two percent of American children live with both parents, while 25 percent live with only their mother. Just 4 percent of children live only with their father.

Most men and women are married. Among the nation's 55 million married couples, 1.4 million are interracial, a figure that has more than doubled since 1980.

■ As the population ages, the nuclear family (husband, wife, and children) will continue to shrink as a share of all households. At the same time, the share of single-person households will grow, possibly becoming the most common household type.

Single-person households are as numerous as nuclear families

(percent distribution of households by type, ranked by share of households, 1996)

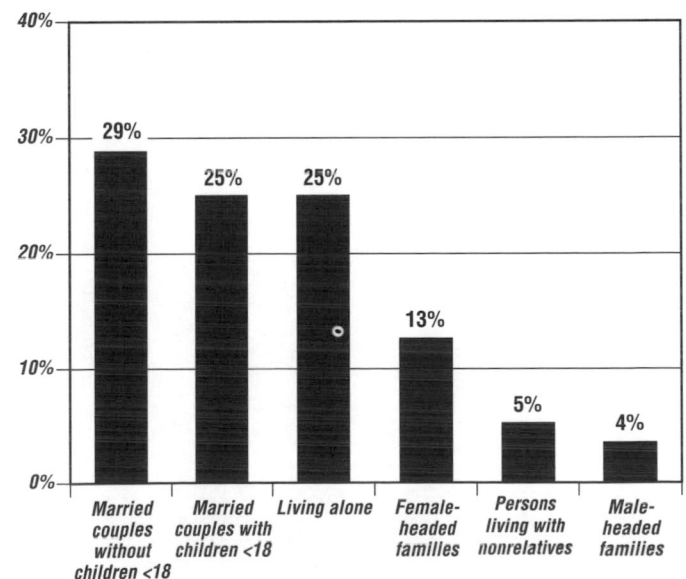

Total Households by Age of Householder, 1996

(number and percent distribution of total households by age of householder, 1996; numbers in thousands)

	number	percent
Total households	**99,627**	**100.0%**
Under age 25	5,282	5.3
Aged 25 to 29	8,354	8.4
Aged 30 to 34	10,871	10.9
Aged 35 to 39	11,788	11.8
Aged 40 to 44	11,439	11.5
Aged 45 to 54	18,008	18.1
Aged 55 to 64	12,401	12.4
Aged 65 to 74	11,908	12.0
Aged 75 or older	9,578	9.6

Source: Bureau of the Census, Household and Family Characteristics: March 1996, *Current Population Reports, P20-495(Update), 1997; calculations by New Strategist*

Total Households by Household Type, 1996

(number and percent distribution of total households by type, 1996; numbers in thousands)

	number	percent
Total households	**99,627**	**100.0%**
Family households	**69,594**	**69.9**
Married-couple families	53,567	53.8
With children under age 18	24,920	25.0
Without children under age 18	28,647	28.8
Female householder, no spouse present	12,514	12.6
With children under age 18	7,656	7.7
Without children under age 18	4,859	4.9
Male householder, no spouse present	3,513	3.5
Nonfamily households	**30,033**	**30.1**
Female householder	16,685	16.7
Living alone	14,612	14.7
Male householder	13,348	13.4
Living alone	10,288	10.3

Source: Bureau of the Census, Household and Family Characteristics: March *1996, Current Population Reports, P20-495(Update), 1997; calculations by New Strategist*

Total Households by Age of Householder and Household Type, 1996

(number and percent distribution of total households by age of householder and household type, 1996; numbers in thousands)

	total	family households				nonfamily households	
		total	married couples	female householder no spouse present	male householder no spouse present	female householder	male householder
Total households, number	**99,627**	**69,594**	**53,567**	**12,514**	**3,513**	**16,685**	**13,348**
Under age 20	598	346	83	173	90	152	100
Aged 20 to 24	4,684	2,670	1,444	920	306	958	1,056
Aged 25 to 29	8,354	5,528	3,852	1,268	407	1,126	1,700
Aged 30 to 34	10,871	8,199	6,108	1,636	455	998	1,674
Aged 35 to 39	11,788	9,262	6,898	1,902	463	897	1,629
Aged 40 to 44	11,439	9,242	6,999	1,759	484	845	1,352
Aged 45 to 49	10,432	8,162	6,463	1,299	400	1,028	1,242
Aged 50 to 54	7,575	5,746	4,698	816	232	980	849
Aged 55 to 59	6,593	4,922	4,213	546	162	964	707
Aged 60 to 64	5,808	4,213	3,528	564	120	1,003	593
Aged 65 to 74	11,908	7,340	6,177	914	249	3,240	1,328
Aged 75 to 84	7,552	3,424	2,753	552	119	3,310	818
Aged 85 or older	2,026	542	351	164	27	1,183	301
Total households, percent	**100.0%**	**69.9%**	**53.8%**	**12.6%**	**3.5%**	**16.7%**	**13.4%**
Under age 20	100.0	57.9	13.9	28.9	15.1	25.4	16.7
Aged 20 to 24	100.0	57.0	30.8	19.6	6.5	20.5	22.5
Aged 25 to 29	100.0	66.2	46.1	15.2	4.9	13.5	20.3
Aged 30 to 34	100.0	75.4	56.2	15.0	4.2	9.2	15.4
Aged 35 to 39	100.0	78.6	58.5	16.1	3.9	7.6	13.8
Aged 40 to 44	100.0	80.8	61.2	15.4	4.2	7.4	11.8
Aged 45 to 49	100.0	78.2	62.0	12.5	3.8	9.9	11.9
Aged 50 to 54	100.0	75.9	62.0	10.8	3.1	12.9	11.2
Aged 55 to 59	100.0	74.7	63.9	8.3	2.5	14.6	10.7
Aged 60 to 64	100.0	72.5	60.7	9.7	2.1	17.3	10.2
Aged 65 to 74	100.0	61.6	51.9	7.7	2.1	27.2	11.2
Aged 75 to 84	100.0	45.3	36.5	7.3	1.6	43.8	10.8
Aged 85 or older	100.0	26.8	17.3	8.1	1.3	58.4	14.9

Source: Bureau of the Census, Household and Family Characteristics: March 1996, *Current Population Reports, P20-495(Update), 1997; calculations by New Strategist*

Total Households by Size, 1996

(number and percent distribution of total households by size, 1996; numbers in thousands)

	number	percent
Total households	**99,627**	**100.0%**
One person	24,900	25.0
Two persons	32,526	32.6
Three persons	16,724	16.8
Four persons	15,118	15.2
Five persons	6,631	6.7
Six persons	2,357	2.4
Seven or more persons	1,372	1.4

Source: Bureau of the Census, Household and Family Characteristics: March 1996, *Current Population Reports, P20-495(Update), 1997; calculations by New Strategist*

Total Married Couples by Presence of Children and Age of Householder, 1996

(number and percent of total married couples by presence and number of own children under age 18 at home and age of householder, 1996; numbers in thousands)

	total	< age 20	20–24	25–29	30–34	35–39	40–44	45–54	55–64	65+
Married couples, number	**53,567**	**83**	**1,444**	**3,852**	**6,108**	**6,898**	**6,999**	**11,161**	**7,741**	**9,281**
Without children <18	28,647	42	578	1,509	1,266	1,081	1,493	6,388	7,113	9,178
With children <18	24,920	41	866	2,343	4,842	5,817	5,507	4,773	628	102
One	9,352	31	541	1,098	1,577	1,359	1,716	2,519	440	71
Two	10,278	10	260	919	2,096	2,622	2,540	1,664	142	24
Three or more	5,290	–	65	327	1,168	1,834	1,250	589	45	8
Married couples, percent	**100.0%**	**100.0%**	**100.0%**	**100.0%**	**100.0%**	**100.0%**	**100.0%**	**100.0%**	**100.0%**	**100.0%**
Without children <18	53.5	50.6	40.0	39.2	20.7	15.7	21.3	57.2	91.9	98.9
With children <18	46.5	49.4	60.0	60.8	79.3	84.3	78.7	42.8	8.1	1.1
One	17.5	37.3	37.5	28.5	25.8	19.7	24.5	22.6	5.7	0.8
Two	19.2	12.0	18.0	23.9	34.3	38.0	36.3	14.9	1.8	0.3
Three or more	9.9	–	4.5	8.5	19.1	26.6	17.9	5.3	0.6	0.1

Note: (–) means sample is too small to make a reliable estimate.
Source: Bureau of the Census, Household and Family Characteristics: March 1996, *Current Population Reports, P20–495(Update), 1997; calculations by New Strategist*

Total Female-Headed Families by Presence of Children and Age of Householder, 1996

(number and percent of total female-headed families by presence and number of own children under age 18 at home and age of householder, 1996; numbers in thousands)

	total	age of householder								
		< age 20	*20–24*	*25–29*	*30–34*	*35–39*	*40–44*	*45–54*	*55–64*	*65+*
Female-headed families, number	12,514	173	920	1,268	1,636	1,902	1,759	2,116	1,111	1,630
Without children <18	4,859	81	117	130	97	181	411	1,199	1,035	1,606
With children <18	7,656	92	802	1,138	1,539	1,720	1,347	916	76	24
One	3,683	65	429	425	549	710	756	662	66	21
Two	2,457	23	209	405	554	638	420	199	8	1
Three or more	1,514	4	165	309	436	372	172	55	2	2
Female-headed families, percent	100.0%	100.0%	100.0%	100.0%	100.0%	100.0%	100.0%	100.0%	100.0%	100.0%
Without children <18	38.8	46.8	12.7	10.3	5.9	9.5	23.4	56.7	93.2	98.5
With children <18	61.2	53.2	87.2	89.7	94.1	90.4	76.6	43.3	6.8	1.5
One	29.4	37.6	46.6	33.5	33.6	37.3	43.0	31.3	5.9	1.3
Two	19.6	13.3	22.7	31.9	33.9	33.5	23.9	9.4	0.7	0.1
Three or more	12.1	2.3	17.9	24.4	26.7	19.6	9.8	2.6	0.2	0.1

Source: Bureau of the Census, Household and Family Characteristics: March 1996, *Current Population Reports, P20-495(Update), 1997; calculations by New Strategist*

Total Single-Person Households by Age of Householder, 1996

(number and percent distribution of single-person households, and single-person households as a percent of total households, by age of householder, 1996; numbers in thousands)

	number	percent	percent of total households
Total households	**24,900**	**100.0%**	**25.0%**
Under age 25	1,072	4.3	20.3
Aged 25 to 29	1,753	7.0	21.0
Aged 30 to 34	1,983	8.0	18.2
Aged 35 to 39	1,970	7.9	16.7
Aged 40 to 44	1,833	7.4	16.0
Aged 45 to 54	3,506	14.1	19.5
Aged 55 to 64	2,941	11.8	23.7
Aged 65 to 74	4,377	17.6	36.8
Aged 75 or older	5,464	21.9	57.0
Median age (years)	56.1	–	–

Source: Bureau of the Census, Household and Family Characteristics: March 1996, *Current Population Reports, P20-495(Update), 1997; calculations by New Strategist*

Living Arrangements of Total Children by Age, 1995

(number and percent distribution of total children by living arrangement, marital status of parent, and age of child, 1995; number in thousands)

	total	under age 6	aged 6 to 11	aged 12 to 17
Number with one or both parents	**67,214**	**23,465**	**22,436**	**21,313**
Living with both parents	48,276	16,740	16,359	15,177
Living with mother only	16,477	5,902	5,309	5,266
Never married	5,862	3,328	1,630	904
Divorced	6,019	1,245	2,190	2,583
Married, spouse absent	3,901	1,227	1,283	1,392
Widowed	695	102	206	387
Living with father only	2,461	823	768	870
Never married	696	487	159	50
Divorced	1,182	207	430	546
Married, spouse absent	447	113	141	193
Widowed	135	16	38	81
Percent with one or both parents	**100.0%**	**100.0%**	**100.0%**	**100.0%**
Living with both parents	71.8	71.3	72.9	71.2
Living with mother only	24.5	25.2	23.7	24.7
Never married	8.7	14.2	7.3	4.2
Divorced	9.0	5.3	9.8	12.1
Married, spouse absent	5.8	5.2	5.7	6.5
Widowed	1.0	0.4	0.9	1.8
Living with father only	3.7	3.5	3.4	4.1
Never married	1.0	2.1	0.7	0.2
Divorced	1.8	0.9	1.9	2.6
Married, spouse absent	0.7	0.5	0.6	0.9
Widowed	0.2	0.1	0.2	0.4

Source: Bureau of the Census, Marital Status and Living Arrangements: March 1995, *Current Population Reports, P20-491, 1996; calculations by New Strategist*

Living Arrangements of Total Men by Age, 1995

(number and percent distribution of total men aged 18 or older by living arrangement and age, 1995; numbers in thousands)

	total	18 to 19	20 to 24	25 to 29	30 to 34	35 to 39	40 to 44	45 to 54	55 to 64	65 to 74	75 or older
Total men, number	**91,999**	**3,522**	**9,023**	**9,689**	**10,900**	**11,041**	**9,931**	**15,022**	**9,878**	**8,097**	**4,906**
Family householder or spouse	56,061	96	1,588	4,238	6,736	7,429	6,222	11,793	7,995	6,528	3,436
Child of householder	12,767	2,848	4,480	1,989	1,177	1,020	595	489	129	12	28
Other member of family household	4,884	242	673	622	504	396	1,376	340	264	228	240
Nonfamily householder	13,177	102	1,144	1,708	1,637	1,620	1,308	1,948	1,322	1,224	1,164
Other member of nonfamily household	5,047	224	1,121	1,115	838	574	430	450	164	105	26
Group quarters*	63	10	17	17	8	2	2	2	4	–	2
Total men, percent	**100.0%**	**100.0%**	**100.0%**	**100.0%**	**100.0%**	**100.0%**	**100.0%**	**100.0%**	**100.0%**	**100.0%**	**100.0%**
Family householder or spouse	60.9	2.7	17.6	43.7	61.8	67.3	62.7	78.5	80.9	80.6	70.0
Child of householder	13.9	80.9	49.7	20.5	10.8	9.2	6.0	3.3	1.3	0.1	0.6
Other member of family household	5.3	6.9	7.5	6.4	4.6	3.6	13.9	2.3	2.7	2.8	4.9
Nonfamily householder	14.3	2.9	12.7	17.6	15.0	14.7	13.2	13.0	13.4	15.1	23.7
Other member of nonfamily household	5.5	6.4	12.4	11.5	7.7	5.2	4.3	3.0	1.7	1.3	0.5
Group quarters*	0.1	0.3	0.2	0.2	0.1	0.0	0.0	0.0	0.0	–	0.0

* The Current Population Survey does not include people living in institutions such as prisons, the military, or college dormitories. It defines people living in group quarters as those in noninstitutional living arrangements that are not conventional housing units, such as rooming houses, staff quarters at a hospital, and halfway houses.
Note: (–) means sample is too small to make a reliable estimate.
Source: Bureau of the Census, Marital Status and Living Arrangements: March 1995, Current Population Reports, P20-491, 1996; calculations by New Strategist

Living Arrangements of Total Women by Age, 1995

(number and percent distribution of total women aged 18 or older by living arrangement and age, 1995; numbers in thousands)

	total	18 to 19	20 to 24	25 to 29	30 to 34	35 to 39	40 to 44	45 to 54	55 to 64	65 to 74	75 or older
Total women, number	**99,590**	**3,494**	**9,119**	**9,712**	**11,088**	**11,200**	**10,163**	**15,672**	**10,878**	**10,117**	**8,147**
Family householder or spouse	66,032	348	3,220	6,172	8,741	9,281	8,529	12,797	8,098	6,156	2,690
Child of householder	8,819	2,560	3,336	1,144	615	418	285	292	104	50	15
Other member of family household	4,685	292	584	519	386	320	247	386	507	515	930
Nonfamily householder	16,489	105	995	1,117	914	863	850	1,896	2,008	3,311	4,430
Other member of nonfamily household	3,485	184	948	749	428	316	252	300	157	78	73
Group quarters*	80	5	36	11	4	2	–	1	4	7	9
Total women, percent	**100.0%**	**100.0%**	**100.0%**	**100.0%**	**100.0%**	**100.0%**	**100.0%**	**100.0%**	**100.0%**	**100.0%**	**100.0%**
Family householder or spouse	66.3	10.0	35.3	63.6	78.8	82.9	83.9	81.7	74.4	60.8	33.0
Child of householder	8.9	73.3	36.6	11.8	5.5	3.7	2.8	1.9	1.0	0.5	0.2
Other member of family household	4.7	8.4	6.4	5.3	3.5	2.9	2.4	2.5	4.7	5.1	11.4
Nonfamily householder	16.6	3.0	10.9	11.5	8.2	7.7	8.4	12.1	18.5	32.7	54.4
Other member of nonfamily household	3.5	5.3	10.4	7.7	3.9	2.8	2.5	1.9	1.4	0.8	0.9
Group quarters*	0.1	0.1	0.4	0.1	0.0	0.0	–	0.0	0.0	0.1	0.1

* The Current Population Survey does not include people living in institutions such as prisons, the military, or college dormitories. It defines people living in group quarters as those in noninstitutional living arrangments that are not conventional housing units, such as roominghouses, staff quarters at a hospital, and halfway houses.

Note: (–) means sample is too small to make a reliable estimate.

Source: Bureau of the Census, Marital Status and Living Arrangements: March 1995, Current Population Reports, P20-491, 1996; calculations by New Strategist

Marital Status of Total Men by Age, 1995

(number and percent distribution of total men aged 15 or older by age and marital status, 1995; numbers in thousands)

	total	never married	married	divorced	widowed
Total men, number	**97,704**	**30,286**	**57,750**	**7,383**	**2,284**
Aged 15 to 19	9,218	9,099	100	17	2
Aged 20 to 24	9,023	7,285	1,638	100	–
Aged 25 to 29	9,689	4,944	4,337	401	6
Aged 30 to 34	10,900	3,075	6,887	927	11
Aged 35 to 39	11,041	2,241	7,561	1,204	35
Aged 40 to 44	9,931	1,390	7,260	1,234	46
Aged 45 to 54	15,022	1,214	11,848	1,807	153
Aged 55 to 64	9,878	494	8,097	1,011	275
Aged 65 to 74	8,097	342	6,549	513	693
Aged 75 to 84	4,066	160	3,042	144	720
Aged 85 or older	840	41	432	24	342
Total men, percent	**100.0%**	**31.0%**	**59.1%**	**7.6%**	**2.3%**
Aged 15 to 19	100.0	98.7	1.1	0.2	0.0
Aged 20 to 24	100.0	80.7	18.2	1.1	–
Aged 25 to 29	100.0	51.0	44.8	4.1	0.1
Aged 30 to 34	100.0	28.2	63.2	8.5	0.1
Aged 35 to 39	100.0	20.3	68.5	10.9	0.3
Aged 40 to 44	100.0	14.0	73.1	12.4	0.5
Aged 45 to 54	100.0	8.1	78.9	12.0	1.0
Aged 55 to 64	100.0	5.0	82.0	10.2	2.8
Aged 65 to 74	100.0	4.2	80.9	6.3	8.6
Aged 75 to 84	100.0	3.9	74.8	3.5	17.7
Aged 85 or older	100.0	4.9	51.4	2.9	40.7

Note: (–) means sample is too small to make a reliable estimate.
Source: Bureau of the Census, Marital Status and Living Arrangements: March 1995, Current Population Reports, P20-491, 1996

Marital Status of Total Women by Age, 1995

(number and percent distribution of total women aged 15 or older by age and marital status, 1995; numbers in thousands)

	total	never married	married	divorced	widowed
Total women, number	**105,028**	**24,693**	**58,984**	**10,270**	**11,082**
Aged 15 to 19	8,934	8,582	330	17	4
Aged 20 to 24	9,119	6,087	2,769	247	17
Aged 25 to 29	9,712	3,429	5,576	689	17
Aged 30 to 34	11,088	2,111	7,758	1,150	69
Aged 35 to 39	11,200	1,408	8,103	1,569	120
Aged 40 to 44	10,163	881	7,519	1,604	159
Aged 45 to 54	15,672	959	11,617	2,441	655
Aged 55 to 64	10,878	467	7,543	1,463	1,405
Aged 65 to 74	10,117	408	5,571	786	3,352
Aged 75 to 84	6,122	255	1,961	264	3,641
Aged 85 or older	2,025	105	235	41	1,643
Total women, percent	**100.0%**	**23.5%**	**56.2%**	**9.8%**	**10.6%**
Aged 15 to 19	100.0	96.1	3.7	0.2	0.0
Aged 20 to 24	100.0	66.8	30.4	2.7	0.2
Aged 25 to 29	100.0	35.3	57.4	7.1	0.2
Aged 30 to 34	100.0	19.0	70.0	10.4	0.6
Aged 35 to 39	100.0	12.6	72.3	14.0	1.1
Aged 40 to 44	100.0	8.7	74.0	15.8	1.6
Aged 45 to 54	100.0	6.1	74.1	15.6	4.2
Aged 55 to 64	100.0	4.3	69.3	13.4	12.9
Aged 65 to 74	100.0	4.0	55.1	7.8	33.1
Aged 75 to 84	100.0	4.2	32.0	4.3	59.5
Aged 85 or older	100.0	5.2	11.6	2.0	81.1

Source: Bureau of the Census, Marital Status and Living Arrangements: March 1995, *Current Population Reports, P20-491, 1996*

Interracial Married Couples, 1980 to 1995

(total number of married couples, number of interracial couples by race, and interracial share of total couples, 1980–95; numbers in thousands)

	total couples	interracial married couples total	black/white total	black/white black husband white wife	black/white white husband black wife	white/ other race	black/ other race
Number							
1995	54,937	1,392	328	206	122	988	76
1994	54,251	1,283	296	196	100	909	78
1993	54,199	1,195	242	182	60	920	33
1992	53,512	1,161	246	163	83	883	32
1991	53,227	994	231	156	75	720	43
1990	53,256	964	211	150	61	720	33
1989	52,924	953	219	155	64	703	31
1988	52,613	956	218	149	69	703	35
1987	52,286	799	177	121	56	581	41
1986	51,704	827	181	136	45	613	33
1985	51,114	792	164	117	47	599	29
1984	50,864	762	175	111	64	564	23
1983	50,665	719	164	118	46	522	33
1982	50,294	697	155	108	47	515	27
1981	49,896	639	132	104	28	484	23
1980	49,714	651	167	122	45	450	34
Percent							
1995	100.0%	2.5%	0.6%	0.4%	0.2%	1.8%	0.1%
1994	100.0	2.4	0.5	0.4	0.2	1.7	0.1
1993	100.0	2.2	0.4	0.3	0.1	1.7	0.1
1992	100.0	2.2	0.5	0.3	0.2	1.7	0.1
1991	100.0	1.9	0.4	0.3	0.1	1.4	0.1
1990	100.0	1.8	0.4	0.3	0.1	1.4	0.1
1989	100.0	1.8	0.4	0.3	0.1	1.3	0.1
1988	100.0	1.8	0.4	0.3	0.1	1.3	0.1
1987	100.0	1.5	0.3	0.2	0.1	1.1	0.1
1986	100.0	1.6	0.4	0.3	0.1	1.2	0.1
1985	100.0	1.5	0.3	0.2	0.1	1.2	0.1
1984	100.0	1.5	0.3	0.2	0.1	1.1	0.0
1983	100.0	1.4	0.3	0.2	0.1	1.0	0.1
1982	100.0	1.4	0.3	0.2	0.1	1.0	0.1
1981	100.0	1.3	0.3	0.2	0.1	1.0	0.0
1980	100.0	1.3	0.3	0.2	0.1	0.9	0.1

Source: Bureau of the Census web site, http://www.census.gov; *calculations by New Strategist*

Interracial and Interethnic Married Couples, 1996

(number and percent distribution of married couples by race and Hispanic origin of husband and wife, 1996; numbers in thousands)

| | total | race of wife | | | origin of wife | |
		white	black	other	non-Hispanic	Hispanic
Married couples, number	**54,664**	**48,584**	**3,684**	**2,396**	**49,940**	**4,724**
Race of husband						
White	48,747	48,056	117	575	44,231	4,517
Black	3,812	220	3,560	32	3,698	113
Other	2,105	309	7	1,789	2,011	94
Origin of husband						
Non-Hispanic	50,149	44,241	3,591	2,317	49,312	836
Hispanic	4,516	4,343	93	79	628	3,888
Married couples, percent	**100.0%**	**88.9%**	**6.7%**	**4.4%**	**91.4%**	**8.6%**
Race of husband						
White	89.2	87.9	0.2	0.1	80.9	8.3
Black	7.0	0.4	6.5	3.3	6.8	0.2
Other	3.9	0.6	0.0	3.3	3.7	0.2
Origin of husband						
Non-Hispanic	91.7	80.9	6.6	4.2	90.2	1.5
Hispanic	8.3	7.9	0.2	0.1	1.1	7.1

Note: Hispanics may be of any race.
Source: Bureau of the Census, Household and Family Characteristics: March 1996, Current Population Reports, P20-495(Update), 1997; calculations by New Strategist

Total Population: Housing

Homeownership is reaching record proportions as the baby-boom generation fills the prime age group of homeownership.

Sixty-five percent of Americans owned their home in 1995. Homeownership is highest in the Midwest, at 70 percent. It is lowest in the West, where just 59 percent of householders are homeowners.

Sixty-two percent of all occupied housing units in the U.S. are single-family detached structures. American homes have a median of 5.5 rooms, and half have more than one bathroom. Most homes have a dishwasher; washing machine; clothes dryer; a porch, deck, balcony, or patio; telephone; and garage or carport.

Fully 74 percent of Americans rate their homes at least an eight on a scale of 1 to 10, with 1 being the worst and 10 the best. This includes 82 percent of homeowners and 59 percent of renters. Only 7 percent of householders think crime is a problem in their area. Homeowners paid a median of $51,305 for their homes, which are currently valued at a median of $92,507.

Sixteen percent of Americans moved between 1995 and 1996. The mobility rate was highest for those aged 20 to 29.

■ Homeownership will continue to increase as boomers age into their 50s and 60s.

Homeownership rates are highest in the Midwest

(percent of householders who own their home, by region, 1995)

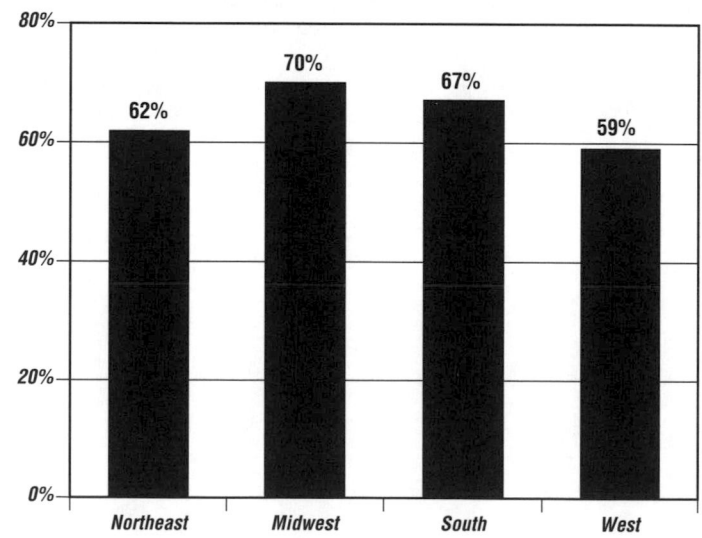

Region of Residence and Metropolitan Status of Total Housing Units, 1995

(number, percent distribution, and percent of total occupied housing units, by regional, metropolitan, and homeownership status, 1995; numbers in thousands)

	total		owner			renter		
	number	percent distrib.	number	percent distrib.	percent of total	number	percent distrib.	percent of total
Total occupied housing units	**97,693**	**100.0%**	**63,544**	**100.0%**	**65.0%**	**34,150**	**100.0%**	**35.0%**
Northeast	19,200	19.7	11,861	18.7	61.8	7,338	21.5	38.2
Midwest	23,662	24.2	16,567	26.1	70.0	7,096	20.8	30.0
South	34,236	35.0	22,959	36.1	67.1	11,277	33.0	32.9
West	20,596	21.1	12,157	19.1	59.0	8,439	24.7	41.0
In metropolitan areas	76,107	77.9	47,688	75.0	62.7	28,398	83.2	37.3
In central cities	30,243	31.0	14,808	23.3	49.0	15,434	45.2	51.0
In suburbs	45,864	46.9	32,880	51.7	71.7	12,964	38.0	28.3
Outside metropolitan areas	21,586	22.1	15,855	25.0	73.5	5,731	16.8	26.5

Source: Bureau of the Census, American Housing Survey for the United States in 1995, *Current Housing Reports, H150/95, 1997; calculations by New Strategist*

Characteristics of Housing Units Occupied by the Total Population, 1995

(number and percent distribution of total occupied housing units, by selected housing characteristics and homeownership status, 1995; numbers in thousands)

	total		owner-occupied		renter-occupied	
	number	percent	number	percent	number	percent
Total occupied housing units	**97,693**	**100.0%**	**63,544**	**100.0%**	**34,150**	**100.0%**
Units in structure						
One, detached	60,826	62.3	52,257	82.2	8,569	25.1
One, attached	5,545	5.7	2,936	4.6	2,609	7.6
Two to four	9,299	9.5	1,734	2.7	7,565	22.2
Five to nine	4,803	4.9	520	0.8	4,283	12.5
10 to 19	4,342	4.4	368	0.6	3,974	11.6
20 to 49	3,244	3.3	342	0.5	2,903	8.5
50 or more	3,470	3.6	550	0.9	2,920	8.6
Mobile home or trailer	6,164	6.3	4,837	7.6	1,328	3.9
Median number of rooms in unit	**5.5**	–	**6.2**	–	**4.2**	–
Median square footage of unit	**1,732**	–	**1,814**	–	**1,270**	–
Number of bathrooms						
None	465	0.5	195	0.3	270	0.8
One	43,777	44.8	19,069	30.0	24,709	72.4
One and one-half	14,780	15.1	11,319	17.8	3,461	10.1
Two or more	38,671	39.6	32,961	51.9	5,710	16.7
Primary heating fuel						
Housing units with heating fuel	96,650	98.9	63,081	99.3	33,569	98.3
Electricity	26,771	27.4	15,485	24.4	11,286	33.0
Piped gas	49,203	50.4	33,438	52.6	15,765	46.2
Bottled gas	4,251	4.4	3,318	5.2	933	2.7
Fuel oil	10,974	11.2	6,871	10.8	4,104	12.0
Kerosene or other liquid fuel	1,055	1.1	756	1.2	298	0.9
Coal or coke	210	0.2	177	0.3	33	0.1
Wood	3,533	3.6	2,708	4.3	825	2.4
Solar energy	16	0.0	13	0.0	3	0.0
Other	637	0.7	315	0.5	321	0.9

(continued)

(continued from previous page)

	total		owner-occupied		renter-occupied	
	number	*percent*	*number*	*percent*	*number*	*percent*
Selected equipment						
Dishwasher	52,508	53.7%	40,236	63.3%	12,272	35.9%
Washing machine	75,745	77.5	60,034	94.5	15,711	46.0
Clothes dryer	70,756	72.4	57,184	90.0	13,571	39.7
Disposal in kitchen sink	42,451	43.5	28,793	45.3	13,659	40.0
Air conditioning	46,577	47.7	34,161	53.8	12,415	36.4
Porch, deck, balcony, or patio	75,657	77.4	54,319	85.5	21,338	62.5
Telephone	91,544	93.7	61,676	97.1	29,868	87.5
Usable fireplace	31,734	32.5	27,280	42.9	4,454	13.0
Garage or carport	57,352	58.7	46,906	73.8	10,446	30.6
Cars and trucks available						
No cars, trucks, or vans	9,583	9.8	2,491	3.9	7,092	20.8
One car, with or without						
trucks or vans	48,263	49.4	30,648	48.2	17,615	51.6
Two or more cars	32,841	33.6	25,736	40.5	7,105	20.8
Overall opinion of housing unit						
1 (worst)	540	0.6	159	0.3	381	1.1
2	399	0.4	122	0.2	276	0.8
3	751	0.8	213	0.3	537	1.6
4	1,088	1.1	379	0.6	709	2.1
5	5,844	6.0	2,374	3.7	3,470	10.2
6	4,738	4.8	2,091	3.3	2,647	7.8
7	10,998	11.3	5,632	8.9	5,366	15.7
8	24,256	24.8	15,274	24.0	8,982	26.3
9	15,173	15.5	10,994	17.3	4,179	12.2
10 (best)	32,826	33.6	25,753	40.5	7,073	20.7

Source: Bureau of the Census, American Housing Survey for the United States in 1995, *Current Housing Reports, H150/95RV, 1997; calculations by New Strategist*

Neighborhood Characteristics of Total Housing Units, 1995

(number and percent distribution of total occupied housing units, by selected neighborhood character-istics and homeownership status, 1995; numbers in thousands)

	total		owner-occupied		renter-occupied	
	number	*percent*	*number*	*percent*	*number*	*percent*
Total occupied housing units	**97,693**	**100.0%**	**63,544**	**100.0%**	**34,150**	**100.0%**
Overall opinion of neighborhood						
1 (worst)	1,349	1.4	447	0.7	902	2.6
2	795	0.8	324	0.5	471	1.4
3	1,208	1.2	482	0.8	726	2.1
4	1,813	1.9	764	1.2	1,049	3.1
5	7,011	7.2	3,387	5.3	3,623	10.6
6	4,919	5.0	2,521	4.0	2,398	7.0
7	10,173	10.4	5,943	9.4	4,230	12.4
8	22,242	22.8	14,692	23.1	7,551	22.1
9	14,361	14.7	10,311	16.2	4,050	11.9
10 (best)	31,623	32.4	23,354	36.8	8,269	24.2
Neighborhood problems						
No problems	60,176	61.6	40,612	63.9	19,563	57.3
With problems*	34,852	35.7	21,308	33.5	13,543	39.7
Crime	6,926	7.1	2,920	4.6	4,007	11.7
Noise	7,396	7.6	3,505	5.5	3,891	11.4
Traffic	7,319	7.5	4,478	7.0	2,842	8.3
Litter or housing deterioration	4,058	4.2	2,680	4.2	1,378	4.0
Poor city or county services	1,179	1.2	777	1.2	402	1.2
Undesirable commerical, institutional, industrial	1,335	1.4	870	1.4	465	1.4
People	11,161	11.4	6,147	9.7	5,013	14.7
Other	9,441	9.7	6,683	10.5	2,758	8.1
Not reported	604	0.6	395	0.6	208	0.6

* Numbers will not add to total because more than one problem could be cited.
Source: Bureau of the Census, American Housing Survey for the United States in 1995, Current Housing Reports, H150/95RV, 1997; calculations by New Strategist

Housing Value and Purchase Price for Total Homeowners, 1995

(number and percent distribution of total homeowners by value of home, purchase price, and major source of down payment, 1995; numbers in thousands)

	number	*percent*
Total homeowners	**63,544**	**100.0%**
Value of home		
Under $50,000	12,960	20.4
$50,000 to $79,999	13,273	20.9
$80,000 to $99,999	8,857	13.9
$100,000 to $149,999	12,725	20.0
$150,000 to $199,999	7,153	11.3
$200,000 to $299,999	5,118	8.1
$300,000 or more	3,459	5.4
Median	$92,507	–
Purchase price*		
Home purchased or built	61,676	97.1
Under $50,000	26,147	41.1
$50,000 to $79,999	9,933	15.6
$80,000 to $99,999	4,902	7.7
$100,000 to $149,999	6,103	9.6
$150,000 to $199,999	2,998	4.7
$200,000 to $299,999	1,946	3.1
$300,000 or more	1,188	1.9
Received as inheritance or gift	1,531	2.4
Median purchase price	$51,305	
Major source of down payment*		
Sale of previous home	18,369	28.9
Savings of cash on hand	28,233	44.4
Sale of other investment	427	0.7
Borrowing, other than mortgage	1,807	2.8
Inheritance or gift	1,391	2.2
Land where building built used for financing	434	0.7
Other	2,819	4.4
No down payment	4,420	7.0

* Numbers may not add to total because "not reported" is not shown.
Source: Bureau of the Census, American Housing Survey for the United States in 1995, *Current Housing Reports, H150/95RV, 1997; calculations by New Strategist*

Geographical Mobility of the Total Population by Age, 1995–96

(total number of persons aged 1 or older and number and percent of those who moved between March 1995 and March 1996, by age of person and type of move; numbers in thousands)

		same house (non-movers)	different house in the U.S.							moved from abroad
					different county					
							different state			
	total		total	same county	total	same state	total	same region	different region	
Number										
Total, 1 or older	260,406	217,868	41,176	26,696	14,480	8,009	6,471	3,113	1,312	1,361
Aged 1 to 4	16,160	12,098	3,923	2,759	1,164	656	508	223	99	140
Aged 5 to 9	20,171	16,443	3,603	2,432	1,171	618	553	237	98	126
Aged 10 to 14	19,449	16,606	2,766	1,871	895	463	431	231	72	77
Aged 15 to 19	18,649	15,796	2,751	1,855	895	521	374	205	75	102
Aged 15 to 17	11,458	10,006	1,406	951	455	266	190	93	43	46
Aged 18 and 19	7,190	5,790	1,344	904	440	256	184	112	32	56
Aged 20 to 24	17,653	11,698	5,730	3,752	1,978	1,135	842	402	190	225
Aged 25 to 29	19,462	13,009	6,245	3,912	2,333	1,283	1,051	484	222	208
Aged 30 to 34	21,457	16,767	4,496	2,800	1,695	873	822	387	147	194
Aged 35 to 39	22,479	18,887	3,465	2,258	1,207	696	511	236	88	128
Aged 40 to 44	20,598	18,126	2,405	1,603	802	460	342	152	90	66
Aged 45 to 49	18,221	16,310	1,872	1,177	696	367	329	185	84	38
Aged 50 to 54	13,363	12,189	1,155	689	466	281	186	115	54	19
Aged 55 to 59	11,300	10,504	787	448	339	193	146	83	33	9
Aged 60 to 64	9,784	9,186	587	321	265	161	105	46	19	11
Aged 60 and 61	4,058	3,811	240	143	97	66	31	14	9	7
Aged 62 to 64	5,726	5,375	347	179	168	94	74	32	11	4
Aged 65 to 69	9,746	9,272	465	278	187	107	80	37	11	10
Aged 70 to 74	8,524	8,188	336	210	126	61	65	32	17	–
Aged 75 to 79	6,485	6,201	280	155	125	61	65	27	3	4
Aged 80 to 84	4,083	3,919	159	94	65	31	33	12	3	5
Aged 85 or older	2,819	2,669	151	81	69	42	28	17	8	–
Median age	34.4	36.7	26.5	25.9	27.4	27.4	27.5	27.7	27.8	25.3

(continued)

(continued from previous page)

		same house (non-movers)	different house in the U.S.		different county			different state			moved from abroad
Percent	total		total	same county	total	same state	total	same region	different region	
Total, aged 1 or older	**100.0%**	**83.7%**	**15.8%**	**10.3%**	**5.6%**	**3.1%**	**2.5%**	**1.2%**	**0.5%**	**0.5%**
Aged 1 to 4	100.0	74.9	24.3	17.1	7.2	4.1	3.1	1.4	0.6	0.9
Aged 5 to 9	100.0	81.5	17.9	12.1	5.8	3.1	2.7	1.2	0.5	0.6
Aged 10 to 14	100.0	85.4	14.2	9.6	4.6	2.4	2.2	1.2	0.4	0.4
Aged 15 to 19	100.0	84.7	14.8	9.9	4.8	2.8	2.0	1.1	0.4	0.5
Aged 15 to 17	100.0	87.3	12.3	8.3	4.0	2.3	1.7	0.8	0.4	0.4
Aged 18 and 19	100.0	80.5	18.7	12.6	6.1	3.6	2.6	1.6	0.4	0.8
Aged 20 to 24	100.0	66.3	32.5	21.3	11.2	6.4	4.8	2.3	1.1	1.3
Aged 25 to 29	100.0	66.8	32.1	20.1	12.0	6.6	5.4	2.5	1.1	1.1
Aged 30 to 34	100.0	78.1	21.0	13.0	7.9	4.1	3.8	1.8	0.7	0.9
Aged 35 to 39	100.0	84.0	15.4	10.0	5.4	3.1	2.3	1.0	0.4	0.6
Aged 40 to 44	100.0	88.0	11.7	7.8	3.9	2.2	1.7	0.7	0.4	0.3
Aged 45 to 49	100.0	89.5	10.3	6.5	3.8	2.0	1.8	1.0	0.5	0.2
Aged 50 to 54	100.0	91.2	8.6	5.2	3.5	2.1	1.4	0.9	0.4	0.1
Aged 55 to 59	100.0	93.0	7.0	4.0	3.0	1.7	1.3	0.7	0.3	0.1
Aged 60 to 64	100.0	93.9	6.0	3.3	2.7	1.6	1.1	0.5	0.2	0.1
Aged 60 and 61	100.0	93.9	5.9	3.5	2.4	1.6	0.8	0.3	0.2	0.2
Aged 62 to 64	100.0	93.9	6.1	3.1	2.9	1.6	1.3	0.6	0.2	0.1
Aged 65 to 69	100.0	95.1	4.8	2.9	1.9	1.1	0.8	0.4	0.1	0.1
Aged 70 to 74	100.0	96.1	3.9	2.5	1.5	0.7	0.8	0.4	0.2	–
Aged 75 to 79	100.0	95.6	4.3	2.4	1.9	0.9	1.0	0.4	0.0	0.1
Aged 80 to 84	100.0	96.0	3.9	2.3	1.6	0.8	0.8	0.3	0.1	0.1
Aged 85 or older	100.0	94.7	5.4	2.9	2.4	1.5	1.0	0.6	0.3	–

Note: (–) means sample is too small to make a reliable estimate.
Source: Bureau of the Census, Geographical Mobility: March 1995 to March 1996, *Current Population Reports, P20–497(Update), 1997; calculations by New Strategist*

Reasons for Moving among Total Households by Homeownership Status, 1995

(number and percent distribution of total households that moved in the past 12 months by reason for move and for choosing new neighborhood and house, and by comparison with previous home and neighborhood, by homeownership status, 1995; numbers in thousands)

	total		owner-occupied		renter-occupied	
	number	percent	number	percent	number	percent
Total movers	**17,655**	**100.0%**	**5,254**	**100.0%**	**12,400**	**100.0%**
Reasons for leaving previous unit*						
Private displacement	926	5.2	226	4.3	700	5.6
Government displacement	192	1.1	27	0.5	165	1.3
Disaster loss	82	0.5	25	0.5	57	0.5
New job or job transfer	2,097	11.9	520	9.9	1,577	12.7
To be closer to work, school, other	1,775	10.1	298	5.7	1,477	11.9
Other, financial or employment-related	854	4.8	158	3.0	697	5.6
To establish own household	2,646	15.0	687	13.1	1,959	15.8
Needed larger house or apartment	2,393	13.6	814	15.5	1,579	12.7
Married	516	2.9	209	4.0	307	2.5
Widowed, divorced, or separated	880	5.0	235	4.5	646	5.2
Other, family or person related	1,860	10.5	491	9.3	1,369	11.0
Wanted better home	2,062	11.7	673	12.8	1,389	11.2
Change from owner to renter	192	1.1	—	–	192	1.5
Change from renter to owner	1,160	6.6	1,160	22.1	–	–
Wanted lower rent or maintenance	1,035	5.9	159	3.0	876	7.1
Choice of present neighborhood*						
Convenient to job	4,195	23.8	918	17.5	3,277	26.4
Convenient to friends or relatives	3,130	17.7	790	15.0	2,340	18.9
Convenient to leisure activities	845	4.8	266	5.1	579	4.7
Convenient to public transportation	632	3.6	119	2.3	513	4.1
Good schools	1,622	9.2	657	12.5	965	7.8
Other public services	384	2.2	132	2.5	252	2.0
Looks or design of neighborhood	3,391	19.2	1,469	28.0	1,923	15.5
House was most important consideration	4,209	23.8	1,613	30.7	2,596	20.9
Neighborhood search						
Looked at just this neighborhood	7,031	39.8	1,647	31.3	5,385	43.4
Looked at other neighborhoods	9,913	56.1	3,293	62.7	6,620	53.4

(continued)

(continued from previous page)

	total		owner-occupied		renter-occupied	
	number	*percent*	*number*	*percent*	*number*	*percent*
Choice of present home*						
Financial reasons	7,153	40.5%	2,109	40.1%	5,043	40.7%
Room layout or design	3,962	22.4	1,736	33.0	2,226	18.0
Kitchen	414	2.3	246	4.7	168	1.4
Size	2,957	16.7	1,055	20.1	1,902	15.3
Exterior appearance	1,455	8.2	739	14.1	716	5.8
Yard, trees, view	1,452	8.2	732	13.9	719	5.8
Quality of construction	1,086	6.2	683	13.0	403	3.3
Only one available	1,976	11.2	192	3.7	1,784	14.4
Other reasons	5,336	30.2	1,405	26.7	3,930	31.7
Comparison to previous home						
Better home	9,034	51.2	3,318	63.2	5,716	46.1
Worse home	3,353	19.0	525	10.0	2,829	22.8
About the same	4,578	25.9	1,098	20.9	3,479	28.1
Comparison to previous neighborhood						
Better neighborhood	6,854	38.8	2496	14.1	4,358	24.7
Worse neighborhood	2,792	15.8	418	2.4	2,375	13.5
About the same	6,254	35.4	1747	9.9	4,507	25.5
Same neighborhood	1,029	5.8	257	1.5	771	4.4

* Numbers may not add to total because more than one category may apply and unreported reasons are not shown.
Note: (–) means not applicable.
Source: Bureau of the Census, American Housing Survey for the United States in 1995, *Current Housing Reports, H150/95RV, 1997; calculations by New Strategist*

Homeownership in the 50 Largest Metropolitan Areas, 1990

(total number of households, percent of total households that are owner occupied, and median value of owner-occupied houses, in the U.S. and in the 50 largest metropolitan areas ranked alphabetically, 1990; numbers in thousands)

	number	owner-occupied percent	owner-occupied median value
Total households	**91,947**	**64.2%**	**$78,300**
Anaheim–Santa Ana, CA	827	60.1	252,700
Atlanta, GA	1,056	62.3	88,300
Baltimore, MD	880	63.7	101,200
Bergen-Passaic, NJ	464	63.9	214,400
Boston, MA	1,081	55.9	186,100
Buffalo, NY	377	63.7	74,100
Charlotte–Gastonia–Rock Hill, NC-SC	441	66.8	72,200
Chicago, IL	2,222	58.6	111,200
Cincinnati, OH	548	63.1	70,700
Cleveland, OH	712	65.4	74,100
Columbus, OH	525	60.1	55,600
Dallas, TX	955	55.1	82,100
Denver, CO	649	61.6	86,800
Detroit, MI	1,619	69.8	68,200
Fort Lauderdale–Hollywood–Pompano Beach, FL	528	68.0	89,800
Fort Worth–Arlington, TX	495	60.3	71,800
Greensboro–Winston-Salem–High Point, NC	372	67.3	71,200
Houston, TX	1,186	54.9	63,900
Indianapolis, IN	480	63.8	66,900
Kansas City, MO-KS	602	65.4	66,100
Los Angeles–Long Beach, CA	2,990	48.2	226,400
Louisville, KY-IN	368	67.5	56,000
Miami–Hialeah, FL	692	54.3	85,300
Milwaukee, WI	538	59.4	76,600
Minneapolis–St. Paul, MN-WI	936	68.7	87,400
Monmouth–Ocean, NJ	366	77.4	150,600
Nashville, TN	376	63.2	75,800
Nassau–Suffolk, NY	856	80.3	187,000

(continued)

(continued from previous page)

	number	owner-occupied	
		percent	*median value*
New Orleans, LA	455	58.0%	$69,800
New York, NY	3,252	33.3	209,000
Newark, NJ	652	59.1	191,400
Norfolk–Virginia Beach–Newport News, VA	494	58.9	85,700
Oakland, CA	780	58.8	224,400
Oklahoma City, OK	368	64.3	53,900
Orlando, FL	402	61.9	83,100
Philadelphia, PA-NJ	1,777	69.6	100,800
Phoenix, AZ	808	63.3	84,300
Pittsburgh, PA	820	69.3	54,800
Portland, OR	487	60.7	72,100
Riverside–San Bernardino, CA	867	65.2	133,900
Rochester, NY	374	67.6	85,600
Sacramento, CA	556	59.0	136,700
San Antonio, TX	451	59.2	56,900
San Diego, CA	887	53.8	186,700
San Francisco, CA	643	48.3	332,400
San Jose, CA	520	59.1	289,400
Seattle, WA	788	60.4	136,700
St. Louis, MO-IL	925	68.5	69,700
Tampa–St. Petersburg–Clearwater, FL	869	69.3	71,100
Washington, DC MD VA	1,459	60.5	166,100

Source: Bureau of the Census, unpublished tables from the 1990 census; calculations by New Strategist

Total Population: Income

The affluence of Americans is close to an all-time high as baby boomers age into their peak earning years.

The median income of American households fell 1 percent between 1990 and 1996, to $35,492 after adjusting for inflation. Despite this decline, median household income in 1996 was 5 percent higher than in 1980, after adjusting for inflation.

Household income peaks for householders aged 45 to 54, at $50,472 in 1996. Among household types, incomes are greatest for married couples, with a median of $49,858. Thirteen percent of married couples had incomes of $100,000 or more in 1996.

For men who work full-time, median earnings stood at $33,538 in 1996. For their female counterparts, the figure was $24,935. Since 1980, the median earnings of men who work full-time has fallen 8 percent, after adjusting for inflation. In contrast, women's median earnings have increased 13 percent. Consequently, the median earnings of women have grown from 61 to 74 percent of the median earnings of men.

Overall, 11 percent of American families were poor in 1996, a slightly larger proportion than in 1990 and 1980. By age, children have the highest poverty rate in the nation—21 percent of people under age 18 are poor versus 14 percent of the population as a whole.

■ American affluence should continue to grow for another decade as boomers fill the 45-to-54 age group.

Household incomes peak in the 45-to-54 age group

(median household income by age of householder, 1996)

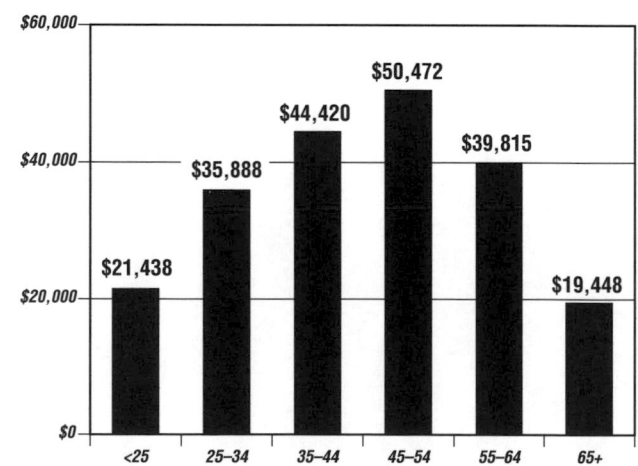

Median Income of Total Households, 1980 to 1996

(median income of total households, 1980–96, and percent change in income for selected years; in 1996 dollars)

	median income
1996	$35,492
1995	35,082
1994	34,158
1993	33,922
1992	34,261
1991	34,705
1990	35,945
1989	36,575
1988	36,108
1987	35,994
1986	35,642
1985	34,439
1984	33,849
1983	32,900
1982	33,105
1981	33,215
1980	33,763
Percent change	
1990–1996	–1.3%
1980–1996	5.1

Source: Bureau of the Census, unpublished tables from the 1997 Current Population Survey; calculations by New Strategist

Income Distribution of Total Households by Age of Householder, 1996

(number and percent distribution of total households by household income and age of householder, 1996; households in thousands as of 1997)

	total	< age 25	25–34	35–44	45–54	55–64	65+
Total households, number	**101,018**	**5,160**	**19,314**	**23,823**	**18,843**	**12,469**	**21,408**
Under $10,000	11,879	1,124	1,790	1,711	1,354	1,422	4,479
$10,000 to $19,999	16,526	1,272	2,681	2,564	1,742	1,751	6,516
$20,000 to $29,999	14,887	1,042	3,279	3,076	1,998	1,690	3,800
$30,000 to $39,999	12,475	691	3,020	3,148	1,996	1,396	2,226
$40,000 to $49,999	10,552	418	2,382	2,886	2,229	1,263	1,374
$50,000 to $59,999	8,763	269	2,014	2,574	1,840	1,196	870
$60,000 to $69,999	6,717	112	1,400	2,208	1,607	856	534
$70,000 to $79,999	5,072	89	955	1,565	1,364	678	421
$80,000 to $89,999	3,447	39	539	1,069	1,043	493	262
$90,000 to $99,999	2,408	30	333	691	782	357	215
$100,000 or more	8,293	76	921	2,330	2,883	1,369	714
Median income	$35,492	$21,438	$35,888	$44,420	$50,472	$39,815	$19,448
Total households, percent	**100.0%**	**100.0%**	**100.0%**	**100.0%**	**100.0%**	**100.0%**	**100.0%**
Under $10,000	11.8	21.8	9.3	7.2	7.2	11.4	20.9
$10,000 to $19,999	16.4	24.7	13.9	10.8	9.2	14.0	30.4
$20,000 to $29,999	14.7	20.2	17.0	12.9	10.6	13.6	17.8
$30,000 to $39,999	12.3	13.4	15.6	13.2	10.6	11.2	10.4
$40,000 to $49,999	10.4	8.1	12.3	12.1	11.8	10.1	6.4
$50,000 to $59,999	8.7	5.2	10.4	10.8	9.8	9.6	4.1
$60,000 to $69,999	6.6	2.2	7.2	9.3	8.5	6.9	2.5
$70,000 to $79,999	5.0	1.7	4.9	6.6	7.2	5.4	2.0
$80,000 to $89,999	3.4	0.8	2.8	4.5	5.5	4.0	1.2
$90,000 to $99,999	2.4	0.6	1.7	2.9	4.2	2.9	1.0
$100,000 or more	8.2	1.5	4.8	9.8	15.3	11.0	3.3

Source: Bureau of the Census, Money Income in the United States: 1996; *Current Population Reports, P60-197, 1997; calculations by New Strategist*

Income Distribution of Total Households by Household Type, 1996

(number and percent distribution of total households by household income and household type, 1996; households in thousands as of 1997)

| | total households | family households | | | | nonfamily households | | | | |
| | | total | married couples | female hh, no spouse present | male hh, no spouse present | total | female hh | | male hh | |
							total	living alone	total	living alone
Total households, number	101,018	70,241	53,604	12,790	3,847	30,777	17,070	14,961	13,707	10,442
Under $10,000	11,879	4,870	1,635	2,939	296	7,009	4,942	4,834	2,066	1,895
$10,000 to $19,999	16,526	8,767	5,096	3,049	622	7,758	4,951	4,657	2,808	2,429
$20,000 to $29,999	14,887	9,650	6,721	2,258	671	5,237	2,688	2,298	2,551	2,058
$30,000 to $39,999	12,475	8,997	6,813	1,606	577	3,478	1,555	1,325	1,924	1,443
$40,000 to $49,999	10,552	8,188	6,617	1,062	508	2,364	987	742	1,375	948
$50,000 to $59,999	8,763	7,138	6,056	685	398	1,624	692	441	933	590
$60,000 to $69,999	6,717	5,754	5,120	403	232	962	381	204	580	200
$70,000 to $79,999	5,072	4,421	3,952	286	184	651	227	130	423	74
$80,000 to $89,999	3,447	2,983	2,712	169	104	462	178	87	286	40
$90,000 to $99,999	2,408	2,118	1,944	103	71	290	121	58	169	195
$100,000 or more	8,293	7,352	6,939	230	183	941	349	185	591	153
Median income	$35,492	$43,082	$49,858	$21,564	$35,658	$20,973	$16,398	$14,626	$27,266	$24,050
Total households, percent	100.0%	100.0%	100.0%	100.0%	100.0%	100.0%	100.0%	100.0%	100.0%	100.0%
Under $10,000	11.8	6.9	3.1	23.0	7.7	22.8	29.0	32.3	15.1	18.1
$10,000 to $19,999	16.4	12.5	9.5	23.8	16.2	25.2	29.0	31.1	20.5	23.3
$20,000 to $29,999	14.7	13.7	12.5	17.7	17.4	17.0	15.7	15.4	18.6	19.7
$30,000 to $39,999	12.3	12.8	12.7	12.6	15.0	11.3	9.1	8.9	14.0	13.8
$40,000 to $49,999	10.4	11.7	12.3	8.3	13.2	7.7	5.8	5.0	10.0	9.1
$50,000 to $59,999	8.7	10.2	11.3	5.4	10.3	5.3	4.1	2.9	6.8	5.7
$60,000 to $69,999	6.6	8.2	9.6	3.2	6.0	3.1	2.2	1.4	4.2	1.9
$70,000 to $79,999	5.0	6.3	7.4	2.2	4.8	2.1	1.3	0.9	3.1	0.7
$80,000 to $89,999	3.4	4.2	5.1	1.3	2.7	1.5	1.0	0.6	2.1	0.4
$90,000 to $99,999	2.4	3.0	3.6	0.8	1.8	0.9	0.7	0.4	1.2	1.9
$100,000 or more	8.2	10.5	12.9	1.8	4.8	3.1	2.0	1.2	4.3	1.5

Source: Bureau of the Census, Money Income in the United States: 1996, *Current Population Reports, P60-197, 1997; calculations by New Strategist*

Income Distribution of Total Men by Age, 1996

(number and percent distribution of total men aged 15 or older by income and age, 1996; men in thousands as of 1997)

	total	< age 25	25–34	35–44	45–54	55–64	65+
Total men, number	**100,159**	**18,539**	**20,040**	**21,793**	**16,119**	**10,265**	**13,404**
Without income	6,720	4,522	686	612	371	299	230
With income	93,439	14,016	19,354	21,181	15,748	9,966	13,173
Under $10,000	19,416	8,536	2,526	2,225	1,664	1,540	2,925
$10,000 to $19,999	20,093	3,374	4,505	3,379	2,162	1,792	4,880
$20,000 to $29,999	16,696	1,413	4,740	3,848	2,472	1,713	2,511
$30,000 to $39,999	12,530	464	3,449	3,701	2,374	1,472	1,072
$40,000 to $49,999	8,268	129	1,863	2,693	2,040	994	548
$50,000 to $74,999	9,912	75	1,655	3,275	2,924	1,287	695
$75,000 to $99,999	3,203	14	315	1,000	1,054	560	260
$100,000 or more	3,319	12	297	1,061	1,057	610	281
Median income of men with income	$23,834	$6,960	$25,179	$32,167	$36,232	$29,526	$16,684
Total men, percent	**100.0%**	**100.0%**	**100.0%**	**100.0%**	**100.0%**	**100.0%**	**100.0%**
Without income	6.7	24.4	3.4	2.8	2.3	2.9	1.7
With income	93.3	75.6	96.6	97.2	97.7	97.1	98.3
Under $10,000	19.4	46.0	12.6	10.2	10.3	15.0	21.8
$10,000 to $19,999	20.1	18.2	22.5	15.5	13.4	17.5	36.4
$20,000 to $29,999	16.7	7.6	23.7	17.7	15.3	16.7	18.7
$30,000 to $39,999	12.5	2.5	17.2	17.0	14.7	14.3	8.0
$40,000 to $49,999	8.3	0.7	9.3	12.4	12.7	9.7	4.1
$50,000 to $74,999	9.9	0.4	8.3	15.0	18.1	12.5	5.2
$75,000 to $99,999	3.2	0.1	1.6	4.6	6.5	5.5	1.9
$100,000 or more	3.3	0.1	1.5	4.9	6.6	5.9	2.1

Source: Bureau of the Census, Money Income in the United States: 1996; *Current Population Reports, P60-197, 1997; calculations by New Strategist*

Income Distribution of Total Women by Age, 1996

(number and percent distribution of total women aged 15 or older by income and age, 1996; women in thousands as of 1997)

	total	< age 25	25–34	35–44	45–54	55–64	65+
Total women, number	**107,076**	**18,115**	**20,217**	**22,167**	**16,894**	**11,210**	**18,474**
Without income	10,518	4,613	1,736	1,530	1,201	990	448
With income	96,558	13,502	18,481	20,637	15,693	10,220	18,026
Under $10,000	39,349	9,232	6,053	6,125	4,418	4,039	9,480
$10,000 to $19,999	24,578	2,988	4,818	4,799	3,758	2,614	5,600
$20,000 to $29,999	15,038	929	4,052	4,066	2,861	1,556	1,575
$30,000 to $39,999	8,137	236	1,976	2,543	1,909	842	632
$40,000 to $49,999	4,237	58	788	1,398	1,235	462	297
$50,000 to $74,999	3,660	39	602	1,139	1,108	506	262
$75,000 to $99,999	833	11	113	310	209	107	82
$100,000 or more	726	7	82	255	195	90	98
Median income of women with income	$12,815	$5,881	$16,384	$18,447	$19,046	$13,316	$9,626
Total women, percent	**100.0%**	**100.0%**	**100.0%**	**100.0%**	**100.0%**	**100.0%**	**100.0%**
Without income	9.8	25.5	8.6	6.9	7.1	8.8	2.4
With income	90.2	74.5	91.4	93.1	92.9	91.2	97.6
Under $10,000	36.7	51.0	29.9	27.6	26.2	36.0	51.3
$10,000 to $19,999	23.0	16.5	23.8	21.6	22.2	23.3	30.3
$20,000 to $29,999	14.0	5.1	20.0	18.3	16.9	13.9	8.5
$30,000 to $39,999	7.6	1.3	9.8	11.5	11.3	7.5	3.4
$40,000 to $49,999	4.0	0.3	3.9	6.3	7.3	4.1	1.6
$50,000 to $74,999	3.4	0.2	3.0	5.1	6.6	4.5	1.4
$75,000 to $99,999	0.8	0.1	0.6	1.4	1.2	1.0	0.4
$100,000 or more	0.7	0.0	0.4	1.2	1.2	0.8	0.5

Source: Bureau of the Census, Money Income in the United States: 1996, *Current Population Reports, P60-197, 1997; calculations by New Strategist*

Median Earnings of Total Persons Who Work Full-Time by Sex, 1980 to 1996

(median earnings of total persons who work year-round, full-time by sex; and female earnings as a percent of male earnings, 1980–96; percent change in earnings and ratio for selected years; in 1996 dollars)

	median earnings		women's earnings as a percent of men's earnings
	men	*women*	
1996	$33,538	$24,935	74.3%
1995	33,150	24,479	73.8
1994	33,468	24,631	73.6
1993	33,744	24,397	72.3
1992	34,480	24,707	71.7
1991	34,941	24,474	70.0
1990	34,788	24,719	71.1
1989	35,959	24,848	69.1
1988	36,263	24,596	67.8
1987	36,851	24,259	65.8
1986	37,069	24,112	65.0
1985	36,453	23,698	65.0
1984	36,249	23,289	64.2
1983	35,457	22,809	64.3
1982	35,540	22,424	63.1
1981	36,033	21,693	60.2
1980	36,552	22,098	60.5
Percent change			
1990–1996	–3.6%	0.9%	4.6%
1980–1996	–8.2	12.8	23.0

Source: Bureau of the Census, Internet web site, http://www.census.gov; *calculations by New Strategist*

Median Earnings of Total Persons Who Work Full-Time by Education and Sex, 1996

(median earnings of total persons aged 25 or older who work year-round, full-time, by educational attainment and sex, 1996)

	men	*women*	*women's earnings as a percent of men's earnings*
Total persons	**$34,463**	**$24,803**	**72.0%**
Less than 9th grade	17,246	13,572	78.7
9th to 12th grade, no diploma	22,206	16,132	72.6
High school graduate	30,090	20,501	68.1
Some college, no degree	33,293	23,832	71.6
Associate's degree	36,072	26,773	74.2
Bachelor's degree or more	50,134	35,129	70.1
Bachelor's degree	43,780	31,910	72.9
Master's degree	56,076	40,415	72.1
Professional degree	78,144	56,431	72.2
Doctoral degree	66,159	51,989	78.6

Source: U.S. Bureau of the Census, Internet web site, http://www.census.gov; *calculations by New Strategist*

Total Families below the Poverty Level, 1980 to 1996

(total number of families, and number and percent below poverty level, by type of family and presence of children under age 18 at home, 1980–96; percent change in numbers and rates for selected years; families in thousands as of March the following year)

	total families			married couples			female hh, no spouse present		
		in poverty			in poverty			in poverty	
	total	number	percent	total	number	percent	total	number	percent
With and without children under age 18									
1996	70,241	7,708	11.0%	53,604	3,010	5.6%	12,790	4,167	32.6%
1995	69,597	7,532	10.8	53,570	2,982	5.6	12,514	4,057	32.4
1994	69,313	8,053	11.6	53,865	3,272	6.1	12,220	4,232	34.6
1993	68,506	8,393	12.3	53,181	3,481	6.5	12,411	4,424	35.6
1992	68,216	8,144	11.9	53,090	3,385	6.4	12,061	4,275	35.4
1991	67,173	7,712	11.5	52,457	3,158	6.0	11,692	4,161	35.6
1990	66,322	7,098	10.7	52,147	2,981	5.7	11,268	3,768	33.4
1989	66,090	6,784	10.3	52,137	2,931	5.6	10,890	3,504	32.2
1988	65,837	6,874	10.4	52,100	2,897	5.6	10,890	3,642	33.4
1987	65,204	7,005	10.7	51,675	3,011	5.8	10,696	3,654	34.2
1986	64,491	7,023	10.9	51,537	3,123	6.1	10,445	3,613	34.6
1985	63,558	7,223	11.4	50,933	3,438	6.7	10,211	3,474	34.0
1984	62,706	7,277	11.6	50,350	3,488	6.9	10,129	3,498	34.5
1983	62,015	7,647	12.3	50,081	3,815	7.6	9,896	3,564	36.0
1982	61,393	7,512	12.2	49,908	3,789	7.6	9,469	3,434	36.3
1981	61,019	6,851	11.2	49,630	3,394	6.8	9,403	3,252	34.6
1980	60,309	6,217	10.3	49,294	3,032	6.2	9,082	2,972	32.7
Percent change									
1990–1996	5.9%	8.6%	2.8%	2.8%	1.7%	−1.8%	13.5%	10.6%	3.6%
1980–1996	16.5	24.0	6.8	8.7	−0.7	−9.7	40.8	40.2	5.8

(continued)

(continued from previous page)

	total families			married couples			female hh, no spouse present		
		in poverty			in poverty			in poverty	
	total	number	percent	total	number	percent	total	number	percent
With children under age 18									
1996	37,204	6,131	16.5%	26,184	1,964	7.5%	8,957	3,755	41.9%
1995	36,719	5,976	16.3	26,034	1,961	7.5	8,751	3,634	41.5
1994	36,782	6,408	17.4	26,367	2,197	8.3	8,665	3,816	44.0
1993	36,456	6,751	18.5	26,121	2,363	9.0	8,758	4,034	46.1
1992	35,851	6,457	18.0	25,907	2,237	8.6	8,375	3,887	46.2
1991	34,861	6,170	17.7	25,357	2,106	8.3	7,991	3,767	47.1
1990	34,503	5,676	16.4	25,410	1,990	7.8	7,707	3,426	44.5
1989	34,279	5,308	15.5	25,476	1,872	7.3	7,445	3,190	42.8
1988	34,251	5,373	15.7	25,598	1,847	7.2	7,361	3,294	44.7
1987	33,996	5,465	16.1	25,464	1,963	7.7	7,216	3,281	45.5
1986	33,801	5,516	16.3	25,571	2,050	8.0	7,094	3,264	46.0
1985	33,536	5,586	16.7	25,496	2,258	8.9	6,892	3,131	45.4
1984	32,942	5,662	17.2	25,038	2,344	9.4	6,832	3,124	45.7
1983	32,787	5,871	17.9	25,216	2,557	10.1	6,622	3,122	47.1
1982	32,565	5,712	17.5	25,276	2,470	9.8	6,397	3,059	47.8
1981	32,587	5,191	15.9	25,278	2,199	8.7	6,488	2,877	44.3
1980	32,773	4,822	14.7	25,671	1,974	7.7	6,299	2,703	42.9
Percent change									
1990–1996	7.8%	8.0%	0.6%	3.0%	–1.3%	–3.8%	16.2%	9.6%	–5.8%
1980–1996	13.5	27.1	12.2	2.0	-0.5	2.6	42.2	38.9	–2.3

Source: Bureau of the Census, Poverty in the United States: 1996, *Current Population Reports, P60-198, 1997*

Total Persons in Poverty by Sex and Age, 1996

(total number of persons, and number and percent below poverty level by sex and age, 1996; persons in thousands as of 1997)

	total	in poverty number	in poverty percent
Total persons	**266,218**	**36,529**	**13.7%**
Under age 18	70,650	14,463	20.5
Aged 18 to 24	24,987	4,466	17.9
Aged 25 to 34	40,256	5,093	12.7
Aged 35 to 44	43,960	4,343	9.9
Aged 45 to 54	33,013	2,516	7.6
Aged 55 to 59	11,579	1,086	9.4
Aged 60 to 64	9,896	1,134	11.5
Aged 65 to 74	18,015	1,580	8.8
Aged 75 or older	13,862	1,848	13.3
Females, total	**135,865**	**20,918**	**15.4**
Under age 18	34,451	7,215	20.9
Aged 18 to 24	12,452	2,665	21.4
Aged 25 to 34	20,217	3,197	15.8
Aged 35 to 44	22,167	2,537	11.4
Aged 45 to 54	16,894	1,450	8.6
Aged 55 to 59	6,003	651	10.9
Aged 60 to 64	5,207	687	13.2
Aged 65 to 74	9,930	1,122	11.3
Aged 75 or older	8,544	1,394	16.3
Males, total	**130,353**	**15,611**	**12.0**
Under age 18	36,199	7,248	20.0
Aged 18 to 24	12,535	1,801	14.4
Aged 25 to 34	20,040	1,896	9.5
Aged 35 to 44	21,793	1,806	8.3
Aged 45 to 54	16,119	1,006	6.6
Aged 55 to 59	5,575	435	7.8
Aged 60 to 64	4,689	447	9.5
Aged 65 to 74	8,085	458	5.7
Aged 75 or older	5,319	454	8.5

Source: Bureau of the Census, Poverty in the United States: 1996, *Current Population Reports, P60-198, 1997*

Total Population: Labor Force

The proportion of Americans in the labor force is at an all-time high now that dual-income couples are the norm.

Sixty-seven percent of Americans aged 16 or older are in the labor force, including 75 percent of men and 60 percent of women. The labor force participation rate peaks for men aged 25 to 44 at 93 percent. Among women, the participation rate peaks at 78 percent for those aged 35 to 44.

Twenty-nine percent of all employed workers are in managerial or professional specialty occupations. A nearly identical proportion are employed in technical, sales, and administrative support jobs. Farming, forestry, and fishing employ fewer than 3 percent of American workers.

Among married couples, 56 percent are dual earners. Just 22 percent are traditional, that is, only the husband works. For 5 percent of couples, the wife is the only worker, while for another 17 percent neither husband nor wife is in the labor force.

Between 1996 and 2006, the number of Americans in the labor force will grow 11 percent. The labor force participation rate for women is projected to rise slightly to 61 percent, while that for men should fall from 75 to 74 percent. The share of workers who are non-Hispanic white men will decline during the next decade from 41 to 38 percent.

■ Women and minorities have made tremendous gains in the workforce over the past few decades. As non-Hispanic white men become a smaller share of workers, those gains are likely to continue.

Most men and women work

(percent of persons aged 16 or older in the labor force, by sex, 1997)

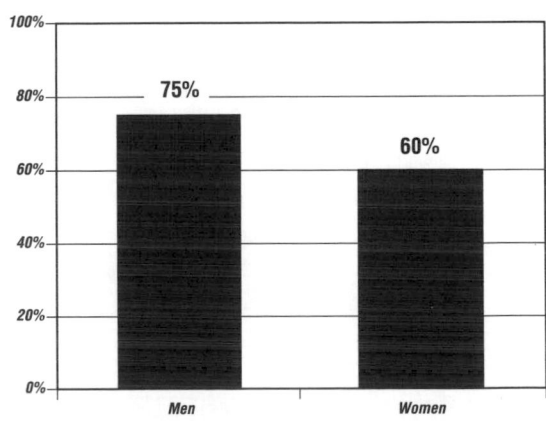

Employment Status of Total Persons by Sex and Age, 1997

(employment status of the civilian noninstitutionalized population aged 16 or older, by sex and age, 1997; numbers in thousands)

		civilian labor force					not in labor force	
	total	percent of population	employed	percent of labor force	unemployed	percent of labor force	total	percent of population
Total persons	**136,297**	**67.1%**	**129,558**	**95.1%**	**6,739**	**4.9%**	**66,837**	**32.9%**
Aged 16 to 19	7,932	51.6	6,661	84.0	1,271	16.0	7,433	48.4
Aged 20 to 24	13,532	77.6	12,380	91.5	1,152	8.5	3,910	22.4
Aged 25 to 34	33,380	84.4	31,809	95.3	1,571	4.7	6,178	15.6
Aged 35 to 44	37,326	85.1	35,908	96.2	1,418	3.8	6,557	14.9
Aged 45 to 54	27,574	82.6	26,744	97.0	830	3.0	5,817	17.4
Aged 55 to 64	12,665	58.9	12,296	97.1	369	2.9	8,840	41.1
Aged 65 or older	3,887	12.2	3,761	96.8	127	3.3	28,102	87.8
Total men	**73,261**	**75.0**	**69,685**	**95.1**	**3,577**	**4.9**	**24,454**	**25.0**
Aged 16 to 19	4,095	52.3	3,401	83.1	694	16.9	3,741	47.7
Aged 20 to 24	7,184	82.5	6,548	91.1	636	8.9	1,521	17.5
Aged 25 to 34	18,110	93.0	17,338	95.7	772	4.3	1,368	7.0
Aged 35 to 44	20,058	92.6	19,327	96.4	732	3.6	1,611	7.4
Aged 45 to 54	14,564	89.5	14,107	96.9	457	3.1	1,712	10.5
Aged 55 to 64	6,952	67.6	6,735	96.9	217	3.1	3,329	32.4
Aged 65 or older	2,298	17.1	2,229	97.0	69	3.0	11,171	82.9
Total women	**63,036**	**59.8**	**59,873**	**95.0**	**3,162**	**5.0**	**42,382**	**40.2**
Aged 16 to 19	3,837	51.0	3,260	85.0	577	15.0	3,691	49.0
Aged 20 to 24	6,348	72.7	5,831	91.9	516	8.1	2,389	27.3
Aged 25 to 34	15,271	76.0	14,471	94.8	800	5.2	4,810	24.0
Aged 35 to 44	17,268	77.7	16,581	96.0	686	4.0	4,947	22.3
Aged 45 to 54	13,010	76.0	12,637	97.1	373	2.9	4,104	24.0
Aged 55 to 64	5,713	50.9	5,561	97.3	152	2.7	5,511	49.1
Aged 65 or older	1,590	8.6	1,532	96.4	58	3.6	16,930	91.4

Note: The civilian labor force equals the number of employed plus the number of unemployed persons. The civilian population equals the number of persons in the labor force plus the number of those not in the labor force.
Source: Bureau of Labor Statistics, Employment and Earnings, *January 1998; calculations by New Strategist*

Total Workers by Occupation, 1997

(number and percent distribution of employed persons aged 16 or older in the civilian labor force by occupation, 1997; numbers in thousands)

	number	*percent*
Total employed	**129,558**	**100.0%**
Managerial and professional specialty	**37,686**	**29.1**
Executive, administrative, and managerial	18,440	14.2
Professional specialty	19,245	14.9
Technical, sales, and administrative support	**38,309**	**29.6**
Technicians and related support	4,214	3.3
Sales occupations	15,734	12.1
Administrative support, including clerical	18,361	14.2
Service occupations	**17,537**	**13.5**
Private household	795	0.6
Protective service	2,300	1.8
Service, except private household and protective	14,442	11.1
Precision production, craft, and repair	**14,124**	**10.9**
Mechanics and repairers	4,675	3.6
Construction trades	5,378	4.2
Other precision production, craft, and repair	4,071	3.1
Operators, fabricators, and laborers	**18,399**	**14.2**
Machine operators, assemblers, and inspectors	7,962	6.1
Transportation and material moving occupations	5,389	4.2
Handlers, equipment cleaners, helpers, and laborers	5,048	3.9
Farming, forestry, and fishing	**3,503**	**2.7**

Source: Bureau of Labor Statistics, Employment and Earnings, *January 1998; calculations by New Strategist*

Total Workers by Industry, 1997

(number and percent distribution of employed persons aged 16 or older in the civilian labor force by industry, 1997; numbers in thousands)

	number	percent
Total employed	**129,558**	**100.0%**
Agriculture	3,399	2.6
Mining	634	0.5
Construction	8,302	6.4
Manufacturing	20,835	16.1
Durable goods	12,437	9.6
Nondurable goods	8,399	6.5
Transportation, communications, and other public utilities	9,182	7.1
Wholesale and retail trade	26,777	20.7
Wholesale trade	4,907	3.8
Retail trade	21,869	16.9
Finance, insurance, and real estate	8,297	6.4
Services	46,393	35.8
Private households	921	0.7
Other service industries	45,472	35.1
Professional and related services	30,935	23.9
Public administration	5,738	4.4

Source: Bureau of Labor Statistics, Employment and Earnings, *January 1998; calculations by New Strategist*

Total Households by Number of Earners, 1996

(number and percent distribution of total households by number of earners, 1996; numbers in thousands)

	number	*percent*
Total households	**101,018**	**100.0%**
No earners	21,228	21.0
One earner	34,026	33.7
Two or more earners	45,764	45.3
Two carners	35,753	35.4
Three earners	7,455	7.4
Four or more earners	2,556	2.5

Source: Bureau of the Census, Money Income: 1996, *Current Population Reports, P60-197, 1997; calculations by New Strategist*

Labor Force Status of Total Married Couples, 1996

(number and percent distribution of total married couples by age of householder and labor force status of husband and wife, 1996; numbers in thousands)

| | total married couples | husband and/or wife in labor force | | | neither husband nor wife in labor force |
		husband and wife	husband only	wife only	
Total couples, number	**53,567**	**29,952**	**11,684**	**2,835**	**9,096**
Under age 20	83	43	33	3	5
Aged 20 to 24	1,444	918	451	37	38
Aged 25 to 29	3,852	2,748	991	75	38
Aged 30 to 34	6,108	4,257	1,666	111	74
Aged 35 to 39	6,898	4,854	1,783	142	119
Aged 40 to 44	6,999	5,046	1,539	275	140
Aged 45 to 49	6,463	4,720	1,333	250	160
Aged 50 to 54	4,698	3,139	1,071	278	211
Aged 55 to 59	4,213	2,278	1,108	408	419
Aged 60 to 64	3,528	1,153	750	546	1,079
Aged 65 to 74	6,177	730	792	596	4,058
Aged 75 to 84	2,753	63	162	105	2,423
Aged 85 or older	351	4	6	10	331
Total couples, percent	**100.0%**	**55.9%**	**21.8%**	**5.3%**	**17.0%**
Under age 20	100.0	51.8	39.8	3.6	6.0
Aged 20 to 24	100.0	63.6	31.2	2.6	2.6
Aged 25 to 29	100.0	71.3	25.7	1.9	1.0
Aged 30 to 34	100.0	69.7	27.3	1.8	1.2
Aged 35 to 39	100.0	70.4	25.8	2.1	1.7
Aged 40 to 44	100.0	72.1	22.0	3.9	2.0
Aged 45 to 49	100.0	73.0	20.6	3.9	2.5
Aged 50 to 54	100.0	66.8	22.8	5.9	4.5
Aged 55 to 59	100.0	54.1	26.3	9.7	9.9
Aged 60 to 64	100.0	32.7	21.3	15.5	30.6
Aged 65 to 74	100.0	11.8	12.8	9.6	65.7
Aged 75 to 84	100.0	2.3	5.9	3.8	88.0
Aged 85 or older	100.0	1.1	1.7	2.8	94.3

Source: Bureau of the Census, Household and Family Characteristics: March 1996, *Current Population Reports, P20-495(Update), 1997; calculations by New Strategist*

Union Membership of Total Workers, 1997

(number of employed wage and salary workers aged 16 or older, number and percent of those who are represented by unions or are union members, and median weekly earnings by union membership status; by sex, 1997; numbers in thousands)

	total	*men*	*women*
Total employed	**114,533**	**59,825**	**54,706**
Represented by unions*	17,923	10,619	7,304
Percent of employed	15.6%	17.7%	13.4%
Members of unions**	16,110	9,763	6,347
Percent of employed	14.1%	16.3%	11.6%
Median weekly earnings, total***	$503	$579	$431
Represented by unions*	632	679	568
Members of unions**	640	683	577
Non-union	478	539	411

* Members of a labor union or an employee association similar to a union as well as workers who report no union affiliation but whose jobs are covered by a union or an employee association contract.
** Members of a labor union or an employee association similar to a union.
*** Full-time wage and salary workers.
Source: Bureau of Labor Statistics, Employment and Earnings, *January 1998*

Workers Entering and Leaving the Labor Force, 1996 to 2006

(number of persons aged 16 or older in the civilian labor force and projected entrants and leavers, by sex, race, and Hispanic origin, 1996 and 2006; numbers in thousands)

	total labor force, 1996	entrants 1996–2006	leavers 1996–2006	total labor force, 2006
Total persons, number	**133,944**	**39,670**	**24,768**	**148,847**
Men	72,087	19,978	13,839	78,226
Women	61,857	19,692	10,929	70,620
White, non-Hispanic	**100,915**	**24,214**	**16,963**	**108,166**
Men	54,451	12,132	9,728	56,856
Women	46,464	12,082	7,236	51,310
Black, non-Hispanic	**14,795**	**6,191**	**5,003**	**15,983**
Men	7,091	2,807	2,550	7,347
Women	7,704	3,384	2,453	8,636
Asian and other, non-Hispanic	**5,459**	**3,346**	**1,508**	**7,296**
Men	2,899	1,674	785	3,788
Women	2,561	1,671	724	3,508
Hispanic	**12,774**	**5,920**	**1,293**	**17,401**
Men	7,646	3,365	776	10,235
Women	5,128	2,555	516	7,166
Total persons, percent	**100.0%**	**100.0%**	**100.0%**	**100.0%**
Men	53.8	50.4	55.9	52.6
Women	46.2	49.6	44.1	47.4
White, non-Hispanic	**75.3**	**61.0**	**68.5**	**72.7**
Men	40.7	30.6	39.3	38.2
Women	34.7	30.5	29.2	34.5
Black, non-Hispanic	**11.0**	**15.6**	**20.2**	**10.7**
Men	5.3	7.1	10.3	4.9
Women	5.8	8.5	9.9	5.8
Asian and other, non-Hispanic	**4.1**	**8.4**	**6.1**	**4.9**
Men	2.2	4.2	3.2	2.5
Women	1.9	4.2	2.9	2.4
Hispanic	**9.5**	**14.9**	**5.2**	**11.7**
Men	5.7	8.5	3.1	6.9
Women	3.8	6.4	2.1	4.8

Source: Bureau of Labor Statistics, Monthly Labor Review, *November 1997*

Labor Force Projections of the Total Population by Sex, 1996 to 2006

(number of persons in the labor force and labor force participation rate in 1996 and 2006, by sex; percent change in number and percentage point change in rate; numbers in thousands)

| | number in labor force | | percent change |
	1996	2006	1996–2006
Total	**133,943**	**148,847**	**11.1%**
Men	72,087	78,226	8.5
Women	61,857	70,620	14.2

| | labor force participation rate | | percentage point change |
	1996	2006	1996–2006
Total	**66.8%**	**67.6%**	**0.8**
Men	74.9	73.6	–1.3
Women	59.3	61.4	2.1

Source: Bureau of Labor Statistics, Monthly Labor Review, *November 1997; calculations by New Strategist*

Total Population: Population

More than one-third of Americans will be non-Hispanic white by 2020.

The U.S. population is projected to grow from 270 million in 1998 to 323 million by 2020, according to the Bureau of the Census. The non-Hispanic white share of the population should fall from 73 to 64 percent during those years. Although U.S. population growth is slowing overall, the minority population is growing much faster than the non-Hispanic white population.

Nearly 25 million Americans, or 9 percent of the total, are foreign born. Among people aged 25 to 34, 14 percent are foreign born. The United States received more than 915,000 immigrants in 1996.

Only 62 percent of the residents of the West are non-Hispanic white, making it the most diverse region. The non-Hispanic white share of the under-age-five population in the West is just 50 percent. In a number of states, the non-Hispanic white share of the population under age 5 is close to or below 50 percent. These are Arizona (55 percent), California (36 percent), Florida (59 percent), Hawaii (22 percent), Louisiana (55 percent), Mississippi (52 percent), New Mexico (38 percent), New York (55 percent), and Texas (45 percent).

Among the 75 largest metro areas, Asians account for the largest share of the population in San Francisco (15 percent), blacks in Greensboro-Winston-Salem-Highpoint, North Carolina (41 percent), Hispanics in El Paso (70 percent), and Native Americans in Tulsa, Oklahoma (7 percent).

■ Because of the differences in diversity by region and state, some parts of the country are already adapting to minority-majority populations while others have not yet begun to address these issues.

Minorities already account for more than one-third of the residents of the West

(percent of total persons who are Hispanic, or non-Hispanic Asian, black, or Native American, by region, 1998)

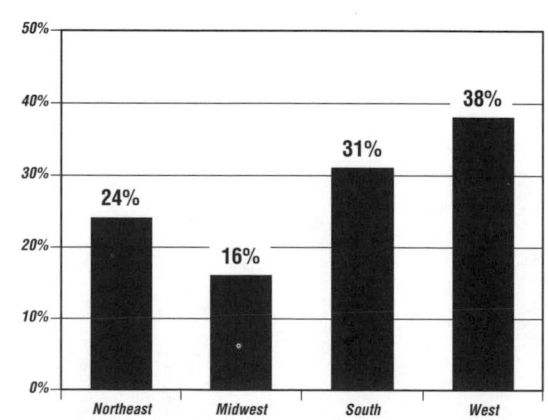

Total Population by Race and Hispanic Origin, 1995 to 2020

(number and percent distribution of persons by race and Hispanic origin, selected years 1995-2020; numbers in thousands)

	1995 number	1995 percent	1998 number	1998 percent	2000 number	2000 percent	2010 number	2010 percent	2020 number	2020 percent
Total persons	262,820	100.0%	270,002	100.0%	274,634	100.0%	297,716	100.0%	322,742	100.0%
White	218,078	83.0	222,648	82.5	225,532	82.1	239,588	80.5	254,887	79.0
Non-Hispanic white	193,566	73.6	195,786	72.5	197,061	71.8	202,390	68.0	207,393	64.3
Black	33,144	12.6	34,537	12.8	35,454	12.9	40,109	13.5	45,075	14.0
Non-Hispanic black	31,598	12.0	32,789	12.1	33,568	12.2	37,466	12.6	41,538	12.9
Asian	9,357	3.6	10,480	3.9	11,245	4.1	15,265	5.1	19,651	6.1
Non-Hispanic Asian	8,788	3.3	9,856	3.7	10,584	3.9	14,402	4.8	18,557	5.7
Native American	2,241	0.9	2,337	0.9	2,402	0.9	2,754	0.9	3,129	1.0
Non-Hispanic Native American	1,931	0.7	2,005	0.7	2,054	0.7	2,320	0.8	2,601	0.8
Hispanic	26,936	11.4	29,565	10.9	31,366	11.4	41,139	13.8	52,652	16.3

Note: Hispanics may be of any race. For a breakdown of the Hispanic composition of racial groups and the racial composition of Hispanics, see the tables in the introduction to this book.

Sources: Bureau of the Census, Population Projections of the United States, by Age, Sex, Race, and Hispanic Origin: 1995 to 2050, Current Population Reports, P25-1130, 1996; calculations by New Strategist

Total Population by Age, 1995 to 2020

(number of persons by age, selected years 1995–2020; percent change 1995–2000 and 2000–2010; numbers in thousands)

	1995	1998	2000	2010	2020	percent change 1995–2000	percent change 2000–2010
Total persons	**262,820**	**270,002**	**274,634**	**297,716**	**322,742**	**4.5%**	**8.4%**
Under age 5	19,591	19,117	18,987	20,012	21,979	–3.1	5.4
Aged 5 to 9	19,213	20,024	19,920	19,489	21,548	3.7	–2.2
Aged 10 to 14	18,918	19,371	20,057	20,231	21,334	6.0	0.9
Aged 15 to 19	18,072	19,426	19,820	21,782	21,364	9.7	9.9
Aged 20 to 24	17,875	17,451	18,257	21,134	21,298	2.1	15.8
Aged 25 to 29	18,981	18,568	17,722	19,710	21,569	–6.6	11.2
Aged 30 to 34	21,881	20,189	19,511	18,582	21,365	–10.8	–4.8
Aged 35 to 39	22,280	22,579	22,180	18,536	20,534	–0.4	–16.4
Aged 40 to 44	20,235	21,811	22,479	19,985	19,078	11.1	–11.1
Aged 45 to 49	17,455	18,813	19,806	21,884	18,376	13.5	10.5
Aged 50 to 54	13,637	15,707	17,224	21,680	19,363	26.3	25.9
Aged 55 to 59	11,089	12,401	13,307	19,068	21,165	20.0	43.3
Aged 60 to 64	10,050	10,261	10,654	16,215	20,549	6.0	52.2
Aged 65 to 69	9,923	9,572	9,410	12,112	17,530	–5.2	28.7
Aged 70 to 74	8,835	8,793	8,726	8,945	13,855	–1.2	2.5
Aged 75 to 79	6,685	7,204	7,415	7,124	9,435	10.9	–3.9
Aged 80 to 84	4,466	4,720	4,900	5,557	5,940	9.7	13.4
Aged 85 or older	3,634	3,996	4,259	5,671	6,460	17.2	33.1
Aged 18 to 24	24,926	25,160	26,258	30,137	29,919	5.3	14.8
Aged 18 or older	194,078	199,773	203,852	225,206	245,138	5.0	10.5
Aged 65 or older	33,543	34,286	34,709	39,408	53,220	3.5	13.5

Source: Bureau of the Census, Population Projections of the United States, by Age, Sex, Race, and Hispanic Origin: 1995 to 2050, *Current Population Reports, P25-1130, 1996; calculations by New Strategist*

Total Population by Age and Sex, 1998

(number of persons by age and sex, and sex ratio by age, 1998; numbers in thousands)

	total	male	female	sex ratio*
Total persons	**270,002**	**131,883**	**138,119**	**95**
Under age 5	19,117	9,780	9,336	105
Aged 5 to 9	20,024	10,252	9,773	105
Aged 10 to 14	19,371	9,920	9,451	105
Aged 15 to 19	19,426	9,955	9,470	105
Aged 20 to 24	17,451	8,853	8,598	103
Aged 25 to 29	18,568	9,279	9,289	100
Aged 30 to 34	20,189	10,046	10,143	99
Aged 35 to 39	22,579	11,246	11,333	99
Aged 40 to 44	21,811	10,798	11,013	98
Aged 45 to 49	18,813	9,225	9,588	96
Aged 50 to 54	15,707	7,635	8,071	95
Aged 55 to 59	12,401	5,957	6,443	92
Aged 60 to 64	10,261	4,847	5,413	90
Aged 65 to 69	9,572	4,378	5,194	84
Aged 70 to 74	8,793	3,846	4,947	78
Aged 75 to 79	7,204	2,983	4,221	71
Aged 80 to 84	4,720	1,747	2,973	59
Aged 85 or older	3,995	1,134	2,862	40
Aged 18 to 24	25,160	12,787	12,373	103
Aged 18 or older	199,773	95,909	103,863	92
Aged 65 or older	34,286	14,089	20,197	70

* The sex ratio is the number of males per 100 females.
Source: Bureau of the Census, Population Projections of the United States, by Age, Sex, Race, and Hispanic Origin: 1995 to 2050, Current Population Reports, P25-1130, 1996; calculations by New Strategist

Characteristics of the Total Foreign-Born Population, 1996

(number and percent distribution of total and foreign-born persons by age, sex, income, and education, 1996; numbers in thousands)

| | total | | foreign-born | | foreign born |
	number	percent	number	percent	share of total
Total persons	**264,314**	**100.0%**	**24,557**	**100.0%**	**9.3%**
Age					
Under age 5	20,069	7.6	292	1.2	1.5
Aged 5 to 15	43,523	16.5	1,887	7.7	4.3
Aged 16 or 17	7,556	2.9	556	2.3	7.4
Aged 18 to 24	24,843	9.4	2,734	11.1	11.0
Aged 25 to 29	19,462	7.4	2,645	10.8	13.6
Aged 30 to 34	21,457	8.1	2,959	12.0	13.8
Aged 35 to 44	43,078	16.3	5,100	20.8	11.8
Aged 45 to 64	52,668	19.9	5,624	22.9	10.7
Aged 65 or older	31,658	12.0	2,761	11.2	8.7
Sex					
Male	129,143	48.9	12,025	49.0	9.3
Female	135,171	51.1	12,532	51.0	9.3
Income in 1995					
Total with income	**186,704**	**100.0**	**19,070**	**100.0**	**10.2**
Under $10,000	59,534	31.9	6,962	36.5	11.7
$10,000 to $19,999	45,270	24.2	5,392	28.3	11.9
$20,000 to $34,999	42,041	22.5	3,646	19.1	8.7
$35,000 to $49,999	20,281	10.9	1,555	8.2	7.7
$50,000 or more	19,578	10.5	1,515	7.9	7.7
Education					
Total aged 25 or older	168,323	100.0	19,088	100.0	11.3
Not a high school graduate	30,724	18.3	6,800	35.6	22.1
High school grad. or some college	97,931	58.2	7,800	40.9	8.0
Bachelor's degree	26,540	15.8	2,845	14.9	10.7
Graduate/professional degree	13,128	7.8	1,643	8.6	12.5

Source: Bureau of the Census, Internet web site, http://www.census.gov; *calculations by New Strategist*

Total Immigrants by Country of Birth, 1996

(number and percent distribution of immigrants to the U.S. by world region and country of origin, 1996; for countries sending at least 5,000 immigrants to the U.S., ranked by number of immigrants within regions)

	number	percent
Total immigrants	**915,900**	**100.0%**
Africa	**52,889**	**6.6**
Nigeria	10,221	1.3
Ethiopia	6,914	0.9
Ghana	6,606	0.8
Egypt	6,186	0.8
Asia	**307,807**	**33.6**
Philippines	55,876	6.1
India	44,859	4.9
Vietnam	42,067	4.6
China, People's Republic	41,728	4.6
Korea	18,185	2.0
Taiwan	13,401	1.5
Pakistan	12,519	1.4
Iran	11,084	1.2
Bangladesh	8,221	0.9
Hong Kong	7,834	0.9
Japan	6,011	0.7
Iraq	5,481	0.6
Europe	**147,581**	**16.1**
Soviety Union, former	62,777	6.9
Ukraine	21,079	2.3
Russia	19,668	2.1
Poland	15,772	1.7
United Kingdom	13,624	1.5
Yugoslavia, former	11,854	1.3
Bosnia-Herzegovina	6,499	0.7
Germany	6,748	0.7

(continued)

(continued from previous page)

	number	*percent*
North America	**340,540**	**37.2%**
Mexico	163,572	17.9
Dominican Republic	39,604	4.3
Cuba	26,466	2.9
Jamaica	19,089	2.1
Haiti	18,386	2.0
El Salvador	17,903	2.0
Canada	15,825	1.7
Guatemala	8,763	1.0
Trinidad and Tobago	7,344	0.8
Nicaragua	6,903	0.8
Honduras	5,870	0.6
Oceania	**5,309**	**0.6**
South America	**61,769**	**6.7**
Colombia	14,283	1.6
Peru	12,871	1.4
Guyana	9,489	1.0
Ecuador	8,321	0.9
Brazil	5,891	0.6

Source: U.S. Immigration and Naturalization Service, 1996 Statistical Yearbook of the Immigration and Naturalization Service, 1997; calculations by New Strategist

Ancestry of the Total Population, 1990

(number and percent distribution of total persons by the 50 largest ancestry groups, ranked by size, 1990; numbers in thousands)

	number	*percent*
Total persons	**248,710**	**100.0%**
German	57,947	23.3
Irish	38,736	15.6
English	32,652	13.1
Afro-American	23,777	9.6
Italian	14,665	5.9
American	12,396	5.0
Mexican	11,587	4.7
French	10,321	4.1
Polish	9,366	3.8
American Indian	8,708	3.5
Dutch	6,227	2.5
Scotch-Irish	5,618	2.3
Scottish	5,394	2.2
Swedish	4,681	1.9
Norwegian	3,869	1.6
Russian	2,953	1.2
French Canadian	2,167	0.9
Welsh	2,034	0.8
Spanish	2,024	0.8
Puerto Rican	1,955	0.8
Slovak	1,883	0.8
White	1,800	0.7
Danish	1,635	0.7
Hungarian	1,582	0.6
Chinese	1,505	0.6
Filipino	1,451	0.6
Czech	1,296	0.5
Portuguese	1,153	0.5
British	1,119	0.4
Hispanic	1,113	0.4
Greek	1,110	0.4
Swiss	1,045	0.4
Japanese	1,005	0.4

(continued)

(continued from previous page)

	number	percent
Austrian	865	0.3%
Cuban	860	0.3
Korean	837	0.3
Lithuanian	812	0.3
Ukrainian	741	0.3
Scandinavian	679	0.3
Acadian/Cajun	668	0.3
Finnish	659	0.3
United States	644	0.3
Asian Indian	570	0.2
Canadian	550	0.2
Croatian	544	0.2
Vietnamese	536	0.2
Dominican	506	0.2
Salvadorian	499	0.2
European	467	0.2
Jamaican	435	0.2

Note: Since those who reported multiple ancestries were included in more than one group, the sum of the persons reporting an ancestry is greater than the total number of persons. Ancestries shown are based on written responses to the 1990 census.
Source: Bureau of the Census, Detailed Ancestry Groups for States, *CP-S-1-2, 1990; calculations by New Strategist*

Total Population by Region and Division, 1995 to 2020

(number and percent distribution of total persons by region and division, selected years 1995–2020; percent change in number and percentage point change in distribution, 1995–2000 and 2000–2010; numbers in thousands)

	1995	2000	2010	2020	percent change 1995–2000	percent change 2000–2010
Number						
UNITED STATES	**262,820**	**274,634**	**297,716**	**322,742**	**4.5%**	**8.4%**
Northeast	**51,465**	**52,107**	**53,692**	**56,104**	**1.2**	**3.0**
New England	13,312	13,580	14,173	14,938	2.0	4.4
Middle Atlantic	38,152	38,527	39,521	41,166	1.0	2.6
Midwest	**61,803**	**63,500**	**65,915**	**68,114**	**2.7**	**3.8**
East North Central	43,458	44,418	45,766	47,064	2.2	3.0
West North Central	18,348	19,082	20,152	21,051	4.0	5.6
South	**91,887**	**97,613**	**107,598**	**117,061**	**6.2**	**10.2**
South Atlantic	46,994	50,146	55,457	60,410	6.7	10.6
East South Central	16,066	16,916	18,124	19,001	5.3	7.1
West South Central	28,827	30,546	34,017	37,647	6.0	11.4
West	**57,596**	**61,412**	**70,514**	**81,466**	**6.6**	**14.8**
Mountain	15,645	17,725	20,219	22,049	13.3	14.1
Pacific	41,951	43,687	50,290	59,415	4.1	15.1

	1995	2000	2010	2020	percentage point change 1995–2000	percentage point change 2000–2010
Percent distribution						
UNITED STATES	**100.0%**	**100.0%**	**100.0%**	**100.0%**	**–**	**–**
Northeast	**19.6**	**19.0**	**18.0**	**17.4**	**–0.6**	**–1.0**
New England	5.1	4.9	4.8	4.6	–0.2	–0.1
Middle Atlantic	14.5	14.0	13.3	12.8	–0.5	–0.7
Midwest	**23.5**	**23.1**	**22.1**	**21.1**	**–0.4**	**–1.0**
East North Central	16.5	16.2	15.4	14.6	–0.3	–0.8
West North Central	7.0	6.9	6.8	6.5	–0.1	–0.1
South	**35.0**	**35.5**	**36.1**	**36.3**	**0.5**	**0.6**
South Atlantic	17.9	18.3	18.6	18.7	0.4	0.3
East South Central	6.1	6.2	6.1	5.9	0.1	–0.1
West South Central	11.0	11.1	11.4	11.7	0.1	0.3
West	**21.9**	**22.4**	**23.7**	**25.2**	**0.5**	**1.3**
Mountain	6.0	6.5	6.8	6.8	0.5	0.3
Pacific	16.0	15.9	16.9	18.4	–0.1	1.0

Note: Numbers may not add to total due to rounding. (–) means not applicable.
Source: Bureau of the Census, Population Projections for States, by Age, Sex, Race, and Hispanic Origin: 1995 to 2025, PPL-47, 1996; calculations by New Strategist

Population of Regions and Divisions
by Age, Race, and Hispanic Origin, 1998

(total number and percent distribution of persons by region, division, age, race, and Hispanic origin, 1998; numbers in thousands)

| | total | | non-Hispanic | | | | |
	number	percent	white	black	Native American	Asian	Hispanic
NORTHEAST							
Total	**51,870**	**100.0%**	**76.3%**	**10.7%**	**0.2%**	**3.6%**	**9.2%**
Under age 5	3,498	100.0	67.6	14.3	0.2	4.3	13.5
Aged 5 to 14	7,221	100.0	70.3	13.2	0.2	4.0	12.3
Aged 15 to 24	6,500	100.0	71.3	12.8	0.2	4.1	11.5
Aged 25 to 34	7,492	100.0	72.5	11.6	0.2	4.6	11.2
Aged 35 to 44	8,662	100.0	76.9	10.2	0.2	4.0	8.7
Aged 45 to 54	6,775	100.0	80.0	9.2	0.2	3.5	7.1
Aged 55 to 64	4,470	100.0	80.9	9.3	0.2	3.0	6.6
Aged 65 to 74	3,814	100.0	85.5	7.7	0.1	1.9	4.7
Aged 75 or older	3,438	100.0	89.9	5.6	0.1	1.0	3.3
New England							
Total	**13,481**	**100.0**	**86.6**	**4.9**	**0.2**	**2.5**	**5.7**
Under age 5	877	100.0	79.7	7.0	0.2	3.6	9.5
Aged 5 to 14	1,859	100.0	81.3	6.6	0.3	3.1	8.7
Aged 15 to 24	1,665	100.0	82.6	6.1	0.3	3.1	7.9
Aged 25 to 34	2,023	100.0	83.7	5.5	0.3	3.4	7.1
Aged 35 to 44	2,320	100.0	87.6	4.6	0.2	2.5	5.0
Aged 45 to 54	1,777	100.0	90.3	3.9	0.2	2.0	3.7
Aged 55 to 64	1,105	100.0	91.4	3.7	0.2	1.6	3.1
Aged 65 to 74	947	100.0	93.8	2.9	0.1	1.1	2.0
Aged 75 or older	908	100.0	95.7	2.0	0.1	0.6	1.7
Middle Atlantic							
Total	**38,389**	**100.0**	**72.6**	**12.8**	**0.2**	**4.0**	**10.4**
Under age 5	2,621	100.0	63.6	16.7	0.2	4.6	14.9
Aged 5 to 14	5,362	100.0	66.5	15.5	0.2	4.2	13.5
Aged 15 to 24	4,835	100.0	67.4	15.2	0.2	4.4	12.8
Aged 25 to 34	5,469	100.0	68.3	13.8	0.2	5.0	12.7
Aged 35 to 44	6,342	100.0	73.0	12.2	0.2	4.6	10.0
Aged 45 to 54	4,998	100.0	76.3	11.1	0.2	4.0	8.4
Aged 55 to 64	3,365	100.0	77.5	11.1	0.2	3.4	7.8
Aged 65 to 74	2,868	100.0	82.8	9.2	0.1	2.2	5.6
Aged 75 or older	2,529	100.0	87.8	6.9	0.1	1.2	3.9

(continued)

(continued from previous page)

	total		non-Hispanic				
MIDWEST	number	percent	white	black	Native American	Asian	Hispanic
Total	**62,864**	**100.0%**	**84.0%**	**10.0%**	**0.6%**	**1.7%**	**3.7%**
Under age 5	4,320	100.0	77.8	13.8	0.8	2.2	5.3
Aged 5 to 14	9,100	100.0	79.4	12.7	0.8	2.1	5.1
Aged 15 to 24	8,790	100.0	81.0	11.7	0.7	1.9	4.7
Aged 25 to 34	8,783	100.0	81.7	10.6	0.6	2.3	4.8
Aged 35 to 44	10,300	100.0	85.0	9.4	0.5	1.7	3.4
Aged 45 to 54	8,024	100.0	87.2	8.3	0.5	1.5	2.5
Aged 55 to 64	5,326	100.0	88.5	7.8	0.4	1.3	2.0
Aged 65 to 74	4,321	100.0	89.9	7.3	0.3	0.8	1.6
Aged 75 or older	3,899	100.0	92.6	5.6	0.2	0.4	1.2
East North Central							
Total	**44,063**	**100.0**	**81.7**	**11.9**	**0.3**	**1.8**	**4.3**
Under age 5	3,061	100.0	75.0	16.3	0.3	2.2	6.2
Aged 5 to 14	6,360	100.0	76.6	15.0	0.4	2.1	5.9
Aged 15 to 24	6,105	100.0	78.3	13.9	0.4	2.0	5.5
Aged 25 to 34	6,248	100.0	79.4	12.3	0.4	2.4	5.5
Aged 35 to 44	7,250	100.0	82.8	11.2	0.3	1.8	3.9
Aged 45 to 54	5,653	100.0	85.0	10.0	0.3	1.7	2.9
Aged 55 to 64	3,739	100.0	86.4	9.5	0.3	1.4	2.4
Aged 65 to 74	3,010	100.0	87.9	9.0	0.2	1.0	1.9
Aged 75 or older	2,637	100.0	90.9	7.0	0.2	0.5	1.4
West North Central							
Total	**18,801**	**100.0**	**89.6**	**5.5**	**1.1**	**1.5**	**2.2**
Under age 5	1,260	100.0	84.7	7.9	1.9	2.4	3.1
Aged 5 to 14	2,740	100.0	85.7	7.3	1.7	2.1	3.2
Aged 15 to 24	2,686	100.0	87.2	6.6	1.5	1.9	2.9
Aged 25 to 34	2,534	100.0	87.2	6.3	1.2	2.3	3.0
Aged 35 to 44	3,051	100.0	90.3	5.4	0.9	1.4	2.0
Aged 45 to 54	2,371	100.0	92.3	4.3	0.8	1.1	1.5
Aged 55 to 64	1,587	100.0	93.4	3.9	0.7	0.9	1.1
Aged 65 to 74	1,311	100.0	94.5	3.5	0.5	0.6	1.0
Aged 75 or older	1,261	100.0	96.1	2.6	0.3	0.3	0.7

(continued)

(continued from previous page)

	total		non-Hispanic				
SOUTH	*number*	*percent*	*white*	*black*	*Native American*	*Asian*	*Hispanic*
Total	**95,383**	**100.0%**	**69.3%**	**18.9%**	**0.6%**	**1.7%**	**9.5%**
Under age 5	6,609	100.0	60.4	23.7	0.6	2.0	13.3
Aged 5 to 14	13,786	100.0	61.9	23.3	0.7	1.9	12.1
Aged 15 to 24	13,226	100.0	63.0	22.8	0.8	1.9	11.5
Aged 25 to 34	13,658	100.0	66.2	20.0	0.6	2.2	11.0
Aged 35 to 44	15,488	100.0	70.0	18.6	0.6	1.9	8.9
Aged 45 to 54	12,214	100.0	74.4	16.0	0.6	1.7	7.3
Aged 55 to 64	8,249	100.0	77.4	14.0	0.5	1.4	6.7
Aged 65 to 74	6,639	100.0	79.9	12.8	0.4	0.9	5.9
Aged 75 or older	5,514	100.0	82.9	11.6	0.4	0.4	4.6
South Atlantic							
Total	**48,928**	**100.0**	**70.4**	**21.1**	**0.4**	**1.9**	**6.2**
Under age 5	3,226	100.0	62.8	27.4	0.4	2.2	7.3
Aged 5 to 14	6,795	100.0	63.5	26.8	0.4	2.1	7.2
Aged 15 to 24	6,379	100.0	64.3	26.1	0.5	2.2	6.9
Aged 25 to 34	7,088	100.0	67.2	22.5	0.4	2.4	7.4
Aged 35 to 44	8,085	100.0	70.3	21.0	0.4	2.1	6.2
Aged 45 to 54	6,361	100.0	74.5	18.0	0.4	1.9	5.2
Aged 55 to 64	4,307	100.0	77.0	15.6	0.3	1.6	5.4
Aged 65 to 74	3,617	100.0	80.3	13.5	0.2	1.0	4.9
Aged 75 or older	3,070	100.0	83.6	11.6	0.2	0.5	4.0
East South Central							
Total	**16,590**	**100.0**	**78.4**	**19.8**	**0.3**	**0.7**	**0.8**
Under age 5	1,114	100.0	71.8	26.1	0.2	0.9	0.9
Aged 5 to 14	2,336	100.0	72.6	25.2	0.3	0.9	1.1
Aged 15 to 24	2,365	100.0	73.5	24.4	0.3	0.8	1.0
Aged 25 to 34	2,362	100.0	77.0	20.6	0.3	1.0	1.1
Aged 35 to 44	2,644	100.0	79.2	18.8	0.3	0.9	0.9
Aged 45 to 54	2,169	100.0	82.6	15.8	0.3	0.7	0.6
Aged 55 to 64	1,501	100.0	85.0	13.7	0.2	0.5	0.5
Aged 65 to 74	1,157	100.0	85.2	13.8	0.2	0.3	0.4
Aged 75 or older	941	100.0	85.2	14.1	0.2	0.1	0.4

(continued)

(continued from previous page)

	total		non-Hispanic				
	number	*percent*	*white*	*black*	*Native American*	*Asian*	*Hispanic*
West South Central							
Total	**29,865**	**100.0%**	**62.5%**	**14.7%**	**1.2%**	**2.0%**	**19.6%**
Under age 5	2,268	100.0	51.4	17.3	1.1	2.3	27.9
Aged 5 to 14	4,655	100.0	54.3	17.3	1.4	2.1	25.0
Aged 15 to 24	4,481	100.0	55.7	17.2	1.4	2.1	23.6
Aged 25 to 34	4,208	100.0	58.3	15.5	1.2	2.5	22.4
Aged 35 to 44	4,759	100.0	64.4	14.5	1.1	2.2	17.9
Aged 45 to 54	3,684	100.0	69.4	12.6	1.1	2.0	14.9
Aged 55 to 64	2,441	100.0	73.5	11.2	1.1	1.5	12.7
Aged 65 to 74	1,865	100.0	75.9	10.8	1.0	1.1	11.3
Aged 75 or older	1,503	100.0	79.8	10.0	1.1	0.5	8.5
WEST							
Total	**59,885**	**100.0**	**62.3**	**4.9**	**1.6**	**8.8**	**22.5**
Under age 5	4,689	100.0	50.1	5.3	2.0	9.5	33.1
Aged 5 to 14	9,289	100.0	53.5	5.5	2.2	9.1	29.8
Aged 15 to 24	8,360	100.0	55.8	5.3	2.0	9.4	27.6
Aged 25 to 34	8,824	100.0	56.1	5.3	1.6	9.7	27.3
Aged 35 to 44	9,940	100.0	64.4	5.2	1.4	8.8	20.1
Aged 45 to 54	7,506	100.0	70.8	4.3	1.3	8.5	15.1
Aged 55 to 64	4,617	100.0	73.0	4.2	1.2	8.2	13.3
Aged 65 to 74	3,591	100.0	76.0	3.6	0.9	8.1	11.4
Aged 75 or older	3,071	100.0	82.6	2.9	0.8	5.5	8.2
Mountain							
Total	**16,930**	**100.0**	**75.7**	**2.9**	**3.2**	**2.0**	**16.3**
Under age 5	1,254	100.0	67.0	3.3	5.0	2.3	22.4
Aged 5 to 14	2,635	100.0	68.5	3.3	4.8	2.1	21.3
Aged 15 to 24	2,514	100.0	71.2	3.2	3.9	2.1	19.6
Aged 25 to 34	2,310	100.0	71.8	3.4	3.5	2.6	18.7
Aged 35 to 44	2,710	100.0	77.2	3.1	2.7	2.1	14.9
Aged 45 to 54	2,155	100.0	81.4	2.4	2.2	1.8	12.2
Aged 55 to 64	1,405	100.0	83.1	2.3	2.0	1.6	11.0
Aged 65 to 74	1,077	100.0	85.5	1.9	1.6	1.4	9.6
Aged 75 or older	870	100.0	89.8	1.3	1.2	0.7	6.9

(continued)

(continued from previous page)

| Pacific | total | | non-Hispanic | | | | |
	number	percent	white	black	Native American	Asian	Hispanic
Total	**42,954**	**100.0%**	**57.0%**	**5.7%**	**0.9%**	**11.5%**	**24.9%**
Under age 5	3,435	100.0	43.9	6.0	1.0	12.2	37.0
Aged 5 to 14	6,654	100.0	47.6	6.3	1.1	11.8	33.1
Aged 15 to 24	5,846	100.0	49.2	6.2	1.1	12.5	31.0
Aged 25 to 34	6,513	100.0	50.5	6.0	0.9	12.2	30.4
Aged 35 to 44	7,230	100.0	59.7	6.0	0.9	11.3	22.1
Aged 45 to 54	5,350	100.0	66.5	5.1	0.9	11.2	16.3
Aged 55 to 64	3,212	100.0	68.6	5.1	0.9	11.1	14.4
Aged 65 to 74	2,513	100.0	71.9	4.4	0.7	10.9	12.1
Aged 75 or older	2,201	100.0	79.7	3.6	0.6	7.4	8.7

Source: Bureau of the Census, Internet web site, http://www.census.gov; *calculations by New Strategist*

Total Population by State, 1995 to 2020

(number of persons by state, selected years 1995–2020; percent change 1995–2020; numbers in thousands)

	1995	2000	2010	2020	percent change 1995–2000	percent change 2000–2010
United States	**262,820**	**274,634**	**297,716**	**322,742**	**4.5%**	**8.4%**
Alabama	4,252	4,451	4,800	5,098	4.7	7.8
Alaska	606	654	744	839	7.9	13.8
Arizona	4,218	4,798	5,522	6,109	13.8	15.1
Arkansas	2,484	2,629	2,839	2,996	5.8	8.0
California	31,589	32,523	37,644	45,278	3.0	15.7
Colorado	3,746	4,168	4,660	5,012	11.3	11.8
Connecticut	3,277	3,285	3,400	3,620	0.2	3.5
Delaware	715	767	816	847	7.3	6.4
District of Columbia	553	520	559	623	-6.0	7.5
Florida	14,164	15,232	17,363	19,633	7.5	14.0
Georgia	7,202	7,874	8,822	9,551	9.3	12.0
Hawaii	1,188	1,256	1,440	1,679	5.7	14.6
Idaho	1,164	1,346	1,558	1,681	15.6	15.8
Illinois	11,831	12,050	12,513	13,121	1.9	3.8
Indiana	5,803	6,044	6,317	6,479	4.2	4.5
Iowa	2,843	2,900	2,976	3,019	2.0	2.6
Kansas	2,566	2,669	2,847	3,027	4.0	6.7
Kentucky	3,859	3,993	4,172	4,281	3.5	4.5
Louisiana	4,342	4,425	4,684	4,990	1.9	5.9
Maine	1,241	1,258	1,322	1,395	1.4	5.1
Maryland	5,042	5,275	5,657	6,070	4.6	7.2
Massachusetts	6,075	6,200	6,433	6,733	2.1	3.8
Michigan	9,551	9,680	9,835	10,000	1.4	1.6
Minnesota	4,607	4,830	5,148	5,407	4.8	6.6
Mississippi	2,695	2,813	2,972	3,090	4.4	5.7
Missouri	5,324	5,540	5,865	6,138	4.1	5.9
Montana	871	950	1,039	1,094	9.1	9.4
Nebraska	1,637	1,706	1,807	1,892	4.2	5.9
Nevada	1,530	1,873	2,131	2,242	22.4	13.8
New Hampshire	1,148	1,224	1,326	1,410	6.6	8.3
New Jersey	7,946	8,176	8,638	9,239	2.9	5.7
New Mexico	1,684	1,861	2,156	2,455	10.5	15.9
New York	18,134	18,147	18,530	19,358	0.1	2.1
North Carolina	7,195	7,779	8,553	9,110	8.1	9.9
North Dakota	638	660	690	715	3.4	4.5

(continued)

(continued from previous page)

	1995	2000	2010	2020	percent change 1995–2000	percent change 2000–2010
Ohio	11,153	11,317	11,504	11,672	1.5%	1.7%
Oklahoma	3,276	3,373	3,638	3,930	3.0	7.9
Oregon	3,140	3,399	3,802	4,177	8.2	11.9
Pennsylvania	12,071	12,201	12,352	12,566	1.1	1.2
Rhode Island	990	997	1,039	1,104	0.7	4.2
South Carolina	3,673	3,857	4,204	4,516	5.0	9.0
South Dakota	729	776	824	854	6.4	6.2
Tennessee	5,254	5,656	6,179	6,529	7.7	9.2
Texas	18,722	20,120	22,857	25,731	7.5	13.6
Utah	1,953	2,208	2,551	2,780	13.1	15.5
Vermont	584	617	652	673	5.7	5.7
Virginia	6,618	6,997	7,627	8,203	5.7	9.0
Washington	5,432	5,857	6,657	7,446	7.8	13.7
West Virginia	1,827	1,840	1,851	1,850	0.7	0.6
Wisconsin	5,121	5,328	5,590	5,789	4.0	4.9
Wyoming	479	524	607	668	9.4	15.8

Note: Numbers may not add to total due to rounding.
Source: Bureau of the Census, Population Projections for States, by Age, Sex, Race, and Hispanic Origin: 1995 to 2025, *PPL-47, 1996; calculations by New Strategist*

Distribution of the Total Population by State, 1995 to 2020

(percent distribution of the total population by state, selected years 1995–2020)

	1995	2000	2010	2020
United States	**100.0%**	**100.0%**	**100.0%**	**100.0%**
Alabama	1.6	1.6	1.6	1.6
Alaska	0.2	0.2	0.3	0.3
Arizona	1.6	1.7	1.9	1.9
Arkansas	0.9	1.0	1.0	0.9
California	12.0	11.8	12.6	14.0
Colorado	1.4	1.5	1.6	1.6
Connecticut	1.2	1.2	1.1	1.1
Delaware	0.3	0.3	0.3	0.3
District of Columbia	0.2	0.2	0.2	0.2
Florida	5.4	5.5	5.8	6.1
Georgia	2.7	2.9	3.0	3.0
Hawaii	0.5	0.5	0.5	0.5
Idaho	0.4	0.5	0.5	0.5
Illinois	4.5	4.4	4.2	4.1
Indiana	2.2	2.2	2.1	2.0
Iowa	1.1	1.1	1.0	0.9
Kansas	1.0	1.0	1.0	0.9
Kentucky	1.5	1.5	1.4	1.3
Louisiana	1.7	1.6	1.6	1.5
Maine	0.5	0.5	0.4	0.4
Maryland	1.9	1.9	1.9	1.9
Massachusetts	2.3	2.3	2.2	2.1
Michigan	3.6	3.5	3.3	3.1
Minnesota	1.8	1.8	1.7	1.7
Mississippi	1.0	1.0	1.0	1.0
Missouri	2.0	2.0	2.0	1.9
Montana	0.3	0.3	0.3	0.3
Nebraska	0.6	0.6	0.6	0.6
Nevada	0.6	0.7	0.7	0.7
New Hampshire	0.4	0.4	0.4	0.4
New Jersey	3.0	3.0	2.9	2.9
New Mexico	0.6	0.7	0.7	0.8
New York	6.9	6.6	6.2	6.0
North Carolina	2.7	2.8	2.9	2.8
North Dakota	0.2	0.2	0.2	0.2

(continued)

(continued from previous page)

	1995	2000	2010	2020
Ohio	4.2%	4.1%	3.9%	3.6%
Oklahoma	1.2	1.2	1.2	1.2
Oregon	1.2	1.2	1.3	1.3
Pennsylvania	4.6	4.4	4.1	3.9
Rhode Island	0.4	0.4	0.3	0.3
South Carolina	1.4	1.4	1.4	1.4
South Dakota	0.3	0.3	0.3	0.3
Tennessee	2.0	2.1	2.1	2.0
Texas	7.1	7.3	7.7	8.0
Utah	0.7	0.8	0.9	0.9
Vermont	0.2	0.2	0.2	0.2
Virginia	2.5	2.5	2.6	2.5
Washington	2.1	2.1	2.2	2.3
West Virginia	0.7	0.7	0.6	0.6
Wisconsin	1.9	1.9	1.9	1.8
Wyoming	0.2	0.2	0.2	0.2

Source: Calculations by New Strategist based on Census Bureau data in Population Projections for States, by Age, Sex, Race, and Hispanic Origin: 1995 to 2025, *PPL-47, 1996*

State Populations by Age, Race, and Hispanic Origin, 1998

(number and percent distribution of persons by state, age, race, and Hispanic origin, 1998; numbers in thousands)

	total number	non-Hispanic				Hispanic	total percent	non-Hispanic				Hispanic
		white	black	Asian	Native American			white	black	Asian	Native American	
ALABAMA												
Total persons	**4,374**	**3,178**	**1,114**	**30**	**17**	**34**	**100.0%**	**72.7%**	**25.5%**	**0.7%**	**0.4%**	**0.8%**
Under age 5	295	193	96	2	1	3	100.0	65.6	32.5	0.8	0.2	0.9
Aged 5 to 14	611	405	193	5	2	6	100.0	66.2	31.6	0.8	0.4	1.0
Aged 15 to 24	617	409	194	5	3	6	100.0	66.3	31.5	0.7	0.6	0.9
Aged 25 to 34	621	443	163	6	2	7	100.0	71.4	26.3	0.9	0.4	1.0
Aged 35 to 44	690	508	168	6	3	6	100.0	73.6	24.3	0.8	0.4	0.8
Aged 45 to 54	569	440	119	4	2	3	100.0	77.3	21.0	0.7	0.4	0.6
Aged 55 to 64	400	322	72	2	1	2	100.0	80.5	18.1	0.5	0.4	0.5
Aged 65 to 74	316	254	59	1	1	1	100.0	80.5	18.6	0.3	0.2	0.4
Aged 75 or older	254	204	49	0	1	1	100.0	80.2	19.1	0.1	0.2	0.3
ALASKA												
Total persons	**634**	**454**	**26**	**37**	**91**	**27**	**100.0**	**71.6**	**4.1**	**5.8**	**14.3**	**4.3**
Under age 5	55	35	2	4	11	3	100.0	63.3	4.5	7.4	19.8	5.0
Aged 5 to 14	111	71	5	7	23	6	100.0	64.1	4.4	6.1	20.4	5.2
Aged 15 to 24	100	68	5	6	15	5	100.0	68.4	4.9	6.1	15.5	5.1
Aged 25 to 34	90	63	5	6	11	5	100.0	70.3	5.7	6.3	12.0	5.7
Aged 35 to 44	115	87	5	6	12	5	100.0	75.6	4.2	5.4	10.8	3.9
Aged 45 to 54	86	69	2	4	9	2	100.0	80.3	2.3	4.8	9.9	2.6
Aged 55 to 64	43	34	1	2	5	1	100.0	79.3	2.0	4.4	11.9	2.3
Aged 65 to 74	23	17	0	1	3	0	100.0	76.4	2.1	5.4	14.0	2.1
Aged 75 or older	12	9	0	1	2	0	100.0	77.2	1.8	4.3	15.3	1.4

(continued)

(continued from previous page)

	total number	non-Hispanic				Hispanic	total percent	non-Hispanic				Hispanic
		white	black	Asian	Native American			white	black	Asian	Native American	
ARIZONA												
Total persons	**4,575**	**3,137**	**141**	**83**	**226**	**988**	**100.0%**	**68.6%**	**3.1%**	**1.8%**	**4.9%**	**21.6%**
Under age 5	348	190	12	6	27	113	100.0	54.5	3.4	1.9	7.7	32.5
Aged 5 to 14	716	407	26	13	55	214	100.0	56.9	3.7	1.8	7.7	29.9
Aged 15 to 24	638	382	23	13	41	179	100.0	59.8	3.6	2.0	6.5	28.0
Aged 25 to 34	627	400	22	15	33	156	100.0	63.9	3.6	2.4	5.3	24.9
Aged 35 to 44	706	500	24	15	29	138	100.0	70.9	3.4	2.1	4.1	19.5
Aged 45 to 54	551	423	15	10	18	86	100.0	76.7	2.7	1.8	3.3	15.5
Aged 55 to 64	384	308	9	6	11	50	100.0	80.3	2.3	1.5	2.9	13.0
Aged 65 to 74	331	280	6	4	7	34	100.0	84.5	1.8	1.2	2.2	10.3
Aged 75 or older	275	247	3	1	4	19	100.0	89.8	1.3	0.5	1.6	6.8
ARKANSAS												
Total persons	**2,574**	**2,109**	**401**	**17**	**15**	**33**	**100.0**	**81.9**	**15.6**	**0.7**	**0.6**	**1.3**
Under age 5	170	128	37	1	1	3	100.0	75.5	21.5	0.8	0.6	1.7
Aged 5 to 14	368	281	75	3	2	7	100.0	76.3	20.5	0.8	0.6	1.8
Aged 15 to 24	364	278	75	3	2	6	100.0	76.3	20.7	0.8	0.6	1.6
Aged 25 to 34	337	271	55	3	2	6	100.0	80.4	16.3	0.9	0.6	1.8
Aged 35 to 44	387	319	57	3	2	5	100.0	82.5	14.9	0.8	0.6	1.3
Aged 45 to 54	331	285	40	2	2	3	100.0	85.9	12.0	0.7	0.6	0.9
Aged 55 to 64	248	219	24	1	1	2	100.0	88.5	9.8	0.5	0.5	0.7
Aged 65 to 74	198	176	19	1	1	1	100.0	88.9	9.8	0.4	0.4	0.6
Aged 75 or older	172	153	18	0	1	1	100.0	88.8	10.3	0.1	0.4	0.4

(continued)

(continued from previous page)

	total number	non-Hispanic				Hispanic	total percent	non-Hispanic				Hispanic
		white	black	Asian	Native American			white	black	Asian	Native American	
CALIFORNIA												
Total persons	**32,100**	**15,956**	**2,153**	**3,752**	**177**	**10,062**	**100.0%**	**49.7%**	**6.7%**	**11.7%**	**0.6%**	**31.3%**
Under age 5	2,689	978	183	318	11	1,199	100.0	36.4	6.8	11.8	0.4	44.6
Aged 5 to 14	5,098	2,026	373	607	27	2,066	100.0	39.7	7.3	11.9	0.5	40.5
Aged 15 to 24	4,360	1,760	313	559	26	1,702	100.0	40.4	7.2	12.8	0.6	39.0
Aged 25 to 34	5,017	2,162	340	620	28	1,867	100.0	43.1	6.8	12.4	0.6	37.2
Aged 35 to 44	5,375	2,830	381	631	31	1,502	100.0	52.7	7.1	11.7	0.6	27.9
Aged 45 to 54	3,843	2,306	242	452	24	819	100.0	60.0	6.3	11.8	0.6	21.3
Aged 55 to 64	2,310	1,449	148	264	14	435	100.0	62.7	6.4	11.4	0.6	18.8
Aged 65 to 74	1,824	1,231	100	195	9	289	100.0	67.5	5.5	10.7	0.5	15.8
Aged 75 or older	1,584	1,213	73	107	7	183	100.0	76.6	4.6	6.8	0.5	11.6
COLORADO												
Total persons	**4,009**	**3,167**	**168**	**89**	**28**	**558**	**100.0**	**79.0**	**4.2**	**2.2**	**0.7**	**13.9**
Under age 5	272	196	14	8	2	51	100.0	72.2	5.2	2.8	0.9	18.9
Aged 5 to 14	578	421	29	14	5	108	100.0	72.9	5.0	2.5	0.9	18.7
Aged 15 to 24	564	418	27	14	5	100	100.0	74.1	4.8	2.5	0.8	17.7
Aged 25 to 34	566	429	28	16	5	88	100.0	75.8	4.9	2.8	0.9	15.6
Aged 35 to 44	710	575	30	15	5	86	100.0	80.9	4.2	2.1	0.7	12.1
Aged 45 to 54	562	473	18	10	3	58	100.0	84.1	3.2	1.8	0.6	10.2
Aged 55 to 64	334	282	11	6	2	33	100.0	84.6	3.3	1.7	0.5	9.9
Aged 65 to 74	235	202	7	4	1	21	100.0	86.2	2.9	1.7	0.4	8.9
Aged 75 or older	188	169	4	2	1	13	100.0	89.9	2.0	0.9	0.3	6.9

(continued)

(continued from previous page)

| | total number | non-Hispanic | | | | | total percent | non-Hispanic | | | | |
		white	black	Asian	Native American	Hispanic		white	black	Asian	Native American	Hispanic
CONNECTICUT												
Total persons	**3,282**	**2,649**	**286**	**70**	**6**	**271**	**100.0%**	**80.7%**	**8.7%**	**2.1%**	**0.2%**	**8.3%**
Under age 5	217	157	25	6	0	28	100.0	72.4	11.7	2.7	0.2	13.0
Aged 5 to 14	454	336	51	11	1	55	100.0	73.9	11.3	2.5	0.2	12.1
Aged 15 to 24	391	291	44	10	1	45	100.0	74.4	11.3	2.6	0.2	11.5
Aged 25 to 34	471	358	49	14	1	49	100.0	76.0	10.3	3.0	0.2	10.4
Aged 35 to 44	568	465	46	13	1	42	100.0	81.9	8.1	2.3	0.2	7.5
Aged 45 to 54	436	372	31	8	1	25	100.0	85.3	7.0	1.9	0.2	5.7
Aged 55 to 64	279	242	19	4	0	13	100.0	86.6	6.9	1.5	0.2	4.8
Aged 65 to 74	235	212	12	2	0	7	100.0	90.5	5.3	0.9	0.1	3.2
Aged 75 or older	231	216	8	1	0	6	100.0	93.5	3.5	0.5	0.1	2.4
DELAWARE												
Total persons	**749**	**572**	**137**	**14**	**2**	**23**	**100.0**	**76.4**	**18.3**	**1.8**	**0.3**	**3.1**
Under age 5	51	36	11	1	0	2	100.0	70.4	22.6	2.1	0.2	4.7
Aged 5 to 14	105	74	24	2	0	4	100.0	70.2	23.3	2.0	0.3	4.3
Aged 15 to 24	98	70	22	2	0	4	100.0	70.9	22.5	2.1	0.3	4.2
Aged 25 to 34	115	85	22	2	0	4	100.0	74.2	19.5	2.2	0.3	3.9
Aged 35 to 44	128	99	23	3	0	4	100.0	77.1	17.7	2.0	0.3	2.9
Aged 45 to 54	94	75	15	2	0	2	100.0	79.6	16.1	1.9	0.3	2.1
Aged 55 to 64	63	52	9	1	0	1	100.0	82.0	14.2	1.7	0.3	1.8
Aged 65 to 74	52	45	6	0	0	1	100.0	86.1	11.5	0.8	0.2	1.3
Aged 75 or older	42	38	4	0	0	0	100.0	88.8	9.7	0.5	0.2	0.8

(continued)

(continued from previous page)

	total number	non-Hispanic				Hispanic	total percent	non-Hispanic				Hispanic
		white	black	Asian	Native American			white	black	Asian	Native American	
DISTRICT OF COLUMBIA												
Total persons	**532**	**153**	**325**	**13**	**1**	**40**	**100.0%**	**28.8%**	**61.1%**	**2.5%**	**0.2%**	**7.4%**
Under age 5	37	6	27	1	0	4	100.0	15.5	71.5	2.1	0.1	10.9
Aged 5 to 14	65	12	45	1	0	7	100.0	18.5	69.1	2.0	0.1	10.2
Aged 15 to 24	71	23	39	2	0	6	100.0	32.5	55.2	3.3	0.2	8.8
Aged 25 to 34	90	33	46	3	0	8	100.0	36.4	51.1	3.4	0.2	9.0
Aged 35 to 44	85	26	50	2	0	6	100.0	30.8	59.1	2.7	0.2	7.3
Aged 45 to 54	67	21	40	2	0	4	100.0	31.9	59.8	2.3	0.2	5.8
Aged 55 to 64	46	13	29	1	0	2	100.0	29.0	63.6	2.2	0.2	5.0
Aged 65 to 74	38	9	27	1	0	1	100.0	24.1	70.4	1.8	0.2	3.5
Aged 75 or older	33	10	22	0	0	1	100.0	29.1	67.1	0.9	0.3	2.6
FLORIDA												
Total persons	**14,812**	**10,256**	**2,082**	**223**	**38**	**2,214**	**100.0**	**69.2**	**14.1**	**1.5**	**0.3**	**14.9**
Under age 5	919	546	197	16	2	158	100.0	59.4	21.4	1.7	0.2	17.2
Aged 5 to 14	1,980	1,196	408	33	5	339	100.0	60.4	20.6	1.6	0.3	17.1
Aged 15 to 24	1,754	1,061	351	32	5	305	100.0	60.5	20.0	1.8	0.3	17.4
Aged 25 to 34	1,906	1,214	300	38	6	349	100.0	63.7	15.7	2.0	0.3	18.3
Aged 35 to 44	2,298	1,576	320	40	7	355	100.0	68.6	13.9	1.8	0.3	15.4
Aged 45 to 54	1,844	1,342	213	31	6	252	100.0	72.8	11.5	1.7	0.3	13.7
Aged 55 to 64	1,400	1,048	136	18	3	194	100.0	74.9	9.7	1.3	0.2	13.9
Aged 65 to 74	1,411	1,145	98	11	2	155	100.0	81.2	6.9	0.8	0.2	11.0
Aged 75 or older	1,300	1,127	60	4	2	107	100.0	86.7	4.6	0.3	0.1	8.2

(continued)

(continued from previous page)

	total number	non-Hispanic					total percent	non-Hispanic				
		white	black	Asian	Native American	Hispanic		white	black	Asian	Native American	Hispanic
GEORGIA												
Total persons	**7,616**	**5,141**	**2,160**	**125**	**15**	**174**	**100.0%**	**67.5%**	**28.4%**	**1.6%**	**0.2%**	**2.3%**
Under age 5	547	328	191	10	1	16	100.0	60.1	35.0	1.9	0.1	3.0
Aged 5 to 14	1,135	691	391	20	2	32	100.0	60.8	34.4	1.8	0.2	2.8
Aged 15 to 24	1,092	675	367	19	2	29	100.0	61.8	33.6	1.7	0.2	2.6
Aged 25 to 34	1,184	771	349	24	3	38	100.0	65.1	29.4	2.0	0.2	3.2
Aged 35 to 44	1,312	893	362	24	3	30	100.0	68.1	27.6	1.8	0.2	2.3
Aged 45 to 54	988	723	232	16	2	15	100.0	73.2	23.5	1.6	0.2	1.5
Aged 55 to 64	604	465	123	8	1	7	100.0	77.0	20.3	1.3	0.2	1.2
Aged 65 to 74	422	332	82	4	1	4	100.0	78.6	19.3	0.9	0.1	1.1
Aged 75 or older	333	263	65	1	0	3	100.0	79.1	19.5	0.4	0.1	0.9
HAWAII												
Total persons	**1,228**	**360**	**26**	**733**	**5**	**104**	**100.0**	**29.3**	**2.1**	**59.7**	**0.4**	**8.5**
Under age 5	97	21	2	61	0	12	100.0	21.9	2.2	62.8	0.5	12.6
Aged 5 to 14	175	40	3	106	1	25	100.0	22.6	1.7	60.7	0.4	14.5
Aged 15 to 24	169	45	6	100	1	17	100.0	26.9	3.6	59.2	0.4	10.0
Aged 25 to 34	174	59	7	92	1	15	100.0	33.7	4.1	53.0	0.5	8.7
Aged 35 to 44	200	67	5	112	1	15	100.0	33.6	2.5	56.1	0.4	7.5
Aged 45 to 54	160	54	2	94	1	9	100.0	34.0	1.1	58.9	0.4	5.7
Aged 55 to 64	99	31	1	62	0	5	100.0	31.0	0.7	62.9	0.3	5.2
Aged 65 to 74	86	22	0	60	0	3	100.0	25.5	0.5	69.9	0.2	4.0
Aged 75 or older	68	20	0	45	0	2	100.0	30.1	0.4	66.8	0.1	2.6

(continued)

(continued from previous page)

	total number	non-Hispanic				Hispanic	total percent	non-Hispanic				Hispanic
		white	black	Asian	Native American			white	black	Asian	Native American	
IDAHO												
Total persons	**1,276**	**1,155**	**5**	**13**	**16**	**86**	**100.0%**	**90.5%**	**0.4%**	**1.1%**	**1.3%**	**6.7%**
Under age 5	94	81	0	1	1	10	100.0	86.0	0.4	1.4	1.6	10.6
Aged 5 to 14	206	180	1	2	3	20	100.0	87.2	0.5	1.1	1.6	9.6
Aged 15 to 24	206	184	1	2	3	16	100.0	89.1	0.5	1.1	1.4	7.8
Aged 25 to 34	163	141	1	3	3	15	100.0	86.9	0.7	1.6	1.7	9.1
Aged 35 to 44	193	175	1	2	2	12	100.0	90.9	0.5	1.1	1.2	6.3
Aged 45 to 54	161	151	0	1	2	7	100.0	93.7	0.3	0.9	1.1	4.1
Aged 55 to 64	107	101	0	1	1	4	100.0	95.0	0.2	0.6	0.9	3.3
Aged 65 to 74	78	75	0	1	1	2	100.0	95.9	0.2	0.7	0.7	2.6
Aged 75 or older	69	68	0	0	0	1	100.0	97.6	0.1	0.4	0.4	1.4
ILLINOIS												
Total persons	**11,966**	**8,582**	**1,796**	**374**	**18**	**1,196**	**100.0**	**71.7**	**15.0**	**3.1**	**0.2**	**10.0**
Under age 5	887	544	181	30	1	132	100.0	61.3	20.4	3.4	0.1	14.8
Aged 5 to 14	1,743	1,123	323	57	3	237	100.0	64.5	18.6	3.3	0.1	13.6
Aged 15 to 24	1,640	1,085	288	56	3	209	100.0	66.1	17.6	3.4	0.2	12.7
Aged 25 to 34	1,734	1,180	260	67	3	224	100.0	68.0	15.0	3.9	0.2	12.9
Aged 35 to 44	1,981	1,456	277	64	3	181	100.0	73.5	14.0	3.2	0.2	9.1
Aged 45 to 54	1,502	1,156	191	49	3	103	100.0	77.0	12.7	3.2	0.2	6.9
Aged 55 to 64	993	781	126	28	1	57	100.0	78.6	12.7	2.8	0.1	5.7
Aged 65 to 74	785	645	89	16	1	34	100.0	82.2	11.4	2.0	0.1	4.3
Aged 75 or older	701	613	59	8	1	20	100.0	87.4	8.5	1.1	0.1	2.9

(continued)

(continued from previous page)

| | non-Hispanic | | | | | | non-Hispanic | | | | |
	total number	white	black	Asian	Native American	Hispanic	total percent	white	black	Asian	Native American	Hispanic
INDIANA												
Total persons	**5,954**	**5,273**	**483**	**53**	**13**	**132**	**100.0%**	**88.6%**	**8.1%**	**0.9%**	**0.2%**	**2.2%**
Under age 5	404	346	42	4	1	11	100.0	85.7	10.4	1.1	0.1	2.7
Aged 5 to 14	841	722	85	8	2	25	100.0	85.8	10.1	1.0	0.2	3.0
Aged 15 to 24	843	726	82	8	2	25	100.0	86.2	9.7	0.9	0.3	2.9
Aged 25 to 34	853	745	71	11	2	23	100.0	87.3	8.4	1.3	0.2	2.7
Aged 35 to 44	971	863	76	10	2	20	100.0	88.9	7.8	1.0	0.2	2.1
Aged 45 to 54	771	699	52	6	2	13	100.0	90.6	6.7	0.8	0.2	1.7
Aged 55 to 64	517	473	33	3	1	7	100.0	91.4	6.4	0.6	0.2	1.3
Aged 65 to 74	406	374	25	2	1	5	100.0	92.0	6.2	0.4	0.2	1.2
Aged 75 or older	347	325	17	1	1	3	100.0	93.9	4.8	0.2	0.2	0.9
IOWA												
Total persons	**2,878**	**2,725**	**58**	**38**	**8**	**50**	**100.0**	**94.7**	**2.0**	**1.3**	**0.3**	**1.7**
Under age 5	182	169	5	3	1	4	100.0	92.4	2.9	1.9	0.4	2.4
Aged 5 to 14	399	369	12	7	2	11	100.0	92.3	2.9	1.7	0.4	2.7
Aged 15 to 24	409	381	11	7	1	10	100.0	93.0	2.6	1.7	0.3	2.4
Aged 25 to 34	377	348	10	9	1	9	100.0	92.4	2.5	2.3	0.3	2.4
Aged 35 to 44	445	422	8	6	1	7	100.0	94.9	1.9	1.3	0.3	1.6
Aged 45 to 54	368	355	5	3	1	4	100.0	96.4	1.5	0.9	0.2	1.1
Aged 55 to 64	258	251	3	2	0	2	100.0	97.1	1.2	0.7	0.2	0.8
Aged 65 to 74	219	214	2	1	0	1	100.0	97.8	1.0	0.4	0.1	0.7
Aged 75 or older	220	217	2	0	0	1	100.0	98.4	0.7	0.2	0.1	0.5

(continued)

(continued from previous page)

		non-Hispanic						non-Hispanic			
	total number	white	black	Asian	Native American	Hispanic	total percent	white	black	Asian	Native American	Hispanic
KANSAS												
Total persons	**2,628**	**2,274**	**161**	**44**	**22**	**128**	**100.0%**	**86.5%**	**6.1%**	**1.7%**	**0.8%**	**4.9%**
Under age 5	183	150	15	4	2	12	100.0	81.9	8.3	2.3	0.9	6.7
Aged 5 to 14	392	323	30	7	4	27	100.0	82.4	7.7	1.9	1.0	7.0
Aged 15 to 24	380	317	27	8	4	24	100.0	83.5	7.2	2.0	1.0	6.3
Aged 25 to 34	356	295	25	9	4	23	100.0	82.8	7.1	2.6	1.0	6.5
Aged 35 to 44	423	368	26	7	3	19	100.0	86.9	6.2	1.6	0.8	4.5
Aged 45 to 54	327	293	15	5	2	11	100.0	89.8	4.7	1.4	0.7	3.3
Aged 55 to 64	212	193	9	2	1	6	100.0	91.2	4.3	1.2	0.7	2.6
Aged 65 to 74	181	168	7	1	1	4	100.0	92.9	3.8	0.7	0.5	2.1
Aged 75 or older	175	167	5	1	1	2	100.0	94.9	3.0	0.3	0.4	1.4
KENTUCKY												
Total persons	**3,943**	**3,602**	**280**	**25**	**6**	**30**	**100.0**	**91.3**	**7.1**	**0.6**	**0.2**	**0.8**
Under age 5	255	228	22	2	0	2	100.0	89.4	8.8	0.8	0.1	0.9
Aged 5 to 14	539	481	47	4	1	6	100.0	89.3	8.8	0.8	0.1	1.0
Aged 15 to 24	564	508	46	4	1	5	100.0	90.1	8.2	0.7	0.2	0.9
Aged 25 to 34	558	503	43	5	1	6	100.0	90.1	7.7	0.8	0.2	1.1
Aged 35 to 44	638	582	45	5	1	5	100.0	91.2	7.1	0.7	0.2	0.8
Aged 45 to 54	526	489	30	3	1	3	100.0	92.9	5.7	0.6	0.2	0.6
Aged 55 to 64	362	340	19	2	0	2	100.0	93.8	5.2	0.4	0.1	0.5
Aged 65 to 74	277	260	15	1	0	1	100.0	93.9	5.3	0.3	0.1	0.4
Aged 75 or older	224	211	12	0	0	1	100.0	94.2	5.3	0.1	0.1	0.3

(continued)

(continued from previous page)

	total number	non-Hispanic				Hispanic	total percent	non-Hispanic				Hispanic
		white	black	Asian	Native American			white	black	Asian	Native American	
LOUISIANA												
Total persons	**4,391**	**2,795**	**1,412**	**54**	**18**	**113**	**100.0%**	**63.6%**	**32.2%**	**1.2%**	**0.4%**	**2.6%**
Under age 5	325	179	133	5	1	6	100.0	55.1	41.1	1.5	0.3	2.0
Aged 5 to 14	682	384	268	9	3	18	100.0	56.3	39.3	1.3	0.4	2.6
Aged 15 to 24	679	390	257	10	3	19	100.0	57.5	37.9	1.4	0.5	2.8
Aged 25 to 34	501	372	198	9	3	19	100.0	61.9	32.9	1.6	0.5	3.1
Aged 35 to 44	579	448	202	9	3	18	100.0	66.0	29.7	1.3	0.4	2.6
Aged 45 to 54	544	375	147	6	2	13	100.0	69.0	27.1	1.1	0.4	2.4
Aged 55 to 64	370	266	90	3	1	9	100.0	71.9	24.4	0.9	0.3	2.4
Aged 65 to 74	288	213	67	2	1	6	100.0	73.7	23.1	0.6	0.3	2.2
Aged 75 or older	225	169	50	1	1	5	100.0	75.0	22.1	0.3	0.3	2.2
MAINE												
Total persons	**1,252**	**1,225**	**4**	**9**	**6**	**9**	**100.0**	**97.8**	**0.4**	**0.7**	**0.5**	**0.7**
Under age 5	75	73	0	1	0	1	100.0	96.9	0.5	1.1	0.5	1.0
Aged 5 to 14	170	165	1	2	1	2	100.0	97.1	0.4	0.9	0.6	1.0
Aged 15 to 24	162	157	1	1	1	1	100.0	97.1	0.5	0.9	0.6	0.9
Aged 25 to 34	168	163	1	2	1	2	100.0	96.9	0.6	1.0	0.5	1.0
Aged 35 to 44	218	213	1	2	1	1	100.0	97.7	0.4	0.7	0.5	0.7
Aged 45 to 54	178	174	0	1	1	1	100.0	98.3	0.3	0.6	0.4	0.5
Aged 55 to 64	109	108	0	0	0	0	100.0	98.7	0.2	0.4	0.3	0.4
Aged 65 to 74	92	91	0	0	0	0	100.0	99.2	0.1	0.3	0.2	0.3
Aged 75 or older	80	80	0	0	0	0	100.0	99.4	0.1	0.1	0.1	0.2

(continued)

(continued from previous page)

		non-Hispanic						non-Hispanic				
	total number	white	black	Asian	Native American	Hispanic	total percent	white	black	Asian	Native American	Hispanic
MARYLAND												
Total persons	**5,189**	**3,369**	**1,412**	**197**	**13**	**198**	**100.0%**	**64.9%**	**27.2%**	**3.8%**	**0.3%**	**3.8%**
Under age 5	361	215	113	15	1	17	100.0	59.5	31.4	4.1	0.2	4.8
Aged 5 to 14	740	441	233	29	2	34	100.0	59.7	31.5	4.0	0.2	4.6
Aged 15 to 24	649	386	203	28	2	30	100.0	59.5	31.2	4.3	0.3	4.7
Aged 25 to 34	791	484	228	35	2	41	100.0	61.2	28.9	4.4	0.3	5.2
Aged 35 to 44	944	608	261	37	3	36	100.0	64.4	27.7	3.9	0.3	3.8
Aged 45 to 54	697	476	174	26	2	19	100.0	68.3	24.9	3.8	0.3	2.8
Aged 55 to 64	424	301	97	15	1	10	100.0	71.0	22.9	3.6	0.3	2.3
Aged 65 to 74	319	243	62	8	1	6	100.0	76.0	19.4	2.5	0.2	1.8
Aged 75 or older	264	215	40	4	0	4	100.0	81.5	15.3	1.4	0.2	1.6
MASSACHUSETTS												
Total persons	**6,151**	**5,201**	**320**	**216**	**10**	**403**	**100.0**	**84.6**	**5.2**	**3.5**	**0.2**	**6.6**
Under age 5	403	308	30	20	1	45	100.0	76.3	7.5	5.0	0.1	11.1
Aged 5 to 14	837	650	61	38	2	87	100.0	77.7	7.2	4.5	0.2	10.4
Aged 15 to 24	758	604	49	34	2	70	100.0	79.6	6.4	4.4	0.2	9.3
Aged 25 to 34	970	792	54	45	2	77	100.0	81.7	5.6	4.6	0.2	7.9
Aged 35 to 44	1,042	892	51	37	2	59	100.0	85.7	4.9	3.6	0.2	5.7
Aged 45 to 54	794	705	34	21	1	32	100.0	88.8	4.3	2.7	0.2	4.1
Aged 55 to 64	496	448	19	11	1	16	100.0	90.4	3.8	2.3	0.2	3.3
Aged 65 to 74	432	402	13	7	1	9	100.0	93.1	3.1	1.6	0.1	2.1
Aged 75 or older	420	400	9	3	1	8	100.0	95.2	2.1	0.8	0.1	1.8

(continued)

(*continued from previous page*)

	total number	non-Hispanic				Hispanic	total percent	non-Hispanic				Hispanic
		white	black	Asian	Native American			white	black	Asian	Native American	
MICHIGAN												
Total persons	**9,634**	**7,790**	**1,396**	**145**	**54**	**248**	**100.0%**	**80.9%**	**14.5%**	**1.5%**	**0.6%**	**2.6%**
Under age 5	672	505	128	11	4	24	100.0	75.2	19.1	1.7	0.6	3.5
Aged 5 to 14	1,416	1,078	253	25	9	50	100.0	76.1	17.9	1.8	0.7	3.6
Aged 15 to 24	1,327	1,030	220	22	10	44	100.0	77.7	16.6	1.7	0.7	3.3
Aged 25 to 34	1,368	1,078	209	28	10	43	100.0	78.8	15.3	2.1	0.7	3.2
Aged 35 to 44	1,600	1,316	213	25	9	37	100.0	82.2	13.3	1.6	0.6	2.3
Aged 45 to 54	1,252	1,046	158	18	6	23	100.0	83.6	12.6	1.4	0.5	1.8
Aged 55 to 64	806	692	90	9	4	12	100.0	85.8	11.1	1.1	0.4	1.5
Aged 65 to 74	645	558	72	4	2	9	100.0	86.5	11.1	0.7	0.3	1.4
Aged 75 or older	550	488	53	2	1	6	100.0	88.6	9.7	0.4	0.2	1.1
MINNESOTA												
Total persons	**4,746**	**4,339**	**140**	**122**	**58**	**87**	**100.0**	**91.4**	**3.0**	**2.6**	**1.2**	**1.8**
Under age 5	319	276	14	14	6	9	100.0	86.4	4.4	4.5	1.9	2.8
Aged 5 to 14	704	612	30	29	14	20	100.0	86.9	4.3	4.1	1.9	2.8
Aged 15 to 24	674	598	26	23	11	16	100.0	88.8	3.8	3.4	1.6	2.4
Aged 25 to 34	658	586	25	21	9	16	100.0	89.2	3.7	3.2	1.4	2.5
Aged 35 to 44	814	755	23	16	8	13	100.0	92.7	2.8	1.9	1.0	1.5
Aged 45 to 54	607	574	12	9	5	7	100.0	94.6	1.9	1.5	0.8	1.1
Aged 55 to 64	382	366	5	5	3	3	100.0	95.8	1.4	1.3	0.7	0.8
Aged 65 to 74	297	287	3	3	1	2	100.0	96.7	1.1	1.0	0.5	0.7
Aged 75 or older	292	285	2	2	1	2	100.0	97.9	0.7	0.6	0.3	0.5

(*continued*)

(*continued from previous page*)

| | | non-Hispanic | | | | | | non-Hispanic | | | |
	total number	white	black	Asian	Native American	Hispanic	total percent	white	black	Asian	Native American	Hispanic
MISSISSIPPI												
Total persons	**2,770**	**1,729**	**993**	**18**	**9**	**22**	**100.0%**	**62.4%**	**35.8%**	**0.7%**	**0.3%**	**0.8%**
Under age 5	204	107	93	2	1	1	100.0	52.4	45.8	0.8	0.4	0.6
Aged 5 to 14	427	231	188	3	2	4	100.0	54.0	44.0	0.7	0.4	0.9
Aged 15 to 24	426	230	188	3	2	4	100.0	54.0	44.1	0.7	0.4	0.9
Aged 25 to 34	389	236	144	3	1	4	100.0	60.7	37.1	0.9	0.3	1.1
Aged 35 to 44	415	268	140	3	1	3	100.0	64.6	33.6	0.7	0.3	0.8
Aged 45 to 54	333	232	96	2	1	2	100.0	69.5	28.9	0.6	0.3	0.6
Aged 55 to 64	237	175	59	1	1	2	100.0	73.9	24.7	0.5	0.2	0.7
Aged 65 to 74	186	138	46	1	0	1	100.0	74.4	24.5	0.3	0.2	0.6
Aged 75 or older	153	112	40	0	0	1	100.0	73.2	26.0	0.1	0.1	0.5
MISSOURI												
Total persons	**5,457**	**4,688**	**607**	**57**	**21**	**84**	**100.0**	**85.9**	**11.1**	**1.0**	**0.4**	**1.5**
Under age 5	364	293	58	5	1	7	100.0	80.7	15.8	1.4	0.3	1.8
Aged 5 to 14	785	644	112	9	3	16	100.0	82.1	14.3	1.1	0.4	2.0
Aged 15 to 24	757	632	98	9	3	15	100.0	83.5	13.0	1.2	0.5	2.0
Aged 25 to 34	743	623	88	12	3	16	100.0	84.0	11.9	1.6	0.5	2.1
Aged 35 to 44	888	767	95	10	3	13	100.0	86.3	10.7	1.1	0.4	1.5
Aged 45 to 54	690	609	63	7	3	8	100.0	88.3	9.2	1.0	0.4	1.1
Aged 55 to 64	481	431	40	4	2	4	100.0	89.6	8.4	0.8	0.3	0.9
Aged 65 to 74	394	358	30	2	1	3	100.0	90.7	7.7	0.5	0.3	0.8
Aged 75 or older	356	330	22	1	1	2	100.0	92.8	6.2	0.2	0.2	0.6

(*continued*)

(continued from previous page)

	total number	non-Hispanic					total percent	non-Hispanic				
		white	black	Asian	Native American	Hispanic		white	black	Asian	Native American	Hispanic
MONTANA												
Total persons	**919**	**836**	**3**	**6**	**55**	**18**	**100.0%**	**90.9%**	**0.3%**	**0.7%**	**6.0%**	**2.0%**
Under age 5	59	50	0	1	6	2	100.0	84.9	0.4	1.1	10.8	2.9
Aged 5 to 14	136	117	0	1	13	4	100.0	86.0	0.4	0.9	9.7	3.0
Aged 15 to 24	133	118	1	1	10	3	100.0	88.6	0.5	0.7	7.7	2.6
Aged 25 to 34	108	96	1	1	8	3	100.0	88.5	0.7	1.1	7.0	2.7
Aged 35 to 44	146	134	1	1	7	3	100.0	92.0	0.4	0.7	5.0	1.9
Aged 45 to 54	129	121	0	1	5	2	100.0	94.0	0.2	0.5	3.9	1.4
Aged 55 to 64	86	81	0	0	3	1	100.0	94.6	0.2	0.4	3.6	1.2
Aged 65 to 74	64	62	0	0	2	1	100.0	96.2	0.2	0.4	2.4	0.8
Aged 75 or older	59	57	0	0	1	0	100.0	97.7	0.1	0.2	1.4	0.6
NEBRASKA												
Total persons	**1,679**	**1,523**	**67**	**20**	**14**	**56**	**100.0**	**90.7**	**4.0**	**1.2**	**0.8**	**3.3**
Under age 5	115	99	6	2	2	6	100.0	86.1	5.5	1.8	1.5	5.0
Aged 5 to 14	249	217	13	4	3	12	100.0	87.2	5.3	1.4	1.3	4.8
Aged 15 to 24	247	219	12	3	3	11	100.0	88.6	4.8	1.3	1.0	4.3
Aged 25 to 34	220	194	11	4	2	10	100.0	88.1	4.8	1.8	0.9	4.4
Aged 35 to 44	265	241	10	3	2	8	100.0	91.3	3.9	1.2	0.6	3.0
Aged 45 to 54	209	196	6	2	1	4	100.0	93.5	3.0	0.9	0.6	2.1
Aged 55 to 64	139	131	4	1	1	2	100.0	94.3	2.8	0.7	0.5	1.7
Aged 65 to 74	119	114	3	1	0	2	100.0	95.4	2.3	0.5	0.3	1.5
Aged 75 or older	115	112	2	0	0	1	100.0	96.9	1.5	0.2	0.2	1.2

(continued)

(continued from previous page)

	total number	non-Hispanic				Hispanic	total percent	non-Hispanic				Hispanic
		white	black	Asian	Native American			white	black	Asian	Native American	
NEVADA												
Total persons	**1,744**	**1,292**	**118**	**68**	**24**	**242**	**100.0%**	**74.1%**	**6.8%**	**3.9%**	**1.4%**	**13.9%**
Under age 5	118	77	10	5	2	24	100.0	65.3	8.5	4.5	1.4	20.2
Aged 5 to 14	244	162	21	10	4	47	100.0	66.6	8.7	4.0	1.7	19.1
Aged 15 to 24	222	151	18	9	4	40	100.0	67.8	8.3	4.3	1.6	18.0
Aged 25 to 34	250	171	19	11	4	46	100.0	68.5	7.4	4.3	1.5	18.2
Aged 35 to 44	302	227	20	12	4	38	100.0	75.3	6.7	3.9	1.3	12.6
Aged 45 to 54	240	193	13	9	3	22	100.0	80.1	5.4	3.9	1.3	9.3
Aged 55 to 64	166	136	9	6	2	13	100.0	82.1	5.2	3.7	1.1	7.9
Aged 65 to 74	122	104	5	4	1	8	100.0	84.8	4.4	3.2	1.0	6.7
Aged 75 or older	80	71	2	1	1	4	100.0	88.7	3.1	1.8	0.9	5.5
NEW HAMPSHIRE												
Total persons	**1,197**	**1,159**	**7**	**13**	**2**	**16**	**100.0**	**96.8**	**0.6**	**1.1**	**0.2**	**1.3**
Under age 5	78	75	1	1	0	1	100.0	96.1	0.7	1.2	0.2	1.9
Aged 5 to 14	174	167	1	2	0	3	100.0	96.0	0.7	1.2	0.2	1.9
Aged 15 to 24	152	146	1	2	0	3	100.0	96.0	0.8	1.3	0.2	1.7
Aged 25 to 34	177	169	1	3	0	3	100.0	95.8	0.7	1.5	0.2	1.7
Aged 35 to 44	224	216	1	3	0	3	100.0	96.8	0.6	1.2	0.2	1.3
Aged 45 to 54	160	156	1	1	0	1	100.0	97.6	0.5	0.9	0.2	0.9
Aged 55 to 64	92	90	0	1	0	0	100.0	98.0	0.5	0.7	0.2	0.7
Aged 65 to 74	74	73	0	0	0	0	100.0	98.7	0.3	0.5	0.1	0.4
Aged 75 or older	67	66	0	0	0	0	100.0	99.2	0.2	0.3	0.1	0.2

(continued)

	total number	non-Hispanic				Hispanic	total percent	non-Hispanic				Hispanic
		white	black	Asian	Native American			white	black	Asian	Native American	
NEW JERSEY												
Total persons	**8,091**	**5,594**	**1,081**	**416**	**14**	**986**	**100.0%**	**69.1%**	**13.4%**	**5.1%**	**0.2%**	**12.2%**
Under age 5	557	339	95	30	1	92	100.0	60.9	17.0	5.4	0.2	16.5
Aged 5 to 14	1,127	710	180	63	2	172	100.0	63.0	15.9	5.6	0.2	15.3
Aged 15 to 24	990	620	162	58	2	148	100.0	62.6	16.4	5.9	0.2	15.0
Aged 25 to 34	1,150	727	172	72	2	177	100.0	63.2	15.0	6.3	0.2	15.4
Aged 35 to 44	1,400	969	177	84	2	166	100.0	69.3	12.7	6.0	0.2	11.9
Aged 45 to 54	1,069	783	123	57	2	104	100.0	73.3	11.5	5.3	0.2	9.7
Aged 55 to 64	705	527	83	29	1	65	100.0	74.8	11.7	4.1	0.2	9.2
Aged 65 to 74	583	474	55	15	1	38	100.0	81.2	9.4	2.6	0.1	6.6
Aged 75 or older	511	444	35	8	1	23	100.0	87.0	6.8	1.5	0.1	4.6
NEW MEXICO												
Total persons	**1,792**	**885**	**33**	**19**	**150**	**704**	**100.0**	**49.4**	**1.8**	**1.1**	**8.4**	**39.3**
Under age 5	142	54	3	2	19	65	100.0	37.8	1.8	1.3	13.1	46.1
Aged 5 to 14	294	116	6	3	34	135	100.0	39.4	2.0	1.0	11.7	45.9
Aged 15 to 24	265	107	5	3	27	123	100.0	40.5	2.0	1.1	10.0	46.5
Aged 25 to 34	236	107	5	3	22	99	100.0	45.3	2.2	1.5	9.2	41.9
Aged 35 to 44	285	149	6	4	20	107	100.0	52.1	2.1	1.2	7.1	37.5
Aged 45 to 54	226	131	4	2	13	75	100.0	58.2	1.6	1.1	5.7	33.4
Aged 55 to 64	147	89	2	1	8	47	100.0	60.6	1.6	0.9	5.3	31.6
Aged 65 to 74	111	71	2	1	5	33	100.0	64.2	1.5	0.7	4.1	29.4
Aged 75 or older	86	62	1	0	3	20	100.0	71.4	1.1	0.3	3.9	23.3

(continued)

(continued from previous page)

	total number	non-Hispanic white	non-Hispanic black	non-Hispanic Asian	non-Hispanic Native American	Hispanic	total percent	non-Hispanic white	non-Hispanic black	non-Hispanic Asian	non-Hispanic Native American	Hispanic
NEW YORK												
Total persons	**18,140**	**11,813**	**2,656**	**918**	**52**	**2,701**	**100.0%**	**65.1%**	**14.6%**	**5.1%**	**0.3%**	**14.9%**
Under age 5	1,298	718	238	72	4	266	100.0	55.3	18.4	5.6	0.3	20.5
Aged 5 to 14	2,581	1,507	446	132	8	488	100.0	58.4	17.3	5.1	0.3	18.9
Aged 15 to 24	2,313	1,362	402	125	8	416	100.0	58.9	17.4	5.4	0.3	18.0
Aged 25 to 34	2,670	1,625	410	163	9	463	100.0	60.8	15.4	6.1	0.3	17.3
Aged 35 to 44	2,975	1,956	417	172	9	420	100.0	65.8	14.0	5.8	0.3	14.1
Aged 45 to 54	2,339	1,623	305	121	6	284	100.0	69.4	13.0	5.2	0.3	12.2
Aged 55 to 64	1,576	1,111	208	72	4	182	100.0	70.5	13.2	4.5	0.2	11.5
Aged 65 to 74	1,282	987	140	41	2	112	100.0	77.0	10.9	3.2	0.2	8.7
Aged 75 or older	1,104	925	88	20	2	69	100.0	83.7	8.0	1.8	0.2	6.3
NORTH CAROLINA												
Total persons	**7,554**	**5,598**	**1,671**	**84**	**90**	**112**	**100.0**	**74.1**	**22.1**	**1.1**	**1.2**	**1.5**
Under age 5	492	330	137	7	7	10	100.0	67.1	27.9	1.4	1.4	2.1
Aged 5 to 14	1,065	722	292	14	16	21	100.0	67.8	27.4	1.3	1.5	2.0
Aged 15 to 24	1,013	696	272	13	15	18	100.0	68.6	26.8	1.2	1.5	1.8
Aged 25 to 34	1,132	820	257	16	15	23	100.0	72.5	22.7	1.4	1.3	2.0
Aged 35 to 44	1,236	924	264	15	14	19	100.0	74.8	21.3	1.2	1.1	1.5
Aged 45 to 54	989	772	186	10	11	10	100.0	78.1	18.8	1.0	1.1	1.0
Aged 55 to 64	673	545	111	5	6	5	100.0	81.1	16.5	0.8	0.9	0.8
Aged 65 to 74	531	437	85	3	4	3	100.0	82.2	16.1	0.5	0.7	0.6
Aged 75 or older	424	351	67	1	3	2	100.0	82.9	15.7	0.3	0.6	0.5

(continued)

(continued from previous page)

	total number	non-Hispanic				Hispanic	total percent	non-Hispanic				Hispanic
		white	black	Asian	Native American			white	black	Asian	Native American	
NORTH DAKOTA												
Total persons	**654**	**607**	**4**	**5**	**30**	**7**	**100.0%**	**92.8%**	**0.7%**	**0.8%**	**4.6%**	**1.0%**
Under age 5	42	37	0	1	4	1	100.0	87.0	1.0	1.2	9.1	1.7
Aged 5 to 14	94	83	1	1	8	1	100.0	88.7	0.7	0.9	8.1	1.6
Aged 15 to 24	102	92	1	1	6	2	100.0	90.5	1.1	0.9	6.1	1.5
Aged 25 to 34	86	78	1	1	4	1	100.0	90.8	1.3	1.3	5.0	1.5
Aged 35 to 44	100	94	1	1	4	1	100.0	94.0	0.7	0.8	3.6	0.8
Aged 45 to 54	79	76	0	1	2	0	100.0	95.7	0.3	0.6	2.8	0.6
Aged 55 to 64	54	52	0	0	1	0	100.0	96.5	0.2	0.5	2.5	0.4
Aged 65 to 74	48	46	0	0	1	0	100.0	97.7	0.1	0.3	1.6	0.3
Aged 75 or older	49	48	0	0	0	0	100.0	98.5	0.1	0.2	0.9	0.3
OHIO												
Total persons	**11,260**	**9,659**	**1,280**	**126**	**20**	**175**	**100.0**	**85.8**	**11.4**	**1.1**	**0.2**	**1.6**
Under age 5	755	617	113	10	1	14	100.0	81.8	15.0	1.3	0.1	1.8
Aged 5 to 14	1,594	1,308	230	20	3	33	100.0	82.1	14.4	1.3	0.2	2.1
Aged 15 to 24	1,548	1,293	203	19	3	32	100.0	83.5	13.1	1.2	0.2	2.0
Aged 25 to 34	1,571	1,330	183	25	3	30	100.0	84.6	11.6	1.6	0.2	1.9
Aged 35 to 44	1,834	1,583	198	22	4	27	100.0	86.3	10.8	1.2	0.2	1.5
Aged 45 to 54	1,456	1,284	137	15	3	17	100.0	88.1	9.4	1.1	0.2	1.2
Aged 55 to 64	984	874	91	8	2	9	100.0	88.8	9.2	0.8	0.2	1.0
Aged 65 to 74	814	727	75	4	1	7	100.0	89.3	9.2	0.5	0.1	0.9
Aged 75 or older	702	643	50	2	1	5	100.0	91.7	7.2	0.3	0.1	0.7

(continued)

(continued from previous page)

		non-Hispanic						non-Hispanic				
	total number	white	black	Asian	Native American	Hispanic	total percent	white	black	Asian	Native American	Hispanic
OKLAHOMA												
Total persons	**3,334**	**2,641**	**266**	**44**	**266**	**116**	**100.0%**	**79.2%**	**8.0%**	**1.3%**	**8.0%**	**3.5%**
Under age 5	222	163	23	4	21	11	100.0	73.5	10.5	1.7	9.3	5.0
Aged 5 to 14	490	354	50	7	52	26	100.0	72.4	10.3	1.4	10.6	5.3
Aged 15 to 24	487	361	47	7	50	22	100.0	74.1	9.6	1.4	10.3	4.6
Aged 25 to 34	433	327	40	9	37	20	100.0	75.5	9.2	2.1	8.5	4.6
Aged 35 to 44	510	410	41	7	35	17	100.0	80.2	8.1	1.5	6.9	3.4
Aged 45 to 54	425	356	27	5	27	10	100.0	83.7	6.3	1.2	6.4	2.3
Aged 55 to 64	308	265	17	3	18	5	100.0	86.2	5.4	0.8	5.9	1.7
Aged 65 to 74	246	217	12	2	13	3	100.0	87.9	4.9	0.6	5.4	1.2
Aged 75 or older	213	189	9	1	13	1	100.0	88.7	4.4	0.3	6.0	0.6
OREGON												
Total persons	**3,299**	**2,922**	**57**	**101**	**43**	**176**	**100.0**	**88.6**	**1.7**	**3.1**	**1.3**	**5.3**
Under age 5	210	175	5	8	3	19	100.0	83.6	2.2	3.8	1.5	8.9
Aged 5 to 14	455	384	10	16	8	37	100.0	84.4	2.3	3.6	1.7	8.1
Aged 15 to 24	443	379	10	16	7	31	100.0	85.6	2.2	3.6	1.6	7.0
Aged 25 to 34	428	359	9	20	7	33	100.0	83.9	2.1	4.7	1.6	7.7
Aged 35 to 44	542	482	10	17	7	26	100.0	89.0	1.8	3.1	1.3	4.9
Aged 45 to 54	475	437	6	11	5	15	100.0	92.0	1.3	2.4	1.1	3.2
Aged 55 to 64	294	273	3	6	3	8	100.0	93.1	1.2	2.1	1.0	2.6
Aged 65 to 74	233	220	2	4	2	4	100.0	94.5	1.0	1.8	0.7	1.9
Aged 75 or older	221	213	2	2	1	3	100.0	96.4	0.7	1.0	0.6	1.3

(continued)

(continued from previous page)

		non-Hispanic						non-Hispanic				
	total number	white	black	Asian	Native American	Hispanic	total percent	white	black	Asian	Native American	Hispanic
PENNSYLVANIA												
Total persons	**12,158**	**10,474**	**1,162**	**195**	**15**	**312**	**100.0%**	**86.1%**	**9.6%**	**1.6%**	**0.1%**	**2.6%**
Under age 5	766	610	106	17	1	32	100.0	79.7	13.8	2.2	0.1	4.2
Aged 5 to 14	1,654	1,351	203	32	2	65	100.0	81.7	12.3	2.0	0.1	3.9
Aged 15 to 24	1,532	1,278	169	29	2	54	100.0	83.4	11.0	1.9	0.1	3.5
Aged 25 to 34	1,649	1,385	171	37	2	54	100.0	84.0	10.4	2.2	0.1	3.3
Aged 35 to 44	1,967	1,705	179	33	3	47	100.0	86.7	9.1	1.7	0.1	2.4
Aged 45 to 54	1,590	1,408	128	23	2	29	100.0	88.6	8.0	1.5	0.1	1.8
Aged 55 to 64	1,084	970	84	13	1	16	100.0	89.5	7.8	1.2	0.1	1.5
Aged 65 to 74	1,002	914	70	7	1	10	100.0	91.3	7.0	0.7	0.1	1.0
Aged 75 or older	914	852	52	3	1	7	100.0	93.2	5.6	0.4	0.1	0.7
RHODE ISLAND												
Total persons	**994**	**857**	**39**	**24**	**4**	**69**	**100.0**	**86.2**	**4.0**	**2.4**	**0.4**	**7.0**
Under age 5	65	49	4	3	1	8	100.0	75.7	6.7	4.3	0.9	12.5
Aged 5 to 14	138	110	8	5	1	14	100.0	79.8	5.7	3.5	0.5	10.5
Aged 15 to 24	122	100	6	4	1	12	100.0	81.6	5.3	3.1	0.5	9.5
Aged 25 to 34	151	126	6	5	1	13	100.0	83.7	4.2	3.0	0.4	8.7
Aged 35 to 44	164	144	6	4	1	10	100.0	87.5	3.9	2.2	0.3	6.1
Aged 45 to 54	124	112	4	2	0	6	100.0	90.3	3.0	1.9	0.3	4.5
Aged 55 to 64	78	72	2	1	0	3	100.0	92.0	2.7	1.4	0.3	3.6
Aged 65 to 74	75	71	2	1	0	2	100.0	94.4	2.1	0.8	0.3	2.5
Aged 75 or older	76	73	1	0	0	2	100.0	96.1	1.0	0.5	0.2	2.2

(continued)

(continued from previous page)

	total number	non-Hispanic				Hispanic	total percent	non-Hispanic				Hispanic
		white	black	Asian	Native American			white	black	Asian	Native American	
SOUTH CAROLINA												
Total persons	**3,786**	**2,577**	**1,131**	**29**	**8**	**41**	**100.0%**	**68.1%**	**29.9%**	**0.8%**	**0.2%**	**1.1%**
Under age 5	257	156	95	2	0	3	100.0	60.8	36.8	0.9	0.2	1.3
Aged 5 to 14	542	330	199	4	1	7	100.0	60.8	36.7	0.8	0.2	1.4
Aged 15 to 24	527	320	194	4	1	7	100.0	60.8	36.9	0.8	0.2	1.3
Aged 25 to 34	553	372	166	5	1	8	100.0	67.3	30.0	0.9	0.3	1.5
Aged 35 to 44	610	422	174	5	1	7	100.0	69.2	28.6	0.9	0.2	1.1
Aged 45 to 54	500	362	129	4	1	4	100.0	72.4	25.8	0.8	0.2	0.8
Aged 55 to 64	335	257	74	2	1	2	100.0	76.5	22.0	0.7	0.2	0.7
Aged 65 to 74	262	203	56	1	0	1	100.0	77.6	21.4	0.4	0.1	0.5
Aged 75 or older	202	156	44	0	0	1	100.0	77.4	21.9	0.2	0.1	0.4
SOUTH DAKOTA												
Total persons	**759**	**684**	**5**	**5**	**57**	**8**	**100.0**	**90.1**	**0.6**	**0.6**	**7.5**	**1.1**
Under age 5	54	44	0	1	8	1	100.0	81.8	0.9	1.0	14.9	1.5
Aged 5 to 14	117	99	1	1	15	2	100.0	84.3	0.7	0.8	12.6	1.6
Aged 15 to 24	116	101	1	1	11	2	100.0	87.3	0.8	0.7	9.8	1.4
Aged 25 to 34	95	85	1	1	8	1	100.0	88.6	1.0	1.1	7.9	1.4
Aged 35 to 44	116	107	1	1	6	1	100.0	92.2	0.6	0.6	5.6	1.0
Aged 45 to 54	91	85	0	0	4	1	100.0	93.8	0.4	0.5	4.7	0.6
Aged 55 to 64	61	58	0	0	2	0	100.0	94.9	0.3	0.3	4.0	0.5
Aged 65 to 74	54	52	0	0	1	0	100.0	96.6	0.2	0.2	2.6	0.4
Aged 75 or older	54	53	0	0	1	0	100.0	97.7	0.2	0.1	1.7	0.4

(continued)

(continued from previous page)

	total number	non-Hispanic					total percent	non-Hispanic				
		white	black	Asian	Native American	Hispanic		white	black	Asian	Native American	Hispanic
TENNESSEE												
Total persons	**5,504**	**4,494**	**895**	**50**	**12**	**53**	**100.0%**	**81.7%**	**16.3%**	**0.9%**	**0.2%**	**1.0%**
Under age 5	361	273	80	4	1	4	100.0	75.5	22.1	1.1	0.2	1.1
Aged 5 to 14	759	579	160	8	2	10	100.0	76.4	21.1	1.1	0.2	1.3
Aged 15 to 24	758	590	150	8	2	9	100.0	77.8	19.8	1.0	0.2	1.2
Aged 25 to 34	794	636	136	9	2	10	100.0	80.1	17.2	1.2	0.2	1.3
Aged 35 to 44	900	736	143	9	2	9	100.0	81.8	15.9	1.0	0.2	1.0
Aged 45 to 54	741	631	97	6	2	5	100.0	85.2	13.0	0.8	0.2	0.7
Aged 55 to 64	502	440	56	3	1	3	100.0	87.6	11.1	0.6	0.2	0.5
Aged 65 to 74	378	333	41	2	1	2	100.0	88.2	10.8	0.4	0.2	0.4
Aged 75 or older	310	276	32	1	0	1	100.0	88.8	10.4	0.2	0.2	0.4
TEXAS												
Total persons	**19,565**	**11,130**	**2,320**	**468**	**59**	**5,588**	**100.0**	**56.9**	**11.9**	**2.4**	**0.3**	**28.6**
Under age 5	1,551	695	199	41	3	613	100.0	44.8	12.8	2.7	0.2	39.5
Aged 5 to 14	3,116	1,507	413	77	8	1,111	100.0	48.4	13.3	2.5	0.3	35.7
Aged 15 to 24	2,952	1,469	390	73	9	1,011	100.0	49.7	13.2	2.5	0.3	34.2
Aged 25 to 34	2,837	1,485	360	84	9	899	100.0	52.3	12.7	2.9	0.3	31.7
Aged 35 to 44	3,184	1,889	388	84	10	813	100.0	59.3	12.2	2.6	0.3	25.5
Aged 45 to 54	2,384	1,543	249	59	8	524	100.0	64.7	10.5	2.5	0.3	22.0
Aged 55 to 64	1,516	1,044	143	29	5	295	100.0	68.8	9.5	1.9	0.3	19.5
Aged 65 to 74	1,132	811	103	16	3	200	100.0	71.6	9.1	1.4	0.3	17.6
Aged 75 or older	892	689	74	6	3	121	100.0	77.2	8.3	0.7	0.3	13.6

(continued)

(continued from previous page)

| | total number | non-Hispanic | | | | Hispanic | total percent | non-Hispanic | | | | Hispanic |
		white	black	Asian	Native American			white	black	Asian	Native American	
UTAH												
Total persons	**2,107**	**1,882**	**16**	**53**	**31**	**125**	**100.0%**	**89.3%**	**0.8%**	**2.5%**	**1.5%**	**5.9%**
Under age 5	188	164	1	6	4	13	100.0	87.4	0.7	3.0	2.0	7.0
Aged 5 to 14	384	335	3	10	8	28	100.0	87.1	0.8	2.7	2.1	7.3
Aged 15 to 24	406	360	3	10	7	26	100.0	88.8	0.8	2.4	1.6	6.3
Aged 25 to 34	299	260	3	10	5	21	100.0	87.0	1.0	3.3	1.6	7.1
Aged 35 to 44	287	257	2	7	4	17	100.0	89.6	0.8	2.6	1.3	5.8
Aged 45 to 54	216	198	1	5	2	10	100.0	91.6	0.6	2.2	1.0	4.6
Aged 55 to 64	138	128	1	3	1	5	100.0	92.9	0.5	1.8	0.8	3.9
Aged 65 to 74	103	97	0	2	1	4	100.0	93.9	0.5	1.6	0.6	3.4
Aged 75 or older	87	84	0	1	0	2	100.0	95.8	0.4	1.0	0.5	2.3
VERMONT												
Total persons	**605**	**590**	**3**	**5**	**2**	**5**	**100.0**	**97.6**	**0.4**	**0.9**	**0.3**	**0.9**
Under age 5	38	37	0	0	0	0	100.0	97.4	0.4	1.2	0.2	0.8
Aged 5 to 14	86	83	1	1	0	1	100.0	96.7	0.6	1.2	0.3	1.1
Aged 15 to 24	80	77	0	1	0	1	100.0	96.7	0.6	1.2	0.4	1.2
Aged 25 to 34	86	84	1	1	0	1	100.0	96.7	0.6	1.3	0.3	1.2
Aged 35 to 44	106	103	0	1	0	1	100.0	97.6	0.4	0.8	0.3	0.9
Aged 45 to 54	86	85	0	0	0	1	100.0	98.2	0.3	0.5	0.3	0.7
Aged 55 to 64	50	49	0	0	0	0	100.0	98.7	0.2	0.4	0.2	0.5
Aged 65 to 74	39	38	0	0	0	0	100.0	98.9	0.1	0.4	0.2	0.4
Aged 75 or older	34	34	0	0	0	0	100.0	99.2	0.1	0.1	0.1	0.4

(continued)

(continued from previous page)

	total number	non-Hispanic				Hispanic	total percent	non-Hispanic				Hispanic
		white	black	Asian	Native American			white	black	Asian	Native American	
VIRGINIA												
Total persons	**6,854**	**5,007**	**1,350**	**236**	**15**	**245**	**100.0%**	**73.0%**	**19.7%**	**3.4%**	**0.2%**	**3.6%**
Under age 5	459	310	108	18	1	22	100.0	67.7	23.6	3.9	0.1	4.7
Aged 5 to 14	935	635	221	35	2	41	100.0	67.9	23.7	3.8	0.2	4.4
Aged 15 to 24	920	631	209	36	2	41	100.0	68.6	22.7	4.0	0.2	4.5
Aged 25 to 34	1,079	761	220	43	3	53	100.0	70.5	20.4	4.0	0.3	4.9
Aged 35 to 44	1,195	873	232	43	3	44	100.0	73.0	19.4	3.6	0.2	3.7
Aged 45 to 54	921	714	150	31	2	24	100.0	77.6	16.3	3.4	0.2	2.6
Aged 55 to 64	576	457	89	17	1	11	100.0	79.4	15.5	3.0	0.2	1.9
Aged 65 to 74	424	340	69	9	1	6	100.0	80.1	16.2	2.1	0.2	1.4
Aged 75 or older	345	286	52	4	1	4	100.0	82.7	15.0	1.1	0.2	1.1
WASHINGTON												
Total persons	**5,693**	**4,782**	**175**	**315**	**93**	**329**	**100.0**	**84.0**	**3.1**	**5.5**	**1.6**	**5.8**
Under age 5	385	300	13	27	8	37	100.0	77.9	3.5	6.9	2.1	9.6
Aged 5 to 14	816	646	30	51	18	71	100.0	79.2	3.7	6.3	2.2	8.6
Aged 15 to 24	775	622	28	50	16	59	100.0	80.3	3.6	6.5	2.1	7.6
Aged 25 to 34	804	644	31	55	14	60	100.0	80.1	3.8	6.8	1.8	7.5
Aged 35 to 44	998	847	33	53	15	50	100.0	84.9	3.3	5.3	1.5	5.0
Aged 45 to 54	786	692	19	37	10	27	100.0	88.1	2.4	4.7	1.3	3.4
Aged 55 to 64	466	417	10	21	6	13	100.0	89.4	2.1	4.5	1.3	2.8
Aged 65 to 74	347	315	6	14	3	8	100.0	90.9	1.8	4.1	0.9	2.2
Aged 75 or older	317	299	4	7	2	4	100.0	94.3	1.4	2.3	0.6	1.4

(continued)

(continued from previous page)

	total number	non-Hispanic				Hispanic	total percent	non-Hispanic				Hispanic
		white	black	Asian	Native American			white	black	Asian	Native American	
WEST VIRGINIA												
Total persons	**1,836**	**1,755**	**57**	**10**	**2**	**11**	**100.0%**	**95.6%**	**3.1%**	**0.5%**	**0.1%**	**0.6%**
Under age 5	105	100	4	1	0	1	100.0	95.2	3.6	0.6	0.1	0.6
Aged 5 to 14	227	215	9	1	0	2	100.0	94.4	3.9	0.7	0.1	0.9
Aged 15 to 24	255	243	9	2	0	2	100.0	95.0	3.6	0.6	0.1	0.7
Aged 25 to 34	238	226	8	2	0	2	100.0	94.9	3.4	0.7	0.1	0.8
Aged 35 to 44	278	265	9	2	0	2	100.0	95.5	3.2	0.6	0.1	0.6
Aged 45 to 54	262	252	6	1	0	1	100.0	96.3	2.5	0.5	0.1	0.5
Aged 55 to 64	187	181	4	1	0	1	100.0	96.7	2.2	0.5	0.1	0.4
Aged 65 to 74	157	151	4	0	0	1	100.0	96.6	2.6	0.2	0.1	0.4
Aged 75 or older	128	123	4	0	0	1	100.0	96.4	3.0	0.1	0.1	0.4
WISCONSIN												
Total persons	**5,249**	**4,690**	**302**	**87**	**44**	**127**	**100.0**	**89.3**	**5.8**	**1.7**	**0.8**	**2.4**
Under age 5	343	284	33	11	4	11	100.0	82.7	9.7	3.2	1.2	3.3
Aged 5 to 14	766	643	65	20	9	28	100.0	84.0	8.5	2.7	1.2	3.6
Aged 15 to 24	747	644	56	15	8	25	100.0	86.2	7.4	2.0	1.1	3.3
Aged 25 to 34	721	631	46	16	7	22	100.0	87.4	6.3	2.2	1.0	3.1
Aged 35 to 44	863	783	44	11	6	19	100.0	90.7	5.2	1.3	0.7	2.2
Aged 45 to 54	672	623	28	7	4	11	100.0	92.7	4.1	1.0	0.6	1.6
Aged 55 to 64	438	412	15	4	2	5	100.0	93.9	3.5	0.8	0.6	1.2
Aged 65 to 74	360	343	10	2	1	3	100.0	95.3	2.8	0.6	0.4	1.0
Aged 75 or older	338	328	6	1	1	2	100.0	97.0	1.6	0.3	0.3	0.7

(continued)

(continued from previous page)

WYOMING

| | total number | non-Hispanic | | | | | total percent | non-Hispanic | | | | |
		white	black	Asian	Native American	Hispanic		white	black	Asian	Native American	Hispanic
Total persons	**507**	**456**	**4**	**4**	**11**	**32**	**100.0%**	**90.0%**	**0.8%**	**0.8%**	**2.1%**	**6.3%**
Under age 5	34	29	0	0	1	3	100.0	85.7	1.1	1.2	3.7	8.3
Aged 5 to 14	77	67	1	1	3	6	100.0	86.5	0.9	0.9	3.3	8.4
Aged 15 to 24	80	71	1	1	2	6	100.0	87.8	0.9	0.8	2.6	7.9
Aged 25 to 34	62	54	1	1	1	5	100.0	87.5	1.1	1.2	2.4	7.8
Aged 35 to 44	81	74	1	1	1	5	100.0	90.9	0.9	0.8	1.7	5.7
Aged 45 to 54	70	65	0	0	1	3	100.0	92.9	0.5	0.6	1.5	4.5
Aged 55 to 64	44	41	0	0	1	2	100.0	93.5	0.4	0.6	1.3	4.2
Aged 65 to 74	33	31	0	0	0	1	100.0	94.7	0.4	0.5	0.9	3.5
Aged 75 or older	26	25	0	0	0	1	100.0	96.0	0.4	0.3	0.6	2.6

Source: Bureau of the Census, Internet web site, http://www.census.gov; calculations by New Strategist

Minority Populations of the 75 Largest Metropolitan Areas, 1990

(total population of the 75 largest metropolitan areas ranked by population, and minority share of the metropolitan population, 1990; numbers in thousands)

		total	Asian	black	Hispanic	Native American
1.	New York–Northern New Jersey–Long Island, NY-NJ-CT-PA	19,342	4.6%	17.8%	14.7%	0.2%
2.	Los Angeles–Riverside–Orange County, CA	14,532	9.2	8.5	32.9	0.6
3.	Chicago–Gary–Kenosha, IL-IN-WI	8,240	3.1	19.0	10.9	0.2
4	Washington–Baltimore, DC-MD-VA-WV	6,727	3.7	25.2	3.9	0.3
5.	San Francisco–Oakland–San Jose, CA	6,253	14.8	8.6	15.5	0.7
6.	Philadelphia–Wilmington–Atlantic City, PA-NJ-DE-MD	5,893	2.0	18.4	3.8	0.2
7.	Boston–Brockton–Nashua, MA-NH-ME-CT	5,455	2.5	4.8	4.4	0.2
8.	Detroit–Ann Arbor–Flint, MI	5,187	1.4	20.5	2.0	0.4
9.	Dallas–Fort Worth, TX	4,037	2.4	14.0	13.0	0.5
10.	Houston–Galveston–Brazoria, TX	3,731	3.5	17.9	20.7	0.3
11.	Miami–Fort Lauderdale, FL	3,193	1.4	18.5	33.3	0.2
12.	Seattle–Tacoma–Bremerton, WA	2,970	6.1	4.5	3.0	1.3
13.	Atlanta, GA	2,960	1.8	25.2	2.0	0.2
14.	Cleveland–Akron, OH	2,860	1.0	15.6	1.9	0.2
15.	Minneapolis–St. Paul, MN-WI	2,539	2.6	3.5	1.5	1.0
16.	San Diego, CA	2,498	7.9	6.4	20.4	0.8
17.	St. Louis, MO-IL	2,493	1.0	17.0	1.1	0.2
18.	Pittsburgh, PA	2,395	0.7	7.5	0.6	0.1
19.	Phoenix–Mesa, AZ	2,238	1.6	3.5	17.0	2.2
20.	Tampa–St. Petersburg–Clearwater, FL	2,068	1.1	9.0	6.7	0.3
21.	Denver-Boulder-Greeley, CO	1,980	2.2	5.0	12.8	0.7
22.	Cincinnati–Hamilton, OH-KY-IN	1,818	0.8	11.2	0.5	0.1
23.	Portland–Salem, OR-WA	1,793	3.2	2.5	4.0	1.0
24.	Milwaukee–Racine, WI	1,607	1.2	13.3	3.8	0.5
25.	Kansas City, MO-KS	1,583	1.1	12.7	2.9	0.5
26.	Sacramento–Yolo, CA	1,481	7.7	6.9	11.6	1.1
27.	Norfolk–Virginia Beach–Newport News, VA-NC	1,443	2.4	28.3	2.3	0.3
28.	Indianapolis, IN	1,380	0.8	13.2	0.9	0.2
29.	Columbus, OH	1,345	1.6	12.1	0.8	0.2
30.	San Antonio, TX	1,325	1.2	6.7	47.4	0.4
31.	New Orleans, LA	1,285	1.7	34.8	4.2	0.3
32.	Orlando, FL	1,225	1.7	12.0	8.2	0.3
33	Buffalo–Niagara Falls, NY	1,189	0.9	10.3	2.0	0.6
34.	Charlotte–Gastonia Rock Hill, NC-SC	1,162	1.0	19.9	0.9	0.4
35.	Hartford, CT	1,158	1.5	8.3	6.9	0.2

(continued)

(continued from previous page)

		total	Asian	black	Hispanic	Native American
36.	Providence–Fall River–Warwick, RI-MA	1,134	1.8%	3.3%	4.2%	0.3%
37.	Salt Lake City–Ogden, UT	1,072	2.4	1.0	5.8	0.8
38.	Rochester, NY	1,062	1.3	8.9	3.0	0.3
39.	Nashville, TN	1,050	0.7	19.3	0.7	0.3
40.	Greensboro–Winston-Salem–High Point, NC	1,007	0.8	40.7	0.8	0.2
41.	Memphis, TN-AR-MS	985	1.0	15.5	0.8	0.2
42.	Oklahoma City, OK	959	1.9	10.5	3.6	4.8
43.	Dayton–Springfield, OH	951	1.0	13.3	0.8	0.2
44.	Louisville, KY-IN	949	0.6	12.9	0.6	0.2
45.	Grand Rapids–Muskegon–Holland, MI	938	0.9	6.9	3.1	0.6
46.	Jacksonville, FL	907	1.7	20.0	2.5	0.3
47.	Richmond–Petersburg, VA	866	1.4	29.2	1.1	0.3
48.	West Palm Beach–Boca Raton, FL	864	1.0	12.5	7.7	0.1
49.	Albany–Schenectady–Troy, NY	861	1.2	4.6	1.7	0.2
50.	Raleigh–Durham–Chapel Hill, NC	856	1.6	24.2	1.3	0.3
51.	Las Vegas, NV-AZ	853	3.1	8.4	10.4	1.1
52.	Austin–San Marcos, TX	846	2.2	9.4	20.9	0.4
53.	Birmingham, AL	840	0.5	28.7	0.4	0.2
54.	Honolulu, HI	836	63.0	3.1	6.8	0.4
55.	Greenville–Spartansburg–Anderson, SC	831	0.6	17.4	0.7	0.1
56.	Fresno, CA	756	7.7	4.8	35.3	1.1
57.	Syracuse, NY	742	1.1	5.7	1.4	0.6
58.	Tulsa, OK	709	0.9	8.2	2.1	6.8
59.	Tucson, AZ	667	1.8	3.1	24.5	3.0
60.	Omaha, NE-IA	640	1.0	8.0	2.6	0.5
61.	Scranton–Wilkes-Barre–Hazelton, PA	638	0.5	0.9	0.6	0.1
62.	Toledo, OH	614	1.0	11.4	3.3	0.2
63.	Youngstown–Warren, OH	601	0.4	9.4	1.3	0.2
64.	Allentown–Bethlehem–Easton, PA	595	1.1	2.0	4.6	0.1
65.	El Paso, TX	592	1.1	3.7	69.6	0.4
66.	Albuquerque, NM	589	1.4	2.5	37.1	5.1
67.	Harrisburg–Lebanon–Carlisle, PA	588	1.1	6.7	1.7	0.1
68.	Springfield, MA	588	1.4	6.3	8.5	0.2
69.	Knoxville, TN	586	0.8	6.1	0.5	0.2
70.	Bakersfield, CA	543	3.0	5.5	28.0	1.3
71.	Little Rock–North Little Rock, AR	513	0.7	19.9	0.8	0.4
72.	Charleston–North Charleston, SC	507	1.2	30.2	1.5	0.3
73.	Sarasota–Bradenton, FL	489	0.5	5.8	3.1	0.2
74.	Wichita, KS	485	1.9	7.6	4.1	1.1
75.	Stockton–Lodi, CA	481	12.4	5.6	23.4	1.1

Source: Bureau of the Census, Statistical Abstract of the United States 1993; *calculations by New Strategist*

Total Population: Wealth

The net worth of Americans rose 7 percent between 1992 and 1995, after adjusting for inflation.

The median net worth (assets minus debts) of American households stood at $56,400 in 1995, but this figure masks sharp differences in net worth by race. The median net worth of non-Hispanic white householders was a lofty $73,900 in 1995, while that of nonwhite and Hispanic householders was a much smaller $16,500. Between 1992 and 1995, the median net worth of non-Hispanic whites rose 3 percent while that of non-whites and Hispanics fell 2 percent, after adjusting for inflation. The net worth of non-Hispanic white households is much higher than that of other households because non-Hispanic whites are much more likely to own a home. Home equity accounts for the largest share of Americans' net worth.

The average householder has only $13,000 in financial assets, with transaction accounts (such as checking accounts) owned by the largest share (87 percent). Forty-three percent have retirement accounts and 31 percent have life insurance. The value of the financial assets held by the average household rose 8 percent between 1992 and 1995, after adjusting for inflation.

Most households are in debt, owing a median of $22,500 in 1995. The debt of the average household rose 15 percent between 1992 and 1995 as homeownership—and mortgage debt—increased.

■ The wealth of Americans should rise substantially in the future as the large baby-boom generation enters the peak ages of homeownership and begins to save seriously for retirement.

Net worth of Americans varies by race and Hispanic origin

(median net worth of households by race and Hispanic origin, 1995)

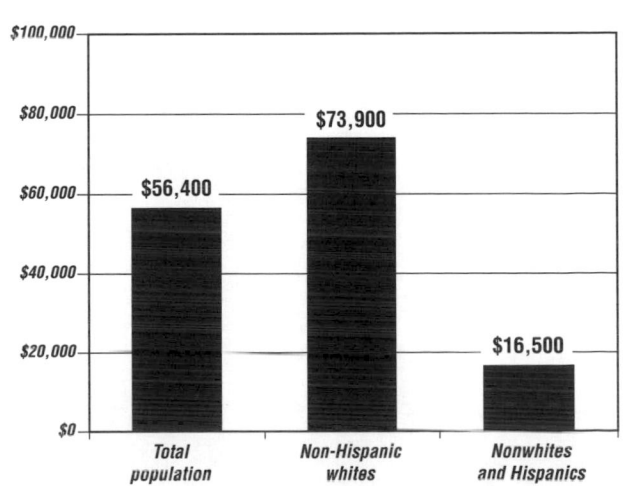

Net Worth of Households by Race and Hispanic Origin, 1992 and 1995

(median net worth of households by race and Hispanic origin of householder, 1992 and 1995; percent change 1992–1995; in 1995 dollars)

	1995	1992	percent change 1992–1995
Total households	**$56,400**	**$52,800**	**6.8%**
Non–Hispanic white	73,900	71,700	3.1
Nonwhite and Hispanic	16,500	16,900	–2.4

Source: Federal Reserve Board, Family Finances in the U.S.: Recent Evidence from the Survey of Consumer Finances, *Federal Reserve Bulletin, January 1997; calculations by New Strategist*

Nonfinancial Assets of Total Households, 1992 and 1995

(percent of total households owning nonfinancial assets, and median value of assets for owners, 1992 and 1995; percentage point change in households with asset and percent change in value of asset, 1992–95; in 1995 dollars)

	1995	1992	percentage point change, 1992–95
Percent owning asset			
Any nonfinancial asset	91.1%	91.0%	0.1
Vehicles	84.2	86.2	–2.0
Primary residence	64.7	63.9	0.8
Investment real estate	17.5	19.3	–1.8
Business	11.0	11.9	–0.9
Other nonfinancial	9.0	8.3	0.7

	1995	1992	percent change 1992–95
Median value of asset for owners			
Any nonfinancial asset	$83,000	$74,200	11.9%
Vehicles	10,000	7,400	35.1
Primary residence	90,000	86,800	3.7
Investment real estate	50,000	48,800	2.5
Business	41,000	65,100	–37.0
Other nonfinancial	10,000	7,600	31.6

Source: Federal Reserve Board, Family Finances in the U.S.: Recent Evidence from the Survey of Consumer Finances, *Federal Reserve Bulletin, January 1997; calculations by New Strategist*

Financial Assets of Total Households, 1992 and 1995

(percent of total households owning financial assets, and median value of assets for owners, 1992 and 1995; percentage point change in households with asset and percent change in value of asset, 1992–95; in 1995 dollars)

	1995	1992	percentage point change, 1992–95
Percent owning asset			
Any financial asset	90.8%	90.3%	0.5
Transaction accounts	87.1	87.0	0.1
Certificates of deposit	14.1	16.7	−2.6
Savings bonds	22.9	22.3	0.6
Bonds	3.0	4.2	−1.2
Stocks	15.3	16.9	−1.6
Mutual funds	12.0	10.4	1.6
Retirement accounts	43.0	37.9	5.1
Life insurance	31.4	34.8	−3.4
Other managed assets	3.8	4.0	−0.2
Other financial assets	11.0	10.8	0.2

	1995	1992	percent change 1992–95
Median value of asset for owners			
Any financial asset	$13,000	$12,000	8.3%
Transaction accounts	2,100	2,500	−16.0
Certificates of deposit	10,000	11,200	−10.7
Savings bonds	1,000	700	42.9
Bonds	26,200	32,600	−19.6
Stocks	8,000	8,700	−8.0
Mutual funds	19,000	17,400	9.2
Retirement accounts	15,600	15,200	2.6
Life insurance	5,000	3,300	51.5
Other managed assets	30,000	21,700	38.2
Other financial assets	3,000	2,700	11.1

Source: Federal Reserve Board, Family Finances in the U.S.: Recent Evidence from the Survey of Consumer Finances, *Federal Reserve Bulletin, January 1997; calculations by New Strategist*

Total Households with Debt, 1992 and 1995

(percent of total households with debt, and median value of debt for those with debts, 1992 and 1995; percentage point change in households with debt and percent change in amount of debt, 1992–95; in 1995 dollars)

	1995	1992	percentage point change, 1992–95
Percent with debt			
Any debt	75.2%	73.6%	1.6
Mortgage and home equity	41.1	39.1	2.0
Installment	46.5	46.1	0.4
Other lines of credit	1.9	2.4	−0.5
Credit card	47.8	43.8	4.0
Investment real estate	6.3	7.8	−1.5
Other debt	9.0	8.8	0.2

	1995	1992	percent change 1992–95
Median value of debt for debtors			
Any debt	$22,500	$19,500	15.4%
Mortgage and home equity	51,000	47,400	7.6
Installment	6,100	5,000	22.0
Other lines of credit	3,500	2,200	59.1
Credit card	1,500	1,100	36.4
Investment real estate	28,000	26,000	7.7
Other debt	2,000	2,700	−25.9

Source: Federal Reserve Board, Family Finances in the U.S.: Recent Evidence from the Survey of Consumer Finances, *Federal Reserve Bulletin, January 1997; calculations by New Strategist*

7

Attitudes

Although the sometimes difficult relations between racial and ethnic groups in the United States are frequently in the news, in fact Americans are more tolerant than ever towards people of other races and ethnicities. Yet they are also concerned that we are an increasingly divided nation. These seemingly contradictory attitudes are revealed by the 1996 General Social Survey, a nationally representative survey of the attitudes of Americans on a wide variety of issues. This survey, taken every two years by the National Opinion Research Center of the University of Chicago, is a window into the hearts and minds of Americans. It reveals a public sharply divided on some diversity issues, but strongly united on others.

Americans agree on what it means to be an American. The majority of whites, blacks, and people of "other" race (a category that includes Asians, Native Americans, and Hispanics—who may be of any race) believe American citizenship and the ability to speak English is very important to being an American. But while the majority of blacks think it is very important to have been born in the U.S., fewer than half of whites and "others" feel this strongly about being born in America. When asked whether racial and ethnic groups should maintain their customs or blend in, a minority of whites, blacks, and "others" favored maintaining distinct customs. A large proportion of people, regardless of race, just don't know the answer to this difficult question.

The biggest disagreements are between whites and blacks over the issues of black progress. While most whites think conditions for blacks have improved in the past few years, a minority of blacks agree. Nearly half of whites profess to thinking that blacks have worse jobs, income, and housing because they lack the motivation to pull themselves out of poverty. Blacks, in contrast, are most likely to blame discrimination. Blacks are much more likely than whites to think the government is obligated to help blacks.

But blacks and whites agree on many black progress issues as well. Whites are almost as likely as blacks to disagree with the statement that blacks shouldn't push themselves where they are not wanted. Most whites favor fair housing laws. And most blacks and whites agree that blacks should work their way up without special favors.

Integration in housing, schools, and the workplace is now widespread and accepted by all. Most whites and blacks say their neighborhoods are integrated. Most would send their children to mixed-race schools. Most work with a mixture of races. But while 83 percent of whites are against the preferential hiring and promotion of blacks, only 46 percent of blacks are. An equal proportion favor affirmative action in the workplace. To whites, reverse discrimination is a real threat. Over 70 percent of whites think it is somewhat or very likely that a white person won't get a job or a promotion while a less qualified black person gets one instead. About half of blacks agree.

Whites are more likely than blacks or people of other race to want immigration reduced. While 57 percent of whites favor decreasing immigration, only 43 percent of blacks and 26 percent of "others" feel that way. The majority of whites and blacks, versus 45 percent of "others," favor stronger efforts to curb illegal immigration. Most blacks, but only 18 percent of "others," think immigrants take jobs away from people who were born in America.

Americans are deeply divided on the impact of immigration on our country. Whites, blacks, and "others" are split on whether immigrants are good for the economy and on whether they increase the crime rate. But a majority of whites and "others" think immigrants make America more open to new ideas and cultures. A 41 percent plurality of blacks agree.

■ Today's children and young adults have been raised to expect and accept diversity. They see people from all racial and ethnic backgrounds in positions of power and leadership, from the President's Cabinet officers to war heroes to movie stars. The American public will increasingly embrace diversity as young people replace less-tolerant older generations.

■ Immigration promises to be a hot-button issue far into the future regardless of the growing tolerance for racial and ethnic diversity. Behind the concerns over immigration is the never-ending quest for an equitable distribution of the nation's limited resources.

Importance of Being American

"How important do you consider the following?"

(percent responding by race, 1996)

	total	white	black	other
To have been born in America				
Very important	39.9%	37.2%	61.3%	26.4%
Fairly important	26.7	27.4	17.7	38.9
Not very important	18.3	19.8	10.8	13.9
Not important	12.0	12.7	5.9	16.7
Can't choose	1.9	1.4	3.8	4.2
To have American citizenship				
Very important	73.7	73.9	75.3	65.3
Fairly important	17.0	16.9	15.1	23.6
Not very important	5.0	4.8	5.4	6.9
Not important	2.3	2.6	0.5	2.8
Can't choose	0.7	0.4	2.7	1.4
To have lived in America for most of one's life				
Very important	42.9	41.3	55.9	34.7
Fairly important	27.9	28.5	21.0	36.1
Not very important	19.8	20.9	13.4	18.1
Not important	6.3	6.7	2.7	9.7
Can't choose	1.5	1.1	3.8	1.4
To be able to speak English				
Very important	69.9	70.3	71.0	61.1
Fairly important	21.2	21.5	17.7	26.4
Not very important	5.0	4.6	5.4	11.1
Not important	1.8	1.7	2.7	1.4
Can't choose	0.8	0.6	2.2	0.0

Note: Numbers may not add to 100 percent because "no answer" is not shown.
Source: 1996 General Social Survey, National Opinion Research Center, University of Chicago

What Does It Mean to Be American?

"Do you agree or disagree that it is impossible for people who do not share American customs and traditions to become fully American?"

(percent responding by race, 1996)

	total	white	black	other
Agree, total	**32.8%**	**31.3%**	**40.9%**	**34.7%**
Agree strongly	8.7	8.1	11.3	11.1
Agree	24.1	23.2	29.6	23.6
Neither	**20.7**	**20.7**	**19.4**	**23.6**
Disagree, total	**39.1**	**40.9**	**29.6**	**36.2**
Disagree	31.5	32.3	26.9	30.6
Disagree strongly	7.6	8.6	2.7	5.6
Can't choose	**3.4**	**2.9**	**6.5**	**2.8**

Note: Numbers may not add to 100 percent because "no answer" is not shown.
Source: 1996 General Social Survey, National Opinion Research Center, University of Chicago

Proud of American Treatment of All Groups?

"How proud are you of the U.S.'s fair and equal treatment of all groups in society?"

(percent responding by race, 1996)

	total	white	black	other
Very proud	17.0%	17.6%	11.8%	22.2%
Somewhat proud	36.6	39.2	23.7	29.2
Not very proud	29.1	29.2	30.6	23.6
Not at all proud	10.7	8.6	21.5	15.3
Can't choose	4.7	3.6	10.8	5.6

Note: Numbers may not add to 100 percent because "no answer" is not shown.
Source: 1996 General Social Survey, National Opinion Research Center, University of Chicago

Racial and Ethnic Unity

"How close do you feel to your ethnic or racial group?"

(percent responding by race, 1996)

	total	white	black	other
Very close	35.8%	31.1%	63.4%	37.5%
Close	34.7	37.6	17.7	33.3
Not very close	15.8	16.9	8.1	19.4
Not at all close	4.9	5.6	2.2	1.4
Can't choose	7.0	7.2	6.5	5.6

Note: Numbers may not add to 100 percent because "no answer" is not shown.
Source: 1996 General Social Survey, National Opinion Research Center, University of Chicago

Melting Pot

"Some people say that it is better for a country if different racial and ethnic groups maintain their distinct customs and traditions. Others say that it is better if groups adapt and blend into the larger society. Which of these views comes closer to your own?"

(percent responding by race, 1996)

	total	*white*	*black*	*other*
Maintain customs	29.2%	28.1%	30.6%	41.7%
Blend in	40.7	43.0	33.9	23.6
Don't know	25.5	24.3	29.6	31.9

Note: Numbers may not add to 100 percent because "no answer" is not shown.
Source: 1996 General Social Survey, National Opinion Research Center, University of Chicago

Should Government Help Maintain Ethnic Identity?

"Should ethnic minorities be given government assistance to preserve their customs and traditions?"

(percent responding by race, 1996)

	total	white	black	other
Agree, total	**15.7%**	**10.5%**	**37.7%**	**37.5%**
Agree strongly	3.4	1.8	10.8	8.3
Agree somewhat	12.3	8.7	26.9	29.2
Neither	**21.4**	**20.6**	**23.1**	**29.2**
Disagree, total	**54.4**	**61.6**	**23.2**	**25.0**
Disagree somewhat	36.7	40.7	19.4	20.8
Disagree strongly	17.7	20.9	3.8	4.2
Can't choose	**4.0**	**2.7**	**11.3**	**5.6**

Note: Numbers may not add to 100 percent because "no answer" is not shown.
Source: 1996 General Social Survey, National Opinion Research Center, University of Chicago

Have Conditions for Blacks Improved?

"In the past few years, do you think conditions for black people have improved, gotten worse, or stayed about the same?"

(percent responding by race, 1996)

	total	*white*	*black*	*other*
Improved	57.6%	62.4%	35.4%	43.4%
Gotten worse	9.3	7.3	20.6	10.4
Stayed the same	29.4	26.4	42.6	39.6
Don't know	3.4	3.7	1.1	5.7

Note: Numbers may not add to 100 percent because "no answer" is not shown.
Source: 1996 General Social Survey, National Opinion Research Center, University of Chicago

Should Blacks Push?

"Blacks shouldn't push themselves where they're not wanted."

(percent responding by race, 1996)

	total	white	black	other
Agree, total	**38.7%**	**39.6%**	**33.3%**	**37.2%**
Agree strongly	16.0	15.8	18.9	10.5
Agree slightly	22.7	23.8	14.4	26.7
Disagree, total	**57.2**	**56.7**	**60.4**	**57.2**
Disagree slightly	24.1	26.4	11.5	22.9
Disagree strongly	33.1	30.3	48.9	34.3
No opinion	**3.7**	**3.2**	**5.9**	**5.7**

Note: Numbers may not add to 100 percent because "no answer" is not shown.
Source: 1996 General Social Survey, National Opinion Research Center, University of Chicago

Should Blacks Work Their Way Up?

"Irish, Italians, Jewish and many other minorities overcame prejudice and worked their way up. Blacks should do the same without special favors—do you agree or disagree?"

(percent responding by race, 1996)

	total	*white*	*black*	*other*
Agree, total	**71.6%**	**75.9%**	**51.9%**	**59.5%**
Agree strongly	43.6	47.2	27.4	32.1
Agree somewhat	28.0	28.7	24.5	27.4
Neither	**11.4**	**10.5**	**12.6**	**21.7**
Disagree, total	**15.1**	**11.8**	**32.5**	**16.9**
Disgree somewhat	9.5	8.1	17.3	9.4
Disagree strongly	5.6	3.7	15.2	7.5
Don't know	**1.7**	**1.6**	**2.5**	**0.9**

Note: Numbers may not add to 100 percent because "no answer" is not shown.
Source: 1996 General Social Survey, National Opinion Research Center, University of Chicago

Why Do Blacks Have It Worse?

"On the average, blacks have worse jobs, income, and housing than white people. Do you think these differences are … "

(percent responding by race, 1996)

	total	white	black	other
A. Mainly due to discrimination?				
Yes	37.5%	32.7%	60.3%	49.1%
No	56.9	62.0	33.6	43.4
Don't know	4.8	4.6	5.8	6.6
B. Because most blacks have less in-born ability to learn?				
Yes	9.8	9.6	10.1	13.2
No	86.6	86.9	87.7	79.2
Don't know	3.3	3.3	2.2	6.6
C. Because most blacks don't have the chance for education that it takes to rise out of poverty?				
Yes	44.5	43.0	52.7	46.2
No	51.9	53.6	45.8	41.5
Don't know	3.3	3.0	1.4	11.3
D. Because most blacks just don't have the motivation or will power to pull themselves out of poverty?				
Yes	47.2	48.6	39.0	49.1
No	46.0	44.7	55.6	40.6
Don't know	6.1	6.1	5.1	9.4

Note: Numbers may not add to 100 percent because "no answer" is not shown.
Source: 1996 General Social Survey, National Opinion Research Center, University of Chicago

Is Government Obligated to Help Blacks?

"On a scale of 1 to 5, how much should government help blacks, from:

1: I strongly agree the government is obligated to help blacks; *to*

5: I strongly agree that government shouldn't give special treatment."

(percent responding by race, 1996)

	total	white	black	other
1 Government obligated to help	8.1%	3.9%	31.1%	14.7%
2	8.5	7.5	14.0	9.5
3 Agree with both	28.7	27.4	33.9	35.8
4	23.0	25.7	7.0	21.1
5 No special treatment	28.0	32.0	8.9	12.6
Don't know	3.3	3.1	3.9	5.3

Note: Numbers may not add to 100 percent because "no answer" is not shown.
Source: 1996 General Social Survey, National Opinion Research Center, University of Chicago

Spending on Improving Conditions for Blacks

"We are faced with many problems in this country, none of which can be solved easily or inexpensively. Do you think we're spending too much money, too little money, or about the right amount of money on improving the conditions of blacks?"

(percent responding by race, 1996)

	total	white	black	other
Too little	31.7%	23.3%	80.5%	28.4%
About right	38.7	42.9	13.7	43.2
Too much	19.2	23.0	1.0	11.1
Don't know	10.1	10.5	4.9	17.3

Note: Numbers may not add to 100 percent because "no answer" is not shown.
Source: 1996 General Social Survey, National Opinion Research Center, University of Chicago

Blacks/Whites in the Neighborhood

"Are there any blacks/whites living in this neighborhood now?"

(percent responding by race, 1996)

	total	white	black	other
Yes	61.0%	57.8%	76.9%	68.6%
No	32.7	35.4	19.2	26.8
Don't know	5.4	6.1	2.2	3.9

Note: Blacks were asked about whites and whites were asked about blacks. Numbers may not add to 100 percent because "no answer" is not shown.
Source: 1996 General Social Survey, National Opinion Research Center, University of Chicago

Can Whites Keep Blacks Out of Their Neighborhoods?

"White people have a right to keep blacks out of their neighborhoods if they want to, and blacks should respect that right."

(percent responding by race, 1996)

	total	*white*	*black*	*other*
Agree, total	**11.5%**	**13.0%**	**3.9%**	**7.4%**
Agree strongly	5.3	6.1	0.8	3.7
Agree slightly	6.2	6.9	3.1	3.7
Disagree, total	**85.5**	**84.1**	**93.0**	**87.0**
Disagree slightly	18.6	20.6	10.1	11.1
Disagree strongly	66.9	63.5	82.9	75.9
No opinion	**2.8**	**2.6**	**3.1**	**5.6**

Note: Numbers may not add to 100 percent because "no answer" is not shown.
Source: 1996 General Social Survey, National Opinion Research Center, University of Chicago

Fair Housing Laws

"Select from:

A. One law says that a homeowner can decide for himself whom to sell his house to, even if he prefers not to sell to blacks; or

B. The second law says that a homeowner cannot refuse to sell to someone because of their race or color."

(percent responding by race, 1996)

	total	white	black	other
Up to owner	28.7%	31.4%	16.4%	17.1%
Can't refuse	66.6	64.8	74.6	75.6
Neither	2.0	1.7	3.0	4.9
Don't know	1.5	1.2	3.7	0.0

Note: Numbers may not add to 100 percent because "no answer" is not shown.
Source: 1996 General Social Survey, National Opinion Research Center, University of Chicago

Integrated Schools

"Would you yourself have any objection to sending your children to a school where a few of the children are whites/blacks?"

(percent responding by race, 1996)

	total	*white*	*black*	*other*
Yes	2.9%	2.4%	4.3%	7.0%
No	96.0	96.7	93.5	91.2
Don't know	0.5	0.5	0.7	0.0

Among those who responded no or don't know to the above question:
"Where half of the children are whites/blacks?"

Yes	14.6	16.9	3.8	7.5
No	82.4	79.8	94.7	90.6
Don't know	1.6	1.9	0.0	0.0

Among those who responded no or don't know to the above question:
"Where more than half of the children are whites/blacks?"

Yes	28.5	32.7	10.9	18.4
No	62.8	58.1	85.2	65.3
Don't know	5.7	6.4	0.0	12.2

Note: Blacks were asked about whites and whites were asked about blacks. Numbers may not add to 100 percent because "no answer" is not shown.
Source: 1996 General Social Survey, National Opinion Research Center, University of Chicago

Busing

"In general, do you favor or oppose the busing of black and white school children from one district to another?"

(percent responding by race, 1996)

	total	*white*	*black*	*other*
Favor	35.3%	31.3%	56.8%	38.6%
Oppose	58.1	62.0	38.8	50.9
Don't know	6.3	6.3	4.3	10.5

Note: Numbers may not add to 100 percent because "no answer" is not shown.
Source: 1996 General Social Survey, National Opinion Research Center, University of Chicago

Integrated Workplace

"If you are employed, are the people who work where you work all white, mostly white, about half and half, mostly black, or all black?"

(percent responding by race, 1996)

	total	white	black	other
All white	25.8%	29.4%	6.2%	21.6%
Mostly white	47.2	49.0	40.2	37.8
About half and half	18.4	15.4	30.9	32.4
Mostly black	3.5	2.6	10.3	0.0
All black	0.9	0.0	6.2	0.0
Don't know	1.1	1.2	1.0	0.0

Note: Numbers may not add to 100 percent because "no answer" is not shown.
Source: 1996 General Social Survey, National Opinion Research Center, University of Chicago

Preferential Hiring and Promotion of Blacks

"Some people say that because of past discrimination, blacks should be given preference in hiring and promotion. Others say that such preference in hiring and promotion of blacks is wrong because it discriminates against others. What about your opinion—are you for or against preferential hiring and promotion of blacks?"

(percent responding by race, 1996)

	total	white	black	other
Favor, total	15.8%	10.4%	46.3%	17.9%
Strongly favor	9.3	4.9	34.7	9.4
Not strongly favor	6.5	5.5	11.6	8.5
Oppose, total	77.0	83.3	46.3	65.1
Not strongly oppose	52.3	57.9	26.4	37.7
Strongly oppose	24.7	25.4	19.9	27.4
Don't know	6.0	5.1	6.9	16.0

Note: Numbers may not add to 100 percent because "no answer" is not shown.
Source: 1996 General Social Survey, National Opinion Research Center, University of Chicago

Reverse Discrimination on the Job

"What do you think the chances are these days that a white person won't get a job or a promotion while a less qualified black person gets one instead?"

(percent responding by race, 1996)

	total	*white*	*black*	*other*
Very likely	24.3%	25.3%	18.4%	25.5%
Somewhat likely	43.5	47.2	30.5	23.5
Not likely	27.8	23.1	48.2	43.1
Don't know	3.4	3.3	2.8	5.9

Note: Numbers may not add to 100 percent because "no answer" is not shown.
Source: 1996 General Social Survey, National Opinion Research Center, University of Chicago

Would You Vote for a Black Presidential Candidate?

"If your party nominated a black for president, would you vote for him if he were qualified for the job?"

(percent responding by race, 1996)

	total	white	black	other
Yes	89.9%	88.7%	95.0%	94.7%
No	6.8	7.9	2.2	1.8
Don't know	2.9	3.1	1.4	3.5

Note: Numbers may not add to 100 percent because "no answer" is not shown.
Source: 1996 General Social Survey, National Opinion Research Center, University of Chicago

Interracial Marriage

"Do you think there should be laws against marriages between blacks and whites?"

(percent responding by race, 1996)

	total	white	black	other
Yes	10.9%	12.5%	4.4%	2.9%
No	86.9	85.3	93.3	94.3
Don't know	2.1	2.1	2.2	2.9

Note: Numbers may not add to 100 percent because "no answer" is not shown.
Source: 1996 General Social Survey, National Opinion Research Center, University of Chicago

Book Banning

"If some people in your community suggested that a book, written by a racist, which said blacks are inferior should be taken out of your public library, would you favor removing this book, or not?"

(percent responding by race, 1996)

	total	white	black	other
Favor	32.4%	30.6%	41.1%	37.1%
Not favor	63.9	66.1	53.0	58.1
Don't know	3.4	3.2	4.8	3.8

Note: Numbers may not add to 100 percent because "no answer" is not shown.
Source: 1996 General Social Survey, National Opinion Research Center, University of Chicago

Free Speech

"Consider a person who believes that blacks are genetically inferior. If such a person wanted to make a speech in your community, claiming that blacks are inferior, should he/she be allowed to speak, or not?"

(percent responding by race, 1996)

	total	*white*	*black*	*other*
Allowed	60.5%	62.0%	54.4%	54.3%
Not allowed	37.1	36.0	42.2	41.0
Don't know	2.2	1.9	3.0	3.8

Note: Numbers may not add to 100 percent because "no answer" is not shown.
Source: 1996 General Social Survey, National Opinion Research Center, University of Chicago

Freedom to Teach

"Should a person who believes that blacks are genetically inferior be allowed to teach in a college or university, or not?"

(percent responding by race, 1996)

	total	white	black	other
Allowed	45.6%	47.5%	36.7%	40.0%
Not allowed	50.0	47.8	60.0	56.2
Don't know	6.0	4.4	3.0	3.8

Note: Numbers may not add to 100 percent because "no answer" is not shown.
Source: 1996 General Social Survey, National Opinion Research Center, University of Chicago

Which Groups Work Hard?

"Do the people in the following groups tend to be hard working or do they tend to be lazy?"

(percent responding by race, 1994)

	total	white	black	other
Whites				
1 Work hard	4.3%	4.0%	5.1%	8.2%
2	10.8	10.9	10.1	12.2
3	23.7	24.6	18.8	24.5
4	42.5	43.4	39.1	38.8
5	11.1	10.7	14.5	8.2
6	2.2	2.0	2.9	2.0
7 Lazy	0.8	0.3	4.3	0.0
Don't know	3.7	3.3	5.1	6.1
Blacks				
1 Work hard	2.2	1.2	7.2	4.1
2	5.1	3.6	13.0	6.1
3	9.9	9.1	15.9	6.1
4	43.8	44.8	43.5	28.6
5	21.6	23.3	11.6	22.4
6	9.8	10.5	3.6	16.3
7 Lazy	2.6	2.7	0.7	6.1
Don't know	4.4	4.1	4.3	10.2

Note: Numbers may not add to 100 percent because "no answer" is not shown.
Source: 1996 General Social Survey, National Opinion Research Center, University of Chicago

Intelligence of Racial Groups

"Do the people in the following groups tend to be unintelligent or do they tend to be intelligent?"

(percent responding by race, 1996)

	total	white	black	other
Whites				
1 Unintelligent	0.7%	0.5%	1.4%	2.0%
2	2.9	2.2	6.5	4.1
3	8.0	8.4	6.5	6.1
4	40.8	40.5	41.3	42.9
5	23.6	24.8	21.0	12.2
6	15.0	15.3	13.0	14.3
7 Intelligent	3.4	3.3	2.2	8.2
Don't know	4.9	4.0	8.0	10.2
Blacks				
1 Unintelligent	0.3	0.3	0.0	2.0
2	3.7	3.8	1.4	8.2
3	12.3	13.6	8.7	2.0
4	50.1	51.7	39.9	53.1
5	19.1	18.7	23.2	14.3
6	6.1	5.0	12.3	6.1
7 Intelligent	2.3	1.3	7.2	4.1
Don't know	5.4	4.7	7.2	10.2

Note: Numbers may not add to 100 percent because "no answer" is not shown.
Source: 1996 General Social Survey, National Opinion Research Center, University of Chicago

How Wealthy Are Racial Groups?

"Where would you rate the wealth of the following groups?"

(percent responding by race, 1996)

	total	*white*	*black*	*other*
Whites				
1 Rich	4.2%	2.7%	10.1%	12.2%
2	6.3	4.7	15.2	6.1
3	25.6	25.7	25.4	24.5
4	50.1	53.6	33.3	40.8
5	8.5	8.7	6.5	10.2
6	1.0	0.9	2.2	0.0
7 Poor	0.2	0.0	1.4	0.0
Don't know	3.5	2.9	5.8	6.1
Blacks				
1 Rich	0.3	0.4	0.0	0.0
2	2.5	2.4	2.9	2.0
3	6.2	6.0	6.5	8.2
4	22.7	21.2	29.7	26.5
5	37.5	39.9	30.4	18.4
6	22.3	22.8	16.7	30.6
7 Poor	4.1	3.2	8.7	6.1
Don't know	3.9	3.5	5.1	8.2

Note: Numbers may not add to 100 percent because "no answer" is not shown.
Source: 1996 General Social Survey, National Opinion Research Center, University of Chicago

Should the Number of Immigrants Be Increased or Decreased?

"Do you think the number of immigrants from foreign countries who are permitted to come to the United States to live should be increased or decreased?"

(percent responding by race, 1996)

	total	white	black	other
Increased, total	**7.2%**	**6.4%**	**8.6%**	**16.7%**
Increased a lot	2.4	1.4	4.8	12.5
Increased a little	4.8	5.0	3.8	4.2
Same	**22.7**	**22.3**	**20.4**	**34.7**
Decreased, total	**53.6**	**57.1**	**43.0**	**26.3**
Decreased a little	24.8	26.1	18.8	19.4
Decreased a lot	28.8	31.0	24.2	6.9
Don't know	**12.6**	**10.2**	**23.7**	**20.8**

Note: Numbers may not add to 100 percent because "no answer" is not shown.
Source: 1996 General Social Survey, National Opinion Research Center, University of Chicago

Should Refugees Be Allowed In?

"Do you agree or disagree that refugees who have suffered political repression in their own country should be allowed to stay in America?"

(percent responding by race, 1996)

	total	white	black	other
Agree, total	**41.4%**	**41.7%**	**39.2%**	**43.1%**
Agree strongly	9.7	9.4	8.6	18.1
Agree somewhat	31.7	32.3	30.6	25.0
Neither	**25.1**	**25.5**	**22.6**	**25.0**
Disagree, total	**22.2**	**23.6**	**17.2**	**13.9**
Disagree somewhat	15.6	17.0	9.1	11.1
Disagree strongly	6.6	6.6	8.1	2.8
Can't choose	**9.4**	**7.7**	**18.8**	**12.5**

Note: Numbers may not add to 100 percent because "no answer" is not shown.
Source: 1996 General Social Survey, National Opinion Research Center, University of Chicago

Stronger Efforts to Curb Illegal Immigration

"Do you agree or disagree that America should take stronger measures to exclude illegal immigrants?"

(percent responding by race, 1996)

	total	*white*	*black*	*other*
Agree, total	**72.2%**	**75.8%**	**61.3%**	**44.5%**
Agree strongly	43.3	46.4	34.4	18.1
Agree somewhat	28.9	29.4	26.9	26.4
Neither	**13.1**	**11.9**	**16.1**	**23.6**
Disagree, total	**8.3**	**6.6**	**12.4**	**23.6**
Disgree somewhat	6.3	5.4	8.6	13.9
Disagree strongly	2.0	1.2	3.8	9.7
Don't know	**5.0**	**4.3**	**8.6**	**5.6**

Note: Numbers may not add to 100 percent because "no answer" is not shown.
Source: 1996 General Social Survey, National Opinion Research Center, University of Chicago

Foreigners Buying Land

"Do you agree or disagree that foreigners should not be allowed to buy land in America?"

(percent responding by race, 1996)

	total	white	black	other
Agree, total	**31.1%**	**31.9%**	**32.3%**	**16.7%**
Agree strongly	10.8	11.4	10.8	1.4
Agree somewhat	20.3	20.5	21.5	15.3
Neither	**25.6**	**26.0**	**24.7**	**22.2**
Disagree, total	**38.4**	**38.2**	**32.8**	**55.6**
Disagree somewhat	29.3	29.2	26.3	38.9
Disagree strongly	9.1	9.0	6.5	16.7
Can't choose	**3.3**	**2.3**	**9.7**	**2.8**

Note: Numbers may not add to 100 percent because "no answer" is not shown.
Source: 1996 General Social Survey, National Opinion Research Center, University of Chicago

Immigrants and Jobs

"Do you agree or disagree with this statement: Immigrants take jobs away from people who were born in America."

(percent responding by race, 1996)

	total	white	black	other
Agree, total	**45.0%**	**45.6%**	**52.6%**	**18.1%**
Agree strongly	12.4	11.4	22.0	4.2
Agree slightly	32.6	34.2	30.6	13.9
Disagree, total	**22.0**	**21.6**	**23.1**	**22.2**
Disagree slightly	4.8	26.8	15.0	56.9
Disagree strongly	21.9	21.9	13.4	45.8
Neither	**26.8**	**4.9**	**1.6**	**11.1**
Can't choose	**2.0**	**1.9**	**3.2**	**1.4**

Note: Numbers may not add to 100 percent because "no answer" is not shown.
Source: 1996 General Social Survey, National Opinion Research Center, University of Chicago

Immigrants and America's Economy

"Do you agree or disagree with this statement: Immigrants are generally good for America's economy."

(percent responding by race, 1996)

	total	white	black	other
Agree, total	**31.0%**	**30.1%**	**26.9%**	**55.6%**
Agree strongly	4.4	3.9	3.8	13.9
Agree slightly	26.6	26.2	23.1	41.7
Disagree, total	**26.4**	**30.4**	**32.3**	**22.2**
Disagree slightly	3.8	31.4	28.5	15.3
Disagree strongly	30.2	27.3	25.8	13.9
Neither	**30.2**	**4.1**	**2.7**	**1.4**
Can't choose	**4.4**	**3.8**	**7.5**	**5.6**

Note: Numbers may not add to 100 percent because "no answer" is not shown.
Source: 1996 General Social Survey, National Opinion Research Center, University of Chicago

Immigrants and Crime

"Do immigrants increase crime rates?"

(percent responding by race, 1996)

	total	white	black	other
Agree, total	**30.9%**	**31.5%**	**29.5%**	**26.4%**
Agree strongly	6.9	6.9	9.1	2.8
Agree slightly	24.0	24.6	20.4	23.6
Neither	**26.9**	**27.9**	**27.4**	**11.1**
Disagree, total	**34.7**	**33.7**	**31.2**	**58.3**
Disagree slightly	28.4	27.6	26.9	44.4
Disagree strongly	6.3	6.1	4.3	13.9
Can't choose	**3.3**	**2.7**	**7.0**	**2.8**

Note: Numbers may not add to 100 percent because "no answer" is not shown.
Source: 1996 General Social Survey, National Opinion Research Center, University of Chicago

Immigrants and Openness to New Ideas

"Do you agree or disagree with this statement: Immigrants make America more open to new ideas and cultures."

(percent responding by race, 1996)

	total	white	black	other
Agree, total	**57.6%**	**59.5%**	**41.4%**	**72.3%**
Agree strongly	11.1	10.4	8.1	30.6
Agree slightly	46.5	49.1	33.3	41.7
Disagree, total	**12.4**	**19.3**	**29.0**	**13.9**
Disagree slightly	2.5	14.7	17.2	11.1
Disagree strongly	20.3	11.9	16.1	9.7
Neither	**14.9**	**2.8**	**1.1**	**1.4**
Can't choose	**3.2**	**2.5**	**8.1**	**1.4**

Note: Numbers may not add to 100 percent because "no answer" is not shown.
Source: 1996 General Social Survey, National Opinion Research Center, University of Chicago

Glossary

adjusted for inflation Income or a change in income that has been adjusted for the rise in the cost of living, or the consumer price index (CPI-U-XI).

ancestry Information on ancestry is based on written responses to the ancestry question on the 1990 census.

Asian In this book, the term "Asian" includes both Asians and Pacific Islanders. The Current Population Survey classifies as Asian or Pacific Islander anyone who identifies his or her race as "Asian or Pacific Islander." The 1990 census goes further, asking respondents to specify their Asian or Pacific Islander ethnic origin, such as Chinese, Filipino, Japanese, Asian Indian, Korean, Vietnamese, Samoan, Tahaitian, and so on. All those who name a Far Eastern or Pacific Island nation as their origin classifies as "Asian or Pacific Islander." The only exception to this definition of Asian is in the immigration tables in the Asian and Total Population sections. The Immigration and Naturalization Service includes people from the Middle East—such as Israel, Lebanon, Iran, and so on—as immigrants from the Asian world region. They are included as Asian immigrants in the immigration tables.

baby boom Americans born between 1946 and 1964.

black The black racial category includes those who identify themselves as "black" on the Current Population Survey, or as "black or Negro" on the 1990 Census, or who wrote in an ancestry or ethnic origin on the 1990 census that included African-American, Jamaican, Nigerian, West Indian, or Haitian.

central cities The largest city in a metropolitan area is called the central city. The balance of the metropolitan area outside the central city is regarded as the "suburbs."

consumer unit For convenience, the term consumer unit and households are used interchangeably in the spending tables of this book, although consumer units are somewhat different from the Census Bureau's households. Consumer units are all related members of a household, or financially independent members of a household. A household may include more than one consumer unit.

dual-earner couple A married couple in which both the householder and the householder's spouse are in the labor force.

earnings A type of income, earnings is the amount of money a person receives from his or her job.

employed All civilians who did any work as a paid employee or farmer/self-employed worker, or who worked 15 hours or more as an unpaid farm worker or in a family-owned business, during the reference period. All those who have jobs but who are temporarily absent from their jobs due to illness, bad weather, vacation, labor management dispute, or personal reasons are considered employed.

expenditure The transaction cost including excise and sales taxes of goods and services acquired during the survey period. The full cost of each purchase is recorded even though full payment may not have been made at the date of purchase. Average expenditure figures may be artifically low for infrequently purchased items such as cars because figures are calculated using all consumer units within a demographic segment rather than just purchasers. Expenditure estimates include money spent on gifts for others.

family A group of two or more people (one of whom is the householder) related by birth, marriage, or adoption and living in the same household.

family household A household maintained by a householder who lives with one or more people related to him or her by blood, marriage, or adoption.

female/male householder A woman or man who maintains a household without a spouse present. May head family or nonfamily households.

full-time, year-round Indicates 50 or more weeks of full-time employment during the previous calendar year.

geographic regions The four major regions and nine census divisions of the United States are the state groupings as shown below:

Northeast:
—New England: Connecticut, Maine, Massachusetts, New Hampshire, Rhode Island, and Vermont
—Middle Atlantic: New Jersey, New York, and Pennsylvania

Midwest:
—East North Central: Illinois, Indiana, Michigan, Ohio, and Wisconsin
—West North Central: Iowa, Kansas, Minnesota, Missouri, Nebraska, North Dakota, and South Dakota

South:
—South Atlantic: Delaware, District of Columbia, Florida, Georgia, Maryland, North Carolina, South Carolina, Virginia, and West Virginia

—East South Central: Alabama, Kentucky, Mississippi, and Tennessee
—West South Central: Arkansas, Louisiana, Oklahoma, and Texas

West:
—Mountain: Arizona, Colorado, Idaho, Montana, Nevada, New Mexico, Utah, and Wyoming
—Pacific: Alaska, California, Hawaii, Oregon, and Washington

Generation X Americans born between 1965 and 1976, also known as the baby-bust generation.

Hispanic The Hispanic statistics in this book include those who identified themselves as Hispanic on the Current Population Survey or on the 1990 census. Hispanics include those who identify themselves as Mexican, Puerto Rican, Cuban, or of "other" Spanish/Hispanic origin. Persons of "other" Hispanic origin include those from Spain, the Spanish-speaking countries of Central and South America, or the Dominican Republic. They also include those who identify themselves as Spanish, Spanish-American, Latino, and so on. The only exception to this definition of Hispanic is in the immigration table in the Hispanic section, where people from Brazil are classified as Hispanic because they are from South America. Persons of Hispanic origin may be of any race. In other words, there are Asian Hispanics, black Hispanics, Native American Hispanics, and white Hispanics.

household All the persons who occupy a housing unit. A household includes the related family members and all the unrelated persons, if any, such as lodgers, foster children, wards, or employees who share the housing unit. A person living alone is counted as a household. A group of unrelated people who share a housing unit as roommates or unmarried partners is also counted as a household. Households do not include group quarters such as college dormitories, prisons, or nursing homes.

household, race/ethnicity of Households are categorized according to the race or ethnicity of the householder only.

householder The householder is the person (or one of the persons) in whose name the housing unit is owned or rented or, if there is no such person, any adult member. With married couples, the householder may be either the husband or wife. The householder is the reference person for the household.

householder, age of The age of the householder is used to categorize households into age groups such as those used in this book. Married couples, for example, are classified according to the age of either the husband or wife, depending on which one identified him or herself as the householder.

housing unit A housing unit is a house, an apartment, a group of rooms, or a single room occupied or intended for occupancy as separate living quarters. Separate living quarters are those in which the occupants do not live and eat with any other persons in the structure and that have direct access from the outside of the building or through a common hall that is used or intended for use by the occupants of another unit or by the general public. The occupants may be a single family, one person living alone, two or more families living together, or any other group of related or unrelated persons who share living arrangements.

income Money received in the preceding calendar year by each person aged 15 or older from each of the following sources: (1) earnings from longest job (or self-employment); (2) earnings from jobs other than longest job; (3) unemployment compensation; (4) workers' compensation; (5) Social Security; (6) Supplemental Security income; (7) public assistance; (8) veterans' payments; (9) survivor benefits; (10) disability benefits; (11) retirement pensions; (12) interest; (13) dividends; (14) rents and royalties or estates and trusts; (15) educational assistance; (16) alimony; (17) child support; (18) financial assistance from outside the household, and other periodic income. Income is reported in several ways in this book. Household income is the combined income of all household members. Income of persons is all income accruing to a person from all sources. Earnings is the amount of money a person receives from his or her job.

industry Refers to the industry in which a person worked longest in the preceding calendar year.

labor force The labor force includes both employed workers and the unemployed—people who are looking for work.

labor force participation rate The percent of a population that is in the labor force, which includes both the employed and unemployed. Labor force participation rates may be shown for sex-age groups or other special populations such as mothers of children of a given age.

married couples with or without children under age 18 Refers to married couples with or without children under age 18 living in the same household. Couples without children under age 18 may be parents of grown children who live elsewhere, or they could be childless couples.

median The median is the amount that divides the population or households into two equal portions: one below and one above the median. Medians can be calculated for income, age, and many other characteristics.

median income The amount that divides the income distribution into two equal groups, half having incomes above the median, half having incomes below the median. The medians for households or families are based on all households or families. The median for persons are based on all persons aged 15 or older with income.

metropolitan area An area qualifies for recognition as a metropolitan area if: (1) it includes a city of at least 50,000 population, or (2) it includes a Census Bureau-defined urbanized area of at least 50,000 with a total metropolitan population of at least 100,000 (75,000 in New England). In addition to the county containing the main city or urbanized area, a metropolitan area may include other counties having strong commuting ties to the central county.

Native American The Native American statistics in this book include people who indicated they were American Indian, Eskimo, or Aleut in the 1990 census. Some of the tables in the Native American chapter do not include Eskimos or Aleuts, a fact noted at the bottom of those tables. The American Indian category includes persons who reported their race as American Indian and/or entered the name of an American Indian tribe. The tribal data shown in this book are from the written entries on the 1990 census questionnaire.

nonfamily household A household maintained by a householder who lives alone or who lives with people to whom he or she is not related.

nonfamily householder A householder who lives alone or with nonrelatives.

non-Hispanic People who did not indicate that they were Hispanic on the Current Population Survey or on the 1990 Census are classified as non-Hispanic.

nonmetropolitan area Counties that are not classified as metropolitan areas.

occupation Occupational classification is based on the kind of work a person did at his or her job during the previous calendar year. If a person changed jobs during the year, the data refer to the occupation of the job held the longest during that year.

occupied housing units A housing unit is classified as occupied if a person or group of persons is living in it or if the occupants are only temporarily absent, for example, on vacation. By definition, the count of occupied housing units is the same as the count of households.

outside central city The portion of a metropolitan county or counties that falls outside of the central city or cities; generally regarded as the suburbs.

part-time or full-time employment Part-time is less than 35 hours of work per week in a majority of the weeks worked during the year. Full-time is 35 or more hours of work per week during a majority of the weeks worked.

percent change The change (either positive or negative) in a measure that is expressed as a proportion of the starting measure. When median income changes from $20,000 to $25,000, for example, this is a 25 percent increase.

percentage point change The change (either positive or negative) in a value which is already expressed as a percentage. When a labor force participation rate changes from 70 percent of 75 percent, for example, this is a 5 percentage point increase.

poverty level The official income threshold below which families and persons are classified as living in poverty. The threshold rises each year with inflation and varies depending on family size and age of householder.

proportion or share The value of a part expressed as a percentage of the whole. If there are 4 million people aged 25 and 3 million of them are white, then the white proportion is 75 percent.

purchase price The purchase price refers to the price of the house or apartment and lot at the time the property was purchased. Closing costs are excluded from the purchase price.

race Race is self-reported and appears in four categories in this book: Asian, black, Native American, and white. A household is assigned the race of the householder.

rounding Percentages are rounded to the nearest tenth of a percent; therefore, the percentages in a distribution do not always add exactly to 100.0 percent. The totals, however, are always shown as 100.0. Moreover, individual figures are rounded to the nearest thousand without being adjusted to group totals, which are independently rounded; percentages are based on the unrounded numbers.

sex ratio The number of men per 100 women.

suburbs *See* Outside central city.

tenure A housing unit is "owner occupied" if the owner lives in the unit, even if it is mortgaged or not fully paid for. A cooperative or condominium unit is "owner occupied" only if the owner lives in it. All other occupied units are classified as "renter occupied."

unemployed Unemployed persons are those who, during the survey period, had no employment but were available and looking for work. Those who were laid off from their jobs and were waiting to be recalled are also classified as unemployed.

value Value is the respondent's estimate of how much his or her house and lot would sell for if it were for sale.

white The white racial category includes those who identify themselves as "white" on the Current Population Survey, or as white on the 1990 census. In addition, those who report an ancestry or ethnic origin that includes Canadian, German, Italian, Lebanese, Near Easterner, Arab, or Polish, or from other countries that are made up primarily of white racial groups. The only exception to this definition of white is in the immigration tables in the Asian and Total Population chapters where the Immigration and Naturalization Service classifies people from the Middle East as from the Asian world region. They are included as Asian immigrants in the immigration tables, though the Census Bureau would classify them as white.

Bibliography

Bureau of the Census

Internet web site, http://www.census.gov

—1990 census STF3 CD-ROM

—1996 and 1997 Current Population Surveys

—*American Housing Survey for the United States in 1995*, Current Housing Reports, H150/95, 1997

—*Asians and Pacific Islanders in the United States*, 1990 Census of Population, 1990 CP-3-5, 1993

—*Characteristics of American Indians by Tribe and Language*, 1990 Census of Population, CP-3-7, 1994

—*Detailed Ancestry Groups for States*, CP-S-1-2, 1990

—*Educational Attainment in the United States: March 1996*, Current Population Reports, P20-493, 1997

—*General Population Characteristics*, 1990 Census of Population, CP-1-1, 1992

—*Geographical Mobility: March 1995 to March 1996*, Current Population Reports, P20-497(Update), 1997

—*Household and Family Characteristics: March 1996*, Current Population Reports, P20-495 (Update), 1997

—*Housing in Metropolitan Areas—Asian or Pacific Islander Households*, Statistical Brief, SB/05-6, 1995

—*Housing in Metropolitan Areas—Black Households*, Statistical Brief, SB/95-5, 1995

—*Housing in Metropolitan Areas—Hispanic Households*, Statistical Brief, SB/95-4, 1995

—*Income, Poverty, and Valuation of Noncash Benefits: 1996*, Current Population Reports, P60-197, 1997

—*Marital Status and Living Arrangements: March 1995*, Current Population Reports, P20-491, 1996

—*Money Income in the United States: 1996*, Current Population Reports, P60-197, 1997

—*Persons of Hispanic Origin in the United States*, 1990 Census of Population, CP-3-3, 1990

—*Population Projections of the United States, by Age, Sex, Race, and Hispanic Origin: 1995 to 2050*, Current Population Reports, P25-1130, 1996

—*Population Projections for States, by Age, Sex, Race, and Hispanic Origin: 1995 to 2025*, PPL-47, 1996

—*Poverty in the United States: 1996*, Current Population Reports, P60-198, 1997

—*School Enrollment—Social and Economic Characteristics of Students: October 1995*, Current Population Reports, P20-492, 1997

—*Statistical Abstract of the United States: 1997* (117th edition) Washington, DC 1997

—*The Asian and Pacific Islander Population in the United States: March 1996* (Update), detailed tables for Current Population Reports P20-503, PPL-77, 1997

Bureau of Labor Statistics

Internet web site, http://www.bls.gov

—1995 Consumer Expenditure Survey

—*Employment and Earnings*, January 1998

—*Monthly Labor Review*, November 1997

Federal Reserve Board

Internet web site, http://www.bog.frb.fed.us

—*Family Finances in the U.S.: Recent Evidence From the Survey of Consumer Finances*, Federal Reserve Bulletin, January 1997

National Center for Education Statistics

Internet web site, http://nces.ed.gov

—*Digest of Education Statistics 1993*, NCES 93-292, 1993

—*Digest of Education Statistics 1997*, NCES 98-015, 1997

National Center for Health Statistics

Internet web site, http://www.cdc.gov/nchswww

—*Advance Report of Final Natality Statistics: 1995*, Monthly Vital Statistics Report, Vol. 45, No. 11(S), 1997

—*Birth Characteristics for Asian or Pacific Islander Subgroups, 1992*, Monthly Vital Statistics Report, Vol. 43, No. 10 Supplement, 1995

—*Births and Deaths: United States, 1996*, Monthly Vital Statistics Report, Vol. 46, No. 1, Supplement 2, 1997

—*Current Estimates from the National Health Interview Survey, 1994*, Series 10, No. 193, 1995

—*Health Status Indicators by Race and Hispanic Origin*, Healthy People 2000 Review, 1995–96

—*Health, United States, 1996–97*

—*Report of Final Mortality Statistics, 1995*, Monthly Vital Statistics Report, 1997, Vol. 46, No. 1, Supplement 2, 1997

National Opinion Research Center

Internet web site, http://www.norc.uchicago.edu

—1996 General Social Survey, unpublished data

TGE Demographics, Inc.

Internet web site, http://www.wessex.com/tgedemographics/

U.S. Immigration and Naturalization Service

Internet web site, http://www.ins.usdoj.gov

—*1996 Statistical Yearbook of the Immigration and Naturalization Service*, 1997

Index

Assets. *See* Wealth.

Attitude toward
  American treatment of all groups, 647
  blacks pushing, 652
  blacks working their way up, 653
  blacks/whites in neighborhood, 657
  book banning, 667
  busing, 661
  condition of blacks, 651
  fair housing laws, 659
  foreigners buying land, 676
  free speech, 668
  freedom to teach, 669
  government helping maintain
     ethnic identity, 650
  government obligation to help blacks, 655
  housing
    black, 129
    Hispanic, 252
    total, 561
  immigration, 673–675, 677–680
  importance of being American, 645
  integrated schools, 660
  integrated workplace, 662
  intelligence of racial and ethnic groups, 671
  interracial marriage, 666
  meaning of being American, 646
  melting pot, 649
  neighborhood
    black, 131
    Hispanic, 254
    total, 562
  preferential hiring of blacks, 663
  racial and ethnic unity, 648
  reverse discrimination on the job, 664
  spending on improving condition of
  blacks, 656
  voting for black presidential candidate, 665
  wealth of racial and ethnic groups, 672
  which groups work hard, 670
  whites keeping black out of
    neighborhood, 658
  why blacks have it worse, 654

Bachelor's degrees earned. *See* Education.

Births. *See* Health.

Central and South American. *See* Ethnicity.

Champus. *See* Insurance, health.

Children
  households with and without
    Asian, 30
    black, 115, 118–119
    Hispanic, 238, 241–242
    Native American, 358
    total, 545, 548–549
    white, 427, 430–431
  in college, families with
    black, 89
    Hispanic, 212
    total, 519
    white, 401
  in poverty
    black, 148–149
    Hispanic, 273–274
    Native American, 369
    total, 579–580
    white, 456–457
  living arrangements of
    Asian, 32
    black, 121
    Hispanic, 244
    total, 551
    white, 433
  number of in family
    black, 118–119
    Hispanic, 241–242
    total, 548–549
    white, 430–431

Chinese. *See* Ethnicity.

College. *See* Education.

Crime in neighborhood
  black, 131
  Hispanic, 254
  total, 562

Cuban. *See* Ethnicity.

Debt. *See* Wealth.

Death. *See* Health.

Disabilities. *See* Health.

Divorce. *See* Marital status.

Doctoral degrees earned. *See* Education.

Earners in household
  Asian, 52
  black, 156
  Hispanic, 283
  Native American, 372
  total, 585
  white, 462

Earnings
  by education
    Asian, 42–43
    black, 146
    Hispanic, 269
    total, 577
    white, 454
  by ethnicity
    Hispanic, 270–271
  by sex
    Asian, 42–43
    black, 145–146
    Hispanic, 268–271
    total, 576–577
    white, 453–454
  by work status
    Asian, 42–43
    black, 145–146
    Hispanic, 268–271
    total, 576–577
    white, 453–454

Education
  attainment
    Asian, 9–11
    black, 83–87
    Hispanic, 205–210
    Native American, 343–345
    total, 513–517
    white, 395–399
  bachelor's degrees earned
    Asian, 14
    black, 93

    Hispanic, 216
    Native American, 347
    total, 523
    white, 405
  by age
    black, 85–86
    Hispanic, 208–209
    total, 515–516
    white, 397–398
  by ethnicity
    Asian, 10
    Hispanic, 206
    Native American, 344
  by region
    black, 86
    Hispanic, 209
    total, 516
    white, 398
  by sex
    Asian, 9–10
    black, 83–85
    Hispanic, 205, 207–208
    Native American, 343
    total, 513–515
    white, 395–397
  by state
    Asian, 11
    black, 87
    Hispanic, 210
    Native American, 345
    total, 517
    white, 399
  college enrollment
    Asian, 8, 13
    black, 90–92
    Hispanic, 213–215
    Native American, 346
    total, 520–522
    white, 402–404
  college graduates
    Asian, 9–11
    black, 83–87
    Hispanic, 205–210
    Native American, 343–345
    total, 513–517
    white, 395–399

doctoral degrees earned
  Asian, 14
  black, 93
  Hispanic, 216
  Native American, 347
  total, 523
  white, 405
earnings by
  Asian, 43
  black, 146
  Hispanic, 269
  total, 577
  white, 454
families with children in college
  black, 89
  Hispanic, 212
  total, 519
  white, 401
fields of study, degrees earned by
  Asian, 14–15
  black, 93–94
  Hispanic, 216–217
  Native American, 347–348
  total, 523–524
  white, 405–406
first-professional degrees earned
  Asian, 15
  black, 94
  Hispanic, 217
  Native American, 348
  total, 524
  white, 406
foreign-born population by
  Asian, 60–61
  Hispanic, 293
  total, 594
high school graduates
  Asian, 9–11
  black, 83–87
  Hispanic, 205–210
  Native American, 343–345
  total, 513–517
  white, 395–399
master's degrees earned
  Asian, 14
  black, 93

  Hispanic, 216
  Native American, 347
  total, 523
  white, 405
poverty by
  Asian, 45
school enrollment
  Asian, 12
  black, 88
  Hispanic, 211
  Native American, 346
  total, 518
  white, 400

Employment. *See* Labor force.

Ethnicity
  ability to speak English by
    Asian, 59
    Hispanic, 291
    Native American, 381
  births by
    Asian, 20–21
    Hispanic, 222–228
  births to teenagers by
    Asian, 19
    Hispanic, 222
  births to unmarried mothers by,
    Asian, 19
  by age
    Hispanic, 292
  by region
    Asian, 63–64
    Hispanic, 295–296
    Native American, 382
  by state
    Asian, 67–72
    Hispanic, 299–304
  earnings by
    Hispanic, 270–271
  educational attainment by
    Asian, 10
    Hispanic, 206
    Native American, 344
  employment status by
    Hispanic, 277

motor vehicle crash deaths
 Asian, 17
 black, 97
 Hispanic, 219
 Native American, 350
 white, 409
physician contacts
 black, 110
 total, 540
 white, 422
status
 black, 96
 total, 526
 white, 408
suicides
 Asian, 17
 black, 97
 Hispanic, 219
 Native American, 350
 white, 409
syphilis
 Asian, 17
 black, 97
 Hispanic, 219
 Native American, 350
 white, 409
tuberculosis
 Asian, 17
 black, 97
 Hispanic, 219
 Native American, 350
 white, 409
work-related injury deaths
 Asian, 17
 black, 97
 Hispanic, 219
 Native American, 350
 white, 409

High school. *See* Education.

Homeownership
 in metropolitan areas
 Asian, 36
 black, 137–138
 Hispanic, 260–261
 non-Hispanic white, 445–446

total, 568–569
 white, 443–444
status
 Asian, 35
 black, 127
 Hispanic, 250
 Native American, 362
 total, 559
 white, 439

Households
 by age of householder
 Asian, 28
 black, 114, 116, 118–120
 Hispanic, 237, 239, 241–243
 total, 544, 546, 548–550
 white, 426, 428, 430–432
 by income
 Asian, 38–40
 black, 140–142
 Hispanic, 263–265
 Native American, 365–367
 non-Hispanic white, 448
 total, 571–573
 white, 448–450
 by number of children
 black, 118
 Hispanic, 241–242
 total, 548
 white, 430–431
 by type
 Asian, 29–30
 black, 115–116, 118–120
 Hispanic, 238–239, 241–243
 Native American, 358
 total, 545–546, 548–550
 white, 427–428, 430–432
 earners, number of
 Asian, 52
 black, 156
 Hispanic, 283
 Native American, 372
 total, 585
 white, 462
 female-headed
 Asian, 29–30, 40
 black, 115–116, 119